On Course

Strategies for Creating Success in College, Career, and Life

Ninth Edition

Skip Downing
Jonathan Brennan

Cengage

Australia • Brazil • Canada • Mexico • Singapore • United Kingdom • United States

Cengage

On Course: Strategies for Success in College, Career, and Life,
Ninth Edition
Skip Downing, Jonathan Brennan

SVP, Higher Education & Skills Product: Erin Joyner

VP, Higher Education & Skills Product: Thais Alencar

Product Director: Laura Ross

Product Manager: Laura Kuhlman

Product Assistant: Celia Smithmier

Learning Designer: Hannah Ells

Content Manager: Jacqueline Czel

Digital Delivery Quality Partner:

Director, Marketing: Neena Bali

Marketing Manager: Danielle Klahr

IP Analyst: Ann Hoffman

IP Project Manager: Kathryn Kucharek

Production Service: Lumina Datamatics

Art Director: Diana Graham

Cover Image: Kwok Design/ ShutterStock.com and iStockphoto. com/clagge

For product information and technology assistance, contact us at
Cengage Customer & Sales Support, 1-800-354-9706 or support.cengage.com.

For permission to use material from this text or product, submit all requests online at
www.copyright.com.

Library of Congress Control Number: 2018953235

Student Edition:
ISBN: 978-0-357-02268-9

Loose-Leaf Edition:
ISBN: 978-0-357-02271-9

Cengage
200 Pier 4 Boulevard
Boston, MA 02210
USA

Cengage is a leading provider of customized learning solutions with employees residing in nearly 40 different countries and sales in more than 125 countries around the world. Find your local representative at **www.cengage.com.**

To learn more about Cengage platforms and services, register or access your online learning solution, or purchase materials for your course, visit **www.cengage.com.**

Printed at CLDPC, USA, 06-22

DEDICATIONS

Skip Downing:

>*To Carol, my compass*

Jonathan Brennan:

>*To all my students, who have taught me
>so many lessons*

Contents

4 Mastering Self-Management   121

6   Gaining Self-Awareness   199

7 Adopting Lifelong Learning   232

8 Developing Emotional Intelligence   276

9   Staying On Course to Your Success   311

Study Skills Plus   321

On Course is intended for college students of any age who want to create success in college, in their career, and in life. Whether students are taking a student success or first-year seminar course, a career course, a writing course, a course in any discipline, or an "inward-looking" course in psychology, self-exploration, or personal growth, *On Course* is an instruction manual for dramatically improving the quality of their outcomes and experiences. Through self-assessments, articles, guided journals, case studies in critical thinking, and inspiring stories from other students, *On Course* empowers students with time-proven strategies for creating a great life—academic, professional, and personal—and honing their study skills. Online resources within MindTap and Cengage Infuse additionally provide students with the opportunity to learn the techniques that have helped hundreds of thousands of students create extraordinary success!

Since its first publication in 1996, *On Course* has become a market leader, standing out in the crowded field of student success texts. Increasingly, educators and researchers are finding (as we have) that engaging and empowering students to become active, responsible learners produces significant increases in both student academic success and retention. In addition, the process empowers them to create great things in their personal and professional lives. Our goal is to make this new edition of *On Course* even more helpful to the success of students and educators alike.

> [*On Course*] is the absolute best approach for a first-year seminar/college success class that there is. The philosophy and textbook are exactly what students need.
>
> Catherine Eloranto, Clinton Community College

> We wanted a curriculum that went beyond study skills to address the foundational needs of first-year college students. *On Course* causes students to examine and reflect on the causes of their successes and setbacks. It challenges students to go beyond the obvious and really delves into their motivations and mindsets. Oh, yeah, and it does a great job addressing study skills too.
>
> Ann Heiny, Armstrong State University

What's New in This Edition of On Course: Highlights

- *On Course* at Work. The ninth edition of *On Course* shows how all the skills learned in this course will help students succeed in their careers. Every career article in the book has been revised and greatly expanded to show students how the same skills that will help them excel in college will help them succeed in the work world. Topics include the contribution to career success of essential soft skills: personal responsibility, self-motivation, self-management, interdependence, self-awareness, lifelong learning, emotional intelligence, and believing in oneself. The technical career preparation and employment skills addressed include choosing a major, selecting a career, résumé and cover letter preparation, seeking mentors, personal branding, interview preparation, performance reviews, networking, maintaining work-life balance, and employee engagement.

- **Healthy Choices**. Making healthy choices can be challenging, especially in college. Appearing in Chapters 2 through 8, these new articles discuss topics that directly affect students' health—and their academic success. Topics include alcohol, drugs, smoking, food, nonalcoholic drinks, exercise, and sleep. Each article provides an overview of the latest scientific research on the topic and ends with wise choices students can make to ensure success—in college, in their career, and in life.

- **Six New "One Student's Stories."** A popular feature in earlier editions, these short essays—now numbering 32 in all—are authored by students who used what they learned from *On Course* to improve the quality of their outcomes and experiences in college and in life. Videos of many of the student-authors reading their essays may be viewed in MindTap.

- **Developing grit**. This article explores the role grit plays in student success. It encourages students to take the Grit Scale, developed by psychologist Angela Duckworth, and offers strategies for how students can increase their grit and, thus, their perseverance in completing a college degree.

- **Discussion on hope theory**. Researcher Charles Snyder has demonstrated that students with higher "hope levels" earn better grades and have higher graduation rates than students with low hope levels. This new content provides specific strategies students can use to raise their hope levels, increasing their motivation to succeed in college.

- **Developing a growth mindset**. Psychologists, inspired by the work of Stanford's Carol Dweck, have confirmed that mindsets influence the choices that learners make and thus shape students' academic outcomes. This revised article guides students to choose a "growth" mindset, proven to help students excel as learners.

- **Information competency**. This newly expanded article encourages students to apply the critical thinking skills they've learned in the book to distinguish between accurate and false information. The article discusses the importance of information competency, how to identify false information (especially from online or social media sources), how to avoid common scams that target college students, and how to improve one's information competency. A revised journal entry asks students to reflect on and apply their new skills in information competency.

- **Tech Tips**. Many websites and apps are available to help students achieve greater success. *On Course* features updated Tech Tips sections that identify free websites and apps that can help students employ the soft skills of personal responsibility, self-motivation, self-management, interdependence, self-awareness, lifelong learning, emotional intelligence, and believing in oneself, as well as hard skills related to effective studying and learning.

I think these are very powerful stories. . . . It's good for students to hear that other students have faced the same struggles that they are going through and they have achieved success.

Kathryn Burk,
Jackson Community
College

On Course has made a huge difference in the students I work with. Most of them see themselves throughout the book, and they are willing to make changes to improve their lives because of the content of *On Course*.

Tanya Stanley,
San Jacinto College

The study skills sections are clear, logically organized and more adaptable as a "how-to" guide than any other texts of similar intent.

Judith Willner, Coppin
State University

- **Toolbox for Active Learners.** Many *On Course* instructors asked that study skills be presented in one section (rather than distributed throughout the book). This edition honors that request with an update made to the ninth edition narrative in 2022. Unlike texts that present a long menu of study options, *On Course* organizes study skills based on the logical learning steps as identified by research on the brain and effective methods for learning. This section begins with a presentation of the CORE Learning Process, the four principles that—consciously or unconsciously—all good learners employ to create deep and lasting learning. Students discover how to use these four principles to learn any subject or skill. Each section of the Toolbox presents effective techniques for one of the study skills covered (reading, taking notes, organizing study materials, rehearsing and memorizing study materials, taking tests, and writing college-level assignments) and ends with an exercise to reinforce the study strategies presented therein. Compared with the regular eighth edition of *On Course*, this ninth edition with Study Skills Plus contains an additional 80 pages of study strategies, along with more examples of their use. Each section ends with an activity in which students are asked to "Do One Different Thing This Week." In this activity, they experiment with one new learning skill for a week and report on their outcomes, experiences, and lessons learned.

What's New in This Edition of *On Course*: Chapter by Chapter

Chapter 1

> There's nothing better than *On Course*, as far as I'm concerned.
>
> Lisa Marks, Ozarks Technical Community College

- At the request of a number of *On Course* instructors, "Money Matters" has been moved to the end of Chapter 1, thus helping students early in the semester to reduce struggles caused by financial difficulties.
- New: *One Student's Story* by Kineesha George, San Juan College, NM.
- Completely revised and expanded: "Soft Skills at Work."
- Updated: "Tech Tips: Money."
- New: *One Student's Story* by Emily Christman, Brigham Young University, ID.

Chapter 2

> Anyone who can teach students personal responsibility is high on my list.
>
> Debbie Unsold, Washington State Community College

- New: *One Student's Story* by Konnie Kellogg, Donnelly College, KS.
- Completely revised and expanded: "Personal Responsibility at Work."
- Updated and expanded: "Tech Tips: Personal Responsibility."
- New: "Healthy Choices: Introduction."

- New: "Healthy Choices: Alcohol."
- Moved: *One Student's Story* by Brandeé Huigens, Northeast Iowa Community College, IA, from Chapter 6.

Chapter 3

- New content: Hope theory and its impact on motivation.
- Completely revised and expanded: "Self-Motivation at Work."
- Updated: "Tech Tips: Self-Motivation."
- New: "Healthy Choices: Drugs."

Chapter 4

- Revised: "Time and Culture" section.
- Revised: Developing Self-Discipline section to focus on "Developing Grit."
- Completely revised and expanded: "Self-Management at Work."
- Updated: "Tech Tips: Self-Management."
- New: "Healthy Choices: Smoking."

Chapter 5

- Revised: "Respecting Cultural Differences" article.
- Completely revised and expanded: "Interdependence at Work."
- Updated: "Tech Tips: Interdependence."
- New: "Healthy Choices: Food."

Chapter 6

- Completely revised and expanded: "Self-Awareness at Work."
- Updated: "Tech Tips: Self-Awareness."
- Revised: "Write Your Own Rules" article.
- Moved: *One Student's Story* by Freddie Davila, The Victoria College, TX, from Chapter 2.
- New: "Healthy Choices: Drinks (Nonalcoholic)."

Chapter 7

- Revised: "Developing a Learning Orientation to Life" to focus on "Developing a Growth Mindset."
- New: Journal Entry 24.
- Revised and expanded: Article on critical thinking and information competency.

On Course is life-changing for my students. I have seen students evolve in ways they never imagined in a matter of a semester thanks to *On Course*. I cannot imagine using another book. No other book encompasses the reflective, introspective, and success attributes that *On Course* does. *On Course* walks students through their journey of self-discovery and allows them to grow into the student they have always wanted to become.

Joselyn Gonzalez,
El Centro College

*O*n several occasions, I have had various members of the same family in different semesters of my [*On Course*] class because they value the learning so much that they recommend it to sisters/brothers/children/uncles.

Sandra Lancaster, Grand Rapids Community College

- Revised: Journal Entry 26.
- Completely revised and expanded: "Lifelong Learning at Work."
- Updated: "Tech Tips: Lifelong Learning."
- New: *One Student's Story* by Dalene Meek, San Juan College, NM.
- New: "Healthy Choices: Physical Activity."
- New: *One Student's Story* by Crystal Kim, California State University–Fullerton, CA.

> I love *On Course*, and I use it in my personal life as well as preaching it in all of my classes…I have even used it with the classes that I teach in a women's shelter. The concept of moving from Victim to Creator puts the individual in charge of their life and I love that mindset.
>
> Pat Grissom,
> San Jacinto College

Chapter 8

- New: *One Student's Story* by Faith Hannah Lea, Daytona State College, FL.
- Completely revised and expanded: "Emotional Intelligence at Work."
- Updated: "Tech Tips: Emotional Intelligence."
- New: "Healthy Choices: Sleep."

Chapter 9

- No changes made.

Study Skills: A Toolbox for Active Learners

- Contains updated coverage from the Study Skills Plus version of *On Course*.

> The [*On Course*] curriculum is written in a way so as to assess study skills and soft skills without intimidation and provides information and exercises to develop them. Most importantly, [it] places emphasis on mastery through reflection and practice and offers a post self-assessment in order for the student and faculty to measure accomplishment and celebrate success!
>
> Jill Beauchamp,
> Washtenaw Community College

What's New in This Edition of On Course: MindTap

MindTap for *On Course*, ninth edition, is the digital learning solution that helps students take charge of their success by encouraging the creation of academic, professional, and personal goals, and prompting regular reflection on progress toward them. With the *On Course* self-assessments, its integrated personal success indicator and early-alert reporting feature, MindTap for *On Course* helps your students assess and improve the specific behaviors, attitudes, and skills that have been proven to lead to college and career success. It also helps you, as an instructor, to easily personalize student learning by seamlessly combining your own assignments, videos, open-source content, and innovative course activities with Cengage's market-leading content into a singular learning path designed to truly elevate student thinking. Ask your Cengage Account Executive for more details:

- **Design Your Path folder.** The Design Your Path folder empowers students to discover their resources, set goals, and plan out their future. In the "Discover Your Resources" activity, students familiarize themselves with the most common campus services for student health, academic success and individual needs. In the "Set Your Goals" activity, students reflect on what's most important to them and set short- and long-term goals for themselves. In the "Create an Academic and Career Plan" activity, students map out the courses, work, and extracurriculars in which they plan to take part to transfer or earn their degree.

- **What Would You Do? activities.** New "What Would You Do?" activities in every chapter tie course concepts to real-world scenarios. At each step, students must decide what they will do when presented with a task or challenge. After every choice, students learn about possible benefits and consequences for their actions, as well as strategies for increasing the likelihood of success.

- **How Transferable Are Your Skills?** activities. New "How Transferable Are Your Skills?" activities in every chapter invite students to connect their personal experiences with skills they will need in the professional world. Presented with a job description, students are tasked with identifying the transferable skills therein, connecting the dots between what they're learning in school and the working world.

- **Study Skills: A Toolbox for Active Learners.** Updated in 2022, this ninth edition MindTap now includes the Toolbox for Active Learners. Originally found in the Study Skills Plus version of *On Course*, students now have access to all the available study skills content in an easy to use, modular-style toolbox. The Study Skills Toolbox in MindTap begins with the Study Skills Self-Assessment, followed by study skill modules, and finally the summative Study Skills Quiz. Each study skill module includes:

  1. Reading: Each reading is focused on key strategies for improving study skills and includes ways to relate study skills to the professional world.

  2. Video Quiz: Each video quiz highlights concrete strategies and techniques students can use to improve their study skills in school and their career. Multiple-choice questions follow each video and test students' understanding of the skill and their ability to apply the strategies and techniques.

  3. Aplia Assignment: Each Aplia Assignment gives students the opportunity to apply what they learned in the reading and video. Aplia provides scenario-based, auto-graded problem sets with robust feedback to keep students on track.

Proven Features of On Course

The ninth edition includes all of the best features of *On Course*, updated and revised from the previous edition:

- **Self-Assessment.** *On Course* begins and ends with a self-assessment questionnaire of important non-cognitive skills ("soft skills"). Scores are provided for self-responsibility, self-motivation, self-management,

[*On Course*] is directed at students who live complicated lives; the One Student's Story feature is always relevant to somebody in the class. The case studies are a great way to start conversations that focus on the most urgent needs of students who are often the first in their family to navigate college.

Michelle Cochran,
Rochester Community and
Technical College

The *On Course* book and class have changed my students' lives; it gives them strategies to make wise choices and decisions that affect their college success, as well as life success. Students who had little hope begin to have hope for their lives and their futures.

Dorothy Collins, Eastern
Gateway Community
College

interdependence, self-awareness, lifelong learning, emotional intelligence, and belief in oneself. Imagine working with students who develop strengths in all of these inner qualities! Imagine how these qualities will affect the choices the students make and the outcomes and experiences they create. By completing the initial questionnaire, students immediately see areas that need strengthening. By completing the concluding questionnaire, students see their semester's growth. Students have the option of completing the self-assessment either in the text or online in MindTap®.

- **Articles on proven success strategies.** Thirty-two short articles explain powerful strategies for creating success in college and in life. Each article presents success strategies from diverse and influential figures in psychology, philosophy, business, sports, politics, and personal and professional growth. In these articles, students learn the "secrets" of extraordinarily successful individuals.

- **Guided journal entries.** A guided journal entry immediately follows each success strategy article, giving students an opportunity to apply the strategy they have just learned to enhance their results in college, career, and life. Many instructors of the course say the guided journal writings are extremely powerful in helping students make new and more effective choices, thus improving their academic success and persistence.

- **CORE Learning System.** All good learners employ four principles that lead to deep and lasting learning. Students learn how to use these four principles to create their own system for learning any subject or skill. The CORE Learning System is now solely offered online with the accompanying MindTap.

- **Case studies in critical thinking.** *On Course* case studies help students apply the strategies they are learning to real-life situations. As such, they help prepare students to make wise choices in the kinds of challenging situations they will likely face in college. These case studies promote critical and creative thinking because there is no clear "right" or "wrong" answer.

- **Focus on diversity.** The challenges and opportunities of interacting with new cultures is introduced in the first chapter ("Understanding the Culture of Higher Education"), is explored within many articles (e.g., Responsibility and Culture), and is more extensively examined in the article "Respecting Cultural Differences."

- ***On Course* principles "at Work."** These greatly expanded sections in each chapter show how important the *On Course* success strategies (soft skills) are for choosing the right career, getting hired, and succeeding in the work world.

I absolutely love these [*Case Studies for Critical Thinking*] and spend a lot of time with each of them. My favorite is "A Fish Story," and [I] start my semester with this one. I get students thinking about professors' expectations, their own expectations, motivation, taking the initiative, being prepared for class, and being organized.

Cindy Thorp, SUNY Alfred, College of Technology

The information about diversity and culture that is integrated throughout the text is a much more authentic way to discuss diversity and ethnicity rather than with a one-chapter focus.

Linda McMeen, North Hennepin Community College

Support Materials for Students and Instructors

For additional information or for help with accessing support materials related to *On Course*, contact your Cengage Account Executive. If you need help finding your account executive, visit *www.cengage.com/repfinder*.

EMBRACING TECHNOLOGY

- **MindTap.** MindTap for *On Course* combines tools like readings, quizzes, and digital activities to guide students through their course, powering them from memorization to mastery. For instructors, MindTap is the only platform that gives you complete ownership of your course. With it, you can challenge every student, build their confidence, and empower them to be unstoppable.

- **Cengage Infuse.** Cengage Infuse for College Success is the first-of-its-kind digital learning platform that fully integrates with your Learning Management System. Students never have to worry about where to find their course materials—no navigation skills required! Instructors can enjoy simple course setup and intuitive management tools with just the right amount of auto-graded content. For course setup, quickly choose assessments, quizzes, and eBook content to insert neatly into your course for worry-free, single point student access.

- **CSFI.** The College Success Factors Index (CSFI) is a personal success indicator that helps students identify their strengths and areas for growth in 10 key factors identified by researchers to affect college success. The CSFI now kicks off MindTap for *On Course*.

SUPPORT FOR STUDENTS

- **Cengage Unlimited.** The first-of-its-kind digital subscription designed specially to lower textbook costs. Students get total access to everything Cengage has to offer on demand—in one place. That's 20,000 eBooks, 2,300 digital learning products, and dozens of study tools across 70 disciplines and over 675 courses. Currently available in select markets. Details at *www.cengage.com/unlimited*.

SUPPORT FOR INSTRUCTORS

- **Revised Facilitator's Manual.** Designed to provide support for instructors new to the course, as well as innovative materials for experienced instructors, the Facilitator's Manual offers suggestions for in-person and online courses, including a complete list of activities from the print book

The At Work sections give students a specific venue to see how the soft skills they acquire will transfer to career success. Semester after semester students will share how their work situation improved as a result of what they learned and tried from the At Work sections. These sections are a natural fit in the *On Course* chapters, and they are packed with pertinent information.

Gail Janecka,
Victoria College

I use *On Course*…because the concepts are all so valuable in the grand scheme of life. In addition, they are presented in a very user-friendly way and the students are encouraged to apply them in college and in life, so results are observable by the end of the semester!

Jill Beauchamp,
Washtenaw Community College

and MindTap, discussion questions, and additional assignments. In it, you can also find a list of chapter objectives, key terms, chapter outlines, and more.

- **Updated Instructor Companion Site.** This free secure website provides educators with many resources to offer a course that empowers students to become active, responsible, and successful learners. Read the Facilitator's Manual, download PowerPoint slides, access a new test bank, and find a useful transition guide and MindTap Educator Guide for educators who used previous editions of *On Course* or are interested in using MindTap. To access the site, follow these steps:

  1. Visit *login.cengage.com.*
  2. If you have not previously created an account, choose "Create Account" and follow the prompts.
  3. If you have created an account previously, log in with your email address and password.
  4. Search for *On Course* to add the available additional digital resources to your bookshelf.

You will always need to return to *login.cengage.com* and enter your email address and password to sign in to access these resources. Use this space to write down your email address and password:

Email Address: _____

Password: _____

- ***On Course* Workshops and National Conference.** Skip Downing and Jonathan Brennan, authors of *On Course*, offer faculty development workshops for all educators who want to learn innovative strategies for empowering students to become active, responsible, and successful learners. These highly regarded professional development workshops are offered at conference centers across the United States, or you can host a one- to four-day event on your own campus. Online graduate courses (3 credits) are available as a follow-up to two of the workshops. Additionally, you are invited to attend the annual *On Course* National Conference, where learner-centered educators gather to share their best practices. For information about these workshops, graduate courses, and the national conference (including testimonials galore), go to *www.oncourseworkshop.com.* Questions? Email *workshop@oncourseworkshop.com* or call 650-365-7623.

- ***On Course* Newsletter.** All college educators are invited to subscribe to the free *On Course* e-Newsletter. Nearly 200,000 educators worldwide receive these emails with innovative, learner-centered strategies for engaging students in deep and lasting learning. To subscribe, simply go to *www.oncourseworkshop.com* and follow the easy, one-click directions. Or you can email a request to *workshop@oncourseworkshop.com.*

I*t is no exaggeration to say this *On Course* Workshop experience was transformative—both professionally and personally. This workshop will long remain a high point of my life. I am feeling energized and eager to start teaching my class next week. I can't wait to use all of my new teaching tools. I will absolutely recommend this workshop to other educators!

Lee Ann Adams, First-Year Seminar Coordinator, Indiana University East

S*ince first attending one of the summer retreats in 1997, I've held nine full On Course staff development trainings for our college, and I plan to offer more. They are invaluable! I strongly recommend this workshop for all faculty, counselors, advisors, administrators, and support staff.

Philip Rodriguez, Director, Student Affairs, Cerritos College

Acknowledgments

This book would not exist without the assistance of an extraordinary group of people. We can only hope that we have returned (or will return) their wonderful support in kind.

At Cengage Learning, we would like to especially thank Rebecca Charles for her wisdom, good cheer, hard work, and commitment to making this edition of *On Course* the best ever. Additionally, our thanks go to Courtney Bryant and Thalia Prum for their unflagging attention to details and encouraging guidance. At *On Course* Workshops, we'd like to thank the extraordinary support and wisdom of our colleagues and friends Robin Middleton, Deb Poese, Eileen Zamora, Mark McBride, LuAnn Wood, Amy Munson, Katherine Orille, and Carolina Williams. Thanks also to the 2,000-plus *On Course* Ambassadors, some of the most dedicated and caring educators in the world, who work tirelessly to empower their students and colleagues with *On Course* principles and practices.

Numerous wise and caring reviewers have made valuable contributions to this book, and many contributed exercises to the Facilitator's Manual, and we thank them for their contributions:

Madeline Adamczeski, San Jose City College
Trisha Alexander, Illinois Central College
Danielle Archambault, Wesley College
Dawn Bartlett, Jefferson Community College
Anitre Bell, Community College of Beaver County Garance
Blanchot-Aboubi, Normandale Community College
Elizabeth Catrini, Centenary University
Essie Childers, Blinn College
Dennis Cliborn, Kilgore College
Christina Davis, Century College
Mary Catherine Denmark, Austin Peay State University
Cami Eastep, Walla Walla Community College
Linda Eckert, Ivy Tech Community College
Lauren Gatto, Truckee Meadows Community College
Betsy Goetz, Riverland Community College
Sherrill Goodlive, Harrisburg Area Community College
Jim Kain, Neumann University
Charlene Latimer, Daytona State College
Lea Beth Lewis, Cal State Fullerton
Margaret Major, Harrisburg Area Community College
Melanie Marine, University of Wisconsin–Oshkosh

Christine McDermott, Wesley College
Venetia Ann Miller, JSU
Kathryn Montalbano, Dominican University
Amber Peplow, Ph.D., University of Cincinnati–Blue Ash College
June Pomann, Union County College
Beverly Russell, College of Southern Maryland
Pratima Sampat-Mar, Pima Medical Institute
Jo Allison Scott, Northeast Wisconsin Technical College
Angela C. Thering, Buffalo State College
Lisa Theriot, El Centro Community College
Kim Thomas, Polk State College
Cheryl Veronda, Centenary University
Bernie Vrona, Hennepin Technical College
Kate Wells, North Country Community College
Gary Williams, Crafton Hills College
LuAnn Wood, Century College
Tami Wooden, American River College

Special thanks to Lauren Hensley of The Ohio State University for updates made in 2022 to Study Skills: A Toolbox for Active Learners for *On Course*. Her ability to enhance this portion of the text by making it more accessible to learners of all types and by increasing its focus on the relevance and importance of study skills will equip students well into their futures. Finally, our deep gratitude goes out to the students who over the years have had the courage to explore and change their thoughts, actions, feelings, and beliefs. We hope, as a result, you have all lived richer, more personally fulfilling lives. We know we have.

On Course is the result of my own quest to live a rich, personally fulfilling life and my strong desire to pass on what I've learned to my students. As such, *On Course* is a very personal book, for me and for you. I invite you to explore in depth what success means to you. I suggest that if you want to achieve your greatest potential in college, your career, and in life, dig deep inside yourself, where you already possess everything you need to make your dreams come true.

During my first two decades of teaching college courses, I consistently observed a sad and perplexing puzzle. Each semester I watched students sort themselves into two groups. One group achieved varying degrees of academic success, from those who excelled to those who just squeaked by. The other group struggled mightily; then they withdrew, disappeared, or failed. But, here's the puzzling part. The struggling students often displayed as much academic potential as their more successful classmates, and in some cases more. What, I wondered, causes the vastly different outcomes of these two groups? And what could I do to help my struggling students achieve greater success?

Somewhere around my 20th year of teaching, I experienced a series of crises in both my personal and professional lives. In a word, I was struggling. After a period of feeling sorry for myself, I embarked on a quest to improve the quality of my life. I read, I took seminars and workshops, I talked with wise friends and acquaintances, I kept an in-depth journal, I saw a counselor, and I even returned to graduate school to add a master's degree in applied psychology to my doctoral degree in English. I was seriously motivated to change my life for the better.

If I were to condense all that I learned into one sentence, it would be this: **People who are successful—by their own definition—consistently make wiser choices than people who struggle.** I came to see that the quality of my life was essentially the result of all of my previous choices. I saw how the wisdom (or lack of wisdom) of my choices influenced, and often determined, the outcomes and experiences of my life. The same, of course, was true for my struggling students.

For three decades, I have continued my quest to identify the inner qualities that empower a person to make consistently wise choices, the very choices that lead to success in college, career, and in life. As a result of what I learned (and continue to learn), I created a course at my college called the College Success Seminar. This course was a departure from traditional student success courses because instead of focusing primarily on study skills and campus resources, it focused on empowering students from the inside out. I had come to believe that most students who struggle in college are perfectly capable of earning a degree and that their struggles go far deeper than not knowing study skills or failing to use campus resources. As a result, I envisioned a course that would empower students to develop their natural inner strengths, the qualities that would help them make the wise choices that would create the very outcomes and experiences they wanted in college . . . and in life. When I couldn't find a book that did this, I wrote *On Course*. A few years later, I created a series of professional development workshops to share what I had learned with other educators who wanted to see their students soar. Then, to provide an opportunity for workshop graduates to continue to exchange their experiences and wisdom, I started a listserv, and this growing group of educators soon named themselves the *On Course* Ambassadors, sharing *On Course* strategies with their students and colleagues alike. Later, I created two online graduate courses that further help college educators learn cutting-edge strategies for empowering their students to be more successful in college and in life. To launch the second decade of *On Course*, the *On Course* Ambassadors hosted the first of many *On Course* National Conferences, bringing together an overflow crowd of educators hungry for new ways to help their students achieve more of their potential in college and in life. Every one of these efforts appeals to a deep place in me because they all have the power to change people's lives for the better. But that's not the only appeal. These activities also help *me* stay conscious of the wise choices I must consistently make to live a richer, more personally fulfilling life.

Now that much of my life is back on course, I don't want to forget how I got here!

Skip Downing

Back when I was a student, I didn't know many of the skills in *On Course,* but I sure could have used them. I made some unwise choices, found myself failing classes, and eventually dropped out of high school. I lost sight of my dream of going to college. It took me years to make my way back to college, but once I did, I learned how to make wiser choices, develop better habits, and take more responsibility for my learning and my future. I completed college and went on to earn four graduate degrees. I've learned a few things on my journey (sometimes the hard way), and I hope you're open to learning some new life lessons too.

In my early years as a professor, I saw many students struggling with the same problems I had. These students had so much potential, but I saw them making unwise choices, failing classes, then dropping out. I really wanted to help these students stay in college and realize their dreams.

Twenty years ago, I began to learn how I could help these students. I had an opportunity to attend a multi-day *On Course* Workshop led by Dr. Skip Downing. Within the first 45 minutes, I was excited to learn that the workshop provided the answers to two questions I had been pondering for many years: (1) Why do so many of my students struggle in my classes, and at the college? and (2) How can I help these students succeed?

Energized and focused, I returned to my college with fresh ideas, a new perspective, and a bold plan. I proposed that we start a student success program, and within one year, we did. In our new success courses, students learned *On Course* skills and how to apply them to make wiser choices. The challenges were significant because many of the students at our college dropped out within their first year. However, after starting our new program, student retention increased by 22 percent! That meant many more students were learning how to be successful in college, in their careers, and in life.

Once I saw what a powerful impact the program had on students in my classes, and on students across the college, I made a commitment: I will significantly increase retention and graduation rates for one million college students. I had no idea how I would make that happen, but nevertheless I committed to it.

I eventually realized that I would need to teach many other educators how to use these strategies with their students. After years of training to become a facilitator of *On Course* Workshops, I began to travel to colleges and universities across North America, eventually working with thousands of educators. I also offered to chair the *On Course* National Conference, where nearly 5,000 educators have come together to learn new success strategies. I calculated how many educators I would need to reach to impact a million students. After 12 years I accomplished my goal, and I promptly reset the goal to impact 10 million students.

Working with Skip as co-author of the *On Course* text is my next step toward reaching my new goal. Please join the over one million students who have used *On Course* to achieve their dreams. I'm pleased with the many new tools we offer in this ninth edition. I hope you will take advantage of the skills you will learn in *On Course*, and that you will use them at college, in the workplace, and for the rest of your life.

So, get on board and travel with us on a new adventure. You'll discover new strengths, develop effective habits, and dream up a great future for yourself.

Getting On Course
to Your Success

Successful Students . . .

▶ **accept personal responsibility,** seeing themselves as the primary cause of their outcomes and experiences.

▶ **discover self-motivation,** finding purpose in their lives by pursuing personally meaningful goals and dreams.

▶ **master self-management,** consistently planning and taking purposeful actions in pursuit of their goals and dreams.

▶ **employ interdependence,** building mutually supportive relationships that help them achieve their goals and dreams (while helping others do the same).

Struggling Students . . .

▶ **see themselves as victims,** believing that what happens to them is determined primarily by external forces such as fate, luck, and powerful others.

▶ **have difficulty sustaining motivation,** often feeling depressed, frustrated, and/or resentful about a lack of direction in their lives.

▶ **seldom identify specific actions needed to accomplish a desired outcome** and, when they do, tend to procrastinate.

▶ **are stubbornly independent,** seldom requesting, even rejecting, offers of assistance from those who could help, and failing to build effective and supportive relationships with others.

College Smart-Start Guide

If you've ever bought a new computer, tablet, or smartphone, you'll recall that it came with a user's manual. The user's manual—whether in print or online—is many pages long and contains all you need to know to get the most from your new device.

Think of *On Course* as your user's manual for higher education. It explains how to get the most out of college. In these pages, you'll discover how to learn effectively, how to get high grades, and how to earn the degree you want. As a bonus, many of the strategies you'll learn will help you achieve success in other key areas of your life, including your career.

Most computers also come with a brief guide that's only a few pages long. This guide describes the essential steps for getting your computer up and running quickly and successfully.

This Smart-Start Guide has that same intention for college. Complete the following actions before the end of your first week in college, and you'll be off to a great start. Some of these actions can be done in a few minutes. Others take longer. You can do them in any order you choose.

So, read and do the following lucky 13 actions. Be smart—complete one of them right now. Do a couple more every day, and you'll have them all done by the end of your first week. By then, you'll be on course to great success in higher education.

WHAT TO DO DURING YOUR FIRST WEEK IN COLLEGE

GET FAMILIAR

1. **Learn your campus.** Find out where things are so you begin to feel comfortable. What's in the various buildings? Where will you find the many services designed to help you succeed? To orient yourself, get a campus map. There's probably one on your college's website.

If your campus offers tours, take one. If not, ask a college employee or an experienced student to show you around. Or ask another first-year student to join you on a self-guided tour. As a last resort, explore on your own. See if you can fill in the location and hours for all of the services listed in Figure 1.1.

Service	Location	Hours
College Bookstore		
Advising Office		
Counseling Office		
Student Activities Office		
Financial Aid Office		
Career Center		
Registrar's Office		
Library		

FIGURE 1.1

Service	Location	Hours
Tutoring or Academic Support		
Computer Center or Lab		
Dining Facilities		
Fitness Center		
Athletic Facilities		
Student Center		
Copy Center		
Public Safety		
Health Services		
Other?		
Other?		

© 2017 Cengage Learning

FIGURE 1.1 (*Continued*)

2. **Locate your classrooms.** Find and visit every room in which you have a class. Nothing ruins your first week like missing classes because you can't find the rooms. You'll likely find a list of your courses and classrooms on the document you received when you registered. Use this information to fill in the first two columns in Figure 1.2.

3. **Learn your instructors' names, office locations, and office hours.** Instructors' names are usually listed on your registration document next to each course. If an instructor is listed as "TBA"—or something other than a name—an instructor has not yet been assigned to the class. (TBA stands for "to be announced.") In that case, you'll need to get your instructor's name at the department office or the first class meeting. In Figure 1.2, record your instructors' names, office locations, and office hours. Office hours are times when instructors are in their office and available for appointments . . . and you'll want to make an appointment soon. This additional information will likely be on the first-day handout for each class. (A first-day handout is often called a "syllabus.")

4. **Study—don't just skim—the first-day handout (syllabus) for each course.** The syllabus is a contract between you and your instructor. In it, your instructor presents essential information about the course. Typically, a syllabus contains:

   a) a course description (usually the same description as in the college catalog);

Course	Classroom	Instructor	Office	Office Hours

FIGURE 1.2

▶

b) learning objectives (what you are expected to learn in the course);

c) homework assignments (possibly every assignment for the entire course);

d) exam schedule (when you'll be tested);

e) how your final grade will be determined (how much each assignment is worth);

f) course rules (what to do and not do, along with consequences);

g) website address (if course materials are posted online); and

h) information about the instructor (name, office location, and office hours).

The syllabus may be the single most important document your instructors provide, so read it carefully. Now is the time to ask questions about the syllabus. Your instructors will assume that if you stay in the course, you understand the syllabus and agree to abide by it.

GET ORGANIZED

5. **Get all your learning supplies.** Every job has both a purpose and essential tools. Job #1 in college is deep learning. Deep learning occurs when you have a thorough understanding of the subject and can carry this knowledge with you for the rest of your life. So, make a list of all the supplies you'll need in order to learn, such as books, a computer/laptop/tablet, calculator, notebooks, three-ring binders, notepaper, pens, monthly calendars, weekly calendars, folders, and flash drives. Of these supplies, arguably the most essential are your textbooks. Required texts are listed in each syllabus (first-day handout). They can be purchased in your campus bookstore and perhaps online as well. Ideally, you'll have your textbooks in hand before your first class meeting. At the latest, get them before the end of Week 1, because any later can sabotage your success. College instructors move quickly and expect you to come to class prepared. If you're just starting to read your assignments in Week 3, your chances of success plunge.

6. **Create a schedule.** Adding college assignments and activities to your life can be overwhelming. A schedule is essential for getting everything important done on time. Whether your schedule is on paper, on your smartphone, online, or you use some other method, tracking your commitments is essential. Make a weekly schedule showing recurring events such as classes, study times, or work. Make a monthly calendar showing due dates for occasional events such as tests, term papers, or meetings with instructors. You'll find weekly and monthly calendars in the section called "Creating a Leak-Proof Self-Management System" in Chapter 4.

7. **Get comfortable with campus technology.** The use of technology is common on college campuses. Check each course syllabus to see what technology your instructors expect you to use. They may send you course updates using campus email. Or expect you to access online resources for their classes. You may be taking a class that is offered partly or entirely online via a course management system (CMS). Some of the more common course management systems are Blackboard (BB), Desire to Learn (D2L), Canvas, and Moodle. It's possible your instructor will arrange some technology help for your class. Regardless, be proactive. Go to your campus computer lab and see if an

▶

orientation is offered. If not, ask someone in the computer lab to help you learn what you need to know (as defined in each course syllabus). Or find a classmate with good technology skills and ask for help.

8. **Manage your money.** Money problems have sabotaged many students' success in college. Some have had to drop out of college to work. Others have tried working full-time while attending college, but they became overwhelmed. An important step toward understanding your financial situation is creating a budget. That will tell you (in case you don't already know) if money is going to be an obstacle to your success in college. If you're serious about your education, there are many options to help you overcome the money obstacle. You'll find many suggestions about money management later in this chapter.

GET SERIOUS

9. **Set goals for each course.** Make a list of your courses. Next to each one, write your target grade for the course. Then write a goal for the most important thing or things you want to learn in the course.

10. **Attend all classes and arrive on time.** Class attendance is essential to success in college. Remember, Job #1 as a student is deep learning, and learning starts in the classroom. Many college instructors do not take attendance, but don't mistakenly think that means you don't need to be there.

11. **Participate in every class.** Active engagement is the key to deep learning. (Remember, deep learning means you've gained a thorough understanding of the subject and can carry this knowledge with you for the rest of your life.) Attend each class having done all assignments beforehand. Ask questions about your homework. Answer questions your instructors ask. When instructors facilitate an activity, they're intending that you learn something important through the experience. Participate at a high level and look for the learning.

12. **Complete and hand in all assignments on time.** Make a list of all assignments and their due dates. Record them, along with test dates, on your monthly calendar so you can see them coming. Check them off as you finish each one. Here's the double benefit. First, you'll learn more when you attend classes having completed all assigned homework. As a bonus, you'll reduce the stress that many first-year college students experience when they fall behind.

13. **Commit to your success.** At the end of your first week, think back over your experiences with each course. Be honest with yourself. Will you make the time necessary to do all of the work? Are you prepared to give the course your best effort? If not, discuss your concerns with your adviser or a counselor. If your concerns continue, now may be the time to drop the course (and perhaps pick up another course in its place). But if your answer is "yes" to doing all of the course work and giving it your very best effort, then write out this solemn commitment and post it where you will see it every day: *I promise myself to give a 100 percent effort every day to every course. Nothing will keep me from achieving success!*

Understanding the Culture of Higher Education

FOCUS QUESTIONS   What is unique about the culture of higher education? How does understanding that culture increase your chances of success in college?

In some ways, enrolling in college is like moving to a foreign country. That's because the culture of higher education is different from other cultures you have known, even that of high school.

"Be prepared to encounter cultural references that we're just not going to get."

Frank Cotham/The New Yorker Collection/The Cartoon Bank

Geert Hofstede, a Dutch psychologist and anthropologist, has studied cultures all over the world. According to Hofstede, culture is "the collective programming of the mind that distinguishes the members of one human group from another." Every culture on Earth is programmed to operate by its own unique software. And this is true of higher education as well. The sooner you understand the culture of higher education, the sooner you will be on course to success.

Some aspects of a culture are obvious and visible, whereas others are subtle and invisible. To understand the distinction between visible and invisible culture, Brooks Peterson, author of *Cultural Intelligence*, suggests picturing an iceberg (see Figure 1.3). Above the waterline are the elements of culture we can perceive with our five senses. "Surface" culture includes such things as food, fashions, language, gestures, games, art, music, holidays, and some customs. For example, when someone speaks with a noticeable accent (different from yours), you know immediately he is from a different culture.

> Toto, I have a feeling we're not in Kansas anymore.
>
> Dorothy, in *The Wizard of Oz*

Below the waterline you'll find the more stable and significant features of "deep culture." Most of these features are invisible to tourists and recent immigrants. Deep culture consists of the shared beliefs, attitudes, norms, rules, opinions, expectations, and taboos of a group of people. For natives, these deep-culture features are usually taken for granted until someone disobeys them. Here's a simple example. When you arrive at a ticket line, what do you do? If you're from a culture that expects to wait or stand in a line, you automatically go to the end of the line. No sign is needed because everyone knows that's what you're supposed to do. You probably don't even think about it unless someone cuts in front of you. When someone defies a cultural rule, others get upset. Cultural programs help a group or society run smoothly by keeping people in line (literally and figuratively).

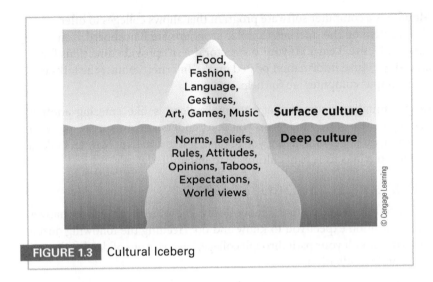

FIGURE 1.3   Cultural Iceberg

Culture, then, is the collection of surface- and deep-level customs and beliefs that are passed on from generation to generation. Each culture provides "approved" choices at significant, and even insignificant, forks in the road. Culture tells us, "This choice is normal and that one is strange." Or, "This choice is right and that one is wrong." Or, "This choice is good and that choice is bad." At each fork in the road, our inner programs give us a nudge in the culturally approved direction.

To put it succinctly, "Culture is the way we do things around here."

THE SURFACE CULTURE OF HIGHER EDUCATION

Because college is a unique culture, expect some challenges as you adapt. But fear not . . . you will adapt and very soon feel comfortable. Most differences in surface culture will be pretty obvious. They include factors such as class sizes; appropriate dress; amount of homework assigned; students' races, ages, religions; holidays observed; courses offered; and methods of teaching. Like all cultures, higher education has its own language, so you'll probably hear words that sound foreign to you. Suppose your instructor announces, "The directions for the assignment are posted in the course syllabus on Moodle." These directions make little sense if you don't know the lingo. But it's not really that complicated. Here's what the natives of college culture know:

- A **syllabus** is a document that most instructors provide at the first class session. It contains essential information about the course such as learning objectives, homework assignments, course rules, and how the course grade is determined. If you recognized the term "syllabus" from the Smart-Start Guide, congratulations. You're already learning to speak "college."

Schools, like ethnic groups, have their own cultures: languages, ways of doing things, values, attitudes toward time, standards of appropriate behavior, and so on. As participants in schools, students are expected to adopt, share, and exhibit these cultural patterns. If they do not or cannot, they are likely to be censured and made to feel uncomfortable in a variety of ways.

Jean Moule, *Cultural Competence*

- **Moodle** is a computer software program that allows colleges to offer class content on the Internet. (Similar programs are Blackboard, Canvas, and Desire2Learn.) If your instructor doesn't provide directions for accessing course information posted on the Internet, contact the folks in your campus computer lab for help.

Keep reminding yourself that entering college is like entering another country. If you hear words and terms you don't understand, be sure to ask what they mean. It won't be long before you're talking like a native. Now let's take a look at a less obvious feature of cultures than unfamiliar words.

ONE DOZEN COLLEGE CUSTOMS

Higher education, like all cultures, has customs. These are the things the natives of higher education expect you to know and do. Heeding the following dozen customs will smooth your path through college, keep you out of dead ends, and speed you on to graduation:

W hat we call customs rest on top and are most apparent. Deepest and least apparent are the cultural values that give meaning and direction to life. Values influence people's perceptions of needs and their choice between perceived alternative courses of action.

Benjamin Paul, anthropologist

1. **Read your college catalog.** Catalogs are usually available in the registrar's or counseling office. Many colleges also post a copy on their website. A catalog contains most of the factual information you'll need to plot a successful journey through higher education. It explains how your college applies many of the customs discussed in this section. So, keep a college catalog on hand and refer to it often. By the way, if a requirement in the catalog changes after you enroll at a college, usually you are bound by only the rules that existed when you first entered. So hold on to your past catalogs.

2. **Create a long-term educational plan.** This plan lists all of the courses you'll take from now until graduation. It assures that you *do* take all required courses and *don't* take any unrequired courses (unless you want to). Colleges provide someone to help you create an educational plan. This person could be an adviser, a counselor, or even an instructor (especially if you have chosen a major—see #5 below). Find out who this person is and make an appointment. It's never too early to map out your straightest route to graduation. Like most plans, it can always be revised.

3. **Complete general education requirements.** Look in your college catalog for a list of general education courses. Almost all colleges and universities require students to complete a minimum number of credits in general education. Your institution may call them something else, such as *core requirements, core curriculum,* or *general curriculum.* Regardless of their name, the purpose of general education requirements is to expose you to a number of broad areas of study—for example, natural sciences, communication, technology, math, languages, humanities, and social and behavioral science. Typically, you'll need to complete a certain number of credits in some or all of these areas. Regardless of how many credits you earn, you can't earn a degree until you've completed all general education

requirements. That's why your long-term educational plan (#2 above) will always include the general education courses you intend to take.

4. **Complete prerequisites and corequisites.** A prerequisite is a course that must be successfully completed before taking a more advanced course. For example, colleges usually require passing algebra before taking calculus. Before you register for courses each semester, check each course description in your college catalog. Any prerequisites will be identified in the course description. Confirm you have completed all prerequisites before registering for a course. A corequisite, which will also be identified in the course description, is a course that must be taken at the same time as another course. Verify and enroll in any corequisites.

5. **Choose a major.** You'll usually choose a major area of study in your first or second year. Examples of majors include nursing, English, mechanical engineering, economics, and commercial art. You'll take many courses in your major, supplemented by general education and elective courses. (An elective is a course you don't have to take but want to.) Having a career goal makes choosing your major easier. If you are undecided about a career, visit your campus career center. There you'll get help identifying careers that fit your interests, talents, and personality. All majors and their required courses are listed in your college catalog. Until you've entered a major, you're wise to concentrate on completing your general education requirements. That will ensure that all the credits you earn will count toward your degree.

6. **Meet with your instructors during their office hours.** Most college instructors have regular office hours. These times are usually included in the course syllabus and may also be posted on the instructor's office door. You can make an appointment before or after class, or you can call the instructor's office. Be sure to show up on time (or call beforehand to reschedule). Arrive with a goal. Maybe you'd like your instructor to clarify a comment she wrote on your English composition. Or you'd like suggestions for how to better prepare for your next math test. Another important reason to meet with your instructors is to establish a friendly relationship and make yourself more than just a name on a course roster. Building such relationships will go a long way to help if you ever need special assistance.

7. **Know the importance of your grade point average (GPA).** Your GPA is the average grade for all of the courses you have taken in college. At most colleges, GPAs range from 0.0 ("F") to 4.0 ("A"). Your GPA affects your future in many ways. At most colleges, a minimum GPA (often 2.0, a "C") is required to graduate, regardless of how many credits you have earned. Students who fall below the minimum GPA may be placed on probation and are usually ineligible for financial aid and cannot play intercollegiate sports. Students with very low GPAs are in danger of academic dismissal. Academic honors (such as the dean's list) and some scholarships are based

on your GPA. Finally, potential employers may look at GPAs to determine if prospective employees have achieved success in college.

8. **Know how to compute your grade point average (GPA).** At most colleges, GPAs are printed on a student's transcript, which is a list of courses completed (with the grades earned). You can get a copy of your transcript from the registrar's office. Transcripts are usually free or available for a nominal charge. You can compute your own grade point average by using the formula in the following box. Or you can do it online at back2college .com/gpa.htm. At most colleges, credits in developmental (basic skills) courses do not count toward graduation, so they may or may not be used by your college for calculating a GPA. For example, if you were taking three courses and one was developmental, your GPA might be determined by only the grades you received in the two nondevelopmental courses. To check your school's policy about this issue, read your college catalog or ask a counselor or adviser.

9. **If you stop attending a class, withdraw officially.** Students are enrolled in a course until they're *officially* withdrawn. Do not assume that someone else will withdraw you from a course if you stop attending. A student who stops attending is still on the class roster at semester's end when grades are assigned, and the instructor will very likely give the nonattending student an "F." That failing grade is now a permanent part of the student's record, lowering his or her GPA. If you decide—for whatever

---

Formula for Computing Your Grade Point Average (GPA)

$$\frac{(G1 \times C1) + (G2 \times C2) + (G3 \times C3) + (G4 \times C4) + \cdots (Gn + Cn)}{\text{Total \# of Credits Attempted}}$$

In this formula, G is the grade in a course and C is number of credits for a course. For example, suppose you had the following grades:

"A" in Math 110 (4 Credits)	G1 ("A") = 4.0
"B" in English 101 (3 Credits)	G2 ("B") = 3.0
"C" in Sociology 101 (3 Credits)	G3 ("C") = 2.0
"D" in Music 104 (2 Credits)	G4 ("D") = 1.0
"F" in Physical Education 109 (1 Credit)	G5 ("F") = 0.0

Here's how to figure the GPA from the grades above:

$$\frac{(4.0 \times 4) + (3.0 \times 3) + (2.0 \times 3) + (1.0 \times 2) + (0.0 \times 1)}{4 + 3 + 3 + 2 + 1} = \frac{16 + 9 + 6 + 2 + 0}{13} = 2.54$$

reason—to stop attending a class, first go to the financial aid office to see if a withdrawal will affect your financial aid. If not, go to the online student portal or the registrar's office to officially withdraw. Make certain that you withdraw before your college's deadline. This date is often about halfway through a course.

10. **Talk to your instructor before withdrawing.** If you're sure you're going to fail a course, withdraw to protect your GPA. But don't withdraw without speaking to your instructor first. Sometimes students think they are doing far worse than they really are. Discuss with your instructor what you need to do to pass the course and make a step-by-step plan. Be sure to discuss your plans with your adviser as well. Advisers might have insights about what will be best for your general education or major requirements. If you discover that failing is inevitable, withdraw officially.

11. **Know your lifetime eligibility for financial aid.** Financial aid sources often restrict the total amount of money you can receive. Pell Grants, for example, limit students to a lifetime maximum of six times their yearly award. If your yearly award is $3,000, then the maximum Pell money you can receive in your lifetime is $18,000 (6 $\times$ $3,000). This means, be careful about failing and/or dropping too many classes. Doing so eats up your award but doesn't move you toward completing your degree. After your financial aid runs out, you're on your own to pay for college—even if you have many more courses to pass in order to graduate. Check on your lifetime eligibility at your college's financial aid office.

12. **Keep a record of important documents.** Forms get lost in large organizations such as colleges and universities. Save everything that may affect your future in a paper file or downloaded into a folder on your desktop or on the cloud. (If you save it on your desktop, make sure it's backed up to an external hard drive or USB device, such as a flash drive, in case your computer crashes.) These include each course syllabus, completed tests and assignments, approved registration forms, scholarship applications, scholarship award notices, transcripts, and paid bills. If you're exempted from a college requirement or course prerequisite, get it in writing and add the document to your files. A year later when a college official says to you, "Sorry, but you can't do that," it's a great feeling to easily find a signed approval letter, and—ta da!—present it to the college official.

WRITE A GREAT LIFE

One of the best things about the culture of higher education is that it offers the perfect opportunity to design a life worth living. A time-tested tool for this purpose is a journal, a written record of your thoughts and feelings, hopes and dreams, life lessons and next steps. Journal writing is a way to explore your life in depth and discover your best "self." This self-awareness will enable you to develop the skills needed for success in college and beyond.

Many people who keep journals do what is called "free writing." They simply write whatever thoughts come to mind. This approach can be extremely valuable for exploring issues present in one's mind at any given moment.

In *On Course*, however, you'll write a guided journal. This approach is like going on a journey with an experienced guide. Your guide takes you places and shows you sights you might never have discovered on your own.

Before writing each journal entry, you'll read an article about proven success strategies. Then you'll apply the strategies to your own life by completing the guided journal entry that follows the article. Here are five guidelines for creating a meaningful journal:

> Journal work is an excellent approach to uncovering hidden truths about ourselves.
>
> Marsha Sinetar

1. **Copy the directions for each step into your journal (just the bold print).** Having the directions in front of you will help keep you focused while writing. Also when you find your journal in a drawer or computer file 20 years from now, having the directions in your journal will help you make sense of what you've written. Underline or bold the directions to distinguish them from your answers.

2. **Be spontaneous.** Write whatever comes to mind in response to the directions. Imagine pouring liquid thoughts into your journal without pausing to edit or rewrite. Unlike public writings, such as an English composition or a history research paper, your journal is a private document written primarily for your own benefit.

3. **Be honest.** As you write, tell yourself the absolute truth; honesty leads to your most significant discoveries about yourself and your success.

4. **Be creative.** Add favorite quotations, sayings, and poems. Use color, drawings, clip art, and photographs. Express your best creative "self."

5. **Dive deep.** When you think you have exhausted a topic, write more. Your most valuable thoughts will often take the longest to surface. So, most of all—DIVE DEEP!

> I write because I don't know what I think until I read what I say.
>
> Flannery O'Connor

Whether you hand-write your journal or compose it on a computer, I* urge you to keep all of your journal entries together in one book or file. If you do, one day many years from now, you'll have the extraordinary pleasure of reading this autobiography of your growing wisdom about creating success in college and in life.

Let me explain why guided journals are worth your best effort. There is a huge gulf between knowledge and achievement. Reading about success strategies in *On Course* will give you knowledge to be successful. But applying the strategies to your life—as you will do in your journal—will *make* you successful. Sure, it would be easier to simply read about the strategies. But that would be like reading about exercising and wondering why you aren't getting in shape. If you're serious about creating success in college, I urge you to dive deep in every journal you write. In the very near future, you'll be very glad you did.

*When you see a first-person pronoun (I, me, my, mine), that is author Skip Downing speaking. When you see a first-person pronoun followed by (JB), that is author Jonathan Brennan speaking.

JOURNAL ENTRY / 1

In this activity, you'll explore various aspects of surface culture and customs you have experienced in school.

> **Remember:** The five guidelines for creating a meaningful journal appear earlier in this section. Please review these guidelines before writing. Especially remember to copy the directions for each step (just the bold print) into your journal before writing . . . and then DIVE DEEP!

1 **Contrast the surface culture of your most recent educational experience (high school, another college or university, or a trade school) with that of your current school.** From the following list, choose *two* or more surface-level features where they differ. Then, in a separate paragraph for each feature, explain how the two are different. Explain the advantages and/or disadvantages you see in your present higher education culture as compared with your previous educational culture(s).

Number of students in a class	Age of students
Race or ethnicity of students	Economic class of students
Courses offered	Amount of homework
Popular out-of-school activities	Teachers' treatment of students
Alcohol	Academic preparation of educators
In-groups	Religions
Clothes	Food
Languages spoken	Dialects spoken
Sports	Amount of writing assigned
Amount of reading assigned	Drugs
Architecture of buildings	Favorite music
Holidays observed	Out-groups
Attendance policy	Methods of teaching
Involvement of parents	Classrooms

Here's how your journal entry might begin if you chose "Age of students" as the topic you'll explore in Step 1 of your journal entry:

> I graduated from high school last year and the ages of students there ranged from about 14 to 18 years old. Here in college the ages of students range from about 18 to 50 or even older. In my math class this semester, I have a mother and daughter who are taking the class together. Overall, students here in college seem to average about 10 years older than students in high school. A couple of the older students that I've talked with went to college before and dropped out. These returning students seem to be more highly motivated and they take their schoolwork more seriously than the younger

▶

My journal from this course is the most valuable possession I own. I will cherish it always.

Joseph Haskins, student

> **JOURNAL ENTRY** ⟩ **1** *continued*

students. For example, they hardly ever miss a class and they always turn in their homework. Maybe what I should do is. . . .

2 **From the section "Understanding the Culture of Higher Education," explore the one college custom with which you feel most uncomfortable.** Address some or all of the following questions: What is the cause of your discomfort? How big a problem do you think this custom will be for you? What additional information do you want to learn about this custom? Where can you find that information? Who could help you feel more comfortable? How do you think other students in your class feel about this custom? For example, if you decide to examine "Choose a major," your journal entry might begin like this:

> I'm a little uncomfortable about choosing a major. The truth is I have no idea what career I want to pursue. I just know I have to make a change. I've been out of high school for 10 years and I've been working construction. I sure don't want to do that for the rest of my life. The work is physically demanding, and it's hard on some of the older guys. I don't want to be 60 years old and going up and down a ladder all day. So I know what I don't want, but not what I do want. I didn't really have any favorite subjects when I was in high school. I did okay academically, but mostly I enjoyed playing sports. A guy in one of my classes says he wants to be a doctor. His father is a doctor, so he has a really good idea what a doctor's life is like. My father sells real estate, but I don't want to do that. He's never home in the evenings or on weekends, so I didn't see him much when I was growing up. When I have a family, I want to be around to see my kids grow up. I hope I don't have to choose a major too soon. If I do, I'll probably wind up changing it a couple of times. I guess that wouldn't be so bad except I heard that by switching I could lose some credits and that could make me take longer to graduate. To pick a good major for me, what I need to find out is . . .

T he heart and soul of school culture is what people believe, the assumptions they make about how school works.

Thomas Sergiovanni

ONE STUDENT'S STORY

KINEESHA GEORGE, *San Juan College, New Mexico*

One question I was always hesitant to answer is "What are your goals?" The honest answer was, "I don't have any." In my first semester at San Juan College,

it didn't bother me not to have goals. I took general studies courses, thinking I would eventually find what I like. But time went by and nothing changed.

I began missing classes, skipping assignments, and dropping or failing classes. My GPA sunk so low I was facing probation and suspension, so I dropped out. While working a minimum-wage cashier job at a Chinese restaurant, I thought a lot about my future. Do I really want this

▶

to be my life? Or, do I want to go back to school and improve my future?

I thought so much about it that I made an appointment with an academic adviser. I realized I was finally ready to face the bad choices I had made the first time I enrolled in college. The adviser helped me register, and one of the classes was the student success course. Actually, I had taken this class before, but I didn't really get into it, fell behind, and failed.

This second time, however, I started the success class with a positive attitude. The instructor assigned us to write two *On Course* journals each week. The first couple of entries I wrote quickly to get them out of the way, just like the first time I had taken the course. Before long, however, I realized I was putting more passion and personality into my journals. I added personal experiences, thoughts, and feelings to each

entry, and my journals became much longer. To be creative, I even decorated my journal entries with pictures, quotes, borders, and anything that related to my writings.

I found that diving deep in my journals opened my mind to things I hadn't thought about before. When we wrote about goals, I got more specific about what I wanted to do with my life. I started writing about being a registered nurse. That made me look on the Internet to learn more about that career, like how long it would take to earn the degree and what I would be doing as a nurse. When we created a life plan, I set short-term goals to get A's in my classes. We also wrote journals about what we do with our time. I discovered that I spend a lot of time doing unimportant things, like watching YouTube videos, when I should be doing my homework or studying for a test. I used to procrastinate on things that

are important to me, but now I schedule what I need to do. I also wrote journal entries about personal things such as how shy I am and that I wanted to speak up more in class. My instructor wrote back saying we could work on that. She started asking me questions in class, and that helped me get out of my shell. In fact, I've even become more bold and courageous in my other classes as well.

The first time I took this course, I just skimmed along and didn't put my heart into it. I didn't learn anything and just wasted my time. The second time in the course, I really took it seriously, especially diving deep in my journals. My advice is if you do this, you'll learn a lot about yourself and how to be successful in college. Maybe you'll even be able to say, as I do, that this turned out to be my favorite class.

Photo: Courtesy of Kineesha George

Understanding the Expectations of College and University Educators

FOCUS QUESTIONS What is the deep culture of higher education? How can this knowledge help you get the most value from your college or university experience?

Having explored elements of the *surface* culture of higher education, you may now be wondering, "What should I know about the *deep* culture of colleges and universities?" Great question! To get authoritative answers, I put that question to nearly 2,000 college and university educators in an online survey.

Well, not exactly *that* question. What I actually asked was, "What are your concerns about student behaviors and/or attitudes?" That's because—although we may not be fully aware of our deep cultural beliefs—we're well aware of what upsets us (such as people cutting in line in front of us). And what upsets us is often a window into our cultural beliefs, into our expectations of how others should think and behave.

What follows are some—but certainly not all—of the important cultural beliefs in higher education. Said another way, these are the expectations of many educators you will encounter on your campus. These expectations reveal what they value and, therefore, what they want you to do. Each of the following eight cultural beliefs or "eight key expectations" includes related taboos—what educators said upsets them and, therefore, what they *don't* want you to do. Let these insights guide your choices in college and you'll increase your chances of success manyfold. With these insights as a foundation, the rest of *On Course* will show you how.

EIGHT KEY EXPECTATIONS

Students are often shocked by the need to take on personal responsibility for so many things: time management, decision making, problem solving, completing assignments, etc. It's time to grow up a bit and learn some adult responsibilities. Some are ready for it and embrace it; others are not.

Steve Schommer
San Diego City College, CA

1. **Educators expect students to be responsible for their education.** As such, they expect students to be mature and accountable for choices they make. Here are some concerns that educators expressed about students who lack personal responsibility:

   - Blaming poor performance on instructors, or the book, or the time a class meets . . . or any number of other reasons other than themselves.

   - Slacking off, not doing all the assigned work and then expecting the instructor to offer second/third/fourth chances.

   - Returning to class after an absence and thinking "I wasn't here last class" is a valid excuse for being unprepared.

   - Emailing to explain an absence, then asking what they missed, when there is a syllabus and a website they can refer to in case they are absent.

   - Believing whatever is going wrong is not their fault, and they have nothing to do with it.

   - Complaining rather than addressing the concern they are complaining about.

2. **Educators expect students to be highly motivated to succeed.** As such, they expect students to make college an important priority in their lives, and, when necessary, to sacrifice other pursuits to complete their academic work. Here are some concerns that educators expressed about students who lack self-motivation:

   - Expecting instructors to motivate them.

   - Having an apathetic, what-does-it-matter attitude in their courses.

   - Not caring that they are failing, or seeming to think that they will always be able to make up work, rewrite or resubmit anything to get better grades. In other words, if they're failing, they still think they can pass the class. This is known as "magical thinking."

- Expressing that everything is boring, that nothing interests them.
- Lacking any interest in making improvements, even when provided extensive feedback and support.
- Assuming that it's the professor's job to make class "interesting." Instructors SHOULD take responsibility for creating engaging classroom experiences and rich content. I work on that every day, every semester. But at the end of the day, we can't do your homework for you. We can't make the class meaningful *for* you.
- Not completing reading assignments because "it's not interesting."
- Asking to do extra credit instead of work that was assigned.

3. **Educators expect students to attend classes regularly and complete all assignments to the best of their ability.** As such, they expect students to apply effective organizational skills so they can complete their work without supervision or handholding. Here are some concerns that educators expressed about students with poor self-management skills:

- Falling way behind in assignments, coming to class unprepared, and expecting to get good grades with little effort.
- Thinking they can do whatever they want because they paid for the class.
- Believing things like, "If this reading is too difficult, then I shouldn't be required to read it," or "If I have something else to do during class time and I don't show up, then the teacher should catch me up on what I missed."
- Constantly being late, not coming to class, or not doing assignments.
- Acting as if they are entitled to pass a course regardless of how little work they do or how poorly it is done.
- Missing class and then coming to my office and asking me to tell them everything they missed.
- Thinking that if they just show up and sit there (and maybe stay awake), they will get credit for seat time, but they don't have to participate or do any work.

4. **Educators expect students to collaborate with peers and make use of available help to achieve academic success.** As such, they expect students to work well with other students and seek assistance from instructors and campus support services such as tutoring, counseling, and advising. Here are some concerns that educators expressed about students who lack interdependence:

- Saying, "I need to do this all on my own." I tell them, no one got through school "on their own." Everyone needs help to get through the day!

My successful students are self-motivated and driven to earn a college degree.

Gerald Headd
Cuyahoga Community
College, OH

The amount of reading and number of assignments a student needs to do in college is much greater than in high school. Students need to study two to three hours for each class session. Instructors expect students to read, save, and consult the course syllabus for deadlines and tests! The first tests are often wake-up calls because they usually cover large amounts of material.

Lea Beth Lewis
California State University,
Fullerton

- Not utilizing the college resources that are all but handed to them on a silver platter.

- Struggling with something, either subject matter or technology, and not asking for help as soon as the struggle begins.

- Not connecting with other students to study.

- Failing to ask questions when they are confused about an assignment, and not saying anything until it's too late.

- Claiming they can't learn anything by working in groups and that I need to tell them what it is they need to know. In other words, if I'm not lecturing, nothing worth learning is happening.

- Waiting until right before a course ends, panicking, and then descending on tutors in the learning center, expecting that someone there will do their work for them.

5. **Educators expect students to change when what they are doing is not working.** As such, they expect students to realize when they are off course, figure out how they got there, and try something new and more effective to get back on course. Here are some concerns that educators expressed about students who lack self-awareness:

- Thinking that what worked in high school will automatically work in college.

- Developing bad new habits like partying, drinking, skipping classes, doing sloppy work, and making other mistakes that come with the newfound freedom of college. They are often unaware of how these habits are hurting them until it's too late.

- Being unable to see different choices that would be more effective or unwilling to make changes when they do see that something is not working.

- Not realizing that negative thoughts about their academic abilities act as anchors holding them back.

- Focusing on their weaknesses rather than developing new strengths.

- Ignoring low test scores or feedback on assignments and then asking, "How am I doing?"

- Repeating behaviors over and over even though they are not working.

6. **Educators expect students to demonstrate a passion for learning.** As such, educators expect students to be intellectually curious, thus pursuing knowledge rather than grades. Here are some concerns that educators expressed about students who aren't enthusiastic lifelong learners:

- Being unaware of what "learning" is and how to go about doing it on purpose. Students expect to walk into the classroom, flip open the top of their heads, and have the teacher pour in the necessary knowledge.

I f students come to me voluntarily and ask for support, usually they succeed. These students might struggle a bit but they accept the fact that we all need help from time to time.

Stephanie Kroon
State University of New
York – Ulster

S truggling students don't recognize when they are behind or not doing well until it is too late to change.

Peter Shull
Pennsylvania State
University

- Believing that everyone is entitled to their own opinion and everyone's opinion is different, so there is no reason/basis to form an opinion or care about having one.

- Not appreciating the advantages of getting an education. They take their financial aid for granted, waste money, and abuse the system!

- Cheating.

- Making grades their primary reason for attending a class rather than a genuine interest in learning, sometimes even in their major field. This attitude is often revealed by the famous and annoying question, "What do I need to do to pass this class?"

- Expecting to be spoon-fed and thinking they have no role in their own learning.

- Not buying and/or reading their textbooks, thinking the instructors will tell them everything they need to know.

7. **Educators expect students to manage their emotions, as well as the emotions of others, in the service of their goals.** As such, educators expect students to experience normal human emotions but resist impulsive or disrespectful choices that will sabotage their success or the success of others. Here are some concerns that educators expressed about students who lack emotional intelligence:

- Letting fear guide their decisions, and not attempting the work because they are afraid of failing.

- Being judgmental and hurtful to other students on purpose, especially those who are different from them.

- Communicating inappropriately with instructors. For example, I dislike when a message from a student begins "Hey . . ." Or they get bad-tempered when I don't reply to a phone message or email immediately.

- Lacking perseverance and grit when the going gets tough.

- Choosing short-term gratification, causing them to wait until the last moment to do homework or study for a test.

- Never speaking during a class discussion for fear of being criticized or judged.

- Being openly rude and indifferent to college staff, teachers, administrators, and fellow students.

8. **Educators expect students to have realistic self-confidence about themselves and their ability to succeed in college.** As such, educators expect students to be self-assured without being arrogant. Here are some concerns that educators expressed about students who believe in themselves too little or too much.

- Pretending they "know it all." They don't, but are afraid to let others know their personal insecurities.

> When my successful students are in class, they are fully engaged in the classroom activities. They expect to learn new things, they don't expect learning to be easy or fast, and they are eager to learn.
>
> Adrienne Peek
> Modesto Junior College

> Some of my students don't attempt the work simply because they are afraid of failing. Successful students who are afraid do the work anyway.
>
> Kimberly Manner
> West Los Angeles College

- Quitting when they encounter the slightest hint that college may be more than they can handle. Some students are too brittle, taking every setback as a reason to give up.
- Being unwilling to struggle with learning, as if it means they are stupid. Many students "got it" so easily in high school that they don't understand what it's like to have to work to learn something.
- Having little belief in themselves, so any disappointment becomes a self-fulfilling prophesy and a cause for dropping out of school.
- Thinking that because they did well in high school, their college instructors must be wrong to offer any criticisms.
- Continuously talking about how they will never succeed in college.
- Talking big, but giving up easily.

TABLE 1.1 Important Differences between High School and College Culture

High School Culture Assumes Immaturity	College Culture Assumes Maturity
Students attend high school because they are required to by their parents or by law.	Students usually attend college because of a personal choice.
Teachers offer students many reminders to complete assignments.	Instructors give assignments and expect students to hand them in on time, done well, and without reminders.
Teachers spend time disciplining students who create disruptions.	Instructors do not tolerate disruptive students and may bar them from the class.
Students typically spend 30 or more hours in class each week, and teachers cover the majority of course content during class.	Students typically spend 15 or fewer hours in class each week, and instructors expect students to learn the majority of course content outside of class. This is why doing all homework, preferably before class, is so important.
Teachers and parents manage much of the students' time.	Students manage their own time.
Teachers are often pressured to "teach to the test" so that students can pass standardized assessments.	Instructors have more "academic freedom" in what and how they teach.
Academic standards are not always high, and savvy students often get good grades with little effort.	Academic standards are usually high, and all students need to figure out how to meet these challenging standards.
Family and friends provide students with advice or solutions for academic, social, and other problems.	Students solve their own problems or seek help at one of many support services provided by the college.
Students' choice of courses is relatively limited by graduation requirements.	Students have greater freedom to choose the courses they take and drop those they don't want to complete.
Teachers and parents minimize distractions that might otherwise hinder students' success.	Students must deal with distractions on their own, including parties, television, video games, Internet surfing, dating, sports, social media, drinking, drugs, road trips, and hanging out.
Educational costs, including textbooks, are paid for by taxpayers.	Educational costs, including textbooks, are paid for by the student, the student's family, and/or by financial aid for which the student applies and, in some cases, must pay back.
Students have few choices.	Students have many choices.

When you entered higher education, you entered into a partnership with college educators. It may be that your only goal in this partnership is to get passing grades and earn a degree. I must admit, that was my only goal when I went to college. Years later I realized that I set my sights woefully low. The educators you have partnered with—because of their culture—want much more for you than just passing grades and a degree (though they certainly want that, too).

The hope of most educators is that you become an effective learner. They want you to develop intellectual skills such as critical thinking, analytical reasoning, and communication skills. And many—including, most likely, your instructor in this course—want you to develop these personal skills: skills such as personal responsibility, self-motivation, self-management, self-awareness, lifelong learning, emotional intelligence, and realistic confidence in yourself. Why? Because personal skills like these shape your choices and empower you to create a rich, personally fulfilling life.

So, once again, welcome to the culture of higher education. If you are open to all it has to offer, you're going to learn more on this journey than you ever thought possible.

> Successful students have the ability to overcome challenge and change by seeking out strategies to help them stay on the learning path and reach their own goals. This involves the willingness to fail and make mistakes and get back up and try something else.
>
> Janeth Franklin
> Glendale Community
> College

JOURNAL ENTRY / 2

In this activity, you will explore aspects of the deep culture of higher education. Make a choice: Write answers to one of the following two questions.

1 Which of the eight key expectations of college educators (explained in the previous pages) is most different from the culture of your most recent educational experience (e.g., high school, another college or university, a trade school)? Explain the differences, using personal examples wherever possible.

2 Which of the eight key expectations of college educators do you think is the most important one for you to fulfill to be successful, and why? Explore how difficult you think it will be for you to fulfill this expectation, and why. Throughout your response, use personal examples wherever possible.

Understanding Yourself

FOCUS QUESTIONS / What does "success" mean to you? What are the essential skills for creating that success? In which essential skills are you strong? In which would you benefit from improvement?

Have you given much thought to your future? Do you have a clear idea about what you want to have in five years, 10 years, 20 years? How about what you want to be doing? And what about the kind of person you will be? In other words, how will you know if you are a success?

WHAT DOES SUCCESS MEAN TO YOU?

I've asked many college graduates, "What did success mean to you when you were an undergraduate?" Here are some typical answers:

When I was in college, success to me was . . .

. . . getting all A's and B's.
. . . making two free throws to win the conference basketball tournament.
. . . having a great social life.
. . . parenting two great kids and still making the dean's list.
. . . being the first person in my family to earn a college degree.

Notice that each response emphasizes *outer success:* high grades, sports victories, popularity, and college degrees. These successes are public, visible achievements that allow the world to assess one's abilities and worth.

I've also asked college graduates, "If you could repeat your college years, what would you do differently?" Here are some typical answers:

If I had a chance to do college over, I would . . .

. . . focus on learning instead of just getting good grades.
. . . major in engineering, the career I had a passion for.
. . . constantly ask myself how I could use what I was learning to enhance my life and the lives of the people I love.
. . . discover my personal values.
. . . learn more about the world I live in and more about myself . . . especially more about myself!

Notice that the focus some years after graduation often centers on *inner success:* enjoying learning, following personal interests, focusing on personal values, and creating more fulfilling lives. These successes are private, invisible victories that offer a deep sense of personal contentment.

Only with hindsight do most college graduates realize that, to be completely satisfying, success must occur both in the visible world and in the invisible spaces within our minds and hearts. This book, then, is about how to achieve both outer and inner success in college and in life.

To that end, I suggest the following simple definition of success for your consideration: **Success is staying on course to your desired outcomes and experiences.** Maybe you'd like to earn a college degree or start your own business or marry and have six kids. Maybe you'd like to experience joy or confidence or love. Maybe you'd like to be seen by others as a "self-made" person who achieved success by your efforts alone. Maybe you'd prefer to experience being a valued member of a group that is loyal and committed to one another. Regardless of what your desired outcomes and experiences may be, following the time-tested strategies presented in *On Course* will help you achieve them.

Start with the end in mind.

Stephen R. Covey

College is a place where a student ought to learn not so much how to make a living, but how to live.

Dr. William A. Nolen

As a college instructor, I've seen thousands of students arrive on campus with dreams, then struggle, fail, and fade away. I've seen thousands more come to college with dreams, pass their courses, and graduate, having done little more than cram their brains with information that's promptly forgotten after the final exam. They've earned degrees, but in more important ways they have remained unchanged.

Our primary responsibility in life, I suggest, is to realize the incredible potential with which each of us is born. All of our experiences, especially those during college, can contribute to the creation of our best selves.

On Course shows how to use your college experience as a laboratory experiment. In this laboratory, you'll learn and apply proven strategies that help you create success—academically, personally, and professionally. I'm not saying it'll be easy, but you're about to learn strategies that have made a difference in the lives of many thousands of students before you. So get ready to change the outcomes of your life and the quality of your experiences along the way! Get ready to create success as *you* define it.

To begin, consider a curious puzzle: Two students enter a college class on the first day of the semester. Both appear to have similar intelligence, backgrounds, talents, interests, and abilities. The weeks slide by, and the semester ends. Surprisingly, one student soars and the other sinks. One fulfills her potential; the other falls short. Why do students with similar aptitudes perform so differently? More important, which of these students is you?

Teachers observe this puzzle in every class. I bet you've seen it, too, not only in school, but wherever people gather. Some people have a knack for achievement. Others wander about confused and disappointed, unable to create the success they claim they want. Clearly, having potential does not guarantee success.

What, then, are the essential ingredients of success?

> There is only one success—to be able to spend your life in your own way.
>
> Christopher Morley

INGREDIENTS OF SUCCESS

For answers, let's revisit those two students mentioned earlier and observe them more closely. For example, let's see what happens when they receive the same low grade on an essay in their English class. The first student goes immediately to the registrar's office and drops the class. The second student goes immediately to the tutoring center and asks for help. The first student's choice eliminates any chance of learning the skills needed to succeed in the course. The second student's choice keeps the possibility of success alive. By seeking tutoring, she improves her chances of learning the writing skills she needs to pass the course and succeed in college.

So, one important ingredient of success is developing the skills necessary to accomplish a particular task. To be successful in a writing class, you need good writing skills. To be successful in a math class, you need good math skills. To be successful in every college class, you need good learning skills. Skills like these are often called "hard" skills, and there are thousands of them. Accountants

> The deepest personal defeat suffered by human beings is constituted by the difference between what one was capable of becoming and what one has in fact become.
>
> Ashley Montagu

need the hard skill of doing taxes. Nurses need the hard skill of taking people's blood pressure. Filmmakers need the hard skill of using editing software. Hard skills are observable, measurable, and learnable. Much of what you go to college for is to learn hard skills.

Hold on, though. There's something else going on with our two students. Remember, we said they both appear to have similar intelligence, backgrounds, talents, interests, and abilities. So why did they make such different choices when confronted by a low grade? Why did one student quit and the other go for tutoring? To find an answer, we need to ponder their inner strengths.

What inner strengths would someone need to seek help rather than drop a course? Inner strengths that come to my mind include *persistence, self-confidence,* and *motivation* (among others). Like writing and math, these three inner qualities are skills, too, but of a different kind. They are often called "soft" skills. Unlike hard skills, soft skills are invisible and difficult to measure. Like hard skills, though, soft skills are learnable.

Both of these skill sets—hard and soft—influence the hundreds, perhaps thousands, of choices we make every day. Because even a few bad choices can send us far off course, it's wise to improve our choice-making ability. In *On Course*, you'll learn how to strengthen your hard skills *and* your soft skills. Both skill sets, as you will see, are essential for making wise choices and achieving great success in higher education . . . and beyond.

In everyday life, we usually learn soft and hard skills together. For example, learning a hard skill (such as touch typing on a computer keyboard) can simultaneously teach us a soft skill (such as patience). These two skill sets are woven into the fabric of our lives. However, for ease of learning, in this course we'll look at them separately. That way, you can focus on and develop one skill at a time. The nine chapters in *On Course* will help you develop *soft* skills. A Toolbox for Active Learners, which is available online with the accompanying MindTap, will help you develop hard skills, especially study skills that will make you a more effective learner. Applying them together will empower you to thrive in the culture of higher education.

ASSESS YOUR SOFT SKILLS FOR COLLEGE SUCCESS

In preparation for exploring the choices of successful students, take a few minutes to complete the self-assessment questionnaire on the next two pages. Your scores will identify soft skills that support your success. They'll also point out soft skills you may want to strengthen to achieve more of your potential in college and in life. Later on, you'll have an opportunity to repeat this self-assessment and compare your two scores. I think you're going to be pleasantly surprised!

This self-assessment is not a test. There are no right or wrong answers. The questions simply give you an opportunity to create an accurate and current self-portrait. Be absolutely honest and have fun with this activity, for it's an important step on a journey to a richer, more personally fulfilling life.

On average, about a third of a person's strengths are innate, built into his or her genetically based temperament, talents, mood, and personality. The other two-thirds are developed over time. You get them by growing them . . . finding out how to grow these strengths inside you could be the most important thing you ever learn.

Rick Hanson,
neuropsychologist

To live is to choose. But to choose well, you must know who you are and what you stand for, where you want to go and why you want to get there.

Kofi Annan, former
secretary-general of the
United Nations

Self-Assessment

Read the following statements and score each one according to how true or false you believe it is about you. To get an accurate picture of yourself, consider what IS true about you (not what you *want* to be true). Remember, there are no right or wrong answers. Assign each statement a number from 0 to 10, as follows:

Totally False ◄ ⓪ ① ② ③ ④ ⑤ ⑥ ⑦ ⑧ ⑨ ⑩ ► **Totally True**

1. _____ I control how successful I will be.
2. _____ I'm not sure why I'm in college.
3. _____ I spend most of my time doing important things.
4. _____ When I encounter a challenging problem, I try to solve it by myself.
5. _____ When I get off course from my goals and dreams, I realize it right away.
6. _____ I'm not sure how I prefer to learn.
7. _____ I know ways to increase my happiness.
8. _____ I'll truly accept myself only after I eliminate my faults and weaknesses.
9. _____ Forces out of my control (such as poor teaching) are the cause of low grades I receive in school.
10. _____ I place great value on getting my college degree.
11. _____ I don't need to write things down because I can remember what I need to do.
12. _____ I have a network of people in my life that I can count on for help.
13. _____ If I have habits that hinder my success, I'm not sure what they are.
14. _____ When I don't like the way an instructor teaches, I know how to learn the subject anyway.
15. _____ When I get very angry, sad, or afraid, I do or say things that create a problem for me.
16. _____ When I think about performing an upcoming challenge (such as taking a test), I usually see myself doing well.
17. _____ When I have a problem, I take positive actions to find a solution.
18. _____ I don't know how to set effective short-term and long-term goals.
19. _____ I am organized.
20. _____ When I take a difficult course in school, I study alone.
21. _____ I'm aware of beliefs I have that hinder my success.
22. _____ I'm not sure how to think critically and analytically about complex topics.
23. _____ When choosing between doing an important school assignment or something really fun, I do the school assignment.
24. _____ I break promises that I make to myself or to others.
25. _____ I make poor choices that keep me from getting what I really want in life.
26. _____ I expect to do well in my college classes.
27. _____ I lack self-discipline.
28. _____ I listen carefully when other people are talking.
29. _____ I'm stuck with any habits of mine that hinder my success.

30. _____   My intelligence is something about myself that I can improve.
31. _____   I often feel bored, anxious, or depressed.
32. _____   I feel just as worthwhile as any other person.
33. _____   Forces outside of me (such as luck or other people) control how successful I will be.
34. _____   College is an important step on the way to accomplishing my goals and dreams.
35. _____   I spend most of my time doing unimportant things.
36. _____   I am aware of how to show respect to people who are different from me (race, religion, sexual orientation, age, etc.).
37. _____   I can be off course from my goals and dreams for quite a while without realizing it.
38. _____   I know how I prefer to learn.
39. _____   My happiness depends mostly on my circumstances.
40. _____   I accept myself just as I am, even with my faults and weaknesses.
41. _____   I am the cause of low grades I receive in school.
42. _____   If I lose my motivation in college, I don't know how I'll get it back.
43. _____   I have a self-management system that helps me get important things done on time.
44. _____   I seldom interact with people who are different from me.
45. _____   I'm aware of the habits I have that hinder my success.
46. _____   If I don't like the way an instructor teaches, I'll probably do poorly in the course.
47. _____   When I'm very angry, sad, or afraid, I know how to manage my emotions so I don't do anything I'll regret later.
48. _____   When I think about performing an upcoming challenge (such as taking a test), I usually see myself doing poorly.
49. _____   When I have a problem, I complain, blame others, or make excuses.
50. _____   I know how to set effective short-term and long-term goals.
51. _____   I am disorganized.
52. _____   When I take a difficult course in school, I find a study partner or join a study group.
53. _____   I'm unaware of beliefs I have that hinder my success.
54. _____   I know how to think critically and analytically about complex topics.
55. _____   I often feel happy and fully alive.
56. _____   I keep promises that I make to myself or to others.
57. _____   When I have an important choice to make, I use a decision-making process that analyzes possible options and their likely outcomes.
58. _____   I don't expect to do well in my college classes.
59. _____   I am a self-disciplined person.
60. _____   I get distracted easily when other people are talking.
61. _____   I know how to change habits of mine that hinder my success.
62. _____   Everyone is born with a certain amount of intelligence, and there's not really much I can do to change that.
63. _____   When choosing between doing an important school assignment or something really fun, I usually do something fun.
64. _____   I feel less worthy than other people.

Transfer your scores to the scoring sheets on the next page. For each of the eight areas, total your scores in columns A and B. Then total your final scores as shown in the sample on the next page.

Self-Assessment Scoring Sheet

SAMPLE

A	B
6. _8_	29. _3_
14. _5_	35. _3_
21. _6_	50. _6_
73. _9_	56. _2_
_28_ + 40 −	_14_ = 54

SCORE #1: Accepting Personal Responsibility

A	B
1. ___	9. ___
17. ___	25. ___
41. ___	33. ___
57. ___	49. ___
___ + 40 −	___ = ___

SCORE #2: Discovering Self-Motivation

A	B
10. ___	2. ___
26. ___	18. ___
34. ___	42. ___
50. ___	58. ___
___ + 40 −	___ = ___

SCORE #3: Mastering Self-Management

A	B
3. ___	11. ___
19. ___	27. ___
43. ___	35. ___
59. ___	51. ___
___ + 40 −	___ = ___

SCORE #4: Employing Interdependence

A	B
12. ___	4. ___
28. ___	20. ___
36. ___	44. ___
52. ___	60. ___
___ + 40 −	___ = ___

SCORE #5: Gaining Self-Awareness

A	B
5. ___	13. ___
21. ___	29. ___
45. ___	37. ___
61. ___	53. ___
___ + 40 −	___ = ___

SCORE #6: Adopting Lifelong Learning

A	B
14. ___	6. ___
30. ___	22. ___
38. ___	46. ___
54. ___	62. ___
___ + 40 −	___ = ___

SCORE #7: Developing Emotional Intelligence

A	B
7. ___	15. ___
23. ___	31. ___
47. ___	39. ___
55. ___	63. ___
___ + 40 −	___ = ___

SCORE #8: Believing in Myself

A	B
16. ___	8. ___
32. ___	24. ___
40. ___	48. ___
56. ___	64. ___
___ + 40 −	___ = ___

Interpreting Your Scores

A score of . . .

0–39	Indicates an area where your choices will **seldom** keep you on course.
40–63	Indicates an area where your choices will **sometimes** keep you on course.
64–80	Indicates an area where your choices will **usually** keep you on course.

Choices of Successful Students

Successful Students . . .

▶ **accept personal responsibility,** seeing themselves as the primary cause of their outcomes and experiences.

▶ **discover self-motivation,** finding purpose in their lives by pursuing personally meaningful goals and dreams.

▶ **master self-management,** consistently planning and taking purposeful actions in pursuit of their goals and dreams.

▶ **employ interdependence,** building mutually supportive relationships that help them achieve their goals and dreams (while helping others do the same).

▶ **gain self-awareness,** consciously employing behaviors, beliefs, and attitudes that keep them on course.

▶ **adopt lifelong learning,** finding valuable lessons and wisdom in nearly every experience they have.

▶ **develop emotional intelligence,** effectively managing their emotions and the emotions of others in support of their goals and dreams.

▶ **believe in themselves,** seeing themselves as capable, lovable, and unconditionally worthy human beings.

Struggling Students . . .

▶ **see themselves as victims,** believing that what happens to them is determined primarily by external forces such as fate, luck, and powerful others.

▶ **have difficulty sustaining motivation,** often feeling depressed, frustrated, and/ or resentful about a lack of direction in their lives.

▶ **seldom identify specific actions needed to accomplish a desired outcome,** and when they do, they tend to procrastinate.

▶ **are stubbornly independent,** seldom requesting, even rejecting, offers of assistance from those who could help, and failing to build effective and supportive relationships with others.

▶ **make important choices unconsciously,** being directed by self-sabotaging habits and outdated life scripts.

▶ **resist learning new ideas and skills,** viewing learning as fearful or boring rather than as mental play.

▶ **live at the mercy of strong emotions,** such as anger, sadness, anxiety, or a need for instant gratification.

▶ **doubt their competence and personal value,** feeling inadequate to create their desired outcomes and experiences.

FORKS IN THE ROAD

Why are these eight inner strengths so important? Because they shape many of the important choices we make. The road of life forks many times each day, and at every fork we need to make a choice. Some of those choices are so significant they will literally change the outcomes and experiences of our lives. In college, students encounter opportunities such as work-study programs, lunch with an instructor, study groups, social events, sports teams, new friends, study-abroad programs, romantic relationships, academic majors, deep conversations, diverse cultures, challenging viewpoints, and field trips, among many others.

Other choices involve dealing with disappointing grades, homesickness, the death of a loved one, conflicts with friends, loneliness, health problems, endless homework, anxiety, broken romances, self-doubt, lousy class schedules, lost motivation, difficult instructors, academic probation, confusing tests, excessive drinking, frustrating rules, mystifying textbooks, conflicting work and school schedules, jealous friends, drugs, test anxiety, learning disabilities, and financial difficulties, to name a few.

In other words, college is just like life. There are always opportunities and obstacles, and the choices we make at each of these forks in the road determine whether we achieve our desired outcomes and experiences. It takes a lot more than potential to excel in college, a career, or in life. And you're about to find out how to succeed in all three . . . despite inevitable challenges. You see, although life is generating a dizzying array of options, successful people are making one wise choice after another.

> I believe that choice—though it can be finicky, unwieldy, and demanding—is ultimately the most powerful determinant of where we go and how we get there.
>
> Sheena Iyengar

A FEW WORDS OF ENCOURAGEMENT

In this course, you'll be taking a personal journey designed to help you develop the empowering beliefs and behaviors that will help you maximize your potential and achieve the outcomes and experiences you desire. However, before we depart, let's see how you're feeling about this upcoming trip. Please choose the following statement that best describes how you feel right now:

1. I'm excited about developing the inner qualities, outer behaviors, and academic skills that have helped others achieve success in college, a career, and in life.

2. I'm feeling okay about this journey because I'll probably learn a few helpful things along the way.

3. I can't say I'm excited, but I'm willing to give it a try.

4. I'm unhappy, and I don't want to go!

In nearly every *On Course* group I've worked with, there have been some reluctant travelers. If that's you, I want to offer some personal words of encouragement. First, I can certainly understand why you might be hesitant. Frankly, I would have been a reluctant traveler on this journey when I was a first-year college student. I can tell you, though, I sure wish I'd known then what you're about to learn now. Many students after completing the course have asked, "Why didn't they teach us this stuff in high school? It sure would have helped!" Even some of the most reluctant travelers have later said, "Every student should be required to take this course!"

I can't promise that you'll feel this way after finishing the course. But I can promise that if you do only the bare minimum or, worse yet, drop out, you'll never know if this course could have helped you improve your life. So, quite frankly, my goal here is to persuade you to give this course a fair chance.

Maybe you're thinking, *I don't need this success stuff. Just give me the information and skills I need to get a good job.* If so, you're going to be pleased to discover that the soft skills you'll learn in this course are highly prized in the work world. In fact, many companies pay corporate trainers huge fees to teach these same skills to their employees. Think of the advantage you'll have when you bring these skills with you to the job.

Or, perhaps you're thinking, *I already know how to be successful. This is just a waste of my time.* I thought this, too, at one time. And I had three academic degrees from prestigious universities and a good job to back up my claim. Hadn't I already proven I could be a success? But when I opened myself to learning the skills that you'll discover in these pages, the quality of both my professional and personal life improved dramatically. I've also taught these skills to successful college educators (perhaps even your own instructor), and many of them have had the same experience I did. You see, there is success . . . and then there is SUCCESS!

Or, maybe you're thinking, *I don't want to examine and write about myself. That's not what college should be about.* I understand this objection! When I was in college, self-examination was about the last thing on my to-do list (right after walking backward to the North Pole in bare feet). Of course I had a "good" reason: Athletes like me didn't look inward. I labeled it "touchy-feely" and dismissed self-exploration. I'm sure you have reasons for your reluctance: shyness, your cultural upbringing, or a host of other explanations that make you uncomfortable when looking within for the keys to your success. I urge you to lower your resistance and give this approach a try. You can learn now what it took me too many years to discover: **Success occurs from inside out, not outside in.** *You* are the key to your success. So, I hope you'll give this course your best effort. Most likely, it's the only college course you'll ever take where the subject matter is YOU. And, believe me, if you don't master the content of this course, every other course you take (both in college and in the University of Life) will suffer. I wish you a great journey. Let the adventure continue!

Intelligence plus character—that is the goal of true education.

Martin Luther King, Jr.

The battles that count aren't the ones for gold medals. The struggles within yourself—the invisible, inevitable battles inside all of us—that's where it's at.

Jesse Owens, winner of four gold medals at the 1936 Olympics

JOURNAL ENTRY / 3

In this activity, you will take an inventory of your personal strengths and weaknesses as revealed by your self-assessment questionnaire.

1 In your journal, write the eight areas of the self-assessment and record your scores for each, as follows:

_____ 1. Accepting personal responsibility

_____ 2. Discovering self-motivation

_____ 3. Mastering self-management

_____ 4. Employing interdependence

_____ 5. Gaining self-awareness

_____ 6. Adopting lifelong learning

_____ 7. Developing emotional intelligence

_____ 8. Believing in myself

Transfer your scores from the self-assessment to the appropriate lines above.

2 **Write about the areas on the self-assessment in which you had your highest scores.** Explain why you think you scored higher in these areas than in others. Were there any surprises? Were there any high scores you disagreed with? If so, why? How do you feel about your higher scores? Your entry might begin, "By doing the self-assessment, I learned that I . . ."

3 **Write about the areas on the self-assessment in which you had your lowest scores.** Explain why you think you scored lower in these areas than in others. Were there any surprises? Did you disagree with any low scores? If so, why? How do you feel about your lower scores? Remember the saying, "If you keep doing what you've been doing, you'll keep getting what you've been getting." With this thought in mind, write about any specific changes you'd like to make in yourself during this course. Your entry might begin, "By doing the self-assessment, I also learned that I . . ."

All glory comes from daring to begin.

Eugene F. Ware

ONE STUDENT'S STORY

JALAYNA ONAGA, *University of Hawaii at Hilo, Hawaii*

It's amazing how fast someone can go from being excited about college to flunking out. A year and a half ago, I received a letter from the University of Hawaii at Hilo informing me that I was being dismissed due to my inability to maintain a GPA of at least 2.0. I wasn't surprised because I had spent the whole semester making one bad choice after another. I hardly ever attended classes. I didn't do much homework. I didn't study for tests. And I never asked anyone for help. Mostly I just hung out with friends who told me I didn't need to go to college. But, fast-forward to today and you'll see a woman who has clear goals for her

▶

ONE STUDENT'S STORY *continued*

future, the motivation to reach those goals, and a plan to carry her to her dreams. However, it took a lot of learning for me to make such a huge change in my life.

After taking courses for a while at a community college, I got permission to re-enroll at the university. I was so nervous! I worried that I'd get dismissed again and I'd never do anything with my life. A counselor suggested that I take the University 101 course, and I'm so thankful I did. While writing the *On Course* journals, I learned so much about myself and how I can succeed. I realized that when I first enrolled at the university, I was taking nursing courses because

my parents wanted me to and I couldn't get motivated. This time I got inspired because my journals helped me look inside myself to figure out my own dreams for the future and to create a plan to reach them. For the first time, the plans I made were coming from my heart, not from someone telling me what I should do. I realized that I really love kids and *my* dream is to teach second- or third-graders. That's when I made a personal commitment to attend every class and learn as much as I could. In later journals I learned that making a schedule and writing everything down helped me get the important things done. I even learned to ask for

help, and when I was absent because my car broke down, I met with the teacher to find out what I had missed. Before tests, I found it inspiring to read over my journal because my own words reminded me of my dreams and why I should study hard to get them.

Best of all, my new choices really paid off. When the semester ended, I had three A's and a B+ and I made the dean's list. My University 101 course and the *On Course* textbook really changed me as a student and as a person. Not long ago, I was a student without a direction. Now I can envision myself in the near future teaching a class full of eager students, watching them learn and grow, just like I was able to do.

SOFT SKILLS / at Work

> The soft stuff is always harder than the hard stuff.
>
> —*Roger Enrico, vice chairman, PepsiCo*

The skills you will learn in *On Course* have been shown to improve college student performance. Not only that, but these same "soft skills" are exactly what employers are looking for when hiring. They'll help you both ace your interview and succeed in your job. New employees often have technical skills ("hard skills"), but not the "soft skills" required for success. These soft skills help you work effectively with others, and also manage your own behaviors and emotions. For a computer engineer position, hard skills include systems

development and networking technology. For a veterinary technician, hard skills include taking blood samples or assisting with animal dental care. Soft skills for both positions include staying motivated, strengthening relationships at work, and learning new information every day.

JOB EXPLORATION

When starting your job exploration, you'll find many ways to learn about career fields and about how to do well in your desired career. You might read job postings to understand what skills employers really want. You can request an informational interview with a company and ask lots of questions. You could also speak with a mentor who is working in the field. In all these efforts, you'll likely find

▶

that you need more than hard skills in your desired position. For example, recent Google job postings emphasize all eight of the *On Course* soft skills desired in their future employees:

- "Accountable and **Responsible**" (see Chapter 2)
- "Demonstrated **Motivation**" (see Chapter 3)
- "Organizational skills; Prioritize and manage" [**Self-Management**] (see Chapter 4)
- "Teamwork skills; Develop lasting relationships" [**Interdependence**] (see Chapter 5)
- "Requires awareness; Maintain situational awareness" [**Self-Awareness**] (see Chapter 6)
- "Desire to learn; Asking questions" [**Lifelong Learning**] (see Chapter 7)
- "High EQ" [**Emotional Intelligence**] (see Chapter 8)
- "Ability to maintain confidence" [**Belief in Self**] (see all chapters)

If you want to get hired, and get ahead in your field, you'll need to strengthen all these skills. The good news is, they are taught in the course you are taking. Because you're reading *On Course*, you'll be ahead of many college graduates when you jump into the job market.

Let's look at how soft skills contribute to success at your job. For a veterinary technician position, you'll need to know more than animal anatomy and clinical procedures. These hard skills won't be enough for you to excel in your career. You'll also need excellent **listening skills**. These will help you follow precise instructions while handling medication orders. You'll be better able to understand and share information with clients and labs. You'll also need to use **empathy**, a part of emotional intelligence. Empathy is your ability to understand how others are feeling. This skill helps you respond to the feelings of anxious pet owners, or calm animals in distress. It also helps you calm yourself when you have a very stressful day at work.

INTERNSHIPS

After reviewing job postings, another excellent way to understand the requirements of your desired career is through an internship. Getting an internship can be an important career step, and soft skills play an essential role. As an intern (paid or unpaid), you'll work as a trainee at a company to get valuable hands-on experience in your field. You'll also have a chance to show an employer that you can do well at their company. Two researchers, Norman Montague and George Violette, surveyed interns at major accounting firms in 2017 ("The Millennial Internship Experience: Balancing Technical Training with Soft Skills"). Before their internship, these students believed that their technical experience alone would help them get an internship. However, after their interviews, most interns realized that communication and interpersonal skills were even more important. Their interviewers wanted to understand how the intern might be a good fit for the team. They asked questions to understand if interns had a **positive attitude** and a strong **work ethic**. They also wanted to see if they showed **flexibility** in decision making, and a **willingness to learn**.

CAREERS

After an internship, of course, you are hoping to get a good job, and naturally you'll also want to excel at your new job. The soft skills you'll need to excel are personal and professional strengths that you, as a highly capable employee, will use every day at work. They include all eight of the *On Course* principles. Learn these skills and you'll be ready to perform. When the Department of Labor surveyed employers on needed workplace skills, the report (SCANS) showed that "personal qualities" were essential to employee success. Employers want employees who are good at time management, teamwork, and assuming personal responsibility. They want employees with diversity skills, high self-esteem, and creativity. The more soft skills you

▶

have, the easier for you to get hired . . . and stay employed!

Did you know that employers in 2017 spent more than $94 billion to teach their employees crucial skills, including soft skills? Does such training work? A recent study examined younger, less experienced leaders right out of college. It showed that leadership development (soft skill) training improved their effectiveness ratings by more than 30 percent. For young women completing the training, 82 percent reported that they were more confident leaders. Another group of employees working in sales were trained in emotional intelligence. They showed more than a 10 percent increase in their total sales revenue compared to other employees at the company. It is clear these skills can be learned and practiced with positive results. Imagine how marketable you'll be to a future employer when they discover that you have already developed a skill like emotional intelligence.

Learning soft skills will help you in any career. They support you in jobs you are working at during college and prepare you for jobs you'll hold after graduating. Technical (hard) skills are often unique to a specific job. But because soft skills are portable, you can take them with you to any new job. Being prepared for a new job is important because like most college graduates, you can expect to hold at least 10 jobs during your lifetime. You can also expect to shift from one career field to an entirely new field more than once. Robotics and other technology advances will drastically transform the job market, changing the types of jobs available today and creating new ones in the future. Regardless of the specific job title you may hold, soft skills will always be essential, keeping you on course in the work world for a lifetime.

Money Matters

If lack of money could be an obstacle to your college success, get your finances in order now . . . not after it's too late. There's no point heading off on a journey if you're worried you'll run out of fuel before reaching your destination.

The good news is that the efforts (even sacrifices) you make now to get an education will pay off in the future. Check out Figure 1.4 to see how level of education affects earnings and unemployment. Clearly, earning a degree increases the likelihood of greater abundance. Unfortunately, however, many students' money problems keep them from completing the very degree that would help them achieve that abundance. They work so many hours that their learning and grades suffer. Still others drop out of college because of lack of money. If money problems threaten your college degree, read on.

In this section, you'll learn some of the basics of money management. There is, of course, much more to know. But if you effectively apply these strategies, you can look forward to building the financial resources that will see you though to graduation . . . and beyond.

Level of Education (% of U.S. population with this degree)	Median Earnings	Unemployment Rate
Less than a high school diploma (34.1%)	$25,636	8.0%
High school diploma, no college (65.9%)	$35,256	5.4%
Some college, no degree (62.0%)	$38,376	5.0%
Associate degree (40.0%)	$41,496	4.3%
Bachelor's degree (32.0%)	$59,124	2.8%
Master's degree (9.3%)	$69,732	2.4%
Doctoral degree (2.0%)	$84,396	1.7%
Professional degree (1.5%)	$89,960	1.7%

FIGURE 1.4 Yearly Salaries and Unemployment Rates by Levels of Education (25 and older)

Source: U.S. Bureau of Labor Statistics, Current Population Survey, 2016.

MANAGING MONEY: THE BIG PICTURE

When I was a new college instructor, a colleague and I were complaining one day about how little money we were making. Both of us had young families, and our salaries barely got us from paycheck to paycheck. One day we decided to stop complaining and do something about it. Boldly, we decided to give ourselves a raise.

To do so, we brainstormed how we could save or earn more money. Our first discovery was that we were both paying about $6 a month for our checking accounts. We switched to free checking and gave ourselves an instant raise of $72 a year. By itself, that was no big thing. But we also thought of 21 other ways to make or save money. All told, our new choices amounted to an increase of nearly $2,000 a year for each of us. That was the beginning of our realization that we had more control over our money than we had thought. What an empowering feeling!

As you examine the following strategies, keep in mind the big picture of managing money. **Do everything legal to increase the flow of money *into* your personal treasury and decrease the flow of money *out*. The better you become at these complementary skills, the more money you will have to enhance your life and the lives of the people you love.** There is great abundance on our planet, and there is no reason why you shouldn't enjoy your share of it.

GET ORGANIZED

1. **Track your spending.** To organize your finances, start with accurate information. Carry a notepad with you for at least a week—preferably longer—and record every penny you receive and spend. (I know, doing this detailed recording is a pain, but the benefit is worth it! You can also try one of the many free money-tracking apps like Goodbudget or Mint.) You need to know where your money is coming from and where it's going. One student, for example, was shocked to discover that he was spending an average of $24 each week ($1,248 per year!) on fast-food lunches; after that he started packing his lunch and saved a lot of money.

2. **Create a budget.** A budget helps you define and achieve your goals. It guides you to make important decisions about the dollars flowing in and out of your life. Beginning your budget is as simple as filling out the *My Financial Plan* worksheet that follows. Obviously, after subtracting all expenses from your income, your goal is to have a positive and growing balance. If you have a negative balance, with each passing month you'll slide deeper into debt. To avoid debt, you need to increase your income, decrease your expenses, or both.

3. **Find a bank or credit union (if you don't have one already).** A bank or credit union helps you manage your money. Your ideal financial institution offers:

   - free checking accounts that require no minimum balance and pay interest.
   - savings accounts with competitive interest rates.
   - free use of its ATMs and those belonging to other banks or credit unions as well.

   If you need to pay for any of these services, seek to minimize the yearly cost. Credit unions typically offer lower rates on these services than do banks. To find credit unions near you, use the search feature at creditunion .coop. Whether your checking account is with a bank or a credit union, be sure to balance your account regularly. To do so, make it a habit to add any deposits and subtract any expenses charged to your account. This will save you the expense of bounced (rejected) checks because of insufficient funds.

INCREASE MONEY FLOWING IN

4. **Apply for grants and scholarships.** These are financial awards that do not have to be repaid. For U.S. residents, a great place for an overview of financial aid sources is online at ed.gov/fund/grants-college.html. The process of applying for financial aid dollars begins with the FAFSA, which stands for Free Application for Federal Student Aid. Using information reported on this form, the government decides what you or your family can

TABLE 1.2 My Monthly Financial Plan
Use this financial plan to keep your budget every month.

Step A: Monthly Income	Amount
Support from family or others	
Scholarships	
Loans	
Investments	
Earned income (after taxes)	
Total Monthly Income (A)	
Step B: Necessary Fixed Monthly Expenses	
Housing (mortgage or rent)	
Transportation (car payment, insurance, bus pass, car pool)	
Taxes (federal and state income, Social Security, Medicare)	
Insurance (house, health, and life)	
Child care	
Tuition	
Bank fees	
Debt payment	
Savings and investments	
Necessary Fixed Monthly Expenses (B)	
Step C: Necessary Variable Monthly Expenses	
Food and personal care items	
Clothing	
Phone	
Gas and electric	
Water	
Transportation (car repairs, maintenance, gasoline, bus, taxi, rideshare)	
Laundry and dry cleaning	
Doctors and medicine	
Books and software	
Computer/Internet access/Wi-Fi	
Total Necessary Variable Monthly Expenses (C)	
Step D: Optional Fixed and Variable Monthly Expenses	
Eating out (including coffee, snacks, lunches)	
Entertainment (movies, theater, night life, optional child care)	
Leisure travel	
Hobbies	
Gifts	
Charitable contributions	
Subscriptions (Amazon Prime, Netflix, Hulu, Cengage Unlimited, etc.)	
Miscellaneous (music, magazines, online, etc.)	
Total Optional Variable Monthly Expenses (D)	
Money Remaining or Owed at End of Month (A − B − C − D = ?)	

afford to pay toward your education and what you may need in the way of financial assistance. Get copies of the form from your college's financial aid office or online at fafsa.ed.gov. You'll find a "forecaster" at this site that will help you estimate the amount of financial aid you can expect to receive. The deadline for completing the FAFSA form is typically the end of June. However, some colleges and states use the information from the FAFSA form to determine their own financial aid, so be sure to check your school's and state's deadline or you could be out of luck (and money) for that year.

The benefit of qualifying for grants and scholarships is that, unlike loans, you don't need to pay them back. Federal Pell Grants provide financial support to students with family incomes up to $50,000; however, most Pell awards go to students with family incomes below $20,000. With a maximum award in 2017–18 of $5,920, the amount of each Pell Grant depends on four factors: (1) financial need, (2) cost of the college, (3) full- or part-time enrollment, and (4) attendance for a full academic year or less. You can receive a Pell Grant for 12 semesters, or approximately six years. Get comprehensive information from the Federal Student Aid Information Center in Washington at studentaid.ed.gov.

You can also search without cost for scholarships at websites such as bigfuture.collegeboard.org/scholarship-search and fastweb.com. Perhaps most important, spend time with a counselor in your college's financial aid office and let him or her help you get your share of the financial support available for a college education. With all of these resources, there's no need to pay a private service to find scholarships for you. Ron Smith, former head of financial aid at Baltimore City Community College, offers this advice: "Students should apply early, provide accurate information, and follow up until an award has been received."

5. **Apply for low-cost loans.** These are financial awards that *do* need to be repaid. As of this writing, the federal government guarantees Stafford Loans (staffordloan.com), so they generally offer the lowest interest rates. Depending on financial need, Stafford Loans may be up to $5,500 per year for eligible, dependent first-year students and up to $9,500 per year for eligible independent students. The maximum total loan is $31,000 for eligible dependent students and $57,500 for eligible independent students. The U.S. government pays interest costs until repayment begins, which is usually after graduation. Unsubsidized Stafford Loans do not depend on financial need, but the interest accumulates while you are in college.

Other federally guaranteed student loans include PLUS loans (made to students' parents) and Perkins Loans (for lower-income students). You may be approved for more loan money than you need and be tempted to borrow it all; just remember that what you take now, you'll need to repay later, plus interest. You don't want to finish your education with the burden of an unnecessarily large debt. The standard repayment plan for student loans is equal monthly payments for 10 years. That's a long time to pay for an earlier bad choice.

Here's one last caution about loans: A report by the Brown Center on Education Policy at the Brookings Institution found that many students didn't realize that money they received was a loan that needed to be repaid. In fact, 28 percent of students who *did* have federal loans reported they did *not* have federal loans and 14 percent reported that they had no loans at all. Confusion about what they've borrowed, the report concludes, is "almost certainly leading some students into decisions that they later come to regret." The lesson? Make sure you know how much money you get for college is a loan and will need to be paid back.

6. **Work**. Even with grants, scholarships, and low-cost loans, many college students need employment to make ends meet. If this is your situation, use your financial plan to figure out how much money you need each month beyond any financial aid. Then set a goal to earn that amount while also getting work experience in your future field of employment. In other words, your purpose for working is both to make money *and* to get valuable employment experience and recommendations. In this way, you make it easier to find employment after college and perhaps even negotiate a higher starting salary. One place that may help you achieve this double goal is your campus job center. Additionally, on some campuses, instructors can hire student assistants to help them with their research.

   If you try but can't find employment that provides valuable work experience (or you're not sure what your future employment plans are), seek work that allows you to earn your needed income in the fewest hours—saving you time to excel in your studies. You may do well by creating a high-paying job for yourself by using skills you already possess (or could easily learn). For example, one student I know noticed that each autumn the rain gutters of houses near his college became clogged with leaves. With a leaf blower and ladder in hand, he knocked on doors and offered to clean gutters for only $20. Few homeowners could resist such a bargain. Averaging two houses an hour, he earned nearly $700 each fall weekend.

   Currently, the FAFSA allows dependent students to earn up to $6,570 a year without decreasing financial aid. For parents, the allowance depends on the number of people in the family and how many are in college. For 2018–19, a married couple with two children in college can earn up to $25,040 without affecting financial aid.

7. **Save and invest**. If you haven't done so already, open a savings account and begin making regular deposits. You can probably save $20 a month by giving up a movie and one jumbo popcorn. Set a goal to accumulate a financial reserve for emergencies equal to three months' living expenses. After that, consider making regular deposits in higher-income investments such as stocks, bonds, and mutual funds. These are topics beyond the scope of this book but well worth your effort to research. To gain practical experience and guidance, you may want to join (or start) an investment club

on your campus. By investing money regularly, you'll benefit from compound interest (earning interest on interest). In this way, even people with modest incomes can accumulate significant wealth. A way to make your savings grow even faster is to invest in a tax-deferred retirement account. The money you deposit isn't taxed until you withdraw it many years later, increasing the amount you can potentially save by thousands of dollars. You can open such an account through your employer (who may even make additional contributions) or by opening an IRA (individual retirement account) on your own. You may think it's too early to be thinking about retirement, but years from now, you'll be mighty glad you did it now.

DECREASE MONEY FLOWING OUT

8. **Avoid the "Let's go out" trap.** Someone calls and says, "Let's go out." You meet for food or drinks and spend $20 . . . or more. Do this a couple times a week and you'll wind up dropping hundreds of dollars a month into a deep, dark hole. One student reported that even after she ran out of money for the month, friends would say, "Oh, c'mon out with us. I'll loan you the money." That meant she was already spending next month's money. By all means, put entertainment money into your monthly financial plan, but, when it's gone, have the self-discipline to stop going out. Instead, invite friends over and make it BYO—Bring Your Own. Or you could make a great choice by staying home and studying. Studying costs you nothing now and makes a great investment in your future income.

9. **Lower transportation expenses.** Cars are expensive. Beyond car payments, vehicles require costs for insurance, registration, regular maintenance, gasoline, repairs, tolls, and parking. And if you're under 25, you'll pay more for insurance than someone over 25 (especially young men, whose rates are greater than those of older men). So, if money is tight, consider getting along without a car for now. If you live on campus, this option should be fairly easy. If you commute, you could use public transportation or offer gas money to a classmate for rides to school.

10. **Use credit cards wisely.** You'll probably be swamped with invitations to open credit card accounts. You're not alone. "These credit card issuers circle the campus like sharks circling a fish," says Elizabeth Warren, senior senator from Massachusetts and former Harvard Law School professor. So, first, consider whether you should even *have* a credit card. Visa, MasterCard, and other credit cards provide you with short-term loans to purchase anything you want up to your credit limit. These companies are counting on you to postpone paying off the loan past the due date. That's when you start paying interest at their high rates. The consequences to your finances can be staggering. Suppose you're 20 years old, you owe $3,500 on a credit card that charges 17 percent interest, and you regularly pay the minimum charge. You won't pay off that debt until you're 53 years old, and the amount you will ultimately pay is nearly $11,000! And if you ever miss a payment,

you'll incur a triple penalty. First, you'll be charged a late fee that can be as much as $35 for being even one day overdue. Next, some banks punish late payers by raising their interest rates to "penalty rates" of 20 percent or more. Finally, late payments can show up on your credit report, making it difficult for you to get loans for a car, house, or other big-ticket items. How serious is the problem of credit card misuse by college students? One widely quoted statement attributed to an administrator at the University of Indiana notes, "We lose more students to credit card debt than to academic failure." So, use a credit card only if you can discipline yourself to pay off most, and preferably all, of your balance every month. If you can't, a wiser choice would be to cut up your credit cards—or not even apply for one in the first place.

11. **Choose credit cards wisely.** If you decide that you do have the discipline to use a credit card wisely, realize that all credit cards are not created equal. Compare your options and choose the one with the lowest interest rates, the longest grace period (time you get to use the money before paying interest), and the lowest annual fee (preferably free). Some cards offer a reward for using them, such as cash back or frequent-flier miles. To find the best deals on credit cards, visit websites such as bankrate.com or cardratings.com.

12. **Use debit and ATM cards wisely.** A debit card is similar to a credit card. The difference? The money comes not as a loan from the credit card company but as a withdrawal from your own checking account. An ATM card is a payment card that allows you to use an automated teller machine (ATM) to perform transactions such as making deposits and cash withdrawals, or obtaining account information. Here's the danger. These cards are so easy to use that some financial experts refer to them as "death cards." Say you withdraw $100 in cash on Monday, and by Thursday the money has dribbled away. So you take out another $100, and that disappears by the weekend. After a couple of weeks like this, your money runs out before the month does, and you're slipping ever deeper into debt. Not only has your money run out, but if you withdraw more money than is in your account, the bank will also charge you an overdraft fee. Ask your bank about overdraft protection to avoid this additional expense. Use a debit or ATM card only if you have the self-discipline to keep from spending money not in your budget. One way to manage this is to set and keep a schedule for how often and how much you will withdraw each time.

13. **Pay off high-rate debt.** Suppose you pay off a loan (such as a credit card balance) that charges 17 percent. That's the same as investing your money at a guaranteed 17 percent rate of return. Better yet, the 17 percent return is tax free, so you're actually earning a much greater return! Compare that to the puny interest rate you'd be earning in a savings account. Don't have extra money in savings to pay off money you owe? A variation is to transfer debt from high-interest loans to lower-interest loans (but watch carefully for hidden transfer costs on some accounts).

14. **Avoid credit blunders.** There are serious consequences for being financially irresponsible. Every time you create a debt, national credit agencies
keep a record, including assigning you a credit score from 300 to 850, with
850 being the best score. When you later apply for credit, potential lenders
can view your credit score and history for at least the past seven years. This
data tells lenders whether you are a good or bad risk. If you're seen as a bad
risk, your application for a car or house loan may be turned down. Or you
may be offered a loan with extremely high interest rates. Your credit report
might even wind up in the hands of a potential landlord or employer. This
information could affect your ability to rent an apartment or even get your
dream job. Bottom line, unwise financial choices in the present may haunt
you for years. To view your present credit report and verify its accuracy,
order a copy from Equifax at 800-685-1111 (equifax.com), Experian at
888-397-3742 (experian.com), or TransUnion at 800-888-4213 (transunion
.com). Depending on where you live, the report will range in cost from free
to about $8. At annualcreditreport.com you can get a free credit report for
all three agencies once a year. Websites such as creditkarma.com will calcu-
late your scores from TransUnion and Equifax for free. If you make a credit
blunder, immediately contact the company you owe and work out a payment schedule. The sooner you clean up your credit report, the sooner your
past choices will stop sabotaging your future. If you need help with debt,
contact the National Foundation for Credit Counseling (NFCC) for low- or
no-cost credit assistance at 800-388-2227 (nfcc.org).

15. **Use tax credits.** Tax credits are expenses you can subtract directly
from your federal income tax. If you're paying for college yourself, you
may be eligible for an American Opportunity Tax Credit of up to $2,500
in your first four years. For details on this tax credit (as well as the
Lifetime Learning Credit), go to irs.gov/uac/Tax-Benefits-for-Education-
Information-Center.

16. **Examine each expense line in your financial plan for possible
reductions.** Here are some of the money-saving options my students
have come up with: Find a roommate to reduce housing costs. Carpool to
share commuting costs. Cut up credit cards. Pack lunches instead of eating
out. Change banks to lower or eliminate monthly checking fees. Exchange
babysitting with fellow students to minimize child care expenses. Shop at
discount clubs and buy nonperishables (such as toilet paper and laundry
detergent) in bulk. Join up with friends and families to get a family plan
for cell phones. Read magazines and newspapers at the library, instead of
buying them. Pay creditors on time to avoid penalty charges. Delay purchases until the item goes on sale (such as right after Christmas). Find other
money-saving ideas at lowermybills.com.

Although college can be costly, by planning carefully and employing these
money management strategies, you can both get your degree and lay a
strong foundation for a positive financial future.

MONEY MANAGEMENT EXERCISE

To help *increase* your flow of money in, make a list of skills you have that you could possibly turn into a self-employment opportunity with a high hourly wage. To help *decrease* your flow of money out, make a list of choices you could make that would each save you $25 or more a year. If you need help, try an Internet search for "saving money" or "budget tips." Compare your two lists with those of classmates to see if you can find additional choices you didn't think of. Add up all the items on your list (income and outflow) and see how much you could improve your financial picture in one year by making these choices. You'll find more wise advice about managing your money at bettermoneyhabits.com.

TECH TIPS: Money

Mint *(online or for Android and iOS)* is the top money management tool (5 out of 5 stars) recommended by *Personal Computing* magazine. The software connects to all your online financial institutions, such as banks and credit unions, which means you must provide your log-in information for each. The program tracks your personal finances and helps you budget your money.

LearnVest *(online or for iOS)*, which provides paid financial planning services, also offers the option to sign up for free email newsletters filled with extensive tips for budgeting, saving money, and other financial topics.

BudgetSimple.com offers an easy-to-use online budget that (unlike Mint) does not need to be linked to your financial institutions. It promises to help you understand where your money is leaking out and ways to cut off the flow. The free plan offers options for creating a budget and reports.

Bettermoneyhabits.com is a website offered by a partnership between Khan Academy and Bank of America. It offers valuable tips on how to create and stick to a budget, repay a student loan,

finance a car, boost your credit score, save for buying a house, and understand your paycheck.

Spreadsheet programs—such as Google's free Google Sheets program and Excel, a program included in the Microsoft Office software suite—can also be used to create effective budgets.

Student loan calculators may be found online by doing an Internet search. These programs figure out your student loan repayments so you can see how easy or challenging it will be for you to pay back your loan(s). StudentLoanHero.com deserves special mention. It offers resources that allow you to see all your student loan information in one location. It also offers tips for managing, and perhaps lowering, your repayment.

GoodBudget.com *(online and for Android and iOS)* uses the envelope approach to budgeting . . . except your money envelopes are online. First you assign money to each envelope, say you assign $75 a month for entertainment. After going to a movie, enter the theater name and how much you spent, and select the entertainment envelope. The money will be subtracted from your envelope, showing you how much is left for the month.

Note: All of these mentioned are free (except for Excel), but some may offer upgraded features for a fee.

This year marked a great shift in my life. It signaled my change into adulthood as I left home to start college more than a thousand miles from my home. I was very excited to start this next chapter in my life, but I was also hesitant about being completely independent and on my own for the first time in my life. The thought of having to cook, clean, manage money, and shop for groceries all by myself was overwhelming. I didn't know if I could handle being a functioning adult when I had relied on my parents for so much when I was in high school. In the first few weeks of college, however, I began reading the *On Course* book where I learned many tips for students like me who are nervous about certain aspects of college and university life. For me, the most important strategy was how to manage money effectively. I am so thankful that I learned this skill during my very first semester of college.

In my first four weeks of college, my professor assigned us to keep a log of our expenses and categorize them by the reason we spent them. Doing this activity taught me that being a college student can be expensive, especially because I didn't want to have a job that would take my focus off getting good grades. Seeing all my expenses on paper helped me realize that I needed to spend less money on superfluous treats and activities and focus more on necessities, especially because I didn't have a stable source of income. Unlike living at home, now I had to pay for everything I wanted.

On Course offered several strategies for saving and spending money effectively, such as choosing a reliable bank or credit union, avoiding credit card blunders, making use of tax credits, and avoiding the "Let's go out" trap. This last idea has been the most difficult for me because there are so many fun things to do in college that cost money, and I like spending time with my new friends. However, it makes sense that even if you only go out and spend money twice a week, over time that leads to the loss of hundreds of dollars that you can't get back. The book recommends saving that money by staying in and hanging out with your friends at your apartment, park, or anywhere that costs no money. I suggested this idea to my friends the next time they wanted to go out, and they said it was a great idea and that they could all benefit from saving some money.

My time here in college has taught me a lot about how to live an independent life as an adult, and I attribute a lot of my success to the *On Course* book. Managing my money was a big worry for me when I first started college, because I didn't know how much to save or spend, and I had no clue how to budget effectively. *On Course* helped me tremendously with how to save and spend money and has in turn helped me with my stress level because now I don't have to worry about having enough money to pay rent and have fun in college.

Photo: Courtesy of Emily Christman.

Accepting Personal Responsibility

Successful Students . . .

▶ **adopt a Creator mindset,** believing that their choices create the outcomes and experiences of their lives.

▶ **master Creator language,** accepting personal responsibility for their results.

▶ **make wise decisions,** consciously designing the future they want.

Struggling Students . . .

▶ **accept a Victim mindset,** believing that external forces determine the outcomes and experiences of their lives.

▶ **use Victim language,** rejecting personal responsibility by blaming, complaining, and excusing.

▶ **make decisions carelessly,** letting the future happen by chance rather than by choice.

I accept responsibility for creating my life as I want it.

CASE STUDY IN CRITICAL THINKING · The Late Paper

Professor Freud announced in her syllabus for Psychology 101 that final term papers had to be in her hands by noon on December 18. No student, she emphasized, would pass the course without a completed term paper turned in on time. As the semester drew to a close, **Kim** had an "A" average in Professor Freud's psychology class, and she began researching her term paper with excitement.

Arnold, Kim's husband, felt threatened that he had only a high school diploma while his wife was getting close to her college degree. Arnold worked the evening shift at a bakery, and his coworker **Philip** began teasing that Kim would soon dump Arnold for a college guy. That's when Arnold started accusing Kim of having an affair and demanding she drop out of college. She told Arnold he was being ridiculous. In fact, she said, a young man in her history class had asked her out, but she had refused. Instead of feeling better, Arnold became even angrier. With Philip continuing to provoke him, Arnold became sure Kim was having an affair, and he began telling her every day that she was stupid and would never get a degree.

Despite the tension at home, Kim finished her psychology term paper the day before it was due. Because Arnold had hidden the car keys and Professor Freud refused to accept assignments sent by email, Kim decided to take the bus to the college and turn in her psychology paper a day early. While she was waiting for the bus, **Cindy**, one of Kim's psychology classmates, drove up and invited Kim to join her and some other students for an end-of-semester celebration. Kim told Cindy she was on her way to turn in her term paper, and Cindy promised she'd make sure Kim got it in on time. "I deserve some fun," Kim decided, and hopped into the car. The celebration went long into the night. Kim kept asking Cindy to take her home, but Cindy always replied, "Don't be such a bore. Have another drink." When Cindy finally took Kim home, it was 4:30 a.m. She sighed with relief when she found that Arnold had already fallen asleep.

When Kim woke up, it was 11:30 a.m., just 30 minutes before her term paper was due. She could make it to the college in time by car, so she shook Arnold and begged him to drive her. He just snapped, "Oh sure, you stay out all night with your college friends. Then, I'm supposed to get up on my day off and drive you all over town. Forget it." "At least give me the keys," she said, but Arnold merely rolled over and went back to sleep. Panicked, Kim called Professor Freud's office and told **Mary**, the administrative assistant, that she was having car trouble. "Don't worry," Mary assured Kim, "I'm sure Professor Freud won't care if your paper's a little late. Just be sure to have it here before she leaves at 1:00." Relieved, Kim decided not to wake Arnold again; instead, she took the bus.

At 12:15, Kim walked into Professor Freud's office with her term paper. Professor Freud said, "Sorry, Kim, you're 15 minutes late." She refused to accept Kim's term paper and gave Kim an F for the course.

The following are characters in this story. Rank them in order of their *responsibility for Kim's failing grade in Psychology 101.* Give a different score to each character. Be prepared to explain your choices.

Most responsible ▶ ① ② ③ ④ ⑤ ⑥ ◀ **Least responsible**

___ **Professor Freud**, the instructor

___ **Kim**, the psychology student

___ **Arnold**, Kim's husband

___ **Philip**, Arnold's coworker

___ **Cindy**, Kim's classmate

___ **Mary**, the administrative assistant

DIVING DEEPER

Is there someone not mentioned in the story who may also be responsible for Kim's failing grade?

Adopting a Creator Mindset

FOCUS QUESTIONS   What is self-responsibility? Why is it a key to creating the life you want?

When psychologist Richard Logan studied people who survived ordeals such as being imprisoned in concentration camps or lost in the frozen Arctic, he found they shared a common belief. They all saw themselves as personally responsible for creating the outcomes and experiences of their lives.

Ironically, responsibility has gotten a bad reputation. Some see it as a heavy burden they have to lug through life. Quite the contrary, personal responsibility is the foundation for creating success. Personal *response-ability* is the ability to respond wisely at each fork in the road, your choices moving you ever closer to your desired outcomes and experiences. The opposite is waiting passively for your fate to be determined by luck or powerful others. Whether your challenge is surviving an Arctic blizzard or excelling in college, accepting personal responsibility empowers you to make the most out of any situation.

I first met Deborah when she was a student in my English 101 class. Deborah wanted to be a nurse, but before she could qualify for the nursing program, she had to pass English 101. She was taking the course for the fourth time.

"Your writing shows fine potential," I told Deborah after I had read her first essay. "You'll pass English 101 as soon as you eliminate your grammar problems."

"I know," she said. "That's what my other three instructors said."

"Well, let's make this your last semester in English 101, then. After each essay, make an appointment with me to go over your grammar problems."

"Okay."

"And go to the Writing Lab as often as possible. Start by studying verb tense. Let's eliminate one problem at a time."

"I'll go this afternoon!"

But Deborah never found time: *No, really. . . . I'll go to the lab just as soon as I . . .*

Deborah scheduled two appointments with me during the semester and missed them both: *I'm so sorry. . . . I'll come to see you just as soon as I . . .*

To pass English 101 at our college, students had to pass one of two essays written at the end of the semester in an exam setting. Each essay was graded by two other instructors.

At semester's end, Deborah once again failed English 101. "It isn't fair!" Deborah protested. "Those exam graders expect us to be professional writers. They're keeping me from becoming a nurse!"

I suggested another possibility: "What if *you* are the one keeping you from becoming a nurse?"

Deborah didn't like that idea. She wanted to believe that her problem was "out there." Her only obstacle was *those* exam graders. All her disappointments were *their* fault. *They* weren't fair. The *test* wasn't fair. *Life* wasn't fair! In the face of this injustice, she was helpless.

The best years of your life are the ones in which you decide your problems are your own. You do not blame them on your mother, the ecology, or the president. You realize that you control your own destiny.

Albert Ellis

The more we practice the habit of acting from a position of responsibility, the more effective we become as human beings, and the more successful we become as managers of our lives.

Joyce Chapman

I reminded Deborah that it was *she* who had not studied her grammar. It was *she* who had not come to conferences. It was *she* who had not accepted personal responsibility for creating her life the way she wanted it.

"Yes, but . . . ," she said.

VICTIM AND CREATOR MINDSETS

Deborah had a problem that was going to keep her from ever passing English 101. But the problem wasn't the exam graders. The problem was her mindset.

A mindset is a collection of beliefs and attitudes. Like the lenses in eyeglasses, a mindset affects the way you see a situation and influences your resulting choices. A **Victim mindset** keeps people from seeing and acting on choices that could help them achieve the life they want. A **Creator mindset** causes people to see multiple options, choose wisely among them, and take effective actions to achieve the life they want.

When you accept personal responsibility, you believe that you create *everything* in your life. This idea doesn't sit well with some people. "Accidents and natural disasters happen," they say. "There are muggings, murders, and wars. People are marginalized, oppressed, and brutalized simply because they are different. Blaming the victims is unfair. To say these people created the terrible things that happened to them is outrageous."

These observations are, as far as they go, true. At times, we *are* all affected by forces beyond our control. If a hurricane destroys my house, I am a victim (with a small "v"). In this case I am victimized by a force *outside* of me. But after the event, if I make unwise choices that prevent me from getting my life back on track, I am acting from a Victim mindset (with a capital "V"). In this case, I am victimized by a force *inside* of me. Whether I am victimized from the outside or from the inside is a crucial distinction. When I have a Victim mindset, I become my own oppressor. When I have a Creator mindset, I refuse to allow inside (or outside) oppression to be in control of my life. Although I may not be able to prevent the outside circumstances from occurring, I can choose a response that keeps me on track to my goals.

Civil rights activist Rosa Parks is an example of this distinction. On the evening of December 1, 1955, Parks was returning home on a bus in Montgomery, Alabama. She had just completed a long day as a seamstress in a department store. When the driver ordered her to give up her seat to a white passenger, Parks refused and was arrested. A few days later, outraged at her arrest, African Americans began a boycott of Montgomery buses that ended 381 days later when the law requiring segregation on public buses was finally lifted. As a result of refusing to obey an unjust law, Parks has been called the "mother of the modern-day civil rights movement." In an interview years later, Parks was asked why she chose to defy the bus driver's order to move. "People always say that I didn't give up my seat because I was tired," she said, "but that isn't true. I was not tired physically, or no more tired than I usually was at the end of a working day. I was not old, although some people have an image of me as being old then. I was 42. No, the only tired I was, was tired of giving in." In the face of an external oppression, Rosa Parks became an inspiring example of what one person with a Creator mindset can achieve.

Every time your back is against the wall, there is only one person that can help. And that's you. It has to come from inside.

Pat Riley, professional basketball coach

I believe that we are solely responsible for our choices, and we have to accept the consequences of every deed, word, and thought throughout our lifetime.

Elisabeth Kübler-Ross

So, is it outrageous to believe that you create everything in your life? Of course it is. But here's a better question: Would it improve your life to act *as if* you create all of the outcomes and experiences in your life? Answer "YES!" and watch a Creator mindset improve your life. After all, if you believe that someone or something out there causes all of your problems, then it's up to "them" to change. What a wait that can be! How long, for example, will Deborah have to wait for "those exam graders" to change?

The benefits to students of accepting personal responsibility have been demonstrated in various studies. Researchers Robert Vallerand and Robert Bissonnette, for example, asked 1,000 first-year college students to complete a questionnaire about why they were attending school. They used the students' answers to assess whether the students were "origin-like" or "pawn-like." The researchers defined *origin-like* students as seeing themselves as the originators of their own behaviors, in other words, Creators. By contrast, *pawn-like* students see themselves as mere puppets controlled by others, in other words, Victims. A year later, the researchers returned to find out what had happened to the 1,000 students. They found that significantly more of the Creator-like students were still enrolled in college than the Victim-like students. If you want to succeed in college (and in a career and in life), having a Creator mindset gives you a big edge.

> Which mistake do you think would be better to make . . . (a) to believe you are in control of your life when you really might not be [or] (b) to believe you are not in control of your life when you really might be?
>
> Brooks Peterson

RESPONSIBILITY AND CULTURE

In the 1950s, American psychologist Julian Rotter set out to study people's beliefs about who or what was responsible for the outcomes and experiences of their lives. He called it a study of "locus of control." *Locus* in Latin means "place" or "location." So, locus of control defines where people believe the power over their lives is located. Since Rotter's study, locus of control has been one of the most examined aspects of human nature. What researchers discovered is that different cultures can see locus of control differently.

People from some cultures (though not everyone inside these cultures) believe they control most, if not all, of their own destiny. Researchers call this

Victim Mindset

Creator Mindset

mindset an *internal* locus of control. People with this mindset believe their outcomes and experiences depend primarily on their own behaviors. Educators at some institutions believe that college students should be guided by an internal locus of control.

However, researchers found that people from some cultures (though not everyone from that cultural group) assign responsibility for their fate to factors beyond their direct control. If you find that you are uncomfortable with the idea of individual responsibility, the cause may be found in your deep culture. For example, some people believe that a higher power is guiding their lives. The Spanish saying *Si Dios quiere* ("God willing") reflects this belief, and so does the Arabic *Insha'Allah* ("God willing" or "if God allows"). Variations of this expression can be found in many languages and cultures. And members of working-class cultures—regardless of their ethnicity—may experience economic frustrations and doubt their ability to create the life of their dreams.

These differences in cultural mindsets highlight both the challenge and importance of deciding where our responsibilities begin and end. On the one hand, accepting too little responsibility is disempowering. We become little more than a feather floating on the breeze. On the other hand, accepting too much responsibility is disempowering as well. In some cases, we can be crushed under the weight of problems not of our creation or in our control. The reality is that some choices truly are futile because of personal limitations or limitations imposed by bad luck or the will of others with more power. Like some kind of cosmic joke, one of our greatest responsibilities, then, is deciding what we are and are not responsible for, what we do and do not have control over. Worse, those decisions may change at the very next fork in the road.

RESPONSIBILITY AND CHOICE

The key ingredient of personal responsibility is **choice.** Animals respond to a stimulus because of instinct or habit. For humans, however, there is a brief, critical moment of decision available between the stimulus and the response. In this moment, we make the choices—consciously or unconsciously—that influence the outcomes of our lives.

Numerous times each day, you come to a fork in the road and must make a choice. There is no escape. Even *not* making a choice is a choice. Some choices have a small impact: Shall I get my hair cut today or tomorrow? Some have a huge impact: Shall I stay in college or drop out? The sum of the choices you make from this day forward will create the eventual outcome of your life. The Responsibility Model in Figure 2.1 shows what the moment of choice looks like.

In that brief moment between stimulus and response, we can choose a Victim mindset or a Creator mindset. When we respond as a Victim, we typically complain, blame, make excuses, and then repeat ineffective behaviors. When we respond as a Creator, we pause at each decision point and ask, "What are

*G*enerally, European-American teachers believe in internal control and internal responsibility—that individuals are in control of their own fate, their actions affect outcomes, and success or failure in life is related to personal characteristics and abilities.

Jean Moule

*B*y imposing too great a responsibility, or rather, all responsibility, on yourself, you crush yourself.

Franz Kafka

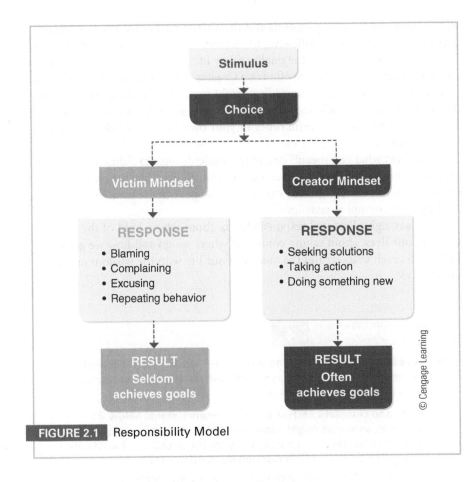

FIGURE 2.1 Responsibility Model

> I do think that the greatest lesson of life is that you are responsible for your own life.
>
> Oprah Winfrey

my options, and which option will best help me create my desired outcomes and experiences?"

The difference between responding to life as a Victim or Creator is how we choose to use our energy. When I'm blaming, complaining, and excusing, my efforts cause little or no improvement. Sure, it may feel good in that moment to claim that I'm a poor Victim and "they" are evil persecutors, but my good feelings are fleeting because afterward my problem still exists. By contrast, when I'm seeking solutions and taking actions, my efforts often (though not always) lead to improvements. At critical forks in the road, Victims waste their energy and remain stuck, whereas Creators use their energy for improving their lives. There is only one situation I can think of where blaming and complaining can be helpful. That's when you use them to generate energy that motivates you to take positive actions. My personal guideline: Up to 10 minutes for griping . . . then on to being a Creator and finding a solution.

But, let's be honest. No one makes Creator choices all the time. I've never met anyone who did, least of all me. Our inner lives feature a perpetual tug of

> When you make the shift to being the predominant creative force in your life, you move from reacting and responding to the external circumstances of your life to creating directly the life you truly want.
>
> Robert Fritz

war between the Creator part of us and the Victim part of us. My own experiences have taught me the following life lesson: The more choices I make as a Creator, the more I improve the quality of my life. That's why I urge you to join me in an effort to choose more often as a Creator. It won't be easy, but it's worth it. You may have to take my word for it right now, but if you experiment with the strategies in this book and continue using the ones that work for you, in a few months you'll see powerful proof in your own life of the value of making Creator choices.

"Oh, I get what you mean!" one of my students once exclaimed as we were exploring this complex issue of personal responsibility, "You're saying that living my life is like traveling in my car. If I want to get where I want to go, I better be the driver and not a passenger."

She was right. Personal responsibility is about taking hold of the steering wheel of our lives, about taking control of where we go and how we get there. Ultimately, each of us creates the quality of our life with the wisdom or folly of our choices.

I am a Shawnee. My forefathers were warriors. Their son is a warrior.... From my tribe I take nothing. I am the maker of my own fortune.

Tecumseh

Life is like a game of cards. The hand you are dealt is determinism; the way you play it is free will.

Jawaharlal Nehru

JOURNAL ENTRY   4

In this activity, you will experiment with the Creator role. By choosing to take responsibility for your life, you will immediately gain an increased power to achieve your greatest potential.

1 **Write and complete each of the five sentence stems below.** For example, someone might complete the first sentence stem as follows: If I take personal responsibility for my education, *I will focus on really learning and not just getting good grades.*

   A.   If I take personal responsibility for my education . . .

   B.   If I take personal responsibility for my career . . .

   C.   If I take personal responsibility for my relationships . . .

   D.   If I take personal responsibility for my health . . .

   E.   If I take personal responsibility for all that happens to me . . .

2 **Make a choice—write about one of the following:**

   A.   What have you learned or relearned in this journal about personal responsibility, and how will you use this knowledge to improve your outcomes and experiences in college . . . and beyond? If you are aware that accepting personal responsibility conflicts with your own cultural or personal beliefs, explore how you will deal with that difference. You might begin, *By reading and writing about personal responsibility, I have learned . . .*

   B.   Share the details of a personal experience in which you did or did not take personal responsibility and explain the effects of this choice on your life.

ONE STUDENT'S STORY

TARYN ROSSMILLER, *Boise State University, Idaho*

I was an honor student in high school, earned a 3.95 GPA, and graduated with scholarships and varsity letters in tennis and marching band. I loved high school, and I knew college was in my future. I entered Boise State University as a music education major with an emphasis in drums and percussion. I had a will to become a music teacher, and my goal was to succeed and excel.

However, in the music department, I was torn apart daily for what seemed like insignificant details. "You're rushing through the music. Your thumb is incorrectly placed. Your technique is all wrong. Have you even practiced?" Although I worked hard to improve, I returned every week to more criticism. The feedback was brutal and deflating. My instructors were commenting on me as a musician, but I took everything personally. After a year of enduring my professors' scrutiny, I stopped attending all of my music courses mid-semester. No matter how hard I worked, I thought my music career was hopeless. So, I felt my only option was to leave my courses and take the F's. As a result, my semester GPA fell to an all-time low of 0.98. I lost my financial aid, got placed on academic probation, and had to improve my academic standing to stay in school. The whole experience was a huge blow to my confidence and self-esteem. I felt I did not belong on "probation." I went from being passionate to becoming petrified about being in college.

Over the summer, I received an email from a professor at my university. She encouraged me to take a special course that was designed for students on academic probation. Although I felt I did not need the class, I enrolled in the Student Success Seminar anyway in hopes of getting right with the university. Still, surely it wasn't my fault that I had come to this academic fate—it was my professors'; it was the music department that was too demanding; it was everyone but me. However, I soon found out in my Student-Success-Seminar-That-I-Didn't-Need that my fate had EVERYTHING to do with me. In fact, I discovered my choices are made by me, my successes depend on me, and my life is my responsibility!

For the first time, I discovered the reality about my future—I am responsible for it, and only I can get myself where I want to go. I came away with many realizations while taking this course, and one of the most important was developing a Creator mindset. This class helped me realize that I demonstrated every aspect of a Victim mindset. I put myself down, I blamed others for my failures, and worst of all—I made excuses when I didn't accomplish a goal that I wanted. I made decisions carelessly, as if it wasn't my fault when things went badly, and my inner conversation didn't help me achieve my goals either.

Thanks to *On Course,* I began seeing my life with fresh eyes. I adopted the following three

steps as my own, and I knew that I could be on my way to achieving academic and personal successes:

1. I will believe that everything I do, whether or not I like my outcomes, is my responsibility,

2. I will believe that everything I do shapes the rest of my life and the experiences I will have, and

3. I will make positive decisions to guide me to what I want out of my life.

The semester after I completed the Student Success Seminar, I finished with a 3.5 GPA and my name on the dean's list. I was no longer on academic probation. With my grades back up, I appealed the loss of my financial aid and got it back. Since then, I changed my major to psychology, time has sped by, and now I will be graduating this May. I plan to pursue a master's degree in counseling and social work.

In the Student Success Seminar, I became empowered. Among other aspects, I learned the importance of developing a Creator mindset, how to build a sense of confidence, and how to stop my Inner Critic and Inner Defender. I no longer blame my professors, the university, or circumstances for my failures. I learned personal responsibility, and I realized that I was not a bad student; I just had a bad start. Overall, I learned I had the power to change my future, and how to take actions to improve my life. I am thrilled to maintain my Creator mindset and leave my Victim side behind. Goodbye, old me. Hello, success!

Photo: Courtesy of Taryn Rossmiller.

Mastering Creator Language

FOCUS QUESTION How can you create greater success by changing your vocabulary?

Have you ever noticed that there is almost always a conversation going on in your mind? Inner voices chatter away, offering commentary about you, other people, and the world. This self-talk is important because what you say to yourself determines the choices you make at each fork in the road.

SELF-TALK

People with a Victim mindset typically pay the most attention to the voice of their Inner Critic or their Inner Defender. By contrast, people with a Creator mindset listen carefully to the voice of their Inner Guide. Let's take a close look at these three inner voices.

The Inner Critic

This is the internal voice that judges us as inadequate: *I'm so uncoordinated. I can't do math. I'm not someone she would want to date. I never say the right thing. My ears are too big. I'm a lousy writer.* The Inner Critic accepts too much responsibility and blames us for whatever goes wrong in our lives: *It's all my fault. I always screw up. I knew I couldn't pass biology. I ruined the project. I ought to be ashamed. I blew it again.* This judgmental inner voice can find fault with anything about us: our appearance, our intelligence, our performance, our personality, our abilities, how others see us, and, in severe cases, even our value as a human being: *I'm not good enough. I'm worthless. I don't deserve to live.* (Although nearly everyone has a critical inner voice at times, if you often think toxic self-judgments like these last three, don't mess around. Get to your college's counseling office immediately and get help revising these hurtful messages so you don't make self-destructive choices.)

Ironically, self-judgments have a positive intention. By criticizing ourselves, we hope to eliminate our flaws and win the approval of others, thus feeling more worthy. Occasionally when we bully ourselves to be perfect, we *do* create a positive outcome, though we make ourselves miserable in the effort. Often, though, self-judgments cause us to give up, as when I tell myself, *I can't pass math,* so I drop the course. What's positive about this? Well, at least I've escaped my problem. Freed from the pressures of passing math, my anxieties float away, and I feel better than I have since the semester started. Of course, I still must pass math to get my degree, so my relief is temporary. The Inner Critic is quite content to trade success in the future for comfort in the present.

Where does an Inner Critic come from? Here's one clue: Have you noticed that its self-criticisms often sound like judgmental adults we have known? It's as if our younger self recorded their judgments and, years later, our Inner Critic replays them over and over. Sometimes you can even trace a self-judgment back

---

The world of self-criticism on the one side and judgment toward others on the other side represents a major part of the dance of life.

Hal Stone & Sidra Stone

A loud, voluble critic is enormously toxic. He is more poisonous to your psychological health than almost any trauma or loss. That's because grief and pain wash away with time. But the critic is always with you—judging, blaming, finding fault.

Matthew McKay & Patrick Fanning

to a specific comment that someone made about you years ago. Regardless of its truth, that judgment can affect the choices you make every day.

During discussions about Inner Critic voices, I have had students say that in their family culture, parents routinely criticize their children. The parents say they do it to help. One student said that if he brought home a test with a grade of 98, his parents would tell him that wasn't good enough. Another student shared that if she gained a pound, her mother would tell her she was fat and no man would ever want to marry her. A third student made a vase in her ceramics class and gave it to her mother as a present. Her mother proudly displayed the vase on the dining table. The next day, she asked, "What grade did you get for the vase?" My student replied that she had gotten a "C." Soon after, the vase disappeared, never to be seen again. I'm inclined to give these parents the benefit of the doubt. I'm willing to believe they thought they were helping their children, even showing love. Whatever their intentions, though, these parents had clearly given great power to their children's Inner Critics.

The Inner Defender

The other side of the Inner Critic is the Inner Defender. Instead of judging ourselves, the Inner Defender judges others: *What a boring teacher. My adviser screwed up my financial aid. Those people are not as good as we are. My roommate made me late to class. No one knows what they're doing around here. It's all their fault!* Inner Defenders accept too little responsibility and, thus, their thoughts and conversations are full of blaming, complaining, accusing, judging, criticizing, and condemning others.

Like Inner Critics, Inner Defenders have a positive intention. They, too, want to protect us from discomfort and anxiety. They, too, want us to feel more worthy. One way they do so is by judging others as wrong or bad or "less than." By tearing others down, the Inner Defender tries to make us feel better about ourselves. In this light, you can perhaps see that prejudice and bias are key tools of the Inner Defender.

Another way Inner Defenders try to help us is by blaming our problems on forces that seem beyond our control, such as other people, bad luck, the

What you're supposed to do when you don't like a thing is change it. If you can't change it, change the way you think about it. Don't complain.

Advice to Maya Angelou
from her grandmother

government, lack of money, uncaring parents, not enough time, or even too much time. The Inner Defender of a college student might say, *I can't pass math because my instructor is terrible. She couldn't teach math to Einstein. Besides that, the textbook stinks and the tutors in the math lab are rude and unhelpful. It's obvious this college doesn't really care what happens to its students.* If I'm that student, I breathe a sigh of relief because now I'm covered. If I drop the course, hey, it's not my fault. If I stay in the course and fail, it's not my fault either. And, if I stay in the course and somehow get a passing grade (despite my terrible instructor, lousy textbook, worthless tutors, and uncaring college), well, then I have performed no less than a miracle! Regardless of how bad things may get, I can find comfort knowing that at least it's not my fault. It's *their* fault!

> The object of teaching personal responsibility is to have the student substitute for the question "Who's to blame?" the question "What needs to be done?"
>
> Nathaniel Branden

And where did this voice come from? Perhaps you've noticed that the Inner Defender's voice sounds like judgmental adults we have known: *You can't trust those people. They're not as good as we are. They are the reason for our problem!* At other times, the Inner Defender sounds like our own voice when we were scared little kids trying to defend ourselves from criticism or punishment by powerful adults. Remember how we'd excuse ourselves from responsibility, shifting the blame for our poor choices onto someone or something else: *He keeps poking me. My dog ate my homework. I didn't have any choice. My sister broke it. He made me do it. It's all their fault!*

Notice what the Inner Critic and Inner Defender have in common. They are both voices of *judgment*. With the Inner Critic, we point the finger of judgment inward at ourselves. With the Inner Defender, we point the finger of judgment outward at someone or something outside of us. We pay a high price for listening to either our Inner Critic or Inner Defender. By focusing on who's to blame, we waste our energy on judgments instead of positive actions. We spin in place instead of moving purposely toward our desired outcomes and experiences. To feel better in the moment, we sabotage creating a better future.

> I used to want the words "She tried" on my tombstone. Now I want, "She did it."
>
> Katherine Dunham

Fortunately, another voice exists within us all.

The Inner Guide

This is the wise inner voice that seeks to make the best of any situation. The Inner Guide knows that judgment doesn't improve difficult situations. So instead, the Inner Guide objectively observes each situation and asks, *Am I on course or off course? If I'm off course, what can I do to get back on course?* Inner Guides tell us the impartial truth (as best they know it at that time), allowing us to be more fully aware of the world around us, other people, and especially ourselves. With this knowledge, we can take actions that will get us back on course.

Some people say, *But my Inner Critic (or Inner Defender) is right!* Yes, it's true that the Inner Critic or Inner Defender can be just as "right" as the Inner Guide. Maybe you really *are* a lousy writer and the tutors in the math lab actually *are* rude and unhelpful. The difference is that Victims expend all their energy in judging themselves or others, whereas Creators use their energy to solve problems. The voice we allow to occupy our thoughts determines our choices, and our choices determine the outcomes and experiences of our lives. So choose your thoughts carefully. As mentioned earlier, I allow myself up to 10 minutes to complain, blame, and make excuses. Then I redirect that energy and look for what I can do to improve the situation.

THE LANGUAGE OF RESPONSIBILITY

Translating Victim statements into the responsible language of Creators moves you from stagnant judgments to dynamic actions. In Table 2.1, the left-hand column presents the Victim thoughts of a student who is taking a challenging college course. Thinking this way, the student's future in this course is easy to predict . . . and it isn't likely to end well.

But, if she changes her inner conversation, as shown in the right-hand column, she'll also change her behaviors. She can learn more in the course and increase her likelihood of passing. More important, she can learn to reclaim control of her life from the judgmental, self-sabotaging thoughts of her Inner Critic and Inner Defender.

As you read these translations, notice two qualities that characterize Creator language. First, Creators accept ownership of their situation. Second, they plan and take actions to improve their situation. So, when you hear *ownership* and a *plan*, you know you're talking to a Creator. At any moment, you can choose either mindset . . . and that choice will shape your destiny.

> You must change the way you talk to yourself about your life situations so that you no longer imply that anything outside of you is the immediate cause of your unhappiness. Instead of saying, "Joe makes me mad," say, "I make myself mad when I'm around Joe."
>
> Ken Keyes

> Excuses rob you of power and induce apathy.
>
> Agnes Whistling Elk

TABLE 2.1

Victims Focus on Their Weaknesses	Creators Focus on How to Improve
I'm terrible in this subject.	I find this course challenging, so I'll start a study group and ask more questions in class.
Victims Make Excuses	**Creators Seek Solutions**
The instructor is so boring he puts me to sleep.	I find it difficult to pay attention in this class, so I'll challenge myself to stay focused and take at least one page of notes each class period.
Victims Complain	**Creators Turn Complaints into Requests**
This course is a stupid requirement.	I don't understand why this course is required, so I'm going to ask my instructor to help me see how it will benefit me in the future. ▶

TABLE 2.1 (*continued*)

Victims Compare Themselves Unfavorably to Others I'll never do as well as John; he's a genius.	**Creators Seek Help from Those More Skilled** I need to do better in this course, so I'm going to ask John if he'll help me study for the exams.
Victims Blame The tests are ridiculous. The professor gave me an F on the first one.	**Creators Accept Responsibility** I got an F on the first test because I didn't read the assignments thoroughly. From now on I'll take detailed notes on everything I read.
Victims See Problems as Permanent Posting comments in our class's discussion forum is impossible. I'll never understand how to do it.	**Creators Treat Problems as Temporary** I've been attempting to post comments on our class's online discussion forum without carefully reading the instructor's directions. I'll read the directions again and follow them one step at a time.
Victims Repeat Ineffective Behaviors Going to the tutoring center is no help. There aren't enough tutors.	**Creators Do Something New** I've been going to the tutoring center right after lunch when it's really busy. I'll start going in the morning to see if more tutors are available then.
Victims Try I'll try to do better.	**Creators Do** To improve, I'll do the following: Attend class regularly, take good notes, ask questions in class, start a study group, and make an appointment with the instructor. If all that doesn't work, I'll think of something else.
Victims Predict Defeat and Give Up I'll probably fail. There's nothing I can do. I can't . . . I have to . . . I should . . . I quit . . .	**Creators Think Positively and Look for a Better Choice** I'll find a way. There's always something I can do. I can . . . I choose to . . . I will . . . I'll keep going . . .

When people choose a Victim mindset, they complain, blame, and make excuses, and they have little energy left over to solve their problems. As a result, they typically remain stuck where they are, telling their sad story over and over to any poor soul who will listen. (Ever hear of a "pity party"?) In this way, Victims exhaust not only their own energy but often drain the energy of the people around them.

By contrast, when people choose a Creator mindset, they use their words and thoughts to improve a bad situation. First, they accept responsibility for creating their present outcomes and experiences, and their words reflect that ownership. Next, they plan and take positive actions to improve their lives. *Ownership* and a *plan*. In this way, Creators energize themselves and the people around them.

> There's no leverage in blaming. Power is rooted in self-responsibility.
>
> Nathaniel Branden

Whenever you feel yourself slipping into Victim language, ask yourself: What do I want in my life—excuses or results? What could I think, say, and do right now that would get me moving toward the outcomes and experiences I want?

JOURNAL ENTRY   5

In this activity, you will practice the language of personal responsibility. By learning to translate Victim statements into Creator statements, you will master the language of successful people.

1 **In your journal, make a copy of Table 2.2, including the 10 Victim statements in the left-hand column.**

2 **In the right-hand column, translate the Victim statements into the words of a Creator.** The two keys to Creator language are taking ownership of a problem and taking positive actions to solve it. *Ownership* and a *plan*. When you respond as if you are responsible for a bad situation, then you are empowered to do something about it (unlike Victims, who must wait for someone else to solve their problems). Use the translations earlier in this section as models.

3 **Write what you have learned or relearned about how you use language: Is it your habit to speak as a Victim or as a Creator? Do you find yourself more inclined to blame yourself (Inner Critic), blame others (Inner Defender), or seek solutions (Inner Guide)?** Be sure to give examples. What is your goal for language usage from now on? How, specifically, will you accomplish this goal? Your paragraph might begin, *While reading about and practicing Creator language, I learned that I . . .*

Remember to DIVE DEEP!

TABLE 2.2

Victim Language	Creator Language
1. If they'd do something about the parking on campus, I wouldn't be late so often.	1.
2. I'm failing my online class because the site is impossible to navigate.	2.
3. I'm too shy to ask questions in class even when I'm confused.	3.
4. She's a lousy instructor. That's why I failed the first test.	4.
5. I hate group projects because people are lazy and I always end up doing most of the work.	5.
6. I wish I could write better, but I just can't.	6.
7. My friend got me so angry that I can't even study for the exam.	7.
8. I'll try to do my best this semester.	8.
9. The financial aid form is too complicated to fill out.	9.
10. I work nights so I didn't have time to do the assignment.	10.

The way you use words has a tremendous impact on the quality of your life. Certain words are destructive; others are empowering.

Susan Jeffers

If you are in shackles, "I can't" has relevance; otherwise, it is usually a roundabout way of saying "I don't want to," "I won't," or, "I have not learned how to." If you really mean "I don't want to," it is important to come out and say so. Saying "I can't" disowns responsibility.

Gay Hendricks &
Kathlyn Hendricks

ALEXSANDR KANEVSKIY, *Oakland University, Michigan*

When I began college, I was unmotivated and chose to blame others for my problems and my shortcomings. I was so much smarter than everyone that I didn't need to do all the work that everyone else did; at least that's what I thought. My favorite pastime was staring blankly at a television, rather than attending lecture or doing assigned homework. I figured everything would take care of itself without my interference. I had carried this uninhibited laziness with me through high school and it, unfortunately, translated into my college career. It was then that the gravitas of my situation hit me; at my current rate I was going to be dismissed from school. I was placed on academic probation my sophomore year and unless I improved, I was out.

This was when I first laid my eyes and hands on the *On Course* book. I didn't think much of it at first, just another guide for the misguided, full of backward theories and advice that wouldn't help me, or anyone else. But from the first reading, I noticed that this book was different. It used different language, language that didn't bore me or induce disinterest. What's funniest, though, was that one of the first journals that I was assigned had the most profound impact on my

changing as a student. Just as *On Course* used innovative and interesting language to teach, this journal was all about changing my own language. Rather than use language that blames others or is blatantly negative, that journal taught me to use positive Creator language. I needed to think and speak in a language that searched for answers and solutions, not a language that kept me unmotivated and helpless. When I rephrased my thinking and speaking, the rest of life followed. All of a sudden, responsibility was in my own hands and the solutions that I needed, but was afraid to search out, became much clearer. Now that I knew there were, in fact, answers and solutions, I didn't look to blame those around me. I realized that it was up to me to find these solutions, that they would not magically appear before my eyes and that nobody else would find them for me. My faults and shortcomings became more apparent than ever, and my arrogance was startling. I saw that I was not smart enough to be exempt from school and from the work of my fellow students. They all searched for solutions and held themselves responsible for these solutions; I never realized this because I had never yearned for these

solutions, and therefore never had responsibility.

I stopped expecting solutions to come to me naturally and started to work, rather than fall asleep at the television. Positive Creator language was only the first step, but what I took from this first lesson carried through to every other lesson in class and in life. I found that I was newly interested in my classes; homework became a pleasure because each assignment was yet another opportunity to learn. Rather than fall asleep at the television, I now fell asleep after studying. And probation? That became a thing of the past. Even in basketball (my sport of choice) I started to take more of an interest in passing, rather than scoring, and helping my teammates, instead of blaming them for mistakes. Among my friends I am now known as the "problem solver," which is just as surprising to me as it is to them. They've noticed a definite change, and I am glad to advise them to read my *On Course* book so that maybe they too will find a lesson that sparks their own improvement. *On Course* provided me with valuable steppingstones that have made me into a student and person who cares enough to take responsibility for his language and his actions, doing what needs to be done to succeed in school and in the outside world.

Making Wise Decisions

FOCUS QUESTIONS   How can you improve the quality of the decisions you make? How can you take personal responsibility for the outcomes and experiences in your life?

Life is a journey with many opportunities and obstacles, and each one requires a choice. Whatever you are experiencing in your life today is, to a great extent, the result of your past choices. More important, the choices you make from this moment on will greatly determine what you'll experience in the future.

This is an exciting thought. If we can make wiser choices, we can more likely create the future we want. On the road to a college degree, you will face important choices such as these:

Shall I . . .

- major in business, science, or creative writing?

- work full-time, part-time, or not at all?

- drop a course that bores me or stick it out?

- experiment with alcohol and drugs?

- study for my exam or go out with friends?

The sum of these choices, plus thousands of others, will determine your degree of success in college and in life. Doesn't it seem wise, then, to develop an effective strategy for choice management?

> The end result of your life here on Earth will always be the sum total of the choices you made while you were here.
>
> Shad Helmstetter

Peter Mueller/The New Yorker Collection/The Cartoon Bank

THE WISE CHOICE PROCESS

In the face of any challenge, you can make a responsible decision by answering the six questions of the Wise Choice Process. This process, you might be interested to know, is actually a variation of a decision-making model used in many career fields. For example, nurses learn a similar process for helping patients that is abbreviated ADPIE. These letters stand for Assess, Diagnose, Plan, Implement, and Evaluate. Counselors and therapists in training may learn a similar process for solving personal problems. William Glasser described this process in his book *Reality Therapy.*

And the *NASA Systems Engineering Handbook* says systems engineering consists of

1. identification and quantification of system goals,

2. creation of alternative system design concepts,

3. performance of design trades,

4. selection and implementation of the best design,

5. verification that the design is properly built and integrated, and

6. post-implementation assessment of how well the system meets (or met) the goals.

In plain English, systems engineers use their version of the Wise Choice Process to achieve their goals.

You are about to learn a decision-making system that will empower you to take greater responsibility for creating your life as you want it to be . . . despite the inevitable challenges that life presents. Here are the six empowering steps of the Wise Choice Process:

1. **What's my present situation?** Begin by identifying your problem or challenge, being sure to define the situation as a Creator, not as a Victim. The important information here is "What exists?" (not "Whose fault is it?"). Quiet your Inner Critic, that self-criticizing voice in your head: *I am a total loser in my history class.* Likewise, ignore your Inner Defender, that judgmental voice that blames everyone else for your problems: *My history instructor is the worst teacher on the planet.* Instead, rely on your Inner Guide, your wise, impartial inner voice that tells the truth as best it can. Consider only the objective facts of your situation, including how you feel about them. For example:

   I stayed up all night studying for my first history test. When I finished taking the test, I hoped for an A. At worst, I expected a B. When I got the test back, my grade was a D. Five other students got A's. I feel depressed and angry.

   By the way, sometimes when we accurately define a troublesome situation, we immediately know what to do. The problem wasn't so much the situation as our muddy understanding of it.

M y choice; my responsibility; win or lose, only I hold the key to my destiny.

Elaine Maxwell

I am the cause of my choices, decisions, and actions. It is I who chooses, decides, and acts. If I do so knowing my responsibility, I am more likely to proceed wisely and appropriately than if I make myself oblivious of my role as source.

Nathaniel Branden

2. **How would I like my situation to be?** You can't change the past, but if you could create your desired outcome in the future, what would it look like?

   I get A's and B's on all my future tests.

3. **What are my possible choices?** Create a list of possible choices that you *could* do, knowing you aren't obligated to do any of them. Compile your list without judgment. Don't say, *Oh, that would never work.* Don't even say, *That's a great idea.* Judgment during brainstorming stops the creative flow. Move from judgments to possibilities, discovering as many creative options as you can. Give yourself time to ponder, explore, consider, think, discover, conceive, invent, imagine. Then dive even deeper. If you get stuck, try one of these options. First, take a different point of view. Think of someone you admire and ask, *What would that person do in my situation?* Or pretend your problem belongs to someone else, and he asks you what he should do. What advice would you offer? Third, incubate. That is, set the problem aside and let your unconscious mind work on a solution while you do other things. Sometimes a great option will pop into your mind while you are brushing your teeth, doing math homework, or even sleeping. Your patience will often pay off with a helpful option that would have remained invisible had you accepted the first idea that came to mind or, worse, given up. For example:

   - *I could complain to my history classmates and anyone else who will listen.*
   - *I could drop the class and take it next semester with another instructor.*
   - *I could complain to the department head that the instructor grades unfairly.*
   - *I could ask my successful classmates for help.*
   - *I could ask the instructor for suggestions about improving my grades.*
   - *I could read about study skills and experiment with some new ways to study.*
   - *I could request an opportunity to retake the test.*
   - *I could take all of the online practice quizzes.*
   - *I could get a tutor.*

4. **What's the likely outcome of each possible choice?** Decide how you think each choice is likely to turn out. If you can't predict the outcome of one of your possible choices, stop this process and gather any additional information you need. For example, if you don't know the impact that dropping a course will have on your financial aid, find out before you take that action. Here are the possible choices from Step 3 and their likely outcomes:

   - *Complain to history classmates: I'd have the immediate pleasure of criticizing the instructor and maybe getting others' sympathy.*

A person defines and redefines who they are by the choices they make, minute to minute.

Joyce Chapman

Destiny is not a matter of chance; it is a matter of choice. It is not a thing to be waited for; it is a thing to be achieved.

William Jennings Bryan

- *Drop the class: I'd lose three credits this semester and have to make them up later.*
- *Complain to the department head: Probably she'd ask if I've seen my instructor first, so I wouldn't get much satisfaction.*
- *Ask successful classmates for help: I might learn how to improve my study habits; I might also make new friends.*
- *Ask the instructor for suggestions: I might learn what to do next time to improve my grade; at least the instructor would learn that I want to do well in this course.*
- *Read about study skills: I would probably learn some strategies I don't know and maybe improve my test scores in all of my classes.*
- *Request an opportunity to retake the test: My request might get approved and give me an opportunity to raise my grade. At the very least, I'd demonstrate how much I want to do well.*
- *Take all of the online practice quizzes: This action wouldn't help my grade on this test, but it would probably improve my next test score.*
- *Get a tutor: A tutor would help, but it would probably take a lot of time.*

What we really mean by free will, of course, is the visualizing of alternatives and making a choice between them.

Jacob Bronowski

5. **Which choice(s) will I commit to doing?** Now create your plan. Decide which choice or choices will likely create your desired outcome; then commit to acting on them. If no favorable option exists, consider which choice leaves you no worse off than before. If no such option exists, then ask which choice creates the least unfavorable outcome. And remember that not making a choice *is* a choice.

I'll talk to my successful classmates, make an appointment with my instructor and ask him to explain what I can do to improve, and I'll request an opportunity to retake the test. I'll read the study skills sections of On Course *and implement at least three new study strategies. If these choices don't raise my next test score to at least a B, I'll get a tutor.*

Each situation will dictate the best options. In this example, if the student had previously failed four tests instead of one, the best choice might be to drop the class. Or, if everyone in the class were receiving D's and F's, and if the student had already met with the instructor, a responsible option might be to see the department head about the instructor's grading policies.

The principle of choice describes the reality that I am in charge of my life. I choose it all. I always have, I always will.

Will Schutz

6. **When and how will I evaluate my plan?** At some future time you will want to assess your results. To do so, compare your new situation with how you want it to be (as you described in Step 2). If the two situations are identical (or close enough), you can call your plan a success. If you find that you are still far from your desired outcome, you have some decisions to make. You might decide that you haven't implemented your new approach long enough, so you'll keep working your plan. Or you may decide that your plan just isn't working, in which case you'll return to Step 1 and work

through Step 5 to design a plan that will work better. However, you're not starting completely over because this time you're smarter than you were when you began: Now you know what doesn't work.

After my next history test, I'll see if I have achieved my goal of getting an A or B. If not, I'll revise my plan.

Here's the bottom line: Our choices reveal what we *truly* believe and value, as opposed to what we *say* we believe and value. When I submissively wait for others to improve my life, I am being a Victim. When I passively wait for luck to go my way, I am being a Victim. When I make choices that take me off course from my future success just to increase my immediate pleasure (such as partying instead of studying for an important test), I am being a Victim. When I make choices that sacrifice my goals and dreams just to reduce my immediate discomfort (such as dropping a challenging course instead of spending extra hours working with a tutor), I am being a Victim.

However, when I design a plan to craft my life as I want it, I am being a Creator. When I carry out my plan even in the face of obstacles (such as when the campus bookstore runs out of a book that I need for class and I keep up with my assignments by reading a copy the instructor has placed on reserve in the library), I am being a Creator. When I take positive risks to advance my goals (such as asking a question in a large lecture class even though I am nervous), I am being a Creator. When I sacrifice immediate pleasure to stay on course toward my dreams (such as resisting the urge to buy a new cell phone so I can reduce my work hours to study more), I am being a Creator.

No matter what your final decision may be, the mere fact that you are defining and making your own choices is wonderfully empowering. By participating in the Wise Choice Process, you affirm your belief that you *can* change your life for the better. You reject the position that you are merely a Victim of outside forces, a pawn in the chess game of life. You insist on being the Creator of your own outcomes and experiences, shaping your destiny through the power of wise choices.

> One's philosophy is not best expressed in words; it is expressed in the choices one makes. In the long run, we shape our lives and we shape ourselves. The process never ends until we die. And, the choices we make are ultimately our own responsibility.
>
> Eleanor Roosevelt

JOURNAL ENTRY   / 6

In this activity, you will apply the Wise Choice Process to improve a difficult situation in your life. Think about a current problem, one that you're comfortable sharing with your classmates and instructor. As a result of this problem, you may be angry, sad, frustrated, depressed, overwhelmed, or afraid. Perhaps this situation has to do with a grade you received, a teacher's comment, or a classmate's action. Maybe the problem relates to a job, a relationship, or money. The Wise Choice Process can help you make an empowering choice in any part of your life.

❶ Write the six questions of the Wise Choice Process and answer each one as it relates to your situation.

▶

JOURNAL ENTRY   **6**   *continued*

The Wise Choice Process

1. What's my present situation? (Describe the problem objectively and completely.)
2. How would I like my situation to be? (What is your ideal future outcome?)
3. What are my possible choices? (Create a long list of specific choices that might create your preferred outcome.)
4. What's the likely outcome of each possible choice? (If you can't predict the likely outcome of an option, stop and gather more information.)
5. Which choice(s) will I commit to doing? (Pick from your list of choices in Step 3.)
6. When and how will I evaluate my plan? (Identify the specific date and criteria by which you will determine the success of your plan.)

2 **Write what you learned or relearned by doing the Wise Choice Process.** Be sure to dive deep. You might begin: *By doing the Wise Choice Process, I learned that I . . .*

Remember, you can enliven your journal by adding pictures you found, drawings of your own, or quotations or song lyrics that appeal to you.

When I see all the choices I really have, it makes the world a whole lot brighter.

Debbie Scott, student

ONE STUDENT'S STORY

KONNIE KELLOGG, *Donnelly College, Kansas*

At the age of 38, I am in prison with 15 months left of my 10-year sentence. Clearly, I have made some bad choices in my life.

I dropped out of high school and got married at 17. At 21, I was unhappy in my marriage, so I called it off and got divorced. In my eyes, we had grown apart, and that was that. Instead of working on our relationship, I couldn't see past my not being happy. Looking back, I wish I had learned how to make the marriage last. For starters, I could have asked for ideas from my parents who were married for 40 years.

A year after my divorce, I was feeling broken, and I started seeing a guy who introduced me to drugs. The drugs, I found, gave me some level of happiness. We ran with a crowd that was also involved with drugs, and we started manufacturing meth. Eventually my boyfriend and I got caught and sent to prison. More bad choices.

After about five years in prison, I saw a flier about an opportunity to take college courses. I really wanted to get a nursing degree, but by this time, I had convinced myself that I wasn't smart enough to take college classes. I believed I was never going to be better than what I was—a prison inmate.

Somehow, though, I found the courage to enroll in one of the college courses, and this was the turning point that changed my life. The textbook was called *On Course,* and who could have been more off course than I was? Through this class, I was challenged to learn about myself, my faults as well as my strengths. I learned a lot of valuable strategies in the course, and one of the most valuable is the Wise Choice

▶

Process, which I've used to make better choices in every aspect of my life.

For example, with my release coming up next year, I need to decide what to do afterward. Using the Wise Choice Process, I asked myself, *How would I like my life to be when I'm released?* I know I want to get a nursing degree and start a new life. I never want to return to prison. What are my choices to make that happen? One option would be returning to my hometown and looking for a job there. Another option is staying here in Topeka.

When I looked at the likely outcomes of going home, I realized it would probably be the

easier option because I know people there who could help me. However, when I looked more deeply, I realized I'd probably get back with my boyfriend, and then I'd wind up involved with drugs again. My other option—staying in Topeka—was scary because I have no one here to be my safety net. Then I realized I've met some people from a church who would provide me with support. I did some more exploring and learned that I could probably get a job here at a hospital or nursing home that are both felon-friendly. The hospital will even reimburse me for college classes, which will let me go to school slowly until I get my

nursing degree. When I realized that, I felt empowered and knew I had found the right choice. I was so confident that I wrote my boyfriend and told him that I couldn't be with him anymore. I had to go cold turkey if I wanted to leave the drug life behind.

The Wise Choice Process made me take the time to really look at the pros and cons of my situation and see the best choice for my future. If I had known this strategy years ago, I wouldn't have made so many rash choices. I would have stayed married, gone to school, and made a much better life for myself and my family. It's time-consuming to do this process, but in the end, it is so worth it.

PERSONAL RESPONSIBILITY / at Work

Failures are going to happen, and how you deal with them may be the most important thing in whether you succeed. You need fierce resolve. You need to take responsibility.

—Jamie Dimon, chairman and CEO of JPMorgan Chase Bank

The foundation of career success is responsibility. Without responsibility, nobody would take action to solve problems at work. Individuals would find someone else to blame instead of fixing the problems. Teams would fall apart without anyone taking ownership for reaching their goals. Companies would never consider the impact of their choices on the community.

According to the *Harvard Business Review*, the most effective CEOs have taken *"personal responsibility* when things went wrong." For example, when someone poisoned bottles of Tylenol on store shelves, company CEO James Burke took immediate responsibility, then rapid action to solve the problem. He recalled 31 million bottles from stores and offered to replace earlier purchases for free. It cost Johnson & Johnson, makers of Tylenol, more than $100 million, but quickly reassured the public, and saved the company from collapse. In many other cases, companies have denied problems with their products, or delayed taking action, resulting in bigger problems and less public trust.

PERSONAL AND SOCIAL RESPONSIBILITY

There are two major categories of responsibility at work: (1) personal responsibility and (2) social

▶

responsibility. You'll need to practice both to be successful.

Personal responsibility means you take ownership for your work choices and the outcomes you create. Responsible employees put all their efforts into doing the best job possible. They invest enough time to do outstanding work. Because they take responsibility for their choices, they are more thoughtful about each choice they make. In preparing for your career, it would be wise for you to practice taking personal responsibility.

In 2014, rising NBA superstar Stephen Curry met with Nike to consider signing another marketing contract. During the meeting, two Nike employees made major mistakes. One representative who met with Curry mispronounced his name, then didn't pay attention to the correction. Another employee charged with the responsibility of creating the slide presentation used an existing marketing slideshow. When updating it, he didn't take responsibility to double-check the final slideshow, overlooking the content on an important slide. That slide still showed another player's name (Kevin Durant, then playing on a rival team) instead of Curry's. Rightfully upset, Curry signed with Under Armour instead. As a result of the actions of two irresponsible employees, Nike lost potential market value that in 2016 was estimated at more than $15 billion.

Because more of our choices today are being shared on social media, it is also important to take responsibility for social media use. Cyber-bullying, spreading false information, or posting someone's personal photos without permission are examples of irresponsible social media use. When current (or future) employees don't take responsibility for managing their personal social media appropriately, an employer often assumes that there will be more unwise choices to follow.

Did you know that more than 70 percent of employers review your public social media history when you apply for a job? Although most states don't allow employers to request password access to your private accounts nor to require you to "friend" an employer, it is easy enough for employers to look up your social media accounts, and most social media users have a long history of public posts and tweets. According to the 2017 CareerBuilder survey, 54 percent of employers found posted content that led them not to hire a candidate. The choices you are making now impact your ability to get hired after graduation. When you are employed, irresponsible posts can also lead to you losing your job. Think carefully before posting or tweeting anything that may demonstrate unprofessional or irresponsible behavior. Do not post sexist, racist, or other biased comments; embarrassing or inappropriate photos; confidential information; or negative statements about your customers or employers. Use your social media to build and maintain a positive image for employers instead.

Personal responsibility also means that you follow professional standards that are expected in your field. For example, lawyers are required to maintain specific standards of behavior in these areas:

1. avoiding conflicts of interest

2. meeting deadlines for filing motions

3. properly handling client fees

4. ensuring confidentiality of client information

Lawyers who violate these standards may have their ability to practice suspended or terminated. Law schools are required to offer a professional responsibility course. After finishing law school, in order to work as a lawyer, you need to pass the state bar exam. The exam tests your understanding of both the law and your professional responsibilities.

▶

Personal responsibility is critical to career success in this and all fields.

One way to begin your exploration of personal responsibility at work is to consider your mindset. At work, do you usually operate with a Creator or Victim mindset? Your current "job" may be part-time or full-time, paid or volunteer, or even being a "professional" student. Take some time to reflect on your patterns at work. Do you respond to challenges by blaming others? Do you frequently complain about problems like difficult customers, coworkers, or classmates? Remember that employees with a Creator mindset seek solutions, take action, and try something new. If you practice this response instead of blaming and complaining, you'll be preparing for a successful career.

The Victim mindset has been described as "reactive" and the Creator mindset as "proactive." When the air conditioning fails at an office complex, a building supervisor might react by complaining about the equipment manufacturer. A proactive supervisor might check the system weekly to make sure it is working properly. Then she can request a service call long before it fails completely. Which choice do you most relate to?

Social responsibility means that you take ownership of your behavior toward others at work. You pay attention to how you interact with your colleagues. You avoid sending negative emails about your coworkers and your boss. When the marketing team doesn't reach its goals, you don't call out one member of your team. You hold the entire team accountable (including yourself). If a new team member didn't do well, you help this new employee learn the skills needed to succeed at the job. If a coworker appears upset, you stop to ask if they're ok. You take consistent action to be an active member of a supportive workplace community.

Social responsibility also means you contribute to others beyond work. Singer Carrie Underwood believes that "successful people have a social responsibility to make the world a better place and not just take from it." Underwood started a foundation in her hometown of Checotah, Oklahoma, where she has also volunteered at the animal shelter. She has donated millions of dollars to the American Red Cross, City of Hope, Global Poverty Project, Habitat for Humanity, Project Clean Water, and the St. Jude Children's Research Hospital. What might you do to make the world a better place? It doesn't take a lot of money to make an impact. Your exploration of social responsibility might begin with your actions at college. Do you belong to any clubs that focus on positive benefits for the campus? What actions might you take to improve your dorm or campus center environment? Your record of social responsibility can be strengthened while you are in college. This will give you an opportunity to develop your résumé and provide clear answers to job interview questions about how you have acted on your social responsibilities.

Another part of social responsibility is corporate responsibility. This effort means your entire company has identified that part of its mission is to contribute value to the surrounding community. It might donate funding for an important social cause. It might reduce the waste it produces in manufacturing. The company might, as did Johnson & Johnson, take immediate responsibility to address any problems with its products, even if the company wasn't the cause. Priscilla Chan, cofounder of the Chan Zuckerberg Initiative, believes that "We—the current generation—have a moral responsibility to make the world better for future generations." Once you are employed at an organization, you become part of its corporate responsibility model. To help you understand corporate responsibility now, you could join a campus community service organization. This will give you experience in having a positive impact on the local community surrounding the college.

▶

COMMITMENT

One of the most powerful responsibility strategies is commitment. A commitment means you follow through on your promises. A commitment to your employer is a promise that you will offer your best effort every day. Research shows that the stronger employees' commitment, the better they do their job. They provide improved customer service, have more consistent job attendance, and stay at their jobs longer than uncommitted employees. They work harder at their jobs and perform more effectively than employees with low commitment. Can you see why a future employer would prefer to hire, retain, and reward responsible employees with high commitment?

Jim Collins is a researcher who explores successful companies. He is the author of many books, including *Good to Great*. After examining 1,435 companies, he observed that some companies made a successful leap from good to great. Being great meant that their financial performance was almost seven times higher than the average performance of competing companies. What was one crucial difference? These companies created an environment where employees were "committed to excellence."

Your challenge is to practice committing to excellence in every role in your life. If you do so, you will be strengthening a skill that will help you bring great results to your company. Here are two strategies to practice commitment:

1. Identify a **personal responsibility commitment** that would also have a positive impact at the workplace. For example, "I am committed to following through when I tell someone I will email them by the end of the day." Practice meeting this commitment consistently. Write down your current commitments so you are prepared to share them during a job interview.

2. Choose a **social responsibility goal**. Then make a commitment to take one small action each day that will help you achieve this goal. Track your actions and keep going until you reach your goal.

LEARNING RESPONSIBILITY

In this course, you're learning about responsibility. But should responsibility even be taught in college? Partnership for 21st Century Learning thinks so. As a coalition of major businesses, education leaders, and policymakers, P21.org wants students to better prepare for career effectiveness. They believe that "today's life and work environments require far more than thinking skills and content knowledge. The ability to navigate the complex life and work environments in the globally competitive information age requires students to pay rigorous attention to developing adequate life and career skills." In other words, practice your career skills now, before your first day on the job. This course offers a great opportunity to do so.

P21.org believes that accountability and responsibility are two of the most important skills you can learn to prepare for a successful career. While responsibility means taking ownership for your choices, accountability means holding oneself responsible for producing results. You can use the Wise Choice Process to improve these two skills. Consider what you would do in the following situation:

Responsibility scenario: You promised your manager that you would take detailed notes at an early morning meeting that she could not attend. The next morning, when the alarm sounds, you hit snooze too many times. Leaving late, you miss the meeting. What are your possible choices?

1. Blame the heavy traffic.

2. Ask a colleague for notes and email them to your manager as though you were actually at the meeting.

3. Email your boss that you couldn't make the meeting due to another commitment.

▶

4. Ask a colleague for notes and email them to your manager. Explain that you overslept, missed the meeting, and then met with a colleague to get her notes. You offer an apology, take responsibility, and promise to follow through in the future.

Consider the outcomes from acting on each of these options. Which option appears to be the most responsible, wisest choice? Success at work doesn't mean never making mistakes. It does mean being responsible and accountable, learning from your mistakes, and making wiser choices the next time. When interviewing you for a position, employers will often ask questions to understand your experience in this area. If you practice responsibility and accountability now, you will be well prepared to share specific examples of when you have made responsible decisions in the past.

By practicing responsibility skills, you'll be investing in a promising future for yourself. You can strengthen these skills in many ways. You can use social media responsibly, adopt a Creator mindset, and be proactive rather than reactive. You can also strengthen your personal and social responsibility to prepare for workplace responsibility. While practicing these skills, don't forget to add them to your résumé. Create a list of the skills you've learned, and practice sharing responsibility examples and stories in a mock interview. Winston Churchill once said, "The price of greatness is responsibility." If you want to move yourself from good to great in your career, responsibility is a powerful place to start.

TECH TIPS: Personal Responsibility

Locus of control is the scientific term that describes the degree to which you believe your outcomes and experiences are the result of your choices or of forces outside your control, such as luck or powerful others. In other words, measuring locus of control is a way to measure the degree to which you take responsibility for your life. To further assess yourself on this important success factor, do an Internet search for "locus of control test." Psychologist Julian Rotter created the first test of this kind in 1966, and you can still find his tests posted online, along with a number of others.

Ahoona.com is an online tool that walks you through a process of making decisions. Funded by a grant from the National Science Foundation, this site was created by Dr. Ali Abbas, a college professor who teaches decision analysis. The decision-making process asks you for important information such as goals, pros and cons, alternatives, and uncertainties. At each step of the decision-making process, it provides information about how to think more deeply. Tools used include pro/con, decision trees, and weight and rate. A social media option also allows you to invite friends or anyone in the world to weigh in on your decision.

ChoiceMap *(iOS)* is an app designed to help make difficult decisions. It asks you to describe your decision and possible options (e.g., *What subject should I major in: biology, English, or math?*) and the factors influencing your decision (e.g., difficulty, time to degree, your interest level, employment outlook). Then you weigh the personal importance of each factor and apply the ratings to each option. ChoiceMap then rates each option, showing how close it comes to being your perfect choice. Use the app to help you make decisions ranging from what to have for breakfast to whom to marry. Although this app does show your "best" options, you are, of course, responsible for your final choice. No fair complaining later that "The app made me do it."

Decision Buddy *(Android)*, like ChoiceMap, is an app that breaks down the decision-making process into little steps that guide you to your final choice.

Note: All of these are free, but some may offer upgraded features for a fee.

BELIEVING IN YOURSELF

Change Your Inner Conversation

FOCUS QUESTION   How can you raise your self-esteem by changing your self-talk?

Imagine this: Three students schedule an appointment with their instructor to discuss a project they're working on together. They go to the instructor's office at the scheduled time, but he isn't there. They wait 45 minutes before leaving. As you learn what they do next, which student do you think has the strongest self-esteem?

Student 1, feeling discouraged and depressed, spends the evening watching television while neglecting assignments in other subjects. Student 2, feeling insulted and furious, spends the evening complaining to friends about the horrible instructor who stood them up. Student 3, feeling puzzled about the mix-up, emails the instructor to see what happened and to set up another meeting; while waiting for a response, this student spends the evening studying for a test in another class.

Which student has the strongest self-esteem?

THE CURSE OF STINKIN' THINKIN'

How is it that three people can have the same experience and respond to it so differently? According to psychologists like Albert Ellis, the answer lies in what each person believes caused the event. Ellis suggested that different responses can be understood by realizing that the activating event (A) plus our beliefs (B) equal the consequences (C) (how we respond). In other words, $A + B = C$. For example:

> It is the mind that maketh good or ill, That maketh wretch or happy, rich or poor.
>
> Edmund Spenser

> Self-esteem can be defined as the state that exists when you are not arbitrarily haranguing and abusing yourself but choose to fight back against those automatic thoughts with meaningful rational responses.
>
> Dr. David Burns

TABLE 2.3

Activating Event	+ Beliefs	= Consequence
Student #1: Instructor didn't show up for a scheduled conference.	My instructor thinks I'm dumb. I'll never get a college degree. I'm a failure in life.	Got depressed and watched television all evening.
Student #2: Same.	My instructor won't help me. Teachers don't care about students.	Got angry and spent the night telling friends how horrible the instructor is.
Student #3: Same.	I'm not sure what went wrong. Sometimes things just don't turn out the way you plan. There's always tomorrow.	Emailed the instructor to see what happened and to set up a new appointment, then studied for another class.

Ellis suggests that our upsets are caused not so much by our problems as by what we *think* about our problems. When our thinking is full of irrational beliefs—what Ellis calls "stinkin' thinkin'"—we feel awful even when the circumstances don't justify it. So, how we *think* about the events in our lives is the key issue. Problems may come and go, but our "stinkin' thinkin'" stays with us. As the old saying goes, "Everywhere I go, there I am."

Stinkin' thinkin' isn't based on reality. Rather, these irrational thoughts are the automatic chatter of the Inner Critic (keeper of negative beliefs about the self) and the Inner Defender (keeper of negative beliefs about other people and the world).

So, what about our three students and their self-esteem? It's not hard to see that Student 1, who got depressed and wasted the evening watching television, has low self-esteem. This student is thrown far off course simply by the instructor's not showing up. A major cause of this self-defeating reaction is the Inner Critic's harsh self-judgments. Here are some common self-damning beliefs held by Inner Critics:

> The Inner Critic keeps us feeling insecure and childlike. When it is operating, we feel like children who have done something wrong and probably will never be able to do anything right.
>
> Hal Stone & Sidra Stone

I'm dumb.
I'm selfish.
I'm a failure.
I'm incapable.
I'm not as good as other people.
I'm worthless.

I'm unattractive.
I'm lazy.
I'm not college material.
I'm weak.
I'm a lousy parent.
I'm unlovable.

People dominated by their Inner Critic often misinterpret events, inventing criticisms that aren't there. A friend says, "Something came up, and I can't meet you tonight." The Inner Critic responds, "I screwed up again! I'll never have any friends!"

The activating event doesn't cause the consequence; rather, the judgmental chatter of the Inner Critic does. A strong Inner Critic is both a cause and an effect of low self-esteem.

What about Student 2, the one who spent the evening telling friends how horrible the instructor was? Though perhaps less apparent, this student's judgmental response also demonstrates low self-esteem. The finger-pointing Inner Defender is merely the Inner Critic turned outward and is just as effective at getting the student off course. Here are some examples of destructive beliefs held by Inner Defenders:

> Everyone has a critical inner voice. But people with low self-esteem tend to have a more vicious and vocal pathological critic.
>
> Matthew McKay & Patrick Fanning

People don't treat me right, so they're rotten.
People don't act the way I want them to, so they're awful.
People don't live up to my expectations, so they're the enemy.
People don't do what I want, so they're against me.
Life is full of problems, so it's terrible.
Life is unfair, so I can't stand it.
Life doesn't always go my way, so I can't be happy.
Life doesn't provide me with everything I want, so it's unbearable.

People dominated by their Inner Defender imagine personal insults and slights in neutral events. A classmate says, "Something came up, and I can't meet you tonight." The Inner Defender responds, "Who do you think you are, anyway? I can find someone a lot better to study with than you!"

The activating event doesn't cause the angry response; rather, the judgmental chatter of the judgmental Inner Defender does. A strong Inner Defender is both a cause and an effect of low self-esteem.

Only Student 3 demonstrates high self-esteem. This student realizes he doesn't know why the instructor missed the meeting. He doesn't blame himself, the instructor, or a rotten world. He considers alternatives: Perhaps the instructor forgot, got sick, or was involved in a traffic accident. Until he finds out what happened and decides what to do next, this student turns his attention to an action that will keep him on course to another goal. The Inner Guide is concerned with positive results, not judging self or others. A strong Inner Guide is both a cause and an effect of high self-esteem.

> Replacing a negative thought with a positive one changes more than just the passing thought—it changes the way you perceive and deal with the world.
>
> Dr. Clair Douglas

DISPUTING IRRATIONAL BELIEFS

How, then, can you avoid stinkin' thinkin'?

First, you can become aware of the chatter of your Inner Critic and Inner Defender. Be especially alert when events in your life go wrong, when your desired outcomes and experiences are thwarted. That's when we are most likely to complain, blame, and excuse. That's when we substitute judgments of ourselves or others for the positive actions that would get us back on course.

Once you become familiar with your inner voices, you can begin a process of separating yourself from your Inner Critic and Inner Defender. To do this, practice disputing your irrational and self-sabotaging beliefs. Here are four effective ways to dispute an irrational belief such as "My instructor doesn't want to help me":

> Does it help to change what you say to yourself? It most certainly does. . . . Tell yourself often enough that you'll succeed and you dramatically improve your chances of succeeding and of feeling good.
>
> Drs. Bernie Zilbergeld & Arnold A. Lazarus

- **Offer evidence that your judgments are incorrect:** *My instructor emailed me last week to see if I needed help with my project, so there's no evidence to believe he won't help me now.*

- **Offer a positive explanation of the problem:** *Sure, my instructor didn't show up, but he may have missed the appointment because of a last-minute problem.*

- **Question the importance of the problem:** *Even if my instructor won't help me, I can still do well on this project, and if I don't, it won't be the end of the world.*

- **If you find that your judgments are true, instead of continuing to criticize yourself or someone else, offer a plan to improve the situation:** *If I'm honest, I have to admit that I haven't done well in this class so far. From now on I'm going to attend every class, take good notes, read my assignments two or three times, and work with a study group before every test.*

According to psychologist Ellis, a key to correcting irrational thinking is changing a "must" into a preference. When we think "must," what follows in our thoughts is typically awful, terrible, and dreadful. For example, my Inner Defender's belief that an instructor "must" meet me for an appointment or he is an awful, terrible, dreadful person is irrational; I'd certainly "prefer" him to meet me for an appointment, but his not meeting me does not make him horrible— in fact, he may have a perfectly good reason for not meeting with me. As another example, my Inner Critic's belief that I "must" pass this course or else I am an awful, terrible, dreadful person is irrational; I'd certainly "prefer" to pass this course, but not doing so does not make me worthless—in fact, not passing this course may lead me to something even better. Believing irrationally that I, another person, or the world "must" be a particular way, Ellis says, is a major cause of distress and misery.

Y ou mainly make yourself needlessly and neurotically miserable by strongly holding absolutist irrational beliefs, especially by rigidly believing unconditional shoulds, oughts, and musts.

Albert Ellis

STEREOTYPE THREAT

Social psychologist Claude Steele of Stanford University has identified a kind of stinkin' thinkin' that afflicts cultural groups: *stereotype threat*. A stereotype is a generalization about members of a particular group, and it is not true. However, stereotypes can still negatively impact cultural groups. Stereotypes include the following: *African Americans are all excellent in sports but they aren't good students . . . or women are all terrific at taking care of children but they are poor at math and science.* Stereotype threat is a fear that your behavior in a particular situation—such as taking a math test—might confirm a negative stereotype about a cultural group to which you belong. The resulting anxiety causes a self-fulfilling prophecy, and you do, indeed, perform down to the stereotype rather than up to your ability.

As an example of the effect of stereotype threat, Steele and his colleagues showed that when race was emphasized, African American college students did less well than their white classmates on a standardized test. However, when race was not emphasized, African American students' scores were equivalent to those of white students. Further studies have shown that stereotype threat can negatively influence the academic success of many cultural groups, including Latinos, females in math, and students of working-class backgrounds.

E veryone experiences stereotype threat. We are all members of some group about which negative stereotypes exist, from white males and Methodists to women and the elderly.

Claude M. Steele

Here's how stinkin' thinkin' seems to contribute to stereotype threat. Let's say a female student sits down to take a math test. That's the activating event. Next come her beliefs: She knows the stereotype—women aren't good at math. She doesn't want to be lumped into or reinforce that stereotype. She becomes anxious, distracted, and can't remember all she studied. The result is a self-fulfilling prophecy. She doesn't do as well on the test as she is capable of, and the culprit is her stinkin' thinkin'.

Besides causing immediate problems in test situations, stereotype threat may even cause people to avoid the threat area altogether. A woman may avoid majoring in math and science. A white man may reject playing basketball. A working-class student may lose motivation and drop out of college.

The strategies for disputing that were mentioned earlier can also be applied to stereotype threat. A woman may **offer evidence that the stereotype is wrong:** *I did well in math and science in high school . . . and I just read that four women recently won Nobel Prizes in science and mathematics.* A white man may **question the importance of the stereotype:** *It really doesn't matter what other people think; I know I have the skills and drive to be an excellent basketball player.* A working-class student may **offer a plan to address the stereotype:** *My English teacher told us her parents were migrant farm workers; I'm going to talk to her about how she kept herself motivated to get a college degree.*

In a study at the University of Arizona, psychologists Michael Johns, Toni Schmader, and Andy Martens suggested another way to reduce the negative impact of stereotype threat. They gave a math test to one group of students and found that female students performed worse than the men. Before giving the math test to a second group, they told students briefly about how stereotype threat could negatively affect the performance of women. Specifically, they announced, "It's important to keep in mind that if you are feeling anxious while taking this test, this anxiety could be the result of these negative stereotypes that are widely known in society and have nothing to do with your actual ability to do well on the test." In this second round of tests, female students did as well as the men. It seems that simply knowing about stereotype threat can reduce its power.

The guiding principle in this section is simple: Choose wisely the thoughts you allow to occupy your mind. Avoid letting automatic, negative thoughts or negative stereotypes undermine your self-esteem or your results. Eliminate stinkin' thinkin' and replace it with thoughts that empower.

> When a woman mathematician enters a room, attends a meeting, goes to a conference, or applies for a job, the first thing that is noticed is that she is a woman . . . As a result, many women talk about feeling 'guilty until proven innocent.'
>
> Claudia Henrion

JOURNAL ENTRY   7

In this activity, you will practice disputing the judgments of your Inner Critic and your Inner Defender. As you become more skilled at seeing yourself, other people, and the world more objectively and without distracting judgments, your self-esteem will thrive.

❶ Write a sentence expressing a recent problem or event that upset you. Think of something troubling that happened in school, at work, or in your personal life. For example, *I got a 62 on my math test.*

❷ Write a list of three or more criticisms your Inner Critic (IC) might level against you as a result of this situation. Have your Inner Guide (IG) dispute each one. Review the four methods of disputing described in the section "Disputing Irrational Beliefs." You only need to use one of them for each criticism. For example:

IC: You failed that math test because you're terrible in math.

IG: It's true I failed the math test, but I'll study harder next time and do better. This was only the first test, and I now know what to expect next time.

▶

3 **Write a list of three or more criticisms your Inner Defender (ID) might level against someone else or life as a result of the same situation. Have your Inner Guide (IG) dispute each one immediately.** Again use one of the four methods for disputing. For example:

ID: You failed that math test because you've got the worst math instructor on campus.

IG: I have trouble understanding my math instructor, so I'm going to make an appointment to talk with him in private. John really liked him last semester, so I bet I'll like him, too, if I give him a chance.

4 **Make a choice—write about one of the following:**

A. **Write what you have learned or relearned about changing your inner conversation.** Your journal entry might begin: *In reading and writing about my inner conversations, I have discovered that . . . .* Wherever possible, offer personal experiences or examples to explain what you learned.

B. **Write a reply to an instructor who said the following:** "While I understand the importance of having students change their inner conversations, I don't think they ever actually apply what they write in their journals to the challenging situations in their lives. In other words, there's a big gap between what they learn and what they do."

ONE STUDENT'S STORY

DOMINIC GRASSETH, *Lane Community College, Oregon*

Enrolling in college at the age of 28 was very intimidating to me. Having dropped out of high school at 15, I had a real problem with confidence. Even though I had a GED and was earning a decent living as a car salesman, I still doubted that I was smart enough to be successful in college. I finally took the leap and enrolled because I want a career where I don't have to work 12 hours a day, six days a week, and never see my family. However, by the second week of the semester, I found myself falling back into old habits. I was sitting in the back of the classroom, asking what homework was due, and talking through most of the class. Negative thoughts constantly ran through my mind: *The teachers won't like me. I can't compete with the 18-year-olds right out of high school. I don't even remember what a "verb" is. I can't do this.*

Then in my College Success class, we read Chapter 2 of *On Course* about becoming a Creator and disputing "stinkin' thinkin'." I realized I had taken on the role of the Victim almost my whole life, and I was continuing to do it now. One day I was on my porch when I caught myself thinking my usual negative thoughts. It occurred to me that I was the only one holding me back, not the teachers, not the other students, not math, not English. If I wanted to be successful in college, I had to quit being scared. I had to change my thinking. So I made a deal with myself that any

▶

ONE STUDENT'S STORY *continued*

time I caught myself thinking negatively, I would rephrase the statement in a way that was more positive. I started to truly pay attention to the thoughts in my head and question the negative things I was telling myself. After that I began sitting up front in my classes and participating more. I've always been kind of scattered, so I started using a calendar and a dry-erase board to keep track of what I had to do.

What amazes me is that I didn't really make that big of a change, yet I finished the semester with a 4.0 average! All I did was realize that what I was saying to myself was my underlying problem. I am responsible for my thoughts, and the choice about whether or not to succeed is mine. These days when I have a ridiculous thought going through my mind and I change it, I smile. It's very empowering.

Photo: Courtesy of Dominic Grasseth.

Healthy Choices: Introduction

Want to live a long, healthy life? Who wouldn't? But maybe you think health and longevity are out of your control . . . defined by forces like genes or luck. If so, think again. You have more influence over your health and how long you live than you may think. Once again, your *choices* shape your future.

Scientific research is finding powerful evidence that certain lifestyle choices make a huge difference in the quality of our health and the length of our lives. Three of these choices are (1) what you put in your body (drugs, food, liquids), (2) how you move your body (exercise), and (3) how you recharge your body (sleep, relaxation). This is empowering news. By being responsible and making wise choices in these areas, you can help your body and brain perform at their best for as long as possible.

Let's look at some of the evidence. A study called the European Prospective Investigation into Cancer and Nutrition (EPIC) followed more than half a million people for 15 years. The findings identified choices that reduced diabetes by 93 percent, strokes by 50 percent, cancers by 36 percent, and heart attacks by 81 percent. The study found four lifestyle habits associated with these health improvements: (1) not smoking, (2) eating a healthy diet, (3) exercising at least three and a half hours a week, and (4) maintaining a healthy weight.

Another study at the Harvard School of Public Health examined the health of 123,239 men and women for more than two decades. Data showed that men who adopted healthy choices lived an average of 12 years longer than men who did not. And women in the healthy-choice group did even better. They lived an average of 14 years longer. What were their secrets to longevity? The study found five lifestyle choices that made the difference: (1) eating a healthy diet, (2) exercising regularly, (3) keeping a healthy body weight, (4) not drinking too much alcohol, and (5) not smoking.

A third study should make you happy you're in college. Two Princeton University economists found that college graduates are healthier and live longer than people who have not attended college. The difference between the two groups, the authors concluded, comes down to two key health choices. College grads are more likely than nongrads to avoid developing problems with drugs and alcohol, thus dodging these potentially serious health hazards.

Making healthy choices can be challenging, especially because some of the benefits (like living a long life) seem so far in the future. However, healthy choices offer immediate benefits as well (like increased energy, decreased stress, and improved self-confidence). Chapters 2 through 8 contain short articles about making wise lifestyle choices. In this chapter, you'll learn what research reveals about healthy choices with alcohol. Additional articles explore research and healthy choices regarding drugs, smoking, food, drinks (nonalcoholic), exercise, and sleep. The choices presented, of course, are not meant to substitute for consulting with your health care provider. Science is always advancing knowledge, so what is believed today may very well be revised tomorrow. What's important is using current knowledge to make healthy choices every day. These choices are the foundation on which you'll build your success in college and for the rest of your life.

If you'd like to see how your present health choices are affecting your health and how long you may live, fill out the free survey at https://apps.bluezones.com/en/vitality. At the end of this course, you can retake the survey and see how the lifestyle changes you've made have affected your health and possible longevity.

Healthy Choices: Alcohol

Like many drugs, alcohol is a tricky substance. In small amounts, it can be beneficial. In large amounts, poison.

Alcohol is classified as a sedative hypnotic drug. That means it depresses your central nervous system, including your brain. At high doses, alcohol slows your breathing. You can slip into a coma and even die. According to the National Institute on Alcohol Abuse and Alcoholism, each year more than 1,800 college students die as a result of alcohol. Plus, an additional 600,000 students are injured in alcohol-related incidents. Alcohol is also involved in more than 100,000 sexual assaults at colleges each year. Could you be one of these devastating statistics some day? Let's make sure the answer is "No!"

Despite the dangers, drinking alcohol is a rite of passage for some college students. Think keg parties, drinking games, and clever T-shirts (*Save Water, Drink Beer*). Weekends often begin with a party, especially for students who live on campus. And partying usually means drinking, even for many who are younger than the legal drinking age of 21. Despite the dangers, it's challenging not to join in. After all, alcohol is glamorized everywhere. Actors and actresses drink alcohol on television and in movies. Alcohol ads fill billboards, sports stadiums, magazines, and the Internet. Alcohol is how we celebrate success and drown our sorrows. And sometimes we drink just to drink. *Hey, it's Thursday. I'll drink to that!*

Of course, there are other reasons to drink. For some, alcohol lowers inhibitions, creates acceptance among other drinkers, and temporarily relieves stress, anxiety, depression, and academic pressures. For others, it satisfies experimentation, relieves peer pressure, enhances fun, and creates attention-getting stories: *Man, I got so wasted on Friday you wouldn't believe!* According to College Drinking Prevention, a United States government website, "The first 6 weeks of freshman year are a vulnerable time for heavy drinking and alcohol-related consequences because of student expectations and social pressures at the start of the academic year." Only the *first* six weeks? Nonsense. For many students, risky drinking goes on . . . and on.

THE LEAST YOU NEED TO KNOW ABOUT ALCOHOL

ALCOHOL—The Positives: Some studies show that drinking alcohol in moderation can improve health. First, though, let's define "moderation." For a woman, moderation means one standard drink per day. For a man, it means two standard drinks per day. (More on this difference in a moment.) A "standard drink" is the amount of alcohol (about 14 grams) found in one 12-ounce beer, one 5-ounce glass of wine, or 1.5 ounces of hard liquor. As an example, one 4-ounce margarita counts as two standard drinks.

In various studies, moderate drinking lowered the risk of heart attack, stroke, cancer, and type 2 diabetes. It also reduced dementia, coronary artery disease, heart failure, gallstones, and it even extended life. In his book *The Science of Drinking*, Dr. Amitava Dasgupta presents research comparing nondrinkers with people who consumed one standard drink a day. The alcohol drinkers showed a 16 percent *lower* risk of death from all causes. A recent six-and-a-half-year study in China followed men who consumed one to two drinks per day and found their risk of death was reduced by about 20 percent. In some studies, the kind of alcohol—beer, wine, or liquor—made no difference in the results. In other studies, red wine achieved the most beneficial results.

ALCOHOL—The Negatives: Now, the bad news. (You knew it was coming, right?) When people consume more than one or two standard drinks per day, alcohol stops being beneficial. Worse, it can become a poison and cause great harm.

To explore the dangers of alcohol, let's first return to the definition of "moderate drinking." Turns out, it's more complicated than just how many grams of alcohol you drink. Many other factors affect your blood alcohol concentration (BAC), which is the ratio of alcohol to blood in your body. As you might imagine, the higher the BAC, the more harmful alcohol is. Two people may drink the same amount of alcohol, but their BAC depends on a number of other factors, including gender, body weight, time spent drinking, interactions with other drugs or medicines, and the presence or absence of food in the stomach. Let's look at each:

- As we've already seen, alcohol affects women and men differently. In fact, a woman who drinks the same amount of alcohol as a man will often have a BAC anywhere from 20 to 30 percent higher. That's because women are usually smaller, their bodies have less water and more fat than men's bodies, and they produce less of an enzyme that breaks down alcohol in the stomach.

- The smaller a person is, the more a standard drink will raise his or her BAC.

- Drinking alcohol while taking drugs or medications can have negative effects. Even combining the painkiller acetaminophen (Tylenol) with alcohol can cause significant liver problems.

- Speed matters. Drinking three standard drinks in one hour raises one's BAC much more than drinking the same amount of alcohol over five hours. It takes about 40 minutes for your BAC to go down just .01 percent.

- Drinking on an empty stomach causes a faster spike in BAC than drinking with a full stomach.

As a student, you need to know that excessive drinking (with the resulting high BAC levels) hinders learning and academic success. In a survey by the National Institute on Alcohol Abuse and Alcoholism, 25 percent of college students reported that drinking caused them to miss classes, fall behind in their work, do poorly on papers or exams, and receive lower grades overall. In their book *Buzzed*, Duke University researchers Cynthia Kuhn, Scott Swartzwelder, and Wilkie Wilson identify the following five areas of mental ability harmed by excessive drinking:

1. **Forming new memories** (as when studying)
2. **Thinking abstractly** (as when interpreting a piece of literature)
3. **Solving problems** (as when deciding on a college major)
4. **Maintaining focus** (as when reading a text or ebook), and
5. **Recognizing the emotions of others** (as when dealing with an upset study group member).

Imagine trying to earn a college degree with these five handicaps!

Given that excessive drinking can harm academic success, is it injuring our brains? In a word, yes. Using brain-imaging technology, researchers saw shrinkage of brain tissue in heavy drinkers. Animal studies reveal that alcohol damages and kills brain cells. Numerous studies show nerve-cell loss in an area of the brain called the hippocampus. This is the region essential in forming new memories. Alcohol also damages the prefrontal cortex. That's the site of our "executive function" where we weigh risks and make wise choices.

Here's another concern. Alcohol reserves its most harmful effects for the still-developing brains of those under 25 years old. This, of course, is the age of most college students. The Duke researchers observe, "While young people do most of the drinking in American society, they are also the ones who need their brains to be functioning at their highest levels because of the intellectual demands of education and career preparation."

Okay, so alcohol handicaps brain function and academic success. What are the effects of alcohol on physical health? See if you can read the next sentence while holding your breath.

In addition to brain damage, excessive drinking causes heart disease, ulcers in the stomach and intestines, increased risk of cancer (esophageal, pancreatic, stomach, rectum, colon, throat, liver, and larynx), kidney failure, liver disease, harm to bones, damage to immune system, increased risk of stroke, epilepsy, anxiety and mood disorders, high blood pressure, hepatitis, diabetes, ulcers, urinary tract infections . . . *still holding your breath?* . . . cirrhosis of the liver, bacterial infections, damage to endocrine system, increased risk of death (up to 49 percent in one study in England), and for men, impotence, decreased semen, and erectile dysfunction, while for pregnant women, risk of miscarriage as well as serious physical, emotional, and mental defects for the baby, with fetal alcohol spectrum disorder (FASD) being the single most preventable cause of intellectual disability in the United States.

Whew! Now *that* is one potent poison . . . the dangers of which, not surprisingly, go unmentioned in ads for booze.

Binge drinking is arguably the greatest danger for college students. According to Dr. Amitava Dasgupta, for men, binge drinking is defined as consuming five or more standard drinks in a short period of time. For women, four or more. To illustrate the dangers of binge drinking, consider that approximately three standard drinks in an hour for a man or two for a woman will likely raise blood alcohol to .08 percent. Symptoms include shaky balance, slurred speech, fuzzy vision, and reduced reaction time. That's the level at which you'll be arrested for drunk driving, although it's unsafe to drive at any level above a .00 percent.

Some people rationalize their binge drinking by abstaining from alcohol all week. Then they drink heavily on Friday or Saturday night. A weekend-only binge is still binge drinking, and the people who do that endanger both their mental and physical health . . . not to mention their academic success. More than a third of binge drinkers admit their schoolwork suffered as a result, according to the Harvard School of Public Health. A study by Karen M. Jennison of the University of Northern Colorado agrees. She followed nearly 2,000 binge-drinking students for 10 years. Bingers, she found, showed "early departure from college and less favorable labor market outcomes." Also troubling, 10 years later, the binge drinkers showed "a much higher risk of becoming dependent on alcohol later in life."

Binge drinking often creates blackouts, with as many as 40 percent of college students reporting them. In one survey, college students reported that after blackouts they learned about troubling behaviors they couldn't remember and wouldn't have done otherwise. These behaviors included fights, sex, and driving a car.

Alcoholism (also called *alcohol use disorder*) is the life-threatening result of excessive drinking. People with alcoholism are unable to stop even when drinking is ruining their lives and the lives of their family and friends. Chances are you're thinking, *This will never happen to me.* Sadly, that's probably what the 10,000,000 or so people with alcoholism in the United States told themselves as well. The Centers for Disease Control (CDC) reports that alcohol abuse kills approximately 75,000 Americans yearly and shortens the lives of those with alcoholism by an average of 30 years. According to Dr. Akikur Mohammad in his book *The Anatomy of Addiction*, alcohol is now the third leading preventable cause of death in the United States. It trails only smoking cigarettes and obesity, each of which we will address later. Both authors of this text have experienced alcoholism in their families, and we strongly hope you will do all you can to spare yourself and your family this misery.

WISE CHOICES: ALCOHOL

- Abstain from drinking alcohol, especially if you are under 25 (your brain is still developing).
- Limit alcohol to one standard drink daily (possibly two for men).
- Drink water and eat food before, during, and after drinking alcohol.
- Consume no more than one standard alcoholic drink per hour.
- Go out with friends who won't push you to drink more.
- Never combine alcohol and drugs.
- Avoid drinking games, challenges, rituals, or initiations.
- If pregnant, drink no alcohol (even one drink can risk your baby's mental, emotional, and physical health).
- Never drive when drinking or let others do it either. Instead, use a designated driver, public transportation, cab, or ride service such as Uber or Lyft.
- If someone drinking heavily passes out and cannot be revived, call 911 immediately. You could be the difference between that person's living or dying.
- If you realize you're drinking too much alcohol and can't cut back or stop, seek help. A starting point is your campus counseling center.

ONE STUDENT'S STORY
BRANDEÉ HUIGENS, *Northeast Iowa Community College, Iowa*

I was never a drinker in high school, but when I turned 21, I started going out to bars with my friends. I found that "liquor courage" made me feel better about myself. When I was drinking, I was funny, had a great time, and I was happy. Then I started having blackouts. One time I woke up in my truck, surrounded by policemen, and I had no idea how I had gotten there or where I had been. Another time, I woke up in my bed and there were traffic citations all over the place. I found out later that I had spent the night in jail and the police had sent me home in a cab, but what made it worse was that I didn't remember a second of it. I had always gotten good grades before, but now I started missing my college classes. I wasn't doing as well as I wanted, especially in my nursing classes, like microbiology. I felt crappy and started putting even more pressure on myself. Then I would drink, and it made me feel better, almost like a good friend. Trouble was, I'd wake up the next day and my life was falling apart. People were telling me that I could get a medical withdrawal, and I started thinking about dropping out of college.

Looking back on it now, I realize that I had completely lost control of my inner core. I've never been a quitter, though, and I started using my journal entries for this course to figure out my challenges and how to fix them. My entries would run on for five or six pages as

▶

I poured myself emotionally into my writing. I was excited because it was a way to express myself positively. About halfway through the semester, I made a new rule for myself and told my class about it: *I will abstain from drinking alcohol.* From day one, it was a rule that took over my life, and I decided to track it with a 32-day commitment. To support my change, I started going to AA meetings, and I got a counselor at the Substance Abuse Services Center. I reread my journals for inspiration, and every day in this class we'd share how we were doing on our commitments. Of course I was tempted to drink at times, but I successfully completed my 32 days, and then I just kept going. In the last six months, I have abstained from drinking every day but one.

Today, I think about how powerful it was to write that little sentence and make a new rule for myself. It set so many other things in motion. Some are obvious, like I got sober and stopped having blackouts. My final grades were awesome, and I even got a B in micro, the hardest course I ever took. I also got a new perspective on grades. I always wanted to be perfect so I could get approval from my family, but now I see a B as a success instead of a failure. Perhaps most of all, I learned that in trying to please everyone else but me, I had lost focus on what is important to me and all I want to accomplish. Now I've created an assertiveness rule. I've started speaking up for myself and saying "no," and I can feel my confidence and self-esteem getting stronger. From this class and from the people I shared it with, I have learned how to stand up for myself. My inner core is not fully complete, but the seed has been planted and it is definitely starting to grow.

Discovering
Self-Motivation

Successful Students . . .

▶ **create inner motivation,** providing themselves with the passion and drive to persist toward their goals and dreams, despite all obstacles.

▶ **design a compelling life plan,** complete with motivating goals and dreams.

▶ **commit to their goals and dreams,** visualizing the successful creation of their ideal future.

Struggling Students . . .

▶ **have little sense of passion and drive,** failing to work their hardest at tasks and often quitting when faced with challenges.

▶ **tend to invent their lives as they live them,** investing little or no time in purposeful life planning.

▶ **wander aimlessly from one activity to another,** lacking both vision and commitment to something important to them.

Once I accept responsibility for creating my own life, I must choose the kind of life I want to create.

I'm motivated to create the outcomes and experiences I've chosen for my life.

CASE STUDY IN CRITICAL THINKING / Popson's Dilemma

Fresh from graduate school, Assistant Professor Popson was midway through his first semester of college teaching when he began to get discouraged. Long gone were the excitement and promise of the first day of class. Now, only about two-thirds of his students were attending, and some of them were barely holding on. When Popson asked a question during class, the same few students answered every time. The rest stared off in bored silence. One student always wore a knit cap with a slender cord slithering from under it to a smartphone in his shirt pocket. With 10 or even 15 minutes remaining in a class period, students would start stuffing notebooks noisily into their backpacks or book bags. Only one student had visited him during office hours, despite Popson's numerous invitations. And when he announced one day that he was canceling the next class to attend a professional conference, a group in the back of the room pumped their fists in the air and hooted with glee. It pained Popson to have aroused so little academic motivation in his students, and he began asking experienced professors what he should do.

Professor Assante said, "Research says that about 70 percent of students enroll in college because they see the degree as their ticket to a good job and fat paycheck. And they're right. College grads earn nearly a million dollars more in their lives than high school grads. Show them how your course will help them graduate and prosper in the work world. After that, most of them will be model students."

Professor Buckley said, "Everyone wants the freedom to make choices affecting their lives, so have your students design personal learning contracts. Let each one choose assignments from a list of options you provide. Let them add their own choices if they want. Even have them pick the dates they'll turn in their assignments. Give them coupons that allow them to miss any three classes without penalty. Do everything you can to give them choices and put them in charge of their own education.

Once they see they're in control of their learning and you're here to help them, their motivation will improve."

Professor Chang said, "Deep down, everyone wants to make a difference. I just read a survey by the Higher Education Research Institute showing that two-thirds of first-year students believe it's essential or very important to help others. Find out what your students want to do to make a contribution, including helping their own family. Tell them how your course will help them achieve those dreams. Even better, engage them in a service learning project. When they see how your course can help them live a life with real purpose, they'll be much more interested in what you're teaching."

Professor Donnelly said, "Let's be realistic. The best motivator for students is grades. It's the old carrot and stick. Start every class with a quiz and they'll get there on time. Take points off for absences and they'll attend regularly. Give extra points for getting assignments in on time. Reward every positive action with points and take off points when they screw up. When they realize they can get a good grade in your class by doing what's right, even the guy listening to the smartphone will get involved."

Professor Egret said, "Most people work harder and learn better when they feel they're part of a team with a common goal, so help your students feel part of a community of learners. Give them interesting topics to talk about in pairs and small groups. Give them team assignments and group projects. Teach them how to work well in groups so everyone contributes their fair share. When your students start feeling like they belong and start caring about one another, you'll see their academic motivation go up."

Professor Fanning said, "Your unmotivated students probably don't expect to pass your course, so they quit trying. Here's my suggestion: Assign a modest challenge at which they can all succeed. And every student *has* to do it. No exceptions. Afterward, give students specific feedback on what they did well and what they can do to improve. Then give them a slightly more challenging assignment and repeat the cycle again and again. Help them *expect* to be successful by *being* successful. At some point they're going to say, 'Hey, I can do this!' and then you'll see a whole different attitude."

Professor Gonzales said, "Learning should be active and fun. I'm not talking about a party; I'm talking engaging students in educational experiences that teach deep and important lessons about your subject. Your students should be thinking, 'I can't wait to get to class to see what we're going to do and learn today!' You can use debates, videos, field trips, group projects, quiz apps, case studies, learning games, simulations,

role-plays, guest speakers, visualizations . . . the possibilities are endless. When learning is engaging and enjoyable, motivation problems disappear."

Professor Harvey said, "I've been teaching for 30 years, and if there's one thing I've learned, it's this: You can't motivate someone else. Maybe you've heard the old saying, 'When the student is ready, the teacher will arrive.' You're just wasting your energy trying to make someone learn before they're ready. Maybe they'll be back in your class in five or ten years and they'll be motivated. But for now, just do the best you can for the students who *are* ready."

Listed below are the eight professors in this story. Based on your experience, rank the quality of their advice on the scale. Give a different score to each professor. Be prepared to explain your choices.

Best advice ▶ ① ② ③ ④ ⑤ ⑥ ⑦ ⑧ ◀ Worst advice

Professor	What Motivates Students
___ Professor Assante	Good job and fat paycheck
___ Professor Buckley	Freedom to make choices
___ Professor Chang	Desire to make a difference
___ Professor Donnelly	Good grades
___ Professor Egret	Feel part of a community
___ Professor Fanning	Expectation of being successful
___ Professor Gonzales	Learning that is engaging and enjoyable
___ Professor Harvey	Can't motivate someone else

DIVING DEEPER

Is there an approach not mentioned by one of the eight professors that would be even more motivating for you?

Creating Inner Motivation

FOCUS QUESTIONS   How important do educators think motivation is to your academic success? What determines how motivated you are? What can you do to keep your motivation consistently high this semester . . . and beyond?

Recently, two extensive surveys asked college and university educators to rank factors that decrease students' success and persistence. These surveys were done by American College Testing (ACT) and the Policy Center on the First Year of College. In both surveys, educators identified *lack of motivation* as the number one barrier to students' success in college.

Lack of motivation has various symptoms: students arriving late to class or being absent, assignments turned in late or not at all, work done carelessly, appointments missed, offers of support ignored, and students not participating in class discussions or activities, to name just a few. But the most glaring symptom of all is the enormous number of students who vanish from college within their first year. According to ACT, about one-third of students in U.S. four-year public colleges and universities fail to return for their second year. In public two-year colleges, it's even worse: Nearly *half* of first-year students don't make it to a second year. Despite these grim statistics, you can be among those who stay and thrive in higher education!

A FORMULA FOR MOTIVATION

The study of human motivation—exploring why we do what we do—is extensive and complex. However, one formula explains much about academic motivation: $V \times E = M$ (where M stands for motivation).

In this formula, "V" stands for value. In terms of your education, value is determined by the benefits you believe you'll obtain from seeking and completing a college degree. The greater the benefits you assign to college outcomes and experiences, the greater will be your motivation. The greater your motivation, the higher the cost you'll be willing to pay in terms of time, money, effort, frustration, inconvenience, and sacrifice. Take a moment to identify the score that presently represents the value you place on seeking and completing a college education. Choose a number from 0 to 10 (where "0" represents no perceived value and "10" represents an extremely high perceived value). Bottom line: To keep your motivation high, you'll need to have a clear sense of the personal value of a college degree to you.

In the formula $V \times E = M$, the "E" stands for expectation. In terms of your education, expectation is determined by how likely you think it is that you can earn a college degree with a reasonable effort. To make that calculation, you need to weigh your abilities (how good a student you are and how strong your previous education is) against the difficulty of achieving your goal

There are three things to remember about education. The first is motivation. The second is motivation. The third is motivation.

Terrell Bell, former U.S. Secretary of Education

Today's theories about motivation emphasize the importance of factors within the individual, particularly the variables of expectancy and value. Students' motivations are strongly influenced by what they think is important (value) and what they believe they can accomplish (expectancy).

K. Patricia Cross

(how challenging the courses are that you will need to take and how much you are willing to sacrifice to be successful). Take a moment to identify the score that presently represents your personal expectation of being able to complete a college degree with a reasonable effort. Choose a number from 0 to 10 (where "0" represents no expectation of success and "10" represents an extremely high expectation of success).

Now take a moment to consider what influences may have swayed your expectations of success in college. For example, consider whether your score reflects the expectation of your parents or others in your life. A young woman in my writing class once told me she knew she was going to fail. It was only the first day of the class and I asked her why she thought that. "I'm from the country," she said, "and people from the country can't write." I asked where she had learned that. "My fifth-grade teacher told us," she replied. And her tone said, "There, that *proves* it."

A growing body of research shows that teacher expectations influence students' own expectations of academic success. Fortunately, many teachers hold very high expectations for their students. Sadly, though, some instructors hold low expectations for all students, while others hold low expectations just for students of a particular culture. If you've had such a teacher or encounter one in college, don't allow a Victim mindset to buy into their disempowering stereotypes. Examples of these stereotypes include "people from the country can't write," or "women can't learn math," or "students with learning disabilities aren't college material," or "older students have lost the ability to learn." Instead, employ a Creator mindset, form your own high expectations, and live up to them.

In short, the $V \times E = M$ formula says that your level of motivation in college is determined by multiplying your value score by your expectation score. For example, if the value you place on a college degree is high (say, a 10), but your expectation of success in college is low (say, a 1), then your motivation score will be very low (10). Similarly, if you put little value on a college degree (say a 2), even if your expectation for success in college is high (say, a 9), then once more, your motivation score will be very low (18). In either case, your low score suggests that you probably won't do what is required to succeed in college: to make goal-directed choices consistently, to give a high-quality effort regularly, and to persist despite inevitable obstacles and challenges. Unless you take action, you could end up joining the many students who exit college without a degree.

Probably you see where all of this leads. To stay motivated in college, first, you need ways to raise (or keep high) the **value** you place on college, including the academic degree you'll earn, the knowledge you'll gain, and the experiences you'll have while enrolled. Second, you need ways to raise (or keep high) the **expectation** you have of being successful in college while making what you consider to be a reasonable effort. Throughout *On Course*, you'll encounter literally hundreds of skills that, when mastered, will contribute greatly to your expectations for success in college.

There is evidence that the time for learning various subjects would be cut to a fraction of the time currently allotted if the material were perceived by the learner as related to his own purposes.

Carl Rogers

Students tend to internalize the beliefs teachers have about their ability and they rise and fall in achieving the level of expectation of their teachers.

Lynn Kell Spradlin

For now, however, we are going to focus on value. Only you can determine how much value a college education holds for you, but let's look at some of the benefits that others have attributed to achieving a degree beyond high school.

VALUE OF COLLEGE OUTCOMES

One of the most widely recognized benefits of a college degree is increased earning power. According to recent U.S. Census Bureau data, high school graduates earn an average of $1.2 million dollars during their working lives. However, if you complete a two-year associate's degree, that lifetime total goes up another $400,000. If you complete a four-year bachelor's degree, you can add another $500,000. That means college graduates earn nearly one million dollars more in their lifetimes than those who end their formal education with a high school degree. Think what that additional money could do to help you (and the people you love) live a good life.

Not only does a college degree offer increased earnings, it also opens doors to employment in many desirable professions. Six out of every 10 jobs now require some postsecondary education and training, according to data reported by the ERIC Clearinghouse on Higher Education. The U.S. Department of Labor reports that the number of jobs requiring advanced skills now grows at twice the rate of those requiring only basic skills.

A college degree confers many additional benefits. According to the Institute for Higher Education Policy and the Carnegie Foundation, college graduates enjoy:

- higher savings levels.
- improved working conditions.
- increased personal and professional mobility.
- improved health and life expectancy.
- improved quality of life for children.
- better consumer decision making.
- increased personal status.
- more hobbies and leisure activities.

> For learning to take place with any kind of efficiency, students must be motivated. To be motivated, they must become interested. And they become interested when they are actively working on projects which they can relate to their values and goals in life.
>
> Gus Tuberville, former president, William Penn College

College grads also become more open-minded, more rational, more consistent, and less authoritarian. As a bonus, these benefits are passed on to their children.

Additionally, attaining a college degree can bring personal satisfaction and accomplishment. I once had a 76-year-old student who inspired our class with her determination "to finally earn the college degree that I cheated myself out of more than 50 years ago." Another valuable outcome of a college degree is the pride and esteem that many enjoy when they walk across the stage to receive their hard-earned diploma. And for some, a college degree is an essential step toward fulfilling a personal vision; such was true for my college roommate who, for as long as he could remember, dreamed of being a doctor (and today he is one).

TABLE 3.1 One Student's Desired Outcomes

Desired Outcomes	Value
Earn a grade point average (GPA) of 3.8 or better and make the dean's list this semester	A high GPA will look great on my transcript when I apply for a job. Also, it will give me a real boost of self-confidence.
In my English class, write at least one essay that contains no more than two nonstandard grammar errors	I want to be able to write so well that my colleagues at work are really impressed by my quarterly reports.
In my Student Success class, learn at least three strategies for managing my time more effectively	Right now I feel overwhelmed and stressed with all I need to do, and learning how to manage my time better will lower my stress level.
Get an A in my accounting class	I want a career in accounting, so doing well in this course is the first step toward success in my profession.
Make three or more new friends	My friends from high school all went to other colleges or they're working. I want to make new friends here so I'll have people to hang out with on the weekends.

> The value of a college education is not the learning of many facts but the training of the mind to think.
>
> Albert Einstein

For some people, long-term goals are too distant to be motivating. They do get fired up, however, by short-term goals, such as outcomes they can create during this semester. Table 3.1 shows the short-term goals that one of my students chose for himself, along with his reasons why.

VALUE OF COLLEGE EXPERIENCES

Value isn't found only in outcomes; it's also found in experiences. In fact, all human beings manage their emotions by doing their best to maximize positive experiences and minimize negative ones. What, for example, is the value of playing an intramural sport, attending a movie, belonging to a fraternity or sorority, dancing, playing a video game, or hanging out with friends? Primarily, all are choices to manage our inner experiences. If done in excess, any one of these choices can get us off course from our desired outcomes. But done in moderation, all of these activities (and many others) can create a positive experience and contribute greatly to academic motivation. That's because if you're enjoying the journey called college, you're much more likely to persist until you reach the destination called graduation.

So, what are your desired experiences in college? If someday in the future you were to tell someone that college was one of the best experiences of your life, what specifically would you have experienced? Many will say "fun." Fair enough. Then make fun happen. Your challenge is to experience fun while staying on course to academic success. And you can do it! Consider these options for fun: Join a club, play a sport, get to know a classmate, attend a party, learn something new that really interests you. Here are other experiences that my students desired: respect, relaxation, connection, self-confidence, an open mind, quiet reflection, passion for learning, total engagement, full-out participation, inspiration, challenge, courage, self-acceptance, joy, pride, freedom, and a new insight (or aha!).

One of the students in my college success class said he wanted to experience "creativity." As an alternative to the final project, he proposed to compose a rap song about the success principles he'd learned in our class. I told him he had my permission as long as he agreed to rap his project to our class on the last day of the semester. Little did I know that he was a professional rapper with a couple of CDs to his credit. As promised, he (and his whole group) showed up on the last day of the semester, handed out the words to "The College Success Rap," and treated us all to a rousing course finale. Best of all, he did a great job of demonstrating that he had learned many of the key principles of success, helping his classmates learn them even more deeply. Afterward he said, "Man, that was a great experience!"

Table 3.2 lists the desired experiences that another of my students identified for herself, along with her reasons why.

German philosopher Friedrich Nietzsche once said, "He who has a *why* to live for can endure almost any *how*." He affirms that few obstacles can stop us when we understand the personal value we place on the outcomes and experiences of our journey. Discover your own motivation, and your chances for success soar!

> Setting specific goals helps learners in at least three ways: The goals focus attention on important aspects of the task; they help motivate and sustain task mastery efforts; and they serve an information function by arming learners with criteria that they can use to assess and if necessary adjust their strategies as they work.
>
> Jere Brophy

TABLE 3.2 One Student's Desired Experiences

Desired Experiences	Value
Fun	My brother dropped out of college because he said it was all work and no play. I know I'm going to have to work hard in college, but I want to have fun, too. I think if I'm enjoying myself, that'll make all the assignments more bearable.
Academic confidence	I've never done particularly well in school, although my teachers have always said I could be a good student if I applied myself more. I want to feel just as smart as any other student in my classes.
Excitement about learning	I didn't really like my classes in high school. I want to get excited about learning in at least one course, so I look forward to the homework and sometimes the class time goes so quickly I can't believe when it's over.
Personal confidence	I have always been a shy person, and I want to become more outgoing so I can do well on future job interviews. I want to be more assertive in my career so I get the promotions I deserve.

> What ultimately counts most for each person is what happens in consciousness: the moments of joy, the times of despair added up through the years determine what life will be like. If we don't gain control over the contents of consciousness, we can't live a fulfilling life.
>
> Mihaly Csikszentmihaly

He who puts in four hours of "want to" will almost always outperform the person who puts in eight hours of "have to."

Roger von Oech

JOURNAL ENTRY | 8

In this journal entry, you'll identify your desired outcomes and experiences for this course and/or this semester. Developing clarity on what you want to create this semester will help you stay motivated and on course until the end. Use the student examples earlier in this section as models, but of course record your own desired outcomes, experiences, and reasons.

① In your journal, create a table like Table 3.1. Fill in three or more of your own desired *outcomes* for this course and/or this semester. Next to each, explain why you value achieving that outcome. Remember, "outcomes" are those things you will take *away* with you at the end of the semester (such as a grade or something you learn). At this point, you don't have to know HOW you will achieve these outcomes; you only need to know WHAT you want and WHY.

② In your journal, create a table like Table 3.2. Fill in three or more of your desired *experiences* for this course and/or this semester. Next to each, explain why you value having that experience. Remember, "experiences" are those things you will have *during* this semester (such as fun or a sense of community). Once again, all that matters here is WHAT you would like to experience and WHY. At this time, you don't need to worry about HOW.

③ Using the formula of $V \times E = M$, write about your level of motivation to be successful in college. Begin as follows: *The value I place on being a success in college is ___ [0–10] and my expectation of being a success in college is ___ [0–10]. Multiplied together, this gives me an achievement motivation score of ___ [0–100].* Then continue by explaining your scores and identifying specific actions you can do to raise it (or keep it high).

Remember, dive deep. When you explore your motivation at a deep level, you improve your chances of having an important insight that can change your life for the better. So dive deep and discover what really motivates you.

Success isn't a result of spontaneous combustion. You must set yourself on fire.

Arnold H. Glasow

ONE STUDENT'S STORY

CHEE MENG VANG, *Inver Hills Community College, Minnesota*

When I got to college, my biggest challenge was staying motivated. I was always going out clubbing with my friends, older sisters, and cousins. I was also shooting pool and hanging out with friends until late at night. I was lazy all the time and couldn't concentrate. I missed classes, fell behind in my homework, and tried to do everything at the last minute. This caused a lot of problems for me, like getting D's on my tests and quizzes. I felt like whatever happened to me was out of my control. I was feeling down and filled with dissatisfaction.

▶

One night I was in a club, watching people drinking and dancing, and I thought, "This is getting boring. I'm tired and this isn't taking me anywhere at all." It was a good thing that College Success was part of my full-time student schedule. Our book was called *On Course,* and it helped me big time. It taught me to see myself as the primary cause of my outcomes and experiences and to find my desires that cause me to act. I was so stupid because my desire was right in front of me. There are so many reasons why it is important that I do well in college. My parents came to the United States from Laos, and all

they ever wanted was a better life for their kids. It was hard for them in a new country, and we never had very much money. I realized I was being a loser and letting them down. Also, I am the first man in my family to go to college and my lovely five little brothers look up to me. I need to show them what a good role model their big brother can be. I want a career that will allow me to help my family, and when I have children, I don't want to be a dad working in McDonald's. My dream is to be a pharmacist, but I was headed in the wrong direction.

I come from a poor family, and I don't ever want to be

like that in the future, so I had to make changes right away. I stopped going out to clubs and started taking responsibility. I became more outgoing in class. I studied two hours or more every day. I started getting A's and B's on my tests and quizzes. I finished the semester by raising my D grades to B's. As you can see, I've gone from being a lazy, unmotivated guy to a responsible, outgoing, I-control-my-destiny man. Now I don't feel like a victim anymore. I've actually started to feel like a hero to my parents, my little brothers, and even to the small community where we live.

Designing a Compelling Life Plan

FOCUS QUESTIONS   If your life were as good as it could possibly be, what would it look like? What would you have, do, and be?

While growing up, Joan dreamed of becoming a famous singer. Following high school, she started performing in nightclubs. She married her manager, and the two of them lived in a motor home, driving from town to town in pursuit of singing jobs. After many exhausting years on the road, Joan recorded a song. It didn't sell, and her dream began to unravel. Marital problems complicated her career. Career problems complicated her marriage. Joan grew tired of the financial and emotional uncertainty in her life. Finally, in frustration, she divorced her husband and gave up her dream of singing professionally.

Although disappointed, Joan started setting new goals. She needed to earn a living, so she set a short-term goal to become a hairdresser. After graduating from cosmetology school, Joan saved enough money to settle some debts, buy a car, and pay for a new long-term goal. She decided to go to a community college (where I met her) and major in dental hygiene.

Two years later, Joan graduated with honors and went to work in a dentist's office. Lacking a dream that excited her, Joan chose another long-term goal: earning her bachelor's degree. Joan worked days in the dentist's office and attended classes at night. After a few years, she again graduated with honors.

The most important thing about motivation is goal setting. You should always have a goal.

Francie Larrieu Smith

Then, she set another long-term goal: earning her master's degree. Earlier in her life, Joan had doubted that she was "college material." With each academic success, her confidence grew. "One day I realized that once I set a goal, it's a done deal," Joan said.

This awareness inspired her to begin dreaming again. As a child, Joan had always imagined herself as a teacher, but her self-doubts had always steered her in other directions. Master's degree now in hand, she returned to our college to teach dental hygiene. A year later, she was appointed department chairperson. In only seven years, Joan went from a self-doubting first-year student to head of our college's dental hygiene department. Despite obstacles and setbacks, she continued to move in a positive direction, ever motivated by the promise of achieving personally valuable goals and dreams.

Your goals are the road maps that guide you and show you what is possible for your life.

Les Brown

ROLES AND GOALS

According to psychologist Brian Tracy, many people resist setting life goals because they don't know how. Let's eliminate this barrier so you, like Joan, can experience the heightened motivation that results from personally meaningful goals.

First, think about the roles you have chosen for your life. A life role is an activity to which we regularly devote more than a few hours weekly. For example, you're presently playing the role of college student. How many of the following roles are you also playing: friend, employee, employer, athlete, brother, sister, church member, son, daughter, roommate, husband, wife, partner, parent, grandparent, tutor, musician, neighbor, volunteer? Do you play other roles as well? Most people identify four to seven major life roles. If you have more than seven, you may be spreading yourself too thin. Consider combining or eliminating one or more of your roles while in college. If you have identified fewer than four roles, assess your life again. You may have overlooked a role or two.

CATHY   **by Cathy Guisewite**

Once you identify your life roles, think about your long-term goals for each one. Identify what you hope to accomplish in this role in the next two to five or even ten years. For example, in your role as a student, ten years from now will you have a two-year associate of arts (AA) degree? A four-year bachelor of arts (BA) or bachelor of science (BS) degree? Will you have attended graduate school to earn a master of arts (MA) or master of science (MS) degree? Or gone even further to obtain a doctor of philosophy (PhD) degree, a medical doctor (MD) degree, or a doctor of jurisprudence (JD) law degree? Any of these future academic goals could be yours.

HOW TO SET A GOAL

To be truly motivating, a goal needs five qualities. You can remember them by applying the DAPPS rule. "DAPPS" is an acronym, a memory device in which each letter of the word stands for one of five qualities of an effective goal: Dated, Achievable, Personal, Positive, and Specific.

Dated

Motivating goals have specific deadlines. A short-term goal usually has a deadline within a few months (like your semester's desired outcomes set in Journal Entry 8). A long-term goal generally has a deadline as far in the future as one year, five years, even ten years (such as the goal you have for your most advanced academic degree). As your target deadline approaches, your motivation typically increases. This positive energy helps you finish strong. If you don't meet your deadline, you have an opportunity to examine what went wrong and create a new plan. Without a deadline, you might stretch the pursuit of a goal over your whole life, never reaching it.

Achievable

Motivating goals are challenging but realistic. It's unrealistic to say you'll run a marathon (26+ miles) next week if your idea of a monster workout has been opening and closing the refrigerator. Still, if you're going to err, do so on the side of optimism. When you set goals at the outer reaches of your present ability, stretching to reach them causes you to grow. Listen to other people's advice, but trust yourself to know what is achievable for you. Apply this guideline: "Is achieving this goal at least 50 percent believable to me?" If so and you *really* value it, go for it!

Personal

Motivating goals are your own. They aren't thrust upon you by someone else. Be aware of pressure to conform to the expectations of others. Maybe you have a passion for graphic design but your parents want you to major in business so you can join the family business. Also be aware of subtle pressure to conform to the norms of your culture at the expense of what you want. For example, all cultures create expectations about what men and women *should*

One day Alice came to a fork in the road and saw a Cheshire cat in a tree. "Which road do I take?" she asked. "Where do you want to go?" was his response. "I don't know," Alice answered. "Then," said the cat, "it doesn't matter."

Lewis Carroll

do, and, interestingly, gender-role stereotypes are similar across cultures. If you're a woman who wants to be an engineer, don't set a goal to be a dental hygienist. If you're a man who wants to be a kindergarten teacher, don't set a goal to be a lawyer. You don't want to be on your deathbed some day and realize you have lived someone else's life. Trust that you know better than anyone else what you want.

Positive

Motivating goals focus your energy on what you *do* want rather than on what you *don't* want. So translate negative goals into positive goals. For example, a negative goal not to fail a class becomes a positive goal to earn a grade of B or better. I recall a race car driver explaining how he miraculously kept his spinning car from smashing into the concrete racetrack wall: "I kept my eye on the track, not the wall." Likewise, focus your thoughts and actions on where you *do* want to go rather than where you *don't* want to go, and you, too, will stay on course.

Specific

Motivating goals state outcomes in specific, measurable terms. It's not enough to say, "My goal is to do better this semester" or "My goal is to work harder at my job." How will you know if you've achieved these goals? What specific, measurable evidence will you have? Revised, these goals become, "I will complete every college assignment this semester to the best of my ability" and "I will volunteer for all offerings of overtime at work." Being specific keeps you from fooling yourself into believing you've achieved a goal when, in fact, you haven't. It also helps you make choices that create positive results.

Through the years, I've had the joy of working with students who have had wonderful and motivating long-term goals: becoming an operating room nurse, writing and publishing a novel, traveling around the world, operating a refuge for homeless children, marrying and raising a beautiful family, playing professional baseball, starting a private school, becoming a college professor, swimming in the Olympics, managing an international mutual fund, having a one-woman art show, becoming a fashion model, getting elected state senator, owning a clothing boutique, and more. How about you? What do you *really* want?

DISCOVER YOUR DREAMS

Perhaps even more than goals do, dreams fuel our inner fire. They give our lives purpose and guide our choices. They provide motivating energy when we run headlong into an obstacle. When Candy Lightner's daughter was killed by a drunk driver, she transformed this tragedy into her dream to stop drunk driving, and her dream became the international organization Mothers Against Drunk Driving (MADD). I found my dream only after 20 years of college teaching: My passion is empowering students with the beliefs and behaviors essential for living a rich and personally fulfilling life. Although it's difficult to define a dream, they're grand in size and fueled by strong emotions. Unlike goals, which

A goal is a dream with a deadline.

Napoleon Hill

I always wanted to be somebody, but now I realize I should have been more specific.

Lily Tomlin

usually fit into one of our life roles, dreams often take over our lives, inspire other people, and take on a life of their own. That's why I sometimes wonder if people have dreams or if dreams have people.

If you presently have a big dream, you know how motivating it is. If you don't have a big dream, you're certainly in the majority. Most people have not found a guiding dream, yet they can still have great lives. College, though, offers a wonderful opportunity to discover or expand your dreams. You'll be exposed to hundreds, even thousands, of new people, ideas, and experiences. With each encounter, be aware of your energy. If you feel it rise, pay attention. Something within you is getting inspired. If you're fortunate enough to find such a dream, consider the advice of philosopher Joseph Campbell: "Follow your bliss."

YOUR LIFE PLAN

Wise travelers use maps to locate their destination and identify the best route to get there. Similarly, Creators identify their goals and dreams and the most direct path there. In creating such a life plan, it helps to start with your destination in mind and work backward. If you have a dream, accomplishing it becomes your ultimate destination. Or maybe your destination is the accomplishment of one or more long-term goals for your life roles. Because you can't complete a long journey in one step, your short-term goals become stepping-stones, and each one completed brings you closer to the achievement of a long-term goal or dream.

Take a look at a page of a life plan that one student, Pilar, designed for herself. Although Pilar recorded her dream, not everyone will be able to do that. Her full life plan includes a page for each of her life roles, all of them with the same dream. Obviously, some life roles are going to make a more significant contribution to her dream than others. Notice that each long- and short-term goal adheres to the DAPPS rule.

> The future belongs to those who believe in the beauty of their dreams.
>
> Eleanor Roosevelt

MY DREAM: *I help families adopt older children (10 years old or older) and create home environments in which the children feel loved and supported to grow into healthy, productive adults.*

MY LIFE ROLE: *College student*

MY LONG-TERM GOALS IN THIS ROLE:

1. *I earn an associate of arts (AA) degree by June 2022.*
2. *I earn a bachelor of arts (BA) degree by June 2024.*
3. *I earn a master of social work (MSW) degree by June 2026.*

MY SHORT-TERM GOALS IN THIS ROLE (THIS SEMESTER):

1. *I achieve an A in English 101 by December 18.*
2. *I write a research paper on the challenges of adopting older children by November 20.*
3. *I achieve an A in Psychology 101 by December 18.*
4. *I learn and apply five or more psychological strategies that will help my family be happier and more loving by November 30.*
5. *I achieve an A in College Success by December 18.*
6. *I dive deep in every* On Course *journal entry, writing a minimum of 500 words for each one.*
7. *I learn five or more new success strategies and teach them to my younger brothers by November 30.*
8. *I take at least one page of notes in every class I attend this semester.*
9. *I turn in every assignment on time this semester.*
10. *I learn to use the college's course management system well enough to submit all of my written assignments by September 15.*

This is the first page of Pilar's six-page life plan. She wrote a similar page for each of her other five life roles: sister, daughter, friend, athlete, and employee at a group home for children.

Consciously designing your life plan, as Pilar did, has many benefits. A life plan defines your desired destinations in life and charts your best route for getting there. It gives your Inner Guide something positive to focus on when the chatter of your Inner Critic or Inner Defender attempts to distract you. And, like all maps, a life plan helps you get back on course if you get lost.

Perhaps most of all, a life plan is your personal definition of a life worth living. With it in mind, you'll be less dependent on someone else to motivate you. Your most compelling motivation will be found within.

W hat is significant about a life plan is that it can help us live our own lives (not someone else's) as well as possible.

Harriet Goldhor Lerner

W e . . . believe that one reason so many high-school and college students have so much trouble focusing on their studies is because they don't have a goal, don't know what all this studying is leading to.

Muriel James & Dorothy Jongeward

JOURNAL ENTRY 9

In this activity, you will design one or more parts of your life plan. To focus your thoughts, glance back at Pilar's life plan and use it as a model.

❶ Title a new page in your journal: MY LIFE PLAN. Below the title, complete the part of your life plan for your role as a student.

My Dream: [If you have a compelling dream, describe it here. If you're not sure what your dream is, you can simply write, "I'm searching."]

▶

My Life Role: Student

My Long-Term Goals in This Role: [These are the outcomes you plan to achieve as a student in the next two to ten years, or even longer if necessary.]

My Short-Term Goals in This Role: [These are the outcomes you plan to achieve as a student this semester; each one achieved brings you closer to your long-term goals as a student. To begin your list of short-term goals, you can write the same desired outcomes that you chose in **Journal Entry 8**; then add other short-term goals as appropriate.]

Remember to apply the DAPPS rule, making sure that each long- and short-term goal is Dated, Achievable, Personal, Positive, and Specific. With this in mind, you may need to revise the desired outcomes that you transfer here from **Journal Entry 8**.

    YOUR CHOICE: If you wish, repeat this process for one or more of your other life roles—employee, parent, athlete, and so on. The more roles you plan, the more complete your vision of life will be. Taken together, these pages map your route to a rich, personally fulfilling life.

    At this time you don't have to know how to achieve your goals and dreams, so don't even think about the method. All you need to know is what you want. In the following chapters, you'll learn dozens of powerful strategies for turning your life plan into reality. For now, keep your eye on your destination!

❷ **Write about what you have learned or relearned by designing your life plan.** In particular, identify any impact this effort has had on your level of motivation to do well in college this semester, or do well in any other parts of your life.

> Many people fail in life, not for lack of ability or brains or even courage but simply because they have never organized their energies around a goal.
>
> Elbert Hubbard

> I started getting successful in school when I saw how college could help me achieve my dreams.
>
> Bobby Marinelli, student

ONE STUDENT'S STORY

BRANDON BEAVERS, *Highland Community College, Kansas*

My older brother had always been my closest friend. When I was a junior in high school, he committed suicide, and I was the one who found his body. That is something no one should ever have to experience. The image haunted me, and my life took a bad turn. Sometimes I felt angry.

Other times I felt numb. Even though I had a 3.7 average in high school and made the all-conference baseball team, I was just going through the motions of life. I quit thinking about long-term goals or anything like that. I felt like giving up, and I lost any sense of a future.

When I got to college, I wasn't thinking about what I wanted in life or where I planned on going. The journal assignments in *On Course* changed that. They made me reflect on things I have done in my life and things that have happened to me. I found out I was never really organized with anything I did; I was always going with the flow and living in the moment. Any goals I had were short-term, ones I knew

▶

I could easily reach. Even though I received a baseball scholarship to play in college, I never really challenged myself to see what I could accomplish. I would always do my work and get good grades, but I never thought about how that would affect my future.

When I first started writing the journals, I would only write about half a page. I just wanted to get them done. Then I realized they were helping me figure out how to improve my life. That's when I started writing two or three pages. Sometimes I would reread my journals at night to see what my progress was. I've never written anything that affected my life like these journals. I went from writing as little as possible to taking my time and seeing what I could get out of each one.

As I wrote my way through the course, I realized that Victim thinking was dragging me down. I began taking responsibility for my own actions in every situation instead of blaming others for my own bad choices. I also realized that my life is my own and I want to live it for me. The course forced me to think seriously about who I am, what I want to do, and how I can achieve it. For the first time I have a plan for my life.

We have a family friend who is a police chief, and he told me about his work. What he said gave me the feeling that law enforcement was something I would enjoy doing. I want to help people and that's what he does every day. I have decided to complete my AA degree and then transfer to Kansas University to major in Criminal Justice with a minor in Psychology. After I get experience in local law enforcement, I plan on switching to the federal side, such as ATF, DEA, or Homeland Security.

In the future, I also plan on being a husband and a father. I will do my very best to shape my children in the positive way this class has shaped me. Life isn't easy. People go through struggles. I will teach them to not just dream, but to make plans, to set goals, and to keep themselves focused!

I'm happy with the way I live now. I'm organized, have a daily routine, and have future goals in mind. I have changed as an individual over the course of this semester by exploring deep down and finding out who I really want to be. I'm more outgoing, focused, and responsible because of this course. I'm not only a better individual but also a better writer. I didn't expect this course to change my life, but I've done a complete 180. I've gone from just going through the motions to having goals that I want to achieve. I'm feeling happier. I'm where I want to be in life.

Photo: Courtesy of Brandon Beavers.

Committing to Your Goals and Dreams

FOCUS QUESTIONS Do you start new projects (such as college) with great enthusiasm, only to lose motivation along the way? How can you keep your motivation strong?

Many people doubt they can achieve what they truly want. When a big, exciting goal or dream creeps into their thoughts, they shake their heads. "Oh, sure," they mumble to themselves, "how am *I* going to accomplish that?"

In truth, you don't need to know how to achieve a goal or dream when you first think of it. What you do need is an unwavering commitment, fueled by a strong desire. Once you promise yourself that you will do whatever it takes to accomplish your goals and dreams, you often discover the method for achieving them in the most unexpected ways.

COMMITMENT CREATES METHOD

A commitment is an unbending intention, a single-mindedness of purpose that promises to overcome all obstacles, regardless of how you may feel at any particular moment. During the summer between my sophomore and junior years in college, I learned the power of commitment.

That summer, I used all of my savings to visit my college roommate in Hawaii. While there, I met a remarkable young woman, and we spent 12 blissful days getting to know each other.

One of my desires was to have a wonderful love relationship, so I promised to return to Hawaii during Christmas break. However, back in college 6,000 miles away, my commitment was seriously tested. I had no idea how, in just three months, I could raise enough money to return to Hawaii. Committed to my dream, though, I spent weeks inventing and rejecting one scheme after another. (Though I didn't realize it at the time, I was actually using the Wise Choice Process to find my best option.)

Then one day, I happened upon a possible solution. I was glancing through *Sports Illustrated* magazine when I noticed an article written by a student athlete from Yale University. Until that moment, all I'd had was a commitment. When I saw that article, I had a plan. A long shot, yes, but a plan, nonetheless: Maybe the editors of *Sports Illustrated* would buy an article about the sport I played, lightweight football (now called "sprint" football). Driven by my commitment, I worked on an article every evening for weeks. Finally, I dropped it in the mail and crossed my fingers.

A few weeks later, my manuscript came back, rejected. On the printed rejection form, however, a kind editor had handwritten, "Want to try a rewrite? Here's how you might improve your article. . . ."

I spent another week revising the article, mailed it directly to my encouraging editor, and waited anxiously. Christmas break was creeping closer. I had just about given up hope of returning to Hawaii in December.

Then one day my phone rang, and the caller identified himself as a photographer from *Sports Illustrated*. "I'll be taking photos at your football game this weekend. Where can I meet you?"

And that's how I learned that my article had been accepted. Better yet, *Sports Illustrated* paid me enough money to return to Hawaii. I spent Christmas on the beach at Waikiki, with my girlfriend on the blanket beside me.

Suppose I hadn't made a commitment to return to Hawaii? Would reading *Sports Illustrated* have sparked such an outrageous plan? Would I, at 20 years of age, have ever thought to earn money by writing a feature article for a national magazine? Doubtful!

What intrigues me as I recall my experience is that the solution for my problem was there all the time; I just couldn't see it until I made a commitment.

> Always bear in mind that your own resolution to succeed is more important than any one thing.
>
> Abraham Lincoln

> When you have a clear intention, methods for producing the desired results will present themselves.
>
> Student Handbook, University of Santa Monica

By committing to our dreams, we program our brains to look for solutions to our problems and to keep us going when the path gets rough. Whenever you're tempted to look for motivation outside yourself, remember this: Motivation surges up from a *commitment* to a passionately held purpose.

VISUALIZE YOUR IDEAL FUTURE

Human beings seek to experience pleasure and avoid pain. Put this psychological truth to work for you by visualizing the pleasure you'll derive when you achieve your goals or dreams.

Cathy Turner explained how she visualized her way to winning two Olympic gold medals in speed skating: "As a little girl, I used to stand on a chair in front of the mirror and pretend I had won a gold medal. I'd imagine getting the medal, I'd see them superimposing the flag across my face just like they did on TV, and I would start to cry. When I really did stand on the podium, and they raised the American flag, it was incredible. I was there representing the United States, all of the United States. The flag was going up and the national anthem was being played, and there wasn't a mirror in front of me and it wasn't a chair I was standing on. I had dreamt that for so long. All my life. And my dream was coming true right then and there."

To make or strengthen your commitment to achieve success in college, do what Cathy Turner did. Visualize yourself accomplishing your fondest goal and imagine the delight you'll experience when it actually happens. Let this desired outcome and the associated positive experiences draw you like a magnet toward a future of your own design.

Some years ago, I happened to glance at a three-ring notebook carried by one of my students. Taped to the cover was a photo showing her in a graduation cap and gown.

"Have you already graduated?" I asked.

"Not yet. But that's what I'll look like when I do."

"How did you get the photo?"

"My sister graduated from college a few years ago," she explained. "After the ceremony, I put on her cap and gown and had my mother take this picture. Whenever I get discouraged about school, I look at this photo and imagine myself walking across the stage to receive my diploma. I hear my family cheering for me, just like we did for my sister. Then I stop feeling sorry for myself and get back to work. This picture reminds me what all my hard work is for."

A few years later at her graduation, I remember thinking, "She looks just as happy today as she did in the photo. Maybe happier."

Life will test our commitments. To keep them strong in times of challenge, we need a clear picture of our desired results. We need a motivating mental image that, like a magnet, draws us steadily toward our ideal future.

The power of visualizing makes sense when you remember that getting anywhere is difficult if you don't know where you're going. A vivid mental image of your chosen destination keeps you on course even when life's adversities conspire against you.

Once a commitment is made without the option of backing out, the mind releases tremendous energy toward its achievement.

Ben Dominitz

From my own experience, there is no question that the speed with which you are able to achieve your goals is directly related to how clearly and how often you are able to visualize your goals.

Charles J. Givens

HOW TO VISUALIZE

Here are four keys to an effective visualization:

1. **Relax.** Visualizing seems to have the most positive impact when experienced during deep relaxation. One way to accomplish deep relaxation is to breathe deeply while you tighten, then relax muscle groups one by one from the tips of your toes to the top of your head.

2. **Use present tense.** Imagine yourself experiencing success *now*. Therefore, use the present tense for all verbs: *I am walking across the stage to receive my diploma.* OR *I walk across the stage.* (Not past tense: *I was walking across the stage*; and not future tense: *I will be walking across the stage.*)

3. **Use all five senses.** Imagine the scene concretely and specifically. Use all of your senses. What do you see, hear, smell, taste, touch?

4. **Feel the feelings.** Events gain power to motivate us when accompanied by strong emotions. Imagine your accomplishment to be just as grand and magnificent as you wish it to be. Then feel the excitement of your success.

Psychologist Charles Garfield notes that athletes have used visualizations to win sports events; psychologist Brian Tracy writes about salespeople using visualizations to succeed in the business world; and Dr. Bernie Siegel, a cancer specialist, has even chronicled patients improving their health with visualizations.

Finally, consider this: The act of *keeping* your commitment may be as important, if not even *more* important, than achieving a particular goal or dream. In this way, you raise your expectations for the success of future commitments, knowing that when you make a promise to yourself, you keep it.

GET MORE HOPEFUL

To achieve or sustain high motivation, you can set DAPPS goals. You can also commit to your goals and visualize yourself achieving them. And, according to "hope theory," there is even more you can do.

You may hear the word *hope* quite often, but what does it really mean? Hope theory refers to a very specific form of hope. According to researcher Charles Snyder, "hope" is a "positive motivational state." It is assessed through a scale that measures **pathway thoughts** and **agency thoughts**. Pathway thoughts are the ones we have that focus on finding multiple choices (paths) to achieve our desired goals. Agency thoughts are beliefs that we can improve our lives. Together, these thoughts increase our motivation to pursue and achieve our goals.

According to the latest research on hope theory, students with high "hope levels" earn better grades and have higher graduation rates than students with low hope levels. In one university study, students with higher hope were 16 percent more likely to graduate than students with lower hope. A second study revealed that learners with higher hope have less test anxiety. Other studies showed that hope was a better predictor of student performance than previous grades, standardized test scores, or intelligence.

I see a Chicago in which the neighborhoods are once again the center of our city, in which businesses boom and provide neighborhood jobs, in which neighbors join together to help govern their neighborhood and their city.

Harold Washington, Chicago's first black mayor

To turn a twist on an old saying, when the going gets tough, the hopeful keep going.

Charles Snyder

All college students encounter obstacles on their journey to graduation. Your hope level affects how well you handle these obstacles. When hope is high, you view obstacles as a challenge to overcome. When hope is low, you give up more easily. The good news is, you can increase your level of hope. In one study, researchers first tested students' hope levels. Then they focused on helping students increase hopeful beliefs. The students who did this process immediately increased their hope levels. They also reported making "significantly more progress" on their goals.

The following four steps can help to increase your hope and therefore your motivation:

1. Establish clear and achievable goals (use the DAPPS rule).

2. Identify many pathways to reach your goals (use the Wise Choice Process, particularly Step 3: What are my possible choices?).

3. Visualize overcoming obstacles and creating inspiring outcomes (use the four steps of visualization from earlier in this section).

4. Identify possible obstacles and view them as challenges to be overcome (be a Creator—seek solutions, take action, and, if unsuccessful, try something new).

Research suggests that regular practice will keep your hope levels higher. After setting your goals, cycle through Steps 2 through 4 weekly. Now you know how to keep the motivation you have and create even more!

> Once you choose hope, anything's possible.
>
> Christopher Reeve

> Until one is committed, there is hesitancy, the chance to draw back, always ineffectiveness. Concerning all acts of initiative (and creation), there is one elementary truth, the ignorance of which kills countless ideas and splendid plans: that the moment one definitely commits oneself, then Providence moves too. All sorts of things occur to help one that would never otherwise have occurred. A whole stream of events issues from the decision, raising in one's favour all manner of unforeseen incidents and meetings and material assistance, which no man could have dreamt would have come his way.
>
> William Hutchison Murray, Scottish mountaineer

JOURNAL ENTRY / 10

In this activity, you will visualize the accomplishment of one of your most important goals or dreams. Once you vividly picture this ideal outcome, you will have strengthened your motivation to achieve it, and you will know how to do the same thing with all of your goals and dreams.

1 **Write a visualization of the exact moment in the future when you are experiencing the accomplishment of your biggest goal or dream in your role as a student.** Describe the scene of your success as if it is happening to you *now*. For example, if your desire is to graduate from a four-year university with a 4.0 average, you might write, *I am dressed in a long, blue robe, the tassel from my graduation cap tickling my face. I look out over the thousands of people in the audience, and I see my mother, a smile spreading across her face. I hear the announcer call my name. I feel a rush of adrenaline, and chills tingle on my back as I take my first step onto the stage. I see the college president smiling, reaching her hand out to me in congratulations. I hear the announcer repeat my name, adding that I am graduating with highest honors, having obtained a 4.0 average. I see my classmates standing to*

▶

applaud me. Their cheers flow over me, filling me with pride and happiness. I walk. . . .

For visual appeal, consider also drawing a picture of your goal or dream in your journal. Or cut pictures from magazines and use them to illustrate your writing. If you are writing your journal on a computer, consider adding digital images that depict your visualization. (If you don't know how, ask someone for help.) Allow your creativity to support your dream.

Remember the four keys to an effective visualization:

1. **Relax** to free your imagination.

2. Use **present-tense verbs** . . . describe the experience as if you are talking to someone on the phone at the very moment you are doing it. *I am going through the door. . . .*

3. Use all **five senses**. What do you see, hear, smell, taste, and touch?

4. Include **emotion**. Imagine yourself feeling fantastic in this moment of grand accomplishment. You deserve to feel fantastic!

Read your visualizations often. Ideal times are right before you go to sleep and when you first awake in the morning. You may even wish to record your visualizations and listen to them often.

ONE STUDENT'S STORY

JAMES TERRELL, *Appalachian State University, North Carolina*

Coming to Appalachian State University was a bit overwhelming for me. It meant that I would be seven hours away from my family. It also meant that I could not just go home whenever I wanted to. In the first week of school, I felt okay and was so glad to be on my own and making my own decisions. Things started to change quickly when I realized that I had to make some important decisions, the ones that my parents usually helped me make. In the back of my mind I kept thinking, I cannot

ask them for help because I am on my own now. I began to get a little depressed because I missed my family, and things were not easy for me. I was ready to quit and enroll in a community college nearer home because I felt that the professors expected too much out of me. I was nearly at the point of telling my parents I was ready to come home because I really did not know why I was here.

That's when we began talking about accepting self-responsibility in my Access

Seminar class. In this lesson, things started to become clear to me. I learned about the different voices everyone has inside of them. I began to realize that it was my Inner Guide talking to me and helping me to stay on course when I was ready to give up. Also, I noticed it was my Inner Critic that was criticizing everything I did to try to stay on course. I had opposing forces trying to get to me.

I continued to listen to my Inner Guide, but I realized there was still something missing. The next week in the class we talked about creating inner motivation. As we began this lesson, I realized that the reason

▶

I was struggling was because I lacked motivation. I did not have a goal in mind that would help me stay on track. This chapter helped me realize that I needed a goal and a dream to stay focused, and in class, we began to do activities that helped us visualize them. In addition to our written journals, our teachers told us to draw a picture of our dreams and to brainstorm obstacles that we might face on the way to our dreams. Before this, I knew I wanted to be a lawyer, and that was about it. Some people would be happy just knowing they wanted to be a lawyer when they finished college. I needed to know a little more, so I visualized various steps to becoming a lawyer. First, I pictured myself graduating from Appalachian State with a degree in political science, next I was graduating from Campbell University with a law degree, and then I saw myself moving to California, where I became a successful entertainment lawyer, living with my family in a nice neighborhood. As I visualized each part of my dream, everything became clear to me. I learned through reading this chapter and talking with the teachers that having our dreams written or drawn on paper can help us stay motivated.

I now feel more confident about staying in school. Every time I go into some of my hard classes, I just keep the mental picture of the day I enter law school and the dream I have plastered inside my head. Every time I get stressed or feel overwhelmed, I just look at the picture of my dream on the wall. I say to myself, "James, did you think this was going to be an easy road to your dream?" Every time the answer is "no," but now I know I'm not going to quit just because of obstacles. I look forward to the next four years of my life because I know that this course has taught me the basics of what I need to know to be a successful college student. I am now encouraged to help other people learn what I have learned, so they can be successful too.

Photo: Courtesy of James Terrell.

SELF-MOTIVATION / at Work

> Motivation comes from working on things we care about. It also comes from working with people we care about.
>
> —*Sheryl Sandberg, chief operating officer, Facebook*

Motivation is essential to your success at work. It's what drives you to persist and excel, even when the work becomes difficult. Motivation keeps you excited about what you do and fully engaged in your work. There are two main categories of motivation: extrinsic (outer) and intrinsic (inner). Extrinsic motivation comes from trying to earn a reward or avoid a negative consequence from someone else. In college, if you are only motivated by achieving high grades or avoiding critical remarks from a professor on an assignment, that's extrinsic motivation. If you attend college only because your family wants you to, even though you don't have much interest, that's also extrinsic motivation. If the only thing that motivates you to go to work is money, that too is extrinsic motivation. It's called extrinsic or "outer" motivation because it comes from someone or something outside of you. The problem is that students and employees who are only extrinsically motivated often lose motivation very quickly. According to motivation researcher Alfie Kohn, author of *Punished by Rewards*, "People's interest in doing what they're

▶

doing typically declines when they are rewarded for doing it . . . scores of studies have confirmed this conclusion . . . what rewards do, and what they do with devastating effectiveness, is smother people's enthusiasm for activities they might otherwise enjoy." In other words, focusing solely on rewards such as high grades or salaries will ultimately lower your motivation instead of increasing it.

A more reliable source of motivation at college or work is intrinsic or inner motivation. Your inner experiences are the source of intrinsic motivation. Examples include experiencing **competence** at your workplace tasks, **fun** while you learn, a sense of **belonging** at your college, or a clear **purpose** for the work you do. Intrinsic motivation is more consistent because you have more control over your inner experiences than you do over external situations. Intrinsic motivation has been shown to persist over the long term. Extrinsic motivation disappears much more quickly.

MOTIVATION AT WORK

Understanding and increasing your motivation are important when exploring a potential career or excelling at your current job. Trying to figure out what kind of career you want can take a long time. Strong motivation helps you keep going when you feel overwhelmed or frustrated. Motivation also keeps you moving forward when you are applying for jobs and interviewing. Sometimes students are highly motivated for the first few weeks of a new term. But soon their motivation drops dramatically. Brand-new employees can also be highly motivated to start strong and do their best. Then they can lose their motivation and their performance drops. These students and employees lose motivation because they are relying on mostly extrinsic motivators (like high grades or salary). However, research shows these motivators don't last very long. Instead, you should plan to focus on intrinsic motivators like belonging or purpose as your primary sources for motivation. This will

allow you to experience consistent motivation for the life of your career.

The benefits of increased motivation at work include:

1. higher job satisfaction;
2. more enjoyment during the work day;
3. greater incentive to continue learning and personal growth; and
4. better performance and more frequent promotions.

MOTIVATION AND CHOOSING A CAREER

What's the best career for you? What role will motivation play in your choice? You can choose from many career options, and they often require very different skill sets. Choosing the right career means understanding your interests, skills, personality, and values. It's important to consider all these areas so you can match your strengths to the needs of the position. When your strengths are a close match for a position or field, you will be more motivated by **competence**, which is an intrinsic motivator. Competence means that you are using your strengths to achieve your intended workplace goals. For example, you might use both your computer design and marketing skills to create a website that draws lots of traffic. Competence is motivating because when you consistently accomplish your goals, you experience more confidence. Higher confidence motivates you to then set and achieve new goals.

Sometimes, students choose a career based solely on how much money they'll make (an extrinsic motivator). That might not be a wise idea. There are many important reasons not to choose a career simply because of salary level or potential bonus pay. If a job is a poor match for your personality type or current skills, you might not enjoy your work. This will decrease your **fun** (an intrinsic motivator). This might also result in your not doing well at your job

▶

or even regretting your career choice. Take the time to investigate a range of career options so you can be sure you find the right fit.

For example, perhaps you're a more introverted person who enjoys working in a quiet, focused environment. A high-paid job in the video gaming industry that requires you to attend packed trade shows and talk to hundreds of people might not fit well. Instead, a job as a technical writer with your own quiet office might be a better fit. A job as an architect that requires excellent attention to detail and strong organizational skills might not work out if you haven't yet strengthened these skills. Do you focus on the big picture instead of small details? Helping a start-up company design an innovative new marketing campaign might be an excellent match. A sales job that consists of making phone calls all day might not be a match if you prefer to talk to people face-to-face. Instead, a job as a real estate agent meeting potential clients in person lets you engage with other people in the way you enjoy.

Sometimes a job might not fit with your personal values or life purpose. If you're asked to sell a product you don't believe in, perhaps even something harmful, all the money in the world might not be enough. If you're asked to hide unethical or illegal activity for greater company profit, you could sacrifice a personal value like integrity. What if a job requires long hours away from your family? If spending significant time with family is your highest priority, it might not be a good fit. If a strong purpose in your life is to eliminate world food shortages, choose a job that helps you meet this purpose, not just one based on salary alone. The point is, consider both your values and life purpose when choosing a career. There's nothing wrong with seeking a high-paying career, just be sure it clearly matches with your skills, values, and purpose. A job based on your strengths, core values, and beliefs will allow you to shine!

ENGAGEMENT AND STRENGTHENING INTRINSIC MOTIVATION

Engaged employees are excited about and deeply committed to their work. Yet, most U.S. workers fall in the "not engaged" category. This results in a major workplace challenge: Many employees lack motivation, a primary part of "employee engagement." A 2012 Gallup report on employee engagement shows that 70 percent of American employees aren't working to their full potential. Only 32 percent of U.S. workers were considered "engaged" in their jobs. More than 50 percent were "not engaged," and over 17 percent were "actively disengaged."

Employees who are not engaged do not give their best effort. They may spend too much of their time surfing the Internet while at work. They might also do only the minimum required to keep from being fired. They often call in sick and are quick to leave the job if something else comes along. They lack creativity and initiative to solve problems. As a result, they perform poorly, get bad evaluations, and receive fewer promotions. When they apply for their next job, they cannot rely on a positive reference from their prior employer.

It should be clear by now that intrinsic motivation is essential to your success at work. It's what drives you to persist, even when the work becomes difficult. It also helps you build your résumé based on a track record of career successes. It may be true that an employer's use of extrinsic motivators could contribute to your disengagement. However, you can do much to increase your own work engagement. To stay engaged at work, you'll need to focus on strengthening your intrinsic motivators. Two of the most important intrinsic motivators are *belonging* and *purpose*.

Belonging

Some people are highly motivated by having a network of positive relationships with other people.

▶

They value belonging, which is a sense of connection to other people at work. Work is where we experience cooperation, teamwork, and community. We feel part of a family or team, welcomed, and welcoming of others.

At some workplaces, employees are encouraged to compete with each other rather than collaborate. You can recognize the difference between competition and collaboration from some of your college classes. If you are collaborating, you might form study teams in preparation for the midterm exam. If the instructor is using grading policies that encourage competition (like grading on a curve), you might instead be competing with classmates. If you are competing with your classmates, you might not share any of your class notes if you think it might result in a lower grade for you.

The same is true at work. Some employers promote competition instead of collaboration because they believe it will produce better results. However, motivation expert Alfie Kohn reviewed a set of 122 studies that took place during the prior 56 years. He found that cooperation in the workplace led to higher employee achievement than competition about 90 percent of the time. Increased cooperation also resulted in better relationships, especially across cultural groups. Not only does collaborating produce better results, and a more tolerant work environment, but it also reinforces the motivational experience of belonging. In a workplace that rewards employees for competing against each other, there won't be as strong a sense of community or teamwork.

Regardless of the choices of your employers or professors, you can do a lot to shift your own focus to intrinsic motivators. For example, you can create more experiences of belonging with the following strategies:

1. **Use active listening skills:** Do less talking and more listening to your coworkers. You'll find out more about their projects, personal lives, concerns, and victories, and they'll come to trust you as a good listener.

2. **Try out other points of view:** Instead of immediately judging someone else's ideas or opinions, delay your response. Take some time to see their perspective. Ask more questions when you find yourself starting to condemn someone else's position. Consider that their position is just a new perspective on an issue important to you.

3. **Socialize and connect with coworkers:** Show up to company social events, both formal and informal. Plan and schedule your own smaller events or activities to get to know coworkers. Network and share posts with coworkers through social media apps.

Purpose

Motivational researcher Daniel Pink notes that top companies identify a "purpose motive" that allows the company to "stand for something and contribute to the world." You can also identify a purpose for your life (*I intend to learn as much as I can during my lifetime*). You can also have a purpose for your career (*I want to help people escape poverty and find meaningful work*). Your purpose guides you in making important decisions, like directional highway signs guide you to your destination. You can create more experiences of purpose with the following strategies:

1. **Clarify a work purpose:** As part of your life purpose, you can develop a more focused work purpose. What outcomes do you intend to create in your role at work? How would you like to show up in your relationship with coworkers and clients? Why have you chosen this career? Modify an unclear purpose like "getting better and learning more" to a clearer purpose like "becoming a more skilled neurosurgeon and learning the latest surgery techniques." Clarify your purpose and then take consistent action to stay in alignment with your work purpose.

▶

continued **SELF-MOTIVATION** / **at Work**

2. **Connect goals to purpose:** Establish goals that are directly connected to your work purpose. Write them down and set them as reminders on your phone. As you review your work goals for each day, ask yourself how each goal is related to your work purpose.

3. **Be of service:** Being of service to others has been shown to increase your happiness, reduce stress, lower your blood pressure, and can even benefit your career. John Reynolds' business book, *The Halo Effect,* asserts that you can renew your purpose and inspiration for your career by volunteering time.

There are many ways to increase your intrinsic motivation at work. If you do so, you'll be more engaged, more productive, more playful, more creative, better compensated, and more satisfied. You can practice many of these strategies as a student in college, and while working part-time on or off campus. As another benefit, the better you understand motivation at work, the more you'll improve your leadership skills to manage and help motivate others. Remember to create consistent experiences of competence, belonging, and purpose. And don't overlook one of the most powerful intrinsic motivators: fun!

Research by Professor Michael Tews (Penn State) and many others demonstrates that having fun at work improves both your performance and your health. The author of *Fish!: A Proven Way to Boost Morale and Improve Results,* Stephen Lundin, uses his observations of employees at Seattle's famous Pike Place Fish Market as an example of the theory that "Work made fun gets done." Although these employees' jobs are tiring, they focus on having fun while at work. Their positive and playful attitude keeps them motivated throughout the day. Fun at your job might include any of the following: an office puppy, a stash of healthy snacks, impromptu dance parties, or quick all-office exercise breaks. Regardless of what type of work you have, how might you make each day more fun?

TECH TIPS: Self-Motivation

42Goals *(Web)* allows you to set and track numerous goals. Log your progress and create charts to show your movement toward goals over time. By making your page public, you can share your progress with friends.

stickK.com uses incentives and accountability to motivate users to achieve a goal. You create a commitment contract by setting a goal and a deadline. For example, "I will study for at least 20 hours every week." Then—and this part is optional—you create the stick (of "carrot and stick" fame). For example, for your stick you could provide your credit card and agree to pay $50 to a group you despise if you don't achieve your goal. (As of this writing, the website claims nearly $20 million are "on the line" as sticks.) If you want, pick a referee who decides if you achieved your goal. You can also link in friends to encourage you.

DoSomething.org might be just what you're looking for if you want to ignite your passion for helping others and (as the site says) "make the world suck less." If you're looking for a service learning project for a class you're taking,

▶

this site provides hundreds of options. Claiming 3.3 million youthful (13- to 25-year-old) members, DoSomething offers members an opportunity to join campaigns to improve life on planet Earth, addressing problems of poverty, violence, and environment, among many others.

Hay House Vision Board *(Android and iOS)* allows you to create a digital vision board, a collection of images that visualize your desired future outcomes and experiences. You simply add images, photos, affirmations, inspiring quotations, and even music. You can create separate vision boards for each goal or role in your life: education, career, relationships, health, and so

on. Carry your inspiration everywhere you go on a mobile device. You can join a Vision Board Community and get inspired by vision boards created by other members of the community.

ThinkUp.me *(Android and iOS)* offers an app for creating and listening to one or many affirmations. You record your own affirmation(s) or choose from a library of affirmations created by experts. You can also record music to play along with your affirmation. The creators of ThinkUp recommend listening to your affirmation at various times during the day, especially before going to sleep. See the following section for more on affirmations.

Note: All of these are free, but some may offer upgraded features for a fee.

Write a Personal Affirmation

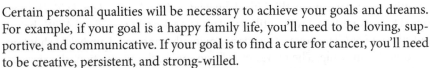

FOCUS QUESTIONS What personal qualities will you need to achieve your dreams? How can you strengthen these qualities?

Certain personal qualities will be necessary to achieve your goals and dreams. For example, if your goal is a happy family life, you'll need to be loving, supportive, and communicative. If your goal is to find a cure for cancer, you'll need to be creative, persistent, and strong-willed.

Think of the short- and long-term goals you have for your education. What are the personal qualities you'll need to accomplish them? Will you need to be intelligent, optimistic, articulate, responsible, confident, goal-oriented, mature, focused, motivated, organized, hardworking, curious, honest, enthusiastic, self-nurturing?

The potential for developing all of these personal qualities, and more, exists in every healthy human being. Whether a particular person fulfills that potential is another matter.

During childhood, a person's judgment of his or her personal qualities seems to be based mostly on what others say. If your friends, family, or teachers told you as a child that you're creative, you probably internalized this quality and labeled yourself "creative." But if no one said you're creative, perhaps you never realized you really are. Worse, someone important may have told you that you are dumb, thus starting the negative mind chatter of your Inner Critic.

W*e are what we imagine ourselves to be.*

Kurt Vonnegut, Jr.

W*e continue to be influenced by our earliest interactions with our parents. We hear their voices as our own internal self-talk. Those voices function like posthypnotic suggestions. They often govern our lives.*

John Bradshaw

How we become the labels that others give us is illustrated by a mistake made at a school in England. A group of students at the school were labeled "slow" by their scores on an achievement test. Because of a computer error, however, their teachers were told these "slow" children were "bright." As a result, their teachers treated them as having high intelligence and great potential. By the time the error was discovered, the academic scores of these "slow" students had risen significantly. Having been treated as if they were bright, the kids started to act bright. Perhaps, like these children, you have positive qualities waiting to blossom.

We continue to be influenced by our earliest interactions with our parents. We hear their voices as our own internal self-talk. Those voices function like posthypnotic suggestions.

As adults, we can consciously choose what we believe. As one of my psychology professors used to say, "In your world, your word is law." In other words, my thoughts create my reality, and then I act according to that reality (regardless of its accuracy). For example, suppose I'm taking a large lecture class and I keep getting confused. Students sitting around me ask questions when they're confused, but I don't because, well, I've just never been comfortable asking questions in a large lecture hall—that's just the way I am. I'm shy. My Inner Defender is fine with this explanation because it protects me from doing something uncomfortable. Or maybe it's part of my deep culture to refrain from questioning authority figures such as an instructor. The trouble is, the questions I don't ask keep popping up on tests, and I'm about to fail the course if I don't do something different.

Another part of me, my Inner Guide, knows I'd benefit from being bolder. In fact, if I want to pass this course, I *have* to be bolder! So I try an experiment. I start telling myself, *I am bold . . . I am bold . . . I am bold.* Of course, life keeps giving me chances to test my claim. A few class sessions later, I have a question, but I don't ask it. This time, though, I'm keenly aware of what I did: I chickened out. Undaunted, I continue my experiment, thinking, *I am bold . . . I am bold . . . I am bold.* The next time I have a question, I wait until after class and ask a fellow student. A little better, but still not *bold*. Then one day in class, I'm totally confused. *I am bold.* I shoot my hand in the air. Gulp. The professor calls on me, I ask my question, she answers, and, amazingly enough, I live to tell about it. Better yet, I get the answer correct on the next test. And best of all, my action finally corresponds with my claim. I came to a fork in the road (one I know so well), I consciously chose the bold path, I got the answer I needed, and I realize: My new thought generated new behaviors that, in turn, changed my outcomes and experiences for the better. And, if I did it once, I can do it again. Any time I need to. Any time I *choose* to!

CLAIMING YOUR DESIRED PERSONAL QUALITIES

An effective way to strengthen desired qualities is to create a personal affirmation. An affirmation is a statement in which we claim desired qualities as if we already have them in abundance. Here are some examples:

- I am bold, joyful, and generous.
- I am confident, creative, and selective.

> I was saying "I'm the greatest" long before I believed it.
>
> Muhammad Ali

> To adopt new beliefs, we can now systematically choose affirming statements, then consciously live in them.
>
> Joyce Chapman

- I am spiritual, wise, and curious, finding happiness in all that I do.
- I am supportive, organized, and secure, and I am creating harmony in my family.

Affirmations help us breathe life into personal qualities that we choose to strengthen. One of my colleagues recalls that whenever she made a mistake as a child, her father would say, "I guess that proves you're NTB." "NTB" was his shorthand for "not too bright." Imagine her challenge of feeling intelligent when she kept getting that message from her father! Today, she doesn't even need her father around; her Inner Critic is happy to remind her that she's NTB. She could benefit from an affirmation that says, "I am VB (very bright) and hardworking, too!"

"*Mother, am I poisonous?*"

What limiting messages did you receive as a child? Perhaps others said you were "ugly," "stupid," "clumsy," or "always screwing up." If so, today you can create an affirmation that empowers your desired qualities. For example, you could say, "I am beautiful, intelligent, and graceful, turning any mistake into a powerful lesson."

Some people report that their positive affirmations seem like lies. The negative messages from their childhood (chanted today by their Inner Critics) feel more like the truth. If so, try thinking of your affirmation as prematurely telling the truth. You may not feel beautiful, intelligent, or graceful when you first begin claiming these qualities, but, just as the "slow" children at the English school responded positively to being treated as bright, you can behave your way into proving the truth of your chosen qualities with each passing day. Using affirmations is like becoming your own parent: You acknowledge the positive qualities that no one has thought to tell you about . . . until now. And then, most important, you act on them, changing your outcomes and experiences in the process.

My "Born to Lose" tattoo was written on my mind long before it was written on my arm. Now I'm telling myself I'm "Born to Win."

Steve R., student

LIVING YOUR AFFIRMATION

Of course, simply creating an affirmation is insufficient to offset years of negative programming. Affirmations need reinforcement to gain influence in your life. Here are three ways to empower your affirmation: Repeat . . . dispute . . . align.

Affirmations have to be supported by the behavior that makes them happen.

Charles Garfield

1. **Repeat your affirmation.** In this way you'll remember the qualities you have chosen to strengthen. One student repeated her affirmation during workouts on a rowing machine. The steady pace of the exercise provided the rhythm to which she repeated her affirmation. What would be a good occasion for you to repeat your affirmation?

2. **Dispute your Inner Critic.** Realize that you already possess the qualities you desire. You already *are* creative, persistent, loving, intelligent . . . or whatever qualities you wish to strengthen. These are your natural human qualities waiting to be re-empowered. To confirm this reality (and quiet your Inner Critic), simply recall a specific event (or many) in your past when you displayed a quality that is in your affirmation.

3. **Align your words and deeds.** At each choice point, be what you affirm. If you say that you're "bold," make a bold choice. If you claim that you're "organized," do what an organized person does. If you assert that you're "persistent," keep going even when you don't feel like it. At some point, you'll have the evidence to assert, "Hey, I really am bold, organized, and persistent!" Your choices will prove the truth of your affirmation and your new outcomes and experiences will be the reward.

So, decide which personal qualities will help you stay on course to your goals and dreams, and prepare to write a personal affirmation that will help you bring them forth!

> An affirmation is self-talk in its highest form.
>
> Susan Jeffers

> The practice of doing affirmations allows us to begin replacing some of our stale, worn out, or negative mind chatter with more positive ideas and concepts. It is a powerful technique, one which can in a short time completely transform our attitudes and expectations about life, and thereby totally change what we create for ourselves.
>
> Shakti Gawain

JOURNAL ENTRY   11

In this activity, you will create a personal affirmation. If you repeat your affirmation often, it will help you make choices that will strengthen the personal qualities needed to achieve your goals and dreams.

1 Write a one-sentence statement of one of your most motivating goals or dreams in your role as a student. You can simply copy one that you wrote in Journal Entry 10 (or create a new one if you prefer).

2 Write a long list of personal qualities that would help you achieve this educational goal or dream. Use adjectives such as *persistent, intelligent, hardworking, loving, articulate, organized, friendly, confident, relaxed,* and so on. Write as many qualities as possible.

3 Circle the three qualities on your list that seem the most essential for you to achieve your goal or dream as a student (the one you identified in Step 1).

4 Write three versions of your personal affirmation. Do this by filling in the blanks in sentence formats A, B, and C below. Fill the blanks with the three personal qualities you circled in Step 3 previously. NOTE: Use the same three personal qualities in each of the three formats.

Format A: I am _____, _____, and _____.

Example: I am strong, intelligent, and persistent.

Format B: I am _____, _____, and_____ , _____ing _____.

▶

Example: I am strong, intelligent, and persistent, creating my dreams.

Format C: I am _____, _____, and _____ , and I _____.

Example: I am strong, intelligent, and persistent, and I love life.

Don't copy the examples, of course; create your own unique affirmation.

⑤ Circle or highlight the sentence from Step 4 that you like best. Say or think your preferred affirmation to yourself until you can do so without looking at your written words. This repetition helps you to begin taking ownership of your affirmation and desired qualities.

⑥ Write three paragraphs—one for each of the three qualities in your affirmation. In each of these paragraphs, write about a specific experience when you displayed your desired quality. For example, if one of your desired qualities is persistence, tell a story about a time in your life when you were persistent (even a little bit!). Write the story like a scene from a book, with enough specific details that readers will feel as though they are seeing what you experienced. Your paragraph might begin: *The first quality from my affirmation is. . . . A specific experience in my life when I demonstrated that quality was. . . .*

You can add creativity to your journal by adding pictures or key words that you found, your own original drawings, or quotations or song lyrics that appeal to you.

ONE STUDENT'S STORY

TINA STEEN, *Chaffey College, California*

When I began dreading every day at work, I knew it was time for a change. I was working in our family's restaurant, and I never had time for myself. Also, I could see how the long hours were aging my mother. I enjoyed keeping the books for the restaurant, so I thought I might like to be an accountant. My mother agreed that I would probably be good at it.

So I enrolled at Chaffey College and took an introductory accounting course. I was anxious because 10 years earlier I had attended college and got a bunch of F's and W's (withdrawals). My GPA was only 0.91 back then, but at the time, I didn't care. I had a job making decent money, so what did I need college for? I wasn't motivated, and my grades showed it. However, when I got a B in the accounting course this time, I was ecstatic.

My feeling of accomplishment didn't last long, though. My past low grades caught up to me, and I was placed on the highest level of academic probation. I was just one step from being officially dismissed from the college, and my B in accounting wasn't nearly enough to pull up my GPA from years long past. I felt the heaviness of this burden weighing me down. I felt defeated and reluctantly enrolled in a

▶

ONE STUDENT'S STORY   *continued*

mandatory guidance class. The class would temporarily protect me from being dismissed and provide a year for me to raise my GPA above 2.0. Along with the Guidance class, I took two accounting classes and one math class.

On the first day of the Guidance class, I looked around at my peers. They looked very young, and I immediately felt out of place. Negative thoughts swirled in my head: *You can't do this. You messed up too much in the past. Do you really think you can raise your GPA enough to be able to stay in school? You're older than most of these students, and you're in a Guidance class with them?* My thoughts shouted how inadequate I was. My Inner Critic was the only voice I heard, though I didn't have a name for it at the time. As the semester progressed, I learned about the different inner voices we hear in our heads. I learned to identify which voice I heard, and I began to harness the voice of my Inner Guide telling me to stay motivated. Then I read about believing in myself and writing a personal affirmation. If I didn't believe in myself, I knew I was going to repeat my previous failures in college. I couldn't let that happen. That's when I came up with an affirmation to help me believe in myself. I would often think or say aloud: *I am capable, loved, valued, wise to learn from my mistakes, and I will persevere by never giving up on myself.* Whenever I heard my Inner Critic's voice, I replaced it with the words of my affirmation.

Throughout the semester, I repeated my affirmation hundreds of times. I spoke these words enough to begin believing them. I used my affirmation to reduce the panic I felt before final exams. It also helped me complete a major project in accounting using Excel. Along with the other tools I learned in the course, I know my affirmation has paid off. I finished my Guidance class with an A+, I earned an overall GPA of 3.785, and I got off probation. All of the knowledge I gained from reading *On Course* and implementing it in my life has contributed to a very successful semester. I know I will reach my goals because this time I am better equipped with tools from the book, and I know how to be a successful student.

I may have begun my college education many years ago being a straight-F student, but I choose to no longer be that unmotivated student. After all, "I am capable, loved, valued, wise to learn from my mistakes, and I will persevere by never giving up on myself."

Photo: Courtesy of Tina Steen.

Healthy Choices: Drugs

Imagine this: You mention to a friend that you sprained your ankle and walking is painful. The next time you see him, he tosses you a little bottle half full of pills. "I broke my arm last year," he explains, "and the doctor prescribed these." The label says *OxyContin*. "Takes the pain away like magic. You can have 'em." You're aware that OxyContin is an opioid, one of the drugs people have been getting addicted to. But you're only going to take a couple. You're not going to get hooked. Right?

Or this: You're meeting with your math study group. Someone pulls out a paper bag and dumps a pile of pills on a table. "You guys all need a major energy boost. Try some Ritalin. It's amazing. If you like what it does, I can get more, and the price is right." Everyone takes one. These are smart people. They wouldn't swallow a pill if it was dangerous. Right?

Or suppose you're at your doctor's office. "I've been feeing anxious all semester," you explain. "I'm so stressed with all the homework and projects and tests. And my grades are really suffering." Your doctor suggests Xanax. If a doctor is prescribing something, it can't be a problem. Right?

Not so fast. As you've probably heard, there's a drug crisis in the United States. And it's creating a huge problem.

In 2016 alone, drugs killed roughly 64,000 people. That's up a staggering 22 percent in just one year, with no slowing in sight. And that doesn't count the millions living with addiction, both those addicted and their suffering families. The U.S. Surgeon General recently estimated that one out of every seven people in the United States may develop a substance addiction. Nearly half of all American adults (46 percent) have a family member or close friend struggling with drug addiction, according to a 2017 survey by the Pew Research Center.

The more you know about drugs, however, the wiser the choices you can make. And the wiser your choices, the more likely you'll stay healthy and on course to your goals and dreams.

People take drugs for many good reasons. They may want to relieve pain, treat a chronic disease, or reduce anxiety and depression. Sometimes, however, the reasons are questionable. They may simply want to escape problems, satisfy curiosity, or fit in with a group. Perhaps the strongest motivation of all is simply to feel better or stop feeling bad. The thing to remember is that many drugs have two potential effects: the one that improves the quality of our life and the other one we never thought could happen to us.

Three drug categories that are especially important to understand are painkillers, stimulants, and depressants. Many of these drugs increase dopamine in the brain. Dopamine is the feel-good chemical that creates pleasure. These positive feelings cause your brain's reward system to perk up and insist, "Oooh, do that again!" So, you take more of the drug to repeat those good feelings . . . but eventually the good feelings fade.

That's when something called "tolerance" kicks in, and here's where you can get in trouble with addiction. Tolerance means your body adapts, and it takes more of the drug to make you feel good. After a while, the drug offers no positive effects, but now you feel lousy without it. So, you take more, trying to recapture the good feelings. Then you start taking the drug to feel normal. And eventually you take it just to stop feeling miserable. Without the drug, you're nervous, irritable, and sick. Experiences that used to make you happy no longer do. Only the drug makes you feel good. Your cravings have taken over. You're addicted.

The National Institute on Drug Abuse defines addiction as a "chronic, relapsing brain disease that is characterized by compulsive drug seeking and use, despite harmful consequences." Attempts to escape addiction are very difficult because of the misery of withdrawal. The need to avoid this misery becomes an even stronger reason to take the drug than the original desire to feel good. The drug is now in charge.

It's tempting to think, "Oh, that could never happen to me." Think again. Dee Owens, former director of the Alcohol/Drug Information Center at Indiana University says, "I've talked to hundreds—no—thousands of people, and not a single person ever meant to become an addict. They just wake up one day—and there they are."

Addiction can happen to anyone. And if you're younger than 25, you're at even greater risk. Human brains continue to develop well into our 20s, and the frontal lobe areas are some of the last to mature. Important tasks of the frontal lobe include planning ahead, mastering complex tasks, and stopping inappropriate or dangerous behaviors . . . like taking drugs. Do you see the problem? Most college students have yet to develop the part of their brains that would stop them from taking the very drugs that will harm their brains. Thus, still-developing brains can be easy prey for drugs.

If you're going to be healthy in today's world, you better have at least a basic knowledge about drugs, their side effects, and alternatives that could help you stay on course.

THE LEAST YOU NEED TO KNOW ABOUT DRUGS

Only a very long book could adequately explore the thousands of legal and illegal drugs that now exist. Here we'll look at three categories of drugs: opioids, stimulants, and depressants. With this knowledge, you'll be better prepared to make healthy choices regarding drugs.

Opioids (Pain Relievers)

This category includes opioid drugs that relieve severe pain. If you've ever had a serious injury or operation, you likely took an opioid. Opioids don't actually eliminate pain; instead they block pain messages before they get to the brain. These drugs are illegal without a doctor's prescription. Opioids include **morphine, codeine, Percodan, OxyContin, Percocet, Vicodin, fentanyl,** and **heroin** (which, of course, is illegal). Opioids are typically taken as pills or intravenous injections. Used as prescribed by a doctor, the pain relief they offer is a blessing. People often describe the experience as trading pain for a pleasant, sleepy state in which all their cares slip away. And then there's the bad news.

Dangers: Abusing opioids can cause grogginess, suppressed breathing, addiction, coma, and death. Because of these dangers, opioids are controlled substances. This means possessing them without a doctor's prescription can lead to serious legal problems, including prison. Opioids are highly addictive, causing people to crave more than they can afford or get legally. That's when heroin may become tempting. Although illegal, heroine is often less expensive and more available than black-market opioids. The problem is, with street drugs you never know what you're getting. Like playing Russian roulette, each time you use a street drug could be the last choice you ever make. Death can happen with a single dose.

Stimulants (Energizers)

This category of drugs is often called "uppers." They are commonly used (or abused) by people wanting to eliminate fatigue, remain alert and focused, get high, or perhaps lose weight. **Concerta, Ritalin,** and **Adderall** are legally prescribed stimulants that help people with attention deficit/hyperactivity disorder (ADHD). Some students use them, instead, as study aids. They take the drug to remain alert, energized, and focused while completing homework and cramming for exams. The idea that these drugs make you smarter, though, is a myth.

Cocaine, crack cocaine (crack), and **methamphetamine (meth)** are stimulant drugs that, like opioids, are illegal to possess unless prescribed by a doctor (which is *very* rare). Cocaine is a powder that is usually snorted or injected. Crack is small rocks of cocaine that are usually smoked in a pipe. It's called "crack" because of the crackling sound it makes when heated. Meth are pills, powders, or chunks that are taken orally, snorted, or injected. These drugs provide an intense high that users often describe as "euphoric" or "blissful." Similar drugs include **Ecstasy** or **Molly,** which are the street names for **MDMA,** a manufactured drug with traits of both stimulants and hallucinogens. It's usually taken orally as a tablet or capsule. Like a stimulant, it creates feelings of increased energy and pleasure. Like a hallucinogen, it also produces experiences in which time and senses are distorted. You may encounter any of these stimulant drugs in a party setting.

Dangers: ADHD drugs have the potential for many unpleasant side effects, especially when misused. Side effects include insomnia, anxiety, stomach pain, nausea, irritability, restlessness, dizziness, and headaches. Dr. David Baron of the Chicago Medical School says, "Taken in too-large doses, [Adderall] has potentially dangerous or even lethal side effects, including hallucinations, other psychotic symptoms, strokes, or heart attacks." When used at unprescribed doses, ADHD drugs have a high potential for dependence and addiction. Withdrawal symptoms include fatigue, depression, and paranoia. Students with a prescription for an ADHD drug may be tempted to give or sell their pills to other students, but think again. Like opioids, these stimulants are controlled substances, and distributing them is a felony punishable by imprisonment.

Cocaine, crack, and meth users eventually crash, and many unpleasant symptoms create strong cravings for more. Physical symptoms include headaches, stomachache, high blood pressure, tremors, restlessness, elevated heart rate, and passing out. Mental and emotional symptoms include memory loss, hallucinations, paranoia, depression, anxiety, panic attacks, hostility, and violence. High doses can cause serious physical danger: seizure, stroke, heart attack, and death. Maybe you're thinking, *I'll just try it once to see what it's like.* If so, consider that death can occur with just one dose. Combining stimulants with alcohol or other drugs—including over-the-counter cold medicines—increases the dangers. And even if you dodge all these health dangers, the police may get you. For small amounts of cocaine, crack, or meth, penalties may be one to two years in prison plus fines. Possession of four or more grams of cocaine may result in drug trafficking charges. Resulting fines can reach $250,000 and prison sentences range from three to fifteen years.

MDMA (Ecstasy or Molly) creates a high that can include muscle cramping, nausea, and blurred vision. Rising body temperatures may cause internal organs to fail, causing death. Whether or not MDMA is addictive is unclear, but other dangerous side effects can last up to a week. These may include depression, anxiety, insomnia, decreased sexual arousal, irritability, aggression, weak attention, and poor memory (obviously not great for students). Worse, taking other drugs or alcohol with Ecstasy will likely heighten these negative effects. And now the really bad news: As with many street drugs, there's no way to know what you're putting in your body. Police report that seized Ecstasy contains many other ingredients. These mystery chemicals include cocaine, caffeine, ketamine, the diet drug ephedrine, meth, and even cough medicine. Some contained no MDMA at all! In short, buyer beware.

Depressants (Sedatives)

This category of drugs is also known as "tranquilizers," "downers," or "benzos" (short for benzodiazepines). Popular drugs in this group include **Xanax, Valium,** and **Prozac.** Another depressant—important for you to know about—is **Rohypnol** (more on why in a moment). All these sedatives require a doctor's prescription and have a similar effect. They slow racing thoughts, soothe a rapid heart, temporarily reduce stress, manage depression, and help calm panic attacks. Users feel relaxed and mellow. Depressants do this by suppressing chemicals in the brain that generate fear. As stress becomes more and more common, sales of these drugs have soared.

Dangers: Depressants have many side effects in common, including blurry vision, insomnia, irritability, and slurred speech. Particularly important for students to know, overuse of depressants can hinder learning and lower grades. According to drug experts at Duke University, ". . . it is unrealistic for someone who needs to learn new information to expect to do so to her full potential if using these drugs." Additionally, depressants are habit forming and powerfully addictive. As with other drugs, long-term use can lead to tolerance. "Tolerance," remember, means that a drug no longer creates the desired effect. Then users need to increase the dose, and the chase begins to reexperience positive feelings. Increased use can lead to fainting spells, mood swings, lost memories, dependence, and addiction. Dangers are greatly increased when depressants are combined with alcohol or other drugs. Withdrawal from depressants is much like withdrawal from alcohol. If not done properly, it can cause serious health risks. For safety, take depressants only as prescribed, which typically limits their use to a month.

Rohypnol, also known as "roofies," is one of several depressants that have been misused to harm others. These "date rape" drugs have been slipped into drinks at parties or bars. Rohypnol causes dizziness, lightheadedness, reduced muscle control, and memory loss. These symptoms can last for several hours, during which a person is extremely vulnerable to sexual assault or other dangers. If you feel any of these symptoms, especially after only moderate drinking, immediately ask someone you trust for help.

WISE CHOICES: DRUGS

- Never buy or use street drugs; there's no way to be sure what you're putting in your body.
- Take prescription drugs—including opioids, stimulants, and depressants—only if prescribed by your doctor; take only the number of pills prescribed for the length of time prescribed. Use common sense and quit taking the drugs if a doctor continues to refill your prescription beyond the time needed for recovery.
- For pain, try alternatives suggested by the Centers for Disease Control, (1) acetaminophen (Tylenol) or ibuprofen (Advil/Motrin); (2) physical therapy; (3) exercise and weight loss; (4) acupuncture; and (5) massage.
- For increased energy and focus, try exercise, more sleep, and modest amounts of caffeinated coffee or tea.
- For anxiety, consider natural means of calming such as deep breathing, meditation, biofeedback, chamomile tea, and exercise.
- Never combine two or more drugs, including alcohol.
- If pregnant, consult with your doctor about the best plan for your health.
- Never buy, sell, or share prescription or illegal drugs.
- At a party or bar, watch your drinks to prevent anyone from adding a dangerous drug. Do not accept a drink handed to you by a stranger.
- If you realize you've developed a drug dependence or addiction, seek help. A starting point is your campus counseling center.

Mastering Self-Management

Successful Students . . .

▶ **act on purpose,** choosing deeds that keep them on course to their goals and dreams.

▶ **employ self-management tools,** regularly planning and carrying out purposeful actions.

▶ **show grit,** demonstrating commitment, focus, and persistence in pursuing their goals and dreams.

Struggling Students . . .

▶ **wait passively for something to happen to them or drift from one unpurposeful activity to another.**

▶ **live disorganized, unplanned lives,** often engaging in urgent and unimportant actions.

▶ **change goals or quit when their actions don't lead to immediate success.**

Once I accept responsibility for choosing and creating the life I want, the next step is taking purposeful actions that will turn my desires into reality.

I am taking all of the actions necessary to achieve my goals and dreams.

CASE STUDY IN CRITICAL THINKING / The Procrastinators

Two students from Professor Hallengren's English composition class sat in the cafeteria discussing the approaching deadline for their fourth essay.

"There's no way I can get this essay done on time," Tracy said. "I've turned in every essay late, and I still owe him a rewrite on the second one. Professor Hallengren is going to be furious!"

"You think you're in trouble!" Ricardo said. "I haven't even turned in the last essay. Now I'm going to be two essays behind."

"How come?" Tracy asked. "I would have thought a young guy right out of high school would have all the time in the world."

"Don't ask me where my time goes," Ricardo answered, shrugging. "Deadlines keep sneaking up on me, and before I know it, I'm weeks behind. I live near campus, so I don't even have a long commute. But something always comes up. Last weekend I was going to write that other English essay and then study for my sociology test, but I had to go to a wedding out of state on Saturday. I was having such a good time, I didn't drive back until Monday morning. Now I'm even further behind."

"So that's why you missed English class on Monday," Tracy said. "Professor Hallengren lectured us because so many students were absent or late."

"I know I miss too many classes. One time I stayed home because I didn't have my essay ready. And sometimes I stay up late texting my girlfriend or playing video games. Then I can't get up in the morning."

"My situation is different," Tracy said. "I'm a single mother. I have three kids: 8, 9, and 12. I work 20 hours a week, and I'm taking four courses. I just can't keep up with it all! Every time I think I'm about to catch up, something goes wrong. Last week one of my kids got sick. Then my refrigerator broke, and I had to work overtime for money to get it fixed. Two weeks ago they changed my schedule at work to weekends, and I had to find a new sitter on Saturdays and Sundays. All my professors act like their class is all I have to do. I wish! The only way I could do everything is give up sleeping, and I'm only getting about five hours a night as it is."

"What are you going to do?" Ricardo asked.

"I don't think I can make it this semester. I'm considering dropping all of my classes."

"Maybe I should drop out, too."

1. **Who do you think has the more challenging self-management problem, Ricardo or Tracy? Be prepared to explain your choice.**
2. **If this person asked for your advice on how to do better in college, what specific self-management strategies would you recommend adopting?**

DIVING DEEPER

Which person's situation, Ricardo's or Tracy's, is more like yours? Explain the similarities, and identify what you do to keep up with all the things you need to do.

Acting on Purpose

FOCUS QUESTIONS   Have you ever noticed how much highly successful people accomplish? How do they make such effective use of their time?

Creators do more than dream. They have developed the skill of translating their desired outcomes into purposeful actions. They make a plan and then take one step after another . . . even when they don't *feel* like it . . . until they achieve their objective. Goals and dreams set your destination, but only persistent, purposeful actions will get you there.

Thomas Edison did more than dream of inventing the lightbulb; he performed more than 10,000 experiments before achieving his goal. Martin Luther King, Jr. did more than dream of justice and equality for people of all races; he spoke and organized and marched and wrote. College graduates did more than dream of their diplomas; they attended classes, read books, wrote essays, met with instructors, rewrote essays, formed study groups, conducted library and online research, asked questions, went to support labs, found tutors, and much, much more!

When we consider the accomplishments of successful people, we may forget that they weren't born successful. Most achieved their success through the persistent repetition of purposeful actions. Creators apply a powerful strategy for turning dreams into reality: **Do important actions first, preferably *before* they become urgent.**

HARNESS THE POWER OF QUADRANT II

The significance of **importance** and **urgency** in choosing our actions is illustrated in Figure 4.1, the Quadrant II Time Management System® (from Stephen Covey's book *The 7 Habits of Highly Effective People*) that follows. This chart shows that our actions fall into one of four quadrants, depending on their importance and urgency.

Only you can determine the importance of your actions. Sure, others (such as friends and relatives) will have their opinions, but they don't really know what you value. If an action will help you achieve what you value, then it's *important* and it would be crazy not to do it. Unfortunately, though, many people fill their time with unimportant actions, thus sabotaging their goals and dreams.

Likewise, only you can determine the urgency of your actions. Sure, others (such as instructors and counselors) will set deadlines for you, but these external finish lines won't be motivating unless you make them personally important. If meeting a short-term deadline that is rapidly approaching will help you achieve something you value, it's both important and *urgent,* and you'd be wise to meet that deadline. Many people miss important, urgent deadlines though, thus sabotaging their goals and dreams.

I've heard all sorts of excuses from students who "couldn't" get an assignment in on time. However, when I asked, "Could you have met the deadline if

Do not confuse a creator with a dreamer. Dreamers only dream, but creators bring their dreams into reality.

Robert Fritz

I am personally persuaded that the essence of the best thinking in the area of time management can be captured in a single phrase: organize and execute around priorities.

Stephen Covey

it was worth a million dollars?" their answer was almost always, "Sure, but it wasn't." So now we know the real problem. It wasn't that they "couldn't" meet the deadline. They just didn't make the deadline valuable enough to do what needed to be done. Creators choose their own goals and meet deadlines (even those set by others) because it's what *they* want, because it's important to creating the life *they* desire.

As you read about the four quadrants, ask yourself, "In which quadrant am I choosing to spend most of my time?" The choice you make will dramatically affect the outcomes and experiences you create.

> N ot all of your daily activities are of equal importance, and your mission is to organize and prioritize all activities into a working plan.
>
> Charles J. Givens

- **QUADRANT I ACTIONS (Important and Urgent)** are important activities done under the pressure of nearing deadlines. These are critical actions that must be done *now* or the consequences may be grim. One of my friends in college began his junior paper (the equivalent of two courses) just three days before it was due. He claimed that success in college was *important* to him, and the impending deadline certainly made this assignment *urgent*. He worked on the paper for 72 hours straight, finally turning it in without proofreading. Although he barely passed the assignment this time, he fell deeper and deeper into this pattern of procrastination. In our senior year he failed too many courses and was dismissed by the university. When you act on low priorities and neglect high priorities, you sabotage your goals and dreams. At the last minute, procrastinators dive desperately into Quadrant I to handle an action that has always been important but is now desperately urgent. People who spend their lives in Quadrant I are constantly dashing about putting out brush fires in their lives. They frantically create modest achievements in the present while sacrificing extraordinary success in the future. Worse, Quadrant I is where people often experience stress, and sometimes develop ulcers and risk nervous breakdowns.

> I t is not enough to be busy … the question is: What are we busy about?
>
> Henry David Thoreau

- **QUADRANT II ACTIONS (Important and Not Urgent)** are important activities done *without* the pressure of looming deadlines. These actions move you a step closer to a personally valuable outcome or experience. When you engage in an important activity with time enough to do it well, you can create your greatest dreams. Lacking urgency, Quadrant II actions are easily postponed. Almost all of the suggestions in this book belong in Quadrant II. For example, you could postpone forever keeping a journal, using the Wise Choice Process, adopting the language of Creators, discovering and visualizing your dreams, designing a life plan, and creating personal affirmations. However, when you do take purposeful actions such as these, you create a rich, full life. Quadrant II is where you will find Creators.

- **QUADRANT III ACTIONS (Not Important and Urgent)** are unimportant activities done with a sense of urgency. How often have you responded to the demand of your ringing phone only to be trapped in a long, unwanted conversation? Or you agree to something because you can't bring yourself to say "no"? When we allow someone else's urgency to talk us into an activity unimportant to our own goals and dreams, we have chosen to be in Quadrant III.

	Urgent	Not Urgent
Important	**Quadrant I** *Example:* Staying up all night cramming for an 8:00 AM test.	**Quadrant II** *Example:* Creating a study group in the first week of the semester.
Not Important	**Quadrant III** *Example:* Attending a hastily called meeting that has nothing to do with your goals.	**Quadrant IV** *Example:* Mindlessly watching television until 4:00 AM.

FIGURE 4.1 Quadrant II Time Management System

> While it is true that without a vision the people perish, it is doubly true that without action the people and their vision perish as well.
>
> Johnnetta B. Cole, former president, Spelman College

- **QUADRANT IV ACTIONS (Not Important and Not Urgent)** are simply time wasters. Everyone wastes some time, so it's not something to judge yourself for, though your Inner Critic may try. Instead, listen to your Inner Guide. Become more conscious of your choices, and minimize wasting the irreplaceable hours of each day. A 2014 Baylor University study showed that college students spend more than half of their waking hours on their smartphones. A college professor I know surveyed his classes and found that many of his students watch more than 40 hours of television per week. How are those many hours contributing to their goals and dreams?

A study in 1961 showed that students in higher education studied an average of 25 hours per week. Twenty years later, in 1981, college students' study time had dropped to 20 hours per week. By 2014, the average dropped again to only 17 hours per week, according to the National Survey of Student Engagement. In a 15-week semester, that's a total drop of 120 hours of studying! These numbers help explain why so many capable students get off course in college. It's difficult to learn complex subjects with so little time spent in Quadrants I and II.

> A vision without a task is but a dream, a task without a vision is drudgery; a vision with a task is the hope of the world.
>
> From a church in Sussex, England, ca. 1730

WHAT TO DO IN QUADRANTS I AND II

So what do Quadrant I and II actions look like? In college, Creators attend class regularly. They take good notes. They do all assignments to the best of their ability. They schedule conferences with their instructors. They create study groups. They organize their notes and study them often. They predict questions that will be on upcoming tests and carry the answers on 3 × 5 study cards. No external urgency motivates them to take these purposeful actions. They create their own urgency by a strong commitment to their valued goals and dreams.

By contrast, Victims spend much of their time in Quadrants III and IV, where they repeat unproductive actions such as complaining, blaming, excusing, and wasting time. Or maybe a well-meaning person helps a friend study while neglecting her own schoolwork. Not surprisingly, these choices move people farther and farther off course each day.

If you want to know which quadrant you are in at any moment, ask yourself this question: "Will what I'm doing now positively affect my life one year from today?" If the answer is "yes," you are in Quadrant I or II. If the answer is "no," you are probably in Quadrant III or IV.

Creators say "no" to Quadrant III and Quadrant IV activities. Sometimes the choice requires saying "no" to other people: *No, I can't drive you to the store right now because I'm headed to my study group. I'll be free at 5:00 if you still need a ride then.* Sometimes this choice requires saying "no" to themselves: *No, I'm not going to sleep late Saturday morning. I'm going to get up early and study for the math test. Then I can go to the movies with my friends without getting off course.*

When we say "no" to Quadrants III and IV, we free up time to say "yes" to Quadrants I and II. Imagine if you spent just 30 additional minutes each day taking purposeful actions. Think how dramatically that one choice could change the outcome of your life!

Remember to reread the visualization of your dream (**Journal Entry 10**) often to help you stay motivated. Also, remember to say your affirmation (**Journal Entry 11**) each day to remind you of the personal qualities that will keep you on course to your dreams! These are both great Quadrant II actions.

JOURNAL ENTRY | **12**

In this activity, you will assess the degree to which you are acting on purpose. *Your* purpose! As you spend more time in Quadrants I and II, you will notice a dramatic improvement in the results you are creating.

1 Write a list of 15 or more specific and observable actions you have taken in the past two days. (The actions are *specific* and *observable* if someone could have recorded you doing them with a camera.)

2 Using an entire journal page, draw a four-quadrant chart like the example in the article.

3 Write each action from your list in Step 1 in the appropriate quadrant on your chart. After each action, put the approximate amount of time you spent in the activity. For example, Quadrant IV might be filled with actions such as these:

1. Watched Netflix (2 hours)
2. Phone call to Terry (1 hour)
3. Checked and posted on Snapchat, Instagram, and Twitter (3 hours)
4. Went to the mall and wandered around (2 hours)
5. Hung out in the cafeteria (2 hours)
6. Played video game (4 hours)

▶

4 Write about what you have learned or relearned concerning your use of time. And as a result, what will you do that you have not been doing? Effective writing anticipates questions that a reader may have and answers these questions clearly. To dive deep in this journal entry, answer questions such as the following:

- In which quadrant do you spend the most time?
- What specific evidence did you use to draw this conclusion?
- If you continue using your time in this way, are you likely to reach your goals and dreams? Why or why not?
- What most often keeps you from taking purposeful actions?
- How do you feel about your discoveries?
- What different choices, if any, do you intend to make about how you use time?

ONE STUDENT'S STORY
JASON POZSGAY, *Oakland University, Michigan*

When I started college as a freshman engineering student, I knew I would have a little trouble with the transition from high school to college. What I didn't know was that my main challenge would come from distractions. There's a mall only five minutes from campus, and when my friends wanted to hang out there, I wouldn't say no. Other times we'd play video games, or go out to dinner, or watch television. There was always something to distract me and no one to tell me to get to work. I was an A/B student in high school, and I was used to things coming easy to me. In college there's a lot more work and it's definitely not work you can do in five minutes and be done like in high school. I always found some excuse not to do my work, and then I'd try

to do it the day it was due. I remember waiting until about 30 minutes before my first chemistry test to start studying. When my grades started dropping, I realized I needed to change, but I wasn't sure how.

That's when we read about self-management in the *On Course* book. In class we did an activity where we divided a paper into four quadrants. Then we put what we had done the last two days onto those quadrants. I only had a few things in Quadrants I and II (Important). But Quadrant IV (Unimportant) was full. I realized I was studying only about 3 hours a week, but I was going to the mall about 5 hours, watching movies and television about 6 to 10 hours, playing video games about 20 hours, and surfing the Internet about 30 hours.

I had never had a high-speed connection before, and things like YouTube and Facebook were consuming a good part of my life.

Now that I had figured out my problem, I needed a solution. I started by hanging up the quadrants in my room with my wasted time on them. I then put up another blank quadrant chart next to it. I decided to try new ways to manage my time over the next week and keep track of how I spent my time every day. I set a goal to reduce my time in Quadrants III and IV to no more than 20 hours per week and increase my time in Quadrants I and II up to 30 or 40 hours. At first I tried to completely cut out everything that was a waste of time, but I found myself stressed out. I was studying so much I thought my brain would explode, and I couldn't remember what I was studying. Then I tried getting all of my work done before I did anything

▶

ONE STUDENT'S STORY *continued*

that could be seen as a waste of time. But, again I was unable to focus on my work. Then I found the strategy that has helped. I put my schedule on a dry erase board and I adjust it to what I have going on that week. I make sure that I put both work and leisure time on the schedule. Also, if I have something important going on, like a test, I write it on my schedule in bold letters so I don't forget. Essentially I have made a reusable planner.

This strategy has helped me out a lot since I put it into effect.

When I filled in the quadrants at the end of the first week, I was about halfway to my goals. Toward the end of the semester, I tracked my time again, and I reached my goals. My new system makes me more aware of what I'm choosing to do. I spend less time on the Internet, and I learned to say no. I remember when a bunch of my friends wanted to go to the movies the night before I had a math test. They asked me to go at least 10 times, but I stayed home and studied. I actually did really

well on the test. Probably the best choice I made was taking my video games home. Since I started writing my important work on the whiteboard, I've missed almost no assignments and my grades have improved in every class. I have found a strategy that arranges my time so that I can get my important work done and still have time for fun things. My reusable planner has helped me a lot in my freshman year, and I plan to keep using it throughout college.

Photo: Courtesy of Jason Pozsgay.

Creating a Leakproof Self-Management System

FOCUS QUESTION   How can you devote more time to creating the outcomes and experiences that matter most to you?

> Time is the coin of your life. It is the only coin you have, and only you can determine how it will be spent.
>
> Carl Sandburg

At the beginning of a class, I asked my students to pass in their assignments. A look of panic came over one man's face. "What assignment?" he moaned. "You mean we had an *assignment* due today?" On another day, I overheard a student ask a friend: "Did you study for the math test today?" "No," the friend replied, "I didn't have time." Not long ago, a student told me, "I'm doing fine in my classes, but that's because I'm letting the rest of my life go down the drain."

Do these situations sound familiar? Do important actions leak through your hands like water? Do you sometimes give a halfhearted effort on important tasks . . . or finish them late . . . or not even do them at all? Do you neglect one important role in your life to do well in another? It's no easy matter getting everything done, especially if you're adding college to an already demanding life. But proven tools can help you work more effectively and efficiently.

Typically these are called *time management* tools, but the term is misleading because no one can actually manage time. No matter what we do, time just keeps on ticking. What we *can* manage, however, is ourselves. More specifically, we can manage the choices we make within the time we have every day.

TIME AND CULTURE

As with so many aspects of life, cultures differ in their beliefs and attitudes about time. In some cultures people tend to be relaxed and informal about time. In such a culture, setting and following a time for an appointment is approximate rather than specific, and those within the culture often expect someone else to arrive during a window *following* the agreed time instead of precisely *at* the agreed time. However, other cultures may view time differently. A common saying is "Time is money." Both are saved, budgeted, invested, spent, and wasted. Time is considered a valuable resource in many cultures, but the currency of time is often spent differently. Time is also a valuable resource when you use it without hurry and move more slowly through the world, perhaps talking with friends and family instead of rushing to your next appointment. It's also true that not everyone within these cultural groups follows the cultural expectations around time, and some even choose behaviors that are the very opposite.

A wise choice in college is to recognize that there are differing views on the use of time. So, be prepared to successfully navigate these differing expectations. When an instructor and student view time differently, it can lead to challenges for both. If a student is more informal about time, and an instructor more formal, the student might be penalized for arriving after the start of class time or late for an appointment during the instructor's office hours. If a student is more formal about time, and an instructor more informal, the student might be upset when an instructor arrives after the start of the scheduled class time or after an agreed office hour appointment time. Look for the syllabus to communicate expectations about your use of time, and even have a dialogue with the instructor and other students about expectations around time and deadlines for assignments, class attendance, break times, exams, and so on. In this way, you ensure that you are able to meet and manage both your own needs and expectations and those of your instructors.

One of the keys to your success in college, then, is having a leakproof self-management system. This is the system in which you record, organize, prioritize, and store all of your important actions. Then you complete one important task after another to the best of your ability. In short, **the secret to effective self-management is making choices that maximize the time you spend in Quadrants I and II.** These are the quadrants, you'll recall, where all of your actions are important because they help you achieve your desired outcomes and experiences. Effectiveness in these quadrants allows you to follow precise deadlines as required and to invest more time in the informal experiences of life without rushing because you have fallen behind in other areas.

Understand that no self-management system is right for everyone. Rather, there are many tools with which to experiment. You'll know you've found your best self-management system when you start achieving more of your desired outcomes and experiences with less stress. As a bonus, when you find the self-management approach that feels right for you, your expectations of success in college (and elsewhere) will go up because now you'll be confident you can get

Unlike many people in dominant culture who may find their days and their lives driven by appointment books, calendars, and to-do lists, Latino cultural values do not emphasize rigid adherence to schedules.

Lynn Kell Spradlin

the required work done. The following are six of the best tools for making sure you spend the bulk of your time creating a great future. You can choose to get organized by using paper versions of these tools, or you can find apps for your smartphone, or websites that perform the same functions electronically. You may even want to combine some of these tools to create a system that works best for you.

WEEKLY CALENDAR: For Tracking Recurring Scheduled Events

Some of the things you need to do happen every week, maybe even on the same day and at the same time. Examples include classes, study time, sports team practice, commuting, work, and recreation. An ideal tool created for managing such actions is a **Weekly Calendar**. On your weekly calendar, record all of your commitments that happen at the same time every week. The value of recording classes, sports team practice, commuting, and work hours on your calendar is probably obvious. However, you may wonder why you should schedule study times. After all, there's no teacher, coach, or boss counting on you to show up to study. Think again. Someone *very* important is waiting for you to show up. *You!* If you're really serious about being a success in college, job number one is learning. And the key to learning is studying. One of the quickest ways to sabotage your college success is to think, *I'll study whenever I have free time.* Study time doesn't just happen. You need to *make* it happen. Schedule it and do it! As a rule of thumb, schedule two hours of study time for each hour of class time you have each week. For example, if you have 12 class hours each week, set aside 24 hours on your weekly calendar to study. If you choose to do something instead of studying at a scheduled time, make sure the substitute activity is more important. *Much* more important. And do this only on rare occasions. Once you get in the habit of trading study time for Quadrant III or IV activities, you're going to be off course in college in no time.

> I think that learning about and using time is a very complicated kind of learning. Many adults still have difficulty with it.
>
> Virginia Satir

MONTHLY CALENDAR: For Tracking One-Time Scheduled Events

Of course, many important actions occur only once, and that date might be far in the future. These actions will happen on a specific day and probably at a specific time. If you miss it, it's gone forever. For such actions, a **Monthly Calendar** provides a chronological list of your upcoming important commitments, appointments, and assignments. Use it to record one-time events such as a tutoring session or conference with an instructor. Also put on your calendar the due dates of tests, research papers, final exams, projects, lab reports, and quizzes. With a monthly planner, one glance will show you all of your one-time events in the days, weeks, even months to come. Never again will you moan the Victim's lament: *What do you mean it's due today?*

In place of paper calendars, many people keep their appointment schedule on a smartphone. They also set reminders about appointments or deadlines.

Weekly Calendar for the Week of _____

	Monday	Tuesday	Wednesday	Thursday	Friday	Saturday	Sunday
7:00 AM							
7:30 AM							
8:00 AM							
8:30 AM							
9:00 AM							
9:30 AM							
10:00 AM							
10:30 AM							
11:00 AM							
11:30 AM							
12:00 PM							
12:30 PM							
1:00 PM							
1:30 PM							
2:00 PM							
2:30 PM							
3:00 PM							
3:30 PM							
4:00 PM							
4:30 PM							
5:00 PM							
5:30 PM							
6:00 PM							
6:30 PM							
7:00 PM							
7:30 PM							
8:00 PM							
8:30 PM							
9:00 PM							
9:30 PM							
10:00 PM							
10:30 PM							
11:00 PM							

Notes:

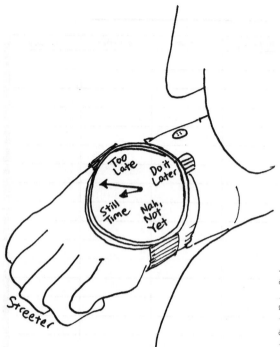

Free electronic calendars are offered as apps and by a number of Internet sites (simply do an Internet search for "online calendar"). A unique advantage of these services is that most allow you to create calendars that can be accessed and updated by members of a group. If you have a project group, a study team, or a large family, an online calendar service might be just the right tool for managing your collective schedules.

Scheduling purposeful actions on your calendar is one thing; actually *doing* them is quite another. Once you have chosen your priorities, let nothing keep you from completing them other than a rare emergency or special opportunity. Make a habit of saying "no" to unscheduled, low-priority alternatives found in Quadrants III and IV.

NEXT ACTIONS LIST: For Tracking Unscheduled Events and Actions

Some important actions don't need to happen on a specific day. They just need to be done as soon as possible. A **Next Actions List** records everything you need to do "next" (as opposed to a calendar, where you schedule actions on a particular day and time). Whenever you have free time that you might otherwise waste, your Next Actions List provides Quadrant I or II actions to complete. Here's how to use one:

1. Write your life roles and corresponding goals, which you defined in Chapter 3, in the shaded boxes. This first step makes your Next Actions List more effective than a to-do list by ensuring that your actions are directed at the accomplishment of *all* of your important goals.

2. List Quadrant I (Important and Urgent) actions for each of your goals. For example, if your short-term goal for Math 107 is to earn an A, your list might contain actions like these:

Role: Math 107 student

Goal: Grade A

- *Read pages 29–41 and complete problems 1–10 on page 40.*

- *Study 2 hours or more for Friday's test on Chapters 1–3.*

Each of these actions is **important** and—with a quickly approaching deadline—is **urgent.** As with a goal set with the DAPPS rule, be specific. Vague items such as *Do homework* provide little help when the time comes to take action. Much more helpful are specific tasks such as *Read pages 29–41 and complete problems 1–10 on page 40.*

In college I learned how to manage more tasks than anyone could possibly finish. Literally. We learned how to keep a lot of balls in the air at the same time. You couldn't study for every class every day, so you had to decide what could be put off till later. The experience taught us to set priorities.

Dennis Hayes, Hayes Microcomputer Products

Betsy Streeter/Cartoon Stock

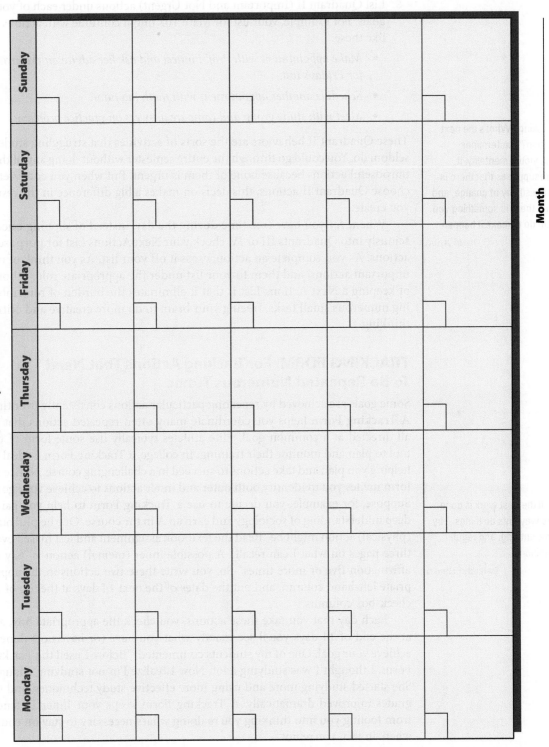

Monthly Calendar

Monday	Tuesday	Wednesday	Thursday	Friday	Saturday	Sunday

Month _____

3. List Quadrant II (Important and Not Urgent) actions under each of your goals. For example, your list for Math 107 might continue with actions like these:

- *Make appointment with Prof. Finucci and ask her advice on preparing for Friday's test.*
- *Schedule another appointment with math lab tutor.*
- *Meet with study group and compare answers on practice problems.*

Asking "What's the next action?" undermines the victim mentality. It presupposes that there is a possibility of change, and that there is something you can do to make it happen.

David Allen

These Quadrant II behaviors are the sorts of activities that struggling students seldom do. You could go through the entire semester without doing any of these purposeful actions because none of them is urgent. But when you consistently choose Quadrant II actions, this decision makes a big difference in the results you create.

Whenever you have free time during the day, instead of slipping unconsciously into Quadrants III or IV, check your Next Actions List for purposeful actions. As you complete an action, cross it off your list. As you think of new important actions, add them to your list under the appropriate role. A bonus of keeping a Next Actions List is that it eliminates the burden of remembering numerous small tasks, freeing your brain to do more creative and critical thinking.

TRACKING FORM: For Tracking Actions That Need To Be Repeated Numerous Times

Some goals are achieved by repeating particular actions consistently over time. A **Tracking Form** helps you coordinate many often-repeated actions that are all directed at a common goal. Elite athletes typically use some form of this tool to plan and monitor their training. In college, a Tracking Form is ideal for helping you plan and take actions to succeed in a challenging course. Notice the form invites you to identify both outer and inner actions to achieve your goals.

All the best work is done the way ants do things—by tiny, untiring, and regular additions.

Lafcadio Hearn

Suppose, for example, you decide to use a Tracking Form to help you gain a deep understanding of sociology and earn an A in the course. One helpful outer (physical) action might be "Read the textbook assignment and test myself every three pages on what I can recall." A possible inner (mental) action is "Say my affirmation five or more times." So, you write these two actions in the appropriate left-hand column, and put the dates of the next 14 days at the top of the check-box columns.

Each day that you take these actions, you check the appropriate box, and at the end of 14 days you'll see exactly what you have (or have not) done to achieve your goal. One of my students commented, "Before I used the Tracking Form, I thought I was studying a lot. Now I realize I'm not studying enough." She started studying more and using more effective study techniques, and her grades improved dramatically. A Tracking Form keeps your Inner Defender from fooling you into thinking you're doing what's necessary to stay on course when, in fact, you're not.

Next Actions List

| Role: | |
| Goal: | |

| Role: | |
| Goal: | |

| Role: | |
| Goal: | |

| Role: | |
| Goal: | |

| Role: | |
| Goal: | |

Phone calls, emails, and texts

Other actions

| Role: | |
| Goal: | |

WAITING-FOR LIST: For Tracking Commitments That Others Have Made To You

Your progress toward a goal will sometimes stall while you wait for someone else to get back to you. Maybe you're waiting to hear from a librarian about when a book you need has become available. Maybe you're waiting to hear from friends about whether they're going to join you at the basketball game on Friday night. Maybe you're waiting for an instructor to tell you whether you can change the topic of your term paper. Each of these items should go on your **Waiting-For List**, along with the date it's added. Glance over the list daily. When an item has been on the list a while, contact the appropriate person and give them a nudge. With this tool, you'll dramatically reduce the number of times your goals get stuck waiting for someone else to take action on something important to you. This can be as simple as recording (1) the date promised, (2) the person you're waiting for, and (3) what you're waiting for. Example: **10/22, Elliott, When to study for math?** If October 22 passes without hearing from Elliott, you can shoot him a text asking again when he'd like to get together to study math.

> Pow much of human life is lost in waiting?
>
> Ralph Waldo Emerson

PROJECT FOLDER: For Tracking and Managing Progress Toward a Large Goal

Some goals take many actions to achieve. For each multistep project, create a separate physical or online **Project Folder**. Suppose your speech instructor assigns a group presentation. Everything related to that large task goes in one folder: the handout describing the assignment, the names and contact information for all group members, a Next Actions List for this project, assignments for each group member, the email address of someone you heard about who knows how to make great PowerPoint slides, research materials you've collected for your part of the presentation, a list of helpful websites, and YouTube videos that might enliven your presentation. Every time you get more information related to this presentation, it goes in the Project Folder. Never again will you utter those woeful words: "I know it's here somewhere."

To keep track of your progress, put a Next Actions List on the outside of the physical folder. You might also use a project collaboration app like Trello to keep track of next actions and team member assignments. Use these tools to record all of the actions you (or others, if it's a group project) are tasked to do. You might even put a due date for each of these actions so you keep the project moving toward completion.

THE REWARDS OF EFFECTIVE SELF-MANAGEMENT

Some people resist using a written self-management system. "These forms and charts are for uptight perfectionists," one student objected. "Everything I need to do, I keep right here in my head." I know this argument well, because I used to make it myself. Then one day, one of my mentors replied, "If you can remember everything you need to do, I guess you're not doing very much." Ouch.

Tracking Form

Role:

Dream:

Long-term goal:

Short-term goals (to be accomplished this semester):

1.

2.

3.

4.

OUTER (Physical) Action Steps

Dates:

INNER (Mental) Action Steps

Dates:

I decided it wouldn't kill me to experiment with self-management tools. Over time, I came up with my own combination of the tools we've been examining. And over more time, my tools migrated more and more into my computer and smartphone. In the process I became aware of how I'd been wasting precious time. With my old self-management system (mostly depending on my memory, with an occasional "note to self"), the best I did was remember to do what was important and urgent. The worst I did was forget something vital. Then I'd waste time cleaning up the mess I'd made.

With my present self-designed system, I almost always complete my Quadrant I actions on time. I also spend large chunks of time in Quadrant II, where I take important actions before they become urgent. I'm better at keeping commitments to myself and to others. I'm less likely to go off course. Relieved of remembering every important task I need to do, my mind is free to think more creatively and boldly. And, most of all, my written self-management system helps me carry out the persistent, purposeful actions necessary to achieve my goals and dreams.

If you're already achieving all of your greatest goals and dreams, then keep using your present self-management system because it's working! However, if your Inner Guide knows you could be more successful than you are now, then maybe it's time to implement a new approach to managing your choices. You'll rarely meet a successful person who doesn't use some sort of written self-management system, whether in the world of work or in college. In fact, researchers at the University of Georgia found that students' self-management skills and attitudes are even better predictors of their grades in college than their Scholastic Assessment Test (SAT) scores.

Consistently using a written or digital self-management system is a habit that takes time to establish. You may begin with great energy, only to find later that a week has gone by without using it. No need for self-judgment. Instead, simply examine where you went astray and begin your plan anew. Experiment until you find the system that works best for your personality and creates the outcomes and experiences you desire. In time, you will excel at using your personally designed self-management system. And then watch how much more you accomplish!

> When the seniors in the College Board study were asked what contributed to a successful and satisfying career in college, 73 percent said the "ability to organize tasks and time effectively."
>
> Tim Walter and Al Siebert

> When people with whom you interact notice that without fail you receive, process, and organize in an airtight manner the exchanges and agreements they have with you, they begin to trust you in a unique way.
>
> David Allen

JOURNAL ENTRY   13

In this activity, you'll explore how you could improve your present self-management system. By using time more effectively and efficiently, you'll complete more important actions and maximize your chances of attaining your goals and dreams.

1 **Write about the system (or lack of system) that you presently use to decide what you will do each day.** There is no "wrong" answer, so don't let your Inner Critic or Inner Defender get involved. Consider questions such as how you know what homework to do, when to prepare for tests, what classes to attend, and what instructor conferences to go to. How do you track what you need

▶

to do in other roles, such as your social or work life? What apps or messaging systems do you use to manage your various life roles? Why do you currently use this approach? How well is your system working (giving examples wherever possible)? How do you *feel* while using this approach to self-management (for example, stressed, calm, energized, frantic, and so on)?

2 **Write about how you *could* use or adapt the self-management tools in this chapter to create a leakproof self-management system and improve your outcomes and experiences. Or, if you do not want to use or adapt any of these tools, explain why.** Consider the Weekly Calendar, the Monthly Calendar, the Next Actions List, the Tracking Form, the Waiting-For List, the Project Folder, and any other apps or tools with which you are familiar. How might you use them separately or in combination? How might you use self-management tools not mentioned here that you may know about? In short, invent your own system for managing your choices that you think will maximize the quality of your outcomes and experiences.

I used to wonder how other students got so much done. Now that I'm using a planner, I wonder how I settled for doing so little.

John Simmons, student

ONE STUDENT'S STORY

ALLYSA LEPAGE, *Sacramento City College, California*

When the fall semester began, I wasn't sure how I was going to fit everything into my schedule. In addition to taking three college courses, I was waitressing 24 hours a week, taking dance classes, teaching dance classes to kids, spending time with my boyfriend, doing housework and errands, hanging out with friends from three different groups (high school, college, and church), and rehearsing two evenings a week for an annual December musical at Memorial Auditorium, an event that draws thousands of people. I'd stay up late to get my homework done, then wake up exhausted. I was struggling in math, and in my heart I knew I could be doing better in my other classes. I'd

forget to turn in homework, I was skimping on preparation for my dance classes, I wasn't calling friends back, and I'd forget to bring costumes and makeup to rehearsals for the musical. I was sick all the time with colds and headaches. I was seriously stressed and not doing full justice to anything.

Before I lost all hope, my Human Career Development class went over self-management tools. I developed my own system and started writing down everything I needed to do. I keep a big calendar by my bed so I see it in the morning, and I carry a smaller calendar in my purse. My favorite tool is a list of everything I have to do put into categories. I make a new list every

day and put important things at the top so it's okay if I don't get to the ones on the bottom. My system helps me see what my priorities are and get them done first so I don't feel so scattered.

By doing important things first, I began having more focus, not rushing as much, and getting more done. Of course I had to let a few lower-priority things go for a while, like doing housework and spending as much time with some of my friends. I started getting more sleep, completing my homework, and getting A's on all of my tests while doing everything else that I needed to do. After a while, I began to accomplish so much more and I realized that I *do* have enough time to fit all of the important things into my schedule. In fact, every once in a while now I actually find myself with a luxury I haven't had in a long while — free time.

Developing Grit

FOCUS QUESTIONS   Do you find yourself procrastinating, slacking off, or even quitting on goals that are important to you? How can you keep taking purposeful actions even when you don't feel like it?

Predicting who will persist through college and earn their degree and who won't is among the most stubborn problems in all of social science.

Angela Duckworth, psychologist

Every year a puzzling thing happens in higher education. Perfectly capable college and university students—millions of them—stop attending, withdraw, drop out, or fail out. Somewhere along the path to their degree, they lose their way. As a result, the number of students dropping out of colleges and universities is disappointingly high.

A psychology professor at the University of Pennsylvania became intrigued with how to help students persist . . . how to help them achieve their potential in college and in life. But before we meet her, let's first explore the dropout problem at a unique institution of higher learning.

Of all the colleges and universities in the world, one of the most difficult to get into is the United States Military Academy (USMA). Applicants immediately face a major hurdle. They must get a nomination to attend the USMA, but not from just anyone. The nomination must come from a member of the Congress, the Senate, or the vice president of the United States. Of the 14,000 or so hopefuls, only about 4,000 receive such a nomination.

These remaining applicants are then rated by the USMA admissions office, using extremely high academic and physical standards. Many, perhaps most, applicants were at the top of their graduating class academically and played varsity sports as well. Many also held leadership positions, such as student government officers or captains of sports teams. But only 1,200 of these highly motivated, highly talented applicants will be accepted. How, then, to choose the lucky few?

For years, the USMA did so using what it called the Whole Candidate Score. Each applicant was given a score based on factors such as high school rank, SAT or ACT scores, leadership potential, and a rigorous physical fitness test. Having considered all this information, the admissions officers accepted only applicants they believed would stick it out, graduate, and become outstanding officers in the United States Army.

However, despite all these efforts to choose the most motivated and talented students, about 20 percent never graduated. In fact, many new cadets quit even before completing the Cadet Basic Training, held during the summer before their first classes. Like many other colleges, the USMA wondered what it could do to improve retention and completion.

Enter psychology professor Angela Duckworth. She had become intrigued with the same problem that puzzled the USMA and so many other colleges and universities. Why do people with the same apparent ability create such different outcomes? Why do some people persevere through challenges and others quit? Why do some people achieve or even exceed their potential while others don't?

Dr. Duckworth's research led her to this theory: It is a "combination of passion and perseverance that made high achievers special. In a word, they had grit." Grit, then, is a combination of two powerful inner qualities: (1) a passion for achieving a specific long-term goal and (2) the perseverance to keep going even in the face of obstacles or disappointments.

To test her theory, Duckworth created a Grit Scale. The scale asks you to rate a statement on how well it describes you. Some statements assess your passion, while others assess your perseverance. You can take the Grit Scale at angeladuckworth.com/grit-scale. Don't worry if your score is lower than you'd hoped. Read on for ways to increase your grit.

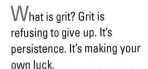

What is grit? Grit is refusing to give up. It's persistence. It's making your own luck.

Peter Diamandis, Greek American engineer, physician, and entrepreneur

Having heard about the puzzling loss of students at the USMA, Duckworth arranged to have brand-new cadets take the Grit Scale. The first finding was that the cadets' Whole Candidate Score and their Grit Score showed little or no relationship. In other words, a cadet getting a high Whole Candidate Score might very well get a low Grit Score. Which score, then, would better predict which students would complete Cadet Basic Training?

The answer to that question was the second important finding. Grit scores proved to be very reliable predictors of which cadets stayed and which ones quit. None of the other factors came close. Duckworth summed up what mattered most: "Not your SAT scores, not your high school rank, not your leadership experience, not your athletic ability. Not your Whole Candidate Score. What matters is grit." In short, grit appears to be even more important to success than talent.

Duckworth went on to show the value of grit for achieving other goals as well. Her Grit Scale successfully predicted all of the following (and others):

- Which people selling vacation time shares would still be around six months later
- Which kids would do well in the finals of the Scripps National Spelling Bee
- Which Chicago public school juniors would graduate a year later
- Which college graduates would go on to achieve advanced degrees

So, let's look more closely at how you can develop the two components of grit: passion and perseverance.

PASSION

In Chapter 3, you read and wrote about creating inner motivation, designing a compelling life plan, and committing to your goals and dreams. Hopefully, in doing so you took a big step toward developing passion about your future. Duckworth offers additional ideas for becoming passionate about your goals and dreams. Let's explore three of them:

Follow your interests. It may seem obvious that you should pursue your interests. However, I've had students tell

me they chose their college majors and future careers based on what their parents wanted them to do. Or based on how much money they would earn. Or which major they thought was the easiest. If you aren't personally interested in pursuing a goal or dream, you're unlikely to persist when inevitable obstacles appear. (That's why one of the P's in the DAPPS Rule stands for Personal.) Research shows that when people are interested in their work, they are both more satisfied and perform better. The same is true when choosing a major. If you're not sure what interests you right now, explore. Expose yourself to as many academic subjects, extracurricular activities, and people as possible. Then follow your interests.

Stay focused. As soon as possible, Duckworth recommends, choose one top-level professional goal and give it your determined effort. The more you focus your energy on a goal, the more likely you are to ignite your own passion. Duckworth says, "What I mean by passion is not just that you have something you care about. What I mean is that you care about that *same* ultimate goal in an abiding, loyal, steady way. . . . Grit is about holding the same top-level goal for a very long time." What about your own top-level goal? Does it inspire a passion that's likely to persist for a very long time? If not, consider staying open to another possible top-level goal.

Contribute. Choose a future in which you are contributing to the well-being of others. The best instructors at your college have done just that. They love seeing their students thrive, laying the foundation for a rich, full life. Some of your classmates may have found that passion. For example, when Michael Moreno was born at a hospital in Corpus Christi, Texas, he had a serious heart problem. Fortunately, surgery healed him. "I knew from the age of 12 what I wanted to do with my life," he said. "That was to go into the medical field, and ultimately to become a nurse." After graduating from the University of Texas School of Nursing, Michael now works in the surgical intensive care unit of Methodist Hospital. There he provides care to patients recovering from heart surgeries, achieving the goal he set many years ago when he was the one being helped. To Dr. Duckworth, "purpose" means "the intention to contribute to the well-being of others." That intention certainly fuels Michael Moreno's passion.

If you have already found your passion, you are in the fortunate minority. If you're still searching, you're not alone, and there are still ways to build grit through perseverance.

PERSEVERANCE

Success takes a willingness to keep doing whatever has to be done to reach your goals and dreams . . . *whether or not you feel like it*. Demonstrating "grit" doesn't mean you can't have fun along the way, but the reality is that success takes persistent effort. People with grit aren't afraid of hard work.

Most students want to be successful, but *wanting* and *doing* are worlds apart. Hanging out with friends is easier than going to class. Playing a video game is easier than reading a challenging textbook. Partying on Saturday night is easier than studying for a test.

You always have to focus in life on what you want to achieve.

Michael Jordan

A dream doesn't become reality through magic; it takes sweat, determination, and hard work.

Colin Powell

Calvin and Hobbes   by Bill Watterson

For many students, grit is essential after mid-semester. The excitement of the new semester has been replaced by a Next Actions List overflowing with assignments. Exams are coming up soon. That's when Inner Defenders start offering excuses to quit: *I've got boring teachers; My schedule is lousy; I'm still getting over the flu; Next semester I could start all over.* Inner Critics chime in: *I never could do math; I'm not as smart as my classmates; I'm too old; I'm too young; I'm not really college material.*

Your Inner Guide, however, knows that Creators finish strong. Their efforts go up as the semester winds down. Your Inner Guide can help you persevere by asking one question: *What are my goals and dreams?* If you need a reminder, revisit your life plan in Journal Entry 9 and the visualization of your biggest academic goals or dream in Journal Entry 10. If your goals and dreams don't provide perseverance, perhaps they need revision.

Here's the thing about perseverance. Although failure is certain if you quit, success isn't guaranteed because you persist. Persistence is more than repeating the same thing over and over while hoping for a better result. If Plan A isn't working, don't quit. But also don't keep doing what isn't working! Learn from your mistakes and change your approach. Move on to Plan B. Or C or even D, if necessary.

One of my students learned just how powerful perseverance and a willingness to try something different can be. When Luanne enrolled in my English 101 class, she had failed the course three times before. She had developed some good writing skills, but she still struggled with Standard English grammar. "I know," she said, "that's what all my other teachers told me." She paused, took a deep breath, and added, "At least I'm not a quitter."

I asked Luanne why she was going to college. As she told me about her dream to work in television, her eyes sparkled, and I saw her passion. I asked if mastering standard grammar would help her achieve her dream. She hesitated, perhaps nervous about where her answer might lead.

Finally she said, "Yes."

Perhaps the most valuable result of all education is the ability to make yourself do the thing you have to do, when it ought to be done, whether you like it or not; it is the first lesson that ought to be learned.

Thomas Henry Huxley

"Great! So, what's one action that, if you did it every day for a month or more, would improve your grammar?" She needed to discover a Quadrant II activity and make it a new habit.

"Probably studying my grammar book."

I handed her a **32-Day Commitment Form** (located in this chapter following Journal Entry 14). "Okay, then, I'm inviting you to make a commitment to study your grammar book for 32 days in a row. Put a check on this form each day that you keep your promise to yourself. Will you do it?"

"I'll try."

"C'mon, Luanne. You've been *trying* for three semesters. My question is, 'Will you commit to studying grammar for at least 30 minutes every day for the next 32 days?'"

She paused again. Her choice at this moment would surely affect her success in college, and probably the outcome of her life.

"Okay," she said, "I'll do it."

And she did. Practically every time I passed the writing lab, I saw Luanne working on grammar. She was there so often the tutors started joking about charging her rent.

But that's not all Luanne did. She attended every English class. She completed every writing assignment. She met with me to discuss her essays. She created flash cards with her problem sentences on one side and corrections on the other. In short, Luanne was putting in the effort. She was persevering! She was demonstrating grit.

To receive a passing grade in English 101, students had to pass one of two exit exam essays graded by other instructors. The first exam that semester brought Luanne some good news: She had gotten her highest score ever. But there was the usual bad news as well: Both exam graders said her grammar errors kept them from passing her.

Luanne was at another important fork in the road. Would she persevere in the face of discouraging news? Would she quit or finish strong?

"Okay," she said, "show me how to correct my errors." We reviewed her essay, sentence by sentence. The next day she went to the writing lab earlier; she left later. She rewrote the exam essay for practice, and we went over it again. Luanne's mastery of grammar continued to improve.

That semester, the second exit exam was given on the Friday before Christmas. To finalize grades, all the English 101 instructors met that evening to grade the essays. I promised to call Luanne with her results.

The room was quiet as two dozen English instructors read one essay after another. At about 10 PM, I received my students' graded essays. I looked quickly through the pile and found Luanne's. She had passed! As I dialed the phone to call her, Luanne's previous instructors told others about her success.

"Merry Christmas, Luanne," I said into the phone, "you passed!"

I heard her delight, and at that moment, two dozen instructors in the room applauded. They were proud of her perseverance. I was, too.

The major difference I've found between the highly successful and the least successful is that the highly successful stick to it. They have staying power. Everybody fails. Everybody takes his knocks, but the highly successful keep coming back.

Sherry Lansing, former CEO, Paramount Pictures

I've never really viewed myself as particularly talented. . . . Where I excel is a ridiculous, sickening work ethic.

Will Smith, Grammy Award–winning musician and Oscar-nominated actor

It seems only right to give the last word to Angela Duckworth: "To be gritty is to keep putting one foot in front of the other. To be gritty is to hold fast to an interesting and purposeful goal. To be gritty is to invest, day after week after year, in challenging practice. To be gritty is to fall down seven times, and rise eight."

JOURNAL ENTRY / **14**

In this activity, you will employ a 32-day commitment to help you achieve a goal in college. Making and keeping a 32-day commitment has a trio of benefits. First, it guarantees that you spend significant time on task, which is essential to success. Second, it helps you make visible progress toward your goal, thus raising your expectations of success and your motivation to persist. And third, it helps you develop grit.

1 From your life plan in Journal Entry 9, copy one of your most important and challenging short-term goals from your role as a *student*.

2 Write and complete the following sentence stem three or more times: I WOULD MOVE STEADILY TOWARD THIS GOAL IF EVERY DAY I . . .

Write three or more different actions that *others can see you do* and that you can do every day of the week, including weekends. So don't write, "I am motivated" or "I attend class." Others cannot see your motivation, and you can't attend class every day for 32 days straight. Instead, if your short-term goal is to earn an A in English, you might complete the sentence with specific actions such as these:

1. **I WOULD MOVE STEADILY TOWARD THIS GOAL IF EVERY DAY**
   I spent at least 15 minutes doing exercises in my grammar book.

2. **I WOULD MOVE STEADILY TOWARD THIS GOAL IF EVERY DAY**
   I wrote at least 200 words in my journal.

3. **I WOULD MOVE STEADILY TOWARD THIS GOAL IF EVERY DAY**
   I revised one of my previous essays, following my instructor's suggestions for improvement.

Chances are, all of these actions will fall in Quadrant II.

3 On a separate page in your journal, create a 32-Day Commitment Form or attach a photocopy of the one following this Journal Entry. Complete the sentence at the top of the form ("Because I know . . .") with ONE action from your list in Step 2. For the next 32 days, put a check beside each day that you keep your commitment.

4 Make a choice—write about one of the following:

A. **Describe your thoughts and feelings as you begin your 32-day commitment.** Develop your journal paragraphs by asking and answering readers' questions, such as, How "gritty" have you been in the past? What is your goal? What were some possible actions you considered? What action

▶

My Daddy used to ask us whether the teacher had given us any homework. If we said no, he'd say, "Well, assign yourself." Don't wait around to be told what to do. Hard work, initiative, and persistence are still the non-magic carpets to success.

Marian Wright Edelman, founder of the Children's Defense Fund

Becoming a world-class figure skater meant long hours of practice while sometimes tolerating painful injuries. It meant being totally exhausted sometimes, and not being able to do all the things I wanted to do when I wanted to do them.

Debi Thomas

did you choose for your 32-day commitment? How will this action, when performed consistently, help you reach your goal? What challenges might you experience in keeping your commitment? How will you overcome these challenges? How do you feel about undertaking this commitment? If you miss a day, what will be your inner conversation? What is your prediction about whether you will succeed in keeping your 32-day commitment?

B. **Some instructors of this course believe that a 32-day commitment is too great a challenge for their students. They worry that students who don't complete an entire 32-day commitment will become discouraged instead of gritty. As such, they prefer to modify the tool, making it a shorter commitment. A popular choice is a seven-day commitment. Write a letter to one of these instructors and offer your opinion about the decision to have students make a seven-day commitment instead of a 32-day commitment.**

ONE STUDENT'S STORY

HOLT BOGGS, *Belmont Technical College, Ohio*

I was a first-year student and enjoying college, but I was having a hard time in my electronics class. The teacher lectured about things like current, watts, volts, and resistance, and even though I read the book, took notes in class, and asked questions, I still wasn't understanding what I needed to. When I got back my first test, I didn't fail but I did pretty badly. I was scared because, if this is what the first test was like, how hard would the rest of them be? This was a new experience for me because I never had to study much to do well in school. I knew that I had to try something different if I was going to pass electronics.

In my Student Learning and Success class, I read about the 32-day commitment, and I decided to give it a try. I decided to read one section from my electronics book twice every day for 32 days. I figured that if I read the section twice, maybe I would understand it better the second time around. However, as the semester went on, I still wasn't doing so hot. At times I felt like quitting my commitment because, even though I was reading every section twice, I still wasn't getting it. By midterm, I was ahead of the class in the book, and when the instructor taught the section, it was all review for me. Then one day he was putting examples on the board, and I realized, "Hey, I know this stuff." Because I already understood most of the material,

I had time to focus on the things that I didn't understand. Everything that was still blurry to me he made clear. On the next chapter test, I got a 93, and in the end I passed the class with a B.

It's amazing what doing one little thing for 32 days can do for you. I never would have thought committing 32 days to reading a section from my book twice would help so much. Before, I'd say, "Yeah, I read it," but I was only skimming. When I read it a second time, I picked up things that I missed the first time through and I really understood what I was reading. In the end, the 32-day commitment was able to help me pass my electronics class, but even more important, this experience gave me a lot more confidence. Now I know that I can pass all of the challenging classes on the way to my degree.

32-Day Commitment

Because I know that this commitment will keep me on course to my goals, I promise myself that every day for the next 32 days I will take the following action:

_____

_____

_____

Day 1		Day 17	
Day 2		Day 18	
Day 3		Day 19	
Day 4		Day 20	
Day 5		Day 21	
Day 6		Day 22	
Day 7		Day 23	
Day 8		Day 24	
Day 9		Day 25	
Day 10		Day 26	
Day 11		Day 27	
Day 12		Day 28	
Day 13		Day 29	
Day 14		Day 30	
Day 15		Day 31	
Day 16		Day 32	

SELF-MANAGEMENT / at Work

Motivation is what gets you started. Habit is what keeps you going.

—*Jim Ryun, Olympic silver medalist*

If you're like most people, sometimes you misplace things, forget to complete an assignment, or miss an appointment. That's why it's essential to have a system to manage your life tasks, both for college and work. For example, you'll need to organize files, respond to emails, and track your projects. However, not everyone uses effective strategies to stay organized. A 2010 Brother International workplace survey showed the average employee spends 38 hours annually (nearly one workweek) just searching for misplaced items. A 2012 Office-Team survey found the average employee wastes over eight hours weekly on personal activities, including email, social media, online shopping, gaming, and watching sports. The time wasted costs employers an estimated $104 billion annually. More importantly, employees could certainly better use that time. When you lose focus on college tasks and miss an assignment deadline, you risk losing points. A missed deadline at work means your entire team may fall behind on an important project. Staying organized, both at college and at work, is essential for success. The consistent use of tools and apps to keep you on track—your self-management system—is how you will accomplish your goals. This includes avoiding distractions, achieving a work–life balance, staying focused on important tasks, and developing productive habits.

SELF-MANAGEMENT AT WORK

Avoiding distractions is not as easy as it sounds, according to researcher Gloria Mark at the University of California, Irvine. On a typical day, most of us (at school or work) switch tasks every three minutes. Every time you switch tasks, you need more time to refocus on the new task. Task distractions at both college and work are very frequent. According to a study by Steelcase, an American office furniture company, the average office worker is interrupted every 11 minutes. After an interruption, an employee takes an average of 23 minutes to get back on task. With so many distractions each day, much of our time is spent just trying to recover our focus. **Self-management** is our ability to identify and maintain our focus on what is most important. It helps us avoid feeling overwhelmed by everything that needs to be done at a busy office. It allows us to shift from procrastinating on important actions to taking action to reach our goals for the day. The benefits of increased self-management skills at work include:

1. Improving your productivity so that you accomplish more

2. Increasing your accuracy on detailed tasks

3. Reducing negative experiences like feeling overwhelmed or stressed

4. Ensuring you reach important deadlines on critical projects

SELF-MANAGEMENT AND WORK/SCHOOL/LIFE BALANCE

How many weekly hours can you expect to work at your job? How about your college work? Can you maintain a healthy work/school/life balance? In some professions, there is still an expectation that employees put in much more than the "standard" 40-hour workweek. For example, working at an investment bank or law firm, at a start-up company, or as a medical resident can demand long hours well past an eight-hour day. However, research from the Australian National University shows that working over 39 hours per week can lead to problems

▶

in mental and physical health. Is it possible to keep your job—and college—responsibilities from taking over your life, or impacting your health?

You might start with your email management. A survey of 1,000 workers by Good Technology revealed that 38 percent of employees checked work email while at home during dinner. Fifty percent checked email while in bed. One definition of work–life balance is that neither intrudes on the other. In other words, you are able to manage your personal life in a way that doesn't negatively impact either your job or your role as a student. You are also able to manage your work and college life in a way that doesn't negatively impact your personal life. If college or work email or tasks distract you from being fully present with family or friends, you may need to make some adjustments. If personal emails distract from your ability to focus at college or work, you may also need to make some adjustments.

Recently, some companies have pushed back against the expectation of working endless hours by shortening the workday. They are relying on research that shows that employee productivity drops dramatically after four to five hours of work. Some offer flexible scheduling for employees, allowing them to choose a more ideal work schedule for themselves. Others ask employees to do some of their work from home. Flextime and working from home can be great but can also create a greater challenge. Once you start working from home, it can blur the boundaries between work life and personal life. If you're not careful, you may end up being "always" at work without stopping for the day. The increase in online education presents a similar challenge, because so many assignments can now be completed almost anywhere. If you're not careful, you'll end up being always at college.

Here are some tips to help maintain a healthy work- and school-life balance:

1. **Recognize that it will never all be done.** There are always endless tasks to be done at work and at college. Accept completing your highest priorities for the day as enough. You can't invent enough hours in a week to accomplish *everything* that could be done. That's why you keep going back to work (and college) the next day. Look at the results you're creating to help you measure your required efforts.

2. **Don't let your home life leak into the workplace or college.** Be sure to use self-management strategies to handle your personal life too. It's not fair to your employer (or college professors) for you to spend much of your day sending personal emails, shopping online, or playing fantasy football. You'll lose out on gaining valuable skills and more experience at your job. You'll miss crucial learning opportunities at college. Find a balance between personal tasks and professional tasks, and don't try to multitask.

3. **Set healthy boundaries for checking and responding to emails.** Avoid getting in the habit of constantly checking work emails, or logging in to check your posted course grades every hour. Eventually you will add hours to every workday. If it's a required part of your job, set a specific time to check email, and set a limit on how long you will take to do so. Limit which types of emails you will read and respond to. They'll be waiting in your inbox tomorrow when you arrive at work. Set a realistic time period each day to complete college tasks like studying and homework. Then be sure to enjoy some restorative personal time away from these tasks. Downtime and rest help you recover from intense efforts. Adequate sleep (seven to eight hours minimum nightly) helps you be better prepared for both work activities and test taking.

4. **Be done with work when you are finished for the day.** Some jobs require you to be on

▶

call as part of the expected workload, but otherwise . . . don't work after work is over. It's true that in some jobs, like many start-up companies, for example, there may be pressure to stay very late and then keep working from home. Set clear expectations with your employer and colleagues early on and stick to your plan. Set similar expectations with your classmates about how and when you will communicate with them. Don't take your phone to bed and check messages late into the night.

5. **Incorporate mindfulness practices into your work life to reduce the impact of a stressful job.** You can try out some of the many apps that promote mindfulness and focus, including Headspace, Calm, or Mindfulness Daily. These will help you stay more balanced at work, college, or at home.

MULTITASKING, TECHNOLOGY, AND WORK

One of the greatest distractions in college and at work is the use of cell phones. Have you ever tried speaking to someone who is busy messaging back and forth with someone else? It's very frustrating to try to hold a conversation when someone is not fully present. Many employees use their cell phones during meetings and lose their focus. Cell phones can also distract users in other critical settings. Have you ever been in a car with a driver who is simultaneously texting, mapping, searching for just the right song, and trying to drive? You probably feel less safe when a driver is "multitasking" instead of paying full-time attention to driving the car. Actually, it's not possible for your brain to multitask. Instead, the brain attempts to rapidly switch back and forth between tasks. This rapid switching reduces your ability to be effective at any one task.

Attempts at multitasking have become very common at the workplace too. Some employees even brag about how many tasks they can juggle at the same time. However, a study by Vanderbilt University looked at the brain function of people engaged in more than one activity at a time. They discovered that when we try to do two tasks at once, a neural network of the brain's frontal lobe creates a delay on the second task. This part of the brain "severely limits our ability to multitask." As Holly Green reports in a *Forbes* magazine article summarizing recent research, "In plain English, humans suck at multitasking." Green also notes that one of the biggest problems is that most people believe they are doing well at multitasking when they are not. There are several important reasons to stay focused on only one task at a time:

Increased Efficiency: When we attempt to multitask, according to Green, our brains switch off the "cognitive rules for the old task and turn on a different set of rules for the new one." Cognitive switching takes time, which reduces productivity, especially among those who multitask on a frequent basis. Focus on a single task simply improves the efficiency for the use of your brain. Another researcher, Richard Gendreau, determined that "workers who switch back and forth between two tasks take 50 percent more time than working on them separately." They also made twice as many errors as those who did the same tasks one at a time. The more complex the task, the greater the inefficiency when multitasking. This can result in "technostress," a response to technology when it introduces distractions instead of helping us accomplish our goals.

Decreased Stress: Multiple studies show that multitaskers can have higher levels of stress hormones. A study in 2006 by business school

▶

professors Andrew Robinson and Clive Small-man concluded that some multitasking workers experience increased stress. Over the long term, multitasking can lead to stress-related injury and illness. Research by professor of Information Science Amanda Spink shows that many employees experience stress "after working in demanding, multitasking-oriented settings."

Increased Creativity: A study by Teresa Amabile at Harvard Business School examined work patterns for thousands of employees. Employees who stayed focused on one task at a time, for a long time, demonstrated more creative thinking. Employees whose days were filled with multitasking, who were "fragmented in their days," engaged in less creative thinking.

SELF-MANAGEMENT AND FOCUS

One answer to all these distractions is to sharpen your ability to focus. Daniel Goleman, the author of *Focus,* and *Promote Yourself: The New Rules for Career Success,* shares research from the new field of "attention science." He describes three types of focus: inner focus (attention and management of your thoughts and feelings), other focus (empathy for and attention to other people), and outer focus (attention to the workplace and the world). The more often our focus is disrupted, the less effective we are at many tasks. For instance, sports researcher Terry Orlick tested college athletes for their level of focus. He found that their ability to maintain focus predicted better performance during the next season.

Goleman argues that "we can strengthen this vital muscle of the mind. . . . Attention works much like a muscle—use it poorly and it can wither; work it well and it grows. Smart practice can further develop and refine the muscle of our attention, even rehab focus-starved brains." You can practice sharpening your muscle of attention to improve focus in all three areas: inner, other, and outer focus. Goleman suggests three main strategies:

1. **Practice paying full attention:** Most people give only partial focus to a task. Practice instead giving your entire focus. Observe the ways you typically distract yourself at work or when you're studying. Do you constantly reach for the phone? Do you check email or social media every few minutes? Let go of those distracting behaviors over time, perhaps by putting your phone in a drawer or muting your notifications. You might also try a concentration app like Isolator or an antidistraction plug-in like Anti-Social. Slowly replace habits of distraction with full task focus. Start with just three minutes of full focus and slowly build up to a longer time.

2. **Get expert feedback:** At college, seek feedback from a professor, counselor, or classmate on your ability to stay focused on a task (for example, demonstrating a skill in a laboratory setting). The feedback on your duration of focus or your improvement in the skill would help you understand if you need to increase or modify your focused attention. At work, ask a coworker or supervisor for frequent feedback. When others can observe you at a task, such as running a meeting, giving a presentation, or working on a project, ask them to rate your level of focus from 1 to 10. Set a goal for better numbers as you keep up this practice.

3. **Put in the time needed:** Like any skill, sharpening focus requires practice. The more you practice, the better your brain becomes at focusing. With focus, you'll learn the tasks at a new job or the subject of a new course more effectively.

Habits and Rules

Once you have increased your focus, you can better implement other strategies to stay organized and efficient at work. Observing and changing your ineffective habits can be one powerful way to

▶

implement new strategies. Charles Duhigg, author of *The Power of Habit,* cites a study from Duke University in 2006 that showed that more than 40 percent of our daily actions are not conscious choices but instead are simply repeated habits. Changing bad habits to better habits will improve important areas of our lives.

Duhigg identifies three parts of a habit: the cue, the routine, and the reward. For example, suppose every day at college or work you find yourself stopping work around 2 PM to check Facebook and Instagram. Suddenly, two hours have gone by. That's the **routine**. The **reward** could be a positive experience (belonging) when you connect with your friends. The routine of your daily two hours on social media while trying to study at college or finish a report at work is just a bad habit. You might benefit from changing this routine to something healthier.

Duhigg argues that our ability to observe the habit loop, seeing all three parts, will allow us to replace unhealthy routines with more desired routines. If you observe yourself, you might discover that just before 2 PM each day, you begin to feel lonely. That could be the **cue** for your routine. Maybe you also notice that your team meetings are in the morning, and you work by yourself in the afternoon.

To change the habit, you observe the cue, then find a new routine that still allows you to experience a reward. For example, perhaps the cue is feeling lonely, the routine is getting on social media, and the reward is the positive experience of feeling connected to others. Once you see the signs for the 2 PM cue (loneliness), shift your routine. You could try taking a much shorter break to connect more deeply with a close friend. You could set up several dinners with family members each week. The reward is the same—increased connection to others. If the cue is feeling lonely, you might also ask to move the morning meeting to the afternoon. You could also visit a colleague for a short time during lunch. We all want our rewards, but we have the power to change our routines once we become aware of the cues that trigger them.

Self-management skills for the workplace can be practiced while still in college. The habits you develop in college will likely remain with you when you arrive at your dream career. You're creating a foundation now for your future self-management practices. Remember, staying organized—at college or work—is very important to your success. By reducing distractions, avoiding multitasking, increasing focus, and modifying habits, you can become much more effective at any task you take on.

TECH TIPS: Self-Management

Google Calendar *(online, Android, and iOS),* among many free online resources Google offers, can be accessed from any device with Internet access. Calendars may be shared so that two or more people can access and update the same calendar. Ideal for project teams at school and busy families at home, Google Calendar might be a way for students to balance home and family life with their school requirements.

Evernote *(online, Android, and iOS)* is a powerful electronic notebook that makes it easy to record and organize all of your lists and notes. You can create to-do lists, record voice

▶

reminders, and organize your daily schedule. You can even add websites to your notes.

Any.do, Workflowy, and **Todoist** *(online, Android, and iOS)* are list-making and task-management tools with different features. Any.do, for example, can send you an email reminder before your tasks are due, while Work-flowy basically just lets you create lists and sublists in an outline format. They all offer the option to collaborate with classmates, friends, and loved ones to accomplish things together. You may wish to experiment with their different approaches to see which works best for you.

MyHomework app *(online, Android, and iOS)* provides a student planner that offers the ability to track assignments, projects, and tests.

Joesgoals.com is a simple website that works very much like an electronic tracking form. You plug in goals, track each action you take toward the goals, and earn points as you take positive actions.

Focus Booster app is a desktop digital timer that helps you avoid distractions and stay on task. You set Focus Booster timer for, say, 25 minutes and then focus diligently on one

task until the timer goes off. Then you reward your efforts as you choose.

RescueTime *(online, Android)* uses another method to help you stop wasting time online. You can set it to track your time on websites and applications (for example, Facebook), generate a weekly email report on how you spend your time, and even limit the time you can spend in certain places if you choose. If you often find yourself in Quadrants III and IV, this could be a big help.

Dontbreakthechain *(online, Android, and iOS)* is a way to track a 32-day (and beyond!) commitment. Simply set a goal to take (or not take) a certain action that will help you achieve a personal, academic, or professional goal. Every day you keep your commitment, you go to the website and click the date on the calendar. The calendar puts the date in a red block . . . and over time a chain of red blocks is formed. The longer the chain, the closer you are to your victory.

iStudiez and My Study Life *(online, Android, and iOS)* are digital planners that give you the ability to track your tasks, assignments, projects, and tests.

Note: All of these are free, but some may offer upgraded features for a fee.

Develop Self-Confidence

FOCUS QUESTIONS In which life roles do you feel most confident? In which do you experience self-doubt? What can you do to increase your overall self-confidence?

On the first day of one semester, a woman intercepted me at the classroom door.

"Can I ask you something?" she said. "How do I know if I'm cut out for college?"

"What's your opinion?" I asked.

"I think I'll do okay."

"Great," I said.

She stood there, still looking doubtful. "But . . . my high school counselor said . . ." She paused.

"Let me guess. Your counselor said you wouldn't do well in college? Is that it?"

She nodded. "I think he was wrong. But how do I know for sure?"

Indeed! How *do* we know? There will always be others who don't believe in us. What matters, however, is that we have confidence in ourselves. Self-confidence is the core belief that *I CAN,* the unwavering trust that I can successfully do whatever is necessary to achieve my realistic goals and dreams.

Ultimately, it matters little whether someone else thinks you can do something. It matters greatly whether *you* believe you can. If you set a DAPPS goal (Dated, Achievable, Personal, Positive, and Specific) for yourself, you'll probably accomplish just about what you believe you can. In this section we'll explore three effective ways to develop greater self-confidence.

CREATE A SUCCESS IDENTITY

Think of a task that you can do easily now, but at one time, you couldn't do. Perhaps it's tying your shoes, writing your name, telling time, or speaking another language. When you first started, you probably struggled. So how did you move from doubt to confidence? Wasn't it by practicing over and over? You built your self-confidence by stacking one small victory upon another. As a result, today you have confidence that you can do these tasks any time you want. By the same method, you can build a success identity in virtually any endeavor.

The life of Nathan McCall illustrates the creation of a success identity under difficult circumstances. It also shows how a Creator mindset can help you overcome any thoughts you have of being "different," such as not being part of the mainstream culture. McCall grew up in a Portsmouth, Virginia ghetto, and he faced prejudice and racism. His involvement with crimes and violence led to imprisonment. After his release, McCall attended college and studied journalism. One of his greatest challenges was self-doubt. But he persevered, tackling each challenge as it came—one more test passed, one more course completed. After graduation, he got a job with a newspaper, and over the years he steadily rose to the position of bureau chief. Recalling his accumulated successes, McCall wrote in his journal, "These experiences solidify my belief that I can do anything I set my mind to do. The possibilities are boundless." Boundless indeed! McCall went from street-gang member and prison inmate to successful and respected reporter for the *Washington Post,* later author of a *New York Times* best seller, and then a faculty member at Emory University in Georgia.

Genuine self-confidence results from a history of success, and a history of success results from persistently taking purposeful actions. That's why a 32-day commitment (Journal Entry 14) is not only an effective self-management tool but also a great way to start building a success identity. After we experience success in one area of our lives, self-confidence begins to seep into every corner of our being, and we begin to believe *I CAN.*

I f people don't feel good about themselves and believe that they'll win a championship, they never will.

Tara VanDerveer, former head coach of the NCAA Championship Stanford University women's basketball team

S uccess brings its own self-confidence.

Lillian Vernon Katz

CELEBRATE YOUR SUCCESSES AND TALENTS

A friend showed me a school assignment that his eight-year-old daughter had brought home. At the top of the page was written: *Nice job, Lauren. Your spelling is very good. I am proud of you.* What made the comments remarkable is this: The teacher had merely put a check on the page; Lauren had added the compliments herself.

At the age of eight, Lauren has much to teach us about building self-confidence. It's great when someone else tells us how wonderful our successes and talents are. But it's even more important that we tell ourselves.

One way to acknowledge your success is to create a success deck: Every day, write at least one success (big or small) on an index card. Add it to your growing stack of successes and read through the deck every day. Or post the cards on a wall where you'll be reminded often of your accomplishments: *Got an 86 on history test. . . . Attended every class on time this week. . . . Exercised for two hours at the gym.* In addition to acknowledging your successes, you can celebrate them by rewarding yourself with something special—a favorite dinner, a movie, a night out with friends.

> Research studies show that people who have high self-esteem regularly reward themselves in tangible and intangible ways. . . . By documenting and celebrating their successes, they ensure that these successes will reoccur.
>
> Marsha Sinetar

VISUALIZE PURPOSEFUL ACTIONS

We can also strengthen our self-confidence, as well as our abilities, by visualizing purposeful actions done well, especially actions outside our comfort zone. Psychologist Charles Garfield once performed an experiment to determine the impact of visualizations on a group of people who were afraid of public speaking. These nervous speakers were divided into three subgroups:

Group 1 read and studied how to give public speeches, but they delivered no actual speeches.

Group 2 read about speech making and also gave two talks each week to small audiences of classmates and friends.

Group 3 read about effective speaking and gave one talk each week to small groups. This group also watched videotapes of effective speakers and, twice a day, *mentally rehearsed* giving effective speeches of their own.

> Peak performers develop powerful mental images of the behavior that will lead to the desired results. They see in their mind's eye the result they want, and the actions leading to it.
>
> Charles Garfield

Experts on public speaking, unaware of the experiment, evaluated the effectiveness of these speakers both before and after their preparation. Group 1 did not improve at all. Group 2 improved significantly. Group 3, the group that had visualized themselves giving excellent speeches, improved the most.

When I first introduce the idea of visualizing to my students, many are skeptical. In particular, young male students are often outspoken. "That's just *stupid,*" one basketball player said. Two things helped change the minds of many. First, they were intrigued to learn that world-class athletes use mental imagery to improve their skills. Three examples are basketball legend Michael Jordan, golf great Tiger Woods, and tennis superstar Roger Federer. Second, like me, many skeptics became believers after they gave visualization a serious try. My conversion occurred after I dramatically improved my backhand in racquetball.

I got a book with still pictures showing each step of a perfect backhand. For weeks, I imagined those steps in my mind . . . and then practiced them on the court. My "aha" came the day that one of my backhands smacked the front wall with a sharp crack (instead of my usual marshmallow-hitting-a-pillow sound).

Mentally rehearsing purposeful actions will not only help you improve your ability to do the action but will also reduce associated fears. Suppose you're feeling anxious about an upcoming test. Your Inner Critic is probably visualizing a disaster: *As soon as I walk into the exam room, my pulse starts racing, I start sweating, I start feeling weak, and my mind goes totally blank. I fail!*

What if you visualized a more positive experience? You could imagine yourself taking the test confidently, creating an ideal outcome. Your revised mental movie might look like this: *I walk into the exam fully prepared. I've attended all of my classes on time, done my very best work on all of my assignments, and studied effectively. Feeling confident, I find a comfortable seat and take a few moments to breathe deeply, relax, and focus myself. I concentrate on the subject matter of this test. I release all my other cares and worries, feeling excited about the opportunity to show how much I have learned. The instructor walks into the room and begins handing out the exams. I know that any question the instructor asks will be easy for me to answer. I glance at the test and see questions that my study group and I have prepared for all semester. Alert and aware, I begin to write. Every answer I write flows easily from the storehouse of knowledge I have in my mind. I work steadily and efficiently, and, after finishing, I check my answers thoroughly. I hand in the exam, and as I leave the room, I feel a pleasant weariness. I am confident that I have done my very best.*

Because you choose the movies that play in your mind, why not choose to star in a movie in which you successfully complete purposeful actions?

Creators know there are many choices that will strengthen self-confidence. When we consciously choose options such as creating a success identity, celebrating our successes and talents, and visualizing the successful completion of purposeful actions, we will soon be able to say with supreme confidence: *I CAN.*

> Mental practice is also referred to as "visualization" or "imagery rehearsal." We start with 20 to 30 minutes of relaxation training, followed by the visualization of some aspect of the athlete's game that needs improvement. It's the mental equivalent of physical practice.
>
> Dr. Richard Suinn, sports psychologist to Olympic athletes

> If we picture ourselves functioning in specific situations, it is nearly the same as the actual performance. Mental practice helps one to perform better in real life.
>
> Dr. Maxwell Maltz

In this activity, you will practice ways to increase your self-confidence. Self-confident people *expect* success, which in turn strengthens their motivation and fuels their energy. If what they are doing isn't working, they don't quit. Instead, they switch to Plan B (or C or D) and persist. Then they finish strong, consistently giving their best to achieve their goals and dreams! In this way, the very success they want and expect often becomes a reality. **Make a choice: Do two of the following four actions:**

1. **List the successes you have created in your life.** The more successes you list, the more you will strengthen your self-confidence. Include small victories as well as big ones.

2. **List your personal skills and talents.** Again, the longer your list, the more you will strengthen your self-confidence. What are you good at doing? What would your friends say are your skills and talents? Don't overlook talents that you use daily. No talent is too insignificant to acknowledge. If listing your personal skills and talents makes you uncomfortable, recall the old saying, "It ain't bragging if it's true!"

3. **List positive risks that you have taken in your life.** When did you stretch your comfort zone and do something despite your fear?

4. **Write a visualization of yourself successfully doing an important action that you presently have some resistance about doing.** For example, maybe you fear asking a question in your biology lecture or you're nervous about going to a scheduled job interview. Remember to use the four keys to effective visualizing discussed in Journal Entry 10:

   A. **Relax.**

   B. **Use present-tense verbs.**

   C. **Be specific and use many senses.**

   D. **Feel the feelings.**

As a model for your writing, reread the positive visualization that appears in the article right before this journal entry.

The way to develop self-confidence is to do the thing you fear and get a record of successful experiences behind you.

William Jennings Bryan

If you have no confidence in self, you are twice defeated in the race of life. With confidence, you have won even before you have started.

Marcus Garvey

ONE STUDENT'S STORY

ASHLEY FREEMAN, *Copper Mountain College, California*

Have you ever walked into a classroom feeling like everyone is staring at you? When you get called upon to read aloud to the class, does your heart beat like a bass drum that you hope others can't hear? When someone talks to you, do you sweat and stumble over your words and end up feeling like a complete fool?

I never wanted to admit that lack of confidence was a problem for me, but in school I was always the person who was extremely shy and quiet,

always keeping to myself, trying to be invisible. When someone asked me a question, I would attempt to answer, but I would lower my eyes and my voice would get very quiet, making it hard to hear what I was saying. The other person probably thought I was rudely ignoring them. The first day of class in college, as I was looking around at all the students coming in, I realized the biggest obstacle I had to face was me. My low self-confidence,

low self-esteem, and my extreme quietness were going to be huge challenges.

When I had decided to attend college, I was a little scared, but I had plenty of love and support from my family and was excited to attend. I knew my grades wouldn't be a problem, as I have really good study habits. Due to health issues, I attended high school through an independent study program. I was able to graduate with good grades, but I never had to be around anyone except my teacher. I lacked social skills with people my own age, but I always had my homework done early and

▶

for all of my hard work, I graduated three months early.

The first day in college, however, I was a nervous wreck, wondering if I had made a huge mistake by enrolling. The teachers announced that we would be doing group activities, partnering with others, reading aloud, and forming study groups to strengthen our skills. I panicked, and all I could do was tell myself not to give up. As the days passed, I said little or nothing during my classes. In my English class, I partnered with Annette, a woman who befriended me the first day despite my quietness. The class uses the *On Course* book, and we started learning strategies that could help us. I was still nervous, but after reading about some of the strategies, I decided to take more actions to get the most out of my college education and experience. I became determined to prove to myself and everyone else that I could succeed in college.

To create what *On Course* calls a "success identity," I made a 32-day commitment to be more outspoken. One promise I made was to talk to at least three people every day. Another was to read out loud in front of the class without having to be asked by my teachers. I also decided to volunteer more in class and share more of my work without being embarrassed. I decided to ask more questions during and after class as well as offer help to my classmates. I even asked my teachers and classmates for written feedback about my efforts to be more self-confident and participate actively in class. Not only did they give me this feedback, some even wrote me inspirational praise.

I'm very proud of myself for all of the changes I've made and that I'm still making every day. I am inspired to continue to grow and reach my full potential, and I'm grateful to

all the people who have been so kind to me and helped me see that I can do it. During the semester, we were asked to write an essay about what we had learned in the course, and my teacher announced that students would be able to read their essays in front of the Copper Mountain College Board of Trustees. I was so proud of the progress I had made that I was the second student in the class to volunteer. As I read my speech, I felt my confidence growing and was even able to make a good amount of eye contact with my audience. After my speech was done, I thanked everyone and as I walked back to my spot I started crying, knowing I had accomplished my goal. Thanks to learning *On Course* strategies and receiving encouragement and motivation from my family, teachers, friends, and classmates, today I have stronger self-confidence and a more positive outlook on my future than ever before.

Photo: Courtesy of Ashley Freeman.

Healthy Choices: Smoking

One summer when I was about 12, I met my friend Pepper at the local baseball field. We were the only ones there. "Look what I've got," he said, holding up a lit cigarette. "Wanna try?"

My mother smoked, and I hated the smell. I guess he saw a "no" on my face. "Chicken!" he mocked. Then he started clucking at me. "All right, all right," I said. I took a puff, then coughed and choked . . . and choked and coughed. I've never smoked another cigarette, and that was one of the best health choices I ever made.

THE LEAST YOU NEED TO KNOW ABOUT SMOKING

Cigarettes

Smoking cigarettes is the number one preventable cause of death in the entire world. What makes these deaths preventable is a simple choice: Don't smoke. In the United States alone, cigarettes cause more than

480,000 deaths yearly, according to the Centers for Disease Control (CDC). That's about 1,315 tobacco deaths per day. Or one death per minute.

Dr. Kevin Hill offers a striking perspective on the danger of cigarettes: "Consider that on average a large jet carries 400 people. Now imagine if in the United States 1,000 such jets crashed *each year*. Would you fly? Wouldn't you be outraged and demand that something be done? That's what we tolerate with legal nicotine."

Fortunately, people today are making wiser choices than they did in the 1960s. Back then, about 40 percent of U.S. adults smoked. Today, only about 15 percent do.

There are, of course, reasons why people smoke. For starters, there's what got me to try: peer pressure and curiosity. For people who keep smoking, the nicotine in cigarettes is a stimulant that briefly increases attention and concentration. For some people it may have the opposite effect, acting as a sedative. Also, many smokers claim that smoking reduces their anxiety. Or it helps them with weight control. Or they simply say, "I like it" or "I'm worried I won't be able to quit." What they may not realize is that nicotine—like cocaine and heroin—increases dopamine in the brain. Dopamine stimulates the brain's pleasure centers, creating a desire to repeat the experience.

Unfortunately, that desire is self-destructive. Research confirms that smoking cigarettes causes many health problems, including nine types of cancer, emphysema, and chronic bronchitis—plus leukemia, asthma, pneumonia, heart disease, and strokes. Studies also show that smoking harms areas of the brain responsible for decision making and impulse control.

Even for nonsmokers, being around secondhand smoke is dangerous. Secondhand smoke is the combination of smoke from a cigarette plus the exhaled smoke from the smoker. According to the CDC, there is no risk-free level of exposure to secondhand smoke. Adults exposed to secondhand smoke are at risk for coronary heart disease, stroke, and lung cancer. Children are additionally vulnerable to asthma attacks, respiratory infections, and sudden infant death syndrome. If a pregnant woman smokes or inhales secondhand smoke, her unborn child risks stunted growth, psychiatric disorders, and sudden infant death syndrome. Worse yet, secondhand smoke causes more than 41,000 deaths per year. And don't forget about thirdhand smoke. This is the residue of nicotine and other chemicals left on your skin, clothes, and indoor surfaces. Like secondhand smoke, it can be harmful to others, especially young children. The CDC estimates that more than 16 million Americans are living with one of the many health issues caused by cigarettes, including the people who don't even smoke themselves.

Dr. Akikur Mohammad, author of *The Anatomy of Addiction*, says tobacco is the most addicting and difficult drug to quit. He notes that for people who smoke cigarettes, the probability of becoming addicted is 32 percent. That's more than twice that of alcohol (15 percent). And quitting is tough. A recent CDC study reported that nearly 70 percent of American smokers want to quit, and more than half have attempted to do so. Quitting, however, leads to powerful cravings, irritability, insomnia, difficulty thinking, and nagging hunger. Together, these withdrawal symptoms drive most people to resume smoking. In fact, only 6 percent of smokers succeed in quitting! A man I know is a perfect example of cigarette addiction. After years of smoking, he was hospitalized for emphysema. His symptoms included coughing fits, severe shortness of breath, and extreme feebleness. While in the hospital, he somehow got hold of a cigarette, and smoked it in the middle of the night. He dropped the cigarette in his bed and was too weak to find it before his bedding caught on fire. To the misery of emphysema, his addiction added the agony of second- and third-degree burns. That is one powerful addiction!

Smokeless Tobacco

What about smokeless chewing tobacco? Users place a piece of tobacco (a "dip") between their lip and cheek. They chew or suck the tobacco, which provides a hit of nicotine. You might think, *At least there's no smoke.* True, but the sugar in smokeless tobacco triggers tooth decay, loose teeth, and painful mouth sores. Worse, chemicals in the tobacco are linked to cancer of the mouth, tongue, cheek, gum, and throat, according to the American Cancer Society. Former Boston Red Sox pitcher Curt Schilling got mouth cancer from chewing tobacco. He told the *Boston Globe,* "I wish I could go back and never have dipped. Not once. It was so painful."

Vaping (E-Cigarettes)

How about e-cigarettes? These smokeless, battery-operated devices have many names: e-cigs, e-hookahs, mods, vape pens, vapes, tank systems, and electronic nicotine delivery systems. They hold a liquid containing nicotine, various other chemicals, and flavorings. The device heats the liquid until it becomes a vapor that smokers inhale. Thus, smoking e-cigarettes is often called "vaping."

E-cigarettes are recent inventions, and the jury is still debating their safety. Dr. Neal Benowitz is a nicotine researcher at the University of California at San Francisco. He says most experts think e-cigs are less dangerous than regular cigarettes. However, Erika Sward, an official at the American Lung Association, has concerns. E-cigs, she says, often contain diacetyl, a chemical that causes lung disease. Kenneth Warner, a tobacco researcher at the University of Michigan, counters. He says e-cigs are somewhere between 50 to 85 percent less dangerous than tobacco cigarettes. But Stanton Glantz, director of tobacco research at the University of California at San Francisco has other worries. He says some chemicals delivered by e-cigs "really raise concern about heart disease and other chronic conditions where inflammation is involved." Other concerns are that e-cigarettes, because of their appealing flavors, will introduce a whole new generation of young people to smoking cigarettes. Bottom line: Though e-cigs might be somewhat safer than cigarettes, they still have dangers, many of which may not yet have been identified. It took many years before the true dangers of smoking cigarettes were finally recognized, and there has been little time to discover the true safety or dangers of e-cigarettes.

Marijuana

Tobacco, of course, isn't the only plant that people smoke. In fact, according to a recent Yahoo News/Marist College poll, about 54 million American adults have tried marijuana. Of them, about 34 million say they use it regularly. Why? Researchers at Duke University found that people's most common experience of marijuana is an elevated mood and relaxation.

Despite its widespread use, if you polled random people about the risks of marijuana, responses would vary widely. Some would insist that marijuana is perfectly safe. Others would say it's a gateway to hell.

This dispute surely contributes to the complex legal status of marijuana. As of this writing, recreational marijuana is legal in the District of Columbia and nine states. An additional 21 states have approved marijuana sales for medical use only. Marijuana remains illegal in the remaining states and at the federal level. In fact, it is listed as a Schedule I narcotic. That means the U.S. government considers marijuana to be a dangerous drug with great potential for abuse and no accepted medical use (like heroin). Stay tuned, however. As of this writing, there's a bill in Congress to end the federal ban on marijuana.

At the center of this debate is the cannabis, or marijuana, plant. Cannabis contains more than 400 chemicals. However, stoking the debate is delta-9-tetrahydrocannabinol (THC). THC is the chemical that gets people high. Setting aside the legal confusion, let's explore what science knows about marijuana.

On the plus side, the medical use of marijuana has important health benefits. In 2017 the National Academies of Sciences, Engineering, and Medicine reviewed 10,000 studies of marijuana. The review—titled "The Health Effects of Cannabis and Cannabinoids"—found conclusive evidence that marijuana "can be an effective treatment for chronic pain." Also, "Cannabis can help treat muscle spasms related to multiple sclerosis and can help prevent or treat nausea and vomiting associated with chemotherapy." Additional studies suggest that marijuana helps with many other health problems. These include epileptic seizures, post-traumatic stress disorder, glaucoma, Alzheimer's, and wasting diseases like AIDS (through appetite stimulation).

Marijuana is less life-threatening than alcohol. Although binge drinking can lead to alcohol poisoning and death, lethal overdoses of marijuana are extremely unlikely. Instead, a heavy dose of marijuana typically puts a person to sleep. However, according to the CDC, possible severe effects of marijuana include "extreme confusion, anxiety, paranoia, panic, fast heart rate, delusions or hallucinations, increased blood pressure, and severe nausea or vomiting. In some cases, these reactions can lead to unintentional injury such as a motor vehicle crash, fall, or poisoning." A great deal of evidence also shows that marijuana use by pregnant women results in pregnancy complications and lower birth weight. Even secondhand marijuana smoke appears to be dangerous. Matthew Springer, a biologist and professor in the division of cardiology at the University of California at San Francisco, has exposed rats to secondhand marijuana smoke. Just a one-minute exposure made it more difficult for the rats' arteries to expand and allow a healthy flow of blood. Springer believes this is just one of many negative effects of secondhand marijuana smoke still to be discovered.

For students, it's important to know that marijuana can hinder the learning and retention of new information. Dr. Nora D. Volkow is director of the National Institute on Drug Abuse. She warns, "Because marijuana impairs short-term memory and judgment and distorts perception, it can impair performance in school or at work. . . ." Dr. Volkow adds that regular use of marijuana by people whose brains are still maturing may have "negative and long-lasting effects on their cognitive development." A recent study measured the IQs of more than 1,000 people at ages 13 and 38. Because IQ measures a person's *ability* to learn (not *what* they have learned), IQ should remain constant throughout life. However, participants in this study who used marijuana regularly during their adolescence saw a loss of about eight points. Eight points may not seem like much. However, that could drop an average IQ score to below-average or drop an above-average score to average. It would seem, therefore, that smoking marijuana could harm your ability to learn in college and beyond, and therefore negatively affect your ability to succeed later in life.

Perhaps you've heard of and wondered about synthetic marijuana (also called "K2" or "spice"). First, synthetic marijuana is *not* marijuana. It is a combination of dried plant material and man-made chemicals. Second, you can never be sure what is in synthetic marijuana or how strong it is. Third, it has many potential harmful effects. These include nausea, vomiting, rapid heart rate, shakes, sweats, violent behavior, paranoia, hallucinations, and panic attacks.

Most troublesome, marijuana is addictive, especially for young people. Psychiatrist Kevin P. Hill specializes in marijuana addiction. He writes, "Data suggest that 9 percent of adults and 17 percent of adolescents who use marijuana develop an addiction to it. . . . The result is that 2.7 million Americans meet criteria for marijuana addiction."

When marijuana addiction occurs, it typically creates negative effects on relationships, school, and/or work. Withdrawal from marijuana has many of the same symptoms as withdrawal from nicotine, including irritability, sleeplessness, and anxiety. Dr. Hill says, "From my clinical experience with patients, it is unlikely, although not impossible, to use marijuana regularly without encountering difficulties in important areas of your life."

WISE CHOICES: SMOKING

- Don't smoke or chew tobacco (especially if you are pregnant).
- Avoid e-cigs until there is more evidence to determine their safety.
- Avoid areas with heavy secondhand smoke.
- Do not use marijuana, especially if you are under 25 years of age (when your developing brain is most vulnerable).
- If you choose to use marijuana, learn and comply with the relevant laws where you live.
- Do not use marijuana while studying or taking tests.
- Do not drive under the influence of marijuana.
- Do not use synthetic marijuana (also known as "K2" or "spice").
- Never use marijuana in combination with any other drug, including alcohol (combining any two drugs can lead to unpredictable and dangerous outcomes).
- Do not smoke cigarettes, e-cigarettes, or marijuana near others, especially infants, children, or pregnant women.
- If you have smoked, change clothes before hugging children as even thirdhand smoke can be harmful to their health.
- Employ healthy ways to stimulate your brain's reward system with dopamine, for example, exercise, yoga, dance, meditation, music, and massage.
- If you are addicted to tobacco or marijuana, seek a referral from a college counselor, physician, or psychologist to an established smoking-cessation program or addiction expert.

Employing Interdependence

Successful Students . . .

▶ **develop mutually supportive relationships,** recognizing that life is richer when giving to and receiving from others.

▶ **strengthen relationships with active listening,** showing their concern for other people's thoughts and feelings.

▶ **respect cultural differences,** understanding how to achieve success in a world of increasing diversity.

Struggling Students . . .

▶ **remain dependent, codependent, or independent** in relation to others, fail to recognize when they need support, and struggle to request help when needed.

▶ **listen poorly,** demonstrating little desire to understand other people's perspective or experience.

▶ **Fear, attack, or judge those who are different** from them as inappropriate, deficient, wrong, or bad.

Once I accept responsibility for taking purposeful actions to achieve my goals and dreams, I then develop mutually supportive relationships that make the journey easier and more enjoyable.

I am employing interdependence in my relationships.

CASE STUDY IN CRITICAL THINKING / Professor Rogers's Trial

Professor Rogers thought her Speech 101 students would enjoy role-playing a real court trial as their last speech for the semester. She also hoped the experience would teach them to work well in teams, a skill much sought after by employers. So, she divided her students into groups of six—a team of three defense attorneys and a team of three prosecuting attorneys—and provided each group with court transcripts of a real murder case. Using evidence from the trial, each team would present closing arguments for the case, after which a jury of classmates would render a verdict. Each team was allowed a maximum of 24 minutes to present its case, and all three team members would receive the same grade.

After class, **Anthony** told his teammates, **Sylvia** and **Donald**, "We'll meet tomorrow at 4:00 in the library and plan a defense for this guy." Sylvia felt angry about Anthony's bossy tone, but she just nodded. Donald said, "Whatever," put headphones on, and strolled away singing louder than he probably realized.

"Look," Anthony said to Sylvia at 4:15 the next day, "we're not waiting for Donald any more. Here's what we'll do. You go first and take about 10 minutes to prove that our defendant had no motive. I'll take the rest of the time to show how it could have been the victim's brother who shot him. I want an A out of this."

Sylvia was furious. "You can't just decide to leave Donald out. Plus, what about the defendant's fingerprints on the murder weapon! We have to dispute that evidence or we'll never win. I'll do that. And I'll go last so I can wrap up all the loose ends. I want to win this trial."

The defense team met twice more before the trial. Donald came to only one of the meetings and spent the entire time texting his girlfriend. He said he wasn't sure what he was going to say, but he'd have it figured out by the day of the trial. Anthony and Sylvia argued about which evidence was most important and who would speak last. At one point, another student threatened to call security when Sylvia lost her temper and started shouting at Anthony that no one had elected him the leader. Sylvia glared at the complaining student and then at Anthony, and without another word, stomped out of the library.

The day before the trial, Sylvia went to Professor Rogers. "It's not fair that my grade depends on my teammates. Donald couldn't care less what happens, and Anthony is always looking for a fight. I'll present alone, but not with them."

"If you were an actual lawyer," Professor Rogers replied, "do you think you could go to the judge and complain that you aren't getting along with your partners? You'll have to figure out how to work as a team. The trial goes on as scheduled, and all three of you will get the same grade."

On the day of the trial, the three student prosecutors presented one seamless and persuasive closing argument. Then Anthony leapt up, saying, "I'll go first for my team." He spoke for 21 minutes, talking as fast as he could to present the entire case, including an explanation of how the defendant's fingerprints had gotten on the murder weapon. Sylvia, greatly flustered, followed with a 7-minute presentation in which she also explained how the defendant's fingerprints had gotten on the murder weapon. At that point, Professor Rogers announced that the defense was already 4 minutes over their time limit. Donald promised to be brief. He assured the jury that the defendant was innocent and then read three unconnected passages from the transcript as "proof." His presentation took 75 seconds. The jury of fellow students deliberated for 5 minutes and unanimously found the defendant guilty. Professor Rogers gave all members of the defense team a D for their speeches.

The following lists the characters in this story. Rank them in the order of their responsibility for the group's grade of "D." Give a different score to each character. Be prepared to explain your answer.

Most ▶ ① ② ③ ④ ◀ **Least**
responsible   **responsible**

___ **Professor Rogers**   ___ **Sylvia**

___ **Anthony**   ___ **Donald**

DIVING DEEPER

Imagine that you have been assigned to a group project in one of your college courses and the student you scored above as most responsible for the group's grade of "D" (Anthony, Sylvia, or Donald) is in your group. What positive actions could you take to help your group be a success despite this person?

Creating a Support System

FOCUS QUESTIONS Why is it important to develop interdependence? What are some effective ways to do this?

All of us make a choice—often unconsciously—about the kinds of relationships we have with other people. And that choice has a huge impact on our success in college and beyond.

People generally engage in four kinds of relationships. The kinds we choose most often reveal the beliefs we have about ourselves and other people. Which of the following sounds most like you?

- *I can't achieve my goals by myself, so I choose to be* ***dependent***.
- *I make helping other people achieve their goals or rescuing them from their problems more important than achieving my own goals, so I choose to be* ***codependent***.
- *By working hard, I can get some of what I want all by myself, so I choose to be* ***independent***.
- *I know I can get some of what I want by working alone, but I'll accomplish more and have more fun if I give and receive help, so I choose to be* ***interdependent***.

In which of these ways do you usually relate to others? More important, which choice will best help you achieve your goals and dreams?

A SIGN OF MATURITY

Moving from dependence or codependence to independence is a major step toward maturity. An exciting part of the college experience for many students is their newfound freedom and independence. And there are certainly times when independence is the best choice.

Dependent people need others to get what they want. Independent people can get what they want through their own effort. Interdependent people combine their own efforts with the efforts of others to achieve their greatest success.

Stephen Covey

We are all interdependent. Do things for others—tribe, family, community—rather than just for yourself.

Chief Wilma Mankiller

However, Creators know that life is often easier and more enjoyable when people collaborate. They are quite capable of being *in*dependent when going it alone is the best choice. But they can also be *inter*dependent when it is necessary, more effective, or simply more enjoyable to work with others. Creators maximize their results in college by seeking assistance from instructors, classmates, librarians, advisers, counselors, community services, and family members, to name just a few. They know that choosing *inter*dependence—at the right times—demonstrates the greatest maturity of all.

Consider my student Martha. Two weeks before the end of a semester, she announced to our class, "I just came today to say goodbye. I have to withdraw from college because my babysitter moved. My baby's only two, and I can't find anyone I trust to stay with her. I wanted to say how much I'll miss you all."

A concerned silence followed Martha's announcement. Her quiet, solid presence had made her a favorite with classmates.

Then one of the women in the class said, "My kids are grown, and this is the only class I'm taking this semester. I can watch your child for the next few weeks if that would help you get through the semester. I'll ask if my sister could watch her during the times I'm in this class since she's at home with her own child. The only thing is, you'll need to bring your baby to my house because I don't have a car."

"I don't have a car either," Martha said. "Thanks anyway."

"Wait a minute," a young man said. "I have a car. I'll drive you and your child back and forth until the semester's over. It's only two weeks!"

Martha sat for a moment, stunned. "Really? You'd do that for me?" In three minutes, Martha's fate had changed from dropping out of school to finishing the semester with the help of two classmates.

Interdependence can help you stay on course in college and support your success in ways you can't even imagine now. By contrast, codependence is among the most destructive relationships. Codependent people are motivated not by their own successes, but by someone else's approval or dependence upon them. Codependent people abandon their own dreams and even endure abuse to keep the approval of others.

John was a bright fellow who had been in college for seven years without graduating. During a class discussion, he related an experience he said was typical of him: He'd been studying for a midterm test in history when a friend called and asked for help with biology. John had already passed biology. John set aside his own studies and spent the evening tutoring his friend. The next day John failed his history exam. In his journal, he wrote, "I've learned that in order to be successful, I need to make my dreams more important than other people's approval. I have to learn to say 'no.'" Codependent people like John often spend time in Quadrant III, engaged in activities that are important to someone else but unimportant to their own goals and dreams.

With codependence, dependence, and independence, giving and receiving are out of balance. Codependent people *give* too much. Dependent people *take* too much. Independent people seldom give *or* receive. By contrast, interdependent people find a healthy balance of giving and receiving, and everyone

---

Nobody but nobody can make it out here alone.

Maya Angelou

Taking on responsibilities that properly belong to someone else means behaving irresponsibly toward oneself.

Nathaniel Branden

benefits. That's why building mutually supportive relation-ships is one of the most important Quadrant II behaviors you'll ever undertake.

My experience is that most students choose indepen-dence far more often than interdependence. Perhaps they think asking for help reveals them as weak. Or they don't feel worthy of the help. Whatever the cause, they avoid using the many resources their colleges provide to help them succeed. Let's consider some choices you can make to create a support system that will help you not only achieve your goals in college but make the journey less stressful as well.

SEEK HELP FROM YOUR INSTRUCTORS

Building positive relationships with your college instructors is a powerful Quadrant II action that can enhance your future success. Your instructors have years of specialized training. You've already paid for their help with your tuition, and all you have to do is ask.

If you haven't done so already, find out your professors' office hours and make an appointment. You might even come with a classmate if that makes you more comfortable. Arrive prepared with questions or requests, and you're very likely to get good help. As a bonus, by getting to know your instructors, you may find a mentor who will help you in college and beyond.

> Until recently, the "old girls" did not know how the "old boys'" network operated.... Women now know that, besides hard work and lots of skill, the move to the top requires a supportive network.
>
> June E. Gabler

GET HELP FROM COLLEGE RESOURCES

Nearly every college spends a chunk of tuition money to provide support ser-vices for students, but these services go to waste unless you use them. Do you know what support services your college offers, where they are, and how to use them? If you completed your College Smart-Start Guide in Chapter 1, you have a list that you may want to expand now.

Confused about Future Courses to Take?

Get help from your adviser or someone in the academic advisement center. Among other things, advisers can help you decide on a major and create a multiyear academic plan that includes all of your required courses and their prerequisites. As you may recall from Chapter 1, such a plan is called a *long-term educational plan.*

Academic Problems?

Get help from your college's learning or tutoring center. Most colleges offer help with reading, writing, and math, as well as many other subjects. Addi-tional sources of academic assistance might include a science learning center or a computer lab. Your college very likely has a diagnostician who tests students for learning disabilities and can suggest strategies for overcoming them.

> For every one of us that succeeds, it's because there's somebody there to show you the way out. The light doesn't always necessarily have to be in your family; for me it was teachers and school.
>
> Oprah Winfrey

Money Problems?

Get help from your college's financial aid office. Money is available in grants and scholarships (which you don't pay back), loans (which you do pay back, usually at low interest rates), and student work programs (which offer jobs on campus). Your college may also have a service that can locate an off-campus job, perhaps one in the very career field you want to enter after graduation. Revisit the "Money Matters" section in Chapter 1 for detailed information about addressing money problems.

Personal Problems?

Get help from your college's counseling office. Trained counselors are available at many colleges to help students through times of emotional upset. It's not unusual for students to experience personal challenges during college. Creators seek assistance.

Health Problems?

Get help from your college's health service. Many colleges have doctors who see students at little or no cost. Health-related products such as aspirin may be available inexpensively or even for free. Your college may even offer low-cost health insurance for students.

Problems Deciding on a Career?

Get help from your college's career office. There you can take aptitude tests, discover job opportunities, explore careers you've never heard of, learn to write or improve your résumé, and practice effective interviewing skills.

Problems Getting Involved Socially at Your College?

Get help from your college's student activities office. Here you'll discover athletic teams, trips, choirs, dances, service projects, student professional organizations, the college newspaper, the campus literary magazine, clubs, and more. All are just waiting for you to get involved.

CREATE A PROJECT TEAM

If you're tackling a big project, why not create a team to help? A project team is formed to accomplish one particular task. For example, one of my students created a project team to help her move. More than a dozen classmates volunteered, including a guy who provided a truck. In one Saturday morning, the team packed and delivered her possessions to a new apartment. Without the help, how long would the move have taken her, how much would it have cost, and how much stress would it have caused her?

What big project do you have that would benefit from the assistance of others? You might find that the only barrier standing between you and a project team is a habit of independence.

No man is an island, entire of itself; every man is a piece of the continent, a part of the main.

John Donne

My driving belief is this: great teamwork is the only way to reach our ultimate moments, to create the breakthroughs that define our careers, to fulfill our lives with a sense of lasting significance.

Pat Riley, former professional basketball coach

I never did anything alone. Whatever was accomplished in this country was accomplished collectively.

Golda Meir

START A STUDY GROUP

A mathematics graduate student at the University of California, Berkeley, showed the value of academic study groups. Philip Uri Treisman had noticed that successful students in calculus met outside of class and, among other things, talked about solving math problems. Struggling students didn't. Because of this observation, Treisman created a program for struggling calculus students. His approach encouraged these students to gather for the purpose of talking about mathematics and solving challenging problems. The program was so successful that it has since been offered at many other colleges and universities. You can create a variation of Treisman's program in any course you want. Simply start a study group with some of your classmates. A study group differs from a project team in two ways. First, a study group is created to help everyone on the team excel in a particular course. Second, a study group meets many times throughout a semester. In fact, some study groups are so helpful that their members stay together throughout college.

Study groups offer important benefits. Participation in study groups increases your active involvement with the course content, which in turn leads to deeper learning and higher grades. The resulting academic success raises your expectations for success and increases your level of motivation. Study group participation helps you develop the skill of working with a group, a skill much sought after by employers. And some study group members may become your lifelong friends. Here are three suggestions for maximizing the value of your study group:

1. **Choose only Creators.** As the semester begins, make a list of potential study group members: classmates who attend regularly, come prepared, and participate actively. Also watch for that quiet student who doesn't say much but whose occasional comments reveal a special understanding of the subject. Invite three or four of them to study with you.

2. **Choose group goals.** Regardless of potential, a study group is only as effective as you make it. Everyone should agree upon common goals. You might say to prospective study group members, "My goal in our math class is to master the subject and earn an A. Is that what you want, too?" Team up with students whose goals match or exceed your own.

3. **Choose group rules.** The last step is establishing team rules. Pat Riley, one of the most successful professional basketball coaches ever, had his players create a "team covenant." Before the season, they agreed on the rules they would follow to stay on course to their goal of a championship. Your team should do the same. Decide where, how often, and at what time you'll meet. Most important, agree on what will happen during the meetings. Many study groups fail because they turn into social gatherings. Yours will succeed if you adopt rules like these:

Rule 1: We meet in the library every Thursday afternoon from 1:00 to 3:00 pm.

None of us is as smart as all of us.

Ken Blanchard

Alone we can do so little; together we can do so much.

Helen Keller

Rule 2: All members bring their study materials, including 20 new questions with answers and sources (e.g., textbook page or class notes).
Rule 3: After a five-minute timed check-in, all study materials are discussed, and all written questions are asked, answered, and understood before any additional socializing.

One of my students took this advice and started a study group in his anatomy and physiology class, a course with a high failure rate. At the end of the semester, he proudly showed me a thank-you card signed by the other four members of his group. "We couldn't have done it without you," they wrote. "Thanks for *making* us get together!" Defying the odds, everyone in the group had passed the course.

> Coming together is a beginning, staying together is progress, and working together is success.
>
> Henry Ford

The people you spend time with will dramatically affect your outcomes and experiences in college. If they place little value on learning or a college degree, it's challenging to resist their negative influence. However, if you associate with highly committed, hardworking students, their encouragement can motivate you to stay on course to graduation even when the road gets rough. A student in my class actually moved when he realized that "friends" from his old neighborhood spent most of their time putting down his efforts to get a college degree. When it comes to selecting your "group" in college, be sure to choose people who want out of life what you do.

Start a contact list of the people you meet in college. You might even want to write a few notes about them: their major or career field, names of family members, hobbies, interests, and especially their strengths. Keep in touch with these people during and after college.

Creators develop mutually supportive relationships in college that continue to support them for years—even for a lifetime. Don't get so bogged down with the daily demands of college that you fail to create an empowering support network.

> If people around you aren't going anywhere, if their dreams are no bigger than hanging out on the corner, or if they're dragging you down, get rid of them. Negative people can sap your energy so fast, and they can take your dreams away from you, too.
>
> Earvin (Magic) Johnson

THE DIFFERENCE BETWEEN HEAVEN AND HELL

A story is told of a man who prayed to know the difference between heaven and hell. An angel came to take the man to see for himself. In hell, the man saw a huge banquet table overflowing with beautifully prepared meats, vegetables, drinks, and desserts. Despite this bounty, the prisoners of hell had withered, sunken looks. Then the man saw why. The poor souls in hell could pick up all the food they wanted, but their elbows would not bend, so they could not place the food into their mouths. Living amid all that abundance, the citizens of hell were starving.

Then the angel whisked the man to heaven, where he saw another endless table heaped with a similar bounty of splendid food. Amazingly, just as in hell, the citizens of heaven could not bend their elbows to feed themselves.

"I don't understand," the man said. "Is heaven the same as hell?"

The angel only pointed. The residents of heaven were healthy, laughing, and obviously happy as they sat together at the banquet tables. Then the man saw the difference.

The citizens of heaven were feeding each other.

JOURNAL ENTRY / 16

In this activity, you will explore your beliefs and behaviors regarding giving and receiving help.

1 **Write and complete the following 10 sentence stems:**

  A. A specific situation when someone assisted me was . . .

  B. A specific situation when I assisted someone else was . . .

  C. A specific situation when I made assisting someone else more important than my own success and happiness was . . .

  D. When someone asks me for assistance, I usually feel . . .

  E. When I think of asking someone else for assistance, I usually feel . . .

  F. What usually gets in the way of my asking for help is . . .

  G. If I often asked other people for assistance, . . .

  H. If I joyfully gave assistance to others, . . .

  I. If I gratefully accepted assistance from others, . . .

  J. One goal that I could use assistance with today is . . .

2 **Write about two (or more) choices you could make to create a stronger support system for yourself in college.** Consider the choices you could make to overcome the challenges and obstacles to your success. Consider also any resistance you may have about taking steps to create a support system. Dive deep as you explore each choice fully.

No matter what accomplishments you make, somebody helped you.

Althea Gibson Darben

Individually, we are one drop.
Together, we are an ocean.

Ryunosuke Satoro

ONE STUDENT'S STORY

MITCH MULL, *Asheville-Buncombe Technical Community College, North Carolina*

The biggest challenge to my success has always been me. Any time I had a problem, I would try to solve it on my own because I didn't want people to think less of me. I probably got this belief from my father, who is very independent. While pursuing an AA degree in Horticulture at Haywood Community College a few years ago, I dropped many classes because I was reluctant to ask for help from fellow students or the instructors. I was able to graduate, but only barely.

Later, while working with a landscaping company, I decided to return to school to advance my career in horticulture. I needed some credits to enter a bachelor's program, so I enrolled at Asheville-Buncombe Technical Community College. In my first semester, I registered for a night chemistry class and an online student success course. When I registered, I was asked if I really wanted to take the chemistry course. They said it's the most dropped class

▶

ONE STUDENT'S STORY *continued*

every semester. With that news, I knew I needed to change my strategies to do better, but I didn't know what I was doing wrong. In the first week of the success course, we took the *On Course* self-assessment, and I scored lowest on interdependence. Needless to say, I wasn't surprised.

The book convinced me that being overly independent and solitary in my studies isn't always a good thing and could possibly keep me from achieving my goals. I decided to commit myself to being more interdependent. I started showing up early for chemistry, which—as I had been warned—was very challenging. I asked the instructor for assistance on homework that I couldn't understand. He'd take a minute to write out an equation on the board or help me see how to get it. After he aimed me in the right direction, it would often click for me. Other chemistry students came to class early and hung around outside. When I overheard them discussing the course, I joined them. It soon turned into a study group, which further helped me to come out of my shell. The online forums in our success class were also good stepping-stones toward

my opening up to others. The online discussions helped me overcome the shyness or nervousness that caused me to avoid most interactions. In both classes I made new friends that I may not have even talked to before. Instead of struggling as I had at Haywood, I got A's in both of my classes. Without the success class and *On Course,* I probably would have struggled with chemistry or dropped it.

Interdependence has also helped me professionally. Working as a supervisor for a local landscape company, I always thought I needed to tackle every task by myself so I'd get praise from my bosses for being efficiently independent. But a lot of times I wasn't achieving the results that my bosses wanted. Employing interdependence was hard for me at first but has become easy. Almost any time I ask for help, I receive it. Recently, I was trying to repair an irrigation line break. I've made the same type of repair many times alone, but it normally took a lot of time. This time, I asked a fellow supervisor to help keep water pumped out of the hole as I made the repair. If I hadn't asked for help, it would have taken much longer and the repair may have

even failed. Then I would have had to fix it again, and my boss wouldn't have been happy. I've also been helping others as much as possible. Some mornings, the nursery manager gets behind in loading trucks, and I pitch in to ensure all the loads are ready before our crews arrive. I've also been working closer with the secretaries to make sure all time logs are returned on time and tracking down any that are missing. There have been big improvements in all these relationships since I've been employing interdependence!

After completing my courses at A-B Tech, I transferred to North Carolina Agricultural and Technical State University as a junior in Agricultural Education. I'm still working full-time with the landscaping company while going to school part-time. I have about a year left to get my bachelor's degree, and then I plan on getting a master's with the goal of working in a state cooperative extension program. At NC A&T, I have all A's and only one B. I was never a big fan of asking for help, but I must say that the benefits of interdependence have made me a believer.

Photo: Courtesy of Mitch Mull.

Strengthening Relationships with Active Listening

FOCUS QUESTIONS   Do you know how to strengthen a relationship with active listening? What are the essential skills of being a good listener?

Once we begin a mutually supportive relationship, we naturally want the relationship to grow. Books on relationships are filled with suggestions on ways to strengthen them. At the heart of all these suggestions is a theme: We must show that we value the other person professionally, personally, or both.

Many ways exist to demonstrate another's value to us. Some of the most powerful methods include keeping promises, giving honest appreciation and approval, resolving conflicts so that both people win, staying in touch, and speaking well of someone when talking to others. However, for demonstrating the high esteem with which you value another person, there may be no better way than active listening.

Few people are truly good listeners. Too often, we're thinking about what we want to say next. Or our thoughts dash off to our own problems, and we ignore what the other person is saying. Or we hear what we *thought* the person was going to say rather than what he or she *actually* said.

Good listeners, by contrast, clear their minds and listen for the entire message, including words, tone of voice, gestures, and facial expressions. No matter how well one person communicates, unless someone else listens actively, both the communication and the relationship are likely to go astray. Imagine the potential problems created if good listening skills are absent when an instructor says to a class, "I need to change the date of the final exam from next Monday to the previous Friday. I just found out that I need to turn in my final grades on Monday." Suppose a student assumes that the instructor said the exam will be moved to the *following* Friday (instead of the *previous* Friday). When that student shows up on the "following" Friday, not only will the exam be long over, but the instructor will have turned in the final course grades as well. Talk about an unpleasant surprise!

Listening actively means accepting 100 percent responsibility for receiving the same message that the speaker sent, uncontaminated by your own thoughts or feelings. That's why active listening begins with empathy, the ability to understand the other person as if, for that moment, you *are* the other person. To empathize doesn't mean that you necessarily agree. Empathy means understanding what the other person is thinking and feeling. And you actively reveal this understanding.

With active listening, you send this message: *I value you so much that I am doing my very best to see the world through your eyes.*

When people talk, listen completely. Most people never listen.

Ernest Hemingway

For the lack of listening, billions of losses accumulate: retyped letters, rescheduled appointments, rerouted shipments, breakdowns in labor management relations, misunderstood sales presentations, and job interviews that never really get off the ground.

Michael Ray and Rochelle Myers

HOW TO LISTEN ACTIVELY

Active listening is a learned skill. You will become an excellent listener if you master the following four steps:

Step 1: Listen to Understand

Listening isn't effective when you're simply waiting for the first opportunity to insert your own opinion. Instead, focus fully on the speaker, activate your empathy, and listen with the intention of fully understanding what the other person thinks and feels.

Step 2: Remain Silent and Focused

Don't be distracted by judgmental chatter from your Inner Critic and Inner Defender. Clear your mind, stay focused, and be quiet. Let your mind listen for thoughts. Let your heart listen for the undercurrent of emotions. Let your intuition listen for a deeper message hidden beneath the words. Let your companion know that you are actively listening. Sit forward. Nod your head when appropriate. Offer verbal feedback that shows you are actively listening: *Mmmmm . . . I see . . . Uh huh. . . .*

Step 3: Ask the Person to Expand or Clarify

Don't make assumptions or fill in the blanks with your own experience. Invite the speaker to share additional information and feelings:

- *Tell me more about that.*
- *Could you give me an example?*
- *Can you explain that in a different way?*
- *How did you feel when that happened?*
- *What happened next?*

Step 4: Reflect the Other Person's Thoughts and Feelings

Don't assume you understand. In your own words, restate what you heard, both the ideas and the emotions. Then verify the accuracy of your understanding:

- To a classmate: *Sounds like you're really angry about the instructor's feedback on your research paper. To you, his comments seem more sarcastic than helpful. Is that it?*
- To a professor: *I want to be clear about the new date for the final exam. You're postponing the exam from Monday to the following Friday. Have I got it right?*

Notice that reflecting adds nothing new to the conversation. Don't offer advice or tell your own experience. Your goal is merely to understand.

USE ACTIVE LISTENING IN YOUR COLLEGE CLASSES

Active listening not only strengthens relationships with people, it strengthens our understanding of new concepts and helps us learn. In class, successful students clear their minds and prepare to hear something of value. They reflect the

> Active listening, sometimes called reflective listening, involves giving verbal feedback of the content of what was said or done along with a guess at the feeling underneath the spoken words or acts.
>
> Muriel James and Dorothy Jongeward

> If I were to summarize in one sentence the single most important principle I have learned in the field of interpersonal relations, it would be this: Seek first to understand, then to be understood.
>
> Stephen Covey

instructor's ideas, confirming the accuracy of what they heard. When confused, they ask the instructor to expand or clarify, either in class or during the instructor's office hours. Using a Creator mindset, these students actively listen to understand. And, ultimately, they record their understanding in their notes. Obviously, the more accurate your class notes, the more you will learn when studying.

So, choose today to master active listening. You'll be amazed at how much this choice will improve your relationships, your learning, and your life.

> What few people realize is that failure to be a good listener prevents us from hearing and retaining vital information, becoming a roadblock to personal and professional success.
>
> Jean Marie Stine

JOURNAL ENTRY / 17

In this activity, you will practice the skill of active listening by writing out a conversation between you and your Inner Guide. As discussed earlier, thoughts are dashing through our minds much of the time. Writing a conversation with your Inner Guide applies this knowledge in a new and powerful way. First, it helps us become more aware of the thoughts that are guiding our choices. Second, writing this conversation encourages us to sort through confusion and find a positive solution. Third, it reminds us that we are not our thoughts and we can change them whenever doing so would benefit us. And, finally, writing this conversation with our Inner Guide gives us practice with an important mental skill used by highly intelligent and adaptive people: *metacognition.*

Metacognition is the skill of thinking about our thinking. Developing metacognition helps us see where our thinking is flawed. It allows us to change our thinking to achieve better outcomes and experiences. If you've ever talked to yourself while working on a problem, you were probably using metacognition. You may find writing this dialogue to be a new (and perhaps unusual) experience. However, the more you practice, the more you'll see what a valuable success skill it is to have a conversation with yourself as an active listener. And, of course, becoming an active listener with others will strengthen those relationships immeasurably.

> Dr. Eliot's listening was not mere silence, but a form of activity. Sitting very erect on the end of his spine with hands joined in his lap, making no movement except that he revolved his thumbs around each other faster or slower, he faced his interlocutor and seemed to be hearing with his eyes as well as his ears. He listened with his mind and attentively considered what you had to say while you said it. . . . At the end of an interview the person who had talked to him felt that he had his say.
>
> Henry James about Charles W. Eliot, former president of Harvard University

1 Write a conversation between you (ME) and your Inner Guide (IG) about a problem you are facing in college. Label each of your IG's responses with the listening skill it uses: silence, expansion, clarification, reflection (remember to reflect feelings as well as thoughts). Let your IG demonstrate the skills of active listening without giving advice.

Here's an example of the beginning of such a conversation:

ME: I've been realizing what a difficult time I have asking for help.

IG: Would you like to say more about that? **(Expansion)**

ME: Well, I've been having trouble in math. I know I should be asking more questions in class, but . . . I don't know, I guess I feel dumb because I can't do the problems myself.

IG: You seem frustrated that you can't solve the math problems without help. **(Reflection)**

ME: That's right. I've always resisted that sort of thing. ▶

JOURNAL ENTRY   17   *continued*

IG: What do you mean by "that sort of thing"? **(Clarification)**

ME: I mean that ever since I can remember, I've had to do everything on my own. When I was a kid, I used to play alone all the time.

IG: Uh-huh. . . . **(Silence)**

ME: As a kid, I never had anyone to help me. And I don't have anyone to help me now.

IG: So, no one is available to help you? Is that how it seems? **(Reflection)**

ME: Well, I guess I could ask Robert for help. He seems really good in math, but I'm kind of scared to ask him.

IG: What scares you about asking him? **(Expansion)** . . . etc.

Imagine that the conversation you create here is taking place over the phone. Don't hang up until you've addressed all aspects of the problem and know what your next action step will be. Let your Inner Guide demonstrate how much it values you by being a great listener.

2 **Write what you learned or relearned about active listening during this conversation with your Inner Guide and what changes, if any, you will make in your communications.** Remember to dive deep to discover a powerful insight. When you think you have written all you can, see if you can write at least one more paragraph.

ONE STUDENT'S STORY

TEROA PASELIO, *Windward Community College, Hawaii*

I grew up in the shadow of my older brother. I was just the little sister of Lafaele Paselio, the all-star football jock, who was one of the popular kids in school. I was never in the spotlight. I felt unimportant. I had no identity of my own. A potato with nothing on it is pretty bland, and that's how I felt. It was really depressing because I knew I have so much to offer.

Stepping into college wasn't as exciting for me as it probably is for most people. Sure it was a new journey, a new experience, but for me, it was just another place to be called Lafaele's little sister. My brother had just finished a year at Windward Community College in Kaneohe, Hawaii, and everyone there knew who he was. Now I was once again in his shadow. Even though my brother had transferred to a university in San Diego, California, I knew I was bound to fall into the same situation I had experienced throughout my life. Once again, I was just Lafaele's little sister.

In my Introduction to College class, we learned tips on how to succeed in college. The class had assignments to write journal entries from the *On Course* book. A journal that was particularly meaningful for me was the one where you wrote a conversation between you and your Inner Guide. Your Inner Guide was supposed to use good listening skills to help you come up with a solution to a problem. It was funny because while I was doing that journal I realized I had the solution right in front of my face, and the conversation with my Inner Guide brought it out. I realized I am in charge of my life. It doesn't matter what others think of me. I fell in love with who I am and what I can do with my life. There are things I'm good at that Lafaele's not good

▶

at. I love my music, and I want to be a high school teacher.

I also saw how good listening skills will help me be the kind of teacher I want to be. I want to make students believe that they matter. I want them to feel important. Some of my teachers have really listened to me and made me feel that I matter. A teacher who doesn't listen sends the message that what the student thinks isn't important. That the *student* isn't important. I remember when I disagreed with my philosophy teacher one time, and he told me to explain why. Then he kept interrupting me and telling me I was wrong without even letting me explain myself. That made me feel angry, and I'm never going to be like him. I'm going to listen to people. I tell my friends if I interrupt you, tell me to stop. I want to listen to the people in my life so they know that what they say is important to me.

With the help of the Introduction to College class, I learned that I can find answers to the problems I face. I just have to listen to my Inner Guide, to myself. It is my choice to let the fact that I am Lafaele's sister get to me or not. I can now say that the person I am today is a lot stronger than the person I was yesterday. I don't have to be the bland potato any more. I am Teroa Paselio, that's it! No one's sister, no one's cousin, no one's namesake, but Teroa Paselio! After writing that journal, I walked into school on Monday singing to myself "I'm feeling like a star, you can't stop my shine!" I can definitely say I'm no longer living in anyone's shadow.

Photo: Courtesy of Teroa Paselio.

Respecting Cultural Differences

FOCUS QUESTION What are some keys to achieving success in a world of increasing diversity?

Nearly anywhere you go these days, you encounter people different from you. And that's a trend you can expect to grow. The Pew Research Center predicts major changes in race and ethnicity in the United States between now and 2050. European Americans will decrease from 67 to 47 percent of the population. Latino/a Americans will increase from 14 to 29 percent. African Americans will remain constant at 13 percent. And Asian Americans will increase from 5 to 9 percent. Other ethnicities such as Native Americans and Arab Americans will add even more to the growing diversity of North America. This remarkable diversity underscores the importance of strengthening your skills in understanding and engaging with people different from yourself.

College enrollment already reflects these changes, according to the *Chronicle of Higher Education*. In the past 40 years, entering European American students decreased from 90.9 to 73.1 percent. Simultaneously, African American students increased from 7.5 to 11 percent. Four decades ago, Asian and Latino/a Americans combined made up only 0.6 percent of new students in higher education, but today the percentage of Asian Americans has increased to 8.9 and Latino/a Americans to 9.7.

Visible differences such as skin color are relatively easy to identify. Others may be less obvious. These differences include religion, economic class, mental and physical ability, sexual and/or gender orientation, age, military experience,

> I am an American; free born and free bred, where I acknowledge no man as my superior, except for his own worth, or as my inferior, except for his own demerit.
>
> Theodore Roosevelt

and learning preferences, to name just a few. If you add deep-culture differences in beliefs, values, attitudes, and norms, the list of possible differences between any two people is long, indeed.

Much has been written about the challenges of interacting effectively with people who are different. If you search "diversity" at Amazon.com, you'll get links to more than 20,000 books. If you search "diversity" at Google.com, you'll get more than a billion results! The complexity of creating harmony in diverse populations has also been explored in college courses, professional journals, newspapers, magazines, conferences, and workshops. The problems explored in these forums range from misunderstandings stemming from differences in cultural beliefs, attitudes, norms, and rules to the horrors of hate crimes, ethnic cleansings, and genocide.

Addressing the complexities of deeply ingrained prejudice and oppression of minorities is beyond the scope of a book about college, career, and life success. My hope is that people empowered by the strategies in this book, like you, will find satisfaction in living up to their potential instead of tearing down the lives of others. And if you are a student who faces prejudice and unfair treatment, my hope is that you will feel empowered to stand in opposition to such injustices. Whether you consider yourself a member of a cultural majority or minority, your success very likely depends on your ability to interact effectively with people who are different from you. In higher education, for example, someone different from you may be your instructor, tutor, counselor, adviser, or classmate. In the workplace, someone different from you may be your employer, supervisor, manager, customer, or coworker.

By themselves, differences are not a problem. But add to them the human tendency to judge, fear, and (in some cases) harm people who are different, and you have the perfect recipe for conflict between individuals, groups, and nations. The antidote is to replace judgments with respect.

Certainly moral arguments can be made for treating everyone with respect, but there is a very practical reason as well. Today, more than ever before, everyone's success is affected by their ability to interact effectively with people who are different from them. Judgments lead to fear, misunderstanding, conflict, discrimination, oppression, and even war. By contrast, respect leads to cooperation, compassion, learning, empowerment, success, and peace. Your choice to judge or show respect will have a profound effect on the outcomes and experiences of your life and those with whom you interact.

> Tolerance, intercultural dialogue and respect for diversity are more essential than ever in a world where peoples are becoming more and more closely interconnected.
>
> Kofi Annan, former secretary-general of the United Nations

SHOWING RESPECT

Here are some ways you can show respect to people who are different from you. They range from the simple to the complex:

1. **Pronounce names correctly.** Few things are more personal to us than our names. In her book, *Stealing Buddha's Dinner*, Bich Minh Nguyen tells of her shame when Americans pronounced her name "bitch" instead of

"Bick." The internationalization of sports is helping mainstream North Americans hear the pronunciation of unfamiliar names such as Yani Tseng (Taiwanese professional golfer), Daisuke Matsuzaka (Japanese professional baseball player), and Siyar Bahadurzada (Afghan mixed martial artist). When you meet someone with an unfamiliar name, simply say, "I want to be sure I'm pronouncing your name correctly. Would you please say it for me?"

2. **Use the preferred term for a person's cultural group.** Close in importance to our names is the name of our cultural group. Thus, using preferred terminology conveys the same sort of respect as does pronouncing a person's name correctly. Complicating the issue, members of some cultures may differ in their preference. So, once again, if in doubt, ask.

For example, *Latino* and *Latina* (and more recently, *Latinx*) are terms preferred by many members of this cultural group. However, some may prefer "Hispanic," a term that others reject as having been thrust upon them by the U.S. Census Bureau. Also, avoid using terminology that excludes a group. For example, if you say to a group of people, "You're welcome to bring your husband or wife," you have excluded gay people and singles living together. Instead, simply say "husband, wife, or partner." When it comes to people with disabilities, remember that the disability is not the person, so separate the two by presenting the person first. Instead of a "disabled person," say "a person with differing abilities." Some members of majority groups resist or condemn this extra effort to come up with the preferred terminology, and they judge it as "political correctness." However, like our personal names, the terms we prefer for our cultural groups are personal as well, and honoring that preference shows respect.

3. **Learn nonverbal behaviors.** Experts in communication say that as much as 90 percent of the message we send is conveyed nonverbally. That's why it's essential to know that two nonverbal languages can be as different as two verbal languages. Remember that while certain gestures, personal space expectations, and eye contact are normal for you, they may be offensive to others. Gestures such as pointing at someone, raising your thumb, or crossing your fingers can be interpreted very differently by different people. In some cultures, it is typical for people to stand several feet away from each other, while in others it's typical for people to stand just inches away. To signal respect for another person, some people will be very careful not to look directly into someone else's eyes, while others will interpret looking away as disrespectful. None of these choices are wrong. They simply represent differing cultural beliefs. It's important to be aware of our own cultural nonverbal behaviors, and open-minded and respectful

[E]thnic group members pay very serious attention to the ways in which they label themselves and are labeled by others. Finding out what term is preferable is a matter of respect. . . .

Jerry V. Diller

When it comes to nonverbal language, we often mistakenly assume that our systems of communicating nonverbally are all the same.

David Matsumoto and Linda Juang

of others' nonverbal behaviors. So whether the difference is in gestures, space, eye contact, or other body language, we can be respectful by realizing that others may speak a different nonverbal language.

4. **See people as individuals (not stereotypes).** The human mind is a pattern-making device. We want to generalize about life to understand, explain, and predict. Knowing that a particular instructor is "easy" or "hard," for example, helps us make decisions about things such as how much to study for a final exam. Unfortunately, once our minds grab onto a generalization, we want to apply it even if it's wrong or doesn't apply in this situation. This is the problem with stereotypes. A stereotype is a generalization about a group of people based on limited or even faulty evidence. Once we accept a generalization as true, we tend to apply it to all individuals we encounter from that group. If you want to see examples of stereotypes you hold about others, simply complete the following sentence stems with the first thought that comes to mind:

Women are. . .	Southerners are. . .
Republicans are. . .	White men are. . .
Jews are. . .	Skateboarders are. . .
Black men are. . .	Rich people are. . .
Muslims are. . .	College instructors are. . .

Stereotypes about any group disrespect individuals from that group, denying them their uniqueness. Knowing cultural tendencies—for example, whether a culture is individualistic or collectivistic—may help to explain why a member of that culture did what he or she did. But using a stereotype to try to predict what a person will do insults that person's uniqueness. As one example of how to employ this idea, don't assume someone either fits a stereotype or can speak for a whole culture: "Emiko, you people are all good in math, right?" Ouch. Instead of stereotyping, see each person for the unique individual he or she is. Just like you.

5. **Avoid the right/wrong game.** Human beings are judgment machines. We think what we do is right, so anything different must be wrong. When we play the right/wrong game with people whose culture is different from ours, it has a fancy name: *ethnocentrism*. Ethnocentrism is the belief that the way *we* do things is superior to the way *they* do things.

6. **Avoid microaggressions.** You think of yourself as a good person. You'd never participate in acts of blatant racism. Yet you may unintentionally disrespect people who are different from you through microaggressions. Microaggressions are brief slights and insults that send demeaning

It is nearly impossible to grow up in a society and not take on its prejudices. Consequently, it is not a matter of whether one is biased. We all are. Rather, it is a question of what negative racial attitudes one has learned so far and what, from this moment on, one is willing to do about them.

Jean Moule

messages to members of minority groups. Jean Moule, an African American professor at Oregon State University, shares some personal examples: "A man saw my face as I walked into the store and unconsciously checked his wallet. On the street, a woman catches my eye a half block away and moves her purse from the handle of her baby's stroller to her side as she arranges the baby's blanket. In the airport, a man signals to his wife to move her purse so it is not over the back of her chair, adjacent to the one I am moving toward. . . . I believe these are examples of 'blink of the eye' racism." The hidden message in each person's response is that African Americans are criminals.

Here's another example. A female student is in a math study group with three men who ignore her efforts to contribute to the discussion of homework problems. The hidden message is that women can't do math. Asian American college professor Derald Wing Sue notes that he is often complimented for speaking English so well. A third-generation American, Sue replies, "I hope so. I was born here." The hidden message is that he will always be a foreigner in the country of his birth.

What makes microaggressions challenging to address is twofold. The senders are often unaware of their bias and the receivers aren't sure if the slight was deliberate. If you believe you were the recipient of a microaggression, use the assertiveness skills you'll learn later in this chapter to address the insult. And if someone tells you that he or she was insulted by something you said or did (a microaggression), set your Inner Defender aside. Use the listening skills you practiced earlier to learn how you can be more respectful of others.

7. **Advocate for respect.** Oppression comes in many guises. Sometimes it shows up as a joke that makes fun of someone who is different. Sometimes oppression escalates to a bigoted comment about something like someone's race, religion, or sexual orientation. Realize that your silence will be interpreted as agreement with these prejudiced views. Be a voice for respect by letting others know that you don't approve of such comments. (You'll learn some great strategies for being assertive later in this chapter.)

Unfortunately, oppression will sometimes escalate to acts of cruelty and violence. Recent examples on college campuses include a swastika scrawled on a bathroom wall near a Jewish studies center and the stabbing of a Nigerian-born student body president. No one can—or should have to—learn in an environment of fear. College offers an opportunity to encounter many points of view so that you can choose the ones that will best support you to create a great life. Don't allow others to deny you or your fellow students of that opportunity because of their prejudices and biases. If you witness or are the target of such hate crimes, report them to campus officials. Follow up to see that something

I see a huge irony. While hate crimes receive the most attention, the greatest damage to the life experiences of people of color is from racial microaggression.

Derald Wing Sue

is done. And, in the spirit of interdependence, consider requesting help from a group that has experience dealing with hate crimes, such as the Southern Poverty Law Center and the Anti-Defamation League. These and other groups that promote social justice can be found online.

Interacting effectively with people from different cultures can be challenging. However, in a world that is becoming more diverse with each passing day, showing respect for others—and insisting upon it for yourself—will help you achieve your goals and dreams while helping others to do the same.

All that is necessary for the triumph of evil is that good men do nothing.

Edmund Burke

JOURNAL ENTRY / **18**

1 **Describe a time when you felt disrespected.** Present the experience as if it is a scene from a novel. Describe the setting where the event took place. Explain who was there. Describe what they did and said. Explain how you felt.

2 **Describe the same experience a second time, but this time revise what people said and did in a way that would have left you feeling fully respected.** In this revision of history, have everyone speak and behave in ways that would have changed the outcomes and experiences for the better, leaving you feeling fully respected.

You demand respect and you'll get it. First of all, you give respect.

Mary J. Blige

INTERDEPENDENCE / **at Work**

> Great things in business are never done by one person; they're done by a team of people.
>
> —Steve Jobs, former CEO of Apple

Success at college requires working well with classmates, professors, and teammates. Just as in college, nearly every job requires that you work well with others, often in project teams or departments. You'll want to get along with colleagues, managers, and clients. You'll also want to create and expand your support network during your career. You'll learn more about that later.

Networking and work style can be different for extroverts and introverts. People who are extroverted recharge their energy by being with other people. People who are introverted recharge their energy through time spent alone. Extroverts typically enjoy interacting with larger groups of people, while introverts appreciate smaller groups or one-on-one conversations. Many people are a combination of both personality types, moving back and forth between them.

If you are more extroverted, you might search for jobs that rely on interaction with many others. For example, as a social media manager, you'd typically collaborate with many departments. You might work with web design, photography/video production, marketing, legal, sales, and many other departments. If you are more introverted, you might research jobs that require much less interaction with

▶

other people. For example, as a data analyst, you may work primarily on your own to collect and examine data to determine consumer habits and behaviors, product efficacy, or sales trends. However, even in a more solitary position, you may be expected to attend team meetings, interact with clients, or discuss projects with your manager. In other words, no matter what you choose to do, it is likely that your job will include interaction with others. Your ability to be interdependent and work well with others will determine your success in your career.

INTERDEPENDENCE AT WORK

A social network is an important part of college and career success. In a Harvard study, researchers Shawn Achor, Phil Stone, and Tal Ben-Shahar found that people at the workplace who offer social support to others were 10 times more engaged at work and 40 percent more likely to be promoted. At the university, social support was also found to be the most important tool to reduce student stress. Teamwork, social support, and social networking are simply essential college and workplace skills. Management and marketing blogger Abhijeet Pratap (cheshnotes, February 18, 2017) argues that teamwork is essential because it improves work quality, employee morale, productivity, and efficiency. It also increases synergy, the added value that results from partnering on a project. It encourages creativity and promotes project success. Work has become increasingly complex. Teamwork is essential because it allows more complex problems to be solved more effectively than if only one person tried to solve them.

Social support is important to develop because a lack of social support has been linked to depression, suicide, alcohol use, cardiovascular disease, early death, and decreased brain function. A 2010 study by researchers Julianne Holt-Lunstad, Timothy Smith, and Bradley Layton concluded that higher levels of social support are as important as regular exercise for a longer life. A lack of social support can be as destructive as high blood pressure. Bottom line: Poor health impacts your capacity to be an effective student and employee. A strong social support network helps you become more resilient when you face challenges in college and in the workplace. The good news is that you can improve your interdependence skills now and start building a strong social network so that you'll be prepared for your career.

Strengthening your interdependence skills in college will better help you succeed at work by:

1. Building a network of experts in critical areas who will help you when you're stuck

2. Increasing your problem-solving skills

3. Improving the chances of being promoted and advancing in your career

4. Becoming a more valued and effective member of project teams

5. Developing a larger client base to produce better results

CAREER SEARCH RESOURCES

Rather than searching for jobs all by yourself, practice interdependence by going to the college's career center. It's one of your most valuable resources on campus. Career centers offer advising and tools to help you explore jobs and industries and analyze your current skills. You can also plan for additional classes to keep you on course to your goals. You'll want to visit the center early, preferably in your first year at college, because a career exploration and job search is a multiyear process. Don't wait until the final term of your senior year! A career center offers in-person and online resources for both current students and alumni. These resources may include:

1. Career advisers and coaches who can guide you in the job preparation and search process

▶

2. Personality and skills assessments that help you determine the best matches in career fields or positions

3. Short workshops and extended training on résumé writing and cover letter preparation

4. Practice in developing interviewing skills

5. Training in developing a LinkedIn profile, identifying appropriate contacts, and networking online

6. Internship opportunities and internship/job application support

7. Search tools for campus jobs, career fairs, and scheduling on-campus job interviews

8. Alumni support for new job searches, career changes, and connecting current students with alumni

Through the career center you can take multiple assessments to learn how your interests connect to specific majors and jobs. You can explore the employment opportunities that are connected with your selected major. Beyond your campus career center and its in-person and online resources, you can also use other online career search websites and apps. These include Indeed, a site where you can search millions of jobs online; Glassdoor, a site where you can read insider reviews about specific companies; The Muse, a site that offers career advice on a wide variety of topics; and Vault, a subscription service that offers in-depth intelligence on what it's really like to work in an industry, company, or profession.

MENTORS

A career mentor is an experienced person in your intended or current field who is willing to advise you. Mentors are enormously valuable because of their years of experience. They can advise you on numerous aspects of preparation for and success during your career, including:

1. Coursework that addresses skills relevant to your intended position

2. Internships that offer valuable work experience

3. Professional conferences and trainings that provide timely and essential skills and information

4. Job openings that may not yet be publicly posted

5. Networking opportunities both inside and outside the company

6. Feedback on performance during a meeting or after a project

IDENTIFYING A MENTOR

How do you find the right mentor? This person might be in your life already. Think about current or past college professors, especially ones with direct experience and contacts in the field. What about your current manager or a family friend? Once you identify someone you'd like as a mentor, make sure you ask them if they would be willing to mentor you. Then set up a regular schedule of meetings.

At the workplace, you might be assigned a mentor, or might request one through the human resources department. Most colleges have mentoring programs that help you connect with a mentor. You can also try mentor websites and apps such as Unibly, Mogul, iCouldBe, iMentor, MentorNet, Find a Mentor, Mentorloop, and MentorCity. LinkedIn not only allows you to develop a professional network, but it also allows you to request mentors.

What are the characteristics of an excellent mentor?

▶

1. Direct and relevant experience in your desired or current field

2. Availability in person, by phone, or email/messaging to answer your questions

3. Willingness and desire to support you in achieving your career goals

WORKING WITH A MENTOR

There are many ways to work with a mentor, but most importantly, you should be responsible, committed, and willing to learn. Respond as quickly as possible when your mentor reaches out. Be prepared with questions whenever you meet with your mentor. Always follow up on your mentor's suggestions to show you recognize the wisdom your mentor has developed over many years of experience. Finally, be sure to demonstrate your appreciation for their help with thoughtful thank-you cards, texts, emails, or a phone call.

NETWORKING

Many career experts argue that networking is your most essential practice in finding a good job and getting ahead at work. Your network is filled with people you've made personal connections with—either by answering their questions or asking them questions. Instead of focusing solely on the number of contacts you can make, consider the quality of each contact in your network. Have you developed at least an initial relationship with this person? Do they trust that you'd be a good candidate to refer for a job opening? Your network may include classmates from college in your major who share similar career goals as you. It may include professors or alumni you've talked to. Most importantly, your network is not just a place to go for help finding jobs. It's a place where you can find social support.

How do you build a network? What's the best way to use that network to reach your goals? You can start with your mentor. Most experienced professionals have a vast network that allows them to identify resources and talent, and solve problems. They may be willing to bring you into this larger network that has taken them decades to develop. Here are other initial steps in building your network:

1. Create a list of your target industries, positions, and professional associations.

2. Identify an inner circle with direct connections to desired employment. Reach out to people who can help you develop wider networks outside this inner circle.

3. Develop a LinkedIn profile (and Google+ or others), and update it as you acquire new skills.

4. Attend multiple social and professional events, and practice sharing your desired career and life goals. Follow up by reaching out to new people in your field.

5. Consider volunteering at positions related to your career goals and personal values that will help you build another network.

Once you have a network in place, you'll need to make good use of it. Identify a small but clear request that will allow you to take the next step in your career search. Perhaps that might be, "Would you be willing to connect me with someone in the Human Resources department so I can ask about potential job openings?" Communicate this request to a few targeted people in your network. Set up some informational interviews to learn more about employer expectations and to meet key players in your intended field. You can prepare for these interviews by developing a set of questions about the company and positions. When you reach out

▶

on LinkedIn, customize your request so it is not generic. Be specific about who you are, how the two of you are connected, your specific interest, and your specific request.

Everyone benefits from strengthening interdependence, both at college and at work. Working well with others can be challenging, but it's worth your time investment to improve these essential skills.

You'll need to develop support networks, both in person and online. Plan to spend lots of time at the career center, and explore their online resources. Start building a LinkedIn profile and try out some of the many online career sites to research career trends and employment conditions. Identify potential mentors and start meeting with them, asking lots of questions. Network, network, network! This may be your single most important practice in finding a job. Most importantly, remember that interdependence is all about communicating and working well with others. You're not alone in this career search!

TECH TIPS: Interdependence

OpenStudy *(online, iOS)* is for students who want to connect with learners studying the same subjects that they are. In addition to working with groups, you can also ask questions and (according to the site) expect an answer in about five minutes. The site says it has 1 million student members from 160 countries and 190 study groups. If you haven't found the right peers at your college with whom to study, this site could be your solution.

Rcampus.com is another source for online groups where students can share files, send messages, and study together. A member can create any number of study groups, and each group comes with its own home page and message center. The person who creates the group then invites others to join by giving them the group ID and access code.

Koofers.com helps students find internships. After you complete an online job profile, Koofers shares this information with companies looking for students qualified for either an internship or full-time career opportunity.

The **Project Implicit website (implicit. harvard.edu)** gives you an opportunity to uncover your hidden biases about people in numerous categories including age, religion, sexuality, skin color, weight, and disabilities. You might be surprised at your results— I was. The project is the work of scientists at a number of universities worldwide, including Harvard.

Dropbox, Box, and Copy *(online, Android, and iOS)* are file-sharing services that allow you to easily share large files with fellow students and across multiple devices.

Google Hangouts *(online, Android,* and *iOS)* allows you to meet with classmates for distance-learning/online study groups.

Note: All of these are free, but some may offer upgraded features for a fee.

Be Assertive

> **FOCUS QUESTION** How can you communicate in a style that strengthens relationships, creates better results, and builds strong self-esteem?

On rare occasions, we may encounter someone who doesn't want us to achieve our goals and dreams. Much more often, though, we run across folks who are too busy or too preoccupied to help. Chances are you might encounter such people in a large organization such as a college or university. How we communicate our desires to them has a profound impact not only on the quality of the relationships and results we create, but on our self-esteem as well.

According to family therapist Virginia Satir, the two most common patterns of ineffective communication are **placating** and **blaming**. Both perpetuate low self-esteem:

- **Placating.** Victims who placate are dominated by their Inner Critic. They place themselves below others, protecting themselves from the sting of criticism and rejection by saying whatever they think will gain approval. Picture placators on their knees, looking up with a pained smile, nodding and agreeing on the outside, while fearfully hiding their true thoughts and feelings within. *"Please, please approve of me,"* they beg as their own Inner Critic judges them unworthy. To gain this approval, placators often spend time in Quadrant III doing what is urgent to others but unimportant to their own goals and dreams. Satir estimated that about 50 percent of people use placating as their major communication style.

- **Blaming.** Victims who blame are dominated by their Inner Defender. They place themselves above others, protecting themselves from disappointment and failure by making others fully responsible for their problems. Picture them sneering down, a finger jabbing judgmentally at those below. Their Inner Defender snarls, *"You never . . . Why do you always . . . ? Why don't you ever . . . ? It's your fault that. . . ."* Satir estimated that about 30 percent of people use blaming as their major communication style.

Either passively placating or aggressively blaming keeps those in a Victim mindset from developing mutually supportive relationships, making the accomplishment of their dreams more difficult. The inner result is damaged self-esteem.

> Once a human being has arrived on this earth, communication is the largest single factor determining what kinds of relationships she or he makes with others and what happens to each in the world.
>
> Virginia Satir

LEVELING

What, then, is the communication style of Creators? Some have called this style *assertiveness:* honestly and respectfully expressing opinions and requests.

Satir calls this communication style *leveling*. Leveling is characterized by a simple, yet profound, communication strategy: asserting the truth as you see it.

Creators boldly express their personal truth without false apology or excuse, without harsh criticism or blame. Leveling requires a strong Inner Guide and a commitment to honesty. Here are three strategies that promote leveling:

1. **Communicate purposefully.** Creators express a clear purpose even in times of emotional upset. Creators who go to a professor to discuss a disappointing grade will be clear whether their purpose is to increase their understanding of the subject, seek a higher grade, question the instructor's grading criteria, or accomplish some other outcome. By knowing their purpose, they have a way to evaluate the success of their communication. Creators state purposefully, *When I saw my grade on this lab report, I was very disappointed. I'd like to go over it with you and learn how to improve my next one.*

2. **Communicate honestly.** Creators candidly express unpopular thoughts and upset feelings in the service of building mutually supportive relationships. Creators say honestly, *I'm angry that you didn't meet me in the library to study for the sociology test as you agreed.*

3. **Communicate responsibly.** Because responsibility lies within, Creators express their personal responsibility with "I" messages. An "I" message allows Creators to take full responsibility for their reaction to anything another person may have said or done. An effective "I" message has four elements:

An observation of the situation:	*When you . . .*
A statement of your reaction:	*I felt/thought/decided . . .*
A request:	*I'd like to ask that you . . .*
An invitation to respond:	*Will you agree to that?*

Let's compare Victim and Creator responses to the same situation. Imagine that you feel sick one day and decide not to go to your history class. You phone a classmate, and she agrees to call you after class with what you missed, especially if a test is announced. But she never calls. At the next history class, the instructor gives a test that was announced the day you were absent, and you fail it. Afterward, your classmate apologizes: "Sorry I didn't call. I was swamped with work." What response do you choose?

Placating: *Oh, don't worry about it. I know you had a lot on your mind. I probably would have failed the test anyway.*

Blaming: *You're the lousiest friend I've ever had! After making me fail that test, you have some nerve even talking to me!*

Leveling: *I'm really upset that you didn't call. I thought I could count on you to keep your word to call me if a test was announced. If we're going to be friends, I need to know if you're going to keep your promises to me in the future. Will you?*

W̲e should replace our alienating, criticizing words with "I" language. Instead of, "You are a liar and no one can trust you," say, "I don't like it when I can't rely on your words—it is difficult for us to do things together."

Ken Keyes, Jr.

I̲ speak straight and do not wish to deceive or be deceived.

Cochise

Notice that the leveling response is the only one of the three that positively addresses the issue, nurtures a relationship of equals, and demonstrates high self-esteem.

MAKING REQUESTS

Making effective requests is another demonstration of both assertiveness and high self-esteem. Creators know they can't reach their greatest goals and dreams alone, so they ask for help. The key to making effective requests is applying the DAPPS rule. Whenever possible, make your requests **D**ated, **A**chievable, **P**ersonal, **P**ositive, and—above all—**S**pecific. Here are some translations of vague Victim requests to specific, clear Creator requests:

Victim Requests	Creator Requests
1. I'm going to be absent next Friday. It sure would be nice if someone would let me know if I miss anything.	1. John, I'm going to be absent next Friday. Would you be willing to call me Friday night and tell me what I missed?
2. I don't suppose you'd consider giving me a few more days to complete this research paper?	2. I'd like to request an extension on my research paper. I promise to hand it in by noon on Thursday. Would that be acceptable?

When you make specific requests, the other person can respond with a clear "yes" or "no." If the person says "no," all is not lost. Try negotiating:

1. *If you can't call me Friday night, could I call you Saturday morning to find out what I missed?*

2. *If Thursday noon isn't acceptable to you, could I turn my paper in on Wednesday by 5:00?*

Creators seek definite yes or no answers. Victims often accept "maybe" or "I'll try" for fear of getting a "no," but it's better to hear a specific "no" and be free to move on to someone who will say "yes."

One of my mentors offered a valuable piece of advice: "If you go through a whole day without getting at least a couple of 'no's,' you aren't asking for enough help in your life."

SAYING "NO"

Saying "no" is another tool of assertive Creators. When I think of the power of saying "no," I think of Monique. One day after class she took a deep breath, sighed, and told me she was exhausted. She complained that everyone at her job kept bringing her tasks to do. As a result, she had virtually no social life, and she was falling behind in college. She wanted advice on how to manage her time better.

Learning to perceive the truth within ourselves and speak it clearly to others is a delicate skill, certainly as complex as multiplication or long division, but very little time is spent on it in school.

Gay and Kathlyn Hendricks

"Sounds like you're working 60 hours a week and doing the work of two people," I observed. She nodded modestly. "Here's an outrageous thought: The next time someone at work brings you more to do, say 'no.'"

"That sounds so rude."

"Okay then, say, 'I'm sorry, but my schedule is full, and I won't be able to do that.'"

"What if my boss asks? I can't say 'no' to her."

"You can say, 'I'll be glad to take that on. But since I have so many projects already, I'll need you to give one of them to someone else. That way I'll have time to do a good job on this new project.'"

Monique agreed to experiment with saying "no." The next time I saw her, she was excited. "I sent my boss a memo telling her I had too much work and I couldn't take on the latest project she had assigned me. Before I'd even talked to her about the memo, one of my coworkers came by. He said our boss had sent him to take over some of my projects. Not only did I not get the new project, I got rid of two others. I just might be able to finish this semester after all."

Monique's voice had a power that hadn't been there before. With one "no" she had transformed herself from exhausted to exhilarated. That's the power of a Creator being assertive.

JOURNAL ENTRY **19**

In this activity, you will explore assertiveness. This powerful way of being creates great results, strengthens relationships, and builds self-esteem.

1 Make a choice—write about one of the following (A or B):

A. **Write three different responses to the instructor described in the following situation.** Respond to the instructor by (1) placating, (2) blaming, and (3) leveling. For an example of this exercise, refer to the dialogues in the section above titled "Leveling."

Situation: You register for a course required in your major. It is the last course you need to graduate. When you go to the first class meeting, the instructor tells you that your name is NOT on the roster. The course is full, and no other sections of the course are being offered. You've been shut out of the class. The instructor tells you that you'll have to postpone graduation and return next semester to complete this required course.

Remember, in each of your three responses, you are writing what you would actually say to the instructor—first as a placator, second as a blamer, and third as a leveler.

B. **Think about one of your most challenging academic goals. Decide who could help you with this goal. Write a letter to this person and request assistance.** You can decide later whether or not you will send the letter.

▶

Here are some possibilities to include in your letter:

- Tell the person your most challenging academic goal for this semester.

- Explain how this goal is a stepping-stone to your dream.

- Describe your dream and explain its importance to you.

- Identify your obstacle, explaining it fully.

- Discuss how you believe this person can help you overcome your obstacle.

- Admit any reluctance or fear you have about asking for assistance.

- Request *exactly* what you would like this person to do for you and persuade him or her to give you helpful assistance.

Remember, for effective requests, use the DAPPS rule.

2 **Write what you have learned or relearned about being assertive.** How assertive have you been in the pursuit of your goals and dreams? How has this choice affected your self-esteem? What changes do you intend to make in communicating (placating, blaming, leveling), making requests, and saying "no"? Be sure to dive deep!

> When things really get difficult, all I can say is, ask for help.
>
> Dr. Bernie Siegel

ONE STUDENT'S STORY
AMY ACTON, *Southern State Community College, Ohio*

I returned fall quarter feeling broken. I had hoped some time off would help my marriage and my mental state. But I felt exhausted and overwhelmed. I barely slept or ate. I was grinding my teeth and having nightmares. In class, I daydreamed because I didn't really want to be there. I already have a bachelor's degree from Wilmington College, but I'm back in school because I want to be a nurse. In the past, my GPA has always been high.

But because of challenges in my marriage, studying was no longer on my A list. Maybe not even on my B or C list. I had to read an assignment several times to get it, and I was definitely not doing my best work. When I got a C on the first test in Anatomy and Physiology, I panicked. The worst part was pretending everything was okay. I couldn't ask for help or admit the level of suffering. Not me. Instead, I smiled my best Pollyanna grin and went

through the motions to keep up the appearance of a healthy life.

I was taking PSYC 1108: College Success because the previous term someone had come into my English class and raved about it. *That sounds like a course I could use,* I thought. In the first week, I took the self-assessment. Ouch. Kick a girl while she's down. I scored remarkably low in interdependence. I was shocked that creating a support system was so important. I'd always valued my independent nature. But I knew I had to do something different. I had to start somewhere.

So I started by asking for help. At first, it made me feel

▶

continued

like vomiting. But it got easier. I trusted *On Course* and decided there must be benefits to interdependence. With practice, it got more comfortable. Now, it's wonderful. I began by asking students who were doing well in Anatomy and Physiology to start a study group. We would meet and go over what we covered in class. They told me about strategies they use to memorize all the bones we had to know. We made study cards and I carried them everywhere. I even started asking for help from coworkers at the hospital where I work. I usually did all of the patient charting, but I started asking others to share the task.

Next, I practiced the art of saying "no." I was raised to say "yes," followed by "please." Saying "no" took some work. I literally broke out in hives at first. I took allergy medicine and kept trying. I've gotten so good at it that now I say it every day,

usually followed by "thank you." My mom is famous for calling me and asking me to pick up something at the store. I finally told her I had to choose activities that were important to my goals, like studying my nursing courses. I even said "no" to cleaning my house all the time. I prefer a clean house, but saying no to cleaning means I can say yes to more important things. The results have been life-changing.

I also made a conscious effort to tell people how I truly feel. Living as my authentic, quirky self feels right. Many relationships where I was doing all the work have disappeared. For example, I asked my husband to help more around the house. He got angry at first, but I told him how important it is to me to get help so I can succeed in school and become a nurse. Now he helps more than he used to. I've finally made living

the life that I want a priority, and the people who really care about me are glad.

I am so happy and grateful that I signed up for this course. Also, that I took it seriously and dove deep. I was off course in September, but the New Year is looking brighter. When I got my grades at the end of the quarter, I had all A's. My marriage is way better and my husband tells me I've changed. He doesn't say how, but I can tell that he likes me better now. This process didn't happen overnight. The journal entries were a valuable tool to inspire healing. While writing the journals, I felt very reserved at first. But soon I realized that I had something to say. I was hearing my voice again . . . *my* voice! Hearing my voice was like running into an old friend. There was a moment when I giggled. I thought, "I remember you. I like you. Where have you been, my old friend?"

Photo: Courtesy of Amy Acton.

Healthy Choices: Food

"Is it okay if I eat my lunch during class?" one of my students pleads. "I have classes straight through until 2:00, and I didn't have time for breakfast."

"Sure," I say, silently predicting what's for lunch. From a fast food bag, the student pulls a cheeseburger, giant fries, and a supersize soda. That's about what I expected. How about you?

Many of us don't think much about the relationship between food, health, learning, and success. Consequently, we may give little thought to the nutritional needs of our bodies and brains. Healthy food choices often lose out to convenience, low cost, and the tasty flavors of highly processed foods full of sugar, salt, fat, white flour, and mysterious additives.

Many colleges offer these unhealthy foods in their campus dining facilities. Plus, college campuses are often surrounded by fast, cheap, and unhealthy food options. Even grocery stores offer many food choices high in calories and low in nutrition. Busy students are particularly vulnerable. They may skip meals to attend classes. Then grab high-calorie, low-nutrition fast food or have it delivered. And the day may end with a late-night study session, fueled by junk food snacks and sugary drinks from campus vending machines. The result? Bad nutrition creates many problems.

For example, have you heard about the "Freshman 15"? That's the problem of college students gaining 15 pounds in their first year. Turns out, most don't actually gain that much, but researchers at Brown University did find that first-year men gained an average of 5.6 pounds, while the women gained 3.6 pounds. Sixteen percent of students in the study gained at least 10 pounds, and 6 percent gained 15 or more pounds. The bigger concern is that the students keep gaining more each year and soon their weight is out of control.

But gaining weight is just the beginning of potential problems for college students who eat poorly. You see, the food we eat has an immediate effect on our energy, concentration, and even our ability to learn and remember. Most of our mental activities are highly affected by our food choices, according to Lisa Mosconi, author of *Brain Food*. She reports that some foods "act as neurotransmitters, the chemical messengers that our brains use for signaling, communicating, and processing information. Neurotransmitters are responsible for how you think, talk, dream, and remember." In other words, healthy foods are not only essential for living a long, healthy, successful life. They are also crucial for learning!

THE WESTERN DIET

Food expert Mark Hyman, MD, says, "I have never seen anyone evolve to be the best version of himself by eating a really crappy diet." One "really crappy diet" is so common these days that it's got its own name. It's called the "Western diet." (Sometimes it's called the standard American diet, appropriately abbreviated "SAD.") This way of eating took hold around 1980, so chances are you've been influenced by it for your whole life. It features highly processed foods, refined grains, unhealthy proteins and fats, and plenty of salt, sugar, and unpronounceable chemicals. In short, lots of calories but little nutrition. Want an example of the Western diet? How about my student's fast food cheeseburger, giant fries, and a supersize soda?

Because of the Western diet, Americans now eat about 500 more calories a day than they did before 1980. The result? In 2017, about 70 percent of Americans were overweight or obese. These numbers are alarming because excess weight increases chronic health problems, including poor bone health, high blood pressure, heart disease, diabetes, stroke, and cancer. More troubling, various studies link unhealthy diets to early death. Researcher Renata Micha reports, "We estimated that nearly half of all deaths from heart disease, stroke, and diabetes—collectively, cardiometabolic diseases—are linked to poor diet. And it wasn't just too much 'bad' in the American diet, it's also not enough 'good.'"

So how do we reduce the "bad" in our diet, and increase the "good"? Well, that's precisely the goal of the Healthy Eating Plate (Figure 5.1), which offers helpful guidance for making wise food choices. The Healthy Eating Plate recommends lots of fresh vegetables and fruits, whole grains, and healthy proteins, along with healthy oils (fats), limited dairy, and plenty of nonsugary liquids, mostly water.

People eating such a diet—combined with exercise—can expect positive outcomes. They'll likely improve their overall health, have more energy, think more clearly, maintain a healthy weight, feel more confident, and even live longer. For students, eating well means your health—especially your brain's health—will support your academic success. Mosconi says, "Science is teaching us that our brain health is highly dependent on the food choices we make."

THE LEAST YOU NEED TO KNOW ABOUT FOOD

With the Healthy Eating Plate as a guide, let's explore what healthy eating looks like.

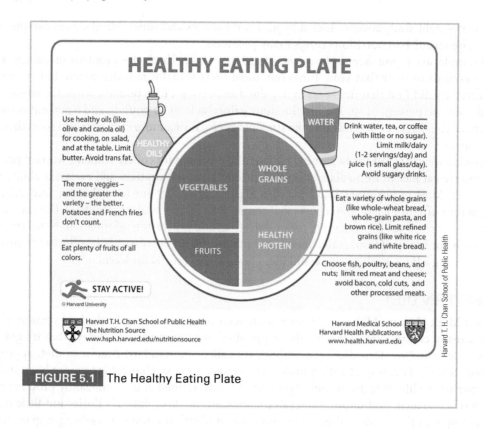

FIGURE 5.1   The Healthy Eating Plate

Vegetables

Vegetables provide carbohydrates, which are your number one source of energy. Your body creates energy by converting the carbs you eat into glucose (blood sugar). Not only does glucose power the cells in your body, it also powers your brain. Registered dietician Keri Gans cautions that if you don't have enough carbs, "your ability to think, learn, and remember stuff will decrease because neurotransmitters in your brain will not have enough glucose to synthesize properly." That said, some carbs are healthier than others. An important difference is how fast our bodies turn a carb into glucose. Slow is better.

Complex (slow) carbs are full of fiber, which is helpful because it passes through the digestive system without being converted into extra sugars. Fiber also slows the absorption of sugars from other foods eaten at the same time. This slow conversion into glucose keeps blood sugar even, helping you feel full and energized longer. Most vegetables are slow carbs and, thus, cause little rise in blood sugar. That's why you can eat pretty much all you want of salad greens, spinach, tomatoes, cucumbers, carrots, celery, bell peppers, kale, broccoli, brussels sprouts, cabbage, cauliflower, eggplant, kohlrabi, asparagus, green beans, mushrooms, snap peas, yellow and green summer squash, collard greens, okra, onions, shallots, garlic, and herbs. To maintain maximum nutrition, cooked veggies are best when steamed for only about four minutes.

Dan Buettner has spent years researching "Blue Zones." These are the areas of the world where people live the longest, healthiest lives, and his research seeks to find out why. He reports that "beans represent the consummate superfood. On average, they are made up of 21 percent protein, 77 percent complex carbohydrates (the kind that deliver a slow and steady energy, rather than the spike you get from refined carbohydrates like white flour), and only a few percent fat. They are also an excellent source of fiber." Not all experts agree that beans are a superfood, but you'll certainly be doing your health a favor if you add a few cups of beans to your weekly diet.

Simple (fast) carbs convert quickly into glucose in our bodies. The result is a spike in blood sugar that causes your body to produce insulin. Insulin's job is to stabilize blood sugar. When there's more glucose than your body can use for energy, insulin stores it as fat. Once insulin does its work, we may experience a sudden drop in energy. That makes us think we need more food, and we may get caught in a vicious cycle. It's wise to limit yourself to two or three one-cup servings a week of the following fast-carb vegetables: beets, parsnips, pumpkin, sweet corn, rutabaga, turnips, winter squash (butternut and acorn), and sweet potatoes. These veggies still have lots of fiber and nutrients, making them nutrient dense and a much healthier choice than foods such as cake or candy.

Fruits

Next on our healthy plate are fruits, and once again the kind of carbs they offer is important. For complex (slow) carbs, a great choice is berries. Because of their high fiber, blueberries, raspberries, blackberries, and strawberries release their sugar content slowly. Plus, berries are filled with vitamins and antioxidants that reduce inflammation, both a health bonus. According to Joel Fuhrman, MD, "Berries are excellent foods for the brain. Substances present in blueberries can both reduce oxidative stress and improve communication between brain cells." Other slow-carb choices among fruits include apples, cherries, plums, peaches, tangerines, pears, oranges, nectarines, grapefruit, kiwi, lemons, pomegranates, and watermelon. As a reminder to eat fruit daily, keep a bowl of your favorites where you'll see them often.

For an occasional quick pickup—such as after strenuous exercise—fast-carb fruits are a healthy option. These include grapes, bananas, pineapple, mango, and papaya. All dried fruits, like raisins, contain fast-release carbs, as do canned fruits that swim in sugary syrup. Avoid fruit juice because it lacks fiber and is very high in sugar and calories.

Wondering how much of all carbs you should eat? Dr. Hyman offers a helpful guideline: "You're better off eating a minimum of 10 servings of plant food each day: seven or eight servings of veggies and no more than two or three servings of fruit." A serving, by the way, is typically about one cup.

Whole Grains

Grains provide another source of carbohydrates, as well as fiber and many other nutrients. You're probably familiar with grains such as wheat, oats, rice, and corn. How about these less familiar grains: amaranth, quinoa, spelt, millet, and buckwheat?

Notice that the Healthy Eating Plate specifies "whole" grains. A grain has three parts—the bran, endosperm, and germ. A grain is considered "whole" only if all three parts are still present in the same proportions as when harvested. Being high in fiber, whole grains help keep blood sugar from spiking and our appetite curbed for longer. However, these benefits are lost with "refined" grains, which have one or more of the three parts removed. Refining (as with white flour) makes the grain more likely to spike blood sugar. Plus, refining removes about 25 percent of the grain's protein and more than 50 percent of other valuable nutrients. So, eat whole grains.

Recommended daily amounts of grains range from three to six ounces for women and three to eight ounces for men. For weight control or loss, stay on the lower ends of these ranges. To put these numbers in perspective, one slice of whole grain bread or a half cup of cooked grains equals one ounce. Cooked grains make a tasty breakfast cereal or addition to salads or soups. Lisa Mosconi in her book *Brain Food* recommends Buddha bowls. These bowls, she explains, "are hearty, filling dishes made of raw or roasted vegetables, legumes such as beans and lentils, and whole grains like spelt or brown rice." Bulk food sections of grocery or health food stores offer a variety of economical whole grains.

Alert: If you eat grains and later experience bloating, stomach upset, and/or diarrhea, see a medical professional. These symptoms may indicate an autoimmune problem called celiac disease. If so, you'll need to avoid grains containing gluten, including wheat, barley, and rye.

An important consideration regarding all vegetables, fruits, and grains is whether to go organic. Sarah Brewer, a registered dietician and nutritionist, reports, "It's estimated that, during the course of one year, those following a nonorganic diet consume around 13 pounds of chemicals such as food additives, colorings, flavorings, preservatives, waxes, fertilizers, pesticides, and herbicide residues." Fortunately, organic foods are grown without these chemicals. Unfortunately, they are often more expensive. However, more and more major grocery stores, including Costco, Safeway, and the online Thrive Market, carry affordable organic products. I've adopted an option that provides me with organic veggies at very little cost: I grow my own.

Healthy Protein

Protein provides the building blocks of the human body. For example, protein is vital for creating and maintaining muscles, bones, organs, cartilage, skin, blood, hair, nails, eyes, enzymes, hormones, and immune system. Like carbs, protein also provides energy. In fact, there's not much that protein doesn't do to keep us healthy. The Healthy Eating Plate suggests making healthy protein about a quarter of your daily diet.

When you eat protein, your digestive system breaks it into smaller units, called amino acids. Humans need 20 different amino acids for good health. Because our bodies can make only 11 of them, we must get the other nine from protein-rich foods. Foods with these nine essential proteins are called *complete proteins*. Those without are called *incomplete proteins*.

Complete Proteins. Food derived from animals—for example, beef, pork, lamb, turkey, chicken, and fish—provides complete protein. Some studies have shown an increase in health problems for meat eaters. However, according to Dr. Hyman, "Three decades of research have shown that grass-fed beef and pasture-raised meat are significantly healthier than grain-fed, factory-farmed meat." As one example, consider the European Prospective Investigation into Cancer and Nutrition (EPIC). With nearly 500,000 participants, this study found no association between unprocessed fresh meat and heart disease or cancer. It did, however, find a link between these diseases and eating processed meat such as bacon, canned meats, hot dogs, and deli meats. These processed meats, then, might well be called "unhealthy protein." Healthy animal protein, some experts like Dr. Hyman say, comes from organic, pastured, grass-fed animals. Additional sources of food proteins from animals include cheese, yogurt, and eggs; all are best consumed in moderation. A few plant foods also provide complete (or nearly complete) protein, including soy, quinoa, amaranth, buckwheat, and hemp and chia seeds.

Incomplete Proteins. Many plants provide some—but not all—of the nine essential amino acids. The following is a list of plants that contain incomplete protein:

- **Vegetables:** Spinach, kale, collards, sun-dried tomatoes, artichokes, broccoli, asparagus, green beans, sweet potatoes, green peas, and brussels sprouts

- **Beans:** Garbanzo (also called chickpeas), peanut (and peanut butter), kidney, black, white, pinto, and tempeh and tofu (both made from soy)

- **Fruit:** Guava, blackberries, nectarines, and bananas
- **Whole grains**: Amaranth, teff, triticale, oatmeal, farro, spelt, and sweet corn
- **Nuts and nut butters:** Almonds, cashews, pistachios, walnuts, pine nuts, pecans, macadamia, and brazil (all are high in calories, so a handful a day is a good guideline)
- **Seeds:** Chia, lentils, hemp, buckwheat, pumpkin, sesame, sunflower, and poppy

As you can see, most plants don't provide all nine essential amino acids. This means, if you're a vegetarian or otherwise limit your diet to plant-based foods, you're wise to combine foods to meet your protein needs. For example, combine corn with beans, brown rice with lentils, or yogurt with walnuts.

Fats *(Oils)*

On the Healthy Eating Plate, oils are placed off to the side, but don't let that fool you into thinking they're unimportant. Oils are fats that are liquid at room temperature, and they are found mostly in vegetables, nuts, seeds, and fish. Together with solid fats (like the fat on a steak), oils are the third major nutrient found in food, along with carbs and protein. There are various kinds of oils and fats, and a dispute continues about which are healthy, which are unhealthy, and how much fat we should eat. What is clear, however, is that we need at least some oils in our diets. As with carbs and protein, fat is an important source of energy. It regulates our body temperature and helps us absorb essential vitamins. Our bodies also use fat to create hormones, cell membranes, and nerve tissues. In fact, the human brain is about 60 percent fat!

Healthy Fats. Consumed in moderation, these fats help improve health. Fats called "omega-3s" are some of the most beneficial. A good source is olive oil, which is packed with omega-3 oils. In her book *Brain Food*, Lisa Mosconi reports, "People who consume omega-3 foods on a regular basis remain mentally clearer and have a lower likelihood of developing cognitive deterioration than those who consume less of these healthy fats." Using extra-virgin olive oil to create your own salad dressings is one way to make it part of a healthy meal. Other plant-based sources of good fats are avocados, seeds, and nuts. Many cold-water fish are also sources of healthy fats (as well as protein). These fish include salmon (preferably wild caught), sardines, mackerel, herring, trout, and anchovies. When it comes to fat from animal sources, experts differ. Although some studies show animal fat to harm health, others contradict those findings. Food writer Michael Pollan summarizes current research: "For most of our food animals, a diet of grass means much healthier fats . . . in their meat, milk, and eggs, as well as appreciably higher levels of vitamins and antioxidants."

Unhealthy Fats. Although scientists vary in their opinions about many fats, they do agree that *trans fats* are unhealthy. Trans fats are manufactured by adding hydrogen to vegetable oil, making it solid at room temperature. Used in processed foods to extend shelf life, trans fats are linked with risks of high blood pressure, coronary heart disease, and obesity. As such, avoid processed foods containing "partially hydrogenated oils" (the food industry's name for trans fats). The danger is great enough that the U.S. Food and Drug Administration has banned trans fats. However, products containing trans fats are likely to be in stores until at least 2020. Joseph Mercola, MD, author of numerous books on healthy eating, advises that we should also avoid canola and soybean oils, along with margarine and shortening. To the list of unhealthy fats, other experts add corn oil, safflower oil, peanut oil, vegetable oil, and butter substitutes. A consensus, however, is hard to find.

WISE CHOICES: FOOD

There's a lot to learn about eating for optimum body and brain health. Remember, though, you don't have to change everything all at once. Instead, you can achieve optimum nutrition by making one small, healthy choice after another:

- Eat mostly slow-carb vegetables, fruits, and whole grains that won't spike your blood sugar.
- Eat small portions of animal-based proteins like meat, fish, eggs, and yogurt—or combine the right vegetables, beans, fruits, nuts, and seeds to provide complete proteins.
- Eat healthy fats, especially oils found in extra-virgin olive oil, nuts, seeds, avocados, and cold-water fish (salmon, herring, trout, sardines, mackerel, and anchovies).
- Whenever possible, eat organically raised plants, and organic, pasture-raised foods from animals.
- Snack healthfully; for example, eat fruit, a whole grain cracker with nut butter, or fresh-popped popcorn sprayed with olive oil (instead of potato chips or ice cream).
- Choose wisely in your college dining facility. For example, add a grilled chicken breast to a large salad and top with a dressing of olive oil and vinegar. Eat desserts only for an occasional treat or reward.
- If your college dining facility provides no healthy options, bring your own food. Also consider a Creator choice: Advocate for a change to healthier food.
- Keep healthy snacks (like fruit and nuts) in your room, and get rid of the junk, especially most packaged foods found in vending machines.
- When hungry, drink water before eating. Sometimes we think we're hungry when we're just thirsty.
- Avoid salt, sugar, trans fats, white flour, processed foods, and most fast foods.

Gaining
Self-Awareness

Successful Students . . .

▶ **recognize when they are off course.**

▶ **identify their self-defeating patterns of thought, emotion, and behavior.**

▶ **rewrite their outdated scripts,** revising limited core beliefs and self-defeating patterns.

Struggling Students . . .

▶ **wander through life unaware of being off course.**

▶ **remain unaware of their self-defeating patterns of thought, emotion, and behavior.**

▶ **unconsciously persist in making choices based on outdated scripts,** finding themselves farther and farther off course with each passing year.

Despite all of my efforts to create success in college and in life, I may still find myself off course. Now is the perfect time to identify and revise the inner obstacles to my success.

I am consciously choosing core beliefs and habit patterns that support my success.

CASE STUDY IN CRITICAL THINKING / Strange Choices

"Do your students make really strange choices?" **Professor Assante** asked.

The other professors looked up from their lunches. "What do you mean?" one asked.

"At the beginning of each class, I give short quizzes that count as 50 percent of the final grade," Professor Assante replied. "One of my students comes late to every class, even though I keep telling her there's no way she can pass the course if she keeps missing the quizzes. But she still keeps coming late! What is she thinking?"

"That's nothing," **Professor Buckley** said. "I've got a really bright student in my online class who came to the in-person orientation, logs in to the course site almost every day, and contributes valuable comments to the discussion forums. But the semester is almost over, and he still hasn't turned in any assignments. At this point, he's too far behind to pass. Now that's what I call a strange choice."

"You think that's strange," **Professor Chang** said, "I'm teaching composition in the computer lab. Last week I sat down next to a woman who was working on her essay, and I suggested a way she could improve her introduction. I couldn't believe what she did. She swore at me, stormed out of the room, and slammed the door."

Professor Donnelly chimed in. "Well, I can top all of you. In my philosophy class, participation counts for one-third of the final grade. I've got a student this semester who hasn't said a word in 12 weeks. Even when I call on him, he just shakes his head and says something under his breath that I can't hear. One day after class, I asked him if he realized that if he didn't participate in class discussions, the best grade he could earn is a D. He just mumbled, 'I know.' Now there's a choice I don't get!"

"How about this!" **Professor Egret** said. "I had a student last semester with a B average going into the final two weeks. Then he disappeared. This semester, I ran into him on campus, and I asked what happened. 'Oh,' he said, 'I got burned out and stopped going to my classes.' 'But you only had two more weeks to go. You threw away 13 weeks of work,' I said. You know what he did? He shrugged his shoulders and walked away. I wanted to say, 'What were you thinking?'"

Professor Fanning said, "Talk about strange choices. Last week I had four business owners visit my marketing class to talk about how they promote their businesses. Near the end of the period, a student asked if the business owners had ever had problems with procrastination. While the panelists were deciding who was going to answer, I joked, 'Maybe they'd rather answer later.' Okay, it was weak humor, but most of the students chuckled, and then one panelist answered the question. The next day I got a call from the dean. The student who'd asked about procrastination told him I'd mocked her in front of the whole class, and now she's going to drop out of college. I had videoed the class, so I asked her if she'd be willing to watch the recording. Later she admitted I hadn't said what she thought I had, but she still dropped out of school. What is it with students today and their self-sabotaging choices?"

Listed below are the six professors' students. Choose the one you think made the strangest choice and speculate on why this student made the choice. Dive deeper than obvious answers such as "He's probably just shy." Why do you suppose he is shy? What past experiences might have made him this way? What might the inner conversation of his Inner Critic and Inner Defender sound like? What emotions might he often feel? What beliefs might he have about himself, other people, or the world? In what other circumstances (e.g., work, relationships, health) might a similar choice sabotage his success?

- **Professor Assante's** student
- **Professor Donnelly's** student
- **Professor Buckley's** student
- **Professor Egret's** student
- **Professor Chang's** student
- **Professor Fanning's** student

DIVING DEEPER

Recall a course you once took in which you made a choice that your instructor might describe as "strange." Explain why you made that choice. Dive deep, exploring what *really* caused your choice.

Recognizing When You Are Off Course

FOCUS QUESTIONS   In which of your life roles are you off course? Do you know how you got there? More important, do you know how to get back on course to your desired outcomes and experiences?

Take a deep breath, relax, and consider your journey so far.

You began by accepting personal responsibility for creating your life as you want it. Then you chose personally motivating goals and dreams that give purpose and direction to your life.

Next, you created a self-management plan and began taking effective actions. Most recently, you developed mutually supportive relationships to help you on your journey. Throughout, you have examined how to believe in yourself.

Despite all these efforts, you may still be off course—in college, in a relationship, in your job, or somewhere else in your life. You just aren't achieving your desired outcomes and experiences. Once again, you have an important choice to make. You can listen to the blaming, complaining, and excusing of your Inner Critic and Inner Defender. Or you can ask your Inner Guide to find answers to important questions such as . . .

- What habits do I have that sabotage my success?
- What beliefs do I have that get me off course?
- How can I consistently make wise choices that will create a rich, personally fulfilling life?

Consider this: If at first you don't succeed, something is blocking your way.

Michael Ray and
Rochelle Myers

THE MYSTERY OF SELF-SABOTAGE

Self-sabotage has probably happened to everyone who's set off on a journey to a better life. Consider my student Jerome. Fresh from high school, Jerome said his dream was to start his own accounting firm by his 30th birthday. He set long-term goals of getting his college degree and passing the CPA (certified public accountant) exam. He set short-term goals of earning an A in every class he took during his first semester. He developed a written self-management system and demonstrated interdependence by starting a study group. But at semester's end, the unthinkable happened: Jerome failed Accounting 101!

Wait a minute, though. Jerome's Inner Guide has more information. You see, Jerome made some strange choices during his first semester. He skipped his accounting class three times to work at a part-time job. On another day, he didn't attend class because he was angry with his girlfriend. Then he missed two Monday classes when he was hungover from weekend parties. He was late five times because parking was difficult to find. Jerome regularly put off doing

Progressively we discover that there are levels of experience beneath the surface, beneath our consciousness, and we realize that these may hold the key both to the problems and the potentialities of our life.

Ira Progoff

homework until the last minute because he was so busy. He didn't hand in an important assignment because he found it confusing. And he stopped going to his study group after the first meeting because . . . well, he wasn't quite sure why. As the semester progressed, Jerome's anxiety about the final exam grew. The night before, he stayed up late cramming, then went to the exam exhausted. During the test, his mind went blank.

Like Jerome, most of us have made choices that worked against our goals and dreams. We take our eyes off the path for just a moment, and some invisible force comes along and pulls us off course. By the time we realize what's happened—if, in fact, we ever do—we can be miles off course and feeling miserable.

What's going on around here, anyway?

UNCONSCIOUS FORCES

One of the most important discoveries in psychology is the existence and power of unconscious forces in our lives. We now know that experiences from our past linger in our unconscious minds long after our conscious minds have forgotten them. As a result, we're influenced in our daily choices by old experiences we don't even recall.

Dr. Wilder Penfield of the Montreal Neurological Institute found evidence that our brains may retain nearly every experience we have ever had. Dr. Penfield performed brain surgery on patients who had local anesthesia but were otherwise fully awake. During the operation, he stimulated brain cells using a weak electric current. At that moment his patients reported once again experiencing long-forgotten events in vivid detail.

Further research by neuroscientist Joseph LeDoux suggests that a part of our brains called the amygdala stores emotionally charged but now unconscious memories. The amygdala, like a nervous watchman, examines every new experience and compares it to past experiences. When a key feature of a new event is similar to a distressing event from the past, it declares a match. Then, *without our conscious knowledge,* the amygdala hijacks our rational thought processes. It causes us to respond to the present event as we learned to respond to the past event. The problem is, the outdated response is often totally inappropriate in our present situation. By the time the amygdala loosens its grip on our decision-making power, we may have made some very bad choices.

If many of the forces that get us off course are unconscious, how can we spot their sabotaging influence? By analogy, the answer appears in a fascinating discovery in astronomy. Years ago, astronomers developed a mathematical formula to predict the orbit of any planet around the sun. However, one planet, Uranus, failed to follow its predicted orbit. Astronomers were baffled as to why Uranus was "off course." Then the French astronomer Le Verrier proposed an ingenious explanation: The gravitational pull of an invisible planet was getting Uranus off course. Sure enough, when stronger telescopes were invented, the planet Neptune was discovered, and Le Verrier was proven correct.

In the entire history of science, it is hard to find a discovery of comparable consequence to the discovery of the power of unconscious belief as a gateway—or an obstacle—to the hidden mind, and its untapped potentialities.

Willis Harman

We know from surgical experiences that electrical stimulation delivered to the temporal area of the brain elicits images of events that occurred in the patient's past. This is confirmation that such memories are "stored," but in most instances they cannot be voluntarily recollected. Thus, all of us "know" more than we are aware that we know.

Richard Restak, MD

Here's the point: Like planets, we all have invisible Neptunes tugging at us every day. For us, these invisible forces are not in outer space. They exist in inner space, in our unconscious minds. As with the planet Uranus, the first clue to spotting the existence of these unconscious forces is recognizing that we are off course. So, be candid. Where are you off course in your life today? School? Relationships? Work? Health? Finances? Elsewhere? What desired outcomes and experiences are you moving away from instead of toward? What goals and dreams seem to be slipping away? Self-awareness allows you to identify that you are off course. Only then can you start making wiser choices that will get you back on course to the life you want to create.

I learned that I could not look to my exterior self to do anything for me. If I was going to accomplish anything in life, I had to start from within.

Oprah Winfrey

JOURNAL ENTRY / 20

Everyone gets off course at times, but only those who are self-aware can make a course correction to improve their lives.

1 **Write about a time when you were off course and took effective actions to get back on course.** Examples include ending an unhealthy relationship, entering college years after high school, changing careers, stopping an addiction, choosing to be more assertive, or changing a negative belief or bias you held about yourself, other people, or the world. Dive deep in your journal entry by asking and answering questions such as the following:

- In what area of my life was I off course?
- What choices had I made to get off course?
- What changes did I make to get back on course?
- What challenges did I face while making this change?
- What personal strengths helped me make this change?
- What benefits did I experience as a result of my change?
- If I hadn't made this change, what would my life be like today?

2 **Write about an area of your life in which you are off course today.** If you need help in identifying an area, review your desired outcomes and experiences from Journal Entry 8 and your goals and dreams from Journal Entry 9. Explain which area of your life is furthest from the way you would like it to be. What choices have you made that got you off course? What will be the effect on your life if you continue to stay off course?

The fact that you've made positive changes in the past is a good reminder that you have the personal strengths to make similar changes whenever you wish. All you need is the awareness that you're off course and the motivation to make new choices.

The truth is that our finest moments are most likely to occur when we are feeling deeply uncomfortable, unhappy, or unfulfilled. For it is only in such moments, propelled by our discomfort, that we are likely to step out of our ruts and start searching for different ways or truer answers.

M. Scott Peck, MD

SARAH RICHMOND, *Missouri University of Science and Technology, Missouri*

I was in the emergency room when it hit me how far off course I was. My friend Matt had driven me to the emergency room because the Student Health Center couldn't supply the antibiotics I needed for a bad sore throat. As we sat in the waiting room talking, I told Matt that I was failing math, and I broke down and cried. I told him I was doing things in college that I had never done at home. When I was in high school, my parents were very strict. They didn't let me go out late during the week, and they'd wake me up in the morning to make sure I went to school. But in college, no one cares if you stay out all night or even if you get up and go to class. I had adopted "Why not?" as my motto, and I started doing things I knew I shouldn't be doing. My weekends had become a blur of boys and parties, and I had even started partying during the week. The parties I went to in high school were mostly small girls' nights, nothing like the drunken fraternity parties I was going to on campus. In high school I was one of the smart kids, and even though

I hardly ever studied, I was an honor student. But college was different. I was doing terrible in math and not much better in biology. It was a shock to not do as well as I had in high school.

I started getting a bleak outlook on life, and I didn't really want to be at the university. I had no idea what I wanted to major in. I thought of myself as lazy and irresponsible. I remember telling one of my friends that I should just get married, have kids, and then I'd probably be divorced by 40. After that I'd spend the rest of my life in a lousy job, struggling to survive. I felt like I couldn't do anything right. I don't know why I let everything bother me so much, but I felt awful.

Talking with Matt in the emergency room, I started realizing how lonely I felt in college. I missed my family, especially my sister. I wasn't getting along with my roommate, and we competed about everything: going out, boys, drinking, staying up late, playing video games, you name it. A lot of the students at my university are really into playing *Halo*. I tried to fit in, but I'm no good

at video games. At my school, if you're not in engineering, they tease you nonstop. One time a guy picked up my *On Course* book and starting teasing me about the class. "So what do you do in that class," he asked, "sit around and talk about your *feelings?*" I didn't bother saying that the course helped me think things out, things I wouldn't have thought about, like all of the mistakes I was making.

That day in the emergency room was my wake-up call. Sitting there talking with Matt, I not only realized that I was way off course, I also realized that deep down I didn't believe in myself, and therefore I couldn't take actions today to improve my tomorrow. After that, I realized I had to make some dramatic changes. I got a new roommate, stopped partying, buckled down, and passed my math class. That was two years ago. Today I'm a junior and my life is very different. I've found a major that I love, I just finished an internship that was great, and my GPA is 3.4. Making positive changes isn't always easy. But my life started to get better that day in the emergency room when I took a good look at myself and realized just how far off course I was.

Photo: Courtesy of Sarah Richmond.

Identifying Your Scripts

What habit patterns in your life get you off course? How did these habit patterns develop?

Once you realize you're off course, you need to figure out how to get back on course. This can be tricky. The forces pulling us off course are often just as invisible to us as the planet Neptune was to Le Verrier and his fellow observers of outer space.

As observers of inner space, psychologists seek to identify what they can't actually see: the internal forces that divert human potential into disappointment. In various psychological theories, these unconscious inner forces have been called names such as ego defenses, conditioned responses, programs, mental tapes, blind spots, schemas, and life traps.

The term I like best to describe our unconscious internal forces was coined by psychologist Eric Berne: **scripts**. In the world of theater, a script tells an actor what words, actions, and emotions to perform onstage. When the actor gets a cue from others in the play, he doesn't make a choice about his response. He responds automatically as his script directs. Performance after performance, he reacts the same way to the same cues.

Responding automatically from a dramatic script is one sure way to succeed as an actor. However, responding automatically from a limiting *life* script is one sure way to struggle as a human being.

> A psychological script is a person's ongoing program for his life drama which dictates where he is going with his life and how he is to get there. It is a drama he compulsively acts out, though his awareness of it may be vague.
>
> Muriel James and
> Dorothy Jongeward

ANATOMY OF A SCRIPT

Everyone has scripts. I do, your instructors do, your classmates do, you do. Some scripts have helped us achieve our present success. Other scripts may be getting us off course from our goals and dreams. Becoming aware of our unique personal scripts helps us make wise choices at each fork in the road, choices that help us create the life we want.

Scripts are composed of two parts. Closest to the surface of our awareness reside the directions for how we are to think, feel, and behave. **Thought patterns** include habitual self-talk such as *I'm too busy, I'm good at math, People different from me are a threat, I always screw up, The way we do things around here is the right way so all other ways must be wrong, I can't write*. **Emotional patterns** include habitual feelings such as anger, excitement, anxiety, sadness, and joy. **Behavior patterns** include habitual actions such as smoking cigarettes, criticizing others, arriving on time, never asking for help, and exercising regularly. When people know us well, they can often predict what we will say, feel, or do in a given situation. This ability reveals their recognition of our patterns.

Deeper in our unconscious mind lies the second, and more elusive, part of our scripts, our **core beliefs**. Early in life, we form core beliefs about the world (*The world is safe* or *The world is dangerous*), about other people (*People can be trusted* or *People can't be trusted*), and about ourselves (*I'm worthy* or *I'm unworthy*). Though we're seldom aware of our core beliefs, these unconscious judgments dictate what we consistently think, feel, and do.

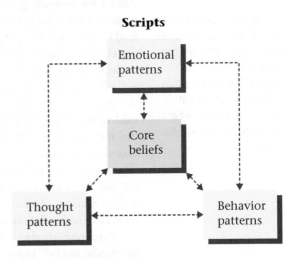

Scripts

Emotional patterns

Core beliefs

Thought patterns

Behavior patterns

These beliefs become the lenses through which we see the world. Whether accurate or distorted, our beliefs dictate the choices we make at each fork in the road. What do you believe that causes you to make choices that other people think are strange? More important, what do you believe that keeps you from creating the outcomes and experiences you want?

HOW WE WROTE OUR SCRIPTS

Though no one knows exactly how we wrote our life scripts as children, reasonable explanations exist. One factor seems to be **how others responded to us**. Imagine this scene: You're two years old. You're feeling lonely and hungry, and you begin to cry. Your mother hurries in to pick you up. "There, there," she croons. "It's all right." She hugs you, feeds you, sings to you. You fall asleep full and content. If this happens often enough, what do you suppose you'd decide about the world, about other people, about yourself? Probably you'd believe *The world is kind; People will help me; I am lovable.* In turn, these beliefs would dictate your thoughts, emotions, and behaviors. With positive beliefs such as these at the core of your scripts, you'd very likely develop optimistic thought patterns (*If I ask, I'll get help*), positive emotional patterns (joy and enthusiasm), and empowering behavior patterns (asking for what you want).

Now imagine the same childhood scene with a different response. You cry but no one comes. You scream louder, but still no one comes. Finally you abandon hope that anyone will respond. You cry yourself to sleep, alone and hungry. Imagine also that being ignored happens often. You'd probably develop core beliefs such as *The world doesn't care about me; People won't help me; I'm not important.* You could very well develop pessimistic thought patterns (*I'm alone*), negative emotional patterns (anxiety and anger), and passive behavior patterns (not asking for what you want).

Now, imagine this scene one more time. As you're crying for attention and food, an adult storms into your room, screams "Shut up!" and slaps your face. After a few wounding experiences like this, you may decide *The world is a dangerous and painful place; People will hurt me; I'm unlovable!* These beliefs may lead to defensive thought patterns (*People are out to get me*), defensive emotional patterns (fear and rage), and defensive behavior patterns (immediately fighting or fleeing at the first sign of danger). Imagine how easily these patterns could get you off course later in life.

A second factor that seems to shape our scripts is **what significant adults said to us**. What did they say about the world: Is it safe or dangerous? What did they say about other people, especially those who are different from us: Can they be trusted or not? And, perhaps most important, what did important adults say about us? Psychologists have a term for qualities that tell us how we "are" or "should be": **attributions**. Common attributions tell us to be *good, quiet, rebellious, devoted, helpful, athletic, sexy, tough, independent, dependent, invisible, macho, dominant, competitive, smart, shy,* or *confident.*

Psychologists also have a term for the qualities that tell us what we "are not" or "should not be": **injunctions**. Common injunctions include *don't be yourself,* *don't talk back, don't feel, don't think, don't be intimate, don't say no, don't say yes, don't get angry, don't trust people who are different from you, don't show your feelings, don't love yourself, don't be happy, don't be weak, don't believe in yourself, don't exist.*

A third way we seem to write our scripts is by **observing the behavior of significant adults**. Children notice, *What did important adults do? If it's right for them, it's right for me.* When children play, we see them trying on adult behaviors, conversations, and emotions. It doesn't take a detective to figure out where they learned them. From significant adults we learn not only our unique personal scripts but our cultural programs as well. For example, some cultures believe we shape our future through our personal choices, whereas other cultures believe our future is determined by forces beyond our direct control. Some cultures place emphasis on future accomplishments, whereas others focus on the present or past. Some cultures are very time sensitive, whereas others are more relaxed about time. Some cultures encourage individuality, whereas others place family and community above all other concerns. Each belief is deeply embedded in the culture and becomes the lens through which its members see the world, influencing their choices, whether or not they are aware of the beliefs.

In these ways we each develop our personal scripts and cultural programs. Each is comprised of core beliefs and their resulting patterns of thoughts, feelings, and behaviors. At critical choice points, especially when we are under stress, we unconsciously default to our personal scripts and cultural programs for guidance.

The good news about our unconscious scripts and programs is that their intention is always positive—always to minimize our pain, always to maximize our pleasure. They help us adapt to the family and society in which we are born. Many of us made it through the mental, emotional, and physical challenges of growing up with the help of our childhood scripts and programs. Some of us would not have survived without them.

But, as you might guess, there is bad news as well: When we make unconscious choices as adults, we often get off course. That's because the scripts and programs we developed in childhood often do not apply to the situations of our present lives. Imagine an adult who can't stop playing a role he or she learned years ago for a grade school play! Many of us do the equivalent of this in our daily lives.

To others, a choice I make may seem strange. To me, it makes perfect sense. The important issue, though, is: Do my habitual choices help or hinder me in the pursuit of the life I want to create? To answer this question, I need to take three steps. First, I need to become aware of my Neptunes, that is, my unconscious beliefs, attitudes, biases, norms, prejudices, and values. Second, I need to assess which of my mindsets help and which hinder me in the pursuit of my goals and dreams. And finally, I need to keep and strengthen the habits that help me while revising or replacing the ones that hinder me. And it all starts with self-awareness.

By the time we are adults, we have learned many cultural rules of behavior and have practiced those rules so much that they are second nature to us. Much of our behavior as adults is influenced by these learned patterns and rules, and we are so well practiced at them that we engage in these behaviors automatically and unconsciously.

David Matsumoto and Linda Juang

The more you are keenly aware of your misery-creating thoughts, feelings, and behaviors, the greater your chances are of ridding yourself of them.

Albert Ellis

SELF-DEFEATING HABIT PATTERNS

Though our unconscious scripts are as invisible to us as the planet Neptune was to early astronomers, we can often see their influence in our lives. Put a check next to any of the following patterns of thought, emotion, and behavior that are often true of you. These habits may reveal the presence of personal scripts or cultural programs that get you off course. In particular, see if you can identify any habits that may have taken you off course in the area you wrote about in Journal Entry 20.

☐ 1. I waste a lot of time doing unimportant things (television, video gaming).

☐ 2. I wonder if I'm "college material."

☐ 3. I easily get upset (angry, sad, anxious, depressed, guilty, frustrated).

☐ 4. I hang out with people who don't support my academic goals.

☐ 5. I believe that most people don't like me.

☐ 6. I often turn in college assignments late.

☐ 7. I don't like to post any of my thoughts in the online class forum because I don't want people to know what I really think.

☐ 8. I worry excessively about doing things perfectly.

☐ 9. I think most of my classmates are smarter than I am.

☐ 10. I quit things that are important to me.

☐ 11. I allow a person in my life to treat me badly.

☐ 12. I don't believe I deserve success as much as other people do.

☐ 13. I miss more college classes than I should.

☐ 14. I'm very critical of myself.

☐ 15. I wait until the last minute to do important college assignments.

☐ 16. I don't ask questions in class or participate in class discussions.

☐ 17. I often break promises I have made to myself or others.

☐ 18. I am addicted to something (caffeine, alcohol, cigarettes, soft drinks, video gaming, social networking websites, drugs).

☐ 19. I experience severe test anxiety.

☐ 20. I feel uncomfortable about asking for help.

☐ 21. I have strong negative feelings about a particular group of people who are different from me.

☐ 22. I often side-talk or daydream in my college classes.

☐ 23. I seldom do my best work on college assignments.

☐ 24. I am very critical of other people.

☐ 25. I get extremely nervous when I speak to a group.

☐ 26. I keep promising to study more in college, but I don't.

☐ 27. I get my feelings hurt easily.

The grooves of mindlessness run deep. We know our scripts by heart.

Ellen J. Langer

☐ **28.** I am a loner.

☐ **29.** I keep enrolling in online classes and then dropping them within the first few weeks of the semester.

☐ **30.** I get defensive when someone gives me feedback that I did something wrong.

☐ **31.** I . . . _____

☐ **32.** I . . . _____

Are you aware of any other of your patterns—mental, emotional, or behavioral? If so, add them to the list.

JOURNAL ENTRY / 21

In this activity, you will explore self-defeating patterns in your life that may reveal unconscious scripts. You're about to embark on an exciting journey into your inner world! There you can discover—and later revise—the invisible forces that have taken you off course from your goals and dreams.

❶ Write about one of your self-defeating *behavior* patterns. Choose a behavior pattern that you checked on the list or identify a self-defeating behavior that isn't on the list but that you do often. Remember, a behavior is something someone else can see you do. Develop your journal paragraphs by anticipating questions that someone reading them might have about this behavior pattern. (Even you might have questions when you read your journal 10 years from now.) For example:

- What exactly is your self-defeating behavior pattern?
- What are some specific examples of when you did this behavior?
- What may have caused this habit?
- What undesirable effects has it had on your life?
- How would your life be improved if you changed it?

One student began by writing, "One of my self-defeating behavior patterns is that I seldom do my best work on college assignments. For example, in my biology lab . . ."

❷ Repeat Step 1 for one of your self-defeating *thought* patterns or for one of your self-defeating *emotional* patterns. Once again, choose a pattern that you checked on the list, or identify a habit that isn't on the list but that you often think or feel. You might begin, *One of my self-defeating thought patterns is that I often wonder if I'm smart enough to be successful in college. I especially think this during exams. For example, last Thursday I . . .* Or . . . *One of my self-defeating emotional patterns is that I often feel frustrated. For example . . .*

It is not true that life is one damn thing after another—it's one damn thing over and over.

Edna St. Vincent Millay,
American poet

All serious daring starts from within.

Eudora Welty

ONE STUDENT'S STORY

JAMES FLORIOLLI, *Foothill College, California*

At different points in my life, I've given up when I ran into a challenge. As a child, I loved baseball, but when I got hit in the face with a ball, I stopped playing. In school, I started having problems with my writing skills, and I was diagnosed with a learning disability. I got all kinds of accommodations, even more than I deserved, and I started goofing off. I convinced myself that success was getting the best grades possible with the least amount of work. After high school, college didn't seem like a viable option, so I joined the Marine Corps Reserve. Boot camp was even harder than I thought it would be. Once again, I used the minimum amount of effort necessary to complete each task, and I failed to achieve the level of success in the Marines that I could have. When I left the Marines to get a civilian job, I defined success as getting maximum compensation for minimum effort.

I got a job at the phone company and at first it seemed perfect. I'm very well paid for very little effort. However, this situation isn't as rewarding as I thought it would be. After a few years I began to want a greater challenge. I knew I needed an education to advance in the workplace, so I started taking college courses part-time. For the first year I avoided classes that involved a lot of writing, as I was still intimidated by past failures in this area. But when poor writing began to affect my grades in other courses, I decided to take a composition class. In that class we read *On Course,* and in the chapter about self-awareness, I began to see how negative scripts could cause problems. I started wondering if there was a script contributing to the frustration I was feeling in my life. An idea kept coming up that at first I was unwilling to accept. I had always thought of myself as a hard worker, but looking back on my life I could not deny there were challenges I had run away from. When baseball had required extra work to get past my fear of the ball, I quit. When school stopped coming easily to me, I quit. When I realized how hard I'd have to work to be a success in the Marines, I quit. Seeing this pattern was powerful for me. Finally, I felt like I understood how I ended up in the situation I am in. I realized that I'll do anything to avoid feeling bad. If I feel down in any way, I'm willing to throw everything out the window to feel better. In the past, I have doubted myself and been afraid to take risks. I overvalued security and undervalued me. I need to believe I am capable of accomplishing anything I want to.

Soon I have to pick my college major. One option is to get a computer science degree and continue working at the phone company. This would probably lead to the greatest profit and security. Or, I could choose a major that would prepare me for my dream job working in the front office of a professional baseball team. Obviously, going for my dream would be very difficult and call for a large initial pay cut. Knowing I have an issue with not following through on my most challenging commitments, I need to set my goals very carefully. No matter what I choose, I hope that when everything is said and done I will be proud of what I have accomplished. This will mean I have successfully revised my negative script of running from important challenges in my life.

Rewriting Your Outdated Scripts

FOCUS QUESTION   How can you revise self-defeating scripts that keep you from achieving your full potential?

Once, in a writing class, I was explaining how to organize an essay when a student named Diana told me she didn't understand. She asked if I'd write an explanation on the board.

Earlier in the class, we'd been talking about the differences between left-brain and right-brain thinking. We'd discussed how the left side of the brain deals with logical, organized information, while the right side deals with more creative, intuitive concepts. "No problem," I said to Diana, "I hear your left brain crying out for some order. Let's see if I can help."

As I turned to write on the blackboard, she screamed, "You have no right to talk to me that way!"

I was stunned. Talk about a strange response! I took a deep breath to compose myself. "Maybe we could talk about this after class," I said.

THE IMPACT OF OUTDATED BELIEFS

Diana and I did talk, and I learned that she was in her late 30s, a single mother of an 8-year-old daughter. Our conversation wandered for a while, then Diana mentioned that she had always disliked school. In elementary school, she had consistently gotten low grades, while her sister consistently earned A's. One day, when Diana was about 12, she overheard her father and mother talking about her poor report card. "I don't know what we're going to do with Diana," her father said. "She's the *half-brain* of the family." (Do you see it yet . . . what got Diana upset with me?)

Diana accepted as a fact other people's belief that she couldn't think or learn. She developed patterns of thought, emotion, and behavior that supported this belief. She decided that school was a waste of time (thought), she exploded when anyone questioned her about schoolwork (emotion), and she was often absent (behavior). Diana barely graduated from high school, then got a menial job that bored her.

For nearly 20 years, Diana heard her Inner Critic (sounding much like her father) telling her that something was wrong with her brain. Finally, another inner voice began to whisper, *Maybe—just maybe.* . . . Then one day she took a big risk and enrolled in college.

"So what happens?" she said, getting angry again. "I get a teacher who calls me a *half-brain!* I knew this would happen. I ought to just quit."

I used my best active listening skills: I listened to understand. I reflected both her thoughts and her anger. I asked her to clarify and expand. I allowed long periods of silence.

Finally, her emotional storm subsided. She took a deep breath and sat back.

I waited a few moments. "Diana, I know you think I called you a 'half-brain.' But what I actually said was *left* brain. Remember we had been talking in class about the difference between left-brain and right-brain thinking? Two different approaches to planning your essay? I was talking about that."

"But I *heard* you!"

"I know that's what you *heard*. But that isn't what I *said*. I've read two of your essays, and I know your brain works just fine. What really matters, though, is what *you* think! You need to believe in your own intelligence. Otherwise, you'll always be ready to hear people call you a 'half-brain' no matter what they really said. Worse, you'll always believe it yourself."

W e don't see things as they are, we see them as we are.

Anaïs Nin

W e are what we think. All that we are arises with our thoughts. With our thoughts, we make the world.

Buddha

Imagine how difficult it is to make wise choices when you hold the core belief "I am a half-brain." Diana had come within an inch of dropping out of college, of abandoning her dreams of a college degree. And all because of her childhood script.

DOING THE REWRITE

Until we revise our limiting scripts, we're less likely to achieve some of our most cherished goals and dreams. That's why realizing we're off course can be a blessing in disguise. By identifying the self-defeating patterns of thought, emotion, and behavior that take us off course, we may be able to discover and revise the underlying core beliefs that are sabotaging our success.

Diana stuck it out and passed English 101. She persevered and graduated with an Associate of Arts degree in early childhood education. When I spoke to her last, she was working at a nursery school and talking about returning to college to finish her bachelor's degree. Like most of us, she'll probably be in a tug-of-war with her scripts for the rest of her life. But now, at least, she knows that she, and not her scripts, can be in charge of making her choices.

One of the great discoveries about the human condition is this: We are not stuck with our personal scripts or cultural programming. We can re-create ourselves. We can keep what works and change what doesn't. By revising outdated scripts, we can get back on course and dramatically improve the outcomes and experiences of our lives.

> In developing our own self-awareness many of us discover ineffective scripts, deeply embedded habits that are totally unworthy of us, totally incongruent with the things we really value in life.
>
> Stephen Covey

JOURNAL ENTRY   22

In this activity, you'll practice revising your scripts, thus taking greater control of your life. As in Journal Entry 17, you'll once again write a conversation with your Inner Guide, a critical thinking skill that empowers you to become your own best coach, counselor, mentor, and guide through challenging times. This practical application of critical thinking greatly enhances your self-awareness, helping you take greater responsibility for making the wise choices necessary to create your desired outcomes and experiences:

1 **Write a dialogue with your Inner Guide that will help you revise your self-sabotaging scripts.**

Have your Inner Guide ask you the following 10 questions. After answering each question, let your Inner Guide use one or more of the active listening skills to help you dive deeper:

- **Silence** (demonstrating that you are paying close attention to the speaker)
- **Reflection** (expressing in your own words what you think the speaker is saying and feeling)

▶

- **Expansion** (requesting examples, evidence, and experiences)
- **Clarification** (asking for an explanation)

Ten questions from your Inner Guide:

1. In what area of your life are you off course?
2. What self-defeating **thought patterns** of yours may have contributed to this situation?
3. What different thoughts could you choose to get back on course?
4. What self-defeating **emotional patterns** of yours may have contributed to this situation?
5. What different emotions could you choose to get back on course?
6. What self-defeating **behavior patterns** of yours may have contributed to this situation?
7. What different behaviors could you choose to get back on course?
8. What limiting **core beliefs** of yours (about the world, other people, or yourself) may have led you to adopt the self-defeating patterns that we've been discussing?
9. What different beliefs could you choose to get back on course?
10. As a result of what you've learned here, what new behaviors, thoughts, emotions, or core beliefs will you adopt?

A sample dialogue follows.

Sample Dialogue with Your Inner Guide

IG: In what area of your life are you off course? (Question 1)

ME: My grades are terrible this semester.

IG: Would you say more about that? **(Expansion)**

ME: In high school I got mostly A's and B's even though I played three sports. My goal this semester is to have at least a 3.5 grade point average, but the way things are going, I'll be lucky if I even get a 2.0.

IG: What self-defeating **thought patterns** of yours may have contributed to this situation? (Question 2)

ME: I guess I tell myself I shouldn't have to work hard to get good grades in college.

IG: Why do you think that? Is there a deeper meaning? **(Clarification)**

ME: If I have to study hard, then I must not be very smart.

IG: That's a good awareness! What different thoughts could you choose to get back on course to your goal of getting at least a 3.5 average? (Question 3)

> It is a marvelous faculty of the human mind that we are also able to stop old programming from holding us back, anytime we choose to. That gift is called conscious choice.
>
> Shad Helmstetter

▶

Until you make the unconscious conscious, it will direct your life and you will call it fate.

Carl Jung

Whatever we believe about ourselves and our ability comes true for us.

Susan L. Taylor,
former editor in chief,
Essence magazine

JOURNAL ENTRY / **22** *continued*

ME: I could remind myself that going to college is like moving from the minor leagues to the major leagues. The challenge is a lot greater, and I better start studying like a major league student or I'm not going to succeed.

IG: What self-defeating **emotional patterns** of yours may have contributed to this situation? (Question 4)

ME: I get really frustrated when I don't understand something right away.

IG: So you want to understand it immediately. **(Reflection)**

ME: Absolutely. When I don't get it right away, I switch to something else.

IG: That's understandable since everything came so easy to you in high school. What different emotion could you choose to get you back on course to your goal of a 3.5 GPA? (Question 5)

ME: I could do the same thing I do in basketball when the coach asks me to shut down the other team's top scorer. I can psych myself up and push myself to study harder. My college degree is worth a lot more to me than winning a basketball game.

IG: What self-defeating **behavior patterns** of yours may have contributed to this situation? (Question 6)

ME: Like I said before, I get frustrated when I don't understand something right away, and then I put it aside. I always plan to come back to it later, but usually I don't.

IG: Are there any other self-defeating behaviors you can think of? **(Expansion)**

ME: I don't ask my teachers for help or go to the tutoring center either. I guess I hate asking for help. It's like admitting that I'm not very smart.

IG: There's that concern again about not being smart enough. **(Reflection)**

ME: I hadn't realized my Inner Critic is so loud!

IG: Now you can prove your Inner Critic wrong. What different behaviors could you choose to get back on course to your goal? (Question 7)

ME: I could ask my teachers for more help and go to the tutoring center. Also, when I set homework aside, I could write on my calendar when I'm going to work on it again. I'm really good about doing things that I write down.

IG: I like it! What limiting **core beliefs** of yours (about the world, other people, or yourself) may have led you to adopt the self-defeating patterns that we've been discussing? (Question 8)

ME: This conversation has made me realize I have some doubts about whether I'm as smart as I think I am. Maybe I don't

▶

believe I can really succeed in college unless studying comes easy for me. Maybe I got a little spoiled and lazy in high school.

IG: What different core belief could you choose to get back on course to your goal? (Question 9)

ME: I can succeed in college if I'm willing to do the work . . . and give it my best.

IG: That's great! Do the work and do your best! As a result of what you've learned here, what new behaviors, thoughts, emotions, or core beliefs will you commit to? (Question 10)

ME: When I feel like putting an assignment aside, I'll work on it for at least 15 more minutes. Then, if I stop before I'm finished, I'll write on my calendar when I'm going to work on it again and I'll go back and finish it later. If I'm still having trouble with the assignment, I'll ask my professor for help. And I'll keep reminding myself, "Do the work and do my best." If that doesn't help, I'll be back to talk to you some more. I *will* get a 3.5 average! Thanks for listening.

Mrs. Turner, my seventh-grade math teacher, lives in my head. I haven't seen her in more than 30 years, but I can still picture her on the day I went up to her desk at the front of the room. She had fair skin, long brown hair, and hazel eyes. I can see her elbows on her big wooden desk, her eyes staring off into the distance, clicking the nail of a finger against the nail on her thumb. When I asked her to help explain the math, she turned and waved my paper at me and told me I was too stupid to learn math. All these years later, I can still hear her words. *I have no idea why you even come to this class, Annette. You're never going to pass math. You're just stupid.* Then she dismissed me with a wave of her hand.

I grew up in Houston, Texas, in the 1970s. College was something that rich, smart people did. It wasn't an option for poor Hispanic children living in the barrio. In our neighborhood, no one talked about going to college. Conversations were about drug dealers, drive-bys, and the latest girl who'd been beaten up by her husband. Our biggest goal in life was to survive. Like many of my friends, I dropped out of school. I got married at 15 and had two children by the time I was 17. After my brother got his GED in the military in 1980, he talked me into getting a GED, too. That diploma qualified me for higher-paying jobs, like working security in a chemical plant or loading

ATM machines. But they were all boring jobs that required physical labor, and I wasn't very happy.

Now fast-forward to 2005. That's when I was diagnosed with rheumatoid arthritis. The doctor said I couldn't work at physical jobs anymore, and I became eligible for a rehabilitation program that offered an opportunity for me to attend college. When I started my first semester at the age of 46, I was overwhelmed and scared. The campus seemed huge. I was intimidated by all of the young students and the academic requirements that I didn't understand. The teachers said, "Here's your syllabus," but I had no idea what a "syllabus" was. My English teacher told us to do our research paper in MLA format, but I had no idea what that meant either. I didn't want to ask because I figured everyone else knew. So I pretended I knew, too. I walked around campus with my head down and watched the cement. If I had a problem and someone didn't say, *Can I help you?* I would just try to figure it out on my own.

One of my courses was called Strategic Learning, where we read *On Course*. In this class I learned to overcome my fears and accept every challenge placed before me. It helped me become armed with the belief that the choices I make and the strategies I use are what will determine what happens to me. I learned to combat the scripts in

my head that were saying *You're not smart enough; You can't do this; You'll never be a good college student.* I replaced those negative thoughts with *I can do this; I will do whatever it takes to get the work done; Only I can change my path.* It's a good thing I had this class, because I was also taking math. Mrs. Turner was still in my head telling me I was stupid and would never pass math. Instead of giving in like I had when I was in her class, I tried my newly learned strategies with determination. One thing I did was take inspirational quotations from *On Course* and write them on my workspace wall at home. When I feel like giving up, I read them out loud. Then I remind myself that I am just as smart as my younger classmates and I can accomplish my dreams just as well as they can. I'm willing to do whatever it takes, even if that means spending 40 hours a week in tutoring. Maybe I'll never be a great math student, but I did pass the course.

I'm now in my fourth semester in college, and I walk across campus with my head up. When I see another student who's confused, I offer to help. I've even used some of the *On Course* techniques to encourage other students who have the same obstacles I had. The course made me a stronger person and helped me change my life. Still, I get sad when I realize that I believed Mrs. Turner for so long. I wasted a lot of years listening to her criticisms in my mind, and for a long time let her steal my thunder of achievement.

Photo: Courtesy of Annette Valle.

SELF-AWARENESS / at Work

Awareness is a key ingredient in success. If you have it, teach it; if you lack it, seek it.

—Michael Kitson, author and founder, OCG Creative, Inc. (branding and marketing agency)

We all make some mistakes, at work and at college. Can they be helpful? Yes, if we have a high level of self-awareness. Self-awareness allows us to benefit from our mistakes, because if we have awareness of the choices we've made in the past, we can learn how to make better choices in the future. Without self-awareness, we'd simply repeat the same mistakes again and again. One reason we repeat mistakes is that we each have blind spots, patterns of behavior of which we are unaware. Blind spots prevent us from seeing all of our choices clearly. The greater our self-awareness, the easier it is to become aware of our blind spots and make wiser choices. Because simple awareness of our patterns doesn't always lead to change, the next step is engaging responsibility to make a different choice the next time. With responsibility, being *self*-aware of our mistakes means we're prepared and willing to learn from them. This type of self-awareness will help ensure your success not just in college, but in getting—and excelling in—your dream career.

SELF-AWARENESS AT WORK

Does self-awareness also improve work performance? In 2013, researchers David Zes and Dana Landis examined 486 companies. They discovered that companies with employees who had higher self-awareness financially outperformed other companies. A 2010 study by Dr. Becky Winkler with Professor John Hausknecht (Cornell University) found that when measuring numerous leadership qualities, a high score on self-awareness was the best predictor of success for top executives.

Strengthening your self-awareness in college will help you succeed at work because you'll be better able to (1) develop a personal "brand" that sets you apart from other applicants, (2) make a strong positive impression in your job interview, and (3) excel on the job, receiving consistently positive performance reviews.

PERSONAL BRANDING

Even before you enter the job market, you can begin developing your own personal "brand." This effort is your first step in separating yourself from the crowd of other applicants for your future dream job. You're probably very familiar with major company brands. The Nike swoosh, a logo that's part of Nike branding, is recognized across the world. People associate Nike with more than shoes and sportswear. They connect the company brand with a lifestyle that includes celebrities, success, and determination to "Just do it." Like Nike, Apple is one of the most famous branded companies. Apple's customers are extremely loyal to Apple products, paying a premium for phones and computers because they feel a personal connection to the brand. They believe in Apple's innovation, and they feel emotional about Apple products and the experience of using its devices. Developing a successful brand is worth billions of dollars in company value.

Developing your personal brand is one of the latest career preparation and success strategies. Like company branding, personal branding will provide tremendous value for you, too. Self-awareness will help you recognize the factors—essentially, your personal brand—that allow you to gain an interview, excel in that interview and get hired, and earn great performance reviews in your job. Your goal in personal branding is to establish yourself as valuable and unique. You want to show that you'll be an asset at your future workplace. You can also brand

▶

yourself at college when you focus on actions that represent you as a student. You can incorporate your personal brand into your résumé, your LinkedIn profile, and other social media sites, as well as in cover letters or scholarship essays. Does personal branding actually help you get a job? According to a 2010 study commissioned by Microsoft, nearly 50 percent of job recruiters report that a positive online reputation has a major influence on their hiring decision. That means that an effective personal brand can help you get hired!

How can you ensure that you are effective at branding? There are four steps to create your personal brand:

1. **Define yourself.** Write down your core values. What are your most essential academic and career goals and dreams? What are your top skills and strengths? (If you're not sure what your top skills and strengths are, ask a manager or instructor who knows you well.) Then choose some powerful adjectives that capture the very core of who you are—your brand. Are you open-minded, resourceful, entrepreneurial? Are you creative, hardworking, persistent? Be accurate and honest in representing and promoting yourself. Once you have written the adjectives down, run them by someone you trust to make sure it's how they see you, too.

2. **Position yourself as unique and valuable.** Determine what sets you apart from others. Each time you reach out to others, promote your strengths and your most compelling attributes. For example, you might capture your brand in a short statement you use with your email signature ("Always looking for new ideas . . ."). Consider how you want others to think of you. Create an argument for why someone should hire you. Use this argument

at college to apply for scholarships or internships. For example, perhaps your argument is "You should hire me because I am innovative and organized." When you apply for scholarships or internships, you can develop your essays/applications with examples of how you're innovative and organized. If you're self-aware, you'll be proactive in demonstrating how your being innovative and organized will provide value to the company where you'd like to work or intern. Having a personal brand and knowing how to articulate it in a scholarship essay, cover letter, or interview will make it easy for someone on a hiring or scholarship selection committee to see your value. There's nobody else like you out there!

3. **Build your brand.** Your brand is constructed by your everyday actions with others and through your social media accounts. You'll want to make consistent, wise choices that align with your personal brand. In your social media postings, showcase your core qualities and desires. For example, if your personal brand is that you are entrepreneurial (ambitious in seeking new business opportunities), you might use social media to post stories or pictures of the tutoring or weekend landscaping business you started. Define yourself with a story that captures your life choices and ambitions. Your story should reveal and illustrate your brand. If your brand is that you're great at communicating with people around the world, you might create your story by posting travel photos from various states or countries that show you interacting with local residents. You could share articles about effective communication skills, or retweet examples of funny (but appropriate) communication breakdowns. You can post updates

▶

about new languages you are learning. By seeking fresh opportunities that illustrate your story, you're actually building your brand! Share your brand with your college and professional networks.

4. **Manage your brand reputation.** Avoid making unwise choices that tarnish your brand in the eyes of others. Be responsible, committed, and reliable in your behavior. Act consistently in alignment with your values and goals. Work hard and maintain a positive attitude. Imagine what others might Yelp about their experiences with you. How many stars might they assign to their interaction with you? Would they say that you delivered what you promised in your branding? Would other students report a favorable interaction with you? Would your coworkers find your actions consistent with your stated intentions? One way to make sure you're managing your brand reputation effectively is to ask for feedback from your instructors, classmates, coworkers, or even social media followers. We'll explore how to use feedback to increase your self-awareness later on.

The former Apple CEO Steve Jobs once said, "The chance to make a memory is the essence of brand marketing." What do others remember about you after you walk away? What are the lasting impressions you want people to have when you interact with them? If you act consistently with what you value most, showing others what you're all about from your actions, you will have developed a powerful personal brand, both at college and at work.

SELF-AWARENESS SKILLS FOR INTERVIEWING

Self-awareness is essential when you interview for jobs. Self-awareness helps you prepare well for the interview process by allowing you to plan what you want to convey during your interview—that you're the best candidate out there for the job! Being self-aware of what message you want to send during your interview also means you have a better chance of actually communicating that message. For example, once you've identified your strengths, being self-aware means you'll know how to show how those strengths will help the company succeed. The following are 10 interview strategies you can employ to improve your chances of getting hired. You can also practice these strategies in college for scholarship or internship interviews:

1. **Research the company.** Visit the company website, read press releases, and review social media posts. Learn about upcoming events or product launches. Research recent news articles about company performance and products. Write down a few actual statistics about the company, like number of stores, last year's revenue, or the number of Facebook followers. Try their products and services yourself. Learn something about competing companies and a few major trends in the industry. Generate a few questions that show you've done your homework. Doing so means that not only are you aware of what the company is doing, you're also self-aware of how you can help the company pursue its goals.

2. **Clarify the interview format.** Request information from the interviewer about the format of the interview. If it's a technical interview, it will be focused on direct, everyday job performance skills. Be prepared to demonstrate specific skills or solve problems. If it's a behavioral interview, it will be focused on soft skills and demonstrating effective interdependence. You'll benefit from self-awareness while preparing examples of your working style, choices you've made under pressure, and how you respond to difficult people. Ask who else will be in attendance during the interview and what their position is. If the interviewer

▶

shares this information, you can learn more about the background of each person and prepare a question for each of them.

3. **Prepare for your interview.** Get clear about why you want the position. Be ready to explain why it's a good match for your interests and strengths. Create a one-page interview preparation sheet that includes company facts, how the position is a good match for you, what your top strengths are (don't forget to prepare brief stories and specific examples to illustrate these strengths!), some areas you're eager to improve, and two to three questions to ask. Sleep well the night before so your brain is sharp.

4. **Practice sharing strengths, telling stories, and answering tough questions.** Engaging in practice interviews can be very helpful to simulate the interview environment. Practice getting across your strengths clearly and concisely. Rehearse several short stories that give examples of these strengths in action. Practice asking questions of the interviewer. Get someone else to ask you some difficult questions. Practice your opening response. Review your interview preparation sheet multiple times. Rehearse your closing comments. The more often you practice, the easier it will be to sound natural and confident about your answers.

5. **Start strong and share your skills.** A quick, positive first impression makes a big difference. Research from the *Journal of Occupational and Organizational Psychology* reveals that 30 percent of hiring decisions are made within the first 5 minutes of the interview, and more than 50 percent between 5 and 15 minutes. Show up early and start with genuine excitement, thanking your interviewer for his or her time. Share a sincere

reason why you'd be thrilled to work with this company. Take the first opportunity to discuss your top three skills that are a match for the position description. One of the most common interview questions is "tell me about yourself." Another is "tell me why we should hire you for this job." Being self-aware and having a personal brand will really help with your answers. Instead of a vague answer about where you go to school, what you like to do, or that the job seems a good fit for you, you'll have prepared a powerful statement about what you believe in and how your values and strengths will help you succeed in this position and benefit the company. Don't forget to dress professionally and look your best.

6. **Connect with your interviewer(s).** Here's where you show your listening and empathy skills. Listen carefully to the interviewers' questions and comments. Respond to their ideas and feelings. Find ways to appreciate the interviewers. You might say, "These are very thoughtful questions and I appreciate the opportunity to answer them." Or "I really appreciate your giving me the chance to learn more about this position and to share some of my strengths." Be sincere in sharing your own feelings and ideas. Look for what you might have in common ("It looks like we're both interested in developing a growth mindset" if the interviewer has a sign about mindset in the office) and communicate your shared beliefs. After asking your questions, listen carefully to the answers, following up if you hear something intriguing. Be your best self.

7. **Think before responding.** It's fine to consider your response before answering a complex question. People with a high level of self-awareness often take time to reflect before

▶

speaking or making important decisions. It's especially important if it's a question asking you to share a failure, or how you responded to a controversial issue, or how you made a difficult decision. You can say, "That's a great question," or "Let me think about that first" before answering. You might also ask for clarification to be sure you understand the question. Before answering, organize your response into two or three main ideas. Then consider skills and strengths you haven't yet mentioned and where you might address them during your response.

8. **Demonstrate self-awareness.** Many interviews include a question asking you to discuss a recent failure. Choose wisely, not revealing anything that shows poor judgment or recklessness. Pick a problem that will allow you to be honest about an area you can benefit from improving. Use the story to show your resilience, determination, and willingness to learn. Make a specific list of your skills and strengths, then do your best to address all of them during the interview. Set aside any judgments from your Inner Critic about your ability that arise during the interview. Dispute these judgments more than once before the next interview.

9. **End strong and share some more.** At the end of the interview, clarify again why you are a good match for the position. Reiterate the top strengths and skills that you bring. Share some of the strengths you were unable to raise earlier in the interview. Discuss what else excites you about working there. Share from your brand another story that shows your commitment to working hard, or that tells them something important about you. Be ready to ask several specific questions about the company and the position from your interview preparation sheet. This is a very

important part of the interview process. It's when you can show your knowledge about the company's products and company culture, and therefore demonstrate excellent self-awareness. Shake hands (if appropriate) and thank them for their time.

10. **Follow through after the interview.** Right after the interview ends, take time to reflect on how it went. Note some important topics that arose. Write down suggestions for improving your performance at the next interview. Add them to your interview preparation sheet. Send a thank you note or email within 24 hours. Address the actual interview experience by mentioning a specific topic that you discussed.

USING FEEDBACK FOR GROWTH

One of the most effective ways to gain more self-awareness is by requesting feedback from others. In college, you receive feedback on your academic performance in the form of grades and comments from instructors. You can also ask your teachers and classmates for additional feedback on how well you're accomplishing your goals. When you're at work, feedback is often formally delivered in a performance review or appraisal from your supervisor, though you can usually request feedback from others as well.

Performance reviews at work are typically scheduled once or twice a year. You are measured on specific goals that were set following the prior review. These goals will include work performance such as completing tasks and larger projects. There are also goals that can be set to measure soft skills such as communicating effectively with coworkers and demonstrating empathy on client phone calls.

Ideally, the review process is used to help you develop as an employee. During a review, you or your manager may indicate that you need to strengthen certain skills. By being self-aware and recognizing that you need to improve these skills,

▶

you're showing your supervisor that you're valuable to the employer. Your manager will be impressed if you then offer concrete ideas for a plan to improve those skills. To help reduce any personal bias that might play a role in an evaluation, it's important to be proactive in setting clear and measurable goals for your own performance. Here's where your knowledge of the DAPPS rule from Chapter 3 will come in handy. Ask for help meeting these goals throughout the review cycle instead of waiting until the next review.

One way to prepare for these performance reviews while in college is by meeting with your college instructors and counselors so they can help you develop an academic development plan. Practice being self-aware by asking for feedback from your instructors and classmates beforehand on areas where they think you can improve. Then come to the meetings with your instructors or counselors with specific ideas on how you think you can develop better skills. Together, you can set clear and measurable goals for grades and units completed toward graduation, as well as development plans for skills like self-management to stay organized and focused.

Sometimes a workplace performance review includes surveys from people on your project team or even from clients. When you seek feedback from a wide circle of people with whom you interact, this process is often called a 360-degree review. The review feedback can help broaden your awareness about your work, allowing others beyond your supervisor to contribute their perspective. You can also confirm if others view you as aligned with your goals and values. One way to prepare for these specific types of reviews while in college is by soliciting feedback from other students on project teams, or lab partners. Feedback from others is important because we each have **blind spots,** behaviors that are invisible to us but seen by others. For example, perhaps we don't recognize that we have a pattern of interrupting other people during class or a meeting. Blind spots can also lead to bias in our decision making because we are using incomplete information. If we don't recognize that we have already formed an opinion before considering all the facts, our decisions may be faulty. To improve decision making, we increase our self-awareness by identifying our blind spots. Only by being self-aware of these blind spots can we overcome them. To truly understand if you've overcome a blind spot, you'll want to ask for more feedback. And so the cycle continues!

Self-awareness is an essential skill for success in college and at work. Luckily, you can start to practice and improve your self-awareness skills right now. The self-awareness you develop in college will remain with you when you arrive at your dream career. You can create a foundation for success by understanding the benefits of being self-aware. Self-awareness will help you create a personal brand that can be leveraged to earn scholarships, create a LinkedIn profile, and effectively interview. Being self-aware of your strengths, lessons learned from your failures, and important achievements, as well as how you personally fit into a company will allow you to create a compelling story. This story—about why you're the best candidate for a job—is key to getting noticed and hired. Finally, understanding how to use feedback from instructors and during your career performance reviews to continually improve your self-awareness will ensure you stay valuable to your supervisor. Not only will you be able to identify your blind spots, you'll also be able to overcome them. This level of self-awareness will prepare you for great success in your career.

TECH TIPS: Self-Awareness

Self-awareness inventories can be found on the Internet. To take one, do an Internet search for "self-awareness test" or "self-awareness inventory." For example, you'll find one at Wisc-online.com, a collaborative effort by the 16 colleges in the Wisconsin Technical College system. Search the site for "Self-Awareness" to take a 24-question test.

Zenify (not to be confused with a drink by the same name; *Android, iOS*) is an app for your mobile device that is designed to help you move out of autopilot and become more aware of what you are thinking, doing, and feeling in every moment. The app delivers seven levels of assignments on a schedule you choose. Most assignments arrive as a text message, though some contain pictures or music. Assignments ask you to focus your awareness on various aspects of your life, including thoughts, emotions, relationships, parents, and friends.

Queendom.com is a website with many self-assessment tests and quizzes that help you learn about yourself. You'll find many other tests on this site that relate to the inner qualities presented in *On Course*, including self-awareness, self-esteem, assertiveness, procrastination, listening skills, anxiety, depression, anger management, and emotional intelligence. *(Brief reports on your results are free; extended reports require a paid membership.)*

Write Your Own Rules

BELIEVING IN YOURSELF

FOCUS QUESTIONS What personal rules do you have that dictate the choices you make daily? Which of these rules help you create high self-esteem?

Few things affect self-esteem more than our sense of personal power. When we feel like mere passengers in life, with no apparent choice in where we're going, self-esteem shrivels. When we feel like the pilots of our lives, with the power to choose wisely and reach our goals and dreams, self-esteem grows.

Unconscious personal scripts and cultural programs can steal our sense of personal power and drag down our self-esteem. When these unconscious forces take over, we essentially give up control of our lives. Then we make those strange choices that can push us far off course and leave us wondering, "How the heck did I get over here?"

Consider, for example, the cultural tradition of *la sufrida* (the woman who suffers), which is an archetype in Latin American culture (and one that can be found in others) that describes the role of a woman, especially the eldest daughter, as surrendering all her own desires and goals to be of service to others, specifically her husband, parents, family, and community.

> I think you're going to be very surprised to discover that you may be living by rules of which you're not even aware.
>
> Virginia Satir

As a member of the Sikh faith, I was constantly keeping track of so many rules: what to wear, what to eat, forbidden behaviors, and my duties to my family. When I added it all up, there wasn't much left for me to decide—so many of my decisions had been made for me.

Sheena Iyengar

If a Latina unconsciously lets these beliefs govern her life, she will be of service to others, but at the likely sacrifice of her own goals. It is a difficult challenge to strike the right balance between this deeply embedded cultural belief system and accomplishing individual goals, but the process begins with self-awareness.

Of course, no one from outside the culture can or should dictate how a Latina will choose to express and act on her own cultural traditions, but unconscious beliefs should not make these decisions for her either. There are always competing cultural narratives within any culture, and all people have the right to select the cultural traditions that speak to them most deeply and that serve their needs. If people unconsciously let cultural rules dictate their choices, they may feel helpless and angry at the life they are living. Imagine, for example, trying to earn a college degree if you are forever setting aside all your dreams to help others achieve what they want. Only when you consciously accept, revise, or replace some of these cultural rules are you likely to feel completely at peace with yourself. The same, of course, is true of the rules embedded in your personal scripts.

As psychologist Virginia Satir pointed out, we are all living by rules, but the important issue is *Have we chosen our own rules?* To answer that question, you'll want to identify and preserve any empowering rules that are keeping you on course. Then you'll want to become conscious of and revise any rules that are holding you back. Finally, you'll want to write new rules that will support you in achieving even greater victories. That's what former First Lady Eleanor Roosevelt did. Here are some of the life rules she created to guide her choices: *"Do whatever comes your way as well as you can. Think as little as possible about yourself; think as much as possible about other people. Since you get more joy out of giving joy to others, you should put a good deal of thought in the happiness that you are able to give."*

THREE SUCCESS RULES

I have polled thousands of college instructors, and they consistently identify three behaviors that their most successful students do consistently. As you'll see, these rules apply just as well to creating great outcomes in other life roles such as your career and relationships. Consider, then, these three rules as the foundation of your personal code of conduct.

Rule 1: I Show Up

The most important thing is to have a code of life, to know how to live.

Hans Selye, MD

Commit to attending every class from beginning to end. Someone once said that 90 percent of success is simply showing up. Makes sense, doesn't it? How can you be successful at something if you're not there? Studies show a direct correlation between attendance and grades (as one measure of success). At Baltimore City Community College, a study found that, on average, as absences went up, grades went down, especially in introductory courses. A study by a business professor at Arizona State University showed that, on average, his students' grades went down one full grade for every two classes they missed. If you can't get motivated to show up, maybe you need new goals and dreams.

Rule 2: I Do My Best Work

Commit to doing your best work on all assignments, including turning them in on time. You'd be amazed at how many sloppily prepared assignments instructors see. But it isn't just students who are guilty. A friend in business has shown me hundreds of job applications so filled with errors that they begged to be tossed in the trash. Doing your best work on assignments is a rule that will propel you to success in all you do.

Rule 3: I Participate Actively

Commit to getting involved. College, like life, isn't a spectator sport. Come to class prepared. Listen attentively. Take notes. Think deeply about what's being said. Ask yourself how you can apply your course work to achieve your goals and dreams. Read ahead. Start a study group. Ask questions. Answer questions. If you participate at this high level, you couldn't keep yourself from learning even if you wanted to.

Some students resist adopting these three basic rules of success. They say, "But what if I get sick? What if my car breaks down on the way to class? What if...?" I trust that by now you recognize the Victim voice of the Inner Defender, the internal excuse maker.

Of course, something may happen to keep you from following your rules. Each rule is simply your strong *intention*. Each rule identifies an action you believe will help you achieve your desired outcomes and experiences. So, you *intend* to be at every class from beginning to end. You *intend* to do your very best work and turn assignments in on time. You *intend* to participate actively. Your promise *to yourself* is never to break your own rules for a frivolous reason. However, you'll always break your own rules if something of a higher value (like your health) demands it. At each fork in the road, the key to your success is being aware of which choice leads to the future you want. When you are a Creator, you make each choice uncontaminated by the past (your scripts), informed by your own rules of conduct, and ultimately determined by which option, in that moment, will best support the achievement of your goals and dreams.

CHANGING YOUR HABITS

Exceptional students not only follow these three basic rules of success, they also create their own rules for college and life. By choosing personal rules, they commit to replacing their limiting scripts and cultural constraints with consciously chosen habits. Here are a few of my own life rules:

- I keep promises to myself and others.
- I seek feedback and make appropriate course corrections.
- I respect others by arriving on time.
- I do my very best work on all projects important to me.
- I play and create joy.

People who lead a satisfying life, who are in tune with their past and with their future—in short, people whom we would call "happy"—are generally individuals who have lived their lives according to rules they themselves created.

Mihaly Csikszentmihalyi

What is hateful to you do not to your neighbor. That is the entire Law; all the rest is commentary.

The Talmud

- I care for my body with exercise, healthy food, and good medical care.
- I am kind.

Do I follow these rules every day of my life? Unfortunately, no. And when I don't, I soon see myself getting off course. Then I can recommit to following my self-chosen rules and avoid sabotaging the life I want to create.

Once we follow our own rules long enough, they're no longer simply rules. They become habits. And once our positive actions, thoughts, and feelings become habits, few obstacles can block the path to our success.

I'll give you the Four Rules of Success:

1. Decide what you want.
2. Decide what you want to give up in order to get what you want.
3. Associate with successful people.
4. Plan your work and work your plan.

Blair Underwood, actor

JOURNAL ENTRY / 23

In this activity, you will write your own rules for success in college and in life. By following your own code of conduct, you will more likely stay on course toward your greatest dreams.

To focus your mind, ask yourself, "What do successful people do consistently? What are their thoughts, attitudes, behaviors, and beliefs?"

1 Title this journal entry "MY PERSONAL RULES FOR SUCCESS IN COLLEGE AND IN LIFE." Below that, write a list of your own rules for achieving your goals in college. Also, consider rules that will benefit your health. List only those actions which you're willing to commit to do consistently. You might want to print your rules on certificate paper and post them where you can see them daily (perhaps right next to your affirmation). Consider adopting the following as your first three rules:

A. I show up.

B. I do my very best work.

C. I participate actively.

2 Write your thoughts and feelings about which of your personal rules is the most important to your success in college and in life, and why.

What if one of your rules was: I dive deep! How much would that rule improve your results in college and in life?

ONE STUDENT'S STORY

FREDDIE DAVILA, *The Victoria College, Texas*

During my first semester of college I noticed a trend among my fellow students. Every time an assignment was due, many of them came to class with excuses instead of their completed work. I took this behavior personally because I had made time to complete all of my homework and prepare for class. I find it extremely disrespectful to the instructors and to those who come to class to learn whenever college students act like helpless children.

▶

Also during my first semester, I happened to be taking "Strategies for Success," a class that introduced me to the *On Course* textbook. When I was invited to identify an important lesson worth sharing in a "One Page of Wisdom" assignment, I felt I needed to explain what I had learned throughout the semester the best way I knew how—through art. I looked back at the Wise Choice Process and the Responsibility Model for inspiration. As I did the preliminary sketches, I kept in mind the excuses I had heard students use over the last few

Courtesy of Freddie Davila

months. I wanted my art to show that by making excuses, they were acting like Victims and were only hurting themselves.

I hope some of the students in my class saw themselves in the drawing; my goal was to make people think about their self-sabotaging habits and bad choices that stand in the way of their success. The road to success is filled with tough obstacles and tempting distractions, but by making wise choices at critical forks in the road, students on the journey will find success to be their ultimate destiny.

Photo: Courtesy of Freddie Davila.

Healthy Choices: Drinks (Nonalcoholic)

It's amazing we don't slosh when we move. After all, water makes up about 60 percent of our bodies and 75 percent of our brains. Without enough water in our bodies, we lack what is called "proper hydration." Without proper hydration, a person's health suffers greatly.

Why? We need water to transport nutrients, remove toxins, digest food, maintain proper temperature, and even lubricate our joints. Proper hydration also combats health issues such as kidney stones, gallstones, liver problems, blood clots, and colon cancer. A University of Illinois study even found that drinking a few extra cups of water daily can reduce calorie intake and promote weight loss. For pregnant women, staying hydrated is essential for avoiding problems such as premature labor and birth defects.

Of importance to students, fluids significantly affect thinking. In her book *Brain Food*, Lisa Mosconi, PhD, says, "Water is undeniably vital to human life and, as it turns out, also to our intelligence." A study by the Human Performance Lab at the University of Connecticut showed that water loss of only 1.36 percent caused problems for learners. Dehydration increased their estimate of a task's difficulty, lowered their ability to concentrate, and triggered headaches. These are not the experiences you want to have while trying to learn! On the plus side, research published in *Frontiers in Human Neuroscience* found that drinking water before a test helped subjects think faster and even perform better.

We're constantly losing fluids from skin evaporation, urine, stool, breathing, and sweating. Surprisingly, though, we may not feel thirsty even when we're low on fluids. In fact, sometimes when we think we're hungry, we're actually thirsty. A good test for gauging hydration is the color of your urine. If it's pale yellow (like weak lemonade), you're sufficiently hydrated. The darker your urine, the more you need fluids even if you don't feel thirsty.

Guidelines differ on how much to drink every day to replace lost fluids. The daily recommendation of the National Academies of Sciences, Engineering, and Medicine is about 124 ounces of fluids for men and 92 for women. Another guideline takes body size into account. It suggests dividing your weight in half to determine how many ounces of fluids to drink daily. For example, if you weigh 150 pounds, drink at least 75 ounces of fluids every day.

THE LEAST YOU NEED TO KNOW ABOUT HYDRATION

Water

Water is the most important liquid on Earth. In fact, water is the chief ingredient in all other drinks. As such, water should be your go-to drink. The key is making sure you're drinking the purest water possible.

The Environmental Protection Agency (EPA) requires community water systems to provide customers with an annual report about the quality of their tap water. Your local water supplier should send you a yearly report by July 1. Didn't get one? You can call the EPA's Safe Drinking Water Hotline (800-426-4791) and request a report on the water supply for your home and/or campus.

Perhaps you've heard about the problem with the safety of tap water in Flint, Michigan. Unhealthy water may contain unsafe chemicals and can happen anywhere. That possibility might motivate you to take greater responsibility for the purity of your drinking water. If so, consider employing a filtration system. This is also a good idea if your water comes from a well. A filtration pitcher or faucet mount system costs between $15 and $50. For even better water filtration, a reverse osmosis system is $150 to $400. If you're buying bottled water now, it won't take long to earn that money back in savings.

Speaking of bottled water, it's become very popular. In fact, sales in the United States in 2016 were just short of 13 billion gallons. The question is . . . how pure is bottled water? Although the EPA is charged with the safety of tap water, the Food and Drug Administration (FDA) is responsible for the quality of bottled water. The FDA requires producers of bottled water to jump through many hoops to assure purity. Unfortunately, these requirements don't apply to water bottled and sold in the same state. For this and other reasons, some bottled water may be even less pure than tap water. In fact, some studies show that up to 25 percent of bottled water *is* tap water. Further, consider the impact of bottled water on the environment. Ever wondered where all those empty bottles go? One place is called the Great Pacific Garbage Patch, a floating garbage dump in the Pacific Ocean. This disgusting island of debris is twice the size of Texas! Much of the debris is plastic, and particles of plastic are now being found in seafood—another reason to purify your own drinking water.

Soda

I love sodas. Especially colas. But when I learned how unhealthy they are, I cut way back. Turns out, I'm not alone. According to beverage-industry data, the last couple of decades have seen the sale of sodas drop more than 25 percent. People seem to be realizing that sodas are bad for their health. The major problem is sugar. A 12-ounce soda contains about 10 teaspoons of sugar, and that much sugar is bad for your health. The American Heart Association advises men to limit their entire daily added sugar to only nine teaspoons and women no more than six teaspoons.

Many studies offer good reasons to limit sugar. Data from the Boston University School of Medicine is of special interest to students. In 2017, researchers studied about 4,200 participants to determine if consuming soft drinks affects thinking and memory. The authors concluded that "higher intake of sugary beverages was associated with lower total brain volume and poorer performance on tests of episodic memory." They also found that drinking sodas was associated with a smaller hippocampus. That's the part of our brain that plays a key role in storing information in memory. So, drinking sodas is unwise, especially when your job is learning.

Damage to thinking and memory, however, are only some of the problems caused by sugar. The Harvard School of Public Health concluded that higher consumption of sugary drinks is associated with development of both obesity and type 2 diabetes. According to Dr. Mark Hyman, "Sugar is more than empty calories: It spurs inflammation, accelerates weight gain (especially belly fat), sets the stage for heart attacks and strokes, and contributes to cancer and Alzheimer's disease."

All this bad news might prompt you to switch to diet sodas. After all, they don't contain sugar, right? Unfortunately, the news here isn't great. Matthew Pase, PhD, is one of the investigators in the Boston University School of Medicine study. He reports, "We also found that people drinking diet soda daily were almost three times as likely to develop stroke and dementia. This included a higher risk of ischemic stroke, where blood vessels in the brain become obstructed, and Alzheimer's disease, the most common form of dementia." And, ironically, other studies have shown that diet drinks actually cause people to gain weight.

Coffee

Many college students depend on coffee to help them study. They say it keeps them awake to study longer. Some claim it even helps them learn better. Well, they're certainly right about caffeinated coffee keeping them awake. Here's how. We have neurotransmitters in our brains called adenosine that, as the day wears on, make us sleepy. Caffeine blocks adenosine, keeping it from doing its job. The result? We stay awake.

But what about the idea that caffeine improves learning? Although evidence of this is thin, a 2014 study at Johns Hopkins University suggests that it can. The key, though, was *when* the caffeine was consumed. Researchers asked two groups to memorize a series of pictures. Afterward, one group was given a caffeine pill while the other group was not. After 24 hours, both groups were tested on the pictures. Those in the caffeine group were significantly better at recalling details. In other words, the experiment showed that caffeine can boost memory when taken *after* studying. Lead researcher Michael Yassa, PhD, said, "We've always known that caffeine has cognitive-enhancing effects, but its particular effects on strengthening memories and making them resistant to forgetting has never been examined in detail in humans. We report for the first time a specific effect of caffeine on reducing forgetting over 24 hours."

In addition to coffee's contributions to studying, researchers have found that it also provides health benefits. These benefits, though, have less to do with caffeine and more to do with other ingredients in coffee. These include antioxidants, magnesium, catechins, chlorogenic acids, flavonoids, and vitamin C. Studies show that coffee lowers the risk of prostate and colon cancer, stroke, skin cancer, and respiratory disease, as well as heart disease, Alzheimer's disease, type 2 diabetes, and Parkinson's disease. In fact, one recent study published in *Circulation* (American Heart Association) found that "Higher consumption of total coffee, caffeinated coffee, and decaffeinated coffee was associated with lower risk of total mortality." In other words, coffee may help you live longer.

That doesn't mean you should overdo caffeinated coffee. The U.S. Dietary Guidelines Advisory Committee considers drinking up to five cups a day to be safe. However, some doctors, like Dr. Hyman, suggest a limit of two cups. Too much coffee may cause stomach upset, nervousness, anxiety, and agitation, any of which could lead to sleep problems. A study in the *Journal of Clinical Sleep Medicine* recommends having no caffeine within the six hours of going to bed. Additionally, Duke researchers warn that stopping caffeine can cause withdrawal symptoms. "Between twelve and twenty-four hours after the last dose of caffeine, users generally experience headaches and fatigue that may persist for several days to a week," they say.

Many experts recommend limiting daily caffeine to 400 milligrams (mg). To put that in perspective, 8 ounces of brewed coffee contain 85 to 165 mg of caffeine. Brewed decaf coffee contains only 2 to 5 mg of caffeine. Other common sources of caffeine include black or green tea, sodas, and energy drinks. Black or green teas contain 25 to 48 mg of caffeine and sodas contain 24 to 46 mg (although citrus sodas typically contain no caffeine). Energy drinks range from 27 to 164 mg of caffeine, though a one-ounce energy shot can contain as much caffeine as an eight-ounce cup of coffee.

One more concern about drinking coffee: calories. Although a black coffee contains no calories, many people add cream, sugar, and other sources of high calories. And then there are the specialty coffees that are ever so tasty and tempting. For example, a grande (16-ounce) Starbuck's Caramel Frappuccino Blended Coffee with whipped cream is 420 calories. Yikes.

Other Drinks

There are, of course, many other drink options besides water, sodas, and coffee. Let's take a quick look at the health effects of some of them.

Milk is a controversial drink. On the plus side, milk from mammals (typically cows and goats) is praised as a good source of calcium. Calcium is noted for building strong bones and teeth. The protein in milk is also said to contribute to healthy muscles. Milk advocates also say it can lower both high blood pressure and the risk of strokes. According to Ruth Kava, director of nutrition at the American Council on Science and Health, "Milk is a nutritious food. It is an excellent source of calcium, phosphorus, riboflavin, and vitamin D and a good source of protein, vitamin A, potassium, and several B vitamins."

However, scientists at the U.S. Department of Agriculture investigated the positive claims about dairy milk. Dr. Hyman summarized some of their findings:

- There's no evidence that dairy strengthens your bones . . . in fact, the animal protein it contains may contribute to bone loss.
- Dairy is linked to prostate cancer.
- Whole milk contains saturated fat and is linked to heart disease.
- Dairy aggravates irritable bowels.
- Dairy causes digestive problems for the 75 percent of people with lactose intolerance (lactose is a sugar present in dairy products).

In our earlier section about food, you learned that deciding what to eat is challenging. That's because of contradictory opinions among experts and ever-changing scientific knowledge. Regarding milk, this challenge appears once again. Since publication of the U.S. Department of Agriculture report summarized above, new evidence reveals that saturated fat in dairy is *not* linked to heart disease or stroke. Additionally, digestive problems attributed to lactose are now thought to be intolerance to A1, a protein found in many commercially produced milks. Fortunately for milk fans, there's now an A2-only milk that helps some people avoid digestive problems.

Despite this good news for milk lovers, criticism of milk persists. For example, a report by the Physicians Committee for Responsible Medicine concluded, "Milk and dairy products are not necessary in the diet and can, in fact, be harmful to health." Dr. Anthony Komaroff of the Harvard Medical School cautions that high milk intake may increase the risk of prostate cancer, ovarian cancer, type 1 diabetes, and multiple sclerosis. Additionally, some people fear the effects of growth hormones and antibiotics given to cows and passed on to people through milk. With warnings like these, you may decide to switch to plant-based milks. You'll find "milk" drinks made from almonds, rice, flax seeds, coconuts, soy, and walnuts. If you choose these alternatives, go with unsweetened varieties to avoid extra sugar. In some cases, these plant-based milks are fortified and contain even more calcium and vitamin D than dairy milk.

Sports drinks such as Gatorade and Powerade not only provide hydration, they also replenish electrolytes and carbohydrates lost through heavy sweating. Electrolytes help cells throughout your body carry electrical impulses. These impulses are essential to keep muscles and other parts of your body working as they should. If your muscles ache, twitch, or feel weak during or after heavy exercise, the cause may be loss of electrolytes. That's why replacing electrolytes is recommended when exercising strenuously for more than an hour. For less than an hour or for less strenuous exercise, water is usually fine. Some experts suggest that coconut water is a good substitute for a sports drink. It replaces lost electrolytes but contains less sugar. The sugar in sports drinks is a source of empty and very expensive calories.

Energy drinks usually contain water, sugar, vitamins, herbal extracts, and about the same amount of caffeine as regular coffee. Because of the caffeine, energy drinks decrease sleepiness and increase alertness. Beyond that, some manufacturers claim benefits such as improved endurance, increased energy, and weight loss. According to the authors of *Lifetime Physical Fitness and Wellness*, "These purported benefits are yet to be proven through scientific research." Do not confuse energy drinks with sports drinks. Energy drinks should not be used for hydration and should never be combined with alcohol. An energy drink will make you feel alert, which could cause you to think you can safely drink more alcohol. The result: You'll be a wide-awake drunk, with all the dangers of intoxication still present.

Fruit juices may contain as much sugar as sodas. For example, a 12-ounce can of Coca-Cola has about 10 teaspoons of sugar and 140 calories. The same amount of orange or apple juice has about 9.8 teaspoons of sugar and 165 calories (25 more calories than Coke!). Health risks of too much fruit juice include obesity, diabetes, and heart disease. Dr. Robert Lustig is the author of *Fat Chance: The Bitter Truth about Sugar*. He says, "When you turn fruit into juice, you are losing the insoluble fiber, which is an essential nutrient and helps delay absorption of the sugar. Take the fiber away and you're just drinking sugar and calories." One option is to water down fruit juices to cut down on sugar. Better yet, skip juice and eat the whole fruit instead.

WISE CHOICES: Drinks (Nonalcoholic)

- Determine your hydration needs by dividing your weight by two; drink at least that many ounces of fluids daily, mostly water.
- Do all you can to ensure that the water you are drinking is pure.
- Carry pure water with you in a steel or glass container and sip all day; avoid bottled water.
- Monitor the color of your urine; if it becomes dark yellow or orange, drink some water.
- Minimize drinking sodas—diet or otherwise.
- Limit daily caffeine to 400 mg/day; that's about two to three cups of brewed regular coffee. Energy drinks, black and green tea, and most soft drinks contribute to your caffeine total.
- Consider nondairy alternatives to milk, especially if you experience digestive problems from dairy milk.
- After strenuous exercise, replace electrolytes with a sports drink or coconut water.
- Avoid fruit juices that are high in sugar; instead eat whole fruits.
- Eat water-rich foods: watermelon, strawberries, cantaloupe, peaches, oranges, cucumber, lettuce, zucchini, celery, tomatoes, bell peppers, cauliflower, cabbage, broths, and soup.

Adopting Lifelong Learning

Successful Students . . .

▶ **develop a growth mindset,** understanding they can learn challenging subjects by increasing their efforts and employing more effective strategies.

▶ **discover their preferred ways of learning,** utilizing strategies that allow them to maximize their learning of valuable new information and skills.

▶ **employ critical thinking,** using probing questions and higher-order reasoning skills to evaluate complex situations, make wise choices, and solve important problems.

Struggling Students . . .

▶ **have a fixed mindset,** believing they were born with a fixed amount of intelligence and talent and there is little or nothing they can do to improve their abilities.

▶ **often experience frustration,** boredom, or resistance when their instructors don't teach the way they like to learn.

▶ **use ineffective thinking skills that result in confusion,** illogical thinking, unwise choices, challenging problems, and even exploitation by others.

As a Creator, I take personal responsibility for learning all the information, skills, and life lessons necessary to achieve my goals and dreams.

I learn valuable lessons from every experience I have.

CASE STUDY IN CRITICAL THINKING / A Fish Story

One September morning, on their first day of college, two dozen first-year students made their way into the biology laboratory. They sat down, six at a lab table, and glanced about for the professor. Because this was their first college class, most of the students were a bit nervous. A few introduced themselves. Others kept checking their watches.

At exactly nine o'clock, the professor, wearing a crisply pressed white lab coat, entered the room. "Good morning," he said. He set a white plate in the middle of each table. On each plate lay a small fish.

"Please observe the fish," the professor said. "Then write down your observations." He turned and left the room.

The students looked at each other, puzzled. This was bizarre! Oh, well. They took out scrap paper and wrote notes such as, *I see a small fish.* One student added, *It's on a white plate.*

Satisfied, they set their pens down and waited. And waited. For the entire class period, they waited. A couple of students whispered that it was a trick. They said the professor was probably testing them to see if they'd do something wrong. Time crawled by. Still they waited, trying to do nothing that would get them in trouble. Finally, one student mumbled that she was going to be late for her next class. She picked up her books and stood. She paused. Others rose as well and began filing out of the room. Some looked cautiously over their shoulders as they left.

When the students entered the biology lab for their second class, they found the same white plates with the same small fish already waiting on their laboratory tables. At exactly nine o'clock, the professor entered the room. "Good morning. Please take out your observations of the fish," he said.

Students dug into their notebooks or backpacks. Many could not find their notes. Those few who could held them up for the professor to see as he walked from table to table.

After visiting each student, the professor said, "Please observe the fish. Write down all of your observations."

"Will there be a test on this?" one student asked. But the professor had already left the room, closing the door behind him. Frustrated, the student blurted, "Why doesn't he just tell us what he wants us to know?"

The students looked at one another, more puzzled. They peered at the fish. Those few who had found their notes glanced from the fish to their notes and back again. Was the professor crazy? What else were they supposed to notice? It was only a stupid fish.

About then, one student spied a book on the professor's desk. It was a book for identifying fish, and she snatched it up. Using the book, she quickly discovered what kind of fish was lying on her plate. She read eagerly, recording in her notes all of the facts she found about her fish. Others saw her and asked to use the book, too. She passed the book to other tables, and her classmates soon found descriptions of their fish. After about 30 minutes the students sat back, very pleased with themselves. Chatter died down. They waited. But the professor didn't return. As the period ended, all of the students carefully put their notes away.

The same fish on the same white plate greeted each student in the third class. The professor entered at nine o'clock. "Good morning," he said. "Please hold up your observations." All of the students held up their notes immediately. They looked at each other, smiling, as the professor walked from table to table, looking at their work. Once again, he walked toward the door. "Please . . . *observe* the fish. Write down *all* of your observations," he said. And then he left.

The students couldn't believe it. They grumbled and complained. *This guy is nuts. When is he going to teach us something? What are we paying tuition for, anyway?* Students at one table, however, began observing their fish more closely. Other tables followed their example.

The first thing all of the students noticed was the biting odor of aging fish. A few students recorded details about the fish's color that they had failed to observe in the previous two classes. They wondered if the colors had been there originally or if the colors had appeared as the fish aged. Each group measured its fish. They poked it and described its texture. One student looked in its mouth and found that he could see light through its gills. Another student found a small balance beam, and each group weighed its fish. They passed around someone's pocket knife. With it, they sliced open the fish and examined its insides. In the stomach of one fish they found a smaller fish. They wrote quickly, and their notes soon overflowed onto three and four sheets of paper. Finally someone shouted, "Hey, class was over 10 minutes ago." They carefully placed their notes in three-ring binders. They said good-bye to their fish, wondering if their finny friends would be there on Monday.

They were, and a vile smell filled the laboratory. The professor strode into the room at exactly nine o'clock. The students immediately thrust their notes in the air. "Good morning," the professor said cheerfully, making his way from student to student. He took longer than ever to examine their notes. The students shifted anxiously in their chairs as the professor edged ever closer to the door. How could they endure the smell for another class period? At the door, the professor turned to the students.

"All right," he said. "Now we can begin."

—Inspired by Samuel H. Scudder,
"Take This Fish and Look at It" (1874)

Based on the events in this case study, rate the professor on the following scale. Be prepared to explain your rating.

Terrier ▶ (1) (2) (3) (4) (5) (6) (7) (8) (9) (10) ◀ Excellent

DIVING DEEPER

If you had been in this biology lab class, what lessons about college and life would you have learned from the experience? When you think you have discovered one life lesson, dive deeper and find another, even more powerful lesson. And then another and another.

Developing a Growth Mindset

FOCUS QUESTION   How can you maximize your learning in college, in your career, and in life?

"Uh-oh," I thought. "I'm in big trouble!"

I was 18 years old at the time, but I recall that scary moment as if it were yesterday. I was about to start my first semester in college. Our entire class was on campus for orientation, and one task was to choose our first-semester classes. I was sitting with one of my new roommates exploring course descriptions. John was going down the reading list for a literature course we were considering.

"I've read this book," he said, ticking the title with the tip of his pen, "and this one . . . and this one . . . and this one . . . and this one." Like many of my classmates, John had gone to a private high school. I had gone to a public high school. John had read every book on the list. I had never even *heard* of any books on the list. That's when I thought: "Uh-oh . . . I'm in big trouble!"

In that moment, I made an unconscious and unfortunate choice. I went into survival mode: *I just want to survive the next four years and graduate.* As a result, I filled my schedule with courses I thought would be easy. One course turned out to be more difficult than I thought, so I dropped it. During classes, I seldom spoke, afraid I would say something stupid. At the end of my first semester, I breathed a sigh of relief. I had passed all my courses. My grades were much lower than they had been in high school, but I had survived. For the next seven semesters, I avoided taking classes with a professor who had a reputation of being "hard." When it came time to pick a major, I chose the one a friend told me was the easiest. My grades crept steadily upward as I got better and better at playing the grade game. After four years, I achieved my goal. I graduated. By most standards I was a success in college. But was I?

FIXED AND GROWTH MINDSETS

It turns out that psychologist Carol Dweck and others have studied the way I approached learning as an undergraduate. Apparently my approach is fairly common. Psychologists call it a "fixed mindset." The opposite is a "growth mindset." As I describe these mindsets, see if they sound familiar.

Learners with a **fixed mindset** believe people are born with a fixed amount of ability and talent. When it comes to intelligence, they've either got it or they don't. If they do well in school, it's because they're smart. If they don't do well in school, it's because they aren't. Dweck found that students with a fixed mindset prefer tasks they can already do well. New challenges are threatening because they fear their intelligence may not be up to the task. Thus, when they encounter a challenge, they tend to avoid it or quit as a method of self-protection. Mistakes and failures scare them because, in their mindset, such outcomes reflect poorly on their fixed level of intelligence. I've seen students complete all the courses they need to graduate except one. That course is inevitably in the subject they fear: perhaps math, writing, or a foreign language. When students with a fixed mindset experience a challenge, setback, or failure, their inner chatter judges them *(I'm just not smart enough)* and they may give up. Does this sound like Victim behavior to you?

By contrast, learners with a **growth mindset** believe that intelligence is like a muscle—it gets stronger the more it's used. Interestingly, this

Too many students are hung up on grades and on proving their worth through grades. Grades are important, but learning is more important.

Carol Dweck

. . . a miracle is just a shift in perception.

Marianne Williamson

mindset is consistent with what we know about how the brain learns. The more we exercise our brains, the more neural networks are created and the "smarter" we become. (See "Becoming an Active Learner" in *A Toolbox for Active Learners* online with the accompanying MindTap for more on this.) A growth mindset encourages us to accept challenges, to work hard, to learn from mistakes, to change course if needed, and to keep going despite setbacks and failures. Learners with this mindset believe their hard work and persistence can overcome initial difficulties in mastering a subject or a skill. If what they are doing isn't working, their Inner Guide explains, "I didn't work hard enough" or "There's a better way to do it," or both. They accept responsibility and they make a new plan. I trust that by now you recognize the response of a Creator.

Dweck has tested her theory about fixed and growth mindsets on students from preschool through college. One was an experiment with premed students at an Ivy League university. These students were taking a very challenging course in organic chemistry. The stakes were high because their grade in the course would play a big role in whether they got into medical school. Students with a growth mindset distinguished themselves from students with a fixed mindset in three important ways: (1) They enjoyed the course more, (2) they bounced back more effectively from setbacks such as poor test scores, and (3) their final grades were higher.

Psychologist Joshua Aronson and colleagues also tested Dweck's theory. They asked Stanford University students to be pen pals with local middle school students and help the younger students stay in school. The experimenters asked the Stanford students to tell their young pen pals things such as, "Humans are capable of learning and mastering new things at any time in their lives." In other words, the Stanford students were encouraging their young pen pals to adopt a growth mindset. What the experimenters actually wanted to see was what impact expressing a growth mindset might have on the Stanford students. When later compared to a control group, the Stanford students in the experiment earned higher grades and reported more often that they enjoyed their academic work.

Dweck and others have explored what causes some people to adopt a fixed mindset while others take on the more empowering growth mindset. One explanation is that fixed mindsets result when important adults (e.g., parents or teachers) praise us for our intelligence: *You did so well in math. You're obviously very smart!* The message here is that success is the result of being smart. The problem is, now we're nervous about trying something new. After all, if we fail that means we're not smart enough . . . and we believe there's no way to get more "smarts." By contrast, a growth mindset is more likely to develop when important adults praise us for our effort (rather than our intelligence): *You did so well in math. You're obviously a hard worker!* The message here is that success is the result of effort. Armed with this belief, we're more likely to respond positively to future challenges because we're confident we can work harder if the outcome or experience is worth it.

> The purpose of learning is growth, and our minds, unlike our bodies, can continue growing as we continue to live.
>
> Mortimer Adler

> If there is no dark and dogged will, there will be no shining accomplishment; if there is no dull and determined effort, there will be no brilliant achievement.
>
> Chinese proverb

Like other mindsets, fixed and growth mindsets seem to be shaped by deep-culture beliefs. For example, some countries' educational systems are more likely to attribute success to a strong effort (growth mindset). They believe that all students can learn if they work hard enough. By contrast, some school systems in the United States are more likely to attribute success to inborn intelligence or ability (fixed mindset). This cultural belief shows up in the American educational system when "gifted" students are given enriched academic programs.

If you've developed a growth mindset, you have a core belief that will help you achieve success in college and beyond. However, if you realize you've developed a fixed mindset, you aren't stuck with it. You can revise your mindset.

HOW TO DEVELOP A GROWTH MINDSET

Here are four ways to develop or strengthen a growth mindset:

Think of Your Brain as a Muscle. Like a muscle, the more you use your brain, the "smarter" and more capable it becomes. The technical term is *neuroplasticity*. Neuroplasticity is the ability of your brain to use new experiences to revise old neural networks and create new ones. This is how learning happens. Once you understand this concept, you'll realize that—with mental effort—your brain is designed to grow and change. The idea that each human brain has a fixed capacity belongs on the scrap heap of faulty beliefs along with "the world is flat." Just because you may be challenged to learn something today doesn't mean that you can't learn it. Because of your brain's neuroplasticity, effort and persistence combined with effective study strategies are the keys to effective learning. For more information about this concept, see "Becoming an Active Learner" in *A Toolbox for Active Learners* online with the accompanying MindTap.

Set Learning Goals . . . As Well As Performance Goals. When I was an undergraduate, I set performance goals. My main goal was to see my grade point average improve every semester. I achieved that goal, but I paid a price. To assure success, I played it safe, wasting many learning opportunities. I avoided courses that might have introduced me to a whole new world. I steered clear of "hard" professors who might have become mentors or guides. By studying only to get grades, I learned just enough to pass tests. Sure, I got a degree and, with it, a ticket into the world of employment . . . but at what cost?

Don't misunderstand, there's nothing wrong with setting a goal to get good grades. Obviously, good grades are the doorway to many future goals, such as a job or graduate school. But we limit ourselves if our *only* goal is to earn a grade. Such a goal limits both our enjoyment and potential. It keeps us from developing knowledge, skills, and wisdom that could help us create a richer, more personally fulfilling life. The solution is to combine both kinds of goals. *Performance goals* provide you with measurable accomplishments (like grades), whereas *learning goals* offer knowledge and skills you can use for the rest of your life.

It's never too late to change your mindset. Mindsets are beliefs—powerful ones and ones that shape our motivation—but beliefs can be changed.

Carol Dweck

We now accept the fact that learning is a lifelong process of keeping abreast of change. And the most pressing task is to teach people how to learn.

Peter Drucker

So, what would a learning goal look like? Suppose you're taking a writing class. A *performance* goal would be to earn an A in the course. A *learning* goal would be to master three ways to write an effective introductory paragraph. Suppose you want to lose weight. A *performance* goal would be to weigh 150 pounds by June 30. A *learning* goal would be to learn three important principles of good nutrition. Suppose you're taking an organic chemistry course. A *performance* goal would be to finish reading your textbook by December 1. A *learning* goal would be to master the ability to read challenging content for at least 20 minutes without losing focus. Notice that performance goals usually give us a defined (often measurable) outcome. By contrast, learning goals help us grow, giving us skills and abilities we can use to achieve future performance goals. Whereas my *performance* goal might be to achieve *x*, my *learning goal* might be to learn five strategies to help me do *x*. Those same five strategies may also help me to achieve other goals for the rest of my life. Look back at the goals you set in Journal Entry 9 and see what kind of goals you created there. If they are mostly performance goals, consider adding a couple of learning goals.

Seek Feedback. Feedback is essential to learning. Luckily, life offers us helpful feedback every day. Sadly, many ignore it . . . especially those with a fixed mindset. At first, feedback taps us politely on the shoulder. If we pay no attention, feedback shakes us vigorously. If we continue to ignore it, feedback may knock us to our knees, creating havoc in our lives. This havoc might be failing out of school, being fired from a job, or getting in trouble with drugs or alcohol. There's usually plenty of feedback long before the failure or firing or addiction if we will only pay attention to its message. Your Inner Defender may see feedback as a threat, but your Inner Guide knows it is vital for success.

In college, think of yourself as an airplane pilot and your instructors as your personal air traffic controllers. When they correct you in class or write a comment on an assignment or give you a grade on a test, what they are really saying is, *You're on course, on course . . . whoops, now you're off course, off course . . . okay, that's right, now you're back on course.* Airplane pilots appreciate such feedback. Without it, they might not get to their destination. They might even crash. Likewise, effective learners welcome their instructors' feedback and use it to stay on course. They pay attention to every suggestion that instructors offer on assignments; they understand the message in their test scores; they request clarification of any feedback they don't understand; and they ask for additional feedback. Maybe the idea of paying attention to feedback sounds obvious to you, but I can't tell you how many students I've known who made the same mistakes over and over, ignoring both my feedback and the reality that when you keep doing what you've been doing, you'll keep getting what you've been getting.

Everywhere in life, heeding feedback is vital to creating the life you want. The feedback may be something said by friends, lovers, spouses, parents,

Once you embrace unpleasant news, not as a negative but as evidence of a need for change, you aren't defeated by it. You're learning from it.

Bill Gates

All human beings are periodically tested by the power of the universe . . . how one performs under pressure is the true measure of one's spirit, heart, and desire.

Spike Lee

children, neighbors, doctors, bosses, coworkers, and even strangers. Or it may be more subtle, coming in the form of an unsatisfying relationship, a boring job, blackouts from drinking too much, or runaway credit card debt. Any areas of discomfort or distress are red flags of warning: *Hey, wake up! You're headed away from your desired outcomes and experiences. You're off course!* And that awareness leads to a fourth way for developing a growth mindset.

Change Course When Needed. It's one thing to realize you are off course. It's quite another to do something about it. Course correction takes courage. You need to admit that what you are doing isn't working, seek alternatives, abandon the familiar, and walk into the unknown. Victims stay stuck. Creators learn, change, and grow.

One of my off-course students was feeling overwhelmed by all she had to do, and then she made a course correction, changing the way she tackled large projects. In her journal she wrote, "When I break a huge task into chunks and do a little bit every day, I can accomplish great things."

Another off-course student discovered he was an expert at blaming his failures in college on other people: his boss, his teachers, his parents, his girlfriend. He decided to change and hold himself more responsible. He learned, "In the past I have spent more energy on getting people to feel sorry for me than I have on accomplishing something worthwhile."

A third off-course student was filled with hate for her father, who she felt had abandoned her, and then she decided to change. She forgave him and moved on with her life. She wrote, "Spending all of my time hating someone leaves me little time to love myself."

A fourth off-course student realized how little effort and care he put into everything he did, including his college assignments. He discovered, "I'm always looking for ways to cut corners, to get out of doing what's necessary. It doesn't work. I have to do my best in order to be successful."

And one more off-course student realized that the only goal he'd ever set in school was to get good grades. As a graduate student, he discovered, "When I focus on learning, my grades take care of themselves. Better yet, I learn things I can use to improve the quality of my life!" He regretted all the learning he had missed out on, but he got excited by all there still is to learn. He started taking courses that excited him. He found new ways to apply what he was learning and created a whole new life for himself. He was grateful that he had given himself the gift of a major course correction, one that changed his outcomes and experiences. In case you haven't guessed, I was this off-course student.

We seldom move toward our goals and dreams in a straight line. With constant course corrections, however, we improve our chances of getting there eventually. And along the way, the University of Life offers us exactly the lessons we need to develop our full potential. We only have to listen, learn, change, and grow.

The capacity to correct course is the capacity to reduce the differences between the path you are on now and the optimal path to your objective.

Charles Garfield

To me, earth is a school. I view life as my classroom. My approach to the experiences I have every day is that I am a student, and that all my experiences have something they can teach me. I am always asking myself, "What learning is available for me now?"

Mary Hulnick,
vice president,
University of Santa Monica

If we don't change direction soon, we'll end up where we're going.

Professor Irwin Corey,
comedian

JOURNAL ENTRY / 24

In this activity, you will explore your mindset(s) about learning. Make a choice—write about one of the following:

A Describe a time when you reacted to a learning challenge with a *fixed* mindset. This challenge can be one at school or any other learning situation. Explain the learning challenge, how you specifically responded to the challenge, and how your learning turned out. Most important, as you look back on this experience, what will you do differently when faced with future learning challenges?

B Describe a time when you reacted to a learning challenge with a *growth* mindset. This challenge can be one at school or any other learning situation. Explain the learning challenge, how you specifically responded to the learning challenge, and how it turned out. Describe as best you can how you think you developed the growth mindset that you used in this situation.

ONE STUDENT'S STORY
JESSIE MAGGARD, *Urbana University, Ohio*

The first friends I made in college were my teammates on the soccer team. After practice we started riding around, shopping, and going to parties. We almost never talked about school or personal problems. To them, play time was more important. I wasn't getting much sleep and I was exhausted all the time. I didn't feel like studying, and when I went to class, I wasn't learning much. Then a couple of things happened that shook me up. First, my English teacher handed back a paper and told me it wasn't very good. I thought all day about what she said and it really bothered me. I'm the first person in my family to go to college, and I started worrying about whether I was going to make it. If I was doing poorly in a class that I thought was easy, what would happen in more difficult classes? Second, I learned that my parents were getting divorced. I tried talking about my feelings with some of my teammates, but they just listened and didn't say anything. I might as well have been talking to a wall, and I realized they weren't really interested in my problems.

The *On Course* book talks about how easy it is to get off course even when you want to be successful. That is so true. By the time soccer season ended, I was *way* off course and I knew I had to make some serious changes. At first I spent more time by myself. I wrote out a schedule and started to get more organized. Then I slowly began spending more time with people in my dorm, and over time I developed friendships with six amazing people who have really touched me. Doing well in school is important to them, too. We started studying together, and my grades began to improve. I even got comments from my teachers about how I had changed. Still, I felt weighed down by my parents' divorce and it was a huge distraction from my schoolwork. One of my new friends had gone through her parents' divorce, and she gave me tips on how she had gotten through it. She encouraged me to sit down with my parents and talk about my feelings. I did, and it helped so much to talk with them and understand why they had fallen out of love with each other.

▶

Through all of this, I've learned that when you get off course, you have to do something different. My soccer friends had different goals. I'm not trying to put them down. Their goals weren't bad; they just weren't my goals. My goal is to get my degree and teach kindergarten, and when I was hanging out with my soccer friends, I was headed in the wrong direction. I totally changed my peer group, and now I am back on course. I know I'm the only person who can change my life. I just need the courage to stand up for myself. At the time, changing seemed so difficult, but now in the big picture, it seems so easy.

Photo: Courtesy of Jessie Maggard.

Discovering Your Preferred Ways of Learning

> **FOCUS QUESTIONS**   What is your preferred way of learning? What can you do when your instructor doesn't teach the way you prefer to learn?

Today, we're well into the information age. That means staying on course to our goals and dreams requires learning vast amounts of information, facts, theories, and skills. Once you master the CORE Learning System explained in *A Toolbox for Active Learners* (available online with the accompanying MindTap), all that learning should be easy, right? Not quite.

You see, in addition to learning approaches that are common to us all, each of us has our own preferred learning experiences. This preference doesn't mean we can't learn in other ways. It simply means that each of us has our own favored ways of taking in and deeply processing our learning experiences. Each of us has our own preferred ways of creating meaning from the rush and jumble of information we encounter in college, at work, at home, and everywhere else in life. Knowing how *you* prefer to learn gives you an advantage everywhere in life, but especially in college when you get an instructor who doesn't teach the way you prefer to learn.

> It is very natural to teach in the same way we learn. It may be difficult for us to believe that others could learn in a way that is foreign and difficult for us.
>
> Carolyn Mamchur

SELF-ASSESSMENT: HOW I PREFER TO LEARN

Before reading on, take the following self-assessment inventory. It will give you insights about how you prefer to gather and process information.

Each of us develops preferred ways of learning. These preferred ways of learning are more pleasurable, require less effort, and usually produce more successful learning than a less-preferred learning experience. For a quick understanding of learning preferences, recall the last time you learned how to play a new video game or assembled something with many parts. Some people prefer to start playing or assembling immediately. They dive right in.

Learning Preference Inventory

In each of the following groups, rank all four answers (A, B, C, D) from the least true of you to the most true of you. Give each possible answer a different score. There are no right or wrong answers; your opinion is all that matters. Remember, items that are MOST TRUE OF YOU get a 4.

Least true of you ▶ ① ② ③ ④ ◀ Most true of you

1. I would prefer to take a college course

_____ A. in science.	_____ B. in business management.	_____ C. in group dynamics.	_____ D. as an independent study that I design.

2. I solve problems by

_____ A. standing back, thinking, and analyzing what is wrong.	_____ B. doing something practical and seeing how it works.	_____ C. leaping in and doing what feels right at the time.	_____ D. trusting my intuition.

3. Career groups that appeal to me are

_____ A. engineer, researcher, financial planner.	_____ B. administrator, city manager, military officer.	_____ C. teacher, social worker, physical therapist.	_____ D. entrepreneur, artist, inventor.

4. Before I make a decision, I need to be sure that

_____ A. I understand all of the relevant ideas and facts.	_____ B. I'm confident my solution will work.	_____ C. I know how my decision will affect others.	_____ D. I haven't overlooked a more creative solution.

5. I believe that

_____ A. life today needs more logical thinking and less emotion.	_____ B. life rewards the practical, hard-working, down-to-earth person.	_____ C. life must be lived with enthusiasm and passion.	_____ D. life, like music, is best composed by creative inspiration, not by rules.

6. I would enjoy reading a book titled

_____ A. *Great Theories and Ideas of the Twenty-first Century.*	_____ B. *How to Organize Your Life and Accomplish More.*	_____ C. *The Keys to Developing Better Relationships.*	_____ D. *Tapping into Your Creative Genius.*

7. I believe the most valuable information for making decisions comes from

_____ A. logical analysis of facts.	_____ B. what has worked in the past.	_____ C. gut feelings.	_____ D. my imagination.

8. I am persuaded by an argument that

_____ A. offers statistical or factual proof.	_____ B. presents the findings of recognized experts.	_____ C. is passionately presented by someone I admire.	_____ D. explores innovative possibilities for future change.

9. I prefer a teacher who

_____ A. lectures knowledgeably about the important facts and theories of the subject.	_____ B. provides practical, step-by-step, hands-on activities with clear learning objectives.	_____ C. stimulates exciting class discussions and group projects.	_____ D. challenges me to think for myself and explore the subject in my own way.

10. People who know me would describe me as

_____ A. logical.	_____ B. practical.	_____ C. emotional.	_____ D. creative.

Total your 10 scores for each letter and record them below:

_____ A. THINKING	_____ B. DOING	_____ C. FEELING	_____ D. INNOVATING

Your scores suggest the following:

30–40	**You have a strong preference to learn this way.**
20–29	**You are capable of learning this way when necessary.**
10–19	**You avoid this way of learning.**

Note: These questions are for educational self-assessment purposes only and do not have any affiliation with the HBDI or any other tests or assessments.

Other people prefer to read the directions first. Only after they digest the written information do they start playing or assembling. Notice that you could approach these learning tasks either way, but you *prefer* one learning experience over the other.

Although there is no preferred way for everyone to learn, there is a preferred way or ways for *you* to learn. Your scores on the self-assessment indicate your order of preference for four different learning approaches: THINKING, DOING, FEELING, and INNOVATING. More specifically, your scores suggest what types of questions motivate you, how you prefer to gather relevant information, and how you prefer to process information to discover meaningful answers.

Traditional college teaching is characterized by lectures and textbook assignments. These learning experiences typically favor the learning preference of Thinkers, and, to a somewhat lesser degree, Doers. However, as more instructors discover the importance of learning preferences, many are adapting their teaching methods to help all learners maximize their academic potential.

As you might guess, you're bound to get instructors whose teaching methods don't match your learning preference(s). When you do, experiment with some of the suggestions that follow. Perhaps most important of all, develop flexibility in how you learn. The more choices you have, the richer your learning experience will be and the greater your success.

In Table 7.1, you'll discover how Thinkers, Doers, Feelers, and Innovators usually prefer to learn. You may want to start by reading the section about your own learning preference(s), based on your self-assessment score. There you'll find options to use when your instructors don't teach as you prefer to learn. By looking at the other learning preferences as well, you'll see additional ways to expand your menu of effective learning strategies. Your goal here is to find deep-processing strategies that are compatible with and supportive of your preferred way(s) of learning as well as to expand your ability to learn in many ways.

Highly effective learners realize that not all instructors will create the kind of learning experiences they prefer. They take responsibility for not only *what* they learn but also *how* they learn it. They are confident that, with smart studying and persistence, their brains are up to the task. They discover deep-processing methods that maximize their learning, regardless of the subject or the way the instructor teaches.

Knowledge of our brain dominance empowers us as individuals and groups to achieve more of our full potential.

Ned Herrmann

Education is our passport to the future, for tomorrow belongs to the people who prepare for it today. . . . Give your brain as much attention as you do your hair and you'll be a thousand times better off.

Malcolm X

TABLE 7.1 Preferred Ways of Learning

	Thinking Learners	Doing Learners	Feeling Learners	Innovating Learners
Motivating questions that energize	**"What?" questions** *What theory supports that claim?* *What does a statistical analysis show?* *What is the logic here?* *What facts do you have?* *What have experts written about this?*	**"How?" questions** *How does this work?* *How can I use this?* *How will this help me or others?* *How did this work in the past?* *How can I do this more efficiently?* *How do experts do this?*	**"Why?" or "Who?" questions** *Why do I want or need to know this subject?* *Who is going to teach me?* *Who is going to learn this with me?* *Why do they want to know this information?* *Who here cares about me?* *Whom here do I care about?*	**"What if?" or "What else?" questions** *What if I tried doing this another way?* *What else could I do with this?* *What if the situation were different?* *What is this similar to?*
Preferred ways of gathering information	• Enjoy pondering facts and theories • Learn well from instructors who present information with lectures, visual aids, and PowerPoint slides; instructor-modeled problem solving; textbook readings; independent library research; and activities that call upon logical skills, such as debates • Benefit from time to reflect on what they are learning	• Enjoy taking action • Learn well from instructors who present factual information and practical skills in a step-by-step, logical manner; who present models or examples from experts in the field; and who allow students to do hands-on work in guided labs or practice applications • Benefit from the opportunity to dive right in and do the work	• Enjoy personal connections and an emotionally supportive environment • Learn well from instructors who are warm and caring; who value feelings as well as thoughts; and who create a safe, accepting classroom atmosphere with activities such as group work, role-playing, and sharing of individual experiences • Benefit from an opportunity to relate personally with both their instructors and classmates	• Enjoy imagining new possibilities and making unexpected connections • Learn well from instructors who encourage students to discover new and innovative applications; who allow students to use their intuition to create something new; and who use approaches such as independent projects, flexible rules and deadlines, and a menu of optional assignments, metaphors, art projects, and visual aids • Benefit from the freedom to work independently and let their imaginations run free
Preferred ways of processing information	• Respect logical arguments supported by documented facts and data • Are uncomfortable with answers that depend on tradition, emotion, personal considerations, or intuition • Excel at analyzing, dissecting, figuring out, and using logic to arrive at reasoned answers	• Honor objective testing of an idea or theory, whether their own or an expert's • Are uncomfortable with answers based on abstract theories, emotion, personal considerations, or intuition • Excel at being unbiased, taking action and observing outcomes, following procedures, and using confirmed facts to arrive at reasoned answers	• Honor their emotions and seek answers that are personally meaningful • Are uncomfortable with answers based on abstract theories or dispassionate facts and data • Excel at responding to emotional currents in groups, empathizing with others, considering others' feelings in making decisions, and using empathy	• Honor personal imagination and intuition • Are uncomfortable with answers based on abstract theories, cold facts, hard data, emotion, or personal considerations • Excel at trusting their inner vision, their intuitive sense of novel and exciting possibilities, and their imaginations

▶

TABLE 7.1 Preferred Ways of Learning *(continued)*

	Thinking Learners	Doing Learners	Feeling Learners	Innovating Learners
	• Like well-organized and well-documented information • Benefit from deep-processing strategies that bring order to complex information, such as creating outlines or comparison charts	• Appreciate well-organized and well-documented information • Benefit from deep-processing strategies that bring order to complex information, such as creating flow charts or a model of the concepts to be learned	and gut feelings to arrive at personally relevant answers	
When your instructor doesn't teach to your preferred style *What you can do:*	• Construct important "What?" questions and search for their answers in class sessions and homework assignments. • Construct and answer other types of questions your instructor might ask: How? Who? Why? What if? • Read all of your textbook assignments carefully, creating well-organized notes that identify the key points. • Resist getting upset if your instructor asks you to work in groups or has students do some of the teaching. • Organize your lecture and reading notes in a logical fashion, using outlines and comparison charts wherever appropriate. • Study with classmates who have different preferred ways of learning from your own, as they may provide insights about how to learn best from your instructor's teaching style.	• Construct important "How?" questions and search for their answers. • Construct and answer other types of questions your instructor might ask: What? Who? Why? What if? • Practice using the course information or skills outside of class. • Find someone who uses the course information or skills in his or her work and shadow that person for a day or more. • Resist getting upset if your instructor seems more interested in theories than in application. • Organize your lecture and reading notes in a step-by-step fashion, using outlines and comparison charts wherever appropriate. • Study with classmates who have preferred ways of learning different from your own, as they may provide insights into how to learn best from your instructor's teaching style.	• Construct important "Who?" and "Why?" questions and search for their answers. • Construct and answer other types of questions your instructor might ask: What? How? What if? • Discover the value of this subject for you personally. • Organize your notes and study materials using concept maps. • Resist feeling upset if your instructor seems distant or aloof. • Practice using the course information or skill with people in your life. • Make friends with classmates and discuss the subject with them outside of class. • Record class sessions (with permission) and listen to the recordings during free time. • Study with classmates who have different preferred ways of learning from your own, as they may provide insights into how to learn best from your instructor's teaching style. • Teach what you are learning to someone else.	• Construct important "What if?" and "What else?" questions and search for their answers. • Construct and answer other types of questions your instructor might ask: What? How? Who? Why? • Resist feeling upset when your instructor or classmates don't immediately see something as you do. • Organize your notes and study materials using concept maps and personally meaningful symbols or pictures. • Think about the content creatively (how could I adapt this? and metaphorically (what is this like?). • Study with classmates who have different preferred ways of learning from your own, as they may provide insights into how to learn best from your instructor's teaching style.

TABLE 7.1 Preferred Ways of Learning (*continued*)

	Thinking Learners	Doing Learners	Feeling Learners	Innovating Learners
Ask your instructor to do the following:	• Answer your important "What?" questions in class or in a conference. • List important points on the board or on handouts. • Provide handouts of PowerPoint presentations. • Allow students time to answer discussion questions in writing before answering them aloud. • Suggest additional readings, especially those written by recognized authorities in the subject. • Provide examples of past test questions. • Demonstrate the step-by-step solution of a math or science problem. • Provide data or other objective evidence that supports theories presented.	• Answer your important "How?" questions in class or in a conference. • Explain practical applications for theories taught in the course. • Provide a visual model of the concept (such as the Scripts Model in Chapter 6). • List important steps on the board or on handouts. • Demonstrate the information or skill in a step-by-step manner. • Invite guest speakers who can explain real-world application of the course information or skill in their daily work. • Observe and give corrective feedback as you demonstrate your hands-on understanding of the subject.	• Answer your important "Who?" and "Why?" questions in class or in a conference. • Explain how you might make a personal application of the course information. • Meet with your instructor outside of class, perhaps for tutoring, so you can get to know one another better and feel more comfortable in the class. • Provide occasional opportunities for small-group activities within the classroom. • Tell stories about how he or she (or someone else) has personally used the information or skills taught in the course. • Let you do some of the course assignments with a partner or in a group. • Allow students time to talk in pairs about discussion questions before answering them in front of the whole class.	• Answer your important "What if?" and "What else?" questions in class or in a conference. • Allow you to design some of your own assignments for the course. • Use visual aids to explain concepts in class. • Recommend a book for you to read by the most innovative or rebellious thinker in the field. • Evaluate your learning with essays and independent projects rather than with objective tests.

Young cat, if you keep your eyes open enough, oh, the stuff you would learn! The most wonderful stuff!

Dr. Seuss

In this activity, you will apply what you have learned about your preferred ways of learning to improve your results in a challenging course:

1 **Write about the most challenging course you are taking this semester.** Using what you just learned about how you prefer to learn, explain why the course may be difficult for you: Consider the subject matter, the teaching methods of the instructor, the textbook, and any other factors that may contribute to making this course difficult for someone with your preferred ways of learning. (If you are not taking a challenging course this semester, write about the most challenging course you have taken at any time in your education.)

2 **Using what you now know about the way you prefer to learn, write about choices you can make that will help you learn this challenging subject more easily.** Refer to the table comparison of Thinking Learners, Doing Learners, Feeling Learners, and Innovating Learners for possible choices.

By choosing different ways of learning in a challenging course, you can avoid the excusing, blaming, and complaining of a Victim and apply the solution-oriented approach of a Creator.

ONE STUDENT'S STORY

MELISSA THOMPSON, *Madison College, Wisconsin*

The challenge for me was chemistry. In lecture, the words were coming at me but the material wasn't sticking. The teacher was dry, standoffish, and intimidating, and he never joked around. I could read the book, reread it, and still wonder what I had just read. I was so frustrated because I needed to pass chemistry to get into my major. Realizing this, I was spending 10 to 12 hours a week studying, and I even started a study group and got a tutor. With all this help, I was doing fine on the homework, but the tests were killing me. I would take one look at them and my mind would go blank. I was stressed and so tempted to drop the course.

About that time I took the self-assessment in *On Course* about how I prefer to learn. I scored highest as a *feeling* learner, with *doing* learner second. I learned it's important for me to relate well personally with my instructors and classmates. Also, I want to see and touch what I'm learning, and I'm not comfortable with abstract theories and dispassionate facts. BINGO! The light went on. My favorite subjects in high school were classes like art and English where I could be creative and hands-on. My favorite teacher was my art teacher, a kind, caring person who told lots of stories that related art to lessons in life. Now I'm in chemistry, which

is exactly the type of subject I'm uncomfortable with, and I have a professor who is distant and intimidating. I knew what I had to do, and I probably wouldn't have done it before taking my College Success class.

I asked my chemistry instructor if I could stay after class to talk with him. I explained what I had discovered about my learning preference and why I was so challenged by chemistry. He agreed to meet with me after every class. During lecture, I'd write questions in the margins of my notes or leave a space wherever I got lost. I'd also highlight things in my book that I didn't understand. Going over my questions with him after class was helpful because everything was fresh in my mind. He would take my

▶

questions and answer them in different ways than he had in class. Then I would tell him what I thought he was saying and he would coach me until I had it right. Once I got to know him, I realized he was actually very friendly and helpful. He's a quiet person, but I could tell how much he loves chemistry.

Before, when I walked into class, I felt intimidated, but before long I felt more comfortable.

Soon after these meetings started, my grades began to come up. I was retaining the information and it showed. I worked hard, and in the end I did pass chemistry. If I hadn't

found out about my learning preference and done something different, I don't think I would have passed. My professor is definitely a "thinker," and he handles things so differently than I do. Once I understood the situation, though, I knew I had to step up and be in control of my life, and I did.

Employing Critical Thinking and Information Competency

FOCUS QUESTIONS   How can you determine the truth in this complex and confusing world? How can you present your truths in a way that is logical and persuasive to others?

Imagine this: While choosing what classes to take next semester, you decide to register for Psychology 101. After checking the various times it will be offered, you're delighted to discover that one section of the course fits perfectly into your schedule. The instructor is Professor Skinner. Because two of your friends are taking the course with Professor Skinner this semester, you wisely ask for their opinions.

One friend says, "Dr. Skinner is terrible. Don't even think about taking his course!" But your second friend says, "Dr. Skinner is the best instructor I've ever had! You should definitely take his class." Darn. Now what do you do?

Before deciding, you'd be smart to apply some critical thinking. The term "critical" derives from the Greek word *kritikos,* which means having the ability to understand or decide by using sound judgment. Critical thinking helps us better understand our complex world, make wise choices, and create more of our desired outcomes and experiences. Because they know the importance of critical thinking in many realms of life, most college educators place it high on the list of skills they want their students to master.

Here's good news. You've already been using a powerful critical thinking skill—the Wise Choice Process. As you've experienced, thoughtfully answering the six questions of the Wise Choice Process guides you through the steps of identifying options, looking at likely outcomes, and choosing the best option(s) available at the time. Making wise choices, then, is a key use of critical thinking.

In addition, critical thinking helps in another important realm: constructing and analyzing persuasive arguments. Think of the countless times others have tried to persuade you to think or do something: *Mathematics is a fascinating subject* (think this), *Let me copy your chemistry notes* (do that), *Global warming is a huge threat* (think this), *Major in accounting* (do that), *My roommate is so*

...[H]igher-order thinking, critical thinking abilities, are increasingly crucial to success in every domain of personal and professional life.

Richard Paul

Intelligence is something we are born with. Thinking is a skill that must be learned.

Edward de Bono

inconsiderate (think this), *Go to graduate school* (do that). And, of course, you're doing the same to them. Think this . . . do that.

Thus, much of life is a mental tug-of-war. Efforts to influence others' thoughts and actions lie at the heart of most human interaction, from conversations to wars. Think this . . . do that. It's no wonder the quality of your life is so greatly affected by your ability to construct and analyze persuasive arguments. You can even use these skills to decide whether or not to register for Professor Skinner's Psychology 101 class.

CONSTRUCTING LOGICAL ARGUMENTS

At many colleges, entire courses, even majors, are devoted to the study of argumentation. Here, we'll focus on two skills that are essential to the construction and analysis of persuasive arguments. The first skill is the ability to **construct a** *logical* **argument**. Three components of a logical argument are (1) reasons, (2) evidence, and (3) conclusions. As the building blocks of a logical argument, these ingredients may be offered in any order. Suppose, for example, someone wants to convince you to participate in your college's Sophomore Year Abroad Program. Here's how she might present her argument: *You should apply for our college's Sophomore Year Abroad Program. It'll change your life. I read an article in our college newspaper about the Sophomore Year Abroad Program. The author surveyed students who have completed the program, and 80 percent rated their experience as "life-changing."*

Here's what this argument looks like when organized by its components:

1. **Reasons** (also called *premises, claims,* or *assumptions*) answer the question "Why?" Reasons explain why the audience should think or do something. Reasons are presented as true, but they may not be.	**Why?** *The Sophomore Year Abroad Program will change your life.*
2. **Evidence** (also called *support*) answers the question "How do you know?" Evidence provides support to explain how the persuader knows the reason(s) to be true. Evidence should be verifiable as true. Three common kinds of evidence are facts, data, and stories.	**How Do I Know?** *I read an article in our college newspaper about the Sophomore Year Abroad Program. The author surveyed students who have completed the program, and 80 percent rated their experience as "life-changing."*
3. **Conclusions** (also called *opinions, beliefs,* or *positions*) answer the question "What?" Conclusions state what the persuader wants the audience to think or do.	**What Should You Think Or Do?** *You should apply for our college's Sophomore Year Abroad Program.*

ASKING PROBING QUESTIONS

Essential to analyzing a logical argument is a second critical thinking skill: **asking probing questions**. A probing question exposes conclusions built on unsound reasons, flawed evidence, and faulty logic. Probing questions are the kind that a good lawyer, doctor, educator, parent, detective, lover, shopper, or

---

The problem with many youngsters today is not that they don't have opinions but that they don't have the facts on which to base their opinions.

Albert Shanker

Always the beautiful answer who asks a more beautiful question.

e. e. cummings

friend asks to expose a hidden truth. The following chart lists some of the questions that critical thinkers might ask of any persuasive argument. Asking and answering the following questions (and others) can help you both construct powerful arguments of your own and analyze the arguments of others.

Questions about Reasons	Sample Probing Questions
• What reasons have been offered to support the conclusion? • Based on your experience and knowledge, do the reasons make sense? • Did the reasons derive from careful reflection and logical thinking, or are they misguided beliefs or prejudices? • Are there important exceptions to the reason? • Are the definitions of all key terms clear? • Are strong emotions being substituted for reasons?	• *When your brother studied for a year in Australia, was the experience life-changing for him?* • *What did the students mentioned in the newspaper article mean by "life-changing"?* • *Does it seem likely that such a program would change my life?* • *Do I even want to change my life?*

Questions about Evidence	Sample Probing Questions
• Is the source of the evidence reliable? • Is the evidence true? • Is the evidence objective and unbiased? • Is the evidence relevant? • Is the evidence current? • Is there enough evidence? • Does contradictory evidence exist? • Is the evidence complete?	• *Could the group of students polled have been specially selected to support the author's point of view about the Sophomore Year Abroad Program?* • *Does the person persuading me stand to gain if I choose to participate in the program?* • *Were enough students polled to make their results significant?* • *What percentage of students from all previous Sophomore Year Abroad groups rated the experience as "life-changing"?*

Questions about Conclusions	Sample Probing Questions
• Why? • Is the conclusion logical, or are there errors in the reasoning? • Could a different conclusion be drawn from the same reasons and/or evidence?	• *Could there be another cause for the students' life-changing experiences besides the Sophomore Year Abroad Program?* • *Did the students who rated their experience as "life-changing" have anything else in common that might have been the cause of their life-changing outcome instead of the program?* • *Is the program today the same program that changed the lives of students in the survey?*

The real value of learning lies in answering questions and questioning answers.

Marty Grothe

Education must enable one to sift and weigh evidence, to discern the true from the false, the real from the unreal, and the facts from the fiction. The function of education, therefore, is to teach one to think intensively and to think critically.

Martin Luther King, Jr.

APPLYING CRITICAL THINKING

Let's observe these critical thinking skills in action. Listen in as two students debate their conclusions about the biology professor described in "A Fish Story" (the case study that opens this chapter). Note how they explain the reasons and evidence that led them to their conclusions. And watch as each uses probing questions to challenge the argument of the other.

The abilities you develop as a critical thinker are designed to help you think your way through all of life's situations.

John Chaffee

I had learned at twenty-one that you couldn't just say a thing is so because it might not be so, and somebody brighter, smarter, and more thoughtful would come out and tell you it wasn't so. Then if you still thought it was, you had to prove it. Well, that was a new thing for me. I cannot, I really cannot describe what that did to my insides and to my head. I thought: I'm being educated finally.

Barbara Jordan

Emiko: I rated the biology professor as "terrible." I'd hate to have him as my instructor. **[Conclusion]**

Frank: Why? **[Probing question]**

Emiko: Are you kidding? College instructors are called "professors" for a reason. They're paid to "profess," and to profess means to *tell*. Professors are supposed to be the experts, so their job is to *tell* students what they need to know. **[Reason]**

Frank: Of course college instructors need to be experts in their subject. But is it really their job to tell students what they need to know? **[Probing question]** I think an instructor's job is to help students learn to think for themselves, not just memorize facts. **[Reason]** I'd love to have an instructor like that. I rated him as "excellent." **[Conclusion]**

Emiko: In the whole first week of the class, all he did was give his students a fish and then leave the room. **[Evidence]** Don't you think an instructor has a responsibility to at least be in the room? **[Probing question]**

Frank: The issue isn't whether the instructor was in the room. The issue is whether he was helping students learn. **[Reason]** The biology instructor did a lot more than give his students a fish and leave the room. He asked students to observe the fish and write down everything they observed. That request got them actively engaged in thinking like biologists on the first day of the course. **[Evidence]** In my opinion, that makes him an excellent instructor. **[Conclusion]**

Emiko: If a professor wants to get students actively engaged in their education, that's fine. But an instructor shouldn't frustrate and make students anxious on their very first day in college. Good instructors make their students feel comfortable. **[Reason]** Look at how anxious they were while waiting for the professor to return. They had no clue what was going on. **[Evidence]** That's why I think this instructor is terrible. **[Conclusion]**

Frank: Maybe the students were a bit anxious, but isn't that a good thing? **[Probing question]** Sometimes we need to be a little uncomfortable to learn something. **[Reason]** The best teacher I ever had in high school made everyone in the class uncomfortable by firing questions at us as fast as she could, especially at people who weren't paying attention or hadn't done the homework. I learned more in that class than in all my other high school classes combined. **[Evidence]** I would rather get a C from a professor who makes me think than get an A from a professor who simply feeds me answers to put on a test. **[Reason]**

Emiko: You wouldn't think that way if you wanted to be a doctor like I do. If I get a couple of C's, I can pretty much forget about getting into a good medical school. **[Reason]** That's why I would avoid this professor like the plague. He's terrible! **[Conclusion]**

Although their arguments aren't airtight, these students deserve credit for using critical thinking skills. They are clearly making an effort to provide reasons and evidence to support their conclusions. Additionally, they're asking probing questions about each other's reasons, evidence, and conclusions. Like all critical thinkers, they are respectful skeptics.

To some, it may appear that the purpose of critical thinking is to win arguments. Although critical thinking can certainly do that, it actually has a loftier goal. Critical thinking helps us seek the truth. That's why, to be an effective critical thinker, you must be willing to abandon your position whenever you find another view that is a better explanation of reality. The ultimate goal of a critical thinker is not victory, then, but learning.

HOW INFORMATION COMPETENCY SUPPORTS CRITICAL THINKING

An important time to apply critical thinking skills is when you're online. Because online sites, emails, tweets, blogs, and Facebook posts are filled with inaccurate, sometimes intentionally misleading information, critical thinking helps you seek the truth—but only if you can distinguish between accurate and false information. That's where information competency comes to the rescue.

According to the American Library Association, information competency consists of the following:

1. recognizing the need for information,
2. acquiring and evaluating information,
3. organizing and maintaining information, and
4. interpreting and communicating information.

In other words, information competency is a crucial skill you'll need to improve lifelong learning. Let's explore why.

Identifying False Information

Have you ever been fooled by false news or false information? It's easy to assume that everything shared over the Internet is true. But what if it's not? How can you tell? And why should you care? Many people think they know if news is true or false information. In fact, a 2018 study by the online learning company MindEdge found that 59 percent of adults ages 18 to 31 have a high level of confidence in their ability to detect false information. However, when tested, 52 percent of the respondents failed to accurately identify the majority of the false information on an Internet test. Only 19 percent of current college students and college graduates scored an "A," which is 5 percent less than the 2017 results! Identifying false news or information is one reason why information competency, also known as information literacy, is so important. Effective critical thinking depends on your having accurate information, and information literacy helps you determine what is accurate and what is false. Only when you have accurate information can you apply critical thinking to make wise choices.

Information literacy is the hyper ability to know when there is a need for information, to be able to identify, locate, evaluate, and effectively use that information for the issue or problem at hand.

United States National Forum on Information Literacy

People tend to quickly download inaccurate or blatantly false statements into memory because it's easier than critically evaluating and analyzing what they've heard.

Doug LaBier, Ph.D.

Applying the following information literacy strategies will help you detect false news or information:

1. **Be wary of headlines.** False news stories will often use catchy headlines to shock you and grab your attention. But are these stories substituting strong emotion for reasoned arguments? Are they filled with misguided beliefs or prejudices? Examine the evidence closely before drawing any conclusions.

2. **Check the link.** Some false news organizations will try to disguise themselves as legitimate news organizations by using a URL that is very similar to the real one. Look up the legitimate news source and compare the links to see if they're the same. If they're not, practice caution.

3. **Research the source (a person or organization).** If you're not familiar with the source, look it up. Check the "About" section on the related website to see if the source seems legitimate. Use probing questions to determine the validity of the source.

4. **Look out for awkward formatting or misspellings.** Not all websites will be free from typos, but false news and information sources may have more than most.

5. **Check the evidence in the article against the evidence at reputable websites.** Is the evidence objective and unbiased? Is there enough evidence, and is the article drawing accurate conclusions?

6. **Review other reports.** Are other news sources reporting this story? If so, and the sources you check are those that you trust, the story is more likely to be true. If not, the story may be false.

Avoiding Scams

Another benefit of information competency skills is avoiding being ripped off by scammers. Imagine getting a phone call two weeks before the start of school, and the caller claims to be a college official. The caller says you need to pay a certain amount of money before the start of school or the college is going to drop you from your classes. What do you do? Or, imagine that you found a great website offering discounted textbooks, and the deal is too good to pass up. Or, what if you get an offer for a fantastic scholarship that would give you enough money to cover your tuition?

By applying both your critical thinking and information competence skills, you can identify a real opportunity and avoid a scam. You can spot an imposter claiming to be a school official by calling your school to ask about the payment. You can research the company selling greatly discounted textbooks before paying any money. To verify the legitimacy of a scholarship offer, you can contact your college's financial aid department or do an Internet search. Other scams, such as those coming by email, may be spotted by looking for misspellings in basic words or a return email address that doesn't match the supposed sender. Don't click on any links in these bogus emails as they may download malware or spyware that can

A reliable source is one that provides a thorough, well-reasoned theory, argument, discussion, etc. based on strong evidence.

from the University of Georgia library website

Technology makes it easy for scammers to fake caller ID information, so the name and number you see aren't always real. If someone calls asking for money or personal information, hang up.

Federal Trade Commission

compromise your personal information or even destroy your computer. The Federal Trade Commission suggests special care with transactions that involve sending cash or wiring money because neither is protected by credit card regulations.

According to the Better Business Bureau, three common scams affect college students: advance fees, taxes, and fake employment. In an advance fee scam, a company makes a too-good-to-be-true offer (such as unusually low interest rates on student loans). But to "qualify," you're required to pay a fee up front. If you send money, that's the last time you'll hear from them. In a scam involving taxes, you may be contacted by a fake "IRS agent," who insists that you immediately pay the government an unpaid tax or be arrested. (By the way, the IRS will never phone you to collect money; instead it will mail tax bills.) In a fake employment scam, you may be offered an "easy" part-time job with high hourly income. For example, you may be asked to deposit checks in your bank account. You then return part of the money to your "employer" and keep the rest for yourself. Sounds good . . . until the checks bounce, and you lose the deposits plus the amount you sent to the scammers. You might even face criminal charges for cashing bad checks.

Online victim losses due to fraud totaled over **$1.4 billion** in 2017.

paraphrased from FBI's 2017 Internet Crime Report

In response to any possible scam offers, combine your critical thinking and information competency skills by conducting research to check the claims and facts:

1. **Ask probing questions.** Lots of questions. If something sounds too good to be true, it probably is.

2. **Research the company.** Look up the company online or search their phone number if you have it. Check the company website and review any articles published about it. Many scams are already reported widely on sites such as fraud.org and snopes.com.

3. **Ask *why* you should provide personal information.** Never give out your social security number, email address, bank or other account information, or any other personal information to people who call you, unless you have verified their identity and the need to submit such information.

Growing tuition costs and high levels of student loan debt are all concerns facing new and seasoned college students. And increasingly, students are falling victims to scam artists that want to prey on these fears.

Jamie Johnson

4. **Consider if the request and reasons for it make sense.** Be aware that you typically do not pay *any* advance "fees" to apply for a job, scholarship, or student loan.

5. **Seek more evidence.** Call your college and ask for more information from an adviser or expert, especially if the call or email is related to tuition, textbooks, or scholarships.

6. **Draw a conclusion, then take action.** If the company or request is fraudulent, report the calls to the Better Business Bureau or Federal Trade Commission to investigate.

Improving Your Information Competency

It's important to improve your information competency, not just to identify false information and scams, but to succeed in your college courses and in your career. In some college classes, for example, you'll be required to develop an argument using research, facts, and expert opinions as evidence. You may need to do the same in a work setting. Here are some strategies to do that effectively:

1. **Work with a librarian.** Librarians often teach information competency classes and workshops. The library typically offers an information or research desk with a specialist who can help you identify accurate and appropriate sources. A librarian can also help you identify false information online and may also be able to help you identify bogus websites.

2. **Learn to conduct searches.** Practice advanced searches in library databases and online search engines, reading abstracts to determine relevant research. Be aware that the top search engine results are often there because companies have paid to have their opinion or product promoted over others. Conducting searches will help you decide whether or not those news stories you read online are real by looking for other sources reporting the same story. You'll also be able to conduct searches on those too-good-to-be-true offers for scholarships or cheap textbooks to see whether or not they're legitimate.

3. **Identify and evaluate sources.** You'll want to determine the validity of the information or evidence you gather to support your ideas. One effective strategy is to ask, "Who is the author?" Ideally, the author is a recognized expert in the subject matter and has nothing to gain by persuading others to believe or act on the information presented. This approach is also important when checking the information you read online. It will help you determine whether or not the information is true.

Evaluating information using critical thinking and information competency skills is essential in both college and the workplace. According to the Santa Barbara City College website, "Information literacy is increasingly important in the contemporary environment of rapid technological change and proliferating information resources. It forms the basis for lifelong learning."

> Subject librarians can help you identify and locate reliable sources, develop effective search strategies for drawing additional information from sources you have found, or assist you in evaluating the reliability of those sources.
>
> from the University of Tennessee Libraries website

> As technology advances and the social landscape shifts, it is crucial for students to become digitally literate citizens.
>
> from the Teaching Tolerance website

JOURNAL ENTRY   26

Make a choice—Write about one of the following:

❶ Revisit the case study "Professor Rogers's Trial" (found at the beginning of Chapter 5). Write a logical argument that explains which character you think is most responsible for the group's grade of D. Be sure to state clearly your conclusion (who is most responsible), your reasons for this conclusion, and evidence from the case study to support your reasons. For example, your journal might begin, *I think the person most responsible for the group's grade of D is . . . The first reason I think this is . . . The evidence in the case study shows that . . . A second reason I think this person is most responsible is . . .* and so on.

▶

2 **Go to the website snopes.com and click on the "Hot 50" (you'll find a link in the banner at the top of the web page). Choose one of the false news stories posted on the "Hot 50" page. Read both the Snopes assessment of the original story as well as the original story itself. Most Snopes articles contain a link to the original story. After reading both the original false story and the Snopes discussion of it, answer the following questions about the original story:**

A. **Headline:** What headline was used for the original story, and why do you think the writer chose it?

B. **Source:** Who/what was the source for the original story? After researching this person or organization, explain if there are reasons to doubt the trustworthiness of this source.

C. **Evidence:** What evidence was used in the original story to support the writer's claims? Is the evidence true? Is there enough evidence?

D. **Questions:** Write three probing questions you might ask the writer of the original story to help you determine if the story is true or false.

Education's purpose is to replace an empty mind with an open one.

Malcolm S. Forbes

LIFELONG LEARNING / at Work

An organization's ability to learn, and translate that learning into action rapidly, is the ultimate competitive advantage.

—*Jack Welch, chairman and CEO, General Electric*

It didn't seem likely that I (JB) would go to college. In my junior year of high school, I was failing most of my courses. I had little interest in learning anything. By my senior year I had dropped out of high school and was parking cars at a restaurant. After two years of parking cars, I looked around one day and asked myself, "Is this it? Is this what I'll do for the rest of my life?" As I anticipated a new future, a small spark of lifelong learning was reignited deep inside me. Maybe I could take a class at the community college. I did. I took one class, then another, and soon I began to find an interest in learning again. Eventually, I would apply to George Washington University, then transfer to University of California, Berkeley. I never looked back, and each year I strengthened my competency of lifelong learning just a little more. I was so excited about learning that I even took classes outside my major. After earning my bachelor's degree, I stayed at the university for both a master's degree and a doctoral degree. I just couldn't stop learning!

As I started my professional career, I stayed curious, always open to learning something new. I took more classes, watched online videos, and apprenticed with more experienced employees. The more I acted as a lifelong learner, the stronger my skill set became. I developed into a more valuable employee, was promoted, earned a higher salary, and enjoyed my job even more because I was constantly using my new skills.

Lifelong learning is the ability to keep learning new things (even enthusiastically) for the rest of your life. Employers strongly value employees who are dedicated lifelong learners. As Mark Cuban,

▶

billionaire owner of the Dallas Mavericks, argues, "I can't say it enough that learning how to learn is one of the greatest skills anyone can have. It's why I advocate that everyone go to college." Being a life-long learner in college and at work will provide you with these benefits, and more:

- Increased opportunities for promotion and increased salary

- Higher level of engagement in and satisfaction with your work

- Stronger motivation to contribute value to your employer

- Greater enjoyment from your pursuit of new ideas

- Increased number of ideas and solutions from your research and new learning

- Enhanced résumé and career portfolio for future job applications

Starting your lifelong learning doesn't have to wait for you to start your career. It can begin with any experience—volunteer opportunities, internships, and so on—that helps you discover your passion for learning more.

First, though, your lifelong learning might start with choosing a major that will go along with the dream career you want.

CHOOSING A MAJOR

How do you go about choosing a major? One place to start is with your interests and values. What ignites your passion and makes you excited to learn more? Do you enjoy helping your friends with their computer problems? Do you find yourself doing extra math problems because you enjoy the logic of numbers? Are you passionate about exercise and being part of a team sport? Next, think about possible careers that match your interests. Be creative! If you like solving problems, what about a career

in engineering? If you enjoy sports, what about a career in nutrition or physical therapy? Once you've identified your interests and possible career options, look at the list of majors your college offers. Do the descriptions of the majors match your interests? If you're struggling to make connections between your interests and a major, talk to someone in your career office, a trusted professor, your adviser, or your mentor. But even if the subjects you like don't immediately suggest a specific career, don't be discouraged. You might love philosophy, but you might not know how to connect philosophy to a career. However, remember that it's not just your major that leads to a career—it's the skills and experiences you learn and gain in your courses that will help you land the career of your dreams. Philosophy majors have skills in critical thinking, persuasive arguments, and writing that can apply to many careers. The important thing to remember is to continue using your lifelong learning skills to explore opportunities in whatever major you choose to help you develop the skills you can later use in your career.

So, how do you take all your lifelong learning and use it to get a new position or a new career? You start with a résumé.

RÉSUMÉ PREPARATION

Whether you are looking to secure an internship, get your first job out of college, or move up in the career you already have, you'll likely need a résumé. Employers look for evidence that new hires are willing to keep learning. After all, you'll need to learn many new skills on the job to succeed. Your résumé is a great place to demonstrate how you've already used your lifelong learning to develop skills. Whether through internships, volunteer experiences, courses you take in college, or previous jobs, these skills will prove to your potential employer that not only will you succeed in this new job, but that you're also the best fit for it.

Your résumé is a brief summary of your professional, educational, and personal skills and experiences. In some fields, job candidates may submit a CV (curriculum vitae) instead. The CV is a much more detailed summary of these same categories of skills and experiences, and would include significant projects, awards, and publications across multiple pages. A résumé should be limited to one page, exceeding that length only for more experienced professionals with many years in the field. You should customize the résumé for each application when the job description is different. Here are the five most important elements of an effective résumé:

- **Contact:** Provide full name, phone number, email, and city (or full mailing address) and Internet/social media sites and contacts that are relevant to the position.

- **Work experience:** List relevant work, internship, and volunteer experience (especially for college students with less direct work experience). Stress what you accomplished in each position rather than just the position title. If you are working now, include your current title/company and previous title/company, and your start and end dates.

- **Hard and soft skills:** Include skills required in the job description (for example, "high proficiency in Microsoft Office software and excellent team building skills"). Add any other skills that will help you stand out as a candidate for the position.

- **Education:** Include all relevant educational degrees or certifications. You can also include any academic honors or awards you have received.

- **Objective or professional résumé summary:** An objective might be *Seeking a position as a financial analyst in the banking industry*. A professional résumé summary represents your brand and focuses on you rather than the desired position. It might be *A responsible, motivated graduate with extensive internship experience in the banking industry*, or *An effective team player with excellent communication skills, client empathy, and deep enthusiasm for finance, statistics, and helping others achieve retirement goals.*

Now that you know what to include on a résumé, how can you organize it to make sure it shows your experience in a way that will be clear to employers? You can organize your résumé in many ways. You can use a chronological method, listing most recent employment and experience first. This is a great way to show you've already advanced in your career and you're ready to use your lifelong learning skills to succeed and progress in a new position. You can also organize your résumé by important skills, where you include relevant experience, such as work, internship, or volunteer experience, to clearly show how you already possess the skills to succeed, despite a lack of direct experience in a career. Remember to be creative when thinking about how your current experience relates to a certain skill. Parking cars isn't a skill required of a college professor, but clear communication is. Whether I was directing a driver how to park to avoid hitting another car or explaining expectations to students in a class, I needed communication skills. Never underestimate the experience you already have—you just need to remember to look for the skills you've learned!

After identifying your organization method and experiences, you'll want to make sure your résumé is tailored to the description of the job for which you're applying. This can be challenging to do. One way to start is by creating a "general résumé" in which you include all of the experiences and skills you've learned in each position. For example, include your coursework, volunteer experience, community service, summer jobs, weekend gigs, internships. Don't leave anything out. Next, review the job description for key skills or required experience. Because a résumé needs to be short— one page—this step is very important. Mark the positions and experiences in your "general" résumé that match these skills and required experience.

▶

Then customize the résumé to the new position, emphasizing the skills and experiences that are a match, those relevant to the job for which you're currently applying.

There are some technical parts of writing a résumé. Studies show that on average, recruiters, hiring managers, and employers only spend 6 to 11 seconds looking at a résumé before deciding on whether to reject or move forward with an applicant. How can you make your résumé stand out?

- Use a readable font, like Times New Roman. Avoid fancy, hard-to-read fonts like Comic Sans or Script. The font size should be easy to read but not too large.

- Keep plenty of open space on your résumé and avoid overcrowding.

- Be concise and avoid repetition.

- Bold keywords that are found in the job description.

- Use strong action verbs, like *coordinated, planned, designed,* or *implemented.*

Writing a résumé takes practice. Search online résumé examples that apply to the career for which you're applying. Also, search for and use words that recruiters love to see on résumés, such as *launched, orchestrated, created,* or *managed* and avoid words they don't like, such as *hard worker, smart, world-class,* or *groundbreaking.* Share your résumé with a trusted friend, mentor, or someone from the career center for feedback on how to improve it. Remember, as a lifelong learner, you'll want to update your general résumé with any new experience so you don't forget it, and to add to future résumés. You never know what opportunities might come up in the future!

COVER LETTER

A cover letter is another way to demonstrate your lifelong learning skills. The purpose of a cover letter is to introduce yourself, encouraging a potential employer to invest more time in reading your résumé. Unlike a résumé, a cover letter isn't always required for a job, but it might be strategic to send one anyway. It's an opportunity to communicate your personal brand, and to persuade a potential employer why you're an excellent fit for the position. You'll want to share more details about experiences listed on your résumé or experiences that you didn't list but that are still applicable.

So what kind of details are helpful? Imagine that you're applying for a teaching job and you've listed your experience of parking cars. The teaching job requires that applicants have excellent communication skills. Here is a great place to detail how your communication skills improved the efficiency of parking cars, and that this experience will therefore help you communicate effectively with students and their parents. As with your résumé, you'll want to pull words and phrases from the job description and relate them directly and specifically to your experience to prove you have the skills to succeed. Check online for cover letter samples for the job you're seeking.

As with a résumé, you'll want to organize your cover letter. At the top of the letter, start with both employer and your own name, address, phone number, email, and the current date. A salutation—for example, "Dear Recruiter Name"—should start the letter. If you can, do some research on who the hiring manager is and address the letter directly to that person—it will help set your cover letter apart from others. Introduce the letter by indicating the job in which you are interested, then state right away why you are an outstanding candidate. Be very specific, making an honest but intriguing claim about yourself. For example, "I feel certain that I'm the right person for this position because ever since I was a child visiting my grandmother, it's been my dream to work with seniors in a nursing home."

In the main body of the letter, promote your personal brand, demonstrate that you are unique, and connect your experiences to the specific requirements in the job description to show that your skills are an excellent fit for the position. In just a few paragraphs, make the most of the cover letter opportunity, acting as though an interviewer had just given you an extra five minutes to showcase yourself. Do everything you can to show more of your human side, engaging the reader's curiosity.

Close your letter by letting the recruiter know that you are grateful that he or she read your letter (and you are, given the research on how little time recruiters typically spend reading job application materials). Make a final point, using a new, persuasive argument about why they should interview you. Ask that the recruiter contact you to arrange a time for an interview. Include your signature.

The technical parts to writing a cover letter are similar to those of a résumé:

- Use the same easy-to-read font you used on your résumé.
- Use proper margins and spacing (review standard business letter templates to identify these if the job description doesn't list their requirements).
- Keep your cover letter to about one page.
- Be concise, using clear and specific examples to illustrate your skills and experience.
- Proofread your letter to ensure it is free from errors; additionally, ask a trusted friend, mentor, or someone at the career center to help you.

When an employer has 100 or more candidates for a single position, nearly anything can lead to a rejection. Take enough time that you have a high level of confidence that you are representing yourself (and your brand) at your best!

Being a lifelong learner while at college will increase your motivation to learn. The increased knowledge and higher GPA you earn will help you more easily get your desired job. Being a lifelong learner at work will make your job more interesting and allow you to grow into increased responsibility (not to mention increased income). To keep learning after college, check out some of the platforms that offer online classes and tutorials. You can try Lynda.com (you can add Lynda's paid "certificate of completion" to your LinkedIn profile). Coursera, edX.org, and Udacity, among others, are also free options that allow you to add a paid certificate to your résumé or LinkedIn profile. Start the habit now of engaging in lifelong learning. Consider the advice of management expert Peter Drucker: "We now accept the fact that learning is a lifelong process of keeping abreast of change. And the most pressing task is to teach people how to learn."

"Even though you're exceptionally well qualified, Kate, I'd say that 'victim' is not a good career choice."

TECH TIPS: Lifelong Learning

Mindsetonline.com is the website of Carol Dweck, originator of the theory of fixed and growth mindsets. Click on the link "Test Your Mindset." Then complete the 16-item online quiz and get immediate results.

Mindsetworks.com offers four assessments related to mindset. As a student, you'll be most interested in the first one: "What's My Mindset?" (for 12 to Adult). This quiz has only eight questions and can be completed in a few minutes. The site also has a couple of videos about fixed and growth mindsets.

VARK-learn.com is an online self-assessment that provides information about your "learning style." Is your preference Visual (seeing), Aural (listening), Read/Write, or Kinesthetic (physically moving)? As with the learning inventory in this chapter, you would be best served by seeing your results on the VARK as indicating a preference for certain learning activities but not an inability to learn in other ways.

EducationPlanner.org allows you to take self-assessments on "What Kind of Student Are You?," "What's Your Learning Style?," "Which Study Habits Can You Improve?," and "How Strong is Your Character?" to help you become a lifelong learner. In addition, this website allows you to submit questions to a counselor about careers, higher education, or paying for college. A career section helps you figure out what careers match your unique skills.

BELIEVING IN YOURSELF

Develop Self-Respect

FOCUS QUESTIONS What is your present level of self-respect? How can you raise your self-respect, and therefore your self-esteem, even higher?

> If you want to be respected by others, the great thing is to respect yourself. Only by that, only by self-respect will you compel others to respect you.
>
> Fyodor Dostoyevsky

Self-respect is the core belief that *I am an admirable person*. If self-confidence is the result of **what** I do, then self-respect is the result of **how** I do it.

Two crucial choices that build up or tear down self-respect are whether or not I live with integrity and whether or not I keep my commitments.

LIVE WITH INTEGRITY (SUCH AS NO CHEATING OR PLAGIARIZING)

The foundation of integrity is my personal value system. What is important to me? What experiences do I want to have? What experiences do I want others to have? Do I prize outer rewards such as cars, clothes, compliments, travel, fame, or money? Do I value inner experiences such as love, respect, excellence, security, honesty, wisdom, or compassion?

Integrity derives from the root word *integer,* meaning "one" or "whole." Thus, we create integrity by choosing words and deeds that are one with our values. Many students say they value their education, but their actions indicate otherwise. They leave assignments undone; they do less than their best work; they miss classes; they come late. In short, their choices contradict what they say they value. Choices that lack integrity tear at an aware person's self-respect.

One of my greatest integrity tests occurred during my first year in college. First, a little background. In the public high school I'd attended, cheating was widespread. You could say it was part of the student culture. As for me, I prided myself on never cheating . . . except in Latin. (Yes, at that time my high school actually offered three levels of Latin.) I knew cheating was wrong, but my Inner Defender was ever ready with excuses: *Everyone cheats. No one uses Latin anymore, so it's a huge waste of time. And if I don't cheat, everyone else will . . . and then my grade will suffer.* I became masterful at writing vocabulary words and verb conjugations on the tiniest pieces of paper imaginable. I got an A. *Mea culpa.*

Now fast-forward to the middle of my first semester in college. All of us were preparing for midterm exams. My Inner Critic, you may recall, had convinced me that I was in serious danger of failing out of college. Every one of my classmates, I believed, was smarter and better prepared than I was. They had read books I hadn't even *heard* of. They had completed courses my high school didn't even *offer.* They could probably talk intelligently about ancient Rome . . . in *Latin.* If I was going to survive in college, I decided, I would have to cheat. As I studied for midterms, I created some of the finest crib notes on planet Earth.

However, I was in for a jolt. When I arrived at my first college exam, the professor told us to write and sign the following statement on the front of our exam booklets: "I pledge my honor that I have neither given nor received assistance on this examination." And then he left the room!

Talk about a fork in the road! There I was with all my cleverly miniaturized crib notes and (1) I had just signed a promise that I would not use them, and (2) there was no instructor present to catch me if I did. Drat. What to do?

Academic integrity is another aspect of the deep culture of higher education. Chances are, your college has a written policy or honor code that upholds the value of academic honesty and condemns cheating. You'll find it in your college's catalog or on its website. Here's part of one from Amherst College: ". . . the College considers it a violation of the requirements of intellectual responsibility to submit work that is not one's own or otherwise to subvert the conditions under which academic work is performed by oneself or by others."

"Academic dishonesty," the Amherst policy explains, "refers to any act that is intended to produce an academic assessment that is not commensurate with an individual's performance, or any act that is intended to unfairly assist or hinder an individual's academic efforts." Because one of the purposes of higher education is to seek truth, stamping out cheating seems like a good idea.

So, you might wonder, how's the "stamping out" going? When I did a recent Google search for "academic integrity," I got "about 165,000,000 results."

Always aim at complete harmony of thought and word and deed.

Mohandas K. Gandhi

I would prefer even to fail with honor than to win by cheating.

Sophocles

Clearly a hot topic. Donald McCabe, a professor at Rutgers University, has studied this topic for years. He surveyed 1,800 students from nine universities. Seventy percent of them admitted to cheating on exams, while 84 percent said they cheated on assignments. Educational Testing Service (ETS) reports that one website that sells term papers averages about 80,000 hits *per day*. Ironically, I found one such website offering a choice of 60 term papers for sale on the topic of academic integrity. In other words, you can cheat by buying a paper that condemns cheating.

So, it would appear that many students cheat. Why not join them? Here are three, among many, reasons.

First, let's be practical. You might get caught. Because cheating is so wide-spread, educators are combating it in many ways. For example, just as students can buy term papers on websites, instructors can check websites to see if a term paper has ever been turned in before. How about consequences? Better check your college's penalties for cheating. Penalties can range from failing the test or assignment, to failing the course, or even to being expelled. Some colleges note the infraction on a student's transcript, a chilling message to all future employers.

Second, you'll learn more. If you're in college only to get a degree and what you learn doesn't matter, you might not care—that is, until you're in a job and need some of the skills you were supposed to learn in that course you cheated your way through. If you're a nursing student, I sure hope I never come under your care. If you're an engineering student, I sure hope I never drive over one of your bridges.

Finally, your self-respect will increase. At least that's what I experienced. You see, at my first college midterm exam many years ago, I decided not to cheat. My first thought was, *With the professor gone, it's too easy.* My second thought was, *If I cheat, I'll never know what I'm capable of . . . maybe it's a lot more than I think.* And then I thought, *It would be wrong. Even if no one else ever finds out, I'll know I cheated.* In that moment, at the ripe old age of 18, I decided that the cost of cheating is too high.

Here's what I learned. Each time we contradict our personal values, we make a withdrawal from our self-respect account. Each time we are true to our personal values, we make a deposit. When you find that your choices are out of alignment with your values, you need to make a change . . . for your own sake. You can't abandon what you hold sacred and still retain your self-respect.

KEEP COMMITMENTS

Now let's consider another choice that influences your self-respect. Imagine that someone has made a promise to you but doesn't keep it. Then he makes and breaks a second promise. And then another and another.

T he willingness to accept responsibility for one's own life is the source from which self-respect springs.

Joan Didion

T his above all; to thine own self be true

And it must follow, as the night the day

Thou canst not then be false to any man.

Polonius, in Shakespeare's *Hamlet*

Wouldn't you lose respect for this person? What do you suppose happens when the person making and breaking all these promises is YOU?

True, your Inner Defender would quickly send out a smoke screen of excuses. But the truth would not be lost on your Inner Guide. The fact remains: You made commitments and broke them. This violation of your word makes a major withdrawal from your self-respect account.

To make a deposit in your self-respect account, keep commitments, especially to yourself. Here's how:

- **Make your agreements consciously.** Understand exactly what you're committing to. Say "no" to requests that will get you off course; don't commit to more than you can handle just to placate others.

- **Use Creator language.** Don't say, "I'll try to do it." Say, "I *will* do it." Or "I *won't* do it."

- **Make your agreements important.** Write them down. Tell others about them.

- **Create a plan; then do everything in your power to carry out that plan.** Use your self-management tools to track your promises to yourself and others.

- **If a problem arises or you change your mind, renegotiate** (don't just abandon your promise).

The person we break commitments with the most is, ironically, our self. How are you doing in this regard? Here's some evidence: How are you doing with the commitment you made to your goals and dream in Journal Entry 10? How are you doing with your 32-Day Commitment from Journal Entry 14?

If you haven't kept these commitments (or others), ask your Inner Guide, *What did I make more important than keeping my commitment to myself?* A part of you wanted to keep your agreement. But another, stronger part of you obviously resisted. Pursue your exploration of this inner conflict with total honesty and you may uncover a self-defeating pattern or limiting core belief that is crying out for a change. After all, our choices reveal what we *really* value.

Keeping commitments often requires overcoming enormous obstacles. That was the case with one of my students. Rosalie had postponed her dream of becoming a nurse for 18 years while raising her two children alone. Shortly after enrolling in college, her new husband asked her to drop out to take care of his two sons from a former marriage. Rosalie agreed, postponing her dream once more. Now back in college 10 years later, she made what she called a "sacred vow" to attend every class on time, to do her very best on all work, and to participate actively. This time she was committed to getting her nursing degree. Finally her time had come.

Then, one night she got a call from her son, who was now married and had a two-year-old baby girl. He had a serious problem: His wife was on drugs. Worse, that day she had bought $200 worth of drugs on credit, and the drug dealers were holding Rosalie's granddaughter until they got paid. Rosalie spent the early evening gathering cash from every source she could, finally delivering

> To me integrity is the bottom line in self-esteem. It begins with the keeping of one's word or doing what you say you will do, when you say you will do it, whether you feel like it or not.
>
> Betty Hatch,
> past president,
> National Council for
> Self-Esteem

> Whenever I break an agreement, I pay the price first. It breaks down my self-esteem, my credibility with myself, my self-trust, my self-confidence. It causes me not to be able to trust myself. If I cannot trust myself, whom can I trust?
>
> Patricia J. Munson

the money to her son. Then, all night she lay awake, waiting to hear if her grandchild would be returned safely.

At six in the morning, Rosalie got good news when her son brought the baby to her house. He asked Rosalie to watch the child while he and his wife had a serious talk. Hours passed, and still Rosalie cared for the baby. Closer and closer crept the hour when her college classes would begin. She started to get angrier and angrier as she realized that once again she was allowing others to pull her off course. And then she remembered that she had a choice. She could stay home and feel sorry for herself, or she could do something to get back on course.

At about nine o'clock, Rosalie called her sister who lived on the other side of town. She asked her sister to take a cab to Rosalie's house, promised to pay the cab fare, and even offered to pay her sister a bonus to watch the baby.

"I didn't get to class on time," Rosalie said. "But I got there. And when I did, I just wanted to walk into the middle of the room and yell, 'YEEAAH! I MADE IT!'"

If you could have seen her face when she told the class about her ordeal and her victory, you would have seen a woman who had just learned one of life's great lessons: When we break a commitment to ourselves, something inside of us dies. When we keep a commitment to ourselves, something inside of us thrives. That something is self-respect.

> You will always be in fashion if you are true to yourself, and only if you are true to yourself.
>
> Maya Angelou

> Character, simply stated, is doing what you say you're going to do. A more formal definition is: Character is the ability to carry out a worthy decision after the emotion of making that decision has passed.
>
> Hyrum W. Smith

JOURNAL ENTRY   27

In this activity, you will explore strengthening your self-respect. People with self-respect honor and admire themselves not just for *what* they do but for *how* they do it.

Make a choice—write about one of the following:

1   **Write about a time when you passed a personal integrity test.** Tell about an experience when you were greatly tempted to abandon one of your important values. Describe how you decided to "do the right thing" instead of giving in to the temptation.

2   **Write about a time when you kept a commitment that was difficult to keep.** Fully explain the commitment you made to yourself or to someone else. Then discuss the challenges—both inner and outer—that made it difficult for you to keep this promise. Explain how you were able to keep the commitment despite these challenges.

Asking probing questions leads to meaningful answers. Anticipate questions a curious reader might ask you about your stories . . . and answer them. For example, what effect did your choice have on your self-esteem?

ONE STUDENT'S STORY

DALENE MEEK, *San Juan College, New Mexico*

I've been going to college for 37 years without earning a degree. In my senior year in high school, I thought about going to Vanderbilt University in Nashville and becoming a teacher, but a stronger dream won out. I wanted to be a wife and a mother, so attending a local college became just a filler until my dream of having a family came true.

Through the years I've held a variety of jobs, married, gotten divorced, raised my daughter, cared for my parents in the last years of their lives, had a granddaughter, and recovered from a serious illness, and all the while I continued to take college courses for pleasure whenever I could. But I never got my degree.

Now I feel like something is unfinished. Every time I took a course and got a good grade, it filled me up with something missing. A voice in my head kept saying, "You silly girl, why didn't you go to college and make a profession for yourself?" I always used the excuse that I wanted to be a mother and a grandmother. Home has always been important to me, but life changed this year.

I'm back in college, and this time my dream is to earn my degree. I only need 16 more credits, and the LRNS III class was part of my required credits. It was my choice to take this class first, and I am so thrilled I did. What a great stepping-stone to get me on the right path. When the semester started,

I was having a hard time, worrying that I might not finish my degree again. Thanks to this course, I have tools to help me achieve my goal, so that is NOT going to happen this time.

From the first day of class, I started finding the young girl I thought was gone forever. The one who loved to learn, the one who got good grades, the one who wasn't afraid. I spent years trying to make life perfect for others, but I left out the most important person: ME. The recording being played over and over in my head was "You're not smart enough, you don't have what it takes to succeed, and you need someone to help you." I didn't respect myself, and it was an awful feeling. NO MORE! Thanks to my inner guide, I have started to change this recording. Every time I hand in an *On Course* journal, complete a quiz, or participate in an activity, I feel wonderful. The recording has started to change: "You can do this, Dalene, and it's fun." Many times during the class, I went out of my comfort zone, and the recording changed even more: "Learning is very rewarding, and I am doing a really good job." In the past, I allowed others and even myself to dummy me down. I didn't respect myself, and it was an awful feeling. Now I spend time building myself up, standing up for myself in ways I never imagined before.

One of my best moments during the class was writing the

letter to someone who could help me academically. It was something I had thought about doing for years. I wrote to a math professor here at San Juan College and asked for his help. I explained that math is a weak spot for me, so when I started college years ago, I wanted to get my math requirement out of the way while my high school math skills were still fresh. I did well in the class and was happy to have those credits finished. However, years later the college recoded the class, and I lost the credits. When I found out, I was scared I couldn't pass math again. In my letter, I explained all of this and how important it was to me to finally finish my degree. Then, I did something I never would have done before this class. I conquered my nervousness, made an appointment with the math professor, and read him my letter. He was more than kind and has gone to bat for me in trying to recover the credits. As of right now the decision is in the hands of the dean of the math department. If I have to start over with math, I will. I now have the confidence to succeed.

I feel proud not only because of what I have accomplished academically, but also for standing up for myself in college and in all areas of my life. I've learned to respect myself, and when we respect ourselves, we'll take care of ourselves just as well as we take care of the people we love. Closed doors have now been opened, and I know it is never too late to start again and finish.

Photo: Courtesy of Dalene Meek.

Healthy Choices: Physical Activity

Now that you've settled into college life, how much do you move?

If your answer is "not much," you're not alone. Most college students are sedentary (inactive) much of the day. They sit in classes, at meals, at the library, while reading, doing assignments, and possibly commuting. They also sit in front of screens: tablets, computers, TVs, video games, cell phones.

And it's not only college students who don't move much. In 2017 a study of 8,000 adults by the Columbia University Department of Medicine revealed just how sedentary Americans are. The study found that participants were inactive about 12.3 hours a day. Now add 8 hours for a good night's sleep. That means for about 85 percent of the day, people weren't moving.

Turns out this inactivity is a risk factor for many health problems, including obesity, several forms of cancer, osteoporosis (weak and brittle bones), depression, anxiety, diabetes, and heart diseases. Diabetes can damage eyes, kidneys, and nerves. Heart problems cause sluggish blood flow, which increases the threat of clots in legs and lungs. Slower blood flow also deprives our brain of needed oxygen, hurting our thinking. A 2018 study by researchers at University of California, Los Angeles, found that sitting too much is associated with thinning of brain regions that are essential to the formation of memories. "This study is interesting," says neuroscientist Tara Swart, "and it contributes to our understanding that being sedentary is bad for your health in many ways, and one of these is that your memory may decline more rapidly."

Worst of all, inactivity has shown a direct link to premature death. That's why the scientific community now calls inactivity the "sitting disease" or "sedentary death syndrome." According to the authors of *Lifetime Physical Fitness and Wellness,* "Excessive sitting is the 'new smoking.'... Sadly, the death rate of 'heavy sitters' nearly matches that of 'heavy smokers.'" (Which makes me quite uneasy as I sit here at my computer writing this. I think I'll get up and take a quick walk!)

An article in the *Journal of Exercise Physiology* reports what we might guess about college students. The majority fail to meet the minimum goals for physical activity set by both the Centers for Disease Control and the American College of Sports Medicine. That's why learning about the value of physical activity could literally save your life.

WHY BE PHYSICALLY ACTIVE?

"If there were a drug with the same benefits as exercise, it would instantly be the standard of care," says Robert Sallis, MD, past president of the American College of Sports Medicine. What are those benefits? Regular physical activity helps our bodies stay healthy, our emotions stay positive, and our brains stay sharp.

Consider the many benefits to our bodies of regular movement:

- Decreased risk for many chronic illnesses, including heart disease, stroke, colon and breast cancer, type 2 diabetes, and osteoporosis
- Lowered "bad" cholesterol (LDL) and increased "good" cholesterol (HDL)
- Enhanced muscle tone, strength, balance, joint flexibility, and endurance
- Reduced chronic back pain
- Improved blood circulation
- Stronger immune system

- Healthier body weight
- Reduced constipation
- Increased energy
- Improved sleep
- Longer life

If you're young, some of these health risks, like heart disease, may seem too far in the future to worry about. Those are problems for old people, right? Not necessarily. Serious health problems can start early in life and go undetected for years. Case in point: Autopsies were done on 3,832 U.S. soldiers who died between 2001 and 2011. These soldiers averaged only 26 years old and all had passed a medical exam to enter the military. Still, autopsies revealed that nearly 9 percent of these young soldiers already had heart-threatening plaque in their arteries. Other studies show that type 2 diabetes, osteoporosis, high blood pressure, and heart disease can all begin early in life. The message is clear. The lifestyle choices you make now will shape both the quality and length of your life.

Regular activity not only contributes to your physical health, it also improves your emotional health. Perhaps you've heard the term "runner's high." During exercise, our bodies release chemicals called endorphins. Endorphins decrease perceptions of pain and increase positive feelings. In 2014, the *Journal of the American Medical Association* published a study that tracked 11,000 people for 50 years. Researchers found that people who often exercised suffered fewer symptoms of depression than those who were inactive. "There's good epidemiological data to suggest that active people are less depressed than inactive people," says James Blumenthal, a clinical psychologist at Duke University. Researchers at Southern Methodist University have used exercise to help people lower anxiety. They provided an exercise program for half a group of people with high anxiety. After only two weeks, members of the exercise group reported a significant drop in anxiety compared to those not in the exercise group.

As if improved physical and emotional health aren't enough, exercise also aids brain health and academic success. According to the authors of *Lifetime Physical Fitness and Wellness,* "Exercise provides the necessary stimulus for brain neurons to interconnect, creating the perfect environment in which the brain is ready and able to learn." The authors report data on a study of more than 2.4 million students in Texas. The data show that "high levels of fitness were associated with better academic grades." Another study at the University of Wisconsin School of Medicine and Public Health found further brain benefits of exercise. People who exercise have more volume in brain areas responsible for executive function and reasoning. "We've done a series of studies showing that increased aerobic capacity boosts brain structure, function, and cognition," said Ozioma Okonkwo, one of the researchers. Summing up the many benefits of physical activity, Dr. Okonkwo added, "Exercise is the full package."

Would you take a free pill that increases your chances of enjoying a long, healthy life? If so, exercise is that pill. According to an article in the *Journal of the American Medical Association,* "There is no drug in current or prospective use that holds as much promise for sustained health as a lifetime program of physical exercise."

THE LEAST YOU NEED TO KNOW ABOUT PHYSICAL ACTIVITY

Physical activity doesn't mean you have to spend your life in a gym. It simply means engaging in activities that cause you to move. And it's never too early or late to get started (after checking with your health care provider, of course).

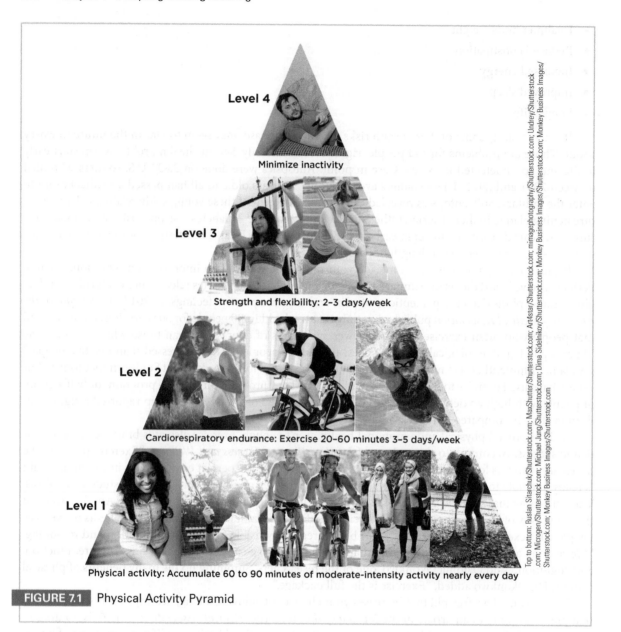

Top to bottom: Ruslan Sitarchuk/Shutterstock.com; MaxShutter/Shutterstock.com; Art4star/Shutterstock.com; mimagephotography/Shutterstock.com; Undrey/Shutterstock .com; Microgen/Shutterstock.com; Michael Jung/Shutterstock.com; Dima Sidelnikov/Shutterstock.com; Monkey Business Images/Shutterstock.com; Monkey Business Images/ Shutterstock.com; Monkey Business Images/Shutterstock.com

FIGURE 7.1   Physical Activity Pyramid

The Physical Activity Pyramid (see Figure 7.1) provides a helpful guide for improving fitness. As you see, the foundation of the pyramid, Level 1, involves daily physical activity. Moving toward greater physical fitness, Level 2 adds activities that improve the endurance of your heart and lungs (cardiorespiratory system). Level 3 adds exercises for strength and flexibility. Ideally, you'll spend the least time in Level 4, the top of the pyramid where you're inactive. If you're on a collegiate sports team, you already spend a lot of time in Levels 2 and 3. Even if you're an accomplished athlete, you'll likely find some tips here that you can use to take your game up a notch (or two).

LEVEL 1: PHYSICAL ACTIVITY

The key to Level 1 can be summed in one word: *Move!* No special skills or equipment are required . . . just a commitment to move, and move often.

If you're presently inactive, here's great news. Studies show that the people who benefit most from increasing physical activity are those who shift from inactive to moderately active. For example, a study published in the *Journal of the American Medical Association* followed 13,344 people for an average of eight years. Those who were most active had the lowest death rates, regardless of their age or risk factors. By contrast, those who were least active had the highest death rates, also regardless of age or risk factors. But the biggest increases in health and decreases in death were achieved by those who went from inactive to moderately active. In other words, if you're presently a couch potato, you have the most to gain from increasing your activity level, even a little.

In Level 1, it doesn't really matter *how* you move. What matters is *that* you move . . . as much as possible. Here are two dozen easy ways to get moving:

Instead of driving for short distances, walk.	Use a stand-up desk.
Park farther away and walk.	Sit on a stability ball instead of a chair.
Stand and walk when on your phone.	Go dancing with friends.
Walk faster than usual.	Take a fitness class.
Take a short walk after each meal or snack.	Swim (see if your campus has a pool).
Invite a friend to go for a walk.	Make use of campus exercise facilities.
Take the stairs (not the elevator or escalator).	Go for a hike with friends.
Every 30 minutes, stand and sit 10 times.	Jump rope.
Exercise while watching television.	Work in the yard or garden.
Take a short walk every 30 minutes.	Join or start an intermural team.
When it's cold outside, walk at an inside mall.	Vacuum your room or house vigorously.
After reading every 10 pages in a book, walk for two minutes.	Join a campus club that offers physical activities, such as canoeing or biking.

Stephanie Green, RDN, advises "The easiest way to add exercise into your life is to schedule a time to go for a walk. . . . Begin with a 5-minute walk if that's all the time or energy you have, and then when you're ready, push it to 10 minutes and so on. Ideally, your goal should be 30 minutes per day for heart health, according to the American Heart Association (AHA)."

Green's advice is also appropriate for pregnant women. According to the Centers for Disease Control and Prevention (CDC), "Healthy women should get at least 150 minutes (2 hours and 30 minutes) per week of moderate-intensity aerobic activity, such as brisk walking, during and after their pregnancy. It is best to spread this activity throughout the week." The CDC adds that pregnant women should "discuss with their health care provider how and when activity should be adjusted over time."

An activity tracker gives you the ability to set another kind of goal: the number of steps you'll take every day. An activity tracker is an electronic device—usually worn as a watch—that will even vibrate when you've been inactive too long. A colleague of mine set a goal of 10,000 steps a day. When her tracker vibrated, she'd stand up in the middle of a meeting, move to the back of the room, and walk in place to get her steps in. Not only did this extra movement help her lose weight, it greatly improved her health. Activity trackers range from $20 for a simple one to hundreds of dollars for one with all the bells and whistles. An activity tracker and a 32-day commitment make powerful partners in helping you move. Imagine the health benefits of taking 10,000 steps every day for 32 days in a row!

LEVEL 2: CARDIORESPIRATORY ENDURANCE

Ready to take your health and fitness up a notch? Developing cardiorespiratory endurance is the answer.

First, let's define our key term: *cardiorespiratory*. "Cardio" refers to the biological system that delivers blood throughout your body. Key parts of the cardio system include your heart and blood vessels. "Respiratory" refers to the system that supplies oxygen to your blood. The key part is your lungs. Developing cardiorespiratory endurance, then, improves your ability to deliver oxygen-rich blood to all parts of your body.

You'll very quickly notice the benefits of cardiorespiratory endurance in your daily activities. For example, you'll carry bags of groceries up a couple flights of stairs without gasping for air. You'll participate actively in recreational activities. You'll find it easier to maintain a comfortable weight, one at which you look your best. According to the Mayo Clinic, building endurance also reduces tension, anxiety, and depression. As a bonus, you'll likely feel more energy throughout the day.

Then there are the invisible health benefits of cardiorespiratory endurance. Like any muscle, a stronger heart does its work more effectively. Your blood pressure and cholesterol levels will likely go down, reducing the odds of a stroke or heart attack. As your body fat goes down, so too does the likelihood of type 2 diabetes. According to the Centers for Disease Control and Prevention, improving fitness also lowers your risk of cancer, kidney failure, and osteoporosis.

How to Build Cardiorespiratory Endurance

The best way to build cardiorespiratory endurance is through aerobic exercise. Aerobic means "with oxygen." Aerobic exercises make you breathe harder, cause your heart to beat faster, and make you sweat. Aerobic fitness increases the delivery of needed oxygen throughout your body. Like any muscle that is exercised, your heart gets stronger, performing its job better and with less effort.

Aerobic exercise is any activity that puts stress on your heart and lungs. Examples include walking (if more than four miles per hour), jogging, running, swimming, fast dancing, cycling, cross-country skiing, elliptical training, and playing sports like basketball, racquetball, and soccer.

One sign of improved cardio strength is a decrease in the number of times your heart beats per minute (BPM). Many pharmacies offer free use of machines that provide you with both your BPM and your blood pressure. To determine your present resting BPM without such a machine, place two fingers of one hand (not your thumb) on the underside of your other wrist directly below your thumb. Count the number of pulses of blood for 60 seconds. That's your resting BPM. To determine your maximum heart rate, subtract your age from 220. For example, if you're 20 years old, your maximum BPM is 200 ($220 - 20 = 200$).

The benefits of aerobic exercise are achieved by pushing your heart to work harder, going from your resting BPM up toward your maximum BPM. To do moderate-intensity exercise (good for beginners), the Centers for Disease Control recommends increasing your BPM to 50 to 70 percent of your maximum heart rate. For vigorous-intensity exercise (good for advanced exercisers), aim for a BPM between

70 to 85 percent of your maximum heart rate. Here's what that would look like for our imaginary 20-year-old with a maximum BPM of 200:

> 50% level: 200 × 0.50 = 100 BPM (low-moderate intensity exercise)
> 70% level: 200 × 0.70 = 140 BPM (high-moderate/low-vigorous intensity exercise)
> 85% level: 200 × 0.85 = 170 BPM (high-vigorous intensity exercise)

The U.S. government's *Physical Activity Guidelines for Americans* provides the following weekly guidelines for aerobic activity (remember, the intensity is determined by your BPM):

- Moderate-intensity aerobic activity for 30 or more minutes on five days per week (goal: 150 or more minutes per week), or
- Vigorous-intensity aerobic activity for 20 to 25 minutes on three days per week (goal: 60 to 75 minutes per week), or
- A combination of moderate-intensity and vigorous-intensity aerobic activity for 20 to 30 minutes on three to five days per week (goal: 60 to 150 minutes per week).
- For very fit exercisers, double the goals above.

Remember, you don't have to start with vigorous-intensity activities. Begin with a goal that is just slightly beyond your comfort zone; then add time and intensity slowly. Importantly, you'll find your fitness goals easier to achieve if you participate in aerobic activities that you enjoy.

LEVEL 3: STRENGTH AND FLEXIBILITY

Round out your fitness efforts with strength training and flexibility exercises. Two or three weekly sessions of each is a good addition to your aerobic workouts. If you're new to exercise or getting more serious about it, a wise choice for avoiding injuries is finding someone qualified to show you proper form. Your campus probably has such coaches, perhaps even teaching credit or noncredit exercise classes in which you can enroll. For flexibility, these might be classes in yoga, tai chi, or Pilates. You can also find YouTube videos with qualified coaches demonstrating strength and flexibility exercises.

Strength training isn't just for bodybuilders. We need muscle fitness for many daily tasks. For example, moving a couch, lifting a child in and out of a car seat, or carrying a backpack full of books up three flights of stairs. Increased strength also improves our ability to enjoy and even excel at recreational or competitive sports. Strength training is great for health. It can lower blood pressure, improve balance and mobility, decrease body fat, and strengthen bones, tendons, and ligaments. Strength training is important for both men and women and isn't necessarily about bulking up. Maintaining muscle mass helps keep bones strong and increases the number of calories your body burns when at rest.

Flexibility allows us to move joints and tendons through their full range of motion while reducing chronic pain. This ability is essential in everyday activities such as twisting to look behind us, bending to pick up something, and reaching to get an item on a high shelf. Flexibility also enhances our ability to enjoy leisure activities like dancing, swimming, and tossing a ball. When we don't regularly stretch, ligaments and muscles shorten, and flexibility is reduced. Inactivity—such as sitting long hours—tightens many muscles, especially those in our lower back. When doing aerobics or strength activities, stretching before and after helps maximize the benefits as well as avoid injury. Stretching afterward is particularly helpful as your muscles are warm, thus giving you greater range of motion and preventing injuries.

WISE CHOICES: PHYSICAL ACTIVITY

- Check with your doctor or medical professional before starting an exercise plan.
- See if your college offers an assessment of your physical fitness.
- Get up and move as often as possible.
- Set goals and use an activity tracker to show how much you have moved.
- Find and participate in activities and sports you enjoy.
- Stretch for 5 to 10 minutes before and after exercising.
- Engage in aerobic activities 3 to 5 days per week, depending on the intensity.
- Do strength and flexibility exercises 2 to 3 days per week. Take physical education classes.
- Find a fitness facility (preferably on-campus and free) where you can work out and get professional guidance regarding proper form.
- Join or start an intermural sports league.
- Schedule a regular time for exercise.
- On days you don't feel like exercising, exercise—or even walk—for just 10 minutes (you may wind up doing more).
- Find one or more friends with whom to exercise.
- If you're pregnant, consult your doctor to find an exercise routine that's safe for you and your baby.
- Keep a record of your exercise and seek to beat your best past efforts.
- Reward yourself when you set a new personal record for exercise.

ONE STUDENT'S STORY

CRYSTAL KIM, *California State University-Fullerton, California*

Healthy living was always a foreign concept to me. Still, I've always wanted to improve my health and have the "perfect body" that every girl dreams of. Most girls, including me, are insecure about their bodies and want to look like the models we see in the media: tiny waist, firm butt, skinny legs, toned arms, and a perky chest. However, I could never get myself to make the necessary life choices to achieve these fitness goals. I was dissatisfied with my body and thought I would never be able to look the way I wanted. My perfect body seemed out of my control, a dream I could never achieve.

In the past, I'd have bursts of motivation and go to the gym. I was determined to get fit, but my commitment never lasted. *I don't have time to exercise today; I'll start next week when I have more time; I've had a stressful week, so I deserve an extra dessert.* These were just some of my excuses. However, working three jobs while being a full-time student was my main excuse. I told myself I was too busy with work and school to add another factor into my already packed schedule. Along with my busy schedule came stress, and what better way to de-stress than go out on the weekends and drown my worries in high-calorie alcohol? This cycle seemed the never-ending story of my life. However, when I decided to take a Career and

▶

Life Planning course, to my surprise it was exactly what I needed to get out of my rut. Our required text, *On Course*, taught me how to discover the self-motivation to finally get fit.

I learned that my dream of having the "perfect body" didn't really motivate me because it was too vague. The solution was setting effective goals using the DAPPS rule. I needed goals that were dated, achievable, personal, positive, and specific. First, I broke my dream of becoming fit into effective short-term goals, such as *I will go to the gym at least three times a week starting January 31, I will cook my own healthy food at least four days out of the week starting February 28, I will do at least 30 minutes of cardio after every workout session* *starting March 31,* and *I will try a new exercise in each workout session starting April 30.* I have achieved these goals and I'm still going.

Making my goals **dated** and **specific** helped me see results, maintain focus, and stay motivated. Because the fitness world is new to me, I didn't start with a goal of going to the gym every day because I knew that would be **unachievable**. Also, I kept my goals **personal** by making them about me, and not for anyone else. They focused **positively** on what I wanted for myself. By replacing my excuses with DAPPS goals, I was able to achieve positive results even sooner than I anticipated. I soon noticed my arms, legs, and butt became firmer and more toned, and I got noticeably stronger.

I also felt less stressed out, my digestive system improved, and my thoughts seemed clearer.

I realize that staying fit is an ongoing process. There will be no point in the future when I will be able to stop and say, "Alright I have reached my goal, I am now officially fit, and I can stop what I've been doing." Fitness is a continuous journey, a lifestyle one must fully commit to. I've also learned that I will never achieve the "perfect body" that I see in the media, so I now have a different vision of what good health and fitness mean to me. Committing to my goals and learning to invest in myself has made me the happiest and healthiest version of myself ever.

Photo: Courtesy of Crystal Kim.

Developing
Emotional Intelligence

Successful Students . . .

▶ **demonstrate emotional intelligence,** using feelings as a compass for staying on course to their goals and dreams.

▶ **effectively reduce stress,** managing and soothing emotions of upset such as anger, fear, and sadness.

▶ **create happiness,** feeling fully and positively engaged in college and the rest of their lives.

Struggling Students . . .

▶ **allow themselves to be hijacked by strong emotions,** making unwise choices that get them off course.

▶ **take no responsibility for managing their emotions,** instead acting irrationally on impulses of the moment.

▶ **frequently experience negative emotions such as boredom,** sadness, anxiety, or anger.

Creating worldly success is meaningless if I am unhappy. That means I must accept responsibility for creating the quality of not only my outcomes but also my inner experiences.

I create my own happiness and peace of mind.

CASE STUDY IN CRITICAL THINKING / After Math

When **Professor Bishop** returned midterm exams, he said, "In 20 years of teaching math, I've never seen such low scores. Can anyone tell me what the problem is?" He ran a hand through his graying hair and waited. No one spoke. "Don't you people even care how you do?" Students fiddled with their test papers. They looked out of the window. No one spoke.

Finally, Professor Bishop said, "Okay, Scott, we'll start with you. What's going on? You got a 35 on the test. Did you even *study?*"

Scott, age 18, mumbled, "Yeah, I studied. But I just don't understand math."

Other students in the class nodded their heads. One student muttered, "Amen, brother."

Professor Bishop looked around the classroom. "How about you, Elena? You didn't even show up for the test."

Elena, age 31, sighed. "I'm sorry, but I have a lot of other things besides this class to worry about. My job keeps changing my schedule, I broke a tooth last week, my roommate won't pay me the money she owes me, my car broke down, and I haven't been able to find my math book for three weeks. I think my boyfriend hid it. If one more thing goes wrong in my life, I'm going to scream!"

Professor Bishop shook his head slowly back and forth. "Well, that's quite a story. What about the rest of you?" Silence reigned for a full minute.

Suddenly **Michael**, age 23, stood up and snarled, "You're a damn joke, man. You can't teach, and you want to blame the problem on us. Well, I've had it. I'm dropping this stupid course. Then I'm filing a grievance. You better start looking for a new job!" He stormed out of the room, slamming the door behind him.

"Okay, I can see this isn't going anywhere productive," Professor Bishop said. "I want you all to go home and think about why you're doing so poorly. And don't come back until you're prepared to answer that question honestly." He picked up his books and left the room. Elena checked her watch and then dashed out of the room. She still had time to catch her favorite reality show in the student lounge.

An hour later, Michael was sitting alone in the cafeteria when his classmates Scott and **Kia**, age 20, joined him. Scott said, "Geez, Michael, you really went off on Bishop! You're not really going to drop his class, are you?"

"Already did!" Michael snapped as his classmates sat down. "I went right from class to the registrar's office. I'm outta here!"

I might as well drop the class myself, Kia thought. Ever since she was denied entrance to the nursing program, she'd been too depressed to do her homework. Familiar tears blurred her vision.

Scott said, "I don't know what it is about math. I study for hours, but when I get to the test, I get so freaked it's like I never studied at all. My mind just goes blank." Thinking about math, Scott started craving something to eat.

"Where do you file a grievance against a professor around here, anyway?" Michael asked.

"I have no idea," Scott said.

"What?" Kia answered. She hadn't heard a word that Michael or Scott had said. All she could think about was how her whole life was ruined because she would never be a nurse.

Michael stood and stomped off to file a grievance. Scott went to buy some French fries. Kia put her head down on the cafeteria table and tried to swallow the burning sensation in her throat.

Listed below are the five characters in this story. Rank them in order of their emotional intelligence. Give a different score to each character. Be prepared to explain your choices.

Least emotionally intelligent ▶ ① ② ③ ④ ⑤ ◀ Most emotionally intelligent

___ **Professor Bishop**   ___ **Elena**   ___ **Kia**

___ **Scott**   ___ **Michael**

DIVING DEEPER

Imagine that you have been asked to mentor the person whom you scored a 1 (least emotionally intelligent). Other than recommending a counselor, how would you suggest that this person handle his or her upset in a more emotionally intelligent manner?

Understanding Emotional Intelligence

FOCUS QUESTIONS   What is emotional intelligence? How can you experience the full range of natural human emotions and still stay on course to a rich, fulfilling life?

During final exam period one semester, I heard a shriek from the nursing education office. Seconds later, a student charged out of the office, screaming, scattering papers in the air, and stumbling down the hall. A cluster of concerned classmates caught up to her and desperately tried to offer comfort. "It's all right. You can take the exam again next semester. It's okay. Really." She leaned against the wall, eyes closed. She slid down the wall until she sat in a limp heap, surrounded by sympathetic voices. Later, I heard that she dropped out of school.

At the end of another semester, I had the unpleasant task of telling one of my hardest-working students that she had failed the writing proficiency exams. Her mother had died during the semester, so I was particularly worried about how she would handle more bad news. We had a conference, and upon telling her the news, I began consoling her. For about a minute, she listened quietly and then said, "You're taking my failure pretty hard. Do you need a hug?" Before I could respond, she plucked me out of my chair and gave me a hug. "Don't worry," she said, patting my back, "I'll pass next semester," and sure enough, she did.

For most of us, life presents a rough road now and then. We fail a college course. The job we want goes to someone else. The person we love doesn't return our affections. Our health gives way to sickness. How we handle these distressing experiences is critical to the outcomes and experiences of our lives.

Success depends on much more than a high IQ and academic success. Karen Arnold and Terry Denny at the University of Illinois studied 81 valedictorians and salutatorians. They found that 10 years after graduation, only 25 percent of these academic stars were at the highest level of their professions when compared with others their age. Actually, many were doing poorly. What seems to be missing for them is **emotional intelligence**.

An experiment during the 1960s shows just how important emotional control is to success. Four-year-old children at a preschool were told they could have one marshmallow immediately. Or if they could wait for about 20 minutes, they could have two. More than a dozen years later, experimenters examined the differences in the lives of the one-marshmallow children who were impulsive and the two-marshmallow children who were able to delay gratification. Among other benefits, the adolescents who as children were able to delay gratification scored an average of 210 points higher on their SATs (Scholastic Assessment Tests). Clearly, the ability to endure some

I know it is hard to accept, but an upset in your life is beneficial, in that it tells you that you are off course in some way and you need to find your way back to your particular path of clarity once again.

Susan Jeffers

In the realm of emotions, many people are functioning at a kindergarten level. There is no need for self-blame. After all, in your formal education, how many courses did you take in dealing with feelings?

Gay and Kathlyn Hendricks

emotional discomfort in the present for greater rewards in the future is a key to success.

FOUR COMPONENTS OF EMOTIONAL INTELLIGENCE

As a relatively new field of study, emotional intelligence is still being defined. However, Daniel Goleman, author of the book *Emotional Intelligence,* identifies four components that contribute to emotional effectiveness. The first two components are personal qualities: the ability to recognize and effectively manage one's own emotions. The second two are social qualities: the ability to recognize and effectively manage the emotions of others:

1. **EMOTIONAL SELF-AWARENESS: Knowing your feelings in the moment.** Self-awareness of one's own feelings as they occur is the foundation of emotional intelligence and is fundamental to effective decision making. Thus, people who are keenly aware of their changing moods are better pilots of their lives. For example, emotional self-awareness helps you deal effectively with feeling overwhelmed instead of using television (or some other distraction) as a temporary escape.

2. **EMOTIONAL SELF-MANAGEMENT: Managing strong feelings.** Emotional self-management enables people to make wise choices despite the pull of powerful emotions. People who excel at this skill avoid making critical decisions during times of high drama. Instead they wait until their inner storm has calmed and then make considered choices that contribute to their desired outcomes and experiences. For example, emotional self-management helps you resist dropping an important class simply because you got angry at the teacher. It also helps you make a choice that offers delayed benefits (e.g., writing a term paper) in place of a choice that promises instant gratification (attending a party).

3. **SOCIAL AWARENESS: Empathizing accurately with other people's emotions.** Empathy is the fundamental "people skill." Those with empathy and compassion are more attuned to the subtle social signals that reveal what others need or want. For example, social awareness helps you notice and offer comfort when someone is overcome by anxiety or sadness.

4. **RELATIONSHIP MANAGEMENT: Handling emotions in relationships with skill and harmony.** The art of relationships depends, in large part, upon the skill of managing emotions in others. People who excel at skills such as listening, resolving conflicts, cooperating, and articulating the pulse of a group do well at anything that relies on interacting smoothly with others. For example, relationship management helps a person resist saying something that might publicly embarrass someone else.

Every great, successful person I know shares the capacity to remain centered, clear and powerful in the midst of emotional "storms."

Anthony "Tony" Robbins

Academic intelligence has little to do with emotional life. The brightest among us can founder on the shoals of unbridled passions and unruly impulses; people with high IQs can be stunningly poor pilots of their private lives.

Daniel Goleman

A common confusion generated by the English language is our use of the word "feel" without actually expressing a feeling. For example in the sentence, "I feel I didn't get a fair deal," the words "I feel" could be more accurately replaced with "I think."

Marshall B. Rosenberg

KNOWING YOUR OWN EMOTIONS

The foundation of emotional intelligence is a keen awareness of our own emotions as they rise and fall. None of the other abilities can exist without this one. Here are some steps toward becoming more attuned to your own emotions.

Build a Vocabulary of Feelings

Learn the names of emotions you might experience. There are hundreds. How many can you name beyond anger, fear, sadness, and happiness?

Be Mindful of Emotions As They Are Happening

Learn to identify and express emotions in the moment. Be aware of the subtleties of emotion, learning to make fine distinctions between feelings that are similar, such as sadness and depression.

Understand What Is Triggering Your Emotion

Look behind the emotion. See when anger is the result of hurt feelings. Notice when anxiety is caused by irrational thoughts. Realize when sadness is caused by disappointments. Identify when happiness is caused by immediate gratification that gets you off course from your long-term goals.

Recognize the Difference Between a Feeling and Resulting Actions

In the midst of great joy do not promise to give a man anything; in the midst of great anger do not answer a man's letter.

Chinese proverb

Feeling an emotion is one thing; acting on the emotion is quite another. Emotions and behaviors are separate experiences—one internal, one external. Note when you tend to confuse the two, as a student did who said, "My teacher made me so angry I had to drop the class." You can be angry with a teacher and still remain enrolled in a class that is important to your goals and dreams. A fundamental principle of emotional intelligence is: ***Never make an important decision while experiencing strong emotions.***

You will never reach your full potential without emotional intelligence. No matter how academically bright you may be, emotional illiteracy will limit your achievements. Developing emotional wisdom will fuel your motivation, help you successfully negotiate emotional storms (yours and those of others), and enhance your chances of creating your greatest goals and dreams.

JOURNAL ENTRY / 28

In this activity, you will explore your ability to understand your own emotions and recognize them as they are occurring. This ability is the foundation for all other emotional intelligence skills.

❶ Write about an experience when you felt one of the following emotions: FRUSTRATION or ANGER, FEAR or ANXIETY, SADNESS or UNHAPPINESS. Describe fully the cause (what happened) and your emotional reaction. Because emotions are difficult to describe, you may want to try a comparison like this: *Anger spread through me like fire in a pile of dry hay, . . .* or *I trembled in fear as though I was the next person to stand before a firing squad,* or *For two days, unhappiness wrapped me in a profound darkness.* Of course, create your own comparison. Your journal entry might begin, *Last week was one of the most frustrating times of my entire life. It all began when. . . .* Most important, be aware of any emotions that you may feel *as* you are writing.

❷ Write about an experience when you felt HAPPINESS or JOY. Once again, describe fully the cause (what happened) and your emotional reaction. A possible comparison: *Joy bubbled like champagne, and I laughed uncontrollably.* Most important, be aware of any emotions that you may feel *as* you are writing.

❸ Write about any emotional changes you experienced as you described each of these two emotions. What did you learn or relearn about how you can affect your emotions? If you weren't aware of any changes in your present emotions as you described past emotions, see if you can explain why. Were you not experiencing any emotions at all? Or could you have been unaware of the emotions you were feeling?

It made me feel better sometimes to get something down on paper just like I felt it. It brought a kind of relief to be able to describe my pain. It was like, if I could describe it, it lost some of its power over me. I jotted down innermost thoughts I couldn't verbalize to anyone else, recorded what I saw around me, and expressed feelings inspired by things I read.

Nathan McCall

ONE STUDENT'S STORY

LINDSEY BECK, *Three Rivers Community College, Connecticut*

When I started college, I had been in an abusive relationship for almost three years. I was terrified to leave this man (I'll call him Henry) because we have a child together and he had convinced me that I had no worth as a human being without him. At 6'4", Henry is a foot taller and

weighs twice as much as I do. He would punch or kick me until I was in so much pain I couldn't go to my classes. When I did go, I'd often leave early because he became convinced I was cheating on him and I didn't want to give him another reason to beat me. I have a fair amount of

academic ability and I did well in high school, but I started allowing my emotions to overrun my intelligence. It was like I had a bunch of emotions in a bowl and I'd just pull one out at random when something happened. One day when my mother expressed concern about my bruises, I got furious at her. But instead of getting angry at Henry for beating me, I'd feel afraid, confused, and depressed. Rather than stepping back and thinking logically about ▶

Photo: Courtesy of Lindsey Beck.

ONE STUDENT'S STORY *continued*

what was going on, I allowed my emotions to control me.

Studying became my escape. In my freshman year experience course, I loved expressing myself in my journals. In Chapter 8, I started writing about my emotions, and for the first time in years, I wasn't ashamed of my feelings. I decided to be totally honest, and I wrote down exactly what was going on and how I *really* felt about it (not how Henry told me I felt about it). Writing the journals really made me look at myself and ask, *What am I doing in this relationship?* When I read about all of the positive

ways I could manage my emotions, I started looking at things as though I wasn't going to take it anymore. I got stronger every day, and then one day I made the decision to leave Henry.

I've always done well at writing papers, studying, and taking tests, but I've never really taken responsibility for my emotions before. I learned that I need to get my emotional life under control if I want the rest of my life to work. I now realize that how I feel at one moment isn't necessarily how I'll feel 10 minutes later. Emotions change. Why let things control me that

are so temporary? By growing emotionally, I'm able to control my emotions instead of letting them control me. I am finally starting to picture a positive life for myself without Henry, and I am growing more confident every day. My dream is to earn a degree in microbiology and make a difference by working for the World Health Organization. Enrolling in this course was the best life decision I will probably ever make. If I hadn't, 10 years from now, I might not have wanted to change my life. However, I have been able to do that, and now I have my whole life ahead of me.

Photo: Courtesy of Lindsey Beck.

Reducing Stress

FOCUS QUESTION   How can you soothe stressful feelings that make life unpleasant and threaten to get you off course?

> The process of living is the process of reacting to stress.
>
> Stanley J. Sarnoff, MD

Changes and challenges are inevitable in our lives; thus, so is the potential for stress. Maybe you waited until the last minute to print your essay for English class and the printer was out of ink. Stress. Or you bounced a $6 check and the bank charged you a $25 penalty. Stress! Or you've got a test coming up in history and you're two chapters behind in your reading. STRESS!

Even life's pleasant events, like a new relationship or a weekend trip with friends, can bring on a positive form of stress called *eustress*. Most of the time, eustress is welcome. However, if we're not careful, even eustress can bump us off course. After all, if you choose to extend a weekend trip with friends instead of studying for a final exam, there's likely to be a price to pay.

WHAT IS STRESS?

The American Medical Association defines stress as any interference that disturbs a person's mental or physical well-being. However, most of us know stress simply as the "wear and tear" that our minds and bodies experience as we attempt to cope with the challenges of life. The body's response to a stressor is much the same today as it was for our ancestors thousands of years ago. As soon as we perceive a threat, our brains release the stress hormones cortisol and epinephrine (also known as adrenaline), and instantly our bodies respond with an increase in heart rate, metabolism, breathing, muscle tension, and blood pressure. We're ready for "fight or flight."

To our ancestors, this stress response literally meant the difference between life and death. After they'd survived a threat (a saber-toothed tiger, perhaps), the stress hormones were gone from their bodies within minutes. In modern life, however, much of our stress comes from worrying about past events, agonizing about present challenges, and fretting about future changes. Instead of stress hormones being active in our bodies for only minutes, they may persist for months or even years. For many of us, then, stress is a constant and toxic companion.

WHAT HAPPENS WHEN STRESS PERSISTS?

Ongoing stress is bad news for our health, damaging almost every bodily system. It inhibits digestion, reproduction, growth, tissue repair, and the responses of our immune system. As just one example of the impact of long-term stress on our health, Carnegie Mellon University researchers exposed 400 volunteers to cold viruses and found that people with high stress in their lives were twice as likely to develop colds as those with low stress.

In fact, the National Institute of Mental Health estimates that 70 to 80 percent of all doctor visits are for stress-related illnesses. Physical symptoms of stress can be as varied as high blood pressure, muscle tension, headaches, backaches, indigestion, irritable bowel, ulcers, chronic constipation or diarrhea, muscle spasms, herpes sores, tics, tremors, sexual dysfunction, fatigue, insomnia, physical weakness, and emotional upsets.

Important to college students is the discovery that stress has a negative impact on memory. It also hinders other mental skills such as creativity, concentration, and attention to details. When you're feeling stressed, you can't do your best academic work, let alone enjoy doing it. So, when you feel stressed, what are your choices?

UNHEALTHY STRESS REDUCTION

When stressed, people in a Victim mindset seek to escape the discomfort as fast as possible. To do so, they often make unwise choices: drinking alcohol to excess, going numb for hours in front of a television or computer, working obsessively, fighting, taking anesthetizing drugs, going on shopping binges, eating too much or too little, smoking excessively, gulping caffeine, or gambling more than they can afford to lose. When confronted with the damage of their self-sabotaging behavior, they typically blame, complain, and make excuses. *Stress made me do it!*

Like the impulsive children in the marshmallow experiment, Victims seek instant gratification. They give little thought to the impact of these choices on their futures. By making one impulsive and ill-considered choice after another, Victims move further and further off course.

Every stress leaves an indelible scar, and the organism pays for its survival after a stressful situation by becoming a little older.

Hans Selye, MD

Of all the drugs and the compulsive behaviors that I have seen in the past twenty-five years, be it cocaine, heroin, alcohol, nicotine, gambling, sexual addiction, or food addiction, all have one common thread. That is the covering up, or the masking, or the unwillingness on the part of the human being to confront and be with his or her human feelings.

Richard Miller, MD

HEALTHY STRESS REDUCTION

People in a Creator mindset find better ways to reduce stress. They realize that managing emotions intelligently means making wise choices that release—not just mask—the grip of stress. Effective at identifying their distressing feelings early, Creators take positive actions to avoid being hijacked by emotional upset. Here's a menu of healthy and effective strategies for managing four of the most common symptoms of stress.

A special note to the highly stressed: Your Inner Defender may take one look at the list of strategies that follows and say something like, "I can't deal with this right now. It's just going to make me even *more* stressed out!" If that's really the case, consider making an appointment at your campus counseling office to get some caring, professional help for your stress.

Victim

Creator

© Cengage Learning

To reduce stress on your own, here's a simple, two-step plan. First, read the following section that addresses your most pressing symptoms of stress: feeling overwhelmed, angry, anxious, or sad. In that section, pick one stress-reduction strategy and make a 32-Day Commitment (see the "Developing Grit" section of Chapter 4) to do it. In little more than a month, you'll likely feel less stressed. Better yet, you'll have proven that *you*, and not stress, are in charge of your life.

Feeling Overwhelmed

Feeling overwhelmed is probably the most common stressor for college students. Its message, if heeded, is valuable: Your life has gotten too complicated, your commitments too many. Feeling overwhelmed warns us that we've lost control of our lives. Creators may notice a tightness or pain in their jaws, shoulders, or lower backs. Or lack of sleep. Or they may notice themselves thinking, *If one more thing goes wrong, I'm going to scream!* Or, maybe they *do* scream! With this awareness, Creators understand it's time to take action. Many positive strategies exist for rescuing your life from the distress of feeling overwhelmed.

Choose New Behaviors. Here are some actions you can take when you feel that your life is stretched a mile wide and an inch thin. As you'll see, many of them are variations of self-management strategies you learned in Chapter 4:

- *Separate from an external stressor.* Perhaps the external stressor is a neighbor's loud music or a demanding job. You can choose to study in the library where it's quiet or find a new job with fewer demands.

- *List and prioritize everything you need to do.* Using a Next Actions List (see "Creating a Leakproof Self-Management System" section in Chapter 4), record all your incomplete tasks according to life roles. Assign priorities to each task: A = Important and Urgent actions

> When you take full responsibility here and now for all of your feelings and for everything that happens to you, you never again blame the people and situations in the world outside of you for any unhappy feelings that you have.
>
> Ken Keyes, Jr.

(do these first); B = Important and Not Urgent actions (do these next); C = All Unimportant actions (do only when all A and B tasks are complete):

- *Delete C's.* Identify where you are wasting time and cross them off your list.
- *Delegate A's and B's.* Where possible, get another person to complete some of your important tasks. Ask a friend to pick up your dry cleaning. Pay someone to clean your apartment. This choice frees up time to do the tasks that only you can do, like your math homework.
  - *Complete remaining A's and B's yourself.* Start with your A priorities, such as a looming term paper or a broken refrigerator. Handle them immediately: Visit the library and take out three books to begin researching your term paper topic. Call an appliance repair shop and schedule a service call. Spend time doing only A and B priorities and watch your overwhelm subside.
- *Discover time-savers.* Consciously make better use of your time. For example, keep an errand list so you can do them all in one trip. Or study flash cards during the hour between classes.
- *Eliminate time-wasters.* Identify and eliminate Quadrant III and IV activities. For example, reduce the time you spend on Facebook and other social media. Cut down on screen time. Stop playing video games.
- *Say "no."* Admit that your plate is full, and politely refuse requests that add to your commitments. If you do agree to take on something new, say "no" to something already on your plate. If saying "no" is difficult for you, do role-plays with a friend to practice. Or put it in writing. (Find more tips on this in the "Saying 'No'" section of Chapter 5.)
- *Keep your finances organized.* A survey of 11,000 adults by *Prevention* magazine revealed that their number one source of stress is worry over personal finances. So curtail unnecessary spending, pay bills when due, balance your checkbook. Use the money-management strategies in Chapter 1 for stress relief as well as debt relief.
- *Exercise.* Aerobic exercise increases the blood levels of endorphins, and these hormones block pain, create a feeling of euphoria (the exercise high), and reduce stress. One caution: Consult your doctor before dramatically changing your level of exercise. For more about exercise, see the section titled "Healthy Choices: Physical Activity" in Chapter 7.
- *Get enough sleep.* If thoughts keep running through your mind, write them down. Breathe deeply and relax. Clear your mind. If sleep eludes you, consider seeing a doctor. You can't learn effectively when deprived of sleep. For more about getting better sleep, see the section titled "Healthy Choices: Sleep" in this chapter.

Choose New Thoughts. Because we create the inner experience of feeling overwhelmed in our mind, we can un-create it. Here's how:

- *Elevate.* See each problem in the bigger picture of your whole life. Notice how little importance it really has. From this new perspective, ask, *Will this problem really matter one year from now?* Often the answer is "no."

Much of the stress that people feel doesn't come from having too much to do. It comes from not finishing what they've started.

David Allen

I like what [exercise] does for my mind. If I've had a bad day, if I'm feeling stressed out, if I'm feeling overwhelmed—it takes it all away.

Kelly Ripa

- *Trust a positive outcome.* How many times have you been upset by something that later turned out to be a blessing in disguise? Because it's possible, expect the blessing.

- *Take a mental vacation.* Picture a place you love (e.g., a white-sand beach, mountain retreat, or forest path) and spend a few minutes visiting it in your mind. Enjoy the peace and rejuvenation of this mini-vacation.

Feeling Angry

Healthy anger declares a threat or injustice against us or someone or something we care about. Perceiving this violation, the brain signals the body to release catecholamines (hormones) that fuel both our strength and our will to fight. Creators become conscious of oncoming anger through changes such as flushed skin, tensed muscles, and increased pulse rates.

With this awareness, Creators can pause and wisely choose what to do next, rather than lashing out impulsively. Emotions don't ask rational questions, so we must. For example, Creators ask, *Will I benefit from releasing my anger, or will it cost me dearly?*

When you perceive a true injustice, use the energy produced by your anger to right the wrong. However, to avoid being hijacked by anger and doing something you will regret later, here are some effective strategies:

Choose New Behaviors. Allow the tidal wave of anger-producing hormones about 20 minutes to recede. Here's how:

- *Separate.* Go off by yourself, allowing enough time to regain your ability to make rational, positive choices.

- *Exercise.* Moving vigorously assists in reducing anger-fueling hormones in your body.

- *Relax.* Slowing down also aids in calming your body, returning control of your decisions to you (as long as you don't spend this time obsessively thinking about the event that angered you).

- *Journal.* Write about your feelings in detail. Rant and rave to your journal. Explore the cause and effect of your anger. Take responsibility for any part you play in creating the anger. Honest expression of emotions can help the dark storm pass and rational thoughts return.

- *Channel your anger into positive actions.* That's what Candy Lightner did when a drunk driver—a repeat offender—killed her 13-year-old daughter, Cari, as she walked through their neighborhood. Lightner turned her anger into action and created Mothers Against Drunk Driving (MADD). Now a nationwide organization, MADD strives to end drunk driving and provide support for its victims. After your anger has subsided, the Wise Choice Process can help you decide on positive actions that you might take.

The sign of intelligent people is their ability to control emotions by the application of reason.

Marya Mannes

I promised myself on the day of Cari's death that I would fight to make this needless homicide count for something positive in the years ahead.

Candy Lightner

Choose New Thoughts. Because thoughts stir emotional responses, revising our anger-producing thoughts can calm us. Here's how:

- *Reframe.* Look at the problem from a different perspective. Search for a benign explanation for the anger-causing event. If you realize you were wronged unknowingly, unintentionally, or even necessarily, you can often see the other person's behavior in a less hostile way.

- *Distract yourself.* Consciously shift your attention to something pleasant, stopping the avalanche of angry thoughts. Involve yourself with uplifting conversations, movies, books, music, video games, puzzles, or similar diversions.

- *Forgive.* Take offending people off the hook for whatever they did, no matter how offensive. Don't concern yourself with whether *they* deserve forgiveness; the question is whether *you* deserve the emotional relief of forgiveness. The reason for forgiveness is primarily to improve *your* life, not theirs. We close the case to free ourselves of the daily self-infliction of poisonous judgments. Of course, forgiveness doesn't mean we forget and allow them to misuse us again.

- *Identify the hurt.* Anger is often built upon hurt: Someone doesn't meet me when she said she would. Below my anger, I'm hurt that she seems to care about me so little. Shift attention from anger to the deeper hurt. Consider expressing the hurt in writing.

Living life as an art requires a readiness to forgive.

Maya Angelou

Feeling Anxious

Healthy anxiety delivers a message that we may be in danger. Our brain then releases hormones that fuel our energy to flee. Many Victims, though, exaggerate dangers, and their healthy concern is replaced by paralyzing anxiety or even terror about what could go wrong.

Creators become conscious of oncoming anxiety through their bodies' clear signals, including shallow breathing, increased pulse rate, and "butterflies" in the stomach. With this awareness, Creators can pause and wisely choose what to do next rather than fleeing impulsively from or worrying constantly about a nonthreatening person or situation.

One of the areas where emotions hinder academic performance is test anxiety. Unless you minimize this distress, you will be unable to demonstrate effectively what you know. Many colleges offer workshops or courses that offer instruction in anxiety-reducing strategies. Here are some wise choices to avoid being hijacked by anxiety, especially anxiety generated by a test.

Anxiety . . . sabotages academic performance of all kinds: 126 different studies of more than 36,000 people found that the more prone to worries a person is, the poorer their academic performance, no matter how measured—grades on tests, grade-point average, or achievement tests.

Daniel Goleman

Choose New Behaviors. As with anger, help the anxiety-producing chemicals to recede. Here's how:

- *Prepare thoroughly.* If your anxiety relates to an upcoming performance (e.g., test or job interview), prepare thoroughly and then prepare some more. Confidence gained through extensive preparation diminishes anxiety. Using your CORE Learning System—explained in the "Toolbox for Active Learners" (offered online with the accompanying MindTap)—is a great way to increase your realistic expectations for success on any test.

- *Relax.* Slowing down helps you reclaim mastery of your thoughts and emotions (but don't spend this time obsessing about the cause of your anxiety).

- *Breathe deeply.* Anxiety and fear constrict. Keep oxygen flowing through your body to reverse the physiological impact of these emotions. Find demonstrations of this kind of breathing by doing a search on YouTube. com for "Diaphragmatic Breathing" or "Belly Breathing."

- *Request accommodations.* Visit your college's disability services to see about making special arrangements, such as a longer time to take tests. Special arrangements usually require a note from a medical professional.

Choose New Thoughts. Changing our thoughts can soothe irrational anxieties. Here's how:

- *Detach.* Once you have prepared fully for an upcoming challenge (such as a test), there's no more you can do. Worrying won't help. So do everything you can to ready yourself for the challenge, then trust the outcome to take care of itself.

- *Reframe.* Ask yourself, *If the worst happens, can I live with it?* If you fail a test, for example, you won't like it, but could you live with it? Of course you could! (If not, consider seeking help to regain a healthy perspective.)

- *Visualize success.* Create a mental movie of yourself achieving your ideal outcomes. Play the movie over and over until the picture of success becomes stronger than your fear. For more on how to visualize effectively, see "Committing to Your Goals and Dreams" in Chapter 3.

- *Assume the best.* Victims often create anxiety through negative assumptions. Suppose your professor says, "I want to talk to you in my office." Resist assuming the conversation concerns something bad. In fact, if you're going to assume, why not assume it's something wonderful?

- *Face the fear.* Do what you fear, in spite of the fear. Most often you will learn that your fear was just a False Expectation Appearing Real.

- *Say your affirmation.* When anxiety-producing thoughts creep into your mind, replace them with the positive words of your affirmation.

Feeling Sad

Sadness is the natural response to the loss of someone or something dear. Fully grieving our loss is essential, for only in this way do we both honor and resolve our loss. Sadness and feeling "down" are also understandable reactions to the academic and social pressures that college students may experience, especially

> If your images are positive, they will support you and cheer you on when you get discouraged. Negative pictures rattle around inside of you, affecting you without your knowing it.
>
> Virginia Satir

in their first year. Unhealthy sadness, however, becomes a lingering, helpless feeling that numbs us. If you feel gripped by such a depression, see a counselor at your college. Help is available!

For bouts with short-term sadness, however, there are numerous ways to bounce back on your own. First, recognize your body's clear signals: low energy, constant fatigue, and lack of a positive will to perform meaningful tasks. With this awareness, take steps to regain a positive experience of college and life. Here are some healthy options for doing so:

Choose New Behaviors. Help your body produce natural, mood-elevating hormones. Here's how:

- *Do something (anything!) toward your goals.* Get moving and produce a result, no matter how small. Accomplishment combats the blues.

- *Exercise.* Moving vigorously helps your body produce endorphins, causing a natural high that brightens your mood.

- *Listen to uplifting music.* Put on a song that picks up your spirits. Avoid sad songs about lost love and misery.

- *Laugh.* Like exercise, laughter is physiologically incompatible with melancholy. So rent a funny movie, go to a comedy club, read joke books or cartoons, or visit your funniest friend.

- *Breathe deeply.* Like fear, sadness constricts. Keep breathing deeply to offset the physiological impact of sadness.

- *Help others in need.* Assisting people less fortunate is uplifting. You experience both the joy of lightening their burden and the reminder that, despite your situation, you still have much to be grateful for.

- *Journal.* Writing about your feelings can help you come to terms with them more quickly and effectively. Often our emotions on paper seem much less distressing than those roaming unexamined in our minds and hearts.

- *Socialize with friends and loved ones.* Isolation usually intensifies gloominess. Socializing reengages you with people who matter and helps you gain a healthier perspective on your situation.

Choose New Thoughts. As with other distressing emotions, changing our thoughts soothes sadness. Here's how:

- *Dispute pessimistic beliefs.* Dark thoughts thrive on pessimism. So challenge negative beliefs that make your present situation seem permanent, pervasive, or personal. Think, instead, how life will improve over time, how the problem is limited to only one part of your life, and how the cause is not a personal flaw in you, but something you can remedy with an action.

- *Distract yourself.* As with anger, consciously replacing gloomy thoughts with pleasant ones will help stop the distress. So involve

Bad things do happen; how I respond to them defines my character and the quality of my life. I can choose to sit in perpetual sadness, immobilized by the gravity of my loss, or I can choose to rise from the pain and treasure the most precious gift I have—life itself.

Walter Anderson

The greatest weapon against stress is our ability to choose one thought over another.

William James

yourself with engaging activities that will take your thoughts on a pleasant diversion.

- *Focus on the positive.* Identify your blessings and successes. Think of all the things for which you are grateful, perhaps even making a list. Appreciate what you *do* have instead of regretting what you don't.

- *Find the opportunity in the problem.* At the very least, learn the lesson life has brought you and move on. At best, turn your loss into a gain.

- *Remind yourself, "This, too, shall pass."* A year from now, you'll be in an entirely different place in your life, and this emotional upset will be only a memory.

- *Identify others who have much more to be sad or depressed about.* Realize by this comparison how fortunate you actually are, changing your focus from your loss to all that you still have.

CHOOSE YOUR ATTITUDE

When dealing with stress, the critical issue is, *Do you manage your emotions or do they manage you?* If you have made an honest effort to manage your emotions and they have defied you still, you may want to seek the help of a counselor or therapist. In some cases, persistent emotional distress is the result of a chemical imbalance that can be treated with prescription drugs. But if it's inspiration you seek, consider Viktor E. Frankl, a psychiatrist imprisoned in the Nazi concentration camps during World War II. In his book *Man's Search for Meaning,* Frankl relates how he and other prisoners rose above their dreadful conditions to create a positive inner experience.

In one example, Frankl tells of a particularly bleak day when he was falling into a deep despair. With terrible sores on his feet, he was forced to march many miles in bitter cold weather to a work site, and there, freezing and weak from starvation, he endured constant brutality from the guards. Frankl describes how he "forced" his thoughts to turn to another subject. In his mind he imagined himself "standing on the platform of a well-lit, warm and pleasant lecture room." Before him sat an audience enthralled to hear him lecture on the psychology of the concentration camp. "By this method," Frankl says, "I succeeded somehow in rising above the situation, above the sufferings of the moment, and I observed them as if they were already of the past."

From his experiences and his observations, Frankl concluded that everything can be taken from us but one thing: "the last of the human freedoms—to choose one's attitude in any given set of circumstances, to choose one's own way."

Creators claim the power to choose their outcomes whenever possible and to choose their inner experiences always. If Viktor Frankl could overcome the stress of his inhumane imprisonment in a concentration camp, surely we can find the strength to overcome the stresses of our own lives.

The greater part of our happiness or misery depends on our dispositions and not our circumstances.

Martha Washington

The greatest discovery of my generation is that human beings, by changing the inner attitudes of their minds, can change the outer aspects of their lives.

William James

In this activity, you will practice identifying positive methods for reducing the stress in your life:

① **Write about a recent time when you felt overwhelmed, angry, sad, or anxious.** Choose an experience different from the one you described in Journal Entry 28. Fully describe the situation that caused your emotional response; then describe the distressing feelings you experienced; finally, explain what you did (if anything) to manage your emotions in a positive way.

② **Identify two or more strategies that you could use in the future when you experience this emotion.** Explain each strategy in a separate paragraph, and remember the power of the 4Es—examples, experiences, explanation, and evidence—to improve the quality of your writing. When you're done, notice if simply writing about your stressors and ways to manage them may have reduced your level of stress. It did for students in a study at Southern Methodist University.

> Emotion comes directly from what we think: Think "I am in danger" and you feel anxiety. Think "I am being trespassed against" and you feel anger. Think "Loss" and you feel sadness.
>
> Martin Seligman

ONE STUDENT'S STORY

JAIME SANMIGUEL, *Miami Dade College, Florida*

I don't consider myself someone who lives in fear, and very few things in life intimidate me. However, the one fear that I could never overcome was my dread of public speaking. When I had to give a speech or read an essay aloud in junior high or high school, I would develop a shaky voice, get sweaty palms, and turn completely red. When I got to college, I took a fundamentals of speech class in which much of our grade depended on two speeches that we had to give using a PowerPoint presentation. My first speech didn't go very well. I hadn't really learned to use PowerPoint, and the slides didn't seem to fit what I was talking about. I began to feel insecure, and I started going all over the place. My teacher said the speech was okay, but I wasn't happy with it, especially because my goal is to work in public relations, where I'll need to be able to speak to groups with confidence.

I was taking SLS 1125, Student Support Seminar, at the same time, and I discovered many helpful hints in *On Course* to overcome my fears. The first thing I did for my next speech was to make sure I was thoroughly prepared. This time I wrote out my whole speech first and then put my key points on index cards. I learned how to work PowerPoint and made sure all of the slides went with what I was talking about. I practiced giving my speech a number of times, with my dog as my audience. Another student in my class gave a great speech on the history of watches, and I visualized myself doing some of the things she had done, like using my hands effectively, looking relaxed, smiling, and being more natural and friendly. I also did some relaxing and deep breathing, and that helped take my mind off my concerns. I used to worry that people would think I didn't know what I was talking about, but I changed these worries by picturing my audience as friends who want to know what I have to say. When I actually gave my speech, I picked out individual students and talked to each of them one at a time. These techniques helped me believe in myself more and not be so self-conscious in front of an audience, and in the end I passed the course with a B.

But just as important, in *On Course* I learned, "If you keep doing what you've been doing, you'll keep getting what you've been getting." I took ownership of the fact that if I want to be successful in a public relations career, I have to face and overcome my fears of giving presentations. I think I'm well on my way to achieving this goal.

Increasing Happiness

FOCUS QUESTIONS Would you like to be happier? Do you know how?

In 1999, scientific researchers started paying more attention to happiness.

We hold these truths to be self-evident, that all men are created equal, that they are endowed by their Creator with certain unalienable Rights, that among these are Life, Liberty and the pursuit of Happiness.

From the United
States Declaration of
Independence

For starters, the first positive psychology summit took place that year in Lincoln, Nebraska. Previously, most psychologists had viewed their role as helping people become less miserable. At the positive psychology summit, psychologists asked, "How can we apply science to help people become more happy?"

Since then, many millions of dollars have been spent on scientific research to answer this important question. In 2002, the first international conference on positive psychology was held to share what the research had found. Since then, dozens of similar conferences have been held around the world.

Meanwhile, happiness courses began popping up on college campuses. In 2006, Harvard University offered a course called "Positive Psychology 1504." An enrollment of 854 students made it Harvard's most popular course. Many other colleges now offer courses in positive psychology. Some offer master's or doctoral degrees in this emerging field as well. Recently a partnership of the Massachusetts Institute of Technology (MIT) and Harvard University offered a free online course called "The Science of Happiness." Nearly 75,000 people worldwide enrolled, including one of your authors, Skip Downing.

The takeaway from all of this attention on happiness seems obvious. People want to be happier. And we want to know how.

The reason to increase happiness may seem obvious: "Happy feels better than unhappy." But research has revealed many other benefits as well. When compared to unhappy people, happy people on average are more productive, likeable, active, friendly, helpful, resilient, and creative. Happy people tend to be healthier, have better relationships, earn higher salaries, and even live longer.

I am more concerned with the Gross National Happiness of my country, than with the Gross National Product.

Jigme Singye Wangchuck,
King of Bhutan

One study of happiness, for example, focused on autobiographical essays written by Catholic nuns in the 1930s and 1940s. Their average age at that time was 22. In 2001, scientists analyzed these essays for expressions of positive emotions. Then they looked to see what happened to the nuns in their study, many of whom have passed away. The findings? Happier nuns outlived less-happy nuns by an average of 10 years. Not only did they live longer, happier nuns were far less afflicted by Alzheimer's disease. So it appears that positive emotions contribute to both longevity and brain health.

LIMITS ON HAPPINESS

Research, unfortunately, has uncovered some bad news about efforts to increase happiness. It turns out we have limited control over our level of happiness. The major reason is heredity. It seems we're born with a happiness set point that's controlled by our genes. By studying identical twins—especially those raised apart—psychologists estimate that about 50 percent of our happiness is genetic. Just as we inherit height from our parents, we also inherit a happiness set point. And no one has figured out how to change the set point for happiness (or height, for that matter).

What about the impact of life circumstances on happiness? you might ask. Surely happiness is raised or lowered by circumstances such as money, health, climate, physical appearance, ethnicity, gender, age, intelligence, and education. Actually, not so much. Research suggests that circumstances like these contribute only about 10 percent to our level of happiness. Sure, we get a burst of happiness when something good happens—like getting an A on a test or receiving a huge raise at work. But then something called **hedonic adaptation** takes over. Here's how it works: After something good happens, we quickly become used to it and slide back down to our happiness set point. In other words, when the *new* good thing becomes the *old* good thing, the thrill is gone. If you've ever had "too much of a good thing," you've experienced hedonic adaptation.

Here's an example of hedonic adaptation. Maybe you've thought, "If only I could win the lottery, then I'd be happy!" Psychologist Philip Brickman and his colleagues decided to find out if that's true. They asked winners of the Illinois State Lottery to rate their happiness. Then they asked nonwinners to do the same. As you might expect, the happiness of lottery winners spiked right after their good fortune. About a year later, however, most of the winners were no happier than the nonwinners. It turns out that once we can take care of basic needs, more money doesn't mean more happiness. That rascal hedonic adaptation tugs us back down to our set point. Think about all of the things you were once thrilled about . . . but now don't seem so great. That's the effect of hedonic adaptation.

Let's recap what we know so far. About 50 percent of our happiness is determined by a genetically fixed set point. And about 10 percent of our happiness is affected by our circumstances, but usually for only a short time. What about the other 40 percent? Here's where scientific research offers good news. It turns out we can make many choices to increase our happiness.

In fact, a number of the choices already discussed in *On Course* are strongly correlated with increasing happiness—for example, pursuing important goals, exercising, and developing positive relationships. Let's look at some other choices that increase happiness.

SAVORING PLEASURES

Pleasures increase happiness. You could experience pleasure by eating a delicious meal, dancing to great music, watching a child play with a kitten, or smelling cinnamon buns right from the oven. One of my pleasures is picking fresh, ripe tomatoes from my garden and adding them to a salad for dinner. Most pleasant experiences, however, fade quickly. Fortunately, there's a way to deepen and prolong pleasure. It's called **savoring**. When we savor an experience, our Inner Guide whispers, "Pay close attention to this . . . stay with it . . . stay with it . . . c'mon, stay with it a little longer." With savoring, we let a pleasant experience linger in our awareness, spreading like sweet cream poured into rich, dark coffee.

Pleasure not only results from a positive experience in the present. It also occurs when we revisit and savor positive events from the past. For example,

> [W]orking toward a meaningful life goal is one of the most important strategies for becoming lastingly happier.
>
> Sonja Lyubomirsky, psychologist

Leo Cullum/The New Yorker Collection/The Cartoon Bank

"But, remember, you're responsible for your own happiness."

By taking just a few extra seconds to stay with a positive experience—even the comfort of a single breath—you'll help turn a passing mental state into lasting neural structure.

Rick Hanson, neuropsychologist

a group of people with severe depression was asked to log onto a website each evening. There they recorded three good things that had happened that day, no matter how small: "I went for a walk." Then, to dive a little deeper, they wrote why this good thing happened: "I decided the weather was too nice to stay inside all day." After 15 days of focusing their attention on and savoring the good things in their lives—no matter how small—94 percent reported improvement in their moods.

Neuropsychologist Rick Hanson reports that savoring pleasures actually changes our brains, making us more able to enjoy future pleasures. Positive experiences increase the release of the hormone dopamine. Dopamine makes you feel good. As you repeatedly create and savor positive experiences, your new neural networks become "stickier" for other positive experiences. The changes in your brain increase your ability to enjoy positive experiences, and enjoying positive experiences makes your brain more receptive to future pleasures.

Hanson suggests helpful strategies to keep hedonic adaptation from ruining this uplifting cycle. First, create a variety of pleasant experiences (not the same one over and over). Second, spread pleasant experience over time (not all at once). And, most of all, fully savor each pleasant experience. Focus your attention on it . . . and stay with it . . . and stay with it.

GRATITUDE

Psychologist Robert Emmons studies the relationship between gratitude and happiness. Gratitude, he says, is "a felt sense of wonder, thankfulness, and appreciation for life." His research, and the research of others, reveals that people who count their blessings on a regular basis experience a number of benefits. Not only are they happier than people who don't express gratitude, they also report greater vitality, optimism, and satisfaction with life. Additionally, grateful people experience lower levels of stress and depression.

Scientists have experimented with many ways of expressing gratitude. One of the most obvious is to make a gratitude list: "I'm alive," "I have food to eat," "I have the opportunity to go to college." When I do this exercise, I find myself listing things I had never thought to appreciate before. For example, I'm grateful to the person who first picked beans off a coffee bush, roasted them, ground them, and poured hot water through them. Not to mention the person who thought of adding sugar and cream.

Another way to generate gratitude is to recall a painful experience from your past, then immediately contrast this past experience with what you are experiencing now. The key is noticing what you feel grateful for now that the pain is in the past: "I lived through it," "I learned who my friends really are," "I'm a much stronger person because of it," "I'm much more willing to take on challenges."

You can also experience gratitude by writing a letter of thanks to someone who has been important in your life. This could be a parent, brother, sister, coach, teacher, employer, or friend. In specific detail, tell this person why you are grateful to him or her. What did he or she say or do? How did it affect your life? How are you different because of him or her? If possible, deliver the letter in person and read the letter together. In one study, these gratitude visits led to large boosts in happiness that lasted anywhere from a week to a month.

> Let us rise up and be thankful, for if we didn't learn a lot today, at least we learned a little, and if we didn't learn a little, at least we didn't get sick, and if we got sick, at least we didn't die; so, let us all be thankful.
>
> **Buddha**

ENGAGEMENT

What these happiness strategies have in common is increasing our awareness of and savoring a positive experience. Ironically, another way to increase happiness is becoming so engaged in an activity that we *lose* awareness of anything beyond what we are doing. It isn't until later that we realize how enjoyable the experience was. Psychologist Mihaly Csikszentmihalyi (pronounced "*chick*-sent-me-hi") calls such times of complete engagement **flow states**. Flow results from total absorption in an activity. During flow, we have no thoughts or concerns about ourselves. Time is distorted, often passing very quickly. We are totally present in the moment.

What if you could experience flow in your college courses? Creators do all they can to maximize that possibility, and how you choose your courses and your instructors is a good first step. Victims typically create their

© Cengage Learning

course schedule based on convenience: *Give me any class at noon because I don't want a two-hour gap in my schedule.*

Creators have a very different approach. They realize that it's worth a sacrifice to get a course with an outstanding instructor, one who creates flow in the classroom. As you plan your schedule for next semester, ask other students to recommend instructors who:

- demonstrate a deep knowledge of their subject,
- show great enthusiasm for the value of their subject,
- set challenging but reasonable learning objectives for their students,
- offer engaging learning experiences that appeal to diverse learning preferences, and
- provide a combination of academic and emotional support that gives their students high expectations of success.

Imagine taking courses with instructors who are knowledgeable, enthusiastic, challenging, engaging, and supportive! These are the instructors who are going to create flow in their classrooms, help you achieve academic success, and inspire you to be a lifelong learner. And if you find a course in which you experience flow, you might very well have found your major . . . and maybe even your ideal career.

CONTRIBUTION

Let's consider one more way to increase your happiness. Start by imagining that scientists are monitoring your brain activity. They give you some money and a choice: You can keep the money or donate it to charity. Which choice do you think will create the greatest activity in your brain's reward center? If you said "donate the money to charity," you're right. Showing kindness to others increases positive emotions.

In a study at the University of California, Riverside, people were asked to perform acts of kindness. They chose such things as doing extra household chores, helping someone carry something, or making breakfast for a special friend. Not only did the participants' happiness go up immediately, the effects were still there a month later. As you might expect, participants who varied their acts of kindness and spread them out over time created even better results than those who did the same thing many times within a short period of time.

So, what kindness could you do today? It could be small (holding a door for someone). Or it could be big (offering to tutor someone who is struggling in a subject you've mastered). Or huge (taking actions to reduce world hunger). As many who help worthy causes will agree, they receive more than they give.

STRAWBERRY MOMENTS

Many of the scientific discoveries about happiness are illustrated by a parable I heard years ago. A man is walking on a narrow, rocky path on the side of a steep mountain when he encounters a hungry tiger. Terrified, the man grabs a vine and dangles over the edge of the cliff. He looks down and sees a second tiger waiting below. Then he feels a vibration in the vine, looks up, and sees a mouse chewing on the vine. As his distress increases, he notices a strawberry plant growing in a crevice on the side of the mountain. Holding the vine with one hand, the man reaches out and plucks a plump, red strawberry. He places it in his mouth and savors how delicious it tastes.

Life is full of difficulties, obstacles, challenges, and pain. At times, life seems to be one problem after another. We wonder, *When will all these problems end?* And yet, among the problems is often a strawberry—if we'll notice it. Maybe the strawberry is creating and savoring a momentary pleasure. Maybe the strawberry is feeling gratitude for what we have rather than distress for what we don't. Maybe the strawberry is engaging in flow. Maybe the strawberry is showing kindness to someone who is also facing one problem after another. The new science of positive psychology is discovering evidence that we can improve our happiness. To do so, we need to find our strawberries.

> The Constitution only gives people the right to pursue happiness. You have to catch it yourself.
>
> Benjamin Franklin

JOURNAL ENTRY / 30

In this activity, you'll experiment with one of two strategies intended to increase happiness. The first was briefly described in the preceding text; the second is new. Assignments similar to both of these have been employed with encouraging results in positive psychology classes at colleges such as the University of Michigan and the University of Pennsylvania:

1. **Complete one of the following:**

    A. **Gratitude letter:** Write a letter to someone who has been an important and positive influence in your life. Pick someone to whom you have never fully expressed your gratitude. In the letter, explain specifically and completely what this person did that you appreciate . . . and how the kindness has positively affected your life. (If you choose to share your letter with the person at a later time, consider getting together in a quiet setting and reading the letter aloud. If a face-to-face meeting isn't possible, you could mail the letter and call later to discuss it.)

    B. **Me at my best:** Describe in detail a time when you successfully faced a difficult situation, one about which you feel proud of the way you handled it. Be sure to discuss fully: (1) what the difficult situation was; (2) how you handled it; and (3) what your handling of this situation shows about your inner strengths and character. Although modesty can be a virtue, please don't let it distort the truth of what you did. Be honest about how you behaved and the inner qualities you demonstrated during a situation in which you were at your best.

2. **Read over what you wrote in Step 1, and take a few moments to savor what you wrote. Then, honestly describe whether or not writing Step 1 of this journal entry lifted your spirits and improved your positive feelings. Explain your reaction as best you can.**

> Don't wait around for other people to be happy for you. Any happiness you get you've got to make yourself.
>
> Alice Walker

▶

| JOURNAL ENTRY | 30 | *continued* |

Remember, activities such as these work for some people but not for others, so you can be truthful about your own unique reaction.

Consider illustrating this journal entry with drawings, stickers, photos, or other images.

ONE STUDENT'S STORY

FAITH HANNAH LEA, *Daytona State College, Florida*

When I start reading a textbook, I'm often interested. But after a few minutes, I usually get bored and start reading mindlessly. When I attend classes, I frequently get bored as well. For example, one of my professors this semester seems to just regurgitate what is in the textbook, so you can imagine how boring it is to listen to her lectures.

As I was getting ready to register for my second semester, I read a section in my *On Course* textbook for my Managing Your Success class about creating flow. The book says that flow results from total absorption in an activity. Since I wasn't experiencing flow in most of my classes, I decided to try one of the book's suggestions to improve my experience for next semester. The suggestion was to identify professors who create flow in their classes and then enroll in their classes.

I started by asking other students which professors they like and why. Unfortunately, I didn't find any helpful information that way, so I decided to be a Creator by using *ratemyprofessor.com*. I started by reading comments from past students about one of my present professors. I found out that she does not (1) offer engaging learning experiences that appeal to diverse learning preferences, or (2) provide a combination of academic and emotional support that gives her students high expectations of success. These are two of the five things that *On Course* says are crucial to create flow in the classroom. No wonder I was really bored in that class!

Next, I looked up comments for professors who would be teaching the English class I planned to take the following semester and read students' comments about them. When I found a professor who had potential, I went to talk to her to see if she did any of the five things that create flow in the classroom. As it turns out, she matched everything on my list and more. She shared that she does all she can to make sure students understand what they are supposed to do, has lots of whole-class and small-group discussions, and spends a lot of time after class helping students. I had finally been successful in finding a good professor for me!

My suggestion to other students is to put more effort into finding professors who will help you experience flow. Talk to other students and ask them who their favorite instructors are and why. Also, check out comments on *ratemyprofessor .com*, and narrow your list of possible professors for each course as much as possible. Finally, before you make up your mind whose class to register for, go and talk with each of your top choices. Find out what they do in their classes. You can even ask what compliments they've gotten from their students. Get all the information you can to decide which professor is likely to engage you at a high level and help you experience flow.

If I hadn't read the *On Course* textbook, I would likely have just gone with the first professor available. Instead, I chose the Creator option and found the best professor I could. I am now confident that next semester will be "flowing" and fun.

Photo: Courtesy of Faith Hannah Lea.

EMOTIONAL INTELLIGENCE / at Work

The aptitudes you need to succeed start with intellectual horsepower—but people need emotional competence, too, to get the full potential of their talents. The reason we don't get people's full potential is emotional incompetence.

—*Doug Lennick, executive vice president, American Express Financial Advisors*

Do you need to be really smart to do well at work? Maybe not. In the past, one's intelligence quotient (IQ) was seen as crucial to a person's success. But it turns out that IQ isn't the most important factor in determining success. According to researcher Daniel Goleman, "IQ alone at best leaves 75 percent of job success unexplained, and at worst 96 percent—in other words, it does not determine who succeeds and fails. For example, a study of Harvard graduates in the fields of law, medicine, teaching, and business found that scores on entrance exams—a surrogate for IQ—had zero or negative correlation with their eventual career success."

So, then, what really does lead to success at work and in college?

Research indicates that emotional intelligence (EQ) has the strongest impact on employee success. Consider the following examples from researcher Joshua Freedman. In 2010, each salesperson at L'Oréal with higher measured emotional intelligence brought in $2.5 million more in annual sales than the average salesperson. AT&T employees with high emotional intelligence were 20 percent more productive. Coca-Cola employees trained in emotional intelligence were 30 percent more effective in reaching performance goals than those without EQ training. Although technical skills are important, Freedman found that high emotional intelligence leads more directly to success on the job.

With these strong findings about the importance of emotional intelligence, it's no wonder that employers look for potential employees with high emotional intelligence. In fact, the 2016 *Future of Jobs Report* from the World Economic Forum ranked emotional intelligence in the top 10 job skills required for 2020 and beyond.

You've already learned about the importance of EQ in your daily life, but how can you use EQ to get a job and be successful in your dream career? It's pretty straightforward. Because many tasks in the workplace depend on collaboration, when we are aware of our emotions and manage them effectively, we get along better with our coworkers. EQ allows us to perform better at our tasks and reach more of our goals. It's an important factor in determining employee success.

The four components of EQ—self-awareness, self-management, social awareness, and relationship management—are essential to workplace success. Becoming more proficient at emotional intelligence in college and at work will provide you with these benefits and more:

1. You'll manage your reactions and responses to difficult classmates, professors, coworkers, customers, and supervisors more effectively.

2. You'll work more effectively on project teams and collaborate more skillfully.

3. You'll demonstrate stronger leadership skills and improve your chances of promotions and positive evaluations.

4. You'll develop a more extensive social network that offers you support and opportunities.

EQ DURING JOB INTERVIEWS

Because nearly every job requires emotional competence and effective teamwork, many employers

▶

now assess potential employees for emotional intelligence skills. Interviewers might use both written tests and in-person interview questions to evaluate a potential employee's emotional intelligence. These questions ask interviewees to describe what they have done in difficult and emotional situations. Employers are looking to determine your awareness of your emotions, how you create and maintain relationships with others, receive feedback, or manage your responses to other people in stressful situations.

These questions might seem scary, but the good news is you can practice answering them before your interview. Plus, your own responses might show you places you can continue to improve your EQ! Try developing both written and spoken responses, and review and revise your responses to showcase your best self. Employers might use some of the following questions to assess your EQ:

1. Please discuss a disagreement you had with a coworker or another student and how you resolved it.

2. Share a time when it was important for you to really understand another person's perspective.

3. Describe a time when you were feeling overwhelmed at work or college. What was going on and what was your response?

4. Have you ever disagreed with a performance evaluation or grade you received? How did you handle it?

5. What is something that has made you very angry at work or at home? How did you deal with the problem and your anger?

6. Discuss an instance when you made a major mistake at work or in college. What did you do next?

7. Share how you have handled a customer complaint about a store policy for returns, or how you would handle one that arose.

8. Tell us about a time when you did something to help another student or employee.

9. What actions have you taken to build strong friendships at college or work?

When crafting your responses, be sure to address your skills in all four EQ components. Take a look at the following question, answer, and analysis:

Question: Describe a time when you were feeling overwhelmed at work or college. What was going on and what was your response?

Answer: A time when I was feeling overwhelmed was when I was studying for finals and trying to work a part-time job. I was struggling to fit in time to study because my boss wanted me to work extra hours for the holiday season. I felt stressed by the amount of work I had, and my friends kept telling me to just call in sick. However, I knew that wasn't what I wanted to do. Instead, I looked at my budget and saw that I didn't need the extra hours that month. I then realized that I was stressing out about money for no reason [**Self-Awareness**]. Once I clearly understood that studying was more in line with my goals and I didn't need the extra money, I felt calmer and less stressed, and set up a meeting with my boss [**Self-Management**]. I explained my situation and that although I liked the job and appreciated the hours, I needed to focus on my schoolwork. I could tell that my manager and coworkers were annoyed that I was trying to work less [**Social Awareness**]. I explained that I understood this would put a strain on my manager and my fellow coworkers and offered to cover some shifts during the holiday break so others could have some time off [**Relationship Management**]. In the end, I was able to focus on studying and passed all my exams. My coworkers were

▶

grateful when I took on their shifts, and my manager saw that I was still committed to doing well.

Analysis: In her answer, this person showed good self-awareness of her emotions during this overwhelming time. She was specific about why she felt stressed—studying for finals and working a part-time job. She then showed self-management by waiting until she felt calmer to come up with a plan and talk with her manager. By showing that she understood her boss's perspective, as well as how her coworkers were upset about the extra hours they had to work, she showed good social awareness. She then demonstrated relationship management by recognizing her boss was annoyed and offering to work extra shifts to help her team out.

Answering the employer's questions isn't the only way you can show emotional intelligence in an interview. Many strategies can show an interviewer your emotional intelligence. You'll want to actively listen to the interviewer. Rather than impulsively jumping in with your prepared answers, listen carefully to what the interviewer is saying. Then, you can better tailor your responses to clearly address the interviewer's questions and concerns. If your interviewer brings up something you're not sure of, don't get flustered. Instead, acknowledge that you don't already know this, but see it as an opportunity to learn! (As a bonus, this answer also shows that you have a growth mindset.) Most interviewers won't expect you to know everything, so don't pretend that you can do it all and risk appearing overconfident and unrealistic. Instead, let the interviewer know that you are willing to do the hard work it takes to develop a high level of competence in the position. Finally, use follow-up questions to demonstrate EQ. Ask about potential trainings in emotional intelligence. You can also ask how current employees collaborate on their projects.

EQ ON THE JOB

Once you land the job, how do you use and continue to develop emotional intelligence? It's tempting to think that once you find your dream career, everything will be smooth sailing. But as in college and life, you're going to run into situations that require high emotional intelligence to succeed.

Consider this study: In 2015, Leadership IQ ran a three-year study surveying 5,247 managers from 312 organizations who had hired over 20,000 employees. The study revealed that within 18 months, 46 percent of newly hired employees failed and only 19 percent demonstrated clear success. The reason for such a high rate of failure? It all depends on the employee's EQ. The study found that 26 percent of new hires failed because they could not accept feedback. Another 23 percent failed because they were unable to understand and manage emotions. Another 15 percent failed for having the wrong "temperament" for the job. Only 11 percent failed because they did not have the necessary technical skills to do the work. Here's even more evidence that EQ is more important than IQ or technical skills in career success.

So how can you avoid these pitfalls and succeed? By practicing emotional intelligence, of course! Following are three common situations you may face on the job and some suggestions for practicing emotional intelligence to ensure success:

1. **You don't get along with your new manager.** What happens if you start a new job and find that you don't get along with your new manager? First, you'll want to take some time to understand your emotions when dealing with your manager. Then, reflect on what is causing that emotion. Are you angry because your boss always expects you to work late so you can't be home with your family? Are you constantly anxious because your boss gives you tight deadlines with little notice? Once you've identified your emotion and what's

▶

causing it, you can make a thoughtful plan to address it. Have a conversation with your manager when you're calm and explain how you're feeling. Be sure not to use accusatory language and remember to listen to your boss's response. Try to see things from his or her perspective. Offer some solutions that address both your needs. Maybe you work late three days instead of five. Or perhaps your boss can give you deadlines ahead of time and help you prioritize.

2. **You receive negative feedback.** It's never easy to receive negative feedback about your performance, but you don't want to show you're upset or ignore it. After receiving feedback, ask for some time to think it over. Then, identify the emotions you're feeling and why you're feeling them. Are you upset because friends have told you before that you weren't always tactful? Are you frustrated because previous coworkers also told you that you didn't know how to delegate? Once you're calm, consider the various areas of feedback and talk honestly with your manager to create a development plan.

3. **You have a bad day.** Everyone has a bad day once in a while. Life happens and we're only human! Sometimes frustrations from life can overflow into work. Have you ever had an extra long commute and then snapped at someone at work? Maybe a fight with a loved one is making it difficult to focus at work. Take time to recognize your emotions and whether what's causing them is not related to work. Apologize to anyone you've snapped at, and make it a point to address your feelings later so you can focus on work.

The best way to prepare yourself for a successful future career is to start now, while still in college. Learn as much as you can about EQ. Practice strengthening all four components. Prepare yourself to address EQ during interviews. Learn to identify and manage distressing emotions like fear, anger, or sadness to help you at college and in the workplace. The more you strengthen your EQ, the higher you will rise in your career. As noted by Chip Conley, Head of Global Hospitality and Strategy for Airbnb, "The most successful business leaders are often experts in emotions."

TECH TIPS: Emotional Intelligence

Awareness *(Android, iOS)* is an app designed by a psychotherapist that randomly "intercepts" your daily routine with a gentle gong sound. You're asked to record what you're doing and feeling at that moment. The app then guides you in a brief meditative exercise to bring your awareness to the present moment. The daily, weekly, and monthly reports help you discover patterns so you can change unwanted habits and lead a more peaceful life.

Gratitude Journal *(Android, iOS)* asks you to write down things for which you are grateful. You can set a timer that will remind you to add to your growing list of things for which you give thanks. For many people, reviewing such a list is uplifting.

Track Your Happiness *(iOS)* begins with a one-time questionnaire. Then you decide when and how often you'd like to be contacted. On your chosen schedule, you'll receive an email or

▶

text and be asked to report what you are doing and how you are feeling. You'll receive periodic reports that identify the factors that increase your happiness.

MindShift *(Android, iOS)*, created especially for teens and young adults, can help you deal with anxiety. The app helps you learn to relax, develop more supportive ways of thinking, and identify specific actions to reduce anxiety. The app offers strategies for dealing with test anxiety, social anxiety, and performance anxiety, among other distressing feelings.

Happify *(online, Android, iOS)* offers activities and games that are based on the scientific study of happiness. These activities help you

strengthen five key happiness skills: Savoring, Thanking, Aspiring, Giving, and Empathizing. The site says it tracks user data and finds that 86 percent of frequent users get happier within two months.

Breathe2Relax *(Android, iOS)* helps you learn diaphragmatic breathing, a relaxation technique for reducing stress and anxiety. After viewing an introductory video with instructions for diaphragmatic breathing, you can complete a guided relaxation exercise complete with a visual timer and audio instructions to help users maintain steady, deep breathing. You can rate your stress, which is recorded and graphed over time so you can see any progress.

Note: All of these are free, but some may offer upgraded features for a fee.

Develop Self-Acceptance

FOCUS QUESTIONS / Why is high self-esteem so important to success? What can you do to raise your self-esteem?

Roland was in his 40s when he enrolled in my English 101 class. He made insightful contributions to class discussions, so I was perplexed when the first two writing assignments passed without an essay from Roland. Both times, he apologized profusely, promising to complete them soon. He didn't want to make excuses, he said, but he was stretched to his limit: He worked at night, and during the day he took care of his two young sons while his wife worked. "Don't worry, though," he assured me, "I'll have an essay to you by Monday. I'm going to be the first person in my family to get a college degree. Nothing's going to stop me."

But Monday came, and Roland was absent. On a hunch, I looked up his academic record and found that he had taken English 101 twice before. I contacted his previous instructors. Both of them said that Roland had made many promises but had never turned in an assignment.

I called Roland, and we made an appointment to talk. He didn't show up. During the next class, I invited Roland into the hall while the class was working on a writing assignment.

The foundation of anyone's ability to cope successfully is high self-esteem. If you don't already have it, you can always develop it.

Virginia Satir

"Sorry I missed our conference," Roland said. "I meant to call, but things have been piling up."

"Roland, I talked to your other instructors, and I learned you never wrote anything for them. I'd love to help you, but you need to take an action. You need to write an essay." Roland nodded silently. "I believe you can do it and so do the instructors I talked to. But I don't know if *you* believe you can do it. It's decision time. What do you say?"

"I'll have an essay to you by Friday."

I looked him in the eye.

"Promise," he said.

I knew that what Roland actually did, not what he promised, would reveal his deepest core beliefs about himself.

> Self-esteem is the reputation we have with ourselves.
>
> Nathaniel Branden

SELF-ESTEEM AND CORE BELIEFS

So it is with us all. Our core beliefs—true or false, real or imagined—form the inner compass that guides our choices.

At the heart of our core beliefs is the statement *I AM ___*. How we complete that sentence in the quiet of our souls has a profound effect on the quality of our lives.

High self-esteem is the fuel that can propel us into the cycle of success. Do we approve of ourselves as we are, accepting our personal weaknesses along with our strengths? Do we believe ourselves capable, admirable, lovable, and fully worthy of the best life has to offer? If so, our beliefs will make it possible for us to choose wisely and stay on course to a rich, full life.

For example, imagine two students: one with high self-esteem, the other with low self-esteem. Picture them just after they get very disappointing test scores. What do they do next? The student with low self-esteem will likely choose options that protect his fragile self-image, options such as dropping the course rather than chancing failure. The student with high self-esteem, on the other hand, will likely choose options that move her toward success, options such as persisting in the course and getting additional help to be successful. Two students, same situation. One focuses on weaknesses. One focuses on strengths. The result: two different choices and two very different outcomes.

The good news is that self-esteem is learned, so anyone can learn to raise his or her self-esteem.

AS SMART AS HE WAS, ALBERT EINSTEIN COULD NOT FIGURE OUT HOW TO HANDLE THOSE TRICKY BOUNCES AT THIRD BASE.

Sidney Harris/ScienceCartoonsPlus.com

KNOW AND ACCEPT YOURSELF

People with high self-esteem know that no one is perfect, and they accept themselves with both their strengths and weaknesses. To paraphrase philosopher Reinhold Niebuhr, successful people accept the things they cannot change, have the courage to change the things they can change, and possess the wisdom to know the difference.

Successful people have the courage to take an honest self-inventory, as you began doing with the self-assessment in Chapter 1. They acknowledge their strengths without false humility, and they admit their weaknesses without stubborn denial. They tell the truth about themselves and take action to improve what they can.

Fortunately for Roland, he decided to do just that. On the Friday after our talk, he turned in his English 101 essay. His writing showed great promise, and I told him so. I also told him I appreciated that he had let go of the excuse that he was too busy to do his assignments. From then on, Roland handed in his essays on time. He met with me in conferences. He visited the writing lab, and he did grammar exercises to improve his editing skills. He easily passed the course.

A few years later, Roland called me. He had transferred to a four-year university and was graduating with a 3.8 average. He was continuing on to graduate school to study urban planning. What he most wanted me to know was that one of his instructors had asked permission to use one of his essays as a model of excellent writing. "You know," Roland said, "I'd still be avoiding writing if I hadn't accepted two things about myself: I was a little bit lazy and I was a whole lot scared. Once I admitted those things about myself, I started changing."

Each of us has a unique combination of strengths and weaknesses. When struggling people become aware of a weakness, they typically blame the problem on others or they beat themselves up for not being perfect. Successful people, however, usually make a different choice: They acknowledge the weakness, accept it without self-judgment, and, when possible, take action to create positive changes. As always, the choices we make determine both where we are headed and the quality of the journey. Developing self-acceptance helps us to make those choices wisely.

> We must do that which we think we cannot.
>
> Eleanor Roosevelt

> Self-esteem is more than merely recognizing one's positive qualities. It is an attitude of acceptance and non-judgment toward self and others.
>
> Matthew McKay and Patrick Fanning

JOURNAL ENTRY / **31**

In this activity, you will explore your strengths and weaknesses and the reputation you have with yourself. This exploration of your self-esteem will allow you to continue revising any limiting beliefs you may hold about yourself. By doing so, you will take an important step toward your success.

1 **In your journal, write a list of 10 or more of your personal strengths.** For example, mentally: *I'm good at math;* physically: *I'm very athletic;* emotionally: *I seldom let anger control me;* socially: *I'm a good friend;* and others: *I'm almost always on time.*

▶

> **JOURNAL ENTRY** / **31**   *continued*
>
> ❷ **Write a list of 10 or more of your personal weaknesses.** For example, mentally: *I'm a slow reader;* physically: *I'm out of shape;* emotionally: *I'm easily hurt by criticism;* socially: *I don't listen very well;* and others: *I'm a terrible procrastinator.*
>
> ❸ **Using the information in Steps 1 and 2, write about the present state of your self-esteem.** When you took the self-assessment in Chapter 1, what was your Score #8 "Believing in Yourself"? What do you think your score will be when you take it again in Chapter 9? If you think your two scores will be different, to what do you attribute the difference? Are you satisfied with where you think your self-esteem is today? If not, what can you do to improve it?
>
> **To create an outstanding journal, remember to use the five suggestions in the section "Write a Great Life" in Chapter 1. Especially remember to dive deep!**

ONE STUDENT'S STORY

WYNDA ALLISON PAULETTE, *National Park College, Arkansas*

When I started back to college, I was 41 years old. I was on a "wing and a prayer." I didn't know if I had it in me to be successful in school, with all the responsibilities I had in my life. I didn't know if I was smart enough or even had the abilities to work on a college level after so many years. But what I did know was that I wanted to succeed. I would do my best. I had managed well in every other facet of my life, and I wanted to prove to myself that I could get a good education and set a good example for my children.

So, there I was in Success Seminar class, reading *On Course.* I read the "One Student's Stories" and began taking a personal inventory of my own life. Some of the journal entries I wrote left me mentally exhausted, because our instructor was always asking us to "dig deeper," and deeper I would go. I would write about subjects that I had left firmly in my past, reopen them, and give myself the opportunity to see them in a whole new light. Eventually, I was able to look at the "horrible" mistakes I had made in my life as lessons instead of failures. I could lay down negative thoughts that I harbored about myself and begin to see the ways I had grown as a human being. I began taking steps unknowingly to practice self-love and acceptance. I learned so much about myself and got so much out of the class that

when the end of the semester came, and we were required to turn in our notebooks, I wrote this poem/story to include for my instructor. It only took a few minutes to write but summed up my journey quite well.

The Friend

I once had a person in my life who
*   I professed to care about; but*
*   the truth is, I didn't like Her*
*   much at all.*

My friends would say how pretty
*   and smart She was; I would*
*   silently disagree.*

I made decisions that would hurt
*   Her . . . choices that would*
*   inconvenience Her and take*
*   Her off track.*

I never worried about Her well-
*   being. In my eyes, She didn't*
*   deserve my love.*

I singlehandedly set that poor
*   girl back 20 years, with all the*
*   unnecessary problems I put in*
*   Her path.*

▶

I silently watched Her go through bad relationships, unproductive friendships, and unnecessary hardships without bothering to intercede.

I saw Her sink farther and farther from Her dreams, and thought She got what She deserved.

I judged Her so harshly, disrespected Her, and felt no remorse. . . .

UNTIL-

One day I looked at that person, REALLY took the time to see Her and started to see the good in Her. . . .

I began to respect Her for the grace with which She handled even the hardest of times . . . and for the optimistic way She viewed the world.

I began to see Her worth shine from within brighter than a whole vault full of gold.

I saw a beauty within Her so great that it made me weep.

I began to encourage Her every day, and assure Her that Her dreams could be realized and that She could accomplish anything She set Her brilliant mind to do.

I fell in love with Her for the first time. I began to admire and respect Her.

I regretted the horrible times I had put Her through: the setbacks, the wrongs. . . .

But now, looking back, I realize that woman I now love would not be the person She is

if She had not traveled the dark paths I led Her through. . . .

. . . Nor would She appreciate the sunshine nearly as much.

For within Her is a well-seasoned, understanding, empathetic,

responsible, caring human being.

That woman is ME.

My story is still ongoing. There will always be struggles; nothing will ever be "laid at my feet." But I also learned through all the hard work I put into Success Seminar, and all of the valuable lessons and information that I was able to reap from the text and the exercises, that life is full of possibility. There are no dead-end roads, only new routes to forge through and lessons to learn. Most of all, we have to learn to love and believe in ourselves.

Photo: Courtesy of Wynda Allison Paulette.

Healthy Choices: Sleep

It's a rare college student who doesn't sometimes—perhaps often—fall behind on sleep. Perhaps to study. Or attend a great social event. Or juggle school and work. Or cope with family problems. Or maybe all of the above.

If any of these situations sounds like you, you're not alone. In a study published in *Nature and Science of Sleep,* 50 percent of college students reported daytime sleepiness, and 70 percent complained of insufficient sleep. Authors of the study explain the risks: "The consequences of sleep deprivation and daytime sleepiness are especially problematic to college students and can result in lower grade point averages, increased risk of academic failure, compromised learning, impaired mood, and increased risk of motor vehicle accidents." In short, to achieve success in college (and beyond), you need to get enough sleep.

So, how much sleep is enough? The National Sleep Foundation recommends seven to nine hours of sleep for adults from 18 to 64 years old. Some researchers urge at least eight hours of sleep for the average person, stating that seven hours is not enough for most people. Not getting enough sleep threatens your brain health and learning. Numerous studies reveal that sleep-deprived students suffer impaired learning, memory, and decision making. A 2014 study by the University of St. Thomas in Minnesota found that the negative effects of sleep deprivation on grades are similar to those caused by binge drinking and drug use. Another study published by the American Academy of Sleep Medicine reports that college students who slept poorly were much more likely to receive lower grades and drop out of classes than peers who slept well.

But that's not all. Sleep deprivation can lead to a host of health problems, including high blood pressure, heart disease, obesity, cancer, and diabetes—as well as weakened immune system, depression, stroke, automobile accidents, and even premature death. The message of hundreds of scientific studies is clear: Get enough sleep or pay a steep price.

THE LEAST YOU NEED TO KNOW ABOUT SLEEP

Sleep is complex and, despite much research, isn't fully understood. Nonetheless, sleep studies have led to important discoveries. Sleep is separated into three distinct stages—light sleep, deep sleep, and dream sleep (also called REM sleep). You cycle through these stages about every 90 minutes. Present research suggests that remembering information and facts (like math formulas or the Wise Choice Process) solidifies during deep sleep. Remembering *how to* do something (like typing or shooting a basketball) solidifies during dream sleep. Bottom line, if you don't get enough sleep, your memory of both information and physical skills is weakened.

Neuroscientist Lisa Mosconi, PhD, explains, "Experts agree that sleeping is crucial for memory consolidation and learning, and that poor sleep negatively affects these much-needed abilities. Without adequate sleep your brain becomes foggy, your attention dwindles, and your memory stalls. This might not be news to anyone who has pulled an all-nighter cramming for a test only to find they couldn't recall most of the information the next day."

Here's another important finding. While awake, our brains build up toxic waste proteins. This is the same harmful waste found in the brains of people with Alzheimer's disease. During sleep, healthy brains call in the cleaning crew (called the glymphatic system) to remove the waste. As Arianna Huffington notes in her book *The Sleep Revolution,* "Sleep is a time of intense neurological activity—a rich time of renewal, memory consolidation, brain and neurochemical cleansing, and cognitive maintenance." Worth repeating: Getting enough sleep is essential to learning and memory.

It's also a key to athletic performance. Shawn Stevenson, in his book *Sleep Smarter,* reports a 2011 study at Stanford University with the men's varsity basketball team. In the study, the athletes increased their sleep time from an average of seven hours per night to eight and a half hours per night. Afterward, their athletic performance improved in many ways. The athletes ran significantly faster, shaving nearly a full second off their full-court sprint times. Their free-throw and three-point shooting improved by 9 percent. They even reported better moods and overall physical well-being. Stevenson concluded, "If you want to perform at your best, then getting great sleep is an absolute must."

ADDRESSING SLEEP PROBLEMS: THE RISKY AND THE SAFE

If you find sleep to be elusive, you may be tempted to turn to alcohol. Don't. A review of 27 studies found that, although alcohol does allow healthy people to fall asleep faster, it reduces dream sleep. This means you miss out on the stage of sleep that strengthens memories and is most healing. Also, if you use alcohol as a sleep aid, the next day you'll likely experience drowsiness and poor concentration.

How about over-the-counter (OTC) sleep aids? These include drugs such as Benadryl, Aleve PM, and ZzzQuil. According to a Mayo Clinic publication, OTC sleep aids can be effective when used for an occasional sleepless night. However, problems occur when you use them often or even become dependent on them for sleep. Problems can include daytime drowsiness, nausea, vomiting, dizziness, headaches, blurred vision, constipation, and urinary retention.

And then there are prescription sleeping pills. Do your best to avoid these as well. But if under a doctor's care, limit use to 7 to 10 days to avoid problems, including addiction. Reported side effects of prescription sleeping pills include headaches, dizziness, unusual thinking, memory loss, and potentially dangerous behaviors while asleep. These behaviors include sleepwalking, cooking food, and driving a vehicle with no memory of doing so afterward. Additionally, a study by researchers at Scripps Clinic found the death rate for people prescribed only 1 to 18 sleeping pills per year was 3.6 times higher than a comparison group, even for teenagers. Additionally, rates of new cancers were 35 percent higher in those who use prescription sleeping pills compared to people not taking them. Sleep expert, Chris Winter, MD, advises, "Sleeping pills are like tigers: I'm not sure either is really suitable to keep in your home long term."

There are safer options for improving sleep. Dr. Winter offers a technique called "sleep restriction." The goal is to work your way up to enjoying eight or more hours of quality sleep. Here's how: Start by setting your alarm for the time you'll get up every day. Then go to bed only five and a half hours before the alarm will go off. Your body, Dr. Winter says, will adapt to this inadequate sleep time with an increase in sleep quality. When you can fall asleep in 15 minutes and stay asleep until your alarm wakes you, go to bed 15 minutes earlier the next night. If you once again experience trouble falling or staying asleep, go to bed 15 minutes later the next night. Keep adjusting your sleep time until you can fall asleep, stay asleep, rise at your chosen time, and feel rested and rejuvenated. I know it seems strange to spend less time in bed when you're trying to get more sleep. However, remember that the goal of sleep restriction is to improve the quality of your sleep so that, over time, you can increase both the time and the quality of your sleep.

If your sleep deprivation is serious, seek help from experts at a sleep clinic. They may find that the problem is a physical disorder called sleep apnea. This potentially serious sleep disorder causes breathing to stop and start during sleep. Symptoms include loud snoring or feeling consistently tired after a night's sleep. Sleep apnea occurs because your throat muscles relax or because your brain isn't correctly controlling your breathing or both. As a result, your breathing stops, depriving your body and brain of oxygen. It's also possible experts will discover that your sleeping problem doesn't have a physical cause. If so, they may recommend cognitive behavioral therapy for insomnia (CBT-I). In 2015, the *Annals of Internal Medicine* published a meta-analysis of numerous sleep studies. The study concluded that CBT-I effectively treats insomnia by improving poor sleep habits, changing sabotaging beliefs, and reducing anxiety.

Whatever the cause, poor sleep is nothing to ignore. Your campus health center may be able to provide a referral to a sleep clinic or specialist. If not, do an Internet search. The value of sleep clinics is indicated by their explosion in numbers. In 1970, there were only three in the United States. In 2016, there were more than 2,500.

Keep in mind that as each semester progresses, time for sleep will slip away if you don't keep up with your academic work. In the self-management chapter, you learned strategies to cope with your flow of schoolwork. Successful students keep up on their assignments, their personal lives, and their sleep. As sleep expert Chris Idzikowski advises, "Remember that sleep is essential to your overall performance in academia—it's worth setting good sleep habits now to maximize what you get out of your education."

WISE CHOICES: SLEEP

Now that we've identified the essential nature of sleep, let's explore recommendations from experts that you can safely institute on your own. The key is consistency. Having a regular routine conditions your brain to sleep and awake on a healthy schedule. Consider putting a check next to the following actions that you already do. Then experiment with unchecked options to improve your sleep.

- Wake up at the same time every day (even weekends), no matter when you went to bed.
- Exercise, preferably in bright natural light; the exercise and light stimulate cortisol, a hormone that makes you alert.

- If needed, nap no more than 30 minutes between noon and 4 p.m.

- Avoid caffeine (coffee, soda, green and black tea, chocolate, energy drinks) six hours before bedtime.

- Eat a healthy dinner at least two hours before bedtime and limit snacking afterward.

- Avoid nicotine and alcohol after dinner; for an evening drink, try chamomile tea.

- Create a relaxing nighttime routine; for example, brush your teeth, take a hot bath, read for pleasure, and write down anything that's causing you anxiety.

- Set an alarm for your regular wake-up time. Then turn the clock so you can't see it. Why? Seeing the time during the night can create stress about not getting enough sleep . . . just trust your alarm to wake you.

- Do no schoolwork in bed; you want to condition your body to associate your bed with sleep (not with work that takes alert focus).

- Ban electronics (TV, computer, smartphone, tablet) from your bedroom. The blue light from the screens disrupts sleeping, and the content on the screens arouses—rather than calms—the brain.

- Make your bedroom completely dark, cool (60 to 67 degrees), and quiet (if needed, try ear plugs or white noise such as a fan or white noise machine).

- Do deep breathing, progressive relaxation, and/or meditation. (Learn how in the section on stress in this chapter.)

- If you lie awake or wake up in the middle of the night, either relax until you sleep or get up and do something (I like to read mystery novels). Most important, don't lie there stressing out. Trust that you'll be just fine even if you miss a little sleep this one night.

- If pregnant, understand that sleep aids may harm your baby. Instead, try strategies that don't include taking drugs, and consult your doctor for additional ways for improving sleep.

Healthy Choices: Continuing Your Healthy Lifestyle

The message of *On Course* is simple: The outcomes and experiences of our lives are greatly influenced by the choices we make. Nowhere is this more true than in the quality of our health and how long we live. As you've seen in the Healthy Choices sections, three lifestyle choices greatly affect our health and longevity: (1) what we put in our bodies (drugs, foods, and liquids), (2) how often and how vigorously we move our bodies (exercise), and (3) how we rest our bodies (relaxation and sleep). Importantly for students, these choices also greatly affect our brains and, therefore, the ability to learn and succeed in college.

In the introduction to the health articles, we encouraged you to take the self-assessment at https://apps.bluezones.com/vitality. Whether or not you took it then, please take it now. Based on your present lifestyle choices, the quiz will estimate how long you'll live. You'll also receive personalized suggestions for living a longer, healthier life. If you did take the self-assessment at the beginning of this course, you'll also receive a comparison of your two scores. In this way, you'll see how any new lifestyle choices you implemented during this course may contribute to a healthier and longer life. Whatever your results, remember that it's never too late to implement new choices to improve your health.

Staying On Course
to Your Success

Successful Students . . .

▶ **gain self-awareness,** consciously employing behaviors, beliefs, and attitudes that keep them on course.

▶ **adopt lifelong learning,** finding valuable lessons and wisdom in nearly every experience they have.

▶ **develop emotional intelligence,** effectively managing their emotions in support of their goals and dreams.

▶ **believe in themselves,** seeing themselves as capable, lovable, and unconditionally worthy human beings.

Struggling Students . . .

▶ **make important choices unconsciously,** being directed by self-sabotaging habits and outdated life scripts.

▶ **resist learning new ideas and skills,** viewing learning as fearful or boring rather than as mental play.

▶ **live at the mercy of strong emotions** such as anger, sadness, anxiety, or a need for instant gratification.

▶ **doubt their competence and personal value,** feeling inadequate to create their desired outcomes and experiences.

Planning Your Next Steps

How have you changed while taking this course? What changes do you still want to make?

Although our travels together are coming to an end, your journey has really just begun. Look out there to your future. What do you want to have, do, or be? What actions do you need to take to achieve your desired outcomes and experiences? Make a plan and go for it!

Sure, you'll get off course at times. But now you have strategies—both outer and inner—to get back on course. Before heading out toward your goals and dreams, take time to review those strategies. Any time you want, you can look over the table of contents of this book for an overview of what you've learned. Read the chapter-opening charts to review the choices of successful and struggling people. Reread a strategy as a reminder. Perhaps most important of all, reread your journal. Once in a while, you can return to *On Course* and to your journal to remind yourself of anything you forget. And, trust us, you *will* forget. You *will* get off course. But you have the power to remember . . . to make wise choices . . . to get back on course . . . and to create the life of your dreams.

Destiny is not a matter of chance; it is a matter of choice. It is not a thing to be waited for; it is a thing to be achieved.

William Jennings Bryan

ASSESS YOURSELF, AGAIN

On the next page is a duplicate of the self-assessment you took in Chapter 1. Take it again. (Don't look back at your previous answers yet.) In Journal Entry 32, you will compare your first scores with your scores today, and you will consider the changes you have made. Acknowledge yourself for your courage to grow. Look, also, at the changes you still need to make to become your best self.

You now have much of what you need to stay on course to the life of your dreams. The rest you can learn on your journey. Be bold! Begin today!

Onward!

It isn't where you came from; it's where you're going that counts.

Ella Fitzgerald

Self-Assessment

Read the following statements and score each one according to how true or false you believe it now is about you. To get an accurate picture of yourself, consider what IS true about you (not what you *want* to be true). Remember, there are no right or wrong answers. Assign each statement a number from 0 to 10, as follows:

Totally False ▶ ⓪ ① ② ③ ④ ⑤ ⑥ ⑦ ⑧ ⑨ ⑩ ◀ Totally True

1. _____ I control how successful I will be.
2. _____ I'm not sure why I'm in college.
3. _____ I spend most of my time doing important things.
4. _____ When I encounter a challenging problem, I try to solve it by myself.
5. _____ When I get off course from my goals and dreams, I realize it right away.
6. _____ I'm not sure how I prefer to learn.
7. _____ I know ways to increase my happiness.
8. _____ I'll truly accept myself only after I eliminate my faults and weaknesses.
9. _____ Forces out of my control (such as poor teaching) are the cause of low grades I receive in school.
10. _____ I place great value on getting my college degree.
11. _____ I don't need to write things down because I can remember what I need to do.
12. _____ I have a network of people in my life that I can count on for help.
13. _____ If I have habits that hinder my success, I'm not sure what they are.
14. _____ When I don't like the way an instructor teaches, I know how to learn the subject anyway.
15. _____ When I get very angry, sad, or afraid, I do or say things that create a problem for me.
16. _____ When I think about performing an upcoming challenge (such as taking a test), I usually see myself doing well.
17. _____ When I have a problem, I take positive actions to find a solution.
18. _____ I don't know how to set effective short-term and long-term goals.
19. _____ I am organized.
20. _____ When I take a difficult course in school, I study alone.
21. _____ I'm aware of beliefs I have that hinder my success.
22. _____ I'm not sure how to think critically and analytically about complex topics.
23. _____ When choosing between doing an important school assignment or something really fun, I do the school assignment.
24. _____ I break promises that I make to myself or to others.
25. _____ I make poor choices that keep me from getting what I really want in life.
26. _____ I expect to do well in my college classes.
27. _____ I lack self-discipline.
28. _____ I listen carefully when other people are talking.
29. _____ I'm stuck with any habits of mine that hinder my success.
30. _____ My intelligence is something about myself that I can improve.

31. _____   I often feel bored, anxious, or depressed.

32. _____   I feel just as worthwhile as any other person.

33. _____   Forces outside of me (such as luck or other people) control how successful I will be.

34. _____   College is an important step on the way to accomplishing my goals and dreams.

35. _____   I spend most of my time doing unimportant things.

36. _____   I am aware of how to show respect to people who are different from me (race, religion, sexual orientation, age, etc.).

37. _____   I can be off course from my goals and dreams for quite a while without realizing it.

38. _____   I know how I prefer to learn.

39. _____   My happiness depends mostly on my circumstances.

40. _____   I accept myself just as I am, even with my faults and weaknesses.

41. _____   I am the cause of low grades I receive in school.

42. _____   If I lose my motivation in college, I don't know how I'll get it back.

43. _____   I have a self-management system that helps me get important things done on time.

44. _____   I seldom interact with people who are different from me.

45. _____   I'm aware of the habits I have that hinder my success.

46. _____   If I don't like the way an instructor teaches, I'll probably do poorly in the course.

47. _____   When I'm very angry, sad, or afraid, I know how to manage my emotions so I don't do anything I'll regret later.

48. _____   When I think about performing an upcoming challenge (such as taking a test), I usually see myself doing poorly.

49. _____   When I have a problem, I complain, blame others, or make excuses.

50. _____   I know how to set effective short-term and long-term goals.

51. _____   I am disorganized.

52. _____   When I take a difficult course in school, I find a study partner or join a study group.

53. _____   I'm unaware of beliefs I have that hinder my success.

54. _____   I know how to think critically and analytically about complex topics.

55. _____   I often feel happy and fully alive.

56. _____   I keep promises that I make to myself or to others.

57. _____   When I have an important choice to make, I use a decision-making process that analyzes possible options and their likely outcomes.

58. _____   I don't expect to do well in my college classes.

59. _____   I am a self-disciplined person.

60. _____   I get distracted easily when other people are talking.

61. _____   I know how to change habits of mine that hinder my success.

62. _____   Everyone is born with a certain amount of intelligence, and there's not really much you can do to change that.

63. _____   When choosing between doing an important school assignment or something really fun, I usually do something fun.

64. _____   I feel less worthy than other people.

Transfer your scores to the scoring sheet on the next page. For each of the eight areas, total your scores in columns A and B. Then total your final scores as shown in the sample on the next page.

Self-Assessment Scoring Sheet

SAMPLE

A	B
6. _8_	29. _3_
14. _5_	35. _3_
21. _6_	50. _6_
73. _9_	56. _2_

_28_ + 40 − _14_ = 54

SCORE #1: Accepting Personal Responsibility

A	B
1. ___	9. ___
17. ___	25. ___
41. ___	33. ___
57. ___	49. ___

___ + 40 − ___ = ___

SCORE #2: Discovering Self-Motivation

A	B
10. ___	2. ___
26. ___	18. ___
34. ___	42. ___
50. ___	58. ___

___ + 40 − ___ = ___

SCORE #3: Mastering Self-Management

A	B
3. ___	11. ___
19. ___	27. ___
43. ___	35. ___
59. ___	51. ___

___ + 40 − ___ = ___

SCORE #4: Employing Interdependence

A	B
12. ___	4. ___
28. ___	20. ___
36. ___	44. ___
52. ___	60. ___

___ + 40 − ___ = ___

SCORE #5: Gaining Self-Awareness

A	B
5. ___	13. ___
21. ___	29. ___
45. ___	37. ___
61. ___	53. ___

___ + 40 − ___ = ___

SCORE #6: Adopting Lifelong Learning

A	B
14. ___	6. ___
30. ___	22. ___
38. ___	46. ___
54. ___	62. ___

___ + 40 − ___ = ___

SCORE #7: Developing Emotional Intelligence

A	B
7. ___	15. ___
23. ___	31. ___
47. ___	39. ___
55. ___	63. ___

___ + 40 − ___ = ___

SCORE #8: Believing in Myself

A	B
16. ___	8. ___
32. ___	24. ___
40. ___	48. ___
56. ___	64. ___

___ + 40 − ___ = ___

Interpreting Your Scores

A score of . . .

0–39	Indicates an area where your choices will **seldom** keep you on course.
40–63	Indicates an area where your choices will **sometimes** keep you on course.
64–80	Indicates an area where your choices will **usually** keep you on course.

Choices of Successful Students

Successful Students . . .

▶ **accept personal responsibility,** seeing themselves as the primary cause of their outcomes and experiences.

▶ **discover self-motivation,** finding purpose in their lives by discovering personally meaningful goals and dreams.

▶ **master self-management,** consistently planning and taking purposeful actions in pursuit of their goals and dreams.

▶ **employ interdependence,** building mutually supportive relationships that help them achieve their goals and dreams (while helping others do the same).

▶ **gain self-awareness,** consciously employing behaviors, beliefs, and attitudes that keep them on course.

▶ **adopt lifelong learning,** finding valuable lessons and wisdom in nearly every experience they have.

▶ **develop emotional intelligence,** effectively managing their emotions and the emotions of others in support of their goals and dreams.

▶ **believe in themselves,** seeing themselves as capable, lovable, and unconditionally worthy human beings.

Struggling Students . . .

▶ **see themselves as victims,** believing that what happens to them is determined primarily by external forces such as fate, luck, and powerful others.

▶ **have difficulty sustaining motivation,** often feeling depressed, frustrated, and/ or resentful about a lack of direction in their lives.

▶ **seldom identify specific actions needed to accomplish a desired outcome,** and when they do, they tend to procrastinate.

▶ **are stubbornly independent,** seldom requesting, even rejecting, offers of assistance from those who could help, and failing to build effective and supportive relationships with others.

▶ **make important choices unconsciously,** being directed by self-sabotaging habits and outdated life scripts.

▶ **resist learning new ideas and skills,** viewing learning as fearful or boring rather than as mental play.

▶ **live at the mercy of strong emotions,** such as anger, sadness, anxiety, or a need for instant gratification.

▶ **doubt their competence and personal value,** feeling inadequate to create their desired outcomes and experiences.

JOURNAL ENTRY / 32

In this activity, you'll examine the changes you have made since the beginning of this course, and you'll plan your next steps toward success in college, career, and life.

1 In your journal, write the eight areas of the self-assessment and transfer your score from the assessment you took in Chapter 1 (first score) and your second score from the assessment you just took here in Chapter 9. Use the following format:

First Score	Second Score	
_____	_____	1. Accepting personal responsibility
_____	_____	2. Discovering self-motivation
_____	_____	3. Mastering self-management
_____	_____	4. Employing interdependence
_____	_____	5. Gaining self-awareness
_____	_____	6. Adopting lifelong learning
_____	_____	7. Developing emotional intelligence
_____	_____	8. Believing in myself

2 **Comparing the results from the two self-assessments, write in depth about the area(s) in which you have raised your score.** Remember to answer questions that a thoughtful reader would have about what you are writing, diving deep by using the 4Es (examples, explanations, experiences, and evidence)!

3 **Further comparing the results from the two self-assessments, write in depth about the area(s) in which you most want to continue improving.** Remember the saying "If you keep doing what you've been doing, you'll keep getting what you've been getting." With this idea in mind, identify the specific changes you'd like to make in your behaviors, thoughts, emotions, and beliefs in the months and years to come.

By the way, if one of your scores went down over the semester, consider that this result may not indicate that you became less effective; rather, it may indicate that you are now more honest with yourself or more aware of what's necessary to excel in this area.

4 **Write one last entry in which you sum up the most important discoveries you've made in this course and plans for a great future. Dive deep!**

In 2002, I hit rock bottom when I moved into a homeless shelter. For the next four years, I cycled in and out of one shelter after another. There, I saw how people can become passive and numb, with no life or hope left in their eyes. They smell bad, walk with their heads down, and are filled with negativity. Their only goal in life is getting a handout. I knew I couldn't allow a sheltered life to become my life.

I was a Detroit police officer from 1985 to 1998. In 1996 I lost my mother and not long after that my 17-year-old son died of an asthma attack. In my mind, crying on someone's shoulder was a sign of weakness, so I kept it all inside. I had been drinking before, but now I started drinking even more. I left the police force in 1998 and started a limo service. Four years later, I was arrested for drunk driving and lost my license. When I couldn't pay rent, the woman I was living with put me out, and I lived in my car for two months. That's when I turned to a homeless shelter for help.

My first concern was to become self-supporting, but I wasn't sure where to start. I went to a state employment service and told a counselor, "I want a college degree, not one of those low-paying jobs

listed in the job bank." She told me about scholarships at the local community college, and with her help, I registered for classes in 2007. I hadn't been a student for 30-plus years, and the thought of attending college scared me. But I had a goal. I wanted to become a computer systems security analyst, a career that starts at about $48,000. The money sure sounded good.

In my English Fundamentals class I encountered *On Course.* The book gave me insights into my past failures and successes and provided specific strategies for achieving success in college and in my life. I realized that many of my past problems were rooted in Victim language. When I was on the police force, I felt that some of the supervisors picked on me. I'd say they didn't like me because I wasn't in the right group. The truth was, I was missing a lot of work, but I always shifted the blame. After reading about Victim/Creator, I told myself, *You have to rebuild yourself. No one else is going to do it for you.* I even started telling people back at the shelter about what I was learning in this class.

My greatest concern about attending college was how to organize my time. The newly discovered Creator in me used the Four-Quadrant Chart to

prioritize my daily tasks. As I used the self-management tools in the book, I developed self-confidence that I would do well in college. I showed the next actions list to others and told them how important it is to have a list to keep you focused. If someone tells you they have tickets to the Detroit Pistons game, you have to say no and do what is important for your goals.

Along with how to organize my time, I discovered the beauty of interdependence. Two of my English classmates and I decided to meet in the writing center after each class and work on our assignments together. We encouraged each other and became teachers as well as students. Our new-found interdependence made us feel valuable and gave us increased confidence and feelings of self-worth. This confidence translated into academic success as well. I earned a 3.88 GPA, high honors, for my first semester.

In the next semester, I got a part-time job in the writing center. I love to see a twinkle in students' eyes when I help them do well on a paper. I also started volunteering at the Washtenaw Literacy program. I continue to use *On Course* principles in my daily life, and I share them at the tutoring center, in my volunteer work, and at the shelter. These principles provide the best hope for people to lead successful, happy, and unsheltered lives. Two of the men from the shelter

▶

are now enrolled at the college, and they come to me when they have a problem. One guy still has a Victim mentality. I tell him, "Why do you blame your woe-is-me on everyone else and not look in the mirror and see yourself as the cause? If I can help you, I will. But you have to help yourself first."

People have to learn to stand on their own two feet, and I now have the skills to help others do that. I've even changed my career goal. I plan to teach elementary school. For me it's no longer about the money. It's about sharing myself. After experiencing the lessons in *On Course*, I feel I have something to share. My fear of failure is gone. Being a Creator, I believe in myself and feel confident that I can solve any problems I face. Now I want to share that feeling with others.

Photo: Courtesy of Stephan J. Montgomery.

STUDY SKILLS
A Toolbox for Active Learners

Becoming an Active Learner

FOCUS QUESTIONS How does the human brain learn? How can you use this knowledge to become a highly effective learner?

Earlier chapters in *On Course* present essential *soft skills* for success in college and beyond. This section presents a toolbox of *hard skills* for becoming an active and highly effective learner.

As mentioned in Chapter 1, both soft skills and hard skills are learnable. Soft skills, however, are invisible and more difficult to measure than hard skills. Some people refer to soft skills as inner strengths, personal qualities, or non-cognitive factors. Examples of soft skills explored in *On Course* are personal responsibility, self-motivation, self-discipline, interdependence, self-awareness, emotional intelligence, and believing in yourself.

Hard skills are more visible and measurable than soft skills. Since your main job as a student is learning, you'll need hard skills that will make you an effective learner. Also called study skills, these hard skills will improve your learning (and grades) in college. But that's not all.

You may have heard the phrase that "College ends. Learning doesn't." After college, these skills will help you in your career and whenever you are facing the 21st-century challenge of lifelong learning. You'd be hard-pressed to find a job in today's economy that doesn't require the ability to learn quickly and effectively. Every time you download a new app, sign a contract, start a new hobby, or travel to a new country, you'll need to employ effective learning skills. And that's just the beginning of all you'll need to learn to create a great life.

Exercise A-1 on page 225 of the Facilitator's Manual demonstrates the importance of being an active learner.

We now accept the fact that learning is a lifelong process of keeping abreast of change. And the most pressing task is to teach people how to learn.

Peter Drucker

ASSESS YOUR STUDY SKILLS FOR COLLEGE SUCCESS

Before we begin an exploration of effective learning skills, take a few minutes to complete the self-assessment questionnaire on the following pages. At the end of this toolbox of learning skills, you'll have an opportunity to repeat this self-assessment and compare your two scores. I think you're going to be impressed by what you've learned about learning!

As you take this self-assessment, be absolutely honest so you can learn the truth about your present learning skills. This valuable information can pave the way to making significant improvements in your future learning efforts.

Study Skills Self-Assessment

Read the following statements and score each one according to how true or false you believe it is about you. To get an accurate picture of yourself, consider what IS true about you (not what you *want* to be true). Remember, there are no right or wrong answers. Assign each statement a number from 0 to 10, as follows:

Totally False ▶ ⓪ ① ② ③ ④ ⑤ ⑥ ⑦ ⑧ ⑨ ⑩ ◀ **Totally True**

1. _____ I understand how the human brain learns, and I use that knowledge to study effectively.
2. _____ When I read an assignment in my textbooks, I have trouble identifying the most important information.
3. _____ I know effective strategies for memorizing important things such as facts, details, and formulas.
4. _____ I don't know how to create graphic or linear organizers.
5. _____ I'm good at figuring out what's important during a class discussion or lecture.
6. _____ After I get a test or quiz back, I check my grade to see how I did and then don't look at it again.
7. _____ When writing a paper, I know how to add supporting details that make my main ideas clear.
8. _____ After I finish taking a test or quiz, I have no idea what kind of grade I will get.
9. _____ While reading an assignment, I have an effective system for marking or writing down important ideas.
10. _____ When I review my notes, they are complete and easy to understand.
11. _____ Before studying for a test, I condense all my class notes, homework, reading assignments, and course handouts into one document, and then I study from this new document.
12. _____ I do most (sometimes all) of my studying on the day before or the day of a test.
13. _____ When I take a test, I feel calm and confident.
14. _____ When I write the answer to an essay question, I find it difficult to organize my ideas.
15. _____ When I study for a test, I use a number of different learning strategies.
16. _____ After reading, I don't recall much of what I just read.
17. _____ My notes include most of the information that later appears on a test.
18. _____ I know at least three different ways to organize my study materials, so the information makes the most sense to me.
19. _____ I study for math tests by looking over the problems I solved for homework and/or the ones the instructor solved.

20. _____   When I take a test, I have a plan to get the most possible points.
21. _____   I usually write one draft of a paper and that's what I turn in.
22. _____   A few days after I take a test or quiz, I don't remember much of what I studied.
23. _____   After reading an assignment, I take time to think, write, or talk with others about the main points of what I just read.
24. _____   I've never learned how to take good notes during a class.
25. _____   I study in a quiet place where I'm not disturbed.
26. _____   I feel unprepared when I take a test because I don't really know how to study effectively.
27. _____   I don't understand how to write a good paper in college.
28. _____   I know how to do well on a test or quiz no matter what kind of questions the instructor asks: multiple-choice, true/false, fill-in-the-blank, matching, problems, or essays.
29. _____   How learning happens is a mystery to me.
30. _____   I'm good at identifying what is important information in a reading assignment.
31. _____   While studying, I make a list of questions that I think will be on a test.
32. _____   During a lecture or presentation, I have trouble staying focused.
33. _____   I'm bad at memorizing important formulas, details, and facts.
34. _____   After I get a test or quiz back, I analyze and correct all the errors I made.
35. _____   My papers are pretty short because I have difficulty adding supporting details that make my main ideas clear.
36. _____   I know how to tell how well I have learned a subject even before I take a test.
37. _____   When I read, I don't write in my book or take separate notes.
38. _____   My class notes are difficult to understand when I look at them a few days later.
39. _____   I study for tests by re-reading my textbooks, class notes, and course handouts.
40. _____   I study each subject frequently, and I spread my study sessions over the whole course.
41. _____   I lose points on tests because of things like spending too much time on one question or taking too much time answering a question that was worth only a few points.
42. _____   The papers I write are well organized.
43. _____   I don't participate in class discussions or activities.
44. _____   When I finish a reading assignment, I remember most of what I read.
45. _____   When I take a test, there are questions about things that weren't in my notes.
46. _____   When I study, there are often distractions, and I can't concentrate.
47. _____   When I study for a math test, I solve many problems of the same kinds that will be on the test.
48. _____   Certain kinds of test questions are difficult for me, and I don't do well on them.
49. _____   I understand and use all four steps of the writing process: Prewriting, Writing, Revising, and Editing.
50. _____   I ask questions in class whenever I'm confused.
51. _____   After reading a textbook, I don't think much about what I read until right before the test.
52. _____   I take good notes during a lecture, video, or presentation.
53. _____   When I take a test, I find questions I didn't study for.
54. _____   I use an effective learning system when I study, so I feel well prepared when I take a test.
55. _____   I know how to write a good paper in college.
56. _____   I feel nervous and my mind goes blank when I take a test.

Transfer your scores to the scoring sheets on the next page. For each of the seven areas, total your scores in columns A and B. Then total your final scores as shown in the sample.

Self-Assessment Scoring Sheet

	SAMPLE	
A		**B**
6. _8_		29. _3_
14. _5_		35. _3_
21. _6_		50. _6_
73. _9_		56. _2_
_28_ + 40 −		_14_ = 54

	SCORE #1: Learning Actively	
A		**B**
1. ___		8. ___
15. ___		22. ___
36. ___		29. ___
50. ___		43. ___
___ + 40 −		___ = ___

	SCORE #2: Reading	
A		**B**
9. ___		2. ___
23. ___		16. ___
30. ___		37. ___
44. ___		51. ___
___ + 40 −		___ = ___

	SCORE #3: Taking Notes	
A		**B**
5. ___		24. ___
10. ___		32. ___
17. ___		38. ___
52. ___		45. ___
___ + 40 −		___ = ___

	SCORE #4: Organizing Study Materials	
A		**B**
11. ___		4. ___
18. ___		39. ___
25. ___		46. ___
31. ___		53. ___
___ + 40 −		___ = ___

	SCORE #5: Rehearsing and Memorizing Study Materials	
A		**B**
3. ___		12. ___
40. ___		19. ___
47. ___		26. ___
54. ___		33. ___
___ + 40 −		___ = ___

	SCORE #6: Taking Tests	
A		**B**
13. ___		6. ___
20. ___		41. ___
28. ___		48. ___
34. ___		56. ___
___ + 40 −		___ = ___

	SCORE #7: Writing	
A		**B**
7. ___		14. ___
42. ___		21. ___
49. ___		27. ___
55. ___		35. ___
___ + 40 −		___ = ___

Interpreting Your Scores

A score of . . .

0–39	Indicates an area where your study skills will **seldom** support deep learning.
40–63	Indicates an area where your study skills will **sometimes** support deep learning.
64–80	Indicates an area where your study skills will **usually** support deep learning.

HOW THE HUMAN BRAIN LEARNS

Much has been discovered, especially in the last few decades, about how human beings learn. To benefit from these discoveries, let's take a quick peek into our brains. The human brain weighs about three pounds and is composed of trillions of cells. About 100 billion of them are neurons, and here's where much of our learning takes place. When a potential learning experience occurs (such as reading this sentence), some neurons send out spikes of electrical activity. This activity causes nearby neurons to do the same. When neurons fire together, they form what is called a "neural network."

I like to picture a bunch of neurons joining hands in my brain, jumping up and down, and having a learning party. If this party happens only once, learning is weak (as when you meet with your instructor to solve a math problem one day and you can't recall how to do it the next). However, if you cause the same collection of neurons to fire repeatedly (as when you solve 10 similar math problems yourself), the result is likely to be a long-term memory. According to David Sousa, author of *How the Brain Learns,* "Eventually, repeated firing of the pattern binds the neurons together so that if one fires, they all fire, ultimately forming a new memory trace."

Here's the takeaway: If you want learning to stick, you need to create strong neural networks. In this way, learning literally changes the structure of your brain. Through autopsies, neuroscientist Robert Jacobs and his colleagues determined that graduate students actually had 40 percent more neural connections

> The human brain has the largest area of uncommitted cortex (no particular required function) of any species on earth. This gives humans extraordinary flexibility and capacity for learning.
>
> Eric Jensen

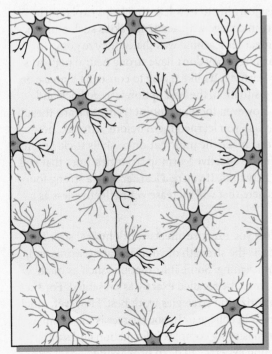

Neurons before learning.

Neurons after learning.

than did students who did not complete high school. Jacobs's research joins many other brain studies to reveal an important fact: **To excel as a learner, you need to create as many neural connections in your brain as possible.**

THREE PRINCIPLES OF DEEP AND LASTING LEARNING

With this brief introduction to what goes on in our brains, let's explore how highly effective learners maximize their learning. Whether they know it or not, effective learners in academic and professional settings have figured out how to create many strong neural connections in their brains. And you can, too.

How? The short answer is: **Become an active learner.** You don't create deep and lasting learning by passively listening to a lecture, casually skimming a textbook, multitasking during class, or having a tutor solve your math problems. In order to create strong neural networks, you've got to participate actively in the learning process.

Now, here's the longer answer. Good learners, consciously or unconsciously, implement three principles for creating deep and lasting learning:

1. **Prior Learning.** Brain research reveals that when you connect what you are learning now to previously stored information (i.e., already-formed neural networks), you learn the new information or skill faster and more deeply. For example, when you review assigned readings or previous notes before class, you activate relevant neural networks that help you make sense of the lecture and identify important content.

   The contribution of past learning to new learning helps explain why some learners have difficulty in college with academic skills such as math, reading, and writing. If their earlier learning was shaky, they're going to have difficulty with new learning. They don't have strong neural networks on which to attach the new learning. It's like trying to construct a house on a weak foundation. In such a situation, the best option is to go back and strengthen the foundation. However, there's no point trying to learn these foundational skills the same way you learned them before. After all, how you learned them before didn't make the information or skills stick. So this time you'll want to employ more effective learning strategies, ones that will create the necessary neural networks. If you're a learner with a strong foundation, you'll find strategies here that will increase your effectiveness as a learner even more.

2. **Quality of Processing.** How you exercise affects your physical strength. Likewise, how you study affects the strength of your neural networks and, therefore, the quality of your learning. Some information (such as math formulas or anatomy terms) must be recalled exactly as presented. For such learning tasks, effective memorization strategies work best. However, much of what you'll be asked to learn in college or in your career is too complex for mere memorization. For mastering complex information and skills, you'll want to use what learning experts call **deep processing**.

   Don't use just one deep-processing strategy, however. Successful athletes know the value of cross training, so they use a variety of training

We're on the edge of an explosion in knowledge about how to learn most effectively.

Jeffrey D. Karpicke,
psychology instructor,
Purdue University

When information goes "in one ear and out the other," it's often because it doesn't have anything to stick to.

Joshua Foer

Mathematics teachers . . . see students using a certain formula to solve problems correctly one day, but they cannot remember how to do it the next day. If the process was not stored, the information is treated as brand new again!

David A. Sousa

strategies. Similarly, successful learners know the value of employing a variety of deep-processing strategies. That's because the more ways you deep-process new learning, the stronger your neural networks become.

When you actively study any information or skill, use many different *and effective deep-processing strategies.* By doing so, you create and strengthen related neural networks and your learning soars.

3. **Quantity of Processing.** The quality of your learning is also affected by how often and how long you study. Here, the most effective approach is **distributed practice.** The human brain learns best when learning efforts are distributed over time. No successful musician waits until the night before a concert to begin practicing. Why, then, do students think they can start studying the night before a test? An all-night cram session may make a deposit in their short-term memories.
It might even allow them to pass a test the next day. However, even students who got good grades have experienced the ineffectiveness of cramming. This effect is sometimes called "learning amnesia." It's the frustrating experience of not being able to remember what was learned in a previous course when you need it. Forgetting happens when we don't create strong neural networks that make learning last. To create strong neural networks, you need to process the target information or skill with *many different* deep-processing strategies and do it *frequently.*

> ### Three Principles of Deep and Lasting Learning
>
> 1. **Prior Learning.** Relate new information to previously learned information.
>
> 2. **Quality of Processing.** Use many different deep-processing strategies.
>
> 3. **Quantity of Processing.** Use frequent practice sessions of sufficient length distributed over time.

In addition to how frequently you use deep-processing strategies to study, also important is the *amount of time* you spend learning. Highly effective learners put in **sufficient time on task.** The traditional guideline for a week's studying is 2 hours for each credit hour. Some students fool themselves by putting in "sufficient time," but spend little of it engaged in effective learning strategies (such as the ones you are about to learn). Instead, they skim complex information in their textbooks. They attempt to memorize information they don't understand. They surf the Internet. They send a couple of text messages, and the next thing they know, it's time to go to bed. When they fail the test the next day, they complain, "But I studied *so long*!"

The reason most students struggle with learning is fully within their control. What you need is a learning system that employs what science has discovered about how the human brain learns.

> Good learners, like everyone else, are living, squirming, questioning, perceiving, fearing, loving, and laughing nervous systems, but they are good learners precisely because they believe and do certain things that less effective learners do not believe and do. And therein lies the key.
>
> Neil Postman & Charles Weingartner

The CORE Learning System

Four general strategies are common to good learners. To remember these strategies, think of the acronym CORE (see **Figure T.1**). CORE stands for **C**ollect, **O**rganize, **R**ehearse, and **E**valuate. The CORE learning system automatically guides you to employ all three of the active learning principles discussed earlier. By applying what is known about how the human brain learns, the CORE learning system helps you create deep and lasting learning. Here's how it works:

Collect: In every waking moment, we're collecting perceptions through our five senses. Without conscious effort, the brain takes in a multitude of sights, sounds, smells, tastes, and physical sensations. Most perceptions disappear within moments. Some, such as our first language, may stick for a lifetime. Thus, much of what we learn in life we do without intention. In college, however, learning needs to be more conscious. That's because instructors expect you to learn specific information and skills. Then, of course, they want you to demonstrate that knowledge on quizzes, tests, exams, term papers, and other forms of evaluation. In college, two of the most important ways you'll collect information and skills are through reading textbooks and attending classes and labs, whether face-to-face or online.

Organize: Once we collect information, we need to make sense of it. When learning in everyday life, we tend to organize collected information in unconscious ways. We don't even realize that we're doing it. However, in a college course, you need to organize information systematically, so it makes sense to you. In fact, *making meaning* from collected information is one of the most important outcomes of studying.

Rehearse: Once we collect and organize our target knowledge, we need to remember it for future use. Rehearsing (also called "practicing") strengthens neural networks and makes learning stick. When you solve

> When something is meaningful it is organized; when it is organized, it is simplified in the mind.
>
> Robert Ornstein

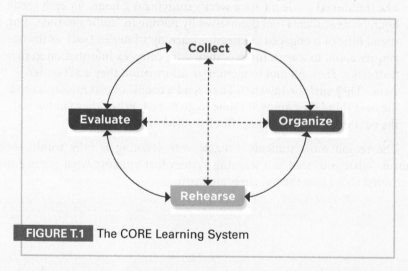

FIGURE T.1   The CORE Learning System

10 challenging math problems, you're rehearsing. Over time, the process of solving becomes easier and more natural. Good learners know how to rehearse information and skills so they can use them, whether on a test, in their career, or in their personal life.

Evaluate: Life is great at giving us informal feedback about the quality of our learning. Maybe you tell a joke and forget the punch line. You know immediately you have more learning to do. Higher education, however, provides us with more formal feedback. Yup, those pesky tests, term papers, quizzes, lab reports, essays, classroom questions, and final exams. Evaluations—whether informal or formal—are an essential component of all learning. That's because without feedback, we can never be sure if our learning is accurate or complete.

> Research has shown that students learn best when they themselves are actively engaged in the subject instead of simply listening to someone else speak.
>
> Barbara Oakley,
> *A Mind for Numbers*

In this "Toolbox for Active Learners," you'll learn proven strategies for

- **C**ollecting key information,
- **O**rganizing that information into effective study materials,
- **R**ehearsing information and skills for future use, and
- **E**valuating how well you have learned.

But learning doesn't occur in a tidy, step-by-step fashion. At any moment while learning, you may need to jump to a different component in the CORE system. For example, while **R**ehearsing, you might realize that some information doesn't make sense to you. So, you stop and **O**rganize it in a different way. At other times you may engage two or more components at once. For instance, when **R**ehearsing study materials, you're probably **E**valuating your mastery of that knowledge at the same time. Thus, you can expect to use the four components of the CORE Learning System in any order and in any combination.

You'll encounter many different strategies in this Toolbox. Your task is to experiment with and find the ones that work best for you. What you'll ultimately construct is a personalized learning system, one you can use for the rest of your life as you further your education, develop new skills and hobbies, and advance in your career.

> Remember, it's not the size of the brain that matters; it's the number of connections between neurons.
>
> David A. Sousa

EXERCISE: ACTIVE LEARNING

Identify one thing you have learned simply because you enjoyed learning it. Then write or discuss answers to each of the following questions.

A. How did you gather the information or skills you needed to learn this? (**C**ollect)

B. What did you do to learn the information or skills needed to learn this? (**O**rganize)

C. What else did you do to learn this? (**R**ehearse—Variety)

D. How often did you engage in learning this? (**R**ehearse—Frequency)

E. When you engaged in learning this, how long did you usually spend? (**R**ehearse—Duration)

F. What feedback did you use to determine how well you had learned this? (**E**valuate)

KASE CORMIER, *Asheville-Buncombe Technical Community College, North Carolina*

At the beginning of my first semester in college, I was overwhelmed. I had been out of school for more than 10 years and wasn't sure how to make the adjustment to being back in school after all that time. In previous attempts at school, I had felt dumb; I had an awful memory and a learning disability that made writing and spelling difficult. While looking over the syllabi for my five classes, I had no idea how I was going to fit all that knowledge into my brain. The information for Anatomy and Physiology was enough by itself; adding in essays, computer projects, and reading assignments from other classes made my head spin. On top of all that, I was required to take a study skills class. A friend who had taken the class before told me it was worth it. Skeptical, I responded, "Are you kidding me? There is no way I'll get anything out of that class, and I have no more time."

The week before classes began, I decided to get a head start on the dizzying amount of reading I had to do. I picked up the *On Course* textbook and skimmed the pages lazily until I got to the section on "Becoming an Active Learner." The information on creating "neural networks" piqued my interest, and I read about the three principles of deep learning: connect new information to things you already know, use a lot of different study techniques, and study often. Although it was interesting at the time, I had too much to do to let it sink in; yet as the semester progressed, those three principles began popping into my head. I could practically feel my neurons firing off faster and faster as I learned new material, trying to find ways to process and retain everything I was being taught. Every class moved quickly, and I found that I only had a short amount of time to learn something. I kept applying those techniques, and as long as I connected new information back to what I already knew, found new and creative ways to learn it, and repeated those activities often, I could fit so much more information into my head. Better than simply cramming for a test, those principles enabled me to do more than just learn new information. They helped me retain it as well.

These three learning principles were extremely important for Anatomy and Physiology because of how much information we were responsible for. Cramming for the next test wouldn't work; every section was laying groundwork for the future, and I needed to retain that information. To create varied learning experiences, I tried out several different study groups, each with a different style of learning, until I finally found a group that I connected with; afterward, I supplemented my primary study group with other groups to have some variety. I worked hard with each group, even making up silly games to explore different ways of learning the material. One game was "flashcard races." We put the names of the cranial nerves on flashcards, shuffled them, and then raced to see who could put them in order first. The more different ways I studied the information, the stronger my neural connections became. I took every opportunity to study in open lab, and in class, I asked lots of questions. My classmates joked with me, saying that I asked "Why?" too much, but I explained that it helped me relate the information to things I already knew. After our final lecture exam (which happened to be on neurons), my study buddies all gave me a hug and thanked me for improving the study sessions with my silly games and constant questioning. We all got As!

The *On Course* principles may seem worthless at first, but don't be fooled. They stay with you and change the way you learn. I am grateful that I took the initiative to read the section on learning before my classes started. In high school, I was a C student, but this semester I earned a 4.0! Connecting information to what I already knew, using a variety of study techniques, and studying often definitely helped make my first semester back in college a success.

Photo: Courtesy of Kase Cormier.

The first step in the CORE Learning System is <u>Collecting</u> knowledge, and one of the most important ways you'll <u>Collect</u> knowledge in college is by reading. During your studies you can expect to read many thousands of pages. You'll read textbooks, reference books, journals, novels, articles, handouts, websites, and more. Many of the tests you'll take will be based on your reading. And so will the essays and research papers you'll write. Obviously, then, reading is one of the most important skills you can have for success in college.

Sadly, according, to American College Testing (ACT), many college-bound students lack this skill. Nearly half of the 1.2 million students who recently took the ACT college entrance test scored low in reading. This is bad news. According to ACT, the ability to read and understand complex texts is essential for college success. And because of all of the reading that is required in college, even students with good reading skills will benefit from becoming more accomplished.

Once your formal education ends, strategies for effective reading will continue to serve you well. Lawyers read judicial opinions to understand precedent and build their arguments. Medical professionals read peer-reviewed journals to stay up to date with advances in diagnosis and treatment. Businesspeople read various reports to understand their product, market, and customer base. Nearly every career path requires that successful professionals engage in ongoing learning, and much of this new knowledge can be <u>Collected</u> through active reading strategies. The learning strategies you'll encounter in this section have one thing in common: they cure **mindless reading**. Mindless reading occurs when you run your eyes over a page only to realize later that you recall little of what you read. The opposite of mindless reading is **active reading**.

Active reading is characterized by intense mental engagement in what you are reading. This highly focused involvement leads to significant neural activity in your brain, assists deep and lasting learning, and (good news for students) leads to high grades.

READING: THE BIG PICTURE

When reading mindfully, you are actively <u>Collecting</u> key concepts, ideas (main and secondary), and supporting details (major and minor). When placed by levels of significance, information you read looks like **Figure T.2**.

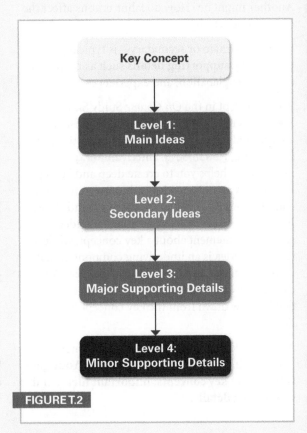

FIGURE T.2

A **key concept** is the main topic you are reading about. Examples of key concepts include *inflation*, *mitosis*, or *World War II*.

Ideas that expand on concepts are divided into main and secondary ideas. A **main idea** (sometimes called a "thesis") is the most important idea the author wants to convey about a key concept. Two authors may write about the same key concept but present different main ideas. For example, they may both write about *inflation* but disagree about its cause. One might say, "The primary cause of inflation is war." The other may say, "The rising cost of production is the main cause of inflation."

A **secondary idea** (sometimes called a "topic sentence") elaborates on a main idea by answering questions that readers may have about it. For example, one question about inflation might be, "What effect do taxes have on rising costs?" Another might be "How do labor unions affect the cost of production?"

Each idea—main or secondary—is typically followed by **supporting details** such as examples, evidence, explanation, and experiences.

A key concept in the *On Course* Study Skills Toolbox is the CORE Learning System. The main idea related to this concept is that <u>C</u>ollecting, <u>O</u>rganizing, <u>R</u>ehearsing, and <u>E</u>valuating information helps you to create deep and lasting learning. A secondary idea is that <u>C</u>ollecting is a conscious effort to gather information and skills. As we can see in this example, the main idea is a summary statement about a key concept, while a secondary idea is an underlying component that helps you better understand the main idea. You can see how these ideas, along with supporting details, flow down from the key concept in **Figure T.#.**

As you look at the following learning strategies, keep in mind the big picture of reading: **Your goal is to <u>C</u>ollect key concepts, important ideas, and supporting details.**

STRATEGIES TO IMPROVE READING

Following you'll find many of the very best strategies for mastering the skill of reading. Keep in mind that the purpose of each strategy is to help you move from mindless reading to active reading. After reading each strategy, pause and decide if it would help you improve your reading skills. If so, mark it in some way, then decide which of these strategies to experiment with to improve your reading.

BEFORE READING

1. Approach reading with a positive attitude. Attitude is a foundation of your success because it influences the choices you make. Realize that reading offers you access to the entire recorded knowledge of the human race. With effective reading skills, you can learn virtually any information or skill you need in order to improve your life, but only if you approach each reading assignment with a positive attitude. Before you sit down to read, consider your "why." Is it making a contribution to society or your family, acquiring knowledge and skills for your career, or enhancing effectiveness in your-day-to-day life? Tuning in to your long- and short-term goals can help you be more attuned to what is important and useful in your readings.

2. Create a distributed reading schedule. A marathon reading session right before an exam is seldom helpful. Instead, spread many shorter sessions over an entire course. A distributed schedule (such as five pages every day) helps you concentrate for your entire reading session and increases how much you recall from what you read.

3. Review past readings. As a warm-up before you read, glance at pages you have previously read. Look at past chapter titles, text headings, and any annotations you've made to jog your memory. Reviewing like this takes advantage of one of the three principles of deep and lasting learning: prior learning. When you connect what you are reading now to previously stored information (i.e., already-formed neural networks), you learn the new information or skill faster and more deeply.

4. Preview before reading. Like observing a valley from a high mountain, previewing a reading assignment provides the big picture of what's to come. You'll see the important ideas and their organization, which increases understanding when you read. Having a big picture understanding also prepares you for class discussion and helps you identify important content in lectures. Preview the pages, taking in chapter titles, chapter objectives, focus questions, text headings, charts, graphs, illustrations, previews, and summaries. Note any words that are specially formatted, such as with CAPITALS, **bold**, *italics*, and so on.

5. Identify the purpose of what you're reading. To keep the big picture in mind, ask yourself, "What's the point of what I'm about to read?" By keeping this purpose in mind, you program yourself to <u>Collect</u> the most important ideas as you read. The purpose of what you are reading right now is to identify strategies that may help you improve your reading comprehension and recall.

6. Create a list of questions. If the author provides focus questions, use them to start this list. Next, turn chapter titles or section headings into questions. For example, if the heading in a computer book reads "HTML Tags," turn this heading into one or more questions: *What is an HTML tag? How are HTML tags created?* The process of reading for answers to questions heightens your concentration, increases your active involvement, and improves your understanding.

7. Plan for online engagement. Because we are so used to scrolling down and swiping through online content, it can be easy to slip into passive reading. Push through this tendency by having a plan for active engagement. Most e-readers have tools that enable you to highlight, mark, and search online readings; preview these tools beforehand and consult a tutorial if needed to become comfortable with them. Then, prepare your note-taking app to record key concepts and questions

that keep you engaged. Set a timer to stay focused for a set amount of time, and plan to take breaks to stay sharp. A common rule of thumb is the 20-20-20 rule. Every 20 minutes, look at something 20 feet away for 20 seconds. If more than your eyes are tired, get up from your study space for a stretch or light physical activity.

WHILE READING

8. Pause to recite. Have you ever finished reading an assignment only to realize you have no idea what you just read? Here's a remedy. Stop at the end of each section and summarize aloud what you understand to be the main ideas and supporting details. The more difficult the reading, the more often you'll want to pause to recite. Each recitation will give you instant feedback about how well you understand the author's ideas. Pause and experiment with this strategy right now. What are the seven reading strategies you have just encountered? How many can you recall? How much do you remember about them?

9. Read for answers to questions on your list. If you've created a list of questions (Strategy 6), now is the time to cash in on that effort. For example, suppose you're about to read a chapter in your accounting book titled "The Double-Entry Accounting System." On your list of questions,

SPEED READING
COURSE
7·00 — 7·05

Mike Flanagan/Cartoon Stock

you've written "What is a double-entry accounting system?" As you read the chapter, look for and underline the answer. Then write the question in the margin. When reading online, take advantage of the built-in tools of your e-reader that allow you to add your questions to the eBook.

10. Mark and annotate your text. As you read, keep asking: *What's the key concept . . . what are the main ideas about the concept . . . and what support is offered?* Once you decide what's important, underline or highlight these ideas in your book. As a guideline, mark only 10–15 percent of your text. That limitation will help you select what is truly important. Additionally, annotate what you read. To *annotate* means to add comments. Annotations could include summaries in your own words, diagrams, or questions. It is tempting to skim or passively read course materials, particularly when they are online. Doing this can hurt you in the future when you are tested on the information, need a strong foundation for an advanced course, or have to draw upon it on the job. Writing your own comments helps you minimize mindless reading, maximize your understanding, and <u>C</u>ollect the most important ideas to learn.

11. Take notes. Start by writing the chapter title at the top of your page in a notebook or note-taking app. Beneath the chapter title, copy the main headings and any subheadings. As you read the chapter, add additional information to clarify these ideas.

12. Look up the definition of key words. Use a dictionary when you don't know the meaning of a key word. Consider starting a vocabulary list as part of your notes. Or create digital flashcards with new words on one side and definitions on the other. Writing the word in a sentence is a good idea, too.

13. Read critically. Not all ideas in print or online are true. Learn to read critically by being a healthy skeptic. Who is the author? What are the author's credentials? Does the author stand to gain (e.g., money and status) by your acceptance

of their opinion? Are the facts accurate and relevant? Is the evidence sufficient? Are the author's positions developed with logic or only strong emotions? Are sources of information identified? Are they believable? Are they current? Are various sides of an issue presented, or only one? Given that anyone can post information on the Internet, reading critically is especially important when assessing information that you encounter online.

14. Apply reading strategies best suited to the subject. Different reading strategies unlock meaning for different subjects (sort of like having different keys for your work, home, and vehicle). For math, you are reading to learn the skill of solving problems. For science, you are reading to understand applications of the scientific method. For literature, you are reading to understand the theme and artistic elements used by the author. To get the most out of these different types of readings, see Figure T.# for a summary of purposeful reading strategies.

AFTER READING

15. Reflect on what you read. Upon finishing a reading assignment, lean back, close your eyes, and ask and answer questions that will help you see the big picture. For example . . .

- What are the key concepts?
- What are the main ideas about those concepts?
- What are the supporting details?
- What do I think and feel about the author's main ideas and supporting details?

Recalling key ideas from what you have just read is one of the most powerful learning strategies you can apply to your reading assignments. This is a learning strategy you can use any time and place. It can be especially helpful when you are reading online because it can help build breaks into your reading and fend off fatigue.

16. Reread difficult passages. On occasion, every reader needs to revisit difficult passages to understand them fully. I recall one author whose writing made me feel stupid. However, somewhere around my fifth or sixth reading (and using strategies in this section), a light went on in my brain and I thought, "Oh . . . so that's what he means! That's not nearly as complicated as I thought!" Trust that by using the strategies presented here, you can comprehend any reading assignment if you stick with it. Developing this attitude now will help you in your career. In fact, patience and perseverance are two of the top skills employers value. Having a growth mindset (explained in Chapter 7) can help greatly in developing this trust in your ability to take on challenges.

17. Recite the marked text. Read aloud the parts of the text you have underlined or highlighted. Attempt to blend the ideas into a flowing statement by adding connecting words between the words in your text. In effect, you'll be summarizing the key points of the material you just read. You may even want to write the summary in your own words because writing is another way to solidify learning.

18. Talk about what you read. Explain the main ideas and supporting details. Especially helpful is having this conversation with another student in your class who has read the same assignment. This study partner can give you feedback on where you may have misunderstood or left out something important.

19. Seek another perspective on the same subject. Sometimes another author or content creator will express the same ideas more clearly. An online video or educational website may provide just the information or explanation you need to make sense of your college textbook.

20. Seek assistance. Still having problems understanding what you read? Ask your instructor to explain muddy points. Or see if your college has a learning, tutoring, or academic success center. For some subjects, there may be dedicated personnel to help. If all else fails, see if your college has a diagnostician who can test you for a possible learning disability. Such a specialist may be able to help you improve your reading skills.

EXERCISE: READING

Choose your most challenging textbook and rate your present comprehension of its content on a scale of 1–10 (with 10 indicating a deep and lasting understanding of what you read). Over the next week, apply new reading strategies when you read this challenging text. At the end of the week, again rate your understanding of the book on the 1–10 scale. Be prepared to explain why you think your rating went up, down, or stayed the same. In particular, is there one reading strategy that was most helpful in your quest to read this challenging text with greater comprehension?

Taking Notes

In this section, we will examine the second most time-consuming way you will **Collect** information while in college: attending classes or engaging in online lectures.

In pursuing a four-year degree, students spend nearly 400 hours in a brick-and-mortar or online classroom. Students seeking a two-year degree spend about half that time in class.

Your instructors, of course, expect you to learn what they cover in these classes. Unless you're motivated and able to take effective notes, however, most of what you hear in class will zip through your short-term memory and be quickly forgotten. More than one hundred years ago, Hermann Ebbinghaus conducted the first studies of memory. He discovered that we lose about 75 percent of what we learn within 24 hours. That's why effective note-taking is an essential skill for achieving academic success in college.

Taking notes in a class is similar to taking notes while reading a textbook. However, taking notes during a class offers additional challenges. For one thing, as you mark or annotate a textbook, you stop reading. Thus, while reading you are in total control of how fast you receive new information. By contrast, when you take notes during a class, the speaker keeps talking. You have little or no control over the speed of information delivery. This situation places greater demands on your ability to identify key concepts, main ideas, and supporting details. Then you need to write them down accurately and completely.

And that's not all. You're likely to encounter instructors who will provide unique obstacles to note-taking: They may speed talk until your head spins. Or . . . drone . . . on . . . so . . . sloooowly . . . you . . . have . . . trouble . . . staying . . . awake. They may be poorly organized. Or all of the above.

Online classes present their own challenges. Synchronous online classes require you to keep up with the live class content while managing the distractions of your study environment, such as noises, other people, and the temptation to switch to another window. Asynchronous online classes provide the flexibility of reviewing lecture content on your own schedule, but this content can quickly pile up if you don't engage with it regularly.

A summary of research on note-taking compiled by Kenneth Kiewra reports sobering news. Lecture notes taken by first-year students contain, on average, only 11 percent of the important ideas presented during a class. The result should be obvious. No matter how well you study, you can't pass tests by studying only 11 percent of the important ideas in a course.

You can choose to complain, blame, and make excuses for why it's impossible to take good notes in a class. Or, you can take full responsibility for your learning outcomes and experiences. Regardless of how many obstacles the instructor or the subject presents, it's your job to take effective notes.

Beyond classes, the ability to take effective notes will pay dividends in the future as you advance in your career. Ongoing learning is part of professional success in fields ranging from accounting to zoology. In any given month, you may be expected to participate in meetings, conferences, and trainings to acquire knowledge related to your role, company, or industry. Just like with lectures, these are all contexts where what you initially learn will quickly be forgotten if you do not first Collect the key ideas through effective note taking. In this section, you'll learn how.

TAKING NOTES: THE BIG PICTURE

To take effective class notes, you need to answer two key questions: *What* should I write in my notes and *how* should I write that information?

First, consider *what* to write in your notes. Despite a popular misconception, the answer is not "everything the instructor says." Even if you could write that fast, having a word-for-word transcript of a class is not the goal of note-taking. As with reading, **the goal of note-taking is Collecting key concepts, main ideas, and supporting details**. Thus, much of what you learned earlier about taking notes while reading also applies to taking class notes . But you'll need some new strategies to compensate for the challenges of writing notes while someone is speaking.

As for *how* to write your notes, a number of note-taking systems have been invented, but essentially, they all fit into one of two categories: linear or graphic. Examples of these methods will be explained shortly. No single method of note-taking works best for everyone, so experiment and personalize a note-taking system that works best for you.

STRATEGIES TO IMPROVE TAKING NOTES

Following, you'll find many of the very best strategies for taking good notes. Keep in mind the purpose of these strategies. They help you Collect key concepts, main ideas, and supporting details, recording them in a way that works best for you. After reading each strategy, pause and decide if it would help you improve your note-taking skills. If so, mark it in some way, then decide which of these strategies to experiment with to improve your note taking.

BEFORE TAKING NOTES

1. Assemble appropriate supplies. Experiment and decide on the best note-taking supplies for you. Find a pen you like writing with. Keep your notes in ring binders, composition books, spiral binders, or a laptop computer. Ring binders are handy because you can add and remove pages easily. This option is helpful when an instructor provides handouts or you revise your notes. If you use one binder for all of your classes, use tabs to separate the notes for each class. If you take digital notes, consider whether you prefer to type your notes or use a digital pen or stylus. Note-taking apps can automatically save your digital notes to the cloud, provide helpful organization through virtual notebook pages and tabs, pull in content from different sources (e.g., slides and links), and help you find previous content quickly via search features. You can also create a more comprehensive record of class content by including attachments or photos of handouts.

2. Complete homework assignments before class. Remember, neural networks created by past learning make present learning easier. That's why you'll benefit from completing reading assignments *before* class. This effort increases your ability to understand lectures and discussions. Also, you'll know better what belongs in your notes. For example, you'll know if the instructor is repeating what was in the reading or adding new information. And, suppose the instructor's presentation style presents a challenge (such as speed talking). Because the information is already familiar, you'll more easily spot key concepts, main ideas, and supporting details. If your homework includes solving problems, complete them before class as well.

3. Attend every class. As obvious as this suggestion may seem, some students don't create good notes simply because they aren't in class. Sure, you can borrow notes from another student. But is it smart to bet your academic success on someone else's note-taking skill? Remember, research reveals that first-year students' notes contain only 11 percent of the important ideas presented during a class. Your notes, after applying the strategies in this chapter, will be far more effective than that! If you are in a synchronous online class, make it a priority to attend the live classes so you keep on track with the course material, stay engaged and focused by having your camera on, and can ask any questions as they arise. (If the class is recorded, you can always go back and rewatch it later, but you can't go back in time to attend a class you've missed.) For asynchronous classes that provide lectures to watch on your own schedule, set aside a regular time each week where you put aside any distractions and give the lectures your full attention. The habit of being present and engaged will give you the edge in many business settings, as well. Your presence both demonstrates your commitment and helps you collect details you may need to land a client, fulfill a business need, or solve a problem for your manager.

4. Be organized. At the end of each term, you'll have note pages galore for each course. To keep them organized, write some or all of the following information at the top of each note page:

- Course name
- Date of the class
- Topic of the class (usually listed in the course syllabus)
- Any associated reading assignments (also usually listed in the course syllabus)
- Page number (in case your notes get mixed up later)

WHILE TAKING NOTES

First, let's consider WHAT to write in your notes.

5. Listen actively. Good notes contain key concepts, main ideas, and supporting details. Collecting this information *accurately* and *completely* takes active listening. When you listen actively, you're able to reflect back what a speaker says. In a conversation with a friend, you might reflect: *Sounds like you had an exciting time white water rafting last weekend.* Or in a music class, you might reflect, *So, you're saying a divertimento is a short musical piece that was popular during the Classical period.* When taking notes, you'd simply write an abbreviated version of this reflection: *Divertimento—short musical piece popular during Classical period.* Inner chatter competes with active listening, so quiet your Inner Critic and Inner Defender during class. Don't judge yourself, and don't judge others. Replace judgments with an active effort to hear all of the speaker's key concepts, main ideas, and supporting details.

6. Ask and answer questions. When you bring questions to class, raise your hand and ask. When your instructor asks a question, raise your hand and answer. When you don't understand an idea, raise your hand and ask: *Excuse me, Professor, what holds atoms together in a molecule?* Or, if you're too confused to formulate a question, simply request more information: *Would you please say more about Kant's idea that metaphysics can be reformed through epistemology?* Many online classes include a discussion board area for posting questions. And in all classes, you can email your instructor at any time. If asking a question isn't an option, leave a space in your notes and write a question in the margin. Many choices exist for later filling in the answer: Listen for the instructor to answer your question during the class. Visit the instructor during their office hours. Look for the missing information in your textbook. Read through the class discussion board. Ask a classmate or study group member for help. Seek assistance at your college's tutoring center.

7. Listen for verbal cues. Instructors often provide verbal cues to introduce a main idea or supporting detail. These cues help you decide *what* to write in your notes. See Figure T.# for common verbal cues that let you know when it's time to record important content.

Now, we'll consider HOW to write your notes.

8. Take notes with an outline. Now that we've looked at ways to determine *what* to put in your notes, let's consider the second critical choice: *how* to write your notes. As mentioned earlier, the two general methods of note-taking are linear and graphic. First, we'll consider linear notes. "Linear" means in a line. When you take notes in a linear

fashion, you record ideas as much as possible in the order they are presented. Outlines are good for this. They record ideas and supporting details on separate lines, using indentations to indicate levels of importance. You can view an example of an informal outline in **Figure T.3**. Note the use of short phrases instead of full sentences to condense what the speaker says. Here's how to take notes with an outline:

Course: Psychology 101
Date: October 5
Topic: Abraham Maslow

Abraham Maslow (1908–1970)
 — Family immigrated to Brooklyn
  — One of seven children
  — Unhappy, neurotic child
 — Taught at Teachers College, Brooklyn College, Brandeis
 — Sought to understand human motivations
 — Became leader of humanistic psychology movement of the
  1950's and 1960's

Maslow's Hierarchy: Theory of Human Motivation (like a pyramid)
 — Physiological needs (the foundation)
  — Food, rest, shelter, etc.
 — Safety needs
  — Security, stability, freedom from fear
 — Psychological needs
  — Belonging, love, affiliation, acceptance, esteem, approval,
   recognition
 — Self-actualization (top of the pyramid)
  — Need to fulfill oneself
   — Maslow: "to become everything that one is capable of
    becoming."

Humanistic psychology
 — Maslow led the "Third Force" in psychology
  — Alternative to...
   — Freudian psychoanalysis
   — Behaviorist psychology
 — Stressed the power of a person to choose how to behave
  — As opposed to...
   — Freudians: Choices controlled by childhood influences
   — Behaviorists: Choices controlled by conditioning
 — Appealed to the individualistic, rebellious college students of the
  1960's

FIGURE T.3 Informal Outline Example

Source: From Kanar, *The Confident Student*, 3e, p. 353, © 1998.

- Write a *key concept* at the top of a page. This information is usually expressed in a word or phrase. This might be the title of a chapter or a key word in the instructor's course outline. For example, the key concept in a history class might be "The Civil Rights Act of 1964," in a biology class it might be "Cell Communication," and in an anthropology class it could be "Margaret Mead."

- Record *main ideas (level 1)* beginning at the left margin.

- Under each main idea, indent a few spaces and record related *secondary ideas (level 2)*.

- Under each secondary idea, indent a few more spaces and record any related *major supporting details (level 3)*.

- If you need to add *minor supporting details (level 4)*, indent those lines a few more spaces.

Outlines are most helpful when instructors present well-organized lectures. If your instructor provides printed lecture notes or uses PowerPoint slides, you've probably got an organized instructor. If, however, your instructor jumps from topic to topic and back again, all is not lost. That's when a concept map can come to the rescue.

9. Take notes with a concept map. In this graphic note-taking method, *where* you place information (key concepts, main ideas, and supporting details) matters. Placement shows both their level of importance and their relationship to one another. In general, the closer an idea is to the middle of a page, the more important it is. **Figure T.4** shows an example of a concept map with content. Here's how to take notes with a concept map:

- Write the *key concept* in the middle of a page. Then underline or circle it. This information is usually just a word or phrase. For example, if the topic of a class session is "Photosynthesis" or "Logical Fallacies" or "Abraham Maslow," that is what you would write in the middle of the page.

- Write *main ideas (level 1)* near the key concept, underline or circle them. Then draw lines connecting them to the key concept.

- Write *secondary ideas (level 2)* near their related main idea, underline or circle them. Then draw lines connecting them to the related main ideas.

- Write *major supporting details (level 3)* near their related secondary idea, underline or circle them. Then draw lines connecting them to the related secondary idea.

- Write *minor supporting details (level 4)* near their related major supporting idea, underline or circle them. Then draw lines connecting them to the related major supporting idea.

Concept maps are helpful when lecturers leap from idea to idea. They are also good for taking notes on class discussions that move back and forth between topics. As a speaker returns to an earlier idea, simply go to that part of the concept map, add the new information, circle or underline it, and draw a line connecting it to related information. The visual nature of a concept map makes it especially appealing to students who like a picture of what they are learning. Concept-mapping apps make it easy to add in new content, color-code, and re-organize your notes—plus, you won't run out of space on your page.

10. Use three-column notes for mathematics. Math instructors spend much class time demonstrating how to solve problems. A three-column approach is extremely helpful for **Collecting** their methods. First, divide your note page into three columns. Title the left-hand column "Problem," the middle column "Solution," and the right-hand column "Explanation." When the instructor presents a problem, write it in the left column. As the instructor demonstrates how to solve the problem, write all steps in the middle column, making sure you understand each one. In the right-hand column, add any explanation that will help you understand how to solve similar problems. For example, you might add an explanation of each step or convert unfamiliar symbols into words.

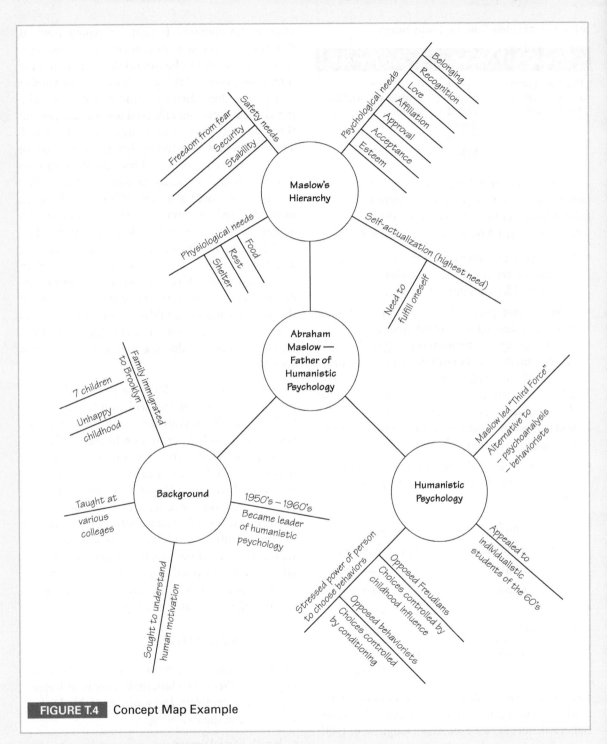

FIGURE T.4   Concept Map Example

Structure of Three-Column Math Notes

Problem	Solution	Explanation
The math problem as presented by the instructor	Step 1 Step 2 Step 3 Step 4 Step 5 Etc.	Elaboration to explain steps of the solution

11. Speed up note-taking. Most speakers talk much faster than you can write (or even type, if using a laptop or tablet), so here are three strategies for speeding up your note-taking:

- *Condense*: Don't attempt to write everything. Paraphrase key concepts, main ideas, and secondary ideas in your own words.

- *Leave a blank space:* When you miss something, skip ahead leaving a few blank lines in your notes. Pick up writing what is being said now. As with unanswered questions, you can return later to fill in the blank space. Options include asking the instructor (in class, if appropriate, or during office hours), a classmate, or a tutor. Or you can review your reading assignment for the missing information.

- *Use abbreviations*: Create your own personal shorthand. The following are some possible abbreviations:

Ex	example	&	and
con't	continued	dept	department
imp	important	→	leads to
#	number	=	equals
1st	first	vs	versus
w/	with	w/o	without
nec	necessary	etc	and other things

You can also shorten names and phrases commonly used in your specific classes. For example, IA for Isabel Allende, FD for Frederick Douglass, or OOF for order of operations. Creating a glossary can help you keep track of your abbreviations.

One of the apparent benefits of typing notes is that you can record more content than if you were writing by hand. But be careful that you do not fall into mindless note-taking. A study by Pam Mueller and Daniel Oppenheimer found that students who typed their notes remembered less lecture content than students who wrote their notes by hand. The researchers concluded that the reduction in learning may have occurred because students who typed their notes tended to write verbatim (that is, word for word) and not differentiate between important and less important content. In contrast, students who wrote by hand tended to write ideas in their own words and had to be more selective about which ideas to include, which resulted in deeper processing. If you choose to type your notes, be sure to keep your mind active as you think about the meaning and value of the content. You may also want to pay extra attention to polishing your notes (strategy 13) and Evaluating your understanding as you study.

12. Record the class. Suppose you try the previous suggestions and still aren't happy with the quality of your notes. Consider asking your instructor for permission to record the class. You can listen to the recording as many times as needed to fill in gaps in your notes or review difficult concepts. *Caution:* Don't procrastinate until you have 45 hours of recorded class sessions and only 24 hours before the final exam. Instead, listen often to short segments. Each time, practice different note-taking strategies until you perfect your own personalized system. Like any skill, the more you practice the better you'll get.

AFTER TAKING NOTES

13. Polish your notes within 24 hours. As soon as possible after each class, make sure your notes are *accurate*, *complete*, and *understandable*. Do some or all of the following:

- Finish partial sentences.
- Expand on key words.

- Fill in blank spaces with missing information.
- Correct misspellings.
- Clarify unreadable words and confusing sentences.
- Delete unnecessary information.
- Revise drawings or charts.
- Correct steps in problem solving.

Afterward, if you still have gaps or confusion in your notes, connect with classmates, a tutor, or your instructor to address the problems. Not only does this action provide you with polished notes, it continues the active process of creating deep and lasting learning.

14. Compare notes. Compare your class notes with those of your study group members or other classmates. See if others have **Collected** any important information that you missed. See where their notes may have different information and decide whose version is more accurate. This effort will help you **Collect** additional information and further polish your notes.

EXERCISE: NOTE-TAKING

In an upcoming class, take notes in a new way. Compare your experimental notes with those of a classmate, seeing which of you has recorded more complete and accurate information for later studying.

Organizing Study Materials

To pass the many quizzes, tests, and exams they will take in college, students need to know how to study but, many do not.

In fact, the study methods of many students—even those who were "good" students in high school—are only marginally effective in college. Even when they pass tests, many students understand and remember only a fraction of what they studied. Imagine the problems this missing knowledge causes when it's needed later in the same course. Or later in a more advanced course. Or even later in a career. Relying on ineffective study skills leads to shallow and short-lived learning. Such ineffective learning is a sure way to undermine academic, professional, and even personal success.

You're about to explore a number of strategies that will help you *learn in a deep and lasting way.* Mastering these strategies will provide you with the ability to improve your learning outcomes and experiences for the rest of your life. And, yes, your grades in college will almost surely go up as well.

ORGANIZING STUDY MATERIALS: THE BIG PICTURE

Effective learners, you'll recall, take advantage of three principles that contribute to deep and lasting learning. First is **prior learning**. This means relating new information to what you already know. Second is the **quality of processing.** This means using many different kinds of deep-processing strategies. And third is the **quantity of processing**. This means using frequent practice sessions of sufficient length distributed over time.

In this chapter we're going to explore study strategies that address the *quality of processing.* As you read about and experiment with the many deep-processing strategies that follow, keep in mind the big picture of the CORE Learning System: **Having Collected knowledge from reading assignments and taking class notes (Step 1), you're now going to Organize it all in ways that are meaningful to you (Step 2). Your goal is the creation of many kinds of effective *study materials.* Engaging in the process of Organizing study materials will greatly enhance how much you understand, learn, and remember.**

STRATEGIES TO IMPROVE ORGANIZING STUDY MATERIALS

Following you'll find many of the very best strategies for mastering the skill of Organizing study materials. After reading each strategy, pause and decide if it would help you improve your ability to create materials that make sense of what you are learning. If so, mark it in some way, then decide which of these strategies to experiment with to improve your study materials.

BEFORE ORGANIZING STUDY MATERIALS

1. **Adopt a growth mindset.** Having positive beliefs about the value of effective studying improves your learning outcomes. According to psychologist Carol Dweck, one important belief is that *the ability to learn can be improved.* Dweck calls this belief a "**growth mindset.**" The opposite mindset is that you're stuck with the learning ability you were born with. The reality? Working hard and using effective learning strategies improves your ability to learn. To begin developing a growth mindset about learning, create an affirming statement about the value of using high-quality study strategies.

2. **Create ideal study spaces.** Design your study area so you enjoy being there. Minimum

requirements include a comfortable chair, plenty of light, room to spread out your course materials, and space to store your books and supplies. Personalize your study area to make it even more inviting. Some studies have shown that we experience more contextual cues that support learning and memory when we study in different places. So, you may want to have a variety of places to study. If you plan to do a lot of work at the computer, take short breaks for physical activity at regular intervals to ward off fatigue and build up energy.

3. Arrange to be undisturbed. Do whatever is necessary to minimize interruptions while you study. A seemingly simple interruption like checking a text can pull you away from your previous state of deep concentration for quite some time. Psychologists have called this phenomenon attention residue, due to the lingering thoughts that occur when a person switches from one task to another. Schedule regular study times and ask friends and relatives not to contact you during those times. Put a Do-Not-Disturb sign on your door. Set your devices to silent to minimize interruptions from phone calls, emails, and text messages. Find places to study where no one can easily disturb you. The steps you take to limit distractions from people and technology will help you make the most of your study time.

4. Create a distributed study schedule. As you know, active learners engage in numerous study sessions spread over time. So refer to your calendar where you have recorded all of the announced tests for your classes (you *have* done this, right?). Then choose a date before each test when you will begin serious studying. As a guideline, start seven days before a regular test and up to fourteen days before a major exam. Plan to use one-quarter to one-third of the days for creating study materials (as you will learn to do in this section). Use the remaining days to Rehearse these materials using the strategies you'll learn in the next section.

5. Gather all course materials. Start with your readings (marked and annotated) and your notes. Add to them all other course documents, such as handouts, study guides, graded tests and essays, and study group notes.

WHILE ORGANIZING STUDY MATERIALS

6. Condense course materials. Since you have already marked and annotated all of your reading assignments and taken detailed notes, you will have a large Collection of information and skills. As a result, you may think you have all you need for studying. Not true. Learning from these raw materials is seldom effective. Instead, good learners condense all of these materials into the key concepts, main ideas, and supporting details of the course. Then they Organize this condensed knowledge into effective *study materials*. But one thing at a time. Here's an effective way to condense:

- Read through the markings, annotations, and notes you added to your course materials. As you do, place a star beside key concepts, main ideas, and supporting details

- Now, reread only the information you marked with a star, find the most important ideas within those, and put a second star beside them.

- Finally, reread just the ideas you have marked with two stars, identify the most important of these, and put a third star beside them.

- Read through all starred information one more time and circle the key concepts.

By doing this process, you should have condensed your course materials by at least half (preferably more) and identified various levels of information:

- Key concepts (circled)
- Level 1: main ideas (three stars)
- Level 2: secondary ideas (two stars)
- Levels 3 and 4: supporting details—major and minor (one star)

Now your goal is to Organize this condensed information in ways that will help you understand it thoroughly. The Organizing options described next fall into one of two broad categories: *linear* or *graphic* (just as with note taking).

7. Create outlines (linear organizer). Now you're ready to use the key concepts, ideas, and supporting details you have just identified with circles and stars. Use them to create an outline using the process described in the "Taking Notes" section of this Toolbox. Outlines make particularly valuable study materials when preparing for essay tests or writing a paper to demonstrate your learning. Knowing how to organize ideas into an outline can also be helpful in the future when preparing for an interview, an important meeting with a client, or a professional presentation.

8. Create test questions (linear organizer). Put yourself in the mind of the instructor preparing a test. What information or skill do they expect you to learn? Write questions that will reveal your understanding of that target knowledge. Some instructors will tell you exactly what to expect if you ask what types of questions will be on the test. Others won't answer your question directly but may offer hints, provide sample questions, or even give you copies of past tests.

Remember, tests are an opportunity to share what you've learned. It's a great feeling to begin a test and find that you have practiced answering nearly every question on it. Likewise, identifying likely questions and practicing your answers can be an excellent way to walk into an interview, important business meeting, or professional presentation with confidence.

9. Create flashcards (linear organizer). On one side of an index card, whether a physical piece of paper or online, virtual flashcard write a question that your instructor might ask on a test. On the back of the card, write the answer. Examples include a. . . .

- date and what happened on that date
- word and its definition
- graph and its meaning
- person's name and what they are noted for
- math problem and its solution
- quotation and who said it

Start creating flashcards early so that you have plenty of time to review them. A number of free websites allow you to create flashcards and even play games with the content. To find such a site,

Front

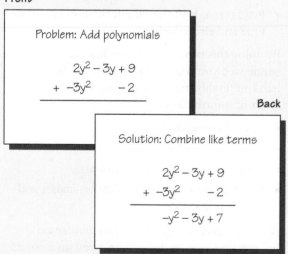

Sample Problem-Solution Flashcards

Source: From Kanar, *The Confident Student*, 3e, p. 353, © 1998.

Front

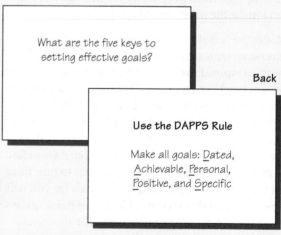

Sample Question-and-Answer Flashcard

simply type "flashcards" into an Internet search engine. Carry flashcards with you everywhere or add a flashcard app to your phone's home screen. Pull them out for a quick review whenever you have a few extra minutes. If you study them only 20 minutes per day, that's over two extra hours of studying each week.

10. Create concept maps (graphic organizer). Whether or not you choose to take class notes with concept maps, strongly consider them for creating study materials. You'll see an example of a concept map and the steps for creating one in the "Taking Notes" section of this Toolbox. Concept maps have a number of benefits when used as study materials. First, they clearly show the relationship among levels of information (i.e., key concepts, main ideas, and supporting details). They aid learning by combining the left brain's verbal and analytical skills with the right brain's spatial and creative abilities. Concept maps are simple to expand, so you can easily add new information from various sources. And they are especially useful when preparing for an essay test or term paper.

11. Create three-column study charts for math (graphic organizer). Begin by dividing blank pages into three columns and titling them: Problem, Solution, and Explanation. Now add one problem at the top of the left-hand column of each page; include problems representing different levels of difficulty:

- **Easy problems:** These could be problems your instructor solved in class that you immediately "got." These might be problems you correctly solved on a test or homework assignment. Or they could even be problems you initially did wrong but have since learned how to solve.

- **Challenging problems:** These might be problems that you got wrong on a test or homework assignment and still don't understand how to solve. Or they might be problems your instructor solved in class but continue to baffle you. Or, they could be sample problems

you haven't tried to solve, but just looking at them, you doubt whether you can. These challenging practice problems could come from sources such as class notes, homework, tests, the tutoring center, or the website for your textbook.

Now do your best to solve each problem in the middle column, while writing explanations (e.g., directions, key terms, and rules) in the right-hand column. Because you are creating study materials, it is essential that you understand each step in the solution as well as its explanation. If you get stuck on a problem, set it aside and save it. You'll learn how to deal with these challenging problems in the next section of this Toolbox. For now, include as many solved problems as you can. **Figure T.5** shows an example of a three-column study chart for math.

12. Create Cornell study sheets. Walter Pauk, an educator at Cornell University, devised a simple and helpful way to organize study materials. Cornell study sheets are very useful when you <u>Rehearse</u> and <u>Evaluate</u> the target knowledge, as you'll learn to do in the next section. Here's how to construct one:

- Create a blank Cornell study sheet by drawing lines on notebook paper to create the three sections depicted in **Figure T.6**. If working on a computer or tablet, conduct a search for a "Cornell Method Template" or use the insert table feature available in many apps.

- In Section A, copy study materials you have already created, such as outlines and concept maps.

- Identify questions you could ask about the information found in Section A. Write each question in Section B.

- Circle or underline key concepts in Section A. Label each key concept in Section B.

- In Section C, write a summary of the key concepts, main ideas, and supporting details that appear in Section A.

Problem	Solution	Explanation
Find an equation of the line with slope 4 that contains the point (2, –1).	Step 1: $y = 4x + b$	Substitute 4 for the "m" in $y = mx + b$; "m" is the slope.
	Step 2: $-1 = 4(2) + b$	Replace x with 2 and y with –1 in the equation.
	Step 3: $-1 = 8 + b$	In ordered pairs, the first value is for x, the second is for y.
	Step 4: $-9 = b$	Multiply to simplify.
	Step 5: Equation: $y = 4x - 9$	Solve for b by subtracting 8 from both sides.
	Step 6: $-1 = 4(2) -9$ Is this true?	Replace the "b" with –9 in the equation $y = 4x + b$.
	Step 7: $-1 = 8 - 9$ YES	Check the answer by substituting the x and y values in the answer.

FIGURE T.5   Three-Column Study Chart for Math

See **Figure T.7** for an example of a completed Cornell study sheet.

AFTER ORGANIZING STUDY MATERIALS

13. Get feedback on your study materials. Share them with classmates and study group members. Show them to a tutor. Show them to your instructor. Ask for their suggestions to improve the accuracy, completeness, and organization of your study materials. The process of asking for feedback helps your performance in professional settings as well, as it can help you identify and correct errors, fill in incomplete information, and demonstrate a commitment to growth.

14. Seek help. If you don't understand something you're studying or need more one-on-one explanations, make an appointment with your instructor. You can also get assistance from the campus tutoring center. If the first tutor you meet with isn't much help, ask for a different tutor the next time. Keep seeking help until you understand the information or skill well enough to create well-**O**rganized study materials.

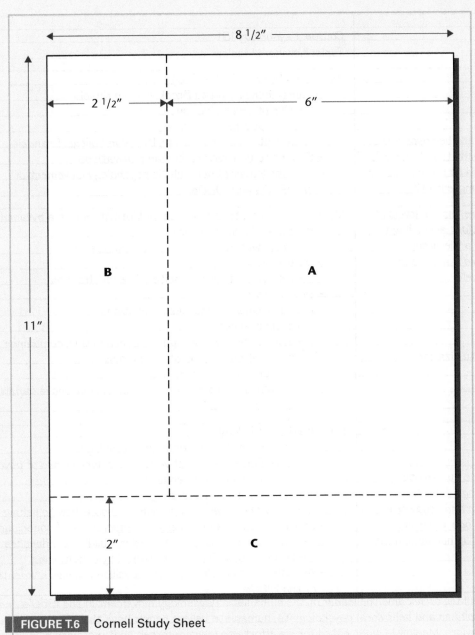

FIGURE T.6   Cornell Study Sheet

Source: From Pauk, *How to Study in College*, 6e, p. 205, © 1997

	Course: Psychology 101
	Topic: Abraham Maslow
	Abraham Maslow (1908–1970)
	– Family immigrated to Brooklyn from Russia
	– One of seven children
	– Unhappy, neurotic child
What was the psychological	– Taught at Teachers College, Brooklyn College, Brandeis
movement that Maslow led?	– Sought to understand human motivations
When did he become leader	– Became leader of humanistic psychology movement of
of this movement?	the 1950s and 1960s.
What are the five levels of	Maslow's hierarch: theory of Human Motivation (like a pyramid)
motivation, according to	– Physical (the foundation)
Maslow's Hierarchy?	– Food, water, air, rest, health, exercise, etc.
What are examples of	– Safety needs
each level?	– Security, stability, shelter, freedom from fear
	– Social needs
	Love, belonging, connection, affiliation
	– Psychological needs
	– self-esteem, power, approval, recognition, confidence
Self-actualization	– Self-actualization (top of the pyramid)
	– Need to fulfill oneself, creation
	– Maslow: "To become everything that one is capable
	of becoming."
	Humanistic psychology
	– Maslow led the "Third Force" in psychology
	– Third Force—alternative to other approaches of psychology
How does humanistic	– Freudian psychoanalysis
psychology differ from	– Behaviorist psychology
Freudian and behavioral	– Stressed the power of a person to choose how to behave
psychology regarding	– Other approaches minimized the importance of conscious choice
"choice" in human behavior?	– Freudians: Choices controlled by childhood influences
	– Behaviorists: Choices controlled by conditioning
	– Appealed to the individualistic, rebellious college students
	of the 1960s

Abraham Maslow became the leader of the humanistic psychology movement in the 1950's and 60's. Unlike Freudian and behavioral psychologists, humanists believe people have the power to choose their own behaviors. Maslow is most noted for his efforts to identify forces that motivate human beings. His "hierarchy" proposes that some needs must be addressed before others. The most primary needs are physical (air, water, food). Next comes safety (freedom from fear, shelter from cold). Then social needs such as love and belonging. Next, psychological needs such as self-esteem, power, approval, recognition and confidence. Self-Actualization sits a top Mazlow's pyramid of motivation.

FIGURE T.7 Cornell Study Sheet Completed Example

EXERCISE: ORGANIZING STUDY MATERIALS

A NOTE ABOUT CORNELL STUDY SHEETS | Many study skills books suggest writing your notes from reading assignments and class sessions directly on Cornell-formatted pages. This approach is usually called the "Cornell note-taking system." By contrast, I recommend that you take your reading and class notes on regular paper or a computer.

Then, do three things to deep process the information you have **Collected**:

1. Polish your notes, making sure they are complete and accurate.

2. Condense your notes, identifying key concepts, ideas, and supporting details.

3. **Organize** the condensed notes, creating effective study materials (e.g., outlines and concept maps) that include information from *all* course materials.

Now, if you wish, copy your polished, condensed, and organized study materials onto a Cornell study sheet.

Here's why I urge you to wait to create Cornell study sheets until you have thoroughly processed your original notes. Let's say you write your original notes on Cornell study sheets. Now you will be tempted to study from them without polishing, condensing, or **Organizing** the information. This means you're skipping essential steps necessary for creating deep and lasting learning. But suppose you do polish, condense, and **Organize** the notes you took on Cornell-formatted pages. Now you need to write them on other pages anyway. So there was no real purpose for taking them on Cornell-formatted pages to begin with. Here's the bottom line: The best use for Cornell-formatted pages is for **Organizing, Rehearsing,** and **Evaluating** (not **Collecting**) what you are learning.

Rehearsing and Memorizing Study Materials

In the previous section, we explored strategies for developing a deep and lasting *understanding* of what we want to learn. To do so, we gathered all of the knowledge we had <u>C</u>ollected from reading assignments and class sessions. Then we <u>O</u>rganized that knowledge to create a variety of helpful study materials. In this way, we continued to build the neural networks that store our knowledge for future use.

In this chapter, we'll take these efforts another step toward creating deep and lasting learning. We'll look at strategies to *remember* what we are learning. To do so, we'll explore effective ways to <u>R</u>ehearse study materials. Here is the learning principle that guides our efforts: *To strengthen neural networks, use many different kinds of <u>R</u>ehearsal strategies and distribute these efforts over time.*

As may be obvious, *understanding* and *remembering* reinforce one another. Thus, efforts to remember also help you understand, just as efforts to understand help you remember. That's why it's so important to include in your CORE Learning System both <u>O</u>rganizing for understanding and <u>R</u>ehearsing for remembering. In fact, I hope you're experiencing confidence that you can learn virtually any information or skill you might need for your life—both in *and* beyond college. The key is choosing effective learning strategies and spending sufficient time on task. You're not only fully responsible for your learning; you're also completely up to the challenge!

REHEARSING AND MEMORIZING STUDY MATERIALS: THE BIG PICTURE

<u>R</u>ehearsal is what learning researchers call efforts to remember something. <u>R</u>ehearsal strategies generally fall into one of two kinds—elaborative and rote. In this chapter, we will look at both.

In most cases, **elaborative rehearsal** will better serve your learning goals in college. These strategies use deep processing that strengthens both understanding *and* remembering. They do so by focusing on meaning, by showing relationships between ideas, and by connecting new knowledge with old. As such, elaborative rehearsal enhances deep and lasting learning.

By contrast, **rote rehearsal** is more about remembering than understanding. As such, it employs surface processing such as memorizing by sheer repetition. There is both good and bad news about rote rehearsal. The good news is that memorized facts and details can be valuable. For example, rote rehearsal is probably how you learned both the alphabet and multiplication tables, and this information has certainly come in handy over the years. But there's bad news as well. Mindlessly memorizing information can fool you into thinking you understand something when you don't. Even if you do pass the test, the knowledge you memorized without understanding will probably be gone when you need it later on.

So, experiment with the many <u>R</u>ehearsal strategies in this chapter. As you do, continue personalizing a CORE Learning System. It will help you create *lasting* learning.

As a bonus, most <u>R</u>ehearsal strategies perform double duty. As you <u>R</u>ehearse, you also get feedback that allows you to <u>E</u>valuate your learning. For example, when you <u>R</u>ehearse by quizzing yourself and get a wrong answer, that's valuable feedback. It prompts you to <u>C</u>ollect more information, <u>O</u>rganize it differently, and/or keep <u>R</u>ehearsing.

While examining the following strategies, keep in mind the big picture of Rehearsing study materials. **Rehearsing, when effective, makes learning stick. First, use** *elaborative* **Rehearsal strategies to learn and remember complex ideas; use** *rote* **Rehearsal strategies to memorize facts and details. Second, employ frequent Rehearsal sessions of sufficient length distributed over time. Third, use feedback about how well you are learning to Evaluate and, if needed, revise your approach.**

STRATEGIES TO IMPROVE REHEARSING AND MEMORIZING STUDY MATERIALS

Following you'll find many of the very best strategies for mastering the skill of Rehearsing and Memorizing Study Materials. After reading each strategy, pause and decide if it would help you improve your ability to learn and remember what you've included in your study materials. If so, mark it in some way, then decide which of these strategies to experiment with to create deep and lasting learning.

BEFORE REHEARSING AND MEMORIZING STUDY MATERIALS

1. Form a study team. Many of the following learning strategies are enhanced by doing them with others. That's why teaming up with fellow Creators can increase the effectiveness of your study time. Follow the suggestions in "Start a Study Group" (Chapter 5) to ensure that your study team functions at top form. Although meeting in person can enhance team dynamics and interactions, consider scheduling some virtual meetings as well to accommodate busy schedules or inclement weather. Look for a video conferencing tool that includes screen sharing and chat to help you connect with the content—and your fellow students—in engaging ways. As a bonus, the interpersonal and organizational skills you develop can be valuable when leading teams in your career.

2. Create a distributed study schedule. Remember: *Learning is enhanced by frequent practice sessions of sufficient length distributed over time.* Here's an example. Suppose two classmates each study 10 hours for a final exam. One classmate crams all 10 hours of their studying into the 24 hours before the test. The other distributes their effort by studying 1 hour each day for 10 days before the test. Both study for the same amount of time. However, the second student will likely experience deeper and longer lasting learning. Their advantage comes from distributing their study time over 10 sessions. Spacing learning over time causes you to think of the content in a new way and use cognitive effort to retrieve the information from your memory. The payoff is improved learning, not to mention better class performance. When creating a distributed study schedule, the first 25–33 percent of time goes to Organizing a variety of effective study materials. The remaining time is used to deep-process the study materials using the Rehearsal strategies that follow. See Figure # for examples of how the many options for Organizing information can be used during Rehearsal.

3. Assemble all study materials. In the previous section, you learned how to create a great variety of study materials. Have all of your study materials handy as you begin this next stage of your learning. You'll understand and remember more of what you study if you Rehearse different kinds of study materials. For example, you might Rehearse with an outline one day, a concept map the next, and flashcards the next. Create these materials by hand, using an app, or a mix of both. You can even take digital photos of your paper-based study tools to review on the go.

WHILE REHEARSING AND MEMORIZING STUDY MATERIALS

4. Review your study materials. *Reviewing* means reading over your study materials silently and with great concentration on the meaning. To avoid mindless reviewing, do the following three steps:

- Review a section of your study materials.
- Look away and ask yourself, *What are the key concepts, main ideas, and supporting details of what I just read?* Think through complete answers.
- Look back at your study materials to confirm the accuracy of your answers.

Repeat these three steps with additional sections of your study materials. Reviewing in this way causes you to make sense of and remember what you have just read. This process also **Evaluates** how well you understand the content of your study materials.

5. Recite your study materials. *Reciting* is similar to reviewing but is done *aloud*.

Pretend you're explaining the information to someone who isn't in the course but is interested in the information. Look back at your study materials and compare the information there with what you have been saying. Repeat the process with each section of your study materials. Continue doing this look-away technique until what you recite captures the essence of what is in your notes. By reciting aloud, you engage multiple senses (sight and sound), thus creating stronger neural networks.

6. Use Cornell study sheets. (See the "While Organizing Study Materials" section of this Toolbox for how to create them.) Remember that Section A of a Cornell study sheet contains information you have **Organized** in your preferred way (e.g., outlines or concept maps). Section B contains key words and questions about the information in Section A. Section C contains a summary of the key concepts and main ideas in Section A. To **Rehearse** information on Cornell study sheets, do the following:

- Study the content of Section A using either reviewing or reciting. Keep rehearsing the content in Section A until you feel confident that you understand it fully.

- Now cover Section A and look at Section B. There you will see the key words and questions you have written. Explain the key words and answer the questions as thoroughly as you can. Afterward, uncover the information in Section A and check the accuracy of your responses.
- Finally, cover the whole page and write a summary of the information. Then, uncover Section C on your Cornell study sheet and compare summaries. As your learning deepens, you may find that your latest summary is even better than the one you wrote earlier.

Note how this process offers both an excellent learning technique and an instant **Evaluation** of your learning.

7. Test yourself. Get out the list of possible test questions you prepared (see the "While Organizing Study Materials" section of this Toolbox for how to prepare questions). Taking a practice test is a great way to both **Rehearse** and **Evaluate** your knowledge. A self-test is a dress **Rehearsal** for the real thing, so do your best to duplicate the actual test situation. For example, practice answering the kinds of questions that will be on the real test (e.g., multiple-choice, short answer, true/false, essay, and problems). If the test will be timed, time your own practice test. If possible, test yourself in the room where you will take the actual test. After taking the practice test, get feedback on your answers by consulting your course materials or asking an instructor, tutor, or classmate.

8. Hold a study team quiz. Here's a variation on a self-test. Ask study team members to share their questions quiz each other. Don't move on until everyone agrees on an answer. If needed, find the correct answer in your course materials. Or set it aside to ask your instructor. To add fun to your efforts, search the Internet for sites that allow you to create learning games such as *Jeopardy* (the television quiz show).

9. Study three-column math charts. (See the "While Organizing Study Materials" section of this Toolbox for an example.) The key to studying mathematics is solving problems, solving problems, and solving more problems. Here's where the three-column math charts you created are so helpful. Take a blank sheet of paper and hide Column 2 (Solution) and Column 3 (Explanation). Now all you can see is the problem in Column 1. Solve the problem on the blank sheet of paper. If you have difficulty solving the problem, give yourself hints by uncovering part of the solution or explanation. After solving the problem, uncover Columns 2 and 3. Then check both your solution and your understanding of the process. If a problem continues to stump you, seek help from your instructor, a tutor, or classmates who excel in math. Trust that with enough practice and enough help, you'll be able to solve even the most difficult problems. Remember, you don't learn to solve math problems by only watching your instructor solve them. You don't learn to solve math problems by only reading how. You learn to solve math problems by *solving* math problems.

10. Study with flashcards. (See the "While Organizing Study Materials" section of this Toolbox for suggestions on creating flashcards.) Carry a deck of flashcards with you at all times, or keep a flashcard app handy on your phone or tablet. Pull them out for a quick review whenever you have a few extra minutes. If you study your flashcards just 15 minutes per day (say in three sessions of 5 minutes each), that's nearly two extra hours of studying each week!

The process is simple. Look at the front side of a flashcard and decide on an answer. Don't skip this step! To make the most of your memory's natural storage and retrieval processes, it's important to attempt an answer on your own rather than just looking at it. Turn the card over. Keep track whenever you get the answer correct, either by adding a checkmark to the card or monitoring progress using a flashcard app. After you have answered a card correctly a few times, set it aside so you can focus. If you go digital, choose a flashcard app that keeps track of your progress so you can spend ample time on the most challenging cards.

11. Memorize by chunks. Occasionally you may find it desirable—or even required—to memorize something for a course (e.g., a poem, a formula, or a summary from your Cornell study sheets). An important thing to know about memorizing is that *reading* information and *recalling* information strengthen different neural connections. Since you need to *recall* the information on a test, you want to strengthen the neural networks that manage recall (not reading). That's why simply reading something over and over is an ineffective way to memorize it. Here is one way to create strong neural networks for recalling information. If you memorize the words with a full understanding of their meaning, you'll be engaged in *elaborative* <u>Rehearsal</u>. However, if all you do is memorize the words like a parrot, you're using *rote* <u>Rehearsal</u>.

- Recite the entire text you want to memorize (e.g., poem, formula, summary, etc.).

- Now recite only the first chunk of information (e.g., line, string of symbols, sentence, etc.) from the text.

- Look away from the text and recite the first chunk.

- Look back at the text and recite the first *and* second chunks.

- Look away and recite this longer chunk aloud without looking at the text.

- Keep adding chunks until you can correctly recite the entire text aloud five times without looking at it.

- Take a 10-minute break and again recite the entire text aloud from memory until you do it correctly five times in a row.

- Thereafter, recite daily the entire text from memory; give extra practice to sections that are a challenge for you to recall.

If you wish, you can substitute writing for reciting in any of the steps. In fact, you'll probably find it helpful to alternate back and forth between reciting and writing.

12. Memorize with acronyms. An acronym is a word made from the first letters of other words that you want to remember. For example, the DAPPS Rule is presented in Chapter 3. DAPPS is an acronym that helps you remember the qualities of an effective goal: **D**ated, **A**chievable, **P**ersonal, **P**ositive, **S**pecific. In this way, remembering one word (the acronym) cues you to recall the words you want to remember. Acronyms can be real words or made-up words.

13. Memorize with acrostics. Acrostics are sometimes called sentence acronyms. Like acronyms, acrostics are made from the first letters of other words. However, you don't create a new word from the initial letters. Instead, you create a sentence. For example, biology students may be required to know the taxonomic classifications: kingdom, phylum, class, order, family, genus, species. Taking the first letter of each word in this list, you can create the sentence "**K**ing **P**eter **c**ame **o**ver **f**or **g**rape **s**oda." An acrostic is an especially helpful tool when you need to remember items in a particular order.

14. Memorize with associations. When you associate something new with something you already know, the new information is easier to recall. Suppose you want to remember the name of your new mathematics teacher, Professor Getty. You could associate your professor's name with the Battle of Gettysburg that you studied in American history. You might even visualize your professor wearing a uniform and carrying a musket. Now you'll remember the name.

15. Memorize with the loci technique. The loci (pronounced *low-sigh*) technique is a variation of association. *Loci* is Latin for "places," so with this strategy, you associate information you want to memorize with familiar places. For example, imagine that you need to remember different scholars you're learning about in your sociology class. Picture yourself walking through a familiar place, such as your home. Picture the front door, the living room, the kitchen, and so on. Place each sociologist you are studying in a different room

and imagine yourself observing or interacting with them. Review this mental image several times a day for two or three days. When you need to recall intersectionality, mentally visit your home, and there's Patricia Hill Collins at the front door. You can now associate other sociologists you need to remember with additional places in your home. Say, isn't that W.E.B. Du Bois sitting on your couch?

AFTER REHEARSING AND MEMORIZING STUDY MATERIALS

16. Review, Review, Review. Repetition strengthens memory. Shortly after a study period, spend a few minutes reviewing your outlines, graphic organizers, flashcards, Cornell study sheets, or whatever study materials you prefer. Two hours later, review again. For the next three days, review your study materials daily. Next, review them weekly. I've found that reviewing before going to sleep and just as I wake up helps me to remember. But the ideal time to review is anytime you can. Try setting a daily reminder on your phone until your habit of review becomes second nature.

17. Teach what you learn. If you ask your instructors when they achieved a deep and lasting understanding of their subject, most will say it was when they started teaching it. Explaining a complex idea requires a thorough understanding. And stumbling over an explanation is clear evidence of incomplete learning. So find people to teach. Say, "Let me tell you something fascinating that I learned in one of my classes." Teaching is also a great activity to do in a study group. Suppose each time your group met, each member gave a five-minute lecture on something important they had learned in the course that week. One student I knew put their children to bed each night in a most ingenious way. Using hand puppets, she delivered animated lectures to her children about what she had learned in college that day. Other teaching possibilities are only limited by your imagination.

EXERCISE: REHEARSING AND MEMORIZING STUDY MATERIALS

Suppose you were going to be tested on the 17 strategies for rehearsing and memorizing study materials presented in this section.

How would you go about studying for the test? Fully describe your methods.

MICHAEL CHAPASKO, *Blinn College, Texas*

When I was a kid, I didn't learn as fast as my classmates. My mom suggested that I go to the public school where she taught because they had a content mastery program that helped kids one-on-one when they needed it. I wasn't happy about it, but I made the move and got prescribed Adderall to help me stay focused. Come to find out I was a very smart kid when I could focus. Being one of the few kids with dyslexia, I felt embarrassed when I had to take my tests in different rooms or needed one-on-one help. When I got to high school, classes were getting harder, and I started to think I couldn't learn at the pace of everyone else, even with the Adderall. I got down on myself and didn't study much. I blamed my problems on my ADHD and dyslexia. Then in the middle of high school, I moved to a new school. Everything about this new school was intimidating. It was one of the top 10 academic high schools in the nation! Even though I didn't study while at my previous high school, my class rank had been 56 in a class of 808. In my new high school,

however, I dropped to number 203 in a class of 480. Then I really got down on my ability to learn, but I still didn't study. After high school, I decided to go to Blinn College, and in my first semester I took an *On Course* class. I didn't expect it to help me the way it did, but it really changed my whole outlook on studying. I got really interested when I read that the human brain is like a muscle. I played football, basketball, and baseball in high school. Now I'm into body building, and I work out every day. I understand how muscles work, and I found it interesting to think of the brain as a muscle. Before, instead of thinking about the brain as a muscle, I just figured you were either born smart or you weren't. I know the harder you work a muscle, the bigger and stronger it gets, but you can't do it all in one day. I also know the more you practice a certain movement or pattern, the better you get at it. When I got a 52 on my first exam in business law, I knew something had to change in the way I studied. So I decided to apply

my new knowledge about how the brain works and use some of the learning strategies in *On Course*.

Just like working out, I started spreading my studying over more time and using different ways to learn. Eventually, I came up with a way of studying that works for me. When I was studying for my first business law test—the one I failed—I quit reading the book when I didn't understand it. With my new approach, I read each assignment completely and got as much out of it as I could. I even tried to stay a couple of weeks ahead in my reading. My professor posted video lectures on our eCampus site, so after reading an assignment, I'd watch a related lecture online. The professor cut the information in the book down to what I really needed to know. When I attended the next class, his lecture would be a review of what I had read and what was on the video. That repetition deepened my understanding of the material because I had already heard it before. When he asked questions in class, I was ready to participate. I also found flashcards to be helpful, especially for introductory courses like business law where you have to learn a lot of new terms. I usually prefer to study alone, but if it's something I don't understand, then I like being in a group with students who understand the course. I often get their explanations better than the instructor's. Another strategy I've found helpful is to look over my past tests. Even glancing at them for a few minutes helps me remember things I need to know for the next test.

By the time I took the second exam in my business law course, I had a whole new way of studying. Using my new strategies, I ended up making a 96! I no longer thought about dropping the class because at that point I knew I could do it! One of my coaches used to say, "Hard work beats talent when talent refuses to work hard." Now I'm not only working hard, I'm working smart.

Photo: Courtesy of Michael Chapasko.

Taking Tests

First, let's review why tests in college are important (as if you didn't know). Tests contribute to your course grade, and that grade becomes a part of your permanent record. If your grades are consistently low, you may be put on probation or dismissed, lose financial aid, or loss eligibility for intercollegiate sports.

However, if your grades are consistently high enough, you'll eventually earn a degree. Then your grades will be of interest to future employers and graduate schools, to name a few.

So tests are important. But your grades do not define you. In fact, researchers have found that college students who focus on learning perform better on tests than students who focus on avoiding a bad grade. In addition to focusing on *learning* as your end goal, you can master the hidden rules of test taking to score the maximum number of points possible. Three factors determine how well you score on tests:

- **Factor 1: How well have you prepared?** If you have diligently completed each step of the CORE Learning System, you are extremely well prepared! Remind yourself that you are as well prepared as your classmates and more prepared than most of them. You have worked hard, used a powerful learning system, and the result is deep and lasting learning. You have every reason to be confident!

- **Factor 2: How well do you take tests?** Most people assume that tests reveal how much you know and maybe even how intelligent you are. In an ideal world, perhaps this would be true. Here on planet Earth, however, another critical factor influences your grades: Your skill at taking tests. Without this skill, your grades may only vaguely represent how much you know or how intelligent

you are. Every game requires special skills for scoring points. In this chapter, you'll learn some of the very best skills for maximizing the number of points you earn on every test.

- **Factor 3: How much have you learned from previous tests?** Every test provides feedback. Self-aware Creators pay attention to feedback and use it to their advantage. If a test score reveals that you're on course, you can confidently keep doing whatever you've been doing. However, if a test score reveals that you are off course, it's time to change tactics.

TAKING TESTS: THE BIG PICTURE

In previous sections you discovered how to be a good learner. Now you'll learn how to be a good "test taker." These skills can help you across all of your courses and can even prepare you for graduate school entrance examinations or licensure exams in fields such as nursing, teaching, social work, psychology, engineering, and law. Here's good news: There are only so many ways an instructor can ask you to demonstrate your knowledge and skills. Your challenge is to determine the most likely ways and prepare accordingly. So, experiment with the following strategies and, as you do, keep in mind the big picture of test taking: **Just as there is an art to learning, so is there an art to taking tests. It's called being** *test smart*.

STRATEGIES TO IMPROVE TAKING TESTS

Following you'll find many of the very best strategies for mastering the skill of taking tests. After reading each strategy, pause and decide if it would help you improve your ability to maximize the points you earn on tests. If so, mark it in

some way, then decide which of these strategies to experiment with to become test smart.

BEFORE TAKING TESTS

1. Actively use the CORE Learning System. This means when you walk into the test room, you have already. . . .

>**C**ollected *complete and accurate information from all reading assignments, course materials, and class sessions,*

>**O**rganized *many different kinds of effective study materials,*

>**R**ehearsed *these study materials with a distributed study schedule, and*

>**E**valuated *to confirm your understanding of all study materials.*

2. Prepare yourself physically and emotionally. Be sure to get a good night's sleep and eat well before a test. You don't want to be distracted by tiredness or hunger. As your instructor hands out the test, breathe deeply and relax. Remind yourself of what health

psychologists such as Stanford's Kelly McGonigal have found: your nervousness can be reframed as excitement. It's a sign that you care (good!) and that your body is preparing you to meet the challenge (great!). Your studying is done. Now it's game time and your goal is simple: Earn the most points possible. You're ready. Repeat your affirmation. Visualize your success. Take another deep breath and get ready to score! You can do this!

WHILE TAKING TESTS

3. Preview the test. Just as previewing a reading assignment is valuable, so is previewing a test. Note the kinds of questions. Note the point value of various questions. Read the directions carefully so you understand the rules of the game. For example, on a multiple-choice test, if the directions ask you to mark *two or more* answers and you mark only one, you'll lose points. Be sure you understand exactly what you are being asked to do. If unsure, ask the instructor to clarify.

4. Make a test-smart plan. The first rule of a test-smart plan is ***Answer easy questions first***. Skim the test and answer any questions you can answer quickly and correctly. Answering easy questions first has three advantages: It makes sure you earn these points. It builds confidence that calms test anxiety. And, while answering the easy questions, you may jog your memory or come across answers to other questions on the test.

The second rule of a test-smart plan is ***Spend time in proportion to points available***. Having answered the easy questions, now answer the remaining questions that are worth the most points. Suppose you're taking a 50-minute test with 50 true/false questions worth two points each. Your plan is obvious. Assign 1 minute to answer each question. Or consider a different situation: You're taking a 50-minute test with 10 true/false questions worth two points each and two short-answer essay questions worth 40 points each. Make sure you get as many of those 80 essay points as possible. Since each essay is worth 40 percent of the total points available, you assign 40 percent of the time available (20 minutes) to each . . . which leaves 10 minutes to answer the true/false questions.

5. Answer true/false questions. Obviously, the best situation is when you know whether the statement is true or false. However, all is not lost if you are unsure. Here are six test-smart strategies:

A. If any part of a statement is false, the answer is false.

B. If the question contains an **unconditional** word (100% with no exception), such as *all, every, only, never,* or *always,* the answer is probably false.

C. If the question contains a **conditional** word (less than 100% with some exceptions), such as *generally, some, a few, occasionally, seldom, usually, sometimes,* or *often,* the answer is probably true.

D. If the statement has two negatives, cross them both out and see if the statement is true or false.

E. If the sentence contains words you've never heard of, guess false. (This suggestion assumes you've studied thoroughly and will recognize key terms.)

F. If you are reduced to taking a pure guess, choose "True." It is easier for instructors to write a true statement; plus, most would prefer that you think about the correct answer.

6. Answer multiple-choice questions. Multiple-choice questions offer a statement or question, and then present alternative ways to complete the statement or answer the question. When you are stumped, here are ways to be test smart. The following options won't always get you the correct answer, but when you are reduced to making pure guesses, they can improve your odds of choosing the correct answer.

A. In the directions, see whether you can choose only one answer or more than one answer for each question.

B. Be sure to read all answers before making a choice. Answer A may be partly true and tempting, but Answer D may be more true and therefore is the answer you should choose.

C. Cross out all obviously incorrect answers, such as those that are intended to be humorous.

D. Cross out answers with unconditional (100%) words like *all, always, never, must,* or *every.*

E. If two answers are similar (e.g., *independent* and *interdependent*), choose one of them as the correct answer.

F. If you know two or more answers are correct, choose "All of the above" as the correct answer. An exception is when the directions allow you to choose more than one correct answer.

G. If one answer has a more thorough answer than the others, choose that answer as correct.

7. Answer fill-in-the-blank questions. Fill-in-the-blank questions present a sentence with one or more words (or phrases) left out. Your task is to insert the correct word or phrase. Being test smart can improve your chances of earning points on fill-in-the-blank questions.

A. Unless the directions say you will be penalized for a wrong answer, always write something in the blank.

B. Make sure your answer fits grammatically into the sentence (e.g., don't insert a noun if the space in the sentence requires a verb).

C. If you see two or more blanks, realize you need to have a different word or phrase in each blank.

D. Since fill-in-the-blank questions usually ask about key concepts, these concepts are often mentioned elsewhere in the test. Keep alert for them as you do other parts of the test.

E. After inserting the answer, read the sentence to make sure it makes sense.

8. Answer short-answer questions. Short-answer questions are mini-essays, usually one paragraph in length. The best approach, then, is to state a main idea. Then offer specific supporting details to demonstrate your understanding of the idea. It's difficult to fake knowledge on a short-answer question, but there are some test-smart strategies that can maximize the number of points you earn.

A. Always write something. Your instructor can't give you points for a blank space.

B. Circle the *guide word* in the writing prompt. (e.g., ⟨Describe⟩ the advantages of using a tracking form.) Guide words reveal the way in which the instructor expects you to develop the topic. See **Figure T.8** for a description of twelve common guide words.

C. Underline the topic in the writing prompt. (e.g., Describe the <u>advantages of</u> using a <u>tracking form.</u>) Referring to the underlined words helps you stay focused on the topic.

D. On a blank sheet of paper or the back of a test page, jot down any related ideas and supporting details you can think of.

E. Begin writing your answer by turning the question or writing prompt into your main idea. Again, imagine that the prompt is "⟨Describe⟩ the <u>advantages of</u> using a <u>tracking form.</u>" Begin your answer, "Using a tracking form has a number of advantages." This beginning helps you stay focused on the topic as you write your paragraph.

F. Develop your paragraph with supporting details such as examples, evidence, explanations, and experiences.

G. The space provided usually indicates how much writing your instructor expects, so plan your answer to fit in that space (unless there's a note such as "Continue your answer on the back of this page").

H. End your paragraph with a wrap-up sentence (e.g., "There are other advantages to using a tracking form, but these are three of the most valuable").

I. Proofread your paragraph. Even if instructors don't consciously take off points for errors, such distractions can undermine an otherwise positive impression of your answer.

9. Answer essay questions. Essay questions require an in-depth discussion of a topic. Essay questions not only test your knowledge of the course content, they also test your writing ability.

Here are some test-smart strategies for answering essay questions:

A. Read the directions carefully. As with short-answer questions, circle guide words in the essay prompt. Words such as *define, compare, contrast, describe, evaluate, summarize,* and *explain the cause* require different sorts of responses. (See **Figure T.8**: One Dozen Common Guide Words.)

B. Underline all key terms in the writing prompt. Suppose the topic says "Describe the following economic theories: Classical, Marxist, and Keynesian." If you do a great job on Classical and Keynesian theories but don't mention Marxist theory, you'll lose many possible points.

C. If the question gives you a choice of topics to write about, be sure to write the correct number of essays. If you write more essays than asked for, you're wasting precious time on questions you didn't need to answer (and probably won't get points for). And if you answer fewer, you'll certainly lose points.

D. Don't start writing immediately. Instead, brainstorm by jotting down ideas related to the topic. If you need more ideas, glance over the rest of the test to see if other questions or answers suggest additional ideas or supporting details to add to your brainstorm.

E. Revise the question or topic and use it as the first sentence of your essay. (See Strategy 8E for how to do this.)

F. Organize your ideas with your preferred method (e.g., outline or concept map). Creating a clear organization helps you maximize points earned. If you have more main ideas in your plan than you have time to write about, cross out the ones for which you have the fewest supporting details.

G. Develop each main idea in a separate paragraph, offering specific support such as examples, evidence, explanations, and experiences. Don't leave information out of your essay because you think the instructor already

Guide Words	What to Do	Example Questions
1. **Analyze**	Identify the parts of something and explain how those parts contribute to the whole.	*Analyze* the skills of a test-smart student. *Analyze* the symbolism of the white whale in Herman Melville's *Moby Dick*.
2. **Compare**	Show similarities of two or more things. (Note: some instructors also want you to show differences as well.)	*Compare* linear and graphic organizers. *Compare* democracy and socialism.
3. **Contrast**	Show differences between two or more things.	*Contrast* Creators and Victims. *Contrast* Flemish and Italian painters during the Renaissance.
4. **Define**	State the meaning of something.	*Define* a self-sabotaging script. *Define* standard deviation.
5. **Describe**	Tell about in some detail.	*Describe* an effective self-management system. *Describe* the efforts of England's King Henry VII to consolidate royal power.
6. **Discuss (or Explain) Why**	Provide a detailed account showing cause.	*Discuss why* it is important to be an active learner. *Explain why* Chebyshev's theorem is important.
7. **Discuss (or Explain) Effect**	Give the results of something.	*Discuss* the long-term *effects* of stress on physical health. *Explain* the *effect* of global warming.
8. **Discuss (or Explain) How**	Provide the details of a process.	*Discuss how* students can maintain or increase their academic motivation. *Explain how* hydrogen and oxygen combine to make water.
9. **Evaluate**	Assess strengths and weaknesses, providing reasons.	*Evaluate* the quality of writing in your first *On Course* journal entry. *Evaluate* a vegetarian diet.
10. **Explain**	Make clear or comprehensible.	*Explain* the three components of a logical argument. *Explain* the health risks of binge drinking.
11. **Illustrate**	Offer an example.	*Illustrate* the use of the Wise Choice Process. *Illustrate* the benefits of using cascading style sheets in the creation of a website.
12. **Summarize**	Provide a condensed version, highlighting main points only.	*Summarize* the reasons that interdependence is important in the workplace. *Summarize* the plot of *Huckleberry Finn* by Mark Twain.

FIGURE T.8   One Dozen Common Guide Words

knows it. Remember, this is not a test to see if your *instructor* can answer the question; the test is to determine if *you* can. (Strategy 14 in the "Writing" section of this Toolbox offers more information on how to develop a paragraph effectively.)

For Better or For Worse® by Lynn Johnston

H. Write a satisfying conclusion, perhaps summarizing the main points you have made. (Strategy 15 in the "Writing" section provides suggestions for concluding your essay.)

I. Save time for revising. As you read over what you have written, identify and answer questions your reader may have about your ideas. For example, readers often want to know "Why?" and "How do you know?" Add additional supporting details (examples, evidence, explanations, and experiences) to undeveloped paragraphs.

J. Proofread carefully for grammar, spelling, and punctuation errors.

K. To make your handwriting easier to read, consider printing (instead of writing in cursive), writing on every other line, and writing on one side of the paper only.

Here are some final tips for maximizing essay points:

• Always write something. Your instructor can't give you points for a blank page.

• Leave three or four blank lines after each answer in case you think of something later that you can add at the end.

• If you can't finish, provide an outline or concept map for what you would have written with more time. You may get some points for your plan.

10. Solve math problems. Mathematics tests usually ask you to solve problems of the type you have been studying. If you have been solving practice problems successfully throughout the course, you are well prepared. Here are some test-smart strategies to apply during a math test:

A. As soon as you get the test, write notes and formulas on the test. If you freeze up later, you'll have access to this essential information.

B. Do a first pass through the test and solve all of the problems you can do easily. You never want to lose points by leaving a problem undone that you could have solved if you'd had more time.

C. Make a second pass through the test to work on the more challenging problems. Begin to solve each problem by estimating the answer.

D. As you do a problem, write out every step of your solution. Even if you get the answer wrong, the instructor may give you some points.

E. When finished with each problem, compare your answer with your estimate. If the two answers are very different, recheck your computations.

F. As time allows, revisit each problem and double-check all calculations.

11. If you get stuck, move on. Don't sit there wasting time on a question you can't answer. If you doubt an answer that you've given or you've given no answer at all, put a light check mark next to the question. If time allows, return later and review your answer with fresh eyes.

12. Review your answers. Start with the sections that offer the most points. Then, check answers in other parts of the test in descending order of points available. For math problems, look for possible errors in each line of your solution.

13. Provide an answer for every question. When you have reviewed all of your answered questions, revisit unanswered questions. Run your finger along the words and read the question carefully. Highlight key words. Close your eyes and see if you can picture the answer in your study materials. Glance through the test to see if the answer may be included in another question. As a final resort, guess. You might just get some points if your guess is close.

AFTER TAKING TESTS

14. Reward yourself. No matter how you think you did on the test, give yourself a treat for your efforts before and during the test—go out to dinner, call an old friend, stream a movie.

15. Study the instructor's feedback. When you get the test back, don't just look at the grade. Read the instructor's comments. For recognition questions (e.g., true/false, multiple-choice, or matching), all you may see are Xs to indicate errors. For recall questions (e.g., essay or math problems), your instructor may provide commentary to explain why you earned or lost points. Whatever feedback the instructor provides, its purpose is to get you on course. Gobble it up. If there's an error or comment you don't understand, make an appointment with your instructor to discuss your confusion. Taking the time to work through feedback helps you to enhance your performance in any future testing situation. Surveys also reveal that employers value

the workplace skill of accepting and acting on feedback.

16. Analyze your errors. By analyzing your errors, you can determine how to score more points on the next test. There are seven problems that typically cost students points on a test. For example, you might have lost points because you studied the wrong material or because you didn't have a test-smart plan. Use the Test Debrief (**Figure T.9**) to identify where you lost points, and make a plan for earning more points on your next test.

17. Get help. Before the next test, seek help from your instructor, tutors, or classmates. Go to the learning center on your campus. If you haven't already created a study group, start one. If offered, attend workshops on test preparation and test anxiety. By seeking help, you can learn the information you got wrong on the previous test and improve your preparation for the next one.

18. Use special tips for online exams. Depending on your classes, some of your exams may take place online. Here are four test-smart tips specifically for online exams.

A. Change your approach based on the nature of the online test. To avoid any unwelcome surprises, ask your instructor ahead of time whether notes will be permitted. Is it an open-resource test? (If so, be sure to have a copy of your best study tools at hand. See the "Organizing Study Materials" section of this Toolbox for specific ideas.) Are outside resources prohibited? (If so, be sure to enact a distributed study plan so that you are well prepared. See the "Rehearsing and Memorizing Study Materials" section of this Toolbox for specific ideas.)

B. Choose the best time to take the exam. Some instructors may specify a narrow window in which the exam must be completed. If that is the case, mark this date and time on your calendar and set a reminder for 10 or so minutes before the test begins. If your instructor allows you to complete the exam at a time of your choosing, select a time when you will be well prepared, alert, and undistracted. To provide yourself flexibility in case of technical difficulties and unexpected changes to your schedule, plan to complete the exam at least one full day before the deadline.

C. Prepare to be undisturbed. Find a quiet location that provides some privacy. If there are others who might reach out to you during this time, communicate that you are not able to be disturbed. To enhance your focus, silence your phone and close any windows or apps that aren't related to the test.

D. Prepare to interact with the test questions. If permitted, have scrap paper, sticky notes, and something to write with in your testing environment. You can use blank paper to jot down key formulas, brainstorm content for short-answer or essay questions, or use process-of-elimination for multiple choice questions. A pile of sticky notes can come in handy for underlining key information on the screen or covering up answers you want to eliminate.

EXERCISE: TEST-TAKING

Create a 25-question test for a course you are now taking; write out your answers to each question. Include five questions each of the following kinds: (1) true/false, (2) matching, (3) fill-in-the-blank, (4) multiple-choice, and (5) short answer or essay. Or, for a mathematics or science course, prepare problems similar to the ones you have been studying. Design your questions so that a student who answers correctly will be demonstrating the essential knowledge/skills covered in this course. Have a meeting with your instructor and ask for feedback on the quality of your questions and answers. Revise them based on what you discover in the conversation with your instructor. BONUS: Exchange tests with a partner and each of you create a test-smart plan for taking the other's test.

TEST DEBRIEF

Directions: *Consider the seven test-taking problems below, and estimate the number of points you lost on the test for each problem. Circle the problem(s) that cost you the most points, and implement the solution(s) as you prepare for the next test.*

Problem 1: I didn't study some of the information or skills covered on the test.
Points lost: _____
Solution: Be more assertive about discovering what content will be covered on the test. Check the course syllabus; ask classmates, tutors, and especially the instructor. Add this material to your CORE Learning System.

Problem 2: I did study the information or skills covered on the test, but I got questions wrong anyway.
Points lost: _____
Solution: Experiment with **O**rganizing new kinds of study materials. Try different ways of **R**ehearsing your study materials. Distribute your studying over longer periods of time and increase your time on task. Implement more **E**valuations to assess your understanding (e.g., have study team members and/or tutors test your knowledge).

Problem 3: I wasn't good at answering the kind of questions the instructor asked.
Points lost: _____
Solution: Do all you can to determine what kind of questions will be on the test. Construct and take practice tests that use those kinds of questions. Have study team members also construct questions of this kind. Show the questions you create and your answers to a tutor or your instructor for feedback. Keep creating and answering these kinds of questions until you become skilled at answering them.

Problem 4: I didn't follow the directions.
Points lost: _____
Solution: Take time to read all of the directions carefully, circle guide words, and underline key terms. When you proofread, confirm that you have done what was asked.

Problem 5: I lost points for questions I could have answered but didn't get to.
Points lost: _____
Solution: Make a test-smart plan that focuses on accumulating the greatest number of points possible. Determine where the easy, point-rich questions are and make a plan to answer those questions first. Set time limits for each section so you don't get stuck and lose points by not answering questions in other parts of the test.

Problem 6: I knew the answers but made careless mistakes.
Points lost: _____
Solution: Move steadily through the test, but don't rush. Think carefully about what each question is asking and about the best way to answer it. Allow time at the end to check all answers and proofread carefully before handing in the test.

Problem 7: I panicked and was too stressed to answer questions, even those for which I knew the answer.
Points lost: _____
Solution: Overlearn the content and take numerous practice tests under "game" conditions to build test-taking skills and confidence. Visualize your success and create a positive affirmation about your test-taking ability. Make and follow a test-smart plan. If you get stuck during the test, don't waste time on a tough question; move on. If you feel anxious, refocus. Keep reminding yourself that taking tests is a game and that your job is simply to earn the most points possible. If test anxiety continues to plague you, consider seeing a counselor for further suggestions and help.

Points lost for the Seven Problems should total the number of points you lost on the test.

FIGURE T.9 Test Debrief

ONE STUDENT'S STORY

ASHLEY E. BENNET, *Heartland Community College, Illinois*

Not long ago, I took my first step onto the Heartland Community College campus as a legitimate college student. Having gone through the placement testing, piles of enrollment paperwork, supply shopping, and various other preparations, I felt ready and eager to begin what I "thought" college would be. However, what I experienced was nowhere near what I expected. Beginning college is a challenging experience for anyone; however for me, adjusting from home schooling to a college campus of roughly 15,000 students was a blind free fall. You see, attending Heartland was the first time I had ever been in a formal classroom. Previously, all of my learning had been done at home. I took my tests on a computer program, and if I got an answer wrong, I used it as feedback. Then I'd study what I got wrong, learn it more thoroughly, and retake the test.

In my first semester in college, I took two courses: algebra and a success course. In math, I had one major difficulty: the terrors of testing. I took tests every Monday, and they were so different from what I was used to. Just thinking about the tests beforehand caused me emotional distress in my day-to-day life. When I studied, I struggled to retain information due to my anxiety. Actually,

anxiety doesn't even begin to describe what I felt. I would breach the threshold of a full on panic attack before I even left for class. At the test, I would sit down, fiddle, get distracted, fiddle some more, and then slip into complete hysteria simply thinking about the time as it continued ticking away, with my test nowhere near finished. For the first couple of weeks, I went through the same panic before and during every test. I thought there was no escaping it . . . fortunately, I was wrong!

When I look back today and consider all that I went through back then, I am amazed and proud of the accomplishments that I have made since. Armed with the *On Course* textbook from my success course, I came across helpful strategies for taking tests. As I began to use the strategies, I gained a great deal of confidence and improved my ability to study and take exams.

First, I began to prepare for tests differently. One thing I did was organize thorough study materials. One kind was a variation of the three-column approach for studying math. I would solve problems and alongside I'd put down key terms so I could remember the formulas. That helped take a pretty major weight of worry off my shoulders. I'm a big tea drinker, and I'd relax while

studying by treating myself to my favorite tea. I also created the following affirmation to help me feel more confident: *I am prepared to do my best on this test.* I would review almost any time and anywhere. For example, sometimes I'd stop when I was leaving the house and see if I could remember a formula or a way to solve a particular problem.

I also used new strategies during tests. I started arriving at the test about 20 minutes early. This gave me time to find a good seat, do some breathing exercises, say my affirmation, and clear my head. When the test began, I worked on the easier problems first and saved the more challenging ones until later. This got my confidence up and set me up for doing my best. The final test in my math class gave me an opportunity to see how helpful these strategies are. I made it through all the questions I knew without looking at the clock. Then I went back to do the harder ones. The strategies I used obviously worked for me because I got an A in math.

My anxiety level on the first math tests I took was about a 7 or 8 on a scale of 10. After I started using my new strategies, my test anxiety went down to a 3. As my first semester is coming to a close, I can say with confidence that I am and will continue to be prepared to do my best on any and every test.

Photo: Courtesy of Ashley E. Bennet.

Writing

Few academic skills support your success in college more than effective writing. In most college courses, you'll be asked to do at least some—and perhaps much—writing. You'll write compositions, lab reports, discussion posts, and research papers. Additionally, you'll take many tests and exams that contain essay questions. Obviously, then, writing well increases your ability to earn good grades in college. But this is only one of writing's many benefits.

After you graduate, writing well can help you acquire and advance in the career of your choice. In fact, you'll likely write more in your career than you ever expected. With the growth of the Internet and a global economy, more and more business is transacted through e-mail and websites. In both your professional and personal life, writing gives you a means to inform, persuade, or even entertain people. While these benefits may be evident, here is one that may be less obvious: **Writing well enhances learning.** Consider what experienced writers say:

- *We do not write in order to be understood; we write in order to understand.* –Robert Cecil Day-Lewis
- *Writing became such a process of discovery that I couldn't wait to get to work in the morning . . . .*–Sharon O'Brien
- *Writing is making sense of life.* –Nadine Gordimer

Among other reasons, writing enhances learning because the process raises questions that require answers. Your effort to Collect, Organize, and write answers to these questions expands your understanding of yourself, other people, and the world. And that is the essence of learning!

Here's another reason why writing enhances learning: Like learning, writing is a process. Most experts recognize four components in the writing process: prewriting, writing, revising, and editing. As you'll see, these four have much in common with the four components of the CORE Learning System. In fact, knowing the CORE Learning System gives you a real advantage when it comes to writing.

- **Prewriting** includes any preparation you do before actually writing. Guiding this process is an awareness of your audience and your purpose for writing. Prewriting activities include Collecting ideas and supporting details. Next comes Organizing these raw materials into a possible structure.

- **Writing** (also called *drafting*) is the act of creation—turning your raw materials into a document that achieves your defined purpose. As you write, your mind both Rehearses the ideas you want to express and Evaluates your understanding of them. Thus, while writing you may realize that you need to Collect more information, re-Organize the information you already have, or both.

- **Revising** (also called *rewriting*) means "seeing again." When revising, you "re-see" in order to Evaluate your present draft. Does it say what you mean? Will it achieve your purpose for writing? With this effort come both a deeper understanding and the ability to express that understanding more effectively in writing.

- **Editing** (also called *proofreading*) eliminates surface problems such as errors in grammar, sentence structure, and spelling. Editing is your final Evaluation of how well your writing will achieve its purpose.

Perhaps now you understand why so many instructors require writing. To write well requires you to be the most active of learners, developing deep and lasting learning. And that, after all, is the goal of all good teaching.

WRITING: THE BIG PICTURE

Experiment with the many writing strategies that follow. As you do, keep in mind the big picture of writing: **The goal of writing is to inform, persuade, or entertain your intended audience. Thus, writing requires that you anticipate and answer the questions that engaged readers will have about your subject. Writing is not only an important means of communication with others. It is also one of the most powerful ways to create deep and lasting learning for ourselves.**

STRATEGIES TO IMPROVE WRITING

Following you'll find many of the best strategies for mastering the skill of writing. After reading each strategy, pause and decide if it would help you improve your ability to write effective compositions and essay tests. If so, mark it in some way, then decide which of these strategies to experiment with to become a better writer.

BEFORE WRITING

1. Create a positive affirmation about writing. Create an affirming statement such as *I use all steps of the writing process to express my ideas clearly and effectively.* Use this affirmation to develop a "growth mindset" about writing. Remember, a "growth mindset" is a core belief that you can improve your academic outcomes by employing effective strategies and hard work.

2. If you get to choose the topic for your writing, select one that truly interests you. You'll enjoy researching and writing about something meaningful to you. Even if your instructor assigns the topic, look for an approach to the topic that appeals to you.

"Write about dogs!"

George Booth/Conde Nast Photos/Illustrations

3. Be ready to <u>C</u>ollect ideas. Once you begin thinking about a subject, ideas will sometimes pop into your mind at the strangest times. Don't think you'll remember the idea later. Pull out your phone and email yourself a note. Or add an audio recording app to your home screen so you can capture your ideas on the fly.

4. Create focus questions. Turn your topic into a list of questions. Use these questions to guide your <u>C</u>ollection of information as you review class notes, readings, and other resources. For example, if you were writing a paper about financial aid, you could look for answers to focus questions such as "What are the secrets to getting the most scholarship money?" and "What mistakes keep students from getting all of the financial aid available to them?"

5. Group your notes. Once you've <u>C</u>ollected notes on your topic, it's almost time to write . . . but not quite yet. First, group your notes into logical categories by either sorting them into piles or cutting and pasting them into clusters of related ideas. For example, you might group ideas together related to your original focus questions or to new categories that emerge, such as the differences between grants, scholarships, and loans.

6. Identify your audience. Every piece of writing has one or more intended readers. Usually the best approach is to write to a general audience. Picture a *general audience* as a group of interested, well-educated readers who know little or nothing about your topic. In this way, you will be more likely to provide all of the ideas and supporting details needed to show your instructors that you have mastered their course content. Sometimes instructors will specify your audience (e.g., readers of your college newspaper). If so, use this information to make choices as you write such as:

- *What tone (formal or informal) to adopt?*
- *What information to include or exclude?*
- *How much evidence is needed to overcome resistance?*

7. Similarly, in work settings, you will want to adjust your approach based on whether you are writing for management, colleagues, supervisees, or clients. **Define your thesis.** A thesis states the most important idea you want to convey to your audience. Everything else you write merely supports this idea by answering questions that an engaged reader might have about your thesis. A thesis is made up of two elements: (1) the **topic** you're writing about and (2) the **claim** you make about the topic. Thus, a thesis statement is usually one sentence and has the following structure:

[Topic] + [Claim].

For example:

[Subprime mortgage loans] + [are those made to borrowers with questionable ability to pay back the money they borrow].

Sometimes you'll know immediately what your thesis is. Other times you may need to think and write for a while before a thesis emerges.

8. Organize your ideas and supporting details. Earlier in this Toolbox, we looked at linear and graphic ways to Organize information. These methods also work well for Organizing

information during prewriting. Let's revisit two of these strategies and introduce a third.

Outline. (For a review of how to create an outline, along with an example, see the "While Taking Notes" section of this Toolbox.) When creating an outline for a writing assignment, place your thesis statement at the top of a page. Below it and flush to the left margin, add each topic group you determined in Strategy 5. These are now your main ideas (Level 1). Use bullets or indentation to add secondary ideas (Level 2) and supporting details beneath each main idea (Levels 3 and 4).

Concept Map. (For a review of how to create a concept map, along with an example, see the "While Taking Notes" section of this Toolbox.) To create a concept map for a writing assignment, write your thesis statement at the top of a page. Then write the key concept in the middle of the page and either underline or circle it. Now draw lines out from the key concept and write the topic of each of the topic groups you determined in Strategy 5; these will be your main ideas (Level 1). Next, draw lines out from your main ideas, and write secondary ideas (Level 2). Farther out from the center of the concept map, write your supporting details (Levels 3 and 4). If you like organizing with concept maps, you may want to experiment with computer software designed for creating them. To find such software, search for "concept map software" using a search engine.

Question Outline. Here's a variation of an outline that's easy, quick, and effective. After determining your thesis, choose the most interesting focus questions from the list you created in Strategy 4. Make sure you have enough information to answer each question thoroughly . . . or Collect more. Use one question as the topic of each body paragraph. Here's what a Question Outline about scripts might look like:

– Introduction (including the thesis)

– What are scripts?

– How do we write our scripts?

– Why do some scripts sabotage our success?

– How can we revise self-sabotaging scripts?

– Conclusion

WHILE WRITING

9. Use an essay blueprint. When you want to assemble something with many parts, a picture can help. Just as there are many blueprints for building a house, so are there many blueprints for writing an essay. But the one in **Figure T.10** is both effective and easy to understand. When one of my students saw this essay blueprint, she exclaimed, "So *that's* what the structure of an essay looks like? I can do *that!*"

Each part in the blueprint is explained in the strategies that follow. As you add these parts to the essay blueprint, realize that the structure is flexible and can be modified. For example, the essay blueprint shows a five-paragraph essay; if you have a different number of main ideas, simply add or delete body paragraphs. If writing a persuasive essay, you could also add a refutation paragraph to present opponents' argument and provide reasons and evidence to weaken that argument. As you become a more skilled writer, you will begin to take more and more liberties with this blueprint.

10. Write a hook. The beginning of your essay should hook your readers' interest. To do so, start with a question, quotation, humor, surprising data, attention-grabbing statement, or fascinating story. For example, I began the section on "Rewriting Your Outdated Scripts" in Chapter 6 with the story of my student Diana screaming at me in class. My hope was that Diana's unexpected outburst would

---

Paragraph 1: Introduction

    Hook
    Thesis
    Agenda

Paragraph 2: Body Paragraph #1

    Transition (presenting Main Idea #1)
    Secondary Ideas and Supporting Details (4E's)

Paragraph 3: Body Paragraph #2

    Transition (presenting Main Idea #2)
    Secondary Ideas and Supporting Details (4E's)

Paragraph 4: Body Paragraph #3

    Transition (presenting Main Idea #3)
    Secondary Ideas and Supporting Details (4E's)

Paragraph 5: Conclusion

    Summary or Echo
    Restatement of Thesis

FIGURE T.10   Essay Blueprint

motivate you to read on to find out more. Even though a *hook* is the first thing your audience reads, you don't have to write it first. In fact, you may think of a good hook only after writing the first draft of your paper.

11. Add your thesis statement. After hooking your reader's attention, present your thesis—the key concept about which you are writing. Your thesis statement may be exactly as you wrote it in Strategy 7, or you may now decide that it needs revision. That's because the writing process helps you learn even more deeply about your topic.

12. Write an agenda. An agenda for a meeting lists the main ideas that will be discussed. Similarly, an agenda for an essay states the main ideas that readers can expect the author to discuss. They can be a great help to keep both your readers and you (the author) focused. For example, suppose your thesis is *Students should get involved in campus activities.* Your agenda might give a list of the reasons: *First, getting involved in campus activities will increase your chances of earning a degree. Second, you'll meet people who may become lifelong friends. And finally, involvement in campus activities offers valuable learning experiences that are unavailable in an academic classroom.* This three-part agenda lets your readers know exactly the points you intend to present. This approach works well not just for college papers but also for proposals, reports, and presentations you may compose as you advance in your career.

13. Use transitions. A transition is a bridge between ideas. Well-chosen words, phrases, or sentences help your readers follow the flow of your ideas. One important place to use a transition is at the beginning of a paragraph. A good transition connects the idea just discussed with a new idea . . . and maybe even includes a reminder of the thesis. For example, suppose your thesis intends to persuade your readers to get involved with campus activities. Further, suppose that you have just completed a paragraph about how involvement in campus activities increases a student's chances of earning a degree. The first sentence of your next paragraph might be: *Not only will getting involved with campus activities increase your chances of earning a degree, you'll also meet people who may very well become lifelong friends.* Notice how the transition does three things:

- It reminds readers of the thesis: *Get involved with campus activities.*

- It reminds readers about the main idea made in the previous paragraph: *Getting involved in campus activities increases your chances of earning a degree.*

- It creates a bridge to the main point of the new paragraph: *By getting involved in campus activities, you'll meet people who may very well become lifelong friends.*

14. Add support. To generate specific and sufficient support, expand each body paragraph with secondary ideas and supporting details. This is easy to do when you remember to use the 4E's. The 4E's represent four questions that almost always need answering as you develop a paragraph:

- Can you give an EXAMPLE of that?

- Can you give an EXPERIENCE to illustrate that?

- Can you EXPLAIN that further?

- Can you give EVIDENCE to support that?

Answering one or more of the 4E's causes you to dive deeper and makes your writing more complete and fully developed. Remember to give credit to the original source where you gathered these ideas by including a citation. Do a web search or contact your campus's writing center to learn more about the two major formats for bibliographies and citations: MLA (Modern Language Association) and APA (American Psychological Association). For formatting help, search the web for "citation generator."

15. Write a satisfying conclusion. One common way to conclude is to summarize the main points you have made. For example, *So, if you want to become an effective learner, become a master of the CORE Learning System.* A more sophisticated conclusion is called an **echo**. An echo restates all or part of an idea presented earlier in your essay. For example, suppose your hook asked, *Do you realize that college graduates earn nearly a million dollars more in their lives than non-grads?* You might echo this thought in your conclusion by ending with: *So, if you want to raise your lifetime earnings by nearly a million dollars, make getting your college degree a high priority.*

AFTER WRITING

16. Incubate. Set your writing aside and do something else . . . in fact, anything else. That's right—don't even think about what you wrote for at least a couple of hours. Better yet, for a couple of days. When you return to your writing later, you'll notice problems and possibilities that earlier were invisible to you. Obviously you can use this strategy only if you make the wise choice to start your writing long before it's due.

17. Revise. "Re-vision" means to "see again." After incubation, you'll be ready to see your writing with new eyes. Consider a revised thesis statement, better organization, additional support (4E's: examples, experience, explanation, evidence), improved transitions, a catchier hook, a stronger conclusion. Perhaps most important, make sure that you have answered all reader questions. Two questions that almost always need answering are "*Why?*" and "*How do you know?*" Other important questions begin with *What? When? Who? Where? How?* and *What if?*

18. Edit carefully. Writing filled with errors is distracting to readers. At best, errors will cause them to think less of what you have to say. At worst, your readers may misunderstand. The challenge with proofreading your own writing is that you know what is *supposed* to be there . . . and that is

what you will often see instead of what is *actually* there. Here's a proofreading trick that can help: Start proofreading with the last sentence. Then proofread the second-to-last sentence. And continue proofreading backward from the end of your writing to the beginning. In this way, you can focus on the surface details of grammar, spelling, and punctuation without being distracted by the flow of ideas. Remember that a computer's spell check will not pick up words used incorrectly but spelled correctly (such as using *there* for *their*). Your computer may also help you identify possible grammar errors that need to be corrected. But be careful, because sometimes it will point out "errors" that aren't errors at all.

19. Keep an Error Log. Some instructors, especially for a writing class, will point out your grammar and punctuation errors. When you get a writing assignment back with errors noted, enter them in an Error Log. An Error Log is a record of every sentence in which you had a grammar or punctuation problem. Below the error sentence, rewrite the sentence correctly. Then, write the relevant grammar or punctuation rule(s) so you can learn to correct all errors of the same kind. You'll find this information in the grammar section of a writing handbook, or you can ask a writing tutor to help you identify the rule. Here's an example:

Error Sentence: I went to the tutoring center, the tutor I was supposed to see wasn't there.

Corrected Sentence: I went to the tutoring center, but the tutor I was supposed to see wasn't there.

Rule: When two complete sentences are joined with only a comma, this error is called a comma splice. There are three ways to correct a comma splice: (1) Replace the comma with a period, capitalize the next word, and create two complete sentences. (2) Replace the comma with a semi-colon. (3) Add a coordinating conjunction (i.e., *and, but, or, nor, for, so,* or *yet*) after the comma.

Keeping an error log is time-consuming at first, but seeing your errors disappear from future papers is a great reward.

20. Rewrite graded papers. Most instructors provide feedback on substantive problems with your writing (e.g., unclear purpose, poor organization, and lack of support). Use this feedback to rewrite and improve your assignment. Revising is the ultimate <u>Rehearsal</u> of your writing skills and can help immensely. Impressed with your effort, most instructors will be glad to meet with you to discuss your revision. Some may raise your grade if your revision shows improvement. Regardless of how your instructor responds to your rewrites, realize that there is as much learning available to you in revising. The insights you gain into effective writing will help you on future assignments. Beyond college, thoughtfully using feedback will help you to fine-tune communication skills that can propel your career success. Clear purpose, effective organization, and supporting evidence will help your resumés, cover letters, emails, and other forms of professional communication stand out in the best possible way.

TIPS FOR EFFECTIVE DISCUSSION POSTS

If you're taking classes with some online component, then you are probably no stranger to discussion boards. Discussion boards allow you to express your ideas in writing as you engage with your classmates and the content. However, many students fail to contribute to online discussions as effectively as they could. The following tips can help your discussion posts deepen your learning and meet instructors' expectations.

A. Read the discussion prompt carefully and identify the specific questions being asked.

B. Organize your discussion post to directly address these questions. Use separate paragraphs or bullet points to make the connections clear. Consider using formatting (e.g., bold) to bring attention to key words or concepts.

C. Use the 4 Es (example, experience, explanation, evidence) to provide support for your answers. If using ideas from another source, be sure to reference the page number from a class reading or provide credit to the outside resource by providing a link or citation.

D. Embrace the discussion as an opportunity to enhance your learning through writing, without the pressure that might be associated with a formal paper. Still, to make sure your ideas are easy to follow, use college-level writing, including separate well developed paragraphs, punctuation and capitalization, and clear organization. Consider composing your draft in a separate document, then posting it in the discussion board when finished.

E. When responding to peers, engage respectfully with their ideas. Specifically indicate where you agree, as well as why. It is okay to not agree completely. In fact, many instructors prefer *not* to see oversimplified responses such as "Great post. I agree!" If you have an area of disagreement or wish to offer a suggestion, be specific and constructive as you provide examples from your own experience or interpretations of course content.

F. Whether you are composing an original discussion post or responding to a peer, always review what you have written for spelling, grammar, organization, tone, and adequate detail. Double check that you have addressed each requirement of the discussion. For instance, did you provide an appropriate number of examples or references to course readings? Is it clear from your response that you have thought deeply about the course

EXERCISE: WRITING

Compare the quality of your writing in Journal Entries 1 and 2 with the quality of your writing in your most recent Journal Entries. In your comparison, address the following questions:

- Has the quality of your writing improved? If so, how? Offer specific examples.

- If your writing has not improved, why do you suppose it hasn't?

- Which of your journal entries do you think is the most well written?

- What could you do to improve the writing in your remaining journal entries?

- How did you feel about writing when you began this course?

- Have your feelings about writing changed while keeping your journal? If so, how? And why?

TECH TIPS: Active Learning

Evernote is an electronic notebook that makes it easy to collect and organize notes. Type notes using your keyboard, record audio notes, and even take pictures. You can create to-do lists, record voice reminders, and organize your daily schedule. You can even add websites to your notes. *(Web, Android, and iOS)*

Google Docs allows you to create and share documents online. Google Docs is especially helpful when you need to collaborate on a group project, research paper, or study materials. Instead of emailing documents back and forth, everyone can work on the same document from separate locations. *(Web)*

My Study Life helps you manage your classes, tasks, and assignments. If you didn't already find a productivity website or app that you like, this might be the one. You can track tasks, add exam dates, manage classes, and receive reminders of upcoming events. The dashboard shows an overview of your entire day plus tasks completed and unfinished. *(Web, Android, and iOS)*

Koofers.com offers more than 2 million practice tests and flashcards to help you prepare for exams. An additional feature in

Koofers offers student-created ratings of more than 600,000 instructors, which could help you make wise choices in selecting future courses. *(Web)*

Quizlet provides an opportunity to study with digital flashcards, either those you make or the many already on the site. You can choose to click a flashcard to reveal the answer. Or you can choose among three engaging study tools (Speller, Learn, and Test) or two interactive games (Scatter and Space Race). You can track your study progress and even compete with others. Heads up, though, when using flashcards created by others; the answers could be wrong! *(Web, Android, and iOS)*

StudyBlue, like Quizlet, lets you make digital flashcards or use ones already created by others. Flashcards can contain pictures as well as text. As you study the flashcards, the program tracks what you have learned and suggests areas in which you need more studying. You can set reminders for upcoming tests so you provide enough time for distributed study. You can also create a StudyBlue community of fellow students by adding them to your contacts. *(Web, Android, and iOS)*

Audacity is a downloadable audio recorder and editor. If you have permission to record a lecture or class discussion, Audacity could be the means. Remember, though, that every hour of recordings will necessitate another hour of listening to get the full value. A good use is listening to recordings while commuting or working at a mindless task. *(Windows and Mac)*

PowerPoint, Prezi, and **HaikuDeck** offer different approaches to creating visually appealing presentations. Use in a speech class or any course that requires you to give a speech or verbal report. *(Web)* (PowerPoint is part of the Microsoft Office Suite, which is available on some campuses free of charge to students.)

Note: All of the above (except as noted) are free, but some may offer upgraded features for a fee.

Assess Your Study Skills
For College Success—Again

You're now familiar with the CORE Learning System as well as many strategies for implementing it. Following is a duplicate of the learning skills self-assessment you took at the beginning of this Study Skills Toolbox. Now take it again. (Don't look back at your previous answers yet.) By comparing your two scores, you'll be able to see your present understanding of how to learn your way to success in college and beyond.

As you take this self-assessment, be absolutely honest so you can learn the truth about where your learning skills are at this time. This valuable information can pave the way to making significant improvements in your future learning efforts.

Study Skills Self-Assessment

Totally False   0 1 2 3 4 5 6 7 8 9 10   Totally True

Read the following statements and score each one according to how true or false you believe it is about you. To get an accurate picture of yourself, consider what IS true about you (not what you *want* to be true). Remember, there are no right or wrong answers. Assign each statement a number from 0 to 10, as follows:

1. _____ I understand how the human brain learns, and I use that knowledge to study effectively.

2. _____ When I read an assignment in my textbook, I have trouble identifying the most important information.

3. _____ I know effective strategies for memorizing important things such as facts, details, and formulas.

4. _____ I don't know how to create graphic or linear organizers.

5. _____ I'm good at figuring out what's important during a class discussion or lecture.

6. _____ After I get a test or quiz back, I check my grade to see how I did and then don't look at it again.

7. _____ When writing a paper, I know how to add supporting details that make my main ideas clear.

8. _____ After I finish taking a test, I have no idea what kind of grade I will get.

9. _____ While reading an assignment, I have an effective system for marking or writing down important ideas.
10. _____ When I review my notes, they are complete and easy to understand.
11. _____ Before studying for a test, I condense all of my class notes, homework, reading assignments, and course handouts into one document and then I study from this new document.
12. _____ I do most (sometimes all) of my studying on the day before or the day of a test.
13. _____ When I take a test, I feel calm and confident.
14. _____ When I write the answer to an essay question, I find it difficult to organize my ideas.
15. _____ When I study for a test, I use a number of different learning strategies.
16. _____ After reading, I don't recall much of what I just read.
17. _____ My notes include most of the information that later appears on a test.
18. _____ I know at least three different ways to organize my study materials so the information makes the most sense to me.
19. _____ I study for math tests by looking over the problems I solved for homework and/or the ones the instructor solved in class.
20. _____ When I take a test, I have a plan to get the most possible points.
21. _____ I usually write one draft of a paper and that's what I turn in.
22. _____ A few days after I take a test, I don't remember much of what I studied.
23. _____ After reading a homework assignment, I take time to think, write, or talk with others about the main points of what I just read.
24. _____ I've never learned how to take good notes during a class.
25. _____ I study in a quiet place where I'm not disturbed.
26. _____ I feel unprepared when I take a test because I don't really know how to study effectively.
27. _____ I don't understand how to write a good paper in college.
28. _____ I know how to do well on a test no matter what kind of questions the instructor asks: multiple-choice, true/false, fill-in-the-blank, matching, problems, or essays.
29. _____ How learning happens is a mystery to me.
30. _____ I'm good at identifying the important information in a reading assignment.
31. _____ While studying, I make a list of questions that I think will be on a test.
32. _____ During a lecture or class discussion, I have trouble staying focused.
33. _____ I'm bad at memorizing important formulas, details, and facts.
34. _____ After I get a test back, I analyze and correct all of the errors I made.
35. _____ My papers are pretty short because I have difficulty adding supporting details that make my main ideas clear.
36. _____ I know how to tell how well I have learned a subject even before I take a test.
37. _____ When I read, I don't write in my book or take separate notes.
38. _____ My class notes are difficult to understand when I look at them a few days later.
39. _____ I study for tests by re-reading my textbooks, class notes, and course handouts.
40. _____ I study each subject frequently, and I spread my study sessions over the whole course.
41. _____ I lose points on tests because of things like spending too much time on one question or taking too much time to answer a question that's worth only a few points.
42. _____ The papers I write are well organized.
43. _____ I don't participate in class discussions or activities.
44. _____ When I finish a reading assignment, I remember most of what I read.

45. _____   When I take a test, there are questions about things that weren't in my notes.
46. _____   When I study, there are often distractions and I can't concentrate.
47. _____   When I study for a math test, I solve many problems of the same kinds that will be on the test.
48. _____   Certain kinds of test questions are difficult for me and I don't do well on them.
49. _____   I understand and use all four steps of the writing process: Prewriting, Writing, Revising, and Editing.
50. _____   I ask questions in class whenever I'm confused.
51. _____   After reading a textbook, I don't think much about what I read until right before the test.
52. _____   I take good notes during a lecture, video, or class discussion.
53. _____   When I take a test, I find questions I didn't study for.
54. _____   I use an effective learning system when I study, so I feel well prepared when I take a test.
55. _____   I know how to write a good paper in college.
56. _____   I feel nervous and my mind goes blank when I take a test.

Transfer your scores to the scoring sheets on the next page. For each of the seven areas, total your scores in columns A and B. Then total your final scores as shown in the sample.

Self-Assessment Scoring Sheet

	SAMPLE		
A		B	
6. _8_		29. _3_	
14. _5_		35. _3_	
21. _6_		50. _6_	
73. _9_		56. _2_	
_28_ + 40 −		_14_ = 54	

SCORE #1: Learning Actively

A		B	
1. ___		8. ___	
15. ___		22. ___	
36. ___		29. ___	
50. ___		43. ___	
___ + 40 −		___ = ___	

SCORE #2: Reading

A		B	
9. ___		2. ___	
23. ___		16. ___	
30. ___		37. ___	
44. ___		51. ___	
___ + 40 −		___ = ___	

SCORE #3: Taking Notes

A		B	
5. ___		24. ___	
10. ___		32. ___	
17. ___		38. ___	
52. ___		45. ___	
___ + 40 −		___ = ___	

SCORE #4: Organizing Study Materials

A		B	
11. ___		4. ___	
18. ___		39. ___	
25. ___		46. ___	
31. ___		53. ___	
___ + 40 −		___ = ___	

SCORE #5: Rehearsing and Memorizing Study Materials

A		B	
3. ___		12. ___	
40. ___		19. ___	
47. ___		26. ___	
54. ___		33. ___	
___ + 40 −		___ = ___	

SCORE #6: Taking Tests

A		B	
13. ___		6. ___	
20. ___		41. ___	
28. ___		48. ___	
34. ___		56. ___	
___ + 40 −		___ = ___	

SCORE #7: Writing

A		B	
7. ___		14. ___	
42. ___		21. ___	
49. ___		27. ___	
55. ___		35. ___	
___ + 40 −		___ = ___	

Interpreting Your Scores

A score of . . .

0–39	Indicates an area where your study skills will **seldom** support deep learning.
40–63	Indicates an area where your study skills will **sometimes** support deep learning.
64–80	Indicates an area where your study skills will **usually** support deep learning.

EXERCISE: ACTIVE LEARNING

In the chart below, transfer your scores from the scoring chart in the "Becoming an Active Learner" section of this Toolbox (first score) and the scoring chart from above (second score):

First Score	Second Score	
————	————	1. Becoming an Active Learner
————	————	2. Reading
————	————	3. Taking Notes
————	————	4. Organizing Study Materials
————	————	5. Rehearsing and Memorizing Study Materials
————	————	6. Taking Tests
————	————	7. Writing

In which study skill(s) have you improved the most?

In which study skill(s) do you want to improve even more?

What is your plan for making that improvement? .

Conversation with the Author

Since the first edition of *On Course* more than two decades ago, a number of students have contacted the author with thoughtful questions. Following are some of those questions and Skip Downing's answers:

Q. What inspired you to write this book?

A. The short answer is I was tired of seeing my students—most of whom had everything necessary to be a success in college (and in life)—sabotage their success. I decided to stop complaining and see what I could do about it. The longer answer, which addresses how I was also in need of help in getting my own life on course, is explained in the "Travel with Me" section early in the *On Course* book.

Q. Of all the strategies in *On Course*, which one helped you the most when you were in college?

A. I'll say self-management, particularly persistence. In my first semester in college, I quickly learned that most of my classmates had better academic preparation than I did. My roommate, for example, had read many books I had never even heard of. Additionally, in my first semester I received discouraging feedback from some of my instructors. I recall one instructor whose only comment on my first assignment was, "This is not a very good way to start your college career." However, experiences like that made me grit my teeth and work even harder. I guess I believed that with hard work I could overcome my obstacles, and that turned out to be a self-fulfilling prophesy.

Q. What inner quality do you wish you had had more of when you were in college?

A. All of them. But if I had to choose one, I would say a passion for lifelong learning. In college I only studied what was assigned and all I cared about was the grade. My regret today is that I didn't squeeze more value from my college experience. I now "study" harder than I ever did in college because I love learning new ideas, particularly in the realm of "what makes us tick." In college, I went to the library to study but hardly noticed the miles of shelved books. Today I go to a library and feel a sense of awe that human beings have learned so much and that through books (and now the Internet), that wealth of knowledge is available any time I want it.

Q. Did you struggle in college and, if so, is that how you created such great tips?

A. I guess my answer depends on what you mean by "struggle." If you mean did I have a difficult time getting passing grades, the answer is no. Even though I had a rough first semester, soon after I figured out how the game of school is played. While I was never a threat to be valedictorian, I got decent grades. However, if by "struggle" you mean having difficulty learning at a deep level and using what I was learning to improve my life, the answer is yes, I struggled. If I could do college over, I would focus on learning instead of grades. Fortunately, I had an opportunity to do just that when I returned to graduate school for the second time when I was in my 40s. That's when I learned to love learning. What a great experience! It was like the universe gave me a do-over. If I had only one wish for my students, it would be that they would fall in love with learning.

Q. Using the first person in a textbook is unusual. What is your reason for using this approach throughout the entire book?

A. I thought long and hard before deciding to use the first person in *On Course.* When I was writing the first draft, I don't believe there were any student success texts that employed the first person. As with all of the textbooks I had read in college, the authors were hidden behind a curtain (like the Wizard of Oz). So, it was going to be a risk. However, I ultimately decided that putting myself in the book was the best way to convey that when it comes to making the most of our lives, all of us—students, instructors…all of us—face similar challenges. I am not a third-person observer of how to create a rich, full life…I am fully engaged as a participant in that quest. I want what you want. We're all in this university of life together; we're all creating our outcomes and experiences by the choices we make every day. Like life, creating success in college isn't easy, but there are ways to make it easier.

Q. In your book, the success skills make sense and seem so easy, but sometimes I can't do it. I wonder what it takes for a person to actually apply these skills.

A. I understand your frustration. I've felt that way at times myself. However, as is so often the case, the answer is found right there in our excuses. Here's your excuse: "Sometimes I *can't* do it." Is that really true? Of course you *can* do it because if sometimes you *can't* do it, then logically sometimes you *can* do it. So, "Sometimes I can't do it" is the kind of subtle excuse we tell ourselves when we're in a Victim mindset. We justify our behaviors and outcomes by telling ourselves an untruth. More bluntly, we lie to ourselves. There is no strategy in *On Course* that you can't do. That's why when you are in a Creator mindset you tell yourself the truth, which is: "Sometimes I *choose* not to

do it." And in that moment of clarity and awareness, you have the option to draw on inner strengths, to choose thoughts and actions that will keep you on course to your desired outcomes and experiences. If you choose anything else (say, missing class or not seeking help on difficult math problems or reading your textbooks mindlessly), you would likely benefit from developing the inner qualities and strategies in *On Course* to help you make wiser choices. What inner quality is needed to go to class even when you don't feel like it? What inner strength is needed to ask for help even though asking for help embarrasses you? What strategy is needed to read actively, even when the subject doesn't interest you? I'm not saying it's easy. Goodness knows, I struggle too…and I'm tempted to justify my lack of success in some endeavor by saying "I can't." But in most cases, my Inner Guide knows, "I'm choosing not to…." And if I'm choosing *not to do* something that advances my life, I can also choose *to do* something that does. And that is more often than not the truth.

Q. What is the purpose of including journal entries in each of the chapters?

A. Reflection deepens learning, and the journals in *On Course* apply this powerful learning strategy. They guide you to take what you have just read about—a success principle or practice—and apply it to your own life. When you dive deep in your journal entries, you begin making the strategies your own. When you use the strategies in your life, you improve your outcomes and experiences. By improving your outcomes and experiences, you begin an upward spiral of success and personal development. Reading the success strategies in *On Course* and not writing the journals would be like only reading about exercising and then wondering why you aren't getting in shape.

Q. How did you come up with all of these strategies?

A. My first exposure to success strategies was in a three-day personal effectiveness seminar that I took because I was struggling in both my personal and professional life. Some of the strategies I learned in the seminar helped me, so I shared them with my students. When I saw the strategies helping my students, too, I went on a quest to learn more of them. I already had my doctoral degree in English, but my new quest motivated me to complete a master's degree in counseling. I was blessed to have awesome instructors in that program, and I learned many more strategies. If it worked for me, I offered it to my students and observed their responses. I kept teaching the strategies that helped them improve their outcomes and experiences in college. Today, *On Course* contains the very best strategies I've come across in a search that spans more than two decades. What makes them "best" is that each strategy works for many students, helping them to achieve more of their potential in college . . . and in life.

Q. Why do you put quotations in the margins?

A. Here are four reasons: (1) I love to learn what people who have given a great deal of thought to an important issue have to say about it, and I hope my readers do, too. (2) Because the quotations express ideas in a different way than I do, they may help clarify a point in the book. (3) I have included quotations from diverse thinkers and cultures to convey the universality of these ideas. (4) As with quotations embedded in an article ("The noted expert Farley Studebaker says, "...."), I hope the quotations demonstrate that the ideas and strategies in the book are not just a whim of mine. Rather the ideas and strategies are the product of thinkers and researchers who have come up with powerful answers to the key question addressed in *On Course*: "How can each of us live up to our potential and create a rich, personally fulfilling life?"

Q. Are the case studies in *On Course* true stories?

A. The case studies are not "true" in the sense that the events happened to real people exactly as they are described. But in another sense they are truer than a narrative of actual events. When case studies in *On Course* work as they intended, they show you students dealing with the kinds of complex challenges that anyone might encounter on the path to a college degree. There are no simple answers to the questions posed by the case studies; there are no right answers in the back of the book. Instead each of us must apply our present beliefs—derived from our own unique experiences—to make sense of each case study. Then, during a discussion with classmates and instructors, we get the opportunity to test our answers against those of others. Thus, by applying critical thinking to the situations faced by characters in the case studies, we have the opportunity to develop new insights that can help us successfully confront similar problems in our own lives.

Q. I did an Internet search for "Goal Setting" and came across dozens of sites that use the acronym S.M.A.R.T. to represent the qualities of an effective goal. Why did you come up with your own acronym (D.A.P.P.S.) instead of using S.M.A.R.T.?

A. I very much wanted to use S.M.A.R.T. because who doesn't want to have a SMART goal? However, the more I looked at the acronym, the more problems I found. First, the acronym has been around a long time and users have begun taking liberties with what the five letters stand for. "S" sometimes stands for "specific" and at other times "simple." "M" is used for both "measurable" and "manageable." "A" is used for both "attainable" and "action-oriented." In various versions, "R" stands for "relevant," "relative," and "realistic." And "T" shows up as "time-bound," "timely," or "tangible." So the first problem is: What do the letters in S.M.A.R.T. stand for? A second problem is that the most common words for the letters "S" and "M" are "specific" and "measurable." In my mind, these are essentially the same quality. If something is *specific* (achieve a 3.5 GPA, for example), it is also *measurable*; that means that these two letters actually represent only one quality. And finally, SMART leaves out two qualities that I believe are essential components of an effective goal: Personal and Positive. If a goal isn't Personal (that is, if it's someone else's goal for you, not your own), you're unlikely to persist when the going gets tough. And if a goal isn't Positive, your best choices can be confusing. For example, if my goal is "not to fail math" (a negative goal), I can simply drop the course…but is that what I really want? If my goal is "to pass math with an A" (a positive goal), then withdrawing is no longer an option. So, while I would have preferred to go with the established acronym, creating D.A.P.P.S. seemed like a smart choice.

Q. One of my classmates said she thought that self-motivation should be the first inner quality presented in the book. She said that without self-motivation, no one would do anything. That started a class discussion in which different students made a case for every one of the eight qualities coming first. Why did you put the eight choices of successful students in the order you did?

A. Over the years, I've heard compelling arguments that each of the eight "Choices of Successful Students" is the most important and, therefore, should come

first. I haven't been able to figure out how to present them all first, so here's my rationale for the present order. For me, **responsibility** is the foundation of our success because until I see myself as shaping my own life by my choices, all of the other inner qualities are likely to be unhelpful. Once I realize that (as one of my students put it), I am driving my own car, the next step is determining my destination. This choice generates **motivation** to move my life in a particular direction. With a destination in mind, now I need **self-management** to keep taking the purposeful actions that propel me toward my goals and dreams. Once I realize that big goals and dreams are difficult (maybe impossible) to achieve alone, I understand the importance of **interdependence**. At this point, I may think I'm doing everything "right," but somehow I'm off course. How did that happen? That's when I need to become more **self-aware** so I can spot the habitual thoughts, behaviors, emotions and beliefs (scripts) that are sabotaging my success. At this point (if not before) I begin to realize how much more I need to learn to achieve my goals, and I become a **lifelong learner**. I also see that I need **emotional intelligence** in order to regulate my emotions as well as deal effectively with the emotions of others or I'm likely to be dragged off course. Because I need to **believe in myself** throughout the journey, I distributed strategies to develop this quality throughout the book. I'm tempted to do that with all eight of the inner qualities, but that seems to create other, more serious problems of organization. So, that's my reasoning. And I'm fine when I hear of instructors who choose to present the chapters in a different order that makes sense to them. Ultimately, it doesn't matter what order you put the tires on a car; what matters is that the car has all of its tires so it can get on the road to success.

Bibliography

Allen, David. *Getting Things Done*. Viking, 2001.

———. *Making It All Work*. Viking, 2009.

Branden, Nathaniel. *The Psychology of Self-Esteem*. Jossey-Bass, 2001.

Bucher, Richard D. *Diversity Consciousness*. Prentice Hall, 2014.

Burka, Jane B., and Lenora M. Yuen. *Procrastination*. DeCapo, 2008.

Burns, David, MD. *Feeling Good*. Harper, 2008.

Bushman, Barbara, ed. *Complete Guide to Fitness and Health*. American College of Sports Medicine, 2017.

Ciarrochi, Joseph, and John H. Beck. *Emotional Intelligence in Everyday Life*. Psychology Press, 2013.

Covey, Stephen R. *7 Habits of Highly Effective People*. Simon and Schuster, 2013.

Csikszentmihalyi, Mihaly. *Flow: The Psychology of Optimal Experience*. Harper & Row, 2008.

Davis, Martha, Elizabeth Robbins Eshelman, and Matthew McKay. *The Relaxation and Stress Reduction Workbook*. New Harbinger, 2008.

Duckworth, Angela. *Grit: The Power of Passion and Perseverance*. Scribner, 2016.

Dweck, Carol. *Mindset: The New Psychology of Success*. Ballantine Books, 2007.

Firestone, Robert W., Lisa Firestone, Joyce Catlett, and Pat Love. *Conquer Your Critical Inner Voice*. New Harbinger, 2002.

Furhman, Joel, MD. *Fast Food Genocide*. Harper Collins, 2017.

Glasser, William. *Reality Therapy*. Harper & Row, 1978.

Goleman, Daniel. *Emotional Intelligence*. Bantam Books, 1995.

———. *Working with Emotional Intelligence*. Bantam Books, 2000.

Green, Stephanie, RDN. *Optimum Nutrition*. Alpha, 2015.

Haidt, Jonathan. *The Happiness Hypothesis*. Basic Books, 2006.

Hanson, Rick. *Hardwiring Happiness*. Harmony Books, 2013.

Herrmann, Ned. *The Creative Brain*. Brain Books, 1989.

Hoeger, Werner, Sharon A. Hoeger, Cherrie I. Hoeger, and Amber Lee Fawson. *Lifetime Physical Fitness and Wellness*. Cengage Learning, 2019.

Howard, Pierce J. *The Owner's Manual for the Brain*. William Morrow, 2014.

Hyman, Mark, MD. *Food: What the Heck Should I Eat?* Little, Brown, and Company, 2018.

Iyengar, Sheena. *The Art of Choosing*. Twelve Publishers, 2011.

Jensen, Eric. *Brain-Based Learning*. Corwin, 2008.

Kahneman, Daniel. *Thinking, Fast and Slow*. Macmillan, 2011.

Kernis, Michael. *Self-Esteem: Issues and Answers*. Psychology Press, 2006.

Klaus, Peggy. *The Hard Truth About Soft Skills: Workplace Lessons Smart People Wish They'd Learned Sooner*. HarperBusiness, 2008.

Kuhn, Cynthia, PhD, Scott Swartzwelder, PhD, Wilkie Wilson, PhD. *Buzzed*. W. W. Norton, 2014.

Lanning, Scott. *Concise Guide to Information Literacy*. Libraries Unlimited, 2017.

Lehrer, Jonah. *How We Decide*. Houghton Mifflin Harcourt, 2009.

Lyubomirsky, Sonja. *The How of Happiness*. Penguin Books, 2007.

Matsumoto, David, and Linda Juang. *Culture and Psychology*. Wadsworth, 2008.

McKay, Matthew, Patrick Fanning, Carole Honeychurch, and Catherine Sutker. *The Self-Esteem Companion*. MJF Books, 2001.

Merlevede, Patrick E., Denis Bridoux, and Rudy Vandamme. *7 Steps to Emotional Intelligence*. Crown House, 2001.

Mohammad, Akikur, MD. *The Anatomy of Addiction*. Perigee (Penguin Random House), 2016.

Mosconi, Lisa. *Brain Food*. Avery, 2018.

Moule, Jean. *Cultural Competence: A Primer for Educators*. Wadsworth/ Cengage, 2012.

Oakley, Barbara. *A Mind for Numbers*. Tarcher, 2014.

Olpin, Michael, and Margie Hesson. *Stress Management for Life*. Cengage Learning, 2015.

Orman, Doc. *The Test Anxiety Cure*. Stress Management Group, 2014.

Peterson, Brooks. *Cultural Intelligence: A Guide to Working with People from Other Cultures*. Intercultural Press, 2004.

Peterson, Christopher. *A Primer in Positive Psychology*. Oxford University Press, 2006.

Pink, Daniel. *Drive: The Surprising Truth about What Motivates Us*. Riverhead, 2009.

Rosenberg, Marshall B. *Nonviolent Communication*. PuddleDancer Press, 2005.

Schiraldi, Glen R., Patrick Fanning, and Matthew McKay. *The Self-Esteem Workbook*. New Harbinger, 2001.

Seligman, Martin. *Learned Optimism*. Alfred A. Knopf, 1991.

——— *Authentic Happiness*. Atria Books, 2003.

Shiota, Michelle N., and James W. Kalat. *Emotion*. Cengage Learning, 2012.

Snyder, Charles R. *Psychology of Hope: You Can Get Here from There*. Free Press, 2003.

Sousa, David A. *How the Brain Learns*. Corwin Press, 2011.

Stone, Hal, and Sidra Stone. *Embracing Your Inner Critic*. HarperCollins, 1993.

Tobias, Sheila. *Overcoming Math Anxiety*. W. W. Norton & Co., 1995.

Wehrenberg, Margaret. *The 10 Best-Ever Anxiety Management Techniques*. W. W. Norton, 2008.

Winter, Chris, MD. *The Sleep Solution*. New American Library, 2017.

Glossary

A

32-day commitment taking action every day for 32 days in order to spend significant time on a task, make visible progress toward a goal, and develop grit

academic accommodations additional support for students with disabilities typically granted by the Disability Services office, such as housing accessibility, classroom accessibility, personal instruction, extended examination time, and note takers

acronym one word created from the first letters of other words that you want to remember

acrostic a sentence created from the first letters of other words that you want to remember

active listening listening with empathy and attention with the goal of receiving the same message that the speaker sent

active reading intense mental engagement in what you are reading that leads to significant neural activity in your brain, assisting deep and lasting learning

advisor an individual within a college or university who offers guidance on areas such as education and careers

affirmations stating to yourself that you have the personal qualities needed to accomplish your goals

agenda part of an essay that states the main ideas that readers can expect the author to discuss

amygdala part of the brain that stores emotionally charged but now unconscious memories, which can hijack our rational thought processes and cause us to respond in a way that is inappropriate in our present situation

annotating adding your own comments to a text by summarizing, drawing, or writing questions

anxiety a feeling of uneasiness, fear, or pain in relation to something that might happen; symptoms may include prolonged doubt, fear, sweating, increased heart rate, trouble in sleeping, and difficulty in breathing

associate's degree an undergraduate degree typically earned after completing 2 years of study

attributions qualities that tell us how we "are" or "should be"

B

bachelor's degree an undergraduate degree typically earned after completing 4 years of study

behavior patterns habitual actions

bibliography a formal list of works cited that tells readers where to find the original sources for your information

blaming a pattern of ineffective communication that involves protecting yourself from disappointment and failure by making others fully responsible for your problems

blind spots—NOTE: may not be inclusive behaviors that are invisible to us but seen to others

C

campus the property or grounds of a college or university

choice a brief, critical moment of decision available between a stimulus and our response

citation crediting the source of an idea or quote used in your essay, expected in college writing

collect the first component of the CORE Learning System: consciously gathering key information and skills through activities such as reading and listening

college catalog a printed or online guide to all the courses offered at a college or university in which students can enroll

commitment following through on your promises

concept map a visual/graphic note-taking method that places information based on level of importance and relationships among ideas

core beliefs unconscious judgments that dictate what we consistently think, feel, and do

CORE Learning System an acronym that reflects four general strategies common to good learners: college, organize, rehearse, and evaluate

Cornell study sheet a study method that contains condensed and well-organized information in the middle of a page, study questions in the margin, and a summary at the bottom

counseling office the office at a college or university in which students can seek therapy and/or aid

creator mindset a collection of beliefs and attitudes that causes people to see multiple options, choose wisely among them, and take effective actions to achieve the life they want

critical thinking an in-depth analysis of a subject or problem in order to make logical conclusions about what to believe, what to do, and/or what decisions to make

D

DAPPS an acronym in which each letter of the word stands for one of the five qualities of an effective goal: Dated, Achievable, Personal, Positive, and Specific

deep processing learning strategies used to master complex information and skills, beyond mere memorization

degree an honor given to a student who has completed the required credits to be considered academically successful in a field of study

department a division within a college or university devoted to a particular discipline or subject

depression a serious medical condition in which a person experiences prolonged sadness and hopelessness; symptoms may include sadness, trouble in sleeping, lack of appetite, difficulty in concentrating, and suicidal thoughts

Disability Services the office at a college or university that offers resources, guidance, and accommodations to students with disabilities

discussion board an online forum that allows students to post their thoughts and communicate electronically with one another

distributed practice an effective approach to learning that involves engaging in frequent study sessions spaced over time, as opposed to all at once

diversity the state of having individuals with different cultures, backgrounds, and viewpoints within one community

dopamine positive experiences increase the release of this feel-good hormone

E

echo a type of conclusion that restates an idea presented earlier in your essay

elaborative rehearsal strategies that employ deep processing by focusing on meaning, showing relationships between ideas, and connecting new knowledge with old

elective a course that a student chooses to take but is not required to take

emotional intelligence the combination of emotional self-awareness, emotional self-management, social awareness, and relationship management

emotional patterns habitual feelings

emotional self-awareness knowing your feelings in the moment

emotional self-management managing strong feelings and not making critical decisions during times of high drama

error log a record of every sentence in which you had a grammar or punctuation problem, including the corrected sentence and explanation of the grammar or punctuation rule

essay blueprint a guide to how to assemble the parts of a paper

evaluate the fourth component of the CORE Learning System: engaging in assessment to gather feedback about how well you understand information and apply skills

expectation how likely you think it is that you can be successful in college while making what you consider to be a reasonable effort

F

FAFSA Free Application for Federal Student Aid, a form completed each year to determine federal financial aid for current or incoming students

financial aid a grant, scholarship, or loan that helps students pay for college expenses such as tuition, textbooks, housing, and meal plans

fixed mindset believing people are born with a fixed amount of ability and talent, which can lead to avoiding challenges as a method of self-protection

flashcards physical or digital index cards that contain a question on the front and an answer on the back

flow states complete engagement or total absorption in an activity, which can cause time to seem to pass very quickly

G

general education courses classes within a number of broad areas of study that all students must complete in order to graduate from college, sometimes referred to as core courses

grade point average (GPA) the average grade for all of the courses you have taken in college

gratitude experiencing wonder, thankfulness, and appreciation

grit a passion for achieving a specific long-term goal combined with the perseverance to keep going even in the face of obstacles or disappointment

growth mindset believing that intelligence is like a muscle—it gets stronger the more it's used

H

hard skills visible and measurable behaviors and capabilities, such as active learning, reading, taking notes, organizing study materials, rehearsing and memorizing study materials, taking tests, and writing

hedonic adaptation the tendency to quickly become used to something good that happens

hook a statement, question, or story written at the beginning of an essay to grab readers' interest

hope a positive motivational state that includes thoughts about finding multiple choices and believing you can improve your life

hypothesis a working assumption that is not yet proven but will be researched and studied for accuracy; typically the first step to forming a theory

I

importance characteristic of an action that will help you achieve what you value

information competency applying critical thinking skills to distinguish between accurate and false information

injunctions qualities that tell us what we "are not" or "should not be"

inner critic the internal voice that judges us as inadequate and accepts too much responsibility

inner defender the internal voice that judges others and accepts too little responsibility

inner guide the internal voice that objectively observes each situation and considers how to get back on course

inner motivation intrinsic motivation where the reason for engagement comes from a sense of interest, enjoyment, or purpose

interdependence combining efforts in a mutual relationship with others because it is necessary, more effective, or more enjoyable to do so

internship a program through an employer or company that allows students to gain professional, practical experience in their field of study

K

key concept the main topic

L

learning amnesia the frustrating experience of not being able to remember what was learned in a previous course when you need it, often the result of cramming

learning preferences our own favored ways of taking in and deeply processing our learning experiences, though we can still learn in many ways

leveling a pattern of effective communication that involves asserting the truth as you see it

life goal a long-term goal that specifies what you hope to accomplish in a given life role

life plan defines your desired destinations in life and charts your best route for getting there

life role an activity to which we regularly devote more than a few hours weekly

lifelong learning the ability to keep learning new things for the rest of your life

locus of control the degree to which you believe your outcomes and experiences are the result of your choices or of forces outside your control

logical argument combination of reasons, evidence, and conclusions

long-term memory retention or storage of information over a long period of time, such as days, weeks, and years

M

main idea the most important idea about a key concept

major a principal focus and/or subject in which college students study and pursue knowledge

marking selecting important information in a text by underlining, highlighting, circling, or adding a symbol or question mark

master's degree a graduate degree typically earned at least 1 year after earning a bachelor's degree

mentor an experienced person in your intended or current field who is willing to advise you

metacognition the skill of thinking about our thinking

mindless reading when you run your eyes over a page only to realize later that you recall little of what you read

minor an optional secondary focus and/or subject in which students pursue a degree, typically requiring fewer credit hours/classes than a major

monthly calendar a tool that provides a chronological list of your upcoming important commitments, appointments, and assignments

multitasking when the brain attempts to rapidly switch back and forth between tasks, reducing your ability to be effective at any one task

N

neural network formed during a potential learning experience when neurons send out spikes of electrical activity and cause nearby neurons to do the same

next actions list a tool for tracking unscheduled events and actions that can be completed during your next free time

O

organize the second component of the CORE Learning System: structuring or categorizing information systematically to develop effective study materials

outer motivation extrinsic motivation where the reason for engagement comes from trying to earn a reward or avoid a negative consequence

outline a linear note-taking method that records ideas and supporting details in the order they are presented, using separate lines with indentations to indicate levels of importance

P

paraphrase to give a synopsis of someone else's words or thoughts using your own words

personal branding separating yourself from the crowd of other applicants by establishing yourself as valuable and unique

personal responsibility taking ownership for your work choices and the outcomes you create

placating a pattern of ineffective communication that involves protecting yourself from the sting of criticism and rejection by saying whatever you think will gain approval

plagiarism failure to credit the source of ideas or words in your essay

planner a document or book that typically includes a calendar or blank pages to record and organize tasks, assignments, events, due dates, and schedules

polishing reviewing notes after class to make them more accurate, complete, and understandable

prerequisite a course that must be successfully completed before taking a more advanced course

prior learning one of the three principles of deep and lasting learning: relate new information to previously learned information

probing questions an inquiry that can expose conclusions built on unsound reasons, flawed evidence, and faulty logic

procrastinate to continuously and intentionally put off doing something that needs to be done

project folder a tool for organizing materials related to a multistep project

project team a group that is formed to accomplish one particular task

Q

quadrant I actions important activities done under the pressure of nearing deadlines

quadrant II actions important activities done without the pressure of looming deadlines

quadrant III actions unimportant activities done with a sense of urgency

quadrant IV actions time-wasting activities that are neither important not urgent

quality of processing one of the three principles of deep and lasting learning: use many different deep-processing strategies

quantity of processing one of the three principles of deep and lasting learning: use frequent practice sessions of sufficient length distributed over time

R

rehearse the third component of the CORE Learning System: practicing target information and skills in order to remember them for future use

relationship management handling emotions in relationships with skill and harmony

rote rehearsal strategies that employ surface processing of information, such as memorizing by sheer repetition

S

savoring letting a pleasant experience linger in our awareness

scripts our unconscious internal forces that provide directions for how we are to think, feel, and behave

search engine an online resource used to help locate websites or web pages containing information related to key words or terms entered by the user

secondary idea elaborates on a main idea by answering potential questions about it

self-confidence the core belief that you can successfully do whatever is necessary to achieve your realistic goals and dreams

self-esteem approving of ourselves as we are and believing ourselves capable, admirable, lovable, and fully worthy of the best life has to offer

self-management managing the choices we make within the time we have every day

self-sabotage making choices that work against our goals and dreams

short-term memory retention or storage of information within the very recent past, often within seconds or minutes

social awareness empathizing accurately with other people's emotions

social responsibility taking ownership of your behavior toward others at work

soft skills inner strengths, personal qualities, or non-cognitive factors such as personal responsibility, self-motivation, self-discipline, interdependence, self-awareness, emotional intelligence, and believing in yourself

stereotype threat a fear that your behavior in a particular situation might confirm a negative stereotype about a cultural group to which you belong

stinkin' thinkin' irrational beliefs that make us feel awful even when the circumstances don't justify it

strawberry moments times when we choose to savor a momentary pleasure, feel gratitude, engage in flow, or show kindness to others, even in the face of **difficulties, obstacles, challenges, and pain**

stress the "wear and tear" that our minds and bodies experience as we attempt to cope with the challenges of life

study group students who gather multiple times to actively engage with course content, with the purpose of helping everyone on the team excel in a particular course

success staying on course to your desired outcomes and experiences

supporting details examples, evidence, explanation, and experiences

syllabus instructor-provided document that contains essential information about the course such as learning objectives, homework assignments, course rules, and how the course grade is determined

T

test debrief a feedback method that helps you to identify where you lost points on a prior examination and determine solutions for addressing your common test-taking problems

thesis a statement about the most important idea you want to convey to your audience, comprises the topic you're writing about and the claim you make about the topic

thought patterns habitual self-talk

three-column method a method for note-taking or studying that involves charting out the problem, solution, and explanation in subjects such as mathematics

tracking form a tool for coordinating goal-related actions that you repeat consistently over time

transcript a record of a student's grades and grade point average while in school; similar to a grade-school report card

transition a bridge between ideas that help readers follow the flow of your essay

tuition the cost of attending a college or university; often differs for students who live in-state and students who live out-of-state

U

unconscious forces being influenced in our daily choices by old experiences we don't even recall

urgency characteristic of an action that has an approaching deadline

V

value the benefits you believe you'll obtain from the academic degree you'll earn, the knowledge you'll gain, and the experiences you'll have while enrolled

victim mindset a collection of beliefs and attitudes that keeps people from seeing and acting on choices that could help them achieve the life they want

visualization picturing yourself accomplishing your fondest goal and imagining the delight you'll experience when it actually happens

W

waiting-for list a tool for tracking commitments that others have made to you

weekly calendar a tool for tracking recurring scheduled events

wise choice process helps you make a responsible decision by considering the present situation, desired situation, possible choices, likely outcomes of each choice, the choice you will commit to doing, and when and how to evaluate your plan

works cited a list of the sources cited in a research paper or article that appears at the end of the paper or article

Index

NOTE: Book titles are shown in *italics*; figures are indicated by an *f*, notes are indicated by an *n*, and tables are indicated by a *t* following the page numbers.